Fodor's

W9-AAF-313

CAPE COD, NANTUCKET & MARTHA'S VINEYARD

29th Edition

Where to Stay and Eat
for All Budgets

Must-See Sights
and Local Secrets

Ratings You Can Trust

Fodor's Travel Publications   New York, Toronto, London, Sydney, Auckland
www.fodors.com

FODOR'S CAPE COD, NANTUCKET & MARTHA'S VINEYARD

Editors: Linda Cabasin, Mark Sullivan

Writers: Sandy MacDonald, Janice Randall Rohlf, Laura V. Scheel

Production Editor: Jennifer DePrima

Maps & Illustrations: David Lindroth and Mark Stroud, *cartographers;* Bob Blake, Rebecca Baer, *map editors;* William Wu, *information graphics*

Design: Fabrizio La Rocca, *creative director;* Guido Caroti, Siobhan O'Hare, *art directors;* Tina Malaney, Chie Ushio, Ann McBride, Jessica Walsh, Nora Rosansky, *designers;* Melanie Marin, *senior picture editor*

Cover Photo: (Lobster restaurant, Wellfleet): age fotostock/SuperStock

Production Manager: Steve Slawsky

29th Edition

ISBN 978–1–4000–0518–5

ISSN 1934–5569

SPECIAL SALES

This book is available at special discounts for bulk purchases for sales promotions or premiums. Special editions, including personalized covers, excerpts of existing books, and corporate imprints, can be created in large quantities for special needs. For more information, write to Special Markets/Premium Sales, 1745 Broadway, MD 6-2, New York, NY 10019, or e-mail specialmarkets@randomhouse.com.

AN IMPORTANT TIP & AN INVITATION

Although all prices, opening times, and other details in this book are based on information supplied to us at press time, changes occur all the time in the travel world, and Fodor's cannot accept responsibility for facts that become outdated or for inadvertent errors or omissions. So **always confirm information when it matters,** especially if you're making a detour to visit a specific place. Your experiences—positive and negative— matter to us. If we have missed or misstated something, **please write to us.** Share your opinion instantly through our online feedback center at fodors.com/contact-us.

PRINTED IN THE UNITED STATES OF AMERICA

10 9 8 7 6 5 4 3 2 1

Be a Fodor's Correspondent

Your opinion matters. It matters to us. It matters to your fellow Fodor's travelers, too. And we'd like to hear it. In fact, we need to hear it.

When you share your experiences and opinions, you become an active member of the Fodor's community. That means we'll not only use your feedback to make our books better, but we'll publish your names and comments whenever possible. Throughout our guides, look for "Word of Mouth," excerpts of your unvarnished feedback.

Here's how you can help improve Fodor's for all of us.

Tell us when we're right. We rely on local writers to give you an insider's perspective. But our writers and staff editors—who are the best in the business—depend on you. Your positive feedback is a vote to renew our recommendations for the next edition.

Tell us when we're wrong. We're proud that we update most of our guides every year. But we're not perfect. Things change. Hotels cut services. Museums change hours. Charming cafés lose charm. If our writer didn't quite capture the essence of a place, tell us how you'd do it differently. If any of our descriptions are inaccurate or inadequate, we'll incorporate your changes in the next edition and will correct factual errors at fodors.com immediately.

Tell us what to include. You probably have had fantastic travel experiences that aren't yet in Fodor's. Why not share them with a community of like-minded travelers? Maybe you chanced upon a beach or bistro or B&B that you don't want to keep to yourself. Tell us why we should include it. And share your discoveries and experiences with everyone directly at fodors.com. Your input may lead us to add a new listing or highlight a place we cover with a "Highly Recommended" star or with our highest rating, "Fodor's Choice."

How to reach us. Share your opinion instantly through our online feedback center at fodors.com/contact-us.

You and travelers like you are the heart of the Fodor's community. Make our community richer by sharing your experiences. Be a Fodor's correspondent.

Happy Traveling!

Tim Jarrell, Publisher

CONTENTS

ABOUT THIS BOOK

Our Ratings

Sometimes you find terrific travel experiences and sometimes they just find you. But usually the burden is on you to select the right combination of experiences. That's where our ratings come in.

As travelers we've all discovered a place so wonderful that its worthiness is obvious. And sometimes that place is so unique that superlatives don't do it justice: you just have to be there to know. These sights, properties, and experiences get our highest rating, **Fodor's Choice**, indicated by orange stars throughout this book.

Black stars highlight sights and properties we deem **Highly Recommended**, places that our writers, editors, and readers praise again and again for consistency and excellence.

By default, there's another category: any place we include in this book is by definition worth your time, unless we say otherwise. And we will.

Disagree with any of our choices? Care to nominate a place or suggest that we rate one more highly? Visit our feedback center at www.fodors.com/feedback.

Budget Well

Hotel- and restaurant-price categories from ¢ to $$$$ are defined in the opening pages of each chapter. For attractions, we always give standard adult admission fees; reductions are usually available for children, students, and senior citizens. Want to pay with plastic? **AE, D, DC, MC, V** after restaurant and hotel listings indicate whether American Express, Discover, Diners Club, MasterCard, and Visa are accepted.

Restaurants

Unless we state otherwise, restaurants are open for lunch and dinner daily. We mention dress only when there's a specific requirement and reservations only when they're essential or not accepted—it's always best to book ahead.

Hotels

Hotels have private bath, phone, TV, and air-conditioning and operate on the European Plan (aka EP, meaning without meals), unless we specify that they use the Continental Plan (CP, with a Continental breakfast), Breakfast Plan (BP, with a full breakfast), or Modified American Plan (MAP, with breakfast and dinner). We always list facilities but not whether you'll be charged an extra fee to use them, so when pricing accommodations, find out what's included.

Many Listings

★	Fodor's Choice
★	Highly recommended
✉	Physical address
✛	Directions or Map coordinates
⌖	Mailing address
☎	Telephone
📠	Fax
⊕	On the Web
✍	E-mail
🎫	Admission fee
☉	Open/closed times
Ⓜ	Metro stations
⊟	Credit cards

Hotels & Restaurants

🏨	Hotel
↵	Number of rooms
⌂	Facilities
🍽	Meal plans
✗	Restaurant
⌕	Reservations
🏛	Dress code
⌇	Smoking
🍸	BYOB

Outdoors

🏌	Golf
⛺	Camping

Other

☾	Family-friendly
⇨	See also
✉	Branch address
☞	Take note

Experience
Cape Cod

WORD OF MOUTH

"On Cape Cod, get out on the water if you can:
a seal watch, a whale watch, or a ferry trip to
Martha's Vineyard or Nantucket will all give you
an entirely different perspective of the Cape. Eat
the local bounty: clams, scallops, oysters, cod,
flounder, lobster, fried anything, and of course ice
cream and more ice cream. Go to an art show,
crafts fair, outdoor band concert, or summer stock
theater performance. Do nothing but sit on the
beach with your feet in the warm sand, gaze out
at the sparkling water, and contemplate the meaning of cold, dismal winters."

—bowsprit

CAPE COD TODAY

The People

Although the Cape swells with visitors in summer, this world-famous vacationland has nearly 220,000 permanent residents, plus another 15,000 on Martha's Vineyard and 10,000 on Nantucket. (In total, that's nearly half as many people as there are in Boston.) And though the Northeast's population has not gained significantly in recent years, the Cape has boomed, having more than tripled since 1960—it's the fastest-growing region in Massachusetts.

Retirees and empty nesters (the region is home to 11 of the state's oldest median-age communities), artists, telecommuters, and small-business owners have contributed to the region's growth. Additionally, the Upper Cape is increasingly home to commuters who work in Boston or just south of the city.

Cape Cod is less racially diverse than other parts of Massachusetts, its population is about 95% Caucasian, 2% African American, and less than 1% each Native American and Asian. That being said, Native Americans have always been a dynamic force on the Cape—Mashpee has a sizable population of members of the Wampanoag nation, as does Martha's Vineyard.

The Economy

Tourism is the Cape's leading industry in terms of both revenue and employment, but business leaders and local chambers of commerce are always searching for new ways to diversify the local economy. Compared with the rest of the state, the Cape has a very high cost of living—yet average wages are significantly lower than elsewhere in Massachusetts. And although the prices of homes on the Cape have dropped dramatically since 2005, it's still a remarkably pricey place to buy a home (with the median price around $350,000).

The region's economic challenges have led to an increased number of older residents (who can better afford to live here) and a steady outflow of younger adults who are unable to find sufficiently high-paying jobs. With these obstacles in mind, the Cape has aggressively encouraged the development of viable and less seasonal industries such as marine science, technology, education, the arts, and alternative energy.

One somewhat controversial development has been a large-scale "wind farm" in Nantucket Sound, comprising some 130 turbines, each about 260 feet tall and located several miles offshore. The project is slowly moving ahead, and 2010 saw the developers signing a lease with the federal government.

The Environment and the Outdoors

Cape Codders are fiercely protective of the environment—despite some occasionally rampant development in a few communities, planners have been careful to preserve nature here and encourage responsible, ecoconscious building. Nearly 30% of the Cape's 412 square mi are protected from development, and another 35% have not yet been developed—on Nantucket and Martha's Vineyard, the percentages of protected land are far higher. It's not surprising, then, that opportunities for sports and recreation abound here, as the Cape is rife with biking and hiking trails, serene beaches, and waterways for boating and fishing.

The Politics

Cape Cod is one of the most liberal Democrat-leaning regions of one of America's most liberal Democrat-leaning states (only 12% of Massachusetts registered

voters are Republicans). Although popular with tourists of all political stripes, the Cape has a year-round population that falls heavily to the left on political issues. There are some slight exceptions—blue-blooded Chatham, preppy Nantucket, and the swanky Martha's Vineyard community of Edgartown are stereotypically, if somewhat teasingly, referred to by some as Republican strongholds.

Make no mistake about it: the Kennedy legacy still looms large here. Cape Cod and the islands general revel in their progressive labels, with the Outer Cape towns of Wellfleet, Truro, and Provincetown (with its highly visible gay community) cultivating an especially artsy, bohemian vibe.

The Cuisine

Cape Cod kitchens have long been closely associated with seafood—the waters off the Cape and the islands yield a bounty of lobsters, clams, scallops, and myriad other fish that make their way into everything from chowders and stews to pasta bowls and leafy salads.

Culturally, the region's strong Italian and Portuguese influences have accounted for the large number of pizza and pasta restaurants; you'll also find quite a few spots serving Portuguese specialties like *bacalau* (salt cod), kale soup, and various Portuguese breads and sweets.

But while culinary traditions remain strong in these parts, the Cape has—like other upmarket parts of the country—experienced a huge influx of restaurants serving globally influenced, contemporary cooking. Menus at the Cape's top eateries now routinely feature such far-flung ingredients as Thai lemongrass, Moroccan *harissa* (hot chili) sauce, and Japanese eggplant. And chefs now routinely source from around the Cape and elsewhere in southern New England for locally (and often organically) raised produce and meat.

The Architecture

Virtually every period style of residential American architecture is well represented on Cape Cod, including—of course—that seminal form named for the very region, the Cape-style house. These low, one-and-a-half-story domiciles with clapboard or shingle (more traditionally the latter in these parts) siding and gable roofs have been a fixture throughout Cape Cod since the late 17th century.

Along the main streets of Wellfleet, Barnstable, Sandwich, Falmouth, Provincetown, Nantucket, and Edgartown, you'll also find grand Georgian and Federal mansions from the colonial era, as well as handsome Greek Revival, Italianate, and Second Empire houses that date to Victorian times. Many of the most prominent residences were built for ship captains and sea merchants.

In recent decades, the region has seen an influx of angular, glassy, contemporary homes, many with soaring windows and skylights and massive wraparound porches that take advantage of their enviable sea views.

WHAT'S WHERE

Numbers refer to chapter numbers.

2 The Upper Cape. This area is the closest to the Massachusetts mainland. Cape Cod's oldest towns are here (Sandwich, for one, was settled in 1637), plus there are fine beaches and little museums. A growing full-time population makes it feel more residential than resortlike. Falmouth, the region's commercial center, has a tidy downtown with brick storefronts housing local businesses.

3 The Mid Cape. The Mid Cape has a bit of a Jekyll-and-Hyde complex. Route 6A is home to sophisticated colonial-era hamlets lined with antiques shops, smart taverns, and romantic bed-and-breakfasts, whereas Route 28 is crammed with motels and miniature golf courses. In the midst of it all sits Hyannis, the Cape's unofficial capital.

4 The Lower Cape. Casual clam shacks, lovely light-houses, funky art galleries—the things typically associated with the Cape are found here in abundance. Chatham has a fine downtown filled with shops, restaurants, and galleries that make it ideal for leisurely strolls. The region's most stellar attractions, though, may be the natural

ones: Monomoy National Wildlife Refuge, Nickerson State Park, and the start of the Cape Cod National Seashore. The beaches in Brewster and Orleans are treasured for long walks at low tide.

5 The Outer Cape. The windswept narrow "forearm" of the Cape—less than 2 mi wide in some places—is famous for its landscape of sand dunes, crashing surf, and scrubby pines. Wellfleet is known for its art galleries; quiet Truro is the Cape's least developed town; and frenetic, fun-loving Provincetown (the peninsula's "fist") is a leading gay getaway.

6 Martha's Vineyard. The Vineyard lies 5 mi off the Cape's southwest tip. The Down-Island towns are the most popular and most populated. But much of what makes this island special is found in its rural Up-Island reaches where dirt roads lead past ponds, cranberry bogs, and conservation lands.

7 Nantucket. Chic and charming, Nantucket is some 25 mi south of Hyannis. Ferries dock in historic Nantucket Town, where tourism services are concentrated. The rest of the island is mostly residential (trophy houses abound), and many roads terminate in tiny beach communities.

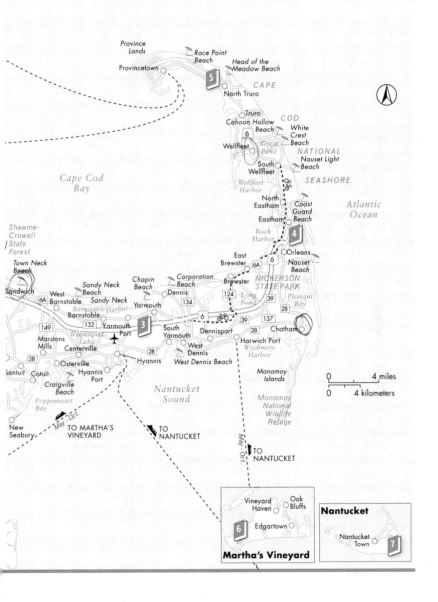

Cape Cod

Province Lands

Provincetown

Race Point Beach

Head of the Meadow Beach

5

North Truro

CAPE

Truro

Cahoon Hollow Beach

White Crest Beach

Wellfleet

Great Pond

COD

NATIONAL

Nauset Light Beach

South Wellfleet

SEASHORE

Wellfleet Harbor

North Eastham

Coast Guard Beach

Atlantic Ocean

Cape Cod Bay

Eastham

Rock Harbor

4

Orleans

Nauset Beach

Shawme-Crowell State Forest

East Brewster

6A

6

Town Neck Beach

Corporation Beach

Brewster

NICKERSON STATE PARK

Sandwich

6A

West Barnstable

Sandy Neck Beach

Chapin Beach

Dennis

134

124

Long Pond

39

Pleasant Bay

Sandy Neck

Barnstable Harbor

Yarmouth

6

39

137

28

149

Barnstable

132

Yarmouth Port

3

South Yarmouth

Dennisport

28

Chatham

Marstons Mills

Wequaquet Lake

West Dennis

Harwich Port

Wychmere Harbor

28

Centerville

Hyannis

West Dennis Beach

Santuit

Cotuit

Osterville

Hyannis Port

Monomoy Islands

Craigville Beach

Popponesset Bay

Nantucket Sound

Monomoy National Wildlife Refuge

0   4 miles

0   4 kilometers

New Seabury

May–Oct.

TO MARTHA'S VINEYARD

TO NANTUCKET

May–Oct.

TO NANTUCKET

Vineyard Haven

Oak Bluffs

Nantucket

Edgartown

6

Martha's Vineyard

Nantucket Town

7

CAPE COD PLANNER

Getting Around

Bus Travel. Cape Cod Regional Transit Authority (☎ 800/352-7155 ⊕ www.capecodtransit.org) provides service throughout the Cape. **Martha's Vineyard Transit Authority** (☎ 508/693-9940 ⊕ www.vineyardtransit.com) is a great way to get around Martha's Vineyard. **Nantucket Regional Transit Authority** (☎ 508/228-7025 ⊕ www.shuttlenantucket.com) circles Nantucket.

Car Travel. Unless you focus your attention on a single community, you'll probably need a car. Be aware that taking a vehicle onto Nantucket and Martha's Vineyard ferries is expensive, as is renting.

Ferry Travel. Freedom Cruise Line (☎ 508/432-8999 ⊕ www.nantucketislandferry.com) travels between Harwich Port and Nantucket. **Hy-Line** (☎ 508/778-2600 or 800/492-8082 ⊕ www.hy-linecruises.com) goes from Hyannis to Martha's Vineyard and Nantucket. **Island Queen** (☎ 508/548-4800 ⊕ www.islandqueen.com) connects Falmouth and Martha's Vineyard. The **Steamship Authority** (☎ 508/477-8600 ⊕ www.steamshipauthority.com) sails from Woods Hole to Martha's Vineyard, and from Hyannis to Nantucket.

Getting Here

For more information about traveling to and around Cape Cod and the Islands, see Travel Smart Cape Cod at the back of the book.

Air Travel. The major air gateways are Boston's Logan International Airport (BOS) and Providence's T. F. Green International Airport (PVD). Smaller municipal airports are located in Barnstable (HYA), Martha's Vineyard (MVY), Nantucket (ACK), and Provincetown (PVC).

Car Travel. Cape Cod is easily reached from Boston via Route 3 and from Providence via I–195. Once you cross Cape Cod Canal, you can follow U.S. 6 all the way to the tip of the Cape. Without any traffic, it takes about an hour to 90 minutes to reach the Upper Cape (the portion nearest to mainland Massachusetts) from either Boston or Providence. Because delays getting onto and off Cape Cod are common throughout summer, allow an extra 30 to 60 minutes' travel time when driving in peak periods. Saturdays, when weekly rentals begin, are a particular challenge.

Bus Travel. The Cape is served by the rather misleadingly named **Plymouth & Brockton Street Railway Company** (☎ 508/746-0378 ⊕ www.p-b.com). The line offers convenient connections from Logan International Airport and other mainland locales.

Ferry Travel. Bay State Cruise Company (☎ 617/748-1428 or 877/783-3779 ⊕ www.baystatecruisecompany.com) operates high-speed ferries between Boston and Provincetown from late spring to mid-October. **Boston Harbor Cruises** (☎ 617/227-4321 or 877/733-9425 ⊕ www.bostonharborcruises.com) is a good option for speedy trips between Boston and Provincetown. **Capt. John Boats** (☎ 508/747-2400 or 800/242-2469 ⊕ www.provincetownferry.com) runs between Plymouth and Provincetown. **New England Fast Ferry** (☎ 866/683-3779 ⊕ www.nefastferry.com) shuttles passengers between New Bedford and Martha's Vineyard. **Vineyard Fast Ferry** (☎ 401/295-4040 ⊕ www.vineyardfastferry.com) runs between North Kingstown, Rhode Island, and Martha's Vineyard.

1

WHEN TO GO

The Cape and islands teem with activity during high season: roughly Memorial Day to Labor Day or, in many cases, until Columbus Day. If you're dreaming of a classic shore vacation with lazy days at the beach, clambakes, and band concerts on the village green, this is prime time.

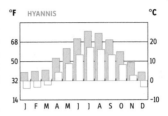

Needless to say, everyone knows it—which translates into daunting crowds and high costs. The good news is that the region is increasingly becoming a year-round destination. In fact, fall has begun to rival summer in popularity, at least on weekends through late October, when the weather is temperate and the scenery remarkable. A growing number of restaurants, shops, and hotels are remaining open in winter, too, making the area desirable even during the coldest months. On the islands and more far-flung sections of the Cape, though, many continue to close down January through March.

Climate

Thanks to the warming effects of the Gulf Stream, the region enjoys fairly moderate weather most of the year, with highs typically in the upper 70s and 80s in summer, and in the upper 30s and lower 40s in winter. Snow and rain are not uncommon during the cooler months, and it can be windy any time. The following are average daily maximum and minimum temperatures for Hyannis. Average temperatures on the islands are similar.

For current local weather, coastal marine forecasts, and tide times, call WQRC's recorded information line in Hyannis (☎ 508/771–5522).

TOP CAPE COD ATTRACTIONS

Even if you haven't already visited Cape Cod and the outer islands, you can likely conjure up a mental picture of "sand dunes and salty air, quaint little villages here and there." But that's just the beginning. On the ground, be sure to check out these superlative sites.

Cape Cod National Seashore. John F. Kennedy certainly knew a good thing when he saw it. During his presidency, Kennedy marked off a magnificent 40-mi swath of the coast from Chatham to Provincetown, protecting it for future generations. Today the seashore—comprising marshlands, uplands, cranberry bogs, and, of course, blissful beaches—remains the Cape's signature site. The preserve and exhibit-filled Salt Pond Visitor Center are open year-round.

Heritage Museums and Gardens. Once a spectacular estate for the Lilly family, Heritage Museums and Gardens in Sandwich is a wonderland. More than 100 acres of grounds are in bloom most of the year—the rhododendrons are extraordinary, as are the hostas and daylilies—and miles of walking paths traverse the property. There are also three galleries devoted to American art, an impressive antique car collection, and a working early-20th-century carousel.

Massachusetts Audubon Wellfleet Bay Wildlife Sanctuary. Scenic trails and a broad selection of naturalist-led programs make the sanctuary a favorite all-season migration stop for Cape vacationers. (It's pretty popular with birds, too.) The 1,100-acre haven is on the North Atlantic flyway, and more than 250 different species have been identified within its borders. Don't forget to bring your binoculars!

Provincetown. Brimming with history—from brigands, whalers, and sea captains to artists, playwrights, and poets—Provincetown is a place of pure exuberance. Past and present live side-by-side here; the town library enfolds a massive replica of a century-old fishing schooner, and the working wharf displays the bounty from a sunken pirate ship. You can enjoy great theater, listen to poets read their work, or visit dozens of excellent art galleries.

Cape Cod Museum of Natural History. No question about it: this museum in Brewster has engaging displays, including a working beehive, a live osprey cam, and tanks filled with an assortment of Cape critters. Yet these account for only part of the facility's appeal. The museum, which sits on an 80-acre property, also boasts its own nature trails, hosts outdoor ecological activities for all ages, and organizes a series of off-site excursions.

Monomoy National Wildlife Refuge. Strike out on one of the trails at Monomoy National Wildlife Refuge, near Chatham, and leave the modern world behind. A major nesting and stopover spot for migrating shorebirds, the region is a favorite of photographers and birdwatchers. Animal lovers will come face-to-face with plenty of gray and harbor seals.

Whaling Museum. You don't have to be a marine biologist, a history buff, or a fan of *Moby-Dick* to appreciate the Whaling Museum in Nantucket. Devoted to the industry on which this island's reputation (and much of its wealth) originally depended, it contains everything from deadly harpoons and delicate scrimshaw carvings to a fully rigged whaleboat. The undisputed star attraction, though, is a 46-foot sperm whale skeleton.

CAPE COD'S TOP EXPERIENCES

If you want to get a genuine sense of local culture, start by sampling these tried-and-true Cape activities.

Visiting Lighthouses

In addition to traditional Cape-style houses, Cape Cod is known for another type of building—the lighthouses that rise along its coast like architectural exclamation marks. Some are active, others decommissioned; a few even offer tours. And a trek to any one of them is truly illuminating. Although each has its own personality, the literal highlight is Truro's Highland Light (the Cape's tallest). Eastham's Nauset Light ranks among the most beautiful, and the Chatham and Nobska Lights afford stellar views. The bluff-top Aquinnah Light on Martha's Vineyard and Nantucket's boldly striped Sankaty Head Light are island options.

Biking the Trails

Well-developed trails and relatively flat terrain make the Cape a magnet for avid and occasional cyclists alike. The Cape Cod Rail Trail from South Dennis to South Wellfleet is the definitive route. Mostly flat, it's an easy ride through woods and past ponds and plenty of pleasant stops.

However, the Cape Cod National Seashore also maintains impressive trails (including an arduous one through undulating dunes), and Falmouth's Shining Sea Trail offers an easy 3½-mi coastal route with sublime views of Vineyard Sound. Truth be told, there are good places to ride and, if need be, rent bikes in just about any town on Cape Cod. Martha's Vineyard and Nantucket—each of which has dedicated bike paths and reliable cycle services—are equally enticing.

Setting Sail

Considering there is "water, water everywhere," it's no wonder that one of the optimal ways to appreciate the Cape and islands is from a boat. Area tour operators and outfitters offer everything from sunset schooner cruises to charter fishing expeditions. Mid-April through October, whale-watching adventures (from Barnstable and Provincetown) are particularly popular. On a good day, Ahab wannabes might spot humpbacks, finbacks, minkes, and more.

Hopping one of the region's many ferries is yet another great way to experience the high seas. Prefer to paddle your own canoe or sail your own Sunfish? Rental companies can set you up with almost any kind of watercraft.

Browsing the Galleries

The Cape was a prominent art colony in the 19th century, and today its concentration of galleries is among the highest in the nation. Spend a few hours idly browsing through them. Or take a more organized approach by following one of the Arts & Artisan Trails on Cape Cod, Martha's Vineyard, and Nantucket.

Be sure to set aside some time for the Provincetown Art Association and Museum. Because it focuses on artists with a Cape connection, local up-and-comers share wall space with A-listers like John Singer Sargent and Andy Warhol. The PAAM also sponsors a variety of classes year-round for the artistically inclined.

CAPE COD'S BEST BEACHES

Each of us defines the "perfect" beach differently, and there are many more to choose from. Cape Cod alone has more than 150—enough to keep the most inveterate beachcomber busy all year long. So whatever your taste, there is one to fit your criteria.

For Traditionalists

Locals contend that Nauset Light, Coast Guard, Marconi, and Race Point, all set within the Cape Cod National Seashore, are the quintessential beaches. And it's hard to argue with that assessment. Combining serious surf, sweeping expanses of sand, magnificent dunes, and mesmerizing views, the four biggies do offer the greatest wow factor.

For Families

Old Silver—a long crescent of soft white sand in North Falmouth—is more than just another pretty beach. Parents love this Buzzards Bay locale for its comparatively calm, warm water, and kids adore poking around the shallow tidal pools full of sea life.

For Photographers

Perhaps no beach in this camera-ready region is more photogenic than that below the Aquinnah Cliffs on Martha's Vineyard. It is especially stunning late in the day because these multicolored clay cliffs face west, allowing for gorgeous shots at sunset.

For Surfers

Wave-blasted White Crest Beach in Wellfleet is one of the preeminent places on the peninsula to Hang 10. If you didn't bring your own board, rentals are readily available at SickDay Surf Shop, Pump House Surf Co., and Nauset Sports.

For Sand Castle Connoisseurs

You can play with a shovel and pail anywhere, but beachgoers with architectural aspirations know Jetties Beach on Nantucket has the finest building material. Hordes gather to prove it during Sandcastle & Sculpture Day, held annually in mid-August.

For History Lovers

In this centuries-old area even a fun-in-the-sun day can double as a history lesson. At Eastham's popular First Encounter Beach, a bronze plaque marks the spot where Myles Standish and his Mayflower buddies first encountered Native Americans in 1620.

For Freshwater Fans

Don't like bathing in brine? Inland, the Cape has dozens of freshwater kettle holes that were carved in the far-distant past by receding glaciers. Aside from warm, salt-free water, some—like Scargo Lake in Dennis—are also blessed with sandy beaches.

For Bird-Watchers

On the barrier beaches of the Monomoy National Wildlife Refuge, accessible only by boat, you're bound to see more sandpipers and plovers than people. Summer through early fall, shorebirds and waterfowl flock here to nest, rest, and feast in tidal flats.

For Night Owls

After hours it's tough to beat Cahoon Hollow Beach in Wellfleet. The water here is chilly. The music at the Beachcomber bar and restaurant is, on the other hand, hot. Bands play for an appreciative crowd most nights from Memorial Day to Labor Day.

CAPE COD'S BEST CLAM SHACKS

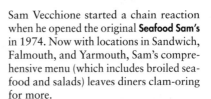

If you are what you eat, then most Cape Codders would be a clam. It should go without saying that a land named for a type of fish would abound with opportunities to sample tasty seafood, and the region does not disappoint.

Some of New England's most talented chefs work in high-end restaurants on the Cape and islands, yet no-frills seafood shacks still have an undeniable appeal. Their food is authentic, their prices are reasonable, and even if their decor can be pretty basic, most serve up dishes with a side order of scenery.

Since 1976 **Cap'n Frosty's** in Dennis Village has been demonstrating just how diverse the humble clam can be. Whether you have a hankering for clam chowder, clam cakes, clam rolls, fried clams, or a high-heaped clam combo plate, you will find them all at this modest spot. It's always packed, even in the middle of the week.

There is more to the **Clam Shack** in Falmouth than those fresh, fat-bellied mollusks for which it is named. Killer lobster rolls, plump scallops cooked to perfection, and a lovely location right on the harbor have all helped solidify its reputation as a Cape Cod institution.

Mac's Seafood in Wellfleet is a hole-in-the-wall take-out joint with perfect views of sailboats and fishing trawlers. For those who can't get enough of its oysters or scallops, Mac's also operates a sit-down restaurant called Mac's Shack, plus several seafood markets.

Don't let the name fool you. Sure the **Kream 'N Kone** serves soft-serve ice cream, but the main course—in fact, the main draw—at this vintage West Dennis eatery is deep-fried seafood. Unless you're concerned about your cholesterol, opt for the clam plate with fries and onion rings.

Sam Vecchione started a chain reaction when he opened the original **Seafood Sam's** in 1974. Now with locations in Sandwich, Falmouth, and Yarmouth, Sam's comprehensive menu (which includes broiled seafood and salads) leaves diners clam-oring for more.

Baxter's Boathouse in Hyannis has been doling out delicious short-order seafood for more than 50 years. Outdoor tables overlook the picturesque harbor, and a passageway also leads to Baxter's Boat House Club, where the same menu is offered in a more upscale atmosphere.

Another memorable place to grab a bite is the **Bite,** a tiny roadside joint on Martha's Vineyard. If the promise of quahog chowder and fresh flounder-and-chips weren't enough to reel you in, the location in the postcard-pretty fishing village of Menemsha would do the trick.

Arnold's Lobster & Clam Bar in Eastham is always busy—and once you see the menu, you will understand why. The standard deep-fried fare here is supplemented with shucked-while-you-wait oysters, raw bar clams, steamed lobsters, and New England "chowdah."

Go for the whole-belly clams at the diminutive **Sir Cricket's Fish and Chips** in Orleans. It sits next to a good fish market, so it's no surprise that catch of the day is incredibly fresh. Table seating is minimal; opt for takeout and head across the road to the grounds of the Orleans windmill, overlooking peaceful Town Cove.

CAPE COD'S BEST ICE CREAM SHOPS

I scream. You scream. We all scream for ice cream. But perhaps nowhere is the collective din heard more clearly than on the Cape and islands. The fascination with ice cream here borders on obsession. Devotees endlessly discuss the merits of traditional hard ice cream versus newfangled gelato, and waffle cones versus sugar ones. Butterfat content is a hotly debated topic, as is the ratio of add-in to ice cream.

Indeed, the only thing aficionados seem to agree on is that the most notable offerings come from mom-and-pop parlors that make their own premium—dare we say artisanal—products. Here's the inside scoop.

The **Ice Cream Smuggler** in Dennis Village prides itself on using only the freshest ingredients, from just-picked berries to spiced apples and rum-soaked raisins. If you're worried about your waistline, frozen yogurts, sorbets, and sugar-free ice cream are on the menu.

In Centerville, **Four Seas Ice Cream** is the sentimental favorite. Established in 1934, this Cape Cod landmark has a retro ambience, efficient service, and back-to-basic flavors (Penuche Pecan is about as fancy as it gets).

Visitors to Martha's Vineyard aren't left out in the cold. They go crazy for **Mad Martha's Ice Cream Parlors** in Edgartown, Vineyard Haven, and Oak Bluffs. Indecisive eaters who can't choose between the two dozen flavors can always request a 12-scoop Pig's Delight.

Not surprisingly, Dennisport's **Sundae School Ice Cream Parlor** specializes in old-school sundaes. Classic hot fudge vies with seasonal options (including fresh blueberry and raspberry) for the "best in class" award. Other locations are in East Orleans and Harwich Port.

The place to go for an ice-cream sandwich is the **Ice Cream Sandwich** in (you guessed it!) Sandwich, where the titular treat consists of a heaping scoop of vanilla wedged between two homemade chocolate chip cookies. Ice-cream cones, cannolis, and cakes are also available.

Need proof that "la vita" really is "dolce" in Provincetown? Just take a look inside the freezer case at **I Dream of Gelato.** More than 160 rotating flavors are made on-site in small batches (amaretto, tiramisu, and sugar-free cappuccino among them), guaranteeing a true taste of Italy.

Since 1889, **Hallet's**—a country drugstore in Yarmouth Port—has served justly famous ice-cream sodas, made from a secret recipe at a marble fountain. Plop yourself down on a swivel stool, place your order; then prepare for a genuine Norman Rockwell moment.

A relative newcomer on the scene, **Cape Cod Creamery** is already challenging established favorites for the "crème de la crème" crown. Located in South Yarmouth, it gives frozen concoctions a local twist, dishing out flavors like Craigville Caramel Crunch and Great Island Grapenut.

The family-run **Ice Cream Café** in Orleans makes a large selection of hard ice cream—favorites include key lime pie, ginger, and dark chocolate almond—and custom-blended yogurts, sorbets, and fruit smoothies. There's even sugar-free ice cream.

CAPE COD WITH KIDS

Cape Cod seems almost purpose-designed for families, and though this is slightly less the case on the islands, you will discover plenty of kid-oriented attractions and activities across the region. Beaches aside, the obvious place to visit is Route 28, from about Hyannis to Harwich Port, as it's lined with arcades and minigolf courses. Local museums are also a reliable bet, because most work overtime to engage young guests. The **Cape Cod Museum of Art** in Dennis Village gives workshops for wee ones; and Nantucket's **Whaling Museum** has its own Children's Discovery Room. Want more? Try these family-tested favorites.

Learning and fun go hand in hand at the hands-on **Cape Cod Children's Museum** in Mashpee. The interactive venue, aimed primarily at the 8-and-under set, comes complete with an indoor planetarium, a puppet theater, and an arghh-rated 30-foot pirate play ship.

Fans of the Peter Cottontail books can see artifacts relating to the author's life—and, in summer, hear readings of some of his timeless stories—at the **Thornton W. Burgess Museum** in Sandwich. On select days fuzzy animals (like those that inspired Burgess) put in an appearance.

Aside from the games themselves, there's plenty of fun to be had while the collegiate players of the **Cape Cod Baseball League** are at bat. Many diamonds have playgrounds, impromptu games of catch, and ice cream trucks. Kids age 6 on up can sign up for weekly baseball clinics with the league's players.

Although most area boat excursions are appropriate for children, some are more engaging than others. The **Viking Princess**, in Provincetown, routinely draws rave reviews because it teaches budding marine

biologists all the tricks of the trade. In the Chatham area, the **Rip Ryder** takes families out for thrilling explorations of seal colonies and nesting areas of such rarely spotted birds as the piping plover.

For more up-close animal encounters visit the **National Marine Fisheries Service Aquarium** in Woods Hole, America's oldest continuously operating research aquarium. Aside from the expected fish tanks, it has cool touch tanks and a seal pool. You're even welcome behind the scenes to watch staffers work.

Get a genuine glimpse of rural life at the **Farm Institute** on Martha's Vineyard. A great variety of programs for kids of all ages introduces little ones to barnyard life of all sorts, from chickens to cows, and teaches about planting and harvesting.

Cue the calliope music. Taking a spin on Oak Bluffs' **Flying Horses Carousel**, built in 1876, lets contemporary kids experience life in the past lane on Martha's Vineyard. Another antique merry-go-round (this one circa 1912) awaits young riders at the **Heritage Museums and Gardens** in Sandwich. The attraction's Hidden Hollow outdoor play area is also popular with kids.

Culture on the Cape isn't for adults only. Productions at the **Harwich Junior Theatre** are tailor-made for younger audiences, and the **Cape Playhouse** and **Cape Cod Melody Tent** (in Dennis and Hyannis respectively) both host a summer children's theater series.

Don't forget to scan **community calendars** for family-friendly events like the Mashpee Powwow, held annually in early July. Three days of dance contests, drumming, fireball games, and clambakes culminate in the crowning of the Mashpee Wampanoag Indian princess.

FREE AND ALMOST FREE

It's easy to spend a fortune on the Cape and islands. It's also unnecessary, because some of the best things in life here actually are free—and you don't have to look far to find them. Take a top-rated site like the **Cape Cod National Seashore.** You may pay to access its swimming beaches (you can buy a seasonal pass)—but the Salt Pond Visitor Center houses a free museum, and the park itself hosts a bevy of free programs ranging from tidal flat forays and fishing demos to alfresco yoga classes. Biking the Cape Cod Rail Trail, window-shopping in Wellfleet, people-watching in P'town, gazing at the stars (whether celestial or cinematic) in Edgartown: these activities are priceless, too. Here are some more options for gratuitous fun:

No-cost **summer concerts**—staged weekly in many communities—are music to parsimonious ears. Chatham's town band strikes up on Friday night in Kate Gould Park. Consult local event calendars for noteworthy alternatives.

You can discover up-and-coming artists during **art openings** at local galleries. Many towns—Provincetown, Wellfleet, and Dennis, to name a few—have designated nights when you can stroll from gallery to gallery and experience an array of artistic styles.

The **Cape Cod Canal Visitor Center**, run by the U.S. Army Corp of Engineers, offers free guided walks and bicycle rides along the canal. You can also relax in a deck chair while watching the boats float past.

Frugal fish lovers will be happy to hear that the **National Marine Fisheries Service Aquarium** in Woods Hole, and **Sandwich Fish Hatchery** both waive entry fees. In peak season, tours of the **Woods Hole Oceanographic Institution** are free as well.

The **Cape Cod Baseball League** is one of the sporting world's best bargains. Mid-June to mid-August, the "Stars of Tomorrow" suit up with one of 10 teams. And since all are nonprofit, the most you'll have to fork over is a small donation.

Taking self-guided tours of the oh-so-fragrant **Cape Cod Lavender Farm** in Harwich when the plants are ready for harvest in June and July and **Mytoi** (a 14-acre Japanese-inspired garden on Chappaquiddick Island) lets you get a double dose of flower power without dropping a dime.

The upwardly mobile are free to drink in divine vistas from the top of the **Scargo Tower** in Dennis. On a clear day, the 30-foot structure offers unsurpassed views of Scargo Lake, Cape Cod Bay, and distant Provincetown.

Penny-pinching oenophiles, rejoice! **Truro Vineyards** and East Falmouth's **Cape Cod Winery** each offer complimentary tours. Tastings are a deal, too, because the $5–$7 fee includes a souvenir glass.

Anyone hungry for information—or just plain hungry—can take a free tour of the **Cape Cod Potato Chip Factory** in Hyannis. You'll learn how the kettle-cooked, über-crunchy chips are made and leave with a sample bag to snack on.

You can peer into the past at **Harris-Black House, Swift-Daley House, Captain Edward Penniman House,** and a handful of other heritage buildings in Brewster and Eastham. Admission is free; however, donations are appreciated.

Put your best foot forward with a free walk around the village of **Sandwich** or along **Nantucket's Black Heritage Trail.** The former is organized by the Sandwich Glass Museum, the latter by the Friends of the African Meeting House.

LIKE A LOCAL

Cape residents always know the best hidden beaches, most reliable seafood shacks, and least-crowded spots for shopping strolls and scenic bike rides. If you want to get to know the heart and soul of Cape Cod, and see some of its most alluring diversions, follow the lead of the year-rounders.

Commune with the Flora and Fauna

Area residents have worked hard to preserve the breathtaking natural beauty and precious wildlife indigenous to the Cape and islands. For sense of this, visit one of parks and preserves favored by locals, from the Tidal Flats Recreation Area on Cape Cod Canal to Mytoi's serene Japanese-inspired garden on Martha's Vineyard. On the Upper Cape, amble over the Sandwich Boardwalk, a wood-planked promontory spanning a salt marsh and sloping rugosa-rose-patch dunes that draw migratory seabirds.

Secret beaches are another locals' draw—try the quietly spectacular Fisher Road Beach in Truro, the tidal pools of secluded Robbin's Hill Beach in Brewster, or dune-backed Chapin Beach in Dennis.

Shop Where the Regulars Go

The most memorable shops on the Cape eschew touristy T-shirts and knickknacks in favor of high-quality, stylish clothing and crafts that appeal to discerning regulars.

Falmouth Center is one of the Cape's top spots for a retail ramble, home to such sophisticated boutiques as Maxwell & Co. and Rosie Cheeks. Main Street in bustling Hyannis is another ground-zero for shopping, having morphed steadily over the years from prosaic to prestigious—check out Oak & Ivory for nautical goods and Puritan of Cape Cod for fine threads.

Provincetown's vaunted Marine Specialties, Inc. is a local institution, thanks to its immense selection of odd lots, salvaged goods, model ships, wooden buoys, and feather boas.

Dine with the Locals

In nearly every town across the Cape and islands, churches host summer suppers to give a healthy boost to the collection plate. These meals start cooking in late June and continue until Labor Day. Menus vary, but most are classic Cape Cod: clam chowder, fish-and-chips, and lobster rolls. There's always an alternative option, usually chicken fingers or hot dogs, to appeal to kids.

Other organizations offer similar meals; the Eastham Elks Lodge sponsors a fish fry every Friday throughout the year. It's a great way to meet locals, get tips on their favorite spots, and enjoy a tasty meal that's easy on the wallet.

Attend a Gallery Opening

Visitors often drop by one of the Cape's dozens of galleries—there are especially large concentrations in Provincetown, Wellfleet, Nantucket, and both Edgartown and Vineyard Haven on Martha's Vineyard.

But for a more meaningful local art experience, and a chance to visit with artists, attend a gallery opening. These are most often held Friday and Saturday evenings, and they sometimes feature live music, art lectures, and hors d'oeuvres and wine. Check local newspapers for listings of upcoming gallery events.

BEST FESTIVALS AND EVENTS

April

Gardeners, this bud's for you! The daffodil—a frilly flower that signals the arrival of spring—takes center stage at Nantucket's **Daffodil Festival Weekend** (☎ 508/228–1700 ⊕ www.nantucketchamber.org). The **Brewster in Bloom Festival** (☎ 800/399–2967 ⊕ www.brewsterinbloom.org) is a "perennial" favorite.

May

The peninsula celebrates all things nautical during **Cape Cod Maritime Days** (☎ 508/362–3225 ⊕ www.capecodmaritimedays.com). Around 75 events, held Cape-wide throughout May, run the gamut from themed lectures and art exhibits to lighthouse tours. More than 100 wineries take part in the annual **Nantucket Wine Festival** (⊕ www.nantucketwinefestival.com).

June

Pilgrims get a lot of press. But they weren't the only European contingent to help shape this region. Provincetown's **Portuguese Festival** (☎ 508/487–0500 ⊕ www.provincetownportuguesefestival.com) honors another with a weekend of food, music, dancing, and fireworks. A boat procession and a blessing of the fleet cap the event.

The standing-room-only **Provincetown International Film Festival** (⊕ www.ptownfilmfest.org) showcases independent films over a four-day period. The **Nantucket Film Festival** (⊕ www.nantucketfilmfestival.org) holds screenwriters in special regard.

July

Barnstable County Fair (☎ 508/563–3200 ⊕ www.barnstablecountyfair.org) in East Falmouth has been a Cape tradition since 1844. Some 90,000 people come for nine days of horse pulls, craft displays, carnival rides, and cotton candy.

August

The **Cape Cod Symphony Orchestra** (☎ 508/362–1111 ⊕ www.capesymphony.org) plays outdoors in Orleans and Falmouth. Top-caliber music is on tap during the **Cape & Islands Chamber Music Festival** (☎ 508/945–8060 ⊕ www.capecodchambermusic.org).

September

There's something fishy about September in Cape Cod. Hyannis hosts the **Oyster Festival** (☎ 508/775–2201 ⊕ www.hyannis.com). Bourne asserts its supremacy with the **Scallop Fest** (☎ 508/759–6000 ⊕ www.bournescallopfest.com).

October

The weekend after Columbus Day is devoted to the famous bivalve during the **Wellfleet OysterFest** (⊕ www.wellfleetoysterfest.org), which includes an exciting oyster shucking contest. Ideal for families, the **Yarmouth Seaside Festival** (⊕ www.yarmouthseasidefeatival.com) has a crafts fair, rides, and fireworks. Get bogged down at the Nantucket Conservation Foundation's one-day **Cranberry Festival** (☎ 508/228–2884 ⊕ www.nantucketconservation.com).

November

See the light at Provincetown's **Pilgrim Monument** (☎ 508/487–1310 ⊕ www.pilgrimmonument.org). On Thanksgiving Eve, the tower is festooned with 5,000 bulbs that remain lighted nightly until the New Year.

December

Many towns celebrate Christmas in grand style, but the monthlong **Nantucket Noel** (☎ 508/228–1700 ⊕ www.nantucketchamber.org)—featuring a "Christmas Stroll"—leads the pack.

RAINY-DAY FUN

You can count on plenty of wonderful things in this region: stunning beaches, fresh seafood, bulging boutiques. Great weather, however, isn't always a sure thing. Cape Cod, for example, averages 3 to 4 inches of rain per month, and extended periods of inclement weather aren't unheard of.

Happily, rain does not have to put a damper on your fun—even if you're a devoted beach bum. Strolling on the sand can be as enjoyable on a stormy morning, when crowds are sparse and the surf intense, as on a sultry afternoon. Plus, once you've gotten a little wet, you may forget about the showers and enjoy the brooding water views more. Be aware that traffic can get heavy when it rains, as everyone else is seeking an alternative to typical activities, too. Be patient.

Prefer to explore the great indoors? Read on.

Honor the region's rich literary heritage by curling up with a good book. If you didn't pack one, don't panic. The Cape and islands are famous for their **public libraries.** Provincetown's is lovely, and holds much more than just books.

There are **movie theaters** where cinephiles can catch a matinee on a dreary afternoon. Come dusk, though, nothing compares with a double feature at the nostalgia-inducing Wellfleet Drive-In. Films are shown nightly, rain or shine, late April to mid-September.

Like **live performances?** Each summer the venerable Cape Playhouse in Dennis stages Broadway-style theatricals, and the Cape Cod Melody Tent in Hyannis hosts pop and comedy acts. Vineyard Playhouse on Martha's Vineyard has year-round offerings. There are any number of shows to see in Provincetown—try a drag show, comedy revue, or dramatic reading.

Say "ahhh" at a **spa.** Top destination spas include the Crowne Pointe Inn (Provincetown), Chatham Bars Inn (Chatham), Cape Codder Resort (Hyannis), Dan'l Webster Inn (Sandwich), and the Wauwinet and White Elephant (both on Nantucket). The region also boasts a selection of day spas.

The chief charm of Sandwich's **Heritage Museums and Gardens** lies in the fact that—like Cape Cod as a whole—it is at once idyllic and idiosyncratic. Nantucket baskets, primitive paintings, antique autos, and toy soldiers are just some of the items on display.

It's easy to pass time on a rainy day visiting local galleries. But for a one-of-a-kind art encounter, drop by the **Sandwich Glass Museum.** It traces the history of Cape Cod's 19th-century glass industry and holds glassblowing demonstrations throughout summer.

Thanks to the Cape's prosperous past as a shipping and whaling center, it has an abundance of fine **antiques shops.** So why not indulge in a little treasure hunting? Route 6A between Sandwich and Brewster is a good place to focus your attention.

When the sun's not shining, you can recapture that "one brief shining moment that was known as Camelot" by visiting the **John F. Kennedy Hyannis Museum.** Archival photos and a brief film tell the story of JFK and his Cape connection.

RIDING THE CAPE COD RAIL TRAIL

In the late 1800s, visitors to Cape Cod could take the train from Boston all the way to Provincetown. However, with the construction of the Sagamore and Bourne bridges in the mid-1930s, the age of the automobile was ushered in. Today, though passenger train service to the Cape has been discontinued, the old railroad right-of-way—now paved and refurbished—is still being put to good use as the peninsula's premier bike path.

Trail Basics

The **Cape Cod Rail Trail** (☎ *508/896–3491* ⊕ *www.mass.gov/dcr/parks/southeast/ ccrt.htm*) offers a scenic ride from South Dennis to South Wellfleet over terrain that is easy-to-moderate in difficulty and generally quite flat. Given the good conditions, Rail Trailers who feel the need for speed can cover its 25-mi length in an hour or two. Yet most go at a more leisurely pace, lingering en route at salt marshes, woodlands, cranberry bogs, beaches, ponds, and Nickerson State Park (which maintains the trail and has its own bike path).

Of course, it isn't mandatory to tackle the trail in its entirety. If you are pressed for time—or prone to saddle sores—simply do a segment, perhaps starting in the middle near Nickerson State Park, then looping to one end and back. If you'd rather return to your starting point by public transportation, the easiest way is to set off from Dennis, ride to Orleans, and catch the bike-rack-equipped H20 Line bus back. The Cape Cod Regional Transit Authority has schedules.

The Cape Cod Rail Trail begins at a parking lot off busy Route 134 south of U.S. 6, near Theophilus Smith Road in South Dennis, and ends in South Wellfleet, with a spur leading westward through Harwich to Chatham. Free maps are available at the Dennis Chamber of Commerce and other locations. In addition to distances, these mark amenities such as strategically placed parking lots and restrooms.

Riding Tips

The trail passes through Dennis, Brewster, Orleans, Eastham, and Wellfleet. Bike shops in these towns can provide rental equipment, plus helpful traveling tips.

Please note that, under Massachusetts law, children 16 and younger are required to wear bike helmets. This applies whether they are drivers or passengers.

Wheels yield to heels, which means cyclists give walkers the right-of-way. Also remember to pass slower traffic on the left, and call out a warning before you pass.

The trail can get crowded at times. So if you prefer solitude (or cooler temperatures), try heading out earlier in the morning or later in the afternoon.

Nonbikers should note that horseback riding, walking, running, and in-line skating are welcome on the trail's broad unpaved shoulder.

GREAT ITINERARIES

CAPE COD IN ONE WEEK: CLASSIC BEACHES AND BUSTLING VILLAGES

Day 1: Falmouth

Begin by crossing the Bourne Bridge and taking Route 28A south through some lovely little towns until you reach Falmouth, an excellent base for exploring the Upper Cape. Here you can stroll around the village green, look into some of the historic houses, and stop at the Waquoit Bay National Estuarine Research Reserve for a walk along the estuary and barrier beach. Take some time to check out the village of Woods Hole, the center for international marine research, and the year-round ferry port for Martha's Vineyard. A small aquarium in town has regional sea-life exhibits, and there are several shops and museums. If you have any extra time, spend it north of here in the lovely old town of Sandwich, known for the Sandwich Glass Museum and the beautiful grounds and collection of antique cars at Heritage Museums and Gardens.

Days 2 and 3: Hyannis

The crowded Mid Cape is a center of activity, and its hub is Hyannis. Here you can take a cruise around the harbor or go on a deep-sea fishing trip. There are shops and restaurants along Main Street and plenty of kid-worthy amusements. Kennedy fans shouldn't miss the JFK Museum. End the day with a concert at the Cape Cod Melody Tent. Spend your second day exploring the northern reaches of the Mid Cape with a drive along scenic Route 6A, which passes through the charming, slow-paced villages of Barnstable, Yarmouth Port, and Dennis. There are beaches and salt marshes, museums, antiques shops and galleries, and old graveyards along this route. Yarmouth Port's Bass Hole Boardwalk makes for a particularly beautiful stroll. In Dennis there are historic houses to tour, and the Cape Museum of Fine Arts merits a stop. End the day by climbing 30-foot Scargo Tower to watch the sun set. At night you can catch a film at the Cape Cinema, on the grounds of the Cape Playhouse in Dennis.

Days 4 and 5: Chatham

Chatham, with its handsome Main Street, is a perfect base for strolling, shopping, and dining. A trip to the nearby Monomoy Islands is a must for bird-watchers and nature lovers. Back in town, you can watch glassblowing at the Chatham Glass Company, visit the Atwood House and Railroad museums, and drive over to take in the view from Chatham Light. Spend your second day detouring up to Brewster to check out the eclectic mix of antiques shops, museums, freshwater ponds for swimming and fishing, and miles of biking and hiking trails through Nickerson State Park. Don't miss the Cape Cod Museum of Natural History. On the way north from Chatham, take the less-commercial end of Route 28 to Orleans, driving past sailboat-speckled views of Pleasant Bay. On the way up toward Provincetown, stop in Eastham at the National Seashore's Salt Pond Visitor Center.

Days 6 and 7: Provincetown

Bustling Provincetown sits at the very tip of the Cape, and there's a lot to see and do here. Catch a whale-watch excursion and take a trolley tour in town or bike through the National Seashore on its miles of trails. Climb the Pilgrim Monument for a spectacular view of the area—on an exceptionally clear day you can see as far as the Boston skyline. Visit

TIPS

❶ Keep in mind that traffic leading onto the Cape is particularly horrendous on Friday afternoon and Saturday morning, and traffic leading off the Cape is rough on Sunday. Try to time your visit to avoid these times, but if you must travel to or from the Cape on these days, cross as early in the day as possible.

❷ If you're traveling with kids, you might want to pass on some of the itinerary's more-adult-oriented highlights described above—such as shopping in Wellfleet and driving along scenic Route 6A from Barnstable to Dennis—and instead set aside some time in the southern sections of Yarmouth and Dennis, where Route 28 passes by countless amusement centers, mini-golf courses, and other kid-friendly amusements.

❸ A car is the best way to explore the Cape, but in the busier town centers—such as Falmouth, Hyannis, Chatham, and Provincetown—you can get around quite easily on foot. Plan to park your car in a lot or at your hotel and avoid using it except to explore less densely populated areas of the Cape.

the museums and shops and art galleries, or spend the afternoon swimming and sunning on one of the beaches. To escape the crowds, spend a day driving south through sleepy but scenic Truro and then park your car in Wellfleet's historic downtown, where you'll find a bounty of intriguing shops and galleries. Continue a bit south to historic Marconi Station, which was the landing point for the transatlantic telegraph early in the 20th century. It's also worth walking the short but stunning White Cedar Swamp Trail.

Alternatives

On Day 2, hop the ferry for a day trip to either Martha's Vineyard or Nantucket. Both islands offer breathtaking scenery and village centers chock-full of great shops and restaurants. And if you're really keen on exploring either island, consider spending the night. Martha's Vineyard requires a shorter ferry ride and is your best choice if time is tight.

GREAT ITINERARIES

MARTHA'S VINEYARD: THE PERFECT THREE-DAY WEEKEND

Day 1: Vineyard Haven and Oak Bluffs

Start your day in downtown Vineyard Haven with a light morning repast of gourmet espresso and a breakfast "eggwich" at the cozy Beetlebung Coffee House, which is right next to the Martha's Vineyard Chamber of Commerce office, a great source of advice and brochures for exploring the island. Spend some time exploring the historic houses that line William Street, and the many shops and eateries along Main Street.

Once you've worked up an appetite, head just a short walk outside of downtown to Net Result for one of the best lobster rolls on the island. In the afternoon, take a quick jaunt out to West Chop for a great view over Vineyard Sound from the lighthouse.

Head back through Vineyard Haven's downtown toward Oak Bluffs via Beach Road. Spend some time wandering the streets of the Oak Bluffs Campground, where tightly packed pastel-painted Victorian-style cottages vie with one another for the fanciest gingerbread trim. Then head into the center of Oak Bluffs for a ride on the Flying Horses, the oldest continuously operating carousel in the country. If you have kids in tow, head to the video arcade across the street. Or unwind at the Offshore Ale brewpub, also in Oak Bluffs, where dart enthusiasts can find formidable foes.

Day 2: Edgartown

Spend your second day on the island exploring historic, dapper Edgartown, where you can start things off with a delicious breakfast at Espresso Love coffeehouse. After downing a vanilla latte and noshing on a homemade raspberry scone, spend the morning browsing the dozens of tony shops and visiting the several museums tracing the town's heritage, including the superb Martha's Vineyard Historical Society and the island's oldest dwelling, the Vincent House Museum.

Grab a lunch at one of the village's many excellent eateries, or grab a hefty sandwich to go from the Edgartown Deli. Then in the afternoon, head to Chappaquiddick Island to visit the Mytoi preserve for a stroll. If conservation areas are your thing, the Cape Poge Wildlife Refuge on the island is a must. You'll need a few hours on Chappaquiddick to make the visit worthwhile. Edgartown abounds with superb dinner options upon your return, with Detente leading the pack.

Day 3: Up-Island

Begin your day with a visit to the West Tisbury farms, some of which have pony rides for kids. Stock up on breakfast snacks at the nostalgic Alley's General Store. Polly Hill Arboretum is a must for horticulture buffs. Then drive out to Aquinnah Cliffs (formerly Gay Head), one of the most spectacular spots on the island. Go to the lookout at the cliffs for the view, or take the boardwalk to the beach and walk back to see the cliffs and Aquinnah Light from below. Spend some time sunning and swimming at this breathtaking spot. (The beach attracts nude sunbathers; though it's technically illegal, the officials usually look the other way.)

You can enjoy a nice lunch at the Aquinnah Restaurant, which has stunning views of the sea, or save your appetite for the return drive through the picturesque fishing village of Menemsha, which is one of the best spots in New England to dine on fresh clams, lobsters, and other seafood. Larsen's and the Bite are both good bets for this.

You could also drop by one of the several notable galleries Up-Island, such as the Granary Gallery at the Red Barn, and Martha's Vineyard Glassworks. As the day comes to an end, either pick up some seafood and take it to Menemsha Beach for a sunset picnic, or opt for a considerably fancier dinner at the elegant restaurant at Lambert's Cove Inn.

Alternatives

If peaceful country lanes and rolling hills bring a smile to your face, skip Oak Bluffs and combine your explorations of Edgartown and Vineyard Haven into one full day. Then spend two days touring Up-Island, allowing extra time to hike the beach below Aquinnah Lighthouse, birdwatch at Sepiessa Point Reservation, or cycle around the part of the island's stunning roads.

Conversely, fans of bustling town centers (and those without a car) might want to skip or drastically shorten any forays Up-Island and instead allocate a full day each for touring Vineyard Haven, Edgartown, and Oak Bluffs. With the extra time in the latter community, you can visit East Chop Lighthouse, and fully avail yourself of the town's growing crop of fine shops.

TIPS

❶ Martha's Vineyard is a sizable island, and for the ultimate freedom to explore the more rural areas Up-Island, it's useful to travel by car. However, the island also has an excellent bus system, and taxis work for getting between the main town centers.

❷ Nature lovers can still find plenty of worthy diversions without venturing Up-Island—just focus your efforts on Chappaquiddick Island, Joseph A. Sylvia State Beach, and Felix Neck Wildlife Sanctuary. Additionally, Island Spirit Sea-Kayak Adventures offers invigorating treks paddles just off-shore.

GREAT ITINERARIES

NANTUCKET: THE PERFECT THREE-DAY WEEKEND

Day 1: An Overview of the Island

If you're new to Nantucket, a great way to spend your first day is simply setting off to explore the different communities on the island, beginning your adventures right in the heart of Nantucket Town, first by enjoying breakfast at the locally revered Fog Island Café on South Water Street. Stroll around town a bit, perhaps treating yourself to a grand view of the harbor and town from Brant Point Light, at the end of Easton Street.

Next head east across the island to Siasconset, just in time for a memorable lunch in the sun at the Summer House beachside bistro. This part of the island is happily free of formal attractions—it's best just to wander about this former fishing village and admire its rose-covered cottages before venturing north a few miles to the even sleepier settlement of Wauwinet. Then head back to Nantucket Town via Polpis Road; along the way you can make detours to check out the Nantucket Shipwreck & Life Saving Museum or Windswept Cranberry Bog. If you still have the time and energy, make the 5-mi trip to the island's western community, Madaket Beach, an absolutely breathtaking perch from which to watch the sunset.

Day 2: Nantucket Town Shopping and Museums

Sophisticated, historic, and relatively bustling—by the peaceful standards of this island—Nantucket Town is an excellent place to spend a full day strolling. There's fine shopping at haute boutiques and esteemed galleries, and a number of museums and historic buildings are within easy walking distance of the village center.

Kick off day with a hearty breakfast at Black-Eyed Susan's before venturing off to see some of the town's excellent museums. Focus on the properties that are part of the outstanding Nantucket Historical Association, with its ambitiously expanded Whaling Museum. If time allows, get a peek inside the magnificent Nantucket Atheneum, a sterling example of Greek Revival architecture, and the stately First Congregational Church.

For lunch, drop by the reasonably priced Slip 14 on Old South Wharf; the local fluke tacos are particularly tasty. Spend your afternoon walking through the commercial district—paying especially close attention to the grid formed by Main, Centre, Broad, and Easy streets—and also drop by the former boathouses of Straight Wharf and Old South Wharf to view the many galleries and boutiques within. The fine shops in this neighborhood proffer everything from whaling artifacts to splashy resort wear to cottage-inspired home furnishings.

Day 3: Getting to Know Nantucket's Natural Side

It may sound a bit ambitious, but if you're a serious fan of nature, you'll want to head out at dawn to see what the birds are up to. The Downyflake, a homey mid-island breakfast joint, starts serving at 5:30 AM most days (6 AM on Sunday). Pick up a couple of homemade doughnuts for carbo-loading on the road.

The best way to bird is on bike. (Rent one from one of the high-quality island shops.) A couple of miles west of Downyflake, the Nantucket Conservation Foundation maintains a 900-acre preserve comprising Sanford Farm, the Woods, and Ram Pasture. To get to here, follow Sparks Avenue to the high school; then it's a scenic zigzag past the Old Mill (consult a bike map, available from the tourism office) to reach the start of the Madaket Bike Path. A few miles farther on the path, just before the intersection with Cliff Road, you'll see a rough-hewn parking lot. From here, 6½ mi of hiking trails (you'll have to ditch your bike—there's a place to lock it up) cross forest and meadow to reach pond and sea, wetlands, and rare sand-plain grassland. Figure on at least two hours of walking and gawking.

After emerging from the preserve, bike another 3 mi west along the bike path to Madaket Beach, known for its unbeatable sunsets. For dinner, retire to Even Keel Cafe in the center of town, where you can dine amid the surprising peace of the patio out back before swooping home on your bike through the cool, starry night.

Alternatives

If you're truly a history buff and less inclined toward biking and the outdoors, skip all of most of the activities described *above* for Day 3 and instead tack on an extra day of museum-hopping in Nantucket Town. If you've already seen most of the properties operated by the Nantucket Historical Association, opt instead to tour the attractions that comprise the Maria Mitchell Association, including the aquarium, natural science museum, and two observatories. You can always just relax among the roses in 'Sconset.

TIPS

❶ For exploring Nantucket Town's museums, consider buying a pass for $20 from the Nantucket Historical Association—this gets you into all of the organization's excellent museums and sites.

❷ It's possible to travel between the different communities by shuttle bus or taxi, but for the freedom to turn down intriguing lanes and go at your own pace, traveling by bike is ideal.

The Upper Cape

WORD OF MOUTH

"Sandwich would be my vote. You can walk or bike along the Cape Cod Canal; no motorized vehicles are allowed on the service road along the canal. Pick it up off the parking place west of the marina. There are several conservation areas with interesting trails in Sandwich, and there are museums such as the Sandwich Glass Museum, with displays of Sandwich glass and glassblowing demonstrations, and the Heritage Museums and Gardens. At the Green Briar Nature Center, check out walking trails. Walk across the boardwalk to the dunes at sunset or sunrise, or go down to the canal at sunrise and watch the working fishing boats unload."

—irishface

Updated by
Janice Randall
Rohlf

The Upper Cape has none of the briny, otherworldly breeziness of the Outer Cape and little of the resort feel of Lower Cape cousins like Chatham. The reason is solidly geographical: The Upper Cape's proximity to the mainland yields slightly less-brutal winters than elsewhere on the Cape and, consequently, a substantial year-round population; the region's beaches are intimate; and more of its attractions—freshwater ponds, conservation areas, and small museums—are inland.

Finding peace and quiet so close to the mainland is an unexpected and much-appreciated pleasure of the Upper Cape. Sandwich, its streets lined with historic houses, is remarkably well preserved. Falmouth is an active year-round community with easy-to-reach beaches that are popular with families. In the villages of North and West Falmouth, tree-lined country lanes lead to sandy coves, and in East Falmouth and Waquoit, narrow spits of land jut into marshy inlets. Woods Hole, on the Cape's southwestern tip, is a center for marine research and the departure point for ferries to Martha's Vineyard.

If you're collecting superlatives, the Upper Cape is fertile. Sandwich is the oldest town on the Cape, Bourne was the Pilgrims' first Cape Cod settlement and an important trading area, and the first Native American reservation in the United States was established in Mashpee, which still has a large Wampanoag population and a tribal-council governing body.

ORIENTATION AND PLANNING

GETTING ORIENTED

On the north shore, Sandwich, gracious and lovely, is the Cape's oldest town. Centered inland, Mashpee is a long-standing Native American township in which Native American–owned land is governed by local Wampanoags. Falmouth, the Cape's second-most-populous town, is still green and historic, if seemingly overrun with strip malls. Woods Hole, the major port for ferries to Martha's Vineyard, is world renowned for its biological research institutions. Along the west coast, in parts of Bourne and West and North Falmouth, you can find wooded areas ending in secluded coves; the south coast has long-established resort communities.

Bourne. A quiet, year-round community, Bourne is the first town you reach on the Upper Cape. With cyclists exploring the Cape Cod Canal Bike Trail and anglers trolling in the waters of Buzzards Bay, Bourne is a diamond in the rough for outdoor enthusiasts.

TOP REASONS TO GO

Relaxing on beautiful beaches: The Upper Cape has beaches for every taste. The southern beaches facing Nantucket Sound are known for their rolling surf and waters warmed by the Gulf Stream. Buzzards Bay has protected coves with sandy stretches. On Cape Cod Bay, the beaches generally have temperate waters and gentle waves.

Riding the bike trails: Several bike trails—including the Shining Sea Bikeway and the Cape Cod Canal Trail—make the Upper Cape a good place for easy rides. Many of the less-traveled roads in Bourne and West and North Falmouth are good for cyclists. The beaches of Buzzards Bay are excellent destinations for leisurely rides.

Taking in summer concerts: In warmer months there's plenty of music on the Upper Cape, including the very popular concerts at

Sandwich's Heritage Museums and Gardens. Bourne, Sandwich, and Falmouth all present summer band concerts in downtown parks. Bring a blanket for a perfect night under the stars.

Going boating and fishing: Canoeing and kayaking are great around the marshy inlets of both Cape Cod Bay and Buzzards Bay and on the Upper Cape's many freshwater ponds. The Cape Cod Canal is a popular destination for anglers. Sign on with a fishing charter if you want some guidance.

Exploring wide-open spaces: You'll find plenty of places to wander on the Upper Cape. Several recreation areas line the Cape Cod Canal, and trails crisscross the region's nature preserves, including the Ashumet Holly sanctuary, the Waquoit Bay National Estuarine Research Reserve, and the Mashpee River Woodlands.

Sandwich. With its streets lined with old homes, Sandwich is a glimpse into the Upper Cape's past. Don't miss the Sandwich Glass Museum, the restored 17th-century Grist Mill, and the 100-acre Heritage Museums and Gardens, featuring the J.K. Lilly III Automobile Collection.

Falmouth. This classic New England town, where sophisticated shopping and dining meet the best of beach and biking opportunities, includes the scientific enclave of Woods Hole, a lovely seaside village and embarkation point for ferries to Martha's Vineyard. East Falmouth and Waquoit have some lovely nature preserves.

Mashpee. Home of the Native American Wampanoag Nation, Mashpee hosts a powwow every July. It draws discerning shoppers to Mashpee Commons and South Cape Village and avid golfers to top-tier courses like Willowbend and New Seabury.

PLANNING

WHEN TO GO

Although summer on the Upper Cape is the quintessential New England–vacation experience, the ideal time of year to visit may be early autumn. You can enjoy the beaches and water activities on Cape Cod Bay, Buzzards Bay, and Nantucket Sound in tranquillity between mid-September and late October, when the summer crowds have left but the weather is still mild. The Bourne Scallop Festival takes place for three days in September.

PLANNING YOUR TIME

Sandwich is an ideal place to base yourself while exploring the Upper Cape. The downtown area has plenty of restaurants and cafés where you can recharge between jaunts around the region. From here you can easily spend head out to some of the walking trails in East Falmouth and Waquoit.

Staying in Falmouth Village, with its own pleasing downtown, is especially convenient if you're planning a trip to Martha's Vineyard. Most hotels will let you leave your car in their lot if you're making a day trip. A trolley takes you right to Woods Hole.

GETTING HERE AND AROUND

BOAT AND FERRY TRAVEL

Year-round ferries to Martha's Vineyard leave from Woods Hole. Seasonal Vineyard ferries leave from Falmouth. *For details ⇨ Boat and Ferry Travel in Travel Smart Cape Cod in the back of this book.*

BUS TRAVEL

Bonanza, run by Peter Pan, offers direct bus service to Bourne, Falmouth, and the Woods Hole steamship terminal from Boston's Logan Airport, downtown Boston, Fall River, New Bedford, and Providence, Rhode Island. Some buses from Boston also make stops in Wareham. Bonanza runs a service between Bourne, Falmouth, and Woods Hole year-round. Plymouth & Brockton Street Railway provides bus service to Provincetown from downtown Boston and Logan Airport, with stops en route. The Logan Direct express service bypasses downtown Boston and stops in Plymouth, Sagamore, Barnstable, and Hyannis.

The Cape Cod Regional Transit Authority's SeaLine, H2O Line, Barnstable Villager, and Hyannis Villager buses travel between the Upper and Lower Cape. Service is not frequent—buses depart once every hour or two, depending on the time of day—so check the schedule before you set out. To travel between Falmouth and Woods Hole, the WHOOSH trolley, also run by the Cape Cod Regional Transit Authority, is convenient. *For more information, see ⇨ Bus Travel in Travel Smart Cape Cod in the back of this book.*

Bus Depots **Bonanza Bus Terminals** (✉ *South Station Bus Terminal, 700 Atlantic Ave., Boston* ☎ *617/720–4110* ✉ *Depot Ave., Falmouth* ☎ *508/548–7588* ⊕ *www.peterpanbus.com* ✉ *Steamship Authority Piers, Woods Hole* ☎ *508/548–5011* ⊕ *www.islandferry.com*). **Hyannis Transportation Center** (✉ *215 Iyannough Rd., Hyannis* ☎ *508/775–8504*). **Plymouth & Brockton Street Railway Terminals** (✉ *South Station Bus Terminal, 700 Atlantic Ave., Boston* ☎ *508/746–0378* ⊕ *www.p-b.com*).

Bus Lines **Bonanza** (☎ *888/751–8800* ⊕ *www.peterpanbus.com*). **Cape Cod Regional Transit Authority** (☎ *800/352–7155* ⊕ *www.capecodtransit.org*). **Plymouth & Brockton Street Railway** (☎ *508/746–0378* ⊕ *www.p-b.com*).

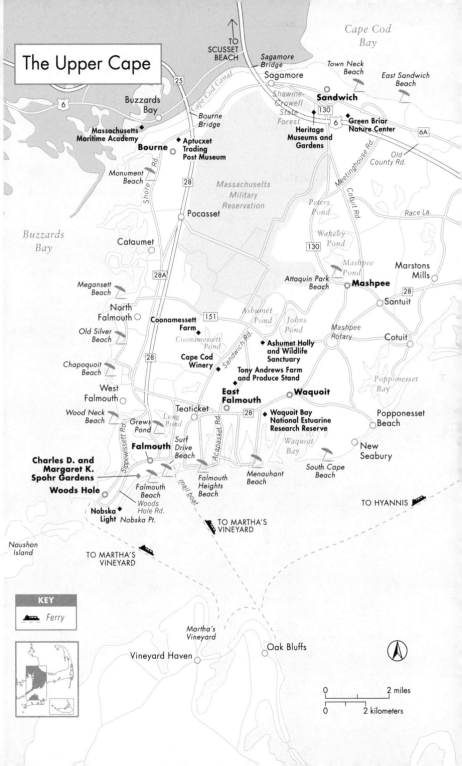

CAR TRAVEL

Unless you're staying in one place, you'll probably need a car while visiting the Upper Cape. Route 28 is one of the main roads through the region. In Falmouth it takes a sharp turn, heading north toward Bourne and the Cape Cod Canal and east toward the Mid Cape. Route 130 slices through the interior, connecting Sandwich with Route 28 around East Falmouth.

TAXI TRAVEL

Taxi Company **Falmouth Taxi** (⊠ *Falmouth* ☎ *508/540–7200*).

RESTAURANTS

Much like the rest of Cape Cod, the Upper Cape's dining scene ranges from basic seafood shacks to contemporary restaurants that draw inspiration from the far corners of the globe—plus everything in between. Overall, the restaurant options tend toward the traditional, with fried clams, baked scrod, and boiled lobster gracing the most popular menus. Restaurants are more widely scattered in the Upper Cape towns—there are few "restaurant rows"—but if you like to wander and check out your dining options, try Main Street in Falmouth Center or Water Street in Woods Hole.

HOTELS

Sandwich and other towns along the north-shore Route 6A Historic District have quiet, traditional villages with an old-Cape feel and charming B&Bs. Along Route 6A you can also find family-friendly motels, ranging from the modest to the better equipped. Historic B&Bs fill the center of Falmouth, and other small inns line the shore and the neighboring streets of Falmouth Heights. Lodging options are fewer in Bourne and West and North Falmouth, but a few B&Bs hidden away on country lanes provide glimpses of old New England. You can also rent modern town houses and condominiums with extensive resort amenities in Mashpee's New Seabury community.

WHAT IT COSTS				
¢	$	$$	$$$	$$$$
Restaurants	under $10	$10–$16	$17–$22	$23–$30	over $30
Hotels	under $90	$90–$140	$141–$200	$201–$260	over $260

Restaurant prices are per person for a main course at dinner. Hotel prices are for a standard double room, excluding 5.7% sales tax (more in some counties) and up to an additional 6% tourist tax.

CONDO AND HOUSE RENTALS

Donahue Real Estate lists both apartments and houses for rent in the Falmouth area. Real Estate Associates lists properties (some pricey) ranging from beach cottages to waterfront estates, with a focus on more-expensive houses. It covers Falmouth, Bourne, and Mashpee.

Local Agents **Donahue Real Estate** (⊠ *Falmouth* ☎ *508/548–5412* ⊕ *www. falmouthhomes.com*). **Real Estate Associates** (⊠ *5 Old Dock Rd., Falmouth* ☎ *508/540–5545* ⊕ *www.uppercaperentals.com*).

VISITOR INFORMATION

The Cape Cod Canal Region Chamber of Commerce staffs a visitor center in Buzzards Bay that is open daily 9–5 from Memorial Day to Columbus Day. The Cape Cod Canal Visitor Center in Sagamore Beach is open year-round, weekdays 8–5 and weekends 9–5.

Tourist Information **Cape Cod Canal Region Chamber of Commerce** (✉ *70 Main St., Buzzards Bay* ☎ *508/759–6000* ⊕ *www.capecodcanalchamber.org).* **Cape Cod Canal Visitor Center** (✉ *1 Meetinghouse La., Sagamore Beach* ☎ *774/413–7475* ⊕ *www.capecodcanalchamber.org).*

BOURNE

The town of Bourne consists of nine villages—Bourne Village, Bournedale, Buzzards Bay, Cataumet, Gray Gables, Monument Beach, Pocasset, Sagamore, and Sagamore Beach—along Buzzards Bay and both sides of the Cape Cod Canal. The villages range from souvenir-shop-dominated commercial districts to bucolic waterfront suburbs. With a mix of year-round and summer residents, the area includes places for learning about the region's marine life and early commercial history, as well as several attractive recreation areas, established and maintained by the U.S. Army Corps of Engineers, for biking, hiking, and fishing along the canal.

The Pilgrims established their first Cape Cod settlement in Bourne in 1627, but back then it was still part of Sandwich; Bourne didn't become a separate town until 1884. By that time it had grown into a popular summer colony whose part-time residents included President Grover Cleveland and *Boston Globe* publisher Charles Taylor. Present-day Bourne's maritime orientation was created by the Cape Cod Canal, which opened in 1914. The 17½-mi canal cut the distance for shipping traffic between Boston and New York by 75 mi and eliminated the often-treacherous journey around the Cape. The U.S. Army Corps of Engineers took over the canal's operation in the late 1920s and embarked on a project to widen it; the current Bourne and Sagamore bridges were built in the 1930s as part of this project.

GETTING HERE AND AROUND

Bourne is about 6 mi southwest of Sandwich, 14 mi north of Falmouth, and 15 mi northwest of Mashpee. If you're coming from Boston, once you cross the Bourne Bridge over the Cape Cod Canal, you will find yourself on Route 28. At the first rotary, take a right and you'll be in downtown Bourne.

EXPLORING

TOP ATTRACTIONS

Aptucxet Trading Post Museum. A monument to the birth of commerce in the New World, this museum was erected on the foundation of the original trading post. Here, in 1627, Plimoth Plantation leaders established a way station between the Native American encampment at Great Herring Pond 3 mi to the northeast, Dutch colonists in New Amsterdam to the south, and English colonists on Cape Cod Bay. The Native Americans traded furs; the Dutch traded linen cloth, metal tools, glass beads, sugar, and other staples; and the Pilgrims traded wool cloth, clay beads, sassafras, and tobacco (which they imported from Virginia). Wampum (beads made from polished shells) was the medium of exchange.

Inside the museum, 17th-century cooking utensils hang from the original brick hearth; beaver and otter skins, arrowheads, tools, and tomahawks are displayed throughout. Also on the grounds are a gift shop in a Dutch-style windmill, a saltworks, herb and wildflower gardens, a picnic area overlooking the canal, and a small Victorian railroad station built for the sole use of President Grover Cleveland, who had a summer home in Bourne. To get here, cross the Bourne Bridge; then take the first right from the rotary onto Trowbridge Road. ⊠ *24 Aptucxet Rd., Bourne Village* ☎ *508/759–9487* ⊕ *www.bournehistoricalsociety.org* ⊠ *$4* ☉ *Late May–Columbus Day, Tues.–Sat. 10–4.*

Ⓒ **National Marine Life Center.** On the mainland near the chamber of commerce office, this facility has a small exhibit area devoted to whales, dolphins, seals, turtles, and other sea creatures. In summer there are marine-life educational programs for children. It includes an expanded facility for rehabilitating injured sea turtles and seals. ⊠ *120 Main St., Buzzards Bay* ☎ *508/743–9888* ⊕ *www.nmlc.org* ⊠ *Free, donations accepted* ☉ *Late May–early Sept., daily 10–5; early Sept.–Columbus Day, weekends 10–5.*

Pairpoint Glass Company. Watch richly colored lead crystal being hand blown at America's oldest glass factory (founded in 1837). The shop sells candlesticks, vases, stemware, sun catchers, cup, plates, lamps, perfume bottles, and reproductions of original Boston and Sandwich glass pieces. ⊠ *851 Rte. 6A, Sagamore* ☎ *508/888–2344* ⊕ *www.pairpoint. com* ⊠ *Free* ☉ *Showroom Mon.–Sat. 10–5, Sun. 11–5. Demonstrations May–Dec., weekdays 9–4; Jan.–Apr., hrs are limited.*

WORTH NOTING

Ⓒ **Cartwheels 2.** Perfect for kids cooped in a car for too many miles, Cartwheels 2 has a go-kart track, a bumper-boat lagoon, 18 holes of miniature golf, Whiffle Ball, batting cages, and an arcade with a snack bar. ⊠ *Rte. 28, 2 mi south of Bourne Bridge, Bourne Village* ☎ *508/743–9930* ⊕ *www.cartwheels2.com* ☉ *July–early Sept., daily 10 AM–11 PM; Apr.–Oct., call for hrs.*

Massachusetts Maritime Academy. Founded in 1891, the Massachusetts Maritime Academy is the oldest such school in the country. Future members of the merchant marine receive their training at its 55-acre campus in Buzzards Bay. The library has nautical paintings and scale models of ships from the 18th century to the present and is open to the public at no charge. For a tour of the academy, call two days in advance. ⊠ *Taylor's Point, Buzzards Bay* ☎ *508/830–5000* ⊕ *www.maritime.edu.*

WHERE TO EAT AND STAY

$$ × **Chart Room.** Located harborside in a former cargo barge, this tra-
SEAFOOD ditional watering hole has been serving seafood classics since 1966.
Clam chowder, lobster rolls, broiled scrod, seafood Newburg, baked
stuffed shrimp—they're all here, as are sirloin steak, broiled lamb
chops, and even grilled cheese-and-tomato sandwiches. ✉ *1 Shipyard
La., at Kingman Yacht Center, Cataumet* ☎ *508/563–5350* ⊕ *www.
chartroomcataumet.com* ▭ *AE, MC, V* ⊗ *Closed mid-Oct.–mid-May
and weekdays mid-May–late June and early Sept.–mid-Oct.*

$ × **Stir Crazy.** Fresh ingredients with lively Cambodian, Thai, and Viet-
ASIAN namese flavors dominate every dish that graces the menu here (owner
Fodor'sChoice Bopha Samms hails from Cambodia). Try the *nhem shross* (a rice roll
★ of vegetables and shrimp) and the refreshing *bar bong* (chilled noodles
topped with pork, egg rolls, and coconut-peanut sauce). ✉ *570 MacAr-
thur Blvd., Pocasset* ☎ *508/564–6464* ⊕ *www.stircrazyrestaurant.
com* ▭ *Reservations not accepted* ▭ *MC, V* ⊗ *Closed Mon. No lunch
Sat.–Thurs.*

$ ⌂ **Wood Duck Inn.** Behind this cozy B&B, a 17-acre working cranberry
bog and acres of conservation land spread out as far as you can see.
The small but comfy Cottage Room has lace curtains and a brass bed
with a floral comforter, and both suites have a bedroom plus a sitting
room that doubles as extra sleeping space. The Garden Suite is done
in romantic florals, and the family-friendly Treetops Suite resembles a
contemporary apartment in forest green and white; it has a tiny but
fully equipped kitchen and sweeping views. The innkeepers deliver
breakfast to your door. **Pros:** private entrances; breakfast brought to
your room; beautiful pastoral views. **Cons:** some stairs; credit cards
not accepted. ✉ *1050 County Rd., Cataumet* ☎ *508/564–6404* ⊕ *www.
woodduckinnbb.com* ⇆ *1 room, 2 suites* ♿ *In-room: a/c, kitchen. In-
hotel: Wi-Fi hotspot* ▭ *No credit cards* ¶ *CP.*

$ ⚠ **Scusset Beach State Reservation.** Encompassing 300 acres adjacent to
the Cape Cod Canal (there's a fishing pier for anglers), the park has
a beach on Cape Cod Bay and 98 RV sites plus five tent sites, some
wooded. There are cold showers on the beach and hot showers in the
campground. **Pros:** popular with anglers; access to bike path. **Cons:**
no dump station, restrooms, or water. ♿ *In-hotel: beachfront, full
hookups* ⇆ *103 sites* ✉ *140 Scusset Beach Rd., off Rte. 3 at Sagamore
Bridge rotary, Sagamore Beach* ☎ *877/422–6762 campsite reserva-
tions, 508/888–0859 general information* ⊕ *www.mass.gov/dcr/parks/
southeast/scus.htm* ▭ *MC, V.*

NIGHTLIFE AND THE ARTS

In Bourne, Thursday evening **town-band concerts** (✉ *Main St., Bourne
Village* ☎ *508/759–6000*) in July and August start at 6:30 in Buzzards
Bay Park.

BEACHES, SPORTS, AND THE OUTDOORS

BASEBALL

The **Bourne Braves** of the collegiate Cape Cod Baseball League play home games at **Upper Cape Tech** (⊠ *220 Sandwich Rd., Bourne Village* ⊕ *www.bournebraves.org*) from mid-June to mid-August. Players and coaches lead youth clinics in summer.

BEACHES

Monument Beach, off Shore Road, is a small but pretty crescent of sand adjacent to the town dock, facing Buzzards Bay just south of Bourne Bridge. The beach has a snack bar, restrooms, and a parking lot, which is restricted in season to those with resident permits. From Shore Road, turn right onto Emmons Road just past the old train depot. ⊠ *Shore Rd., Bourne Village*.

Sagamore's **Scusset Beach State Reservation** is a pleasant place for a swim, walk, or bike ride near the mainland side of the Sagamore Bridge. The beach sweeps along Cape Cod Bay, and its pier and canal breakwater are popular for fishing and viewing boat traffic; other activities include hiking, picnicking, and camping. There's a parking fee from mid-April to mid-October. ⊠ *140 Scusset Beach Rd., off Rte. 3 at Sagamore Bridge rotary, Sagamore Beach* ☎ *508/888–0859* ⊕ *www.mass.gov/dcr* ⊠ *Mid-Apr.–mid-Oct., parking $7* ⊙ *Daily 8–8.*

BICYCLING

An easy, straight trail stretches on either side of the **Cape Cod Canal**, 6½ mi on the south side, 7 mi on the north, with views of the bridges and ship traffic on the canal.

Run by the U.S. Army Corps of Engineers, the **Herring Run Recreation Area** (⊠ *U.S. 6, Bournedale* ☎ *508/759–4431* ⊕ *www.nae.usace.army. mil/recreati/ccc/ccchome.htm*) has access to the canal bike path. There's also a herring run through which the fish travel during spawning in May. The visitor center is on the mainland side of the canal, between the bridges.

Tidal Flats Recreation Area (⊠ *Shore Rd., Bournedale* ☎ *508/759–4431* ⊕ *www.nae.usace.army.mil/recreati/ccc/ccchome.htm*) is a small but peaceful canal-side park near the Cape railroad bridge. Managed by the U.S. Army Corps of Engineers, it has access to the canal bike path. On weekdays in late afternoon you can often watch the bridge lower to allow a service train to cross the canal. To reach the recreation area, cross the Bourne Bridge and follow Trowbridge Road to Shore Road.

FISHING

The Cape Cod Canal is a great place to fish—from the service road on either side—for the big blues and striped bass making their way through the passage seasonally (April through November). You don't need a fishing license for saltwater angling, though you will need one for freshwater fishing.

HIKING AND WALKING

Herring Run Recreation Area (⊠ *U.S. 6, Bournedale* ☎ *508/759–4431* ⊕ *www.nae.usace.army.mil/recreati/ccc/ccchome.htm*) has short self-guided walking trails through the woodland.

ICE-SKATING

John Gallo Ice Arena (⊠ *231 Sandwich Rd., Bourne Village* ☎ *508/759–8904 www.galloarena.com*) is the place to go for ice skating year-round (except May). Lessons are offered and skate rental is available; admission is $3.

SHOPPING

Christmas Tree Shops (⊠ *Rte. 6A, Exit 1 off Rte. 6, Sagamore* ☎ *508/888–7010* ⊕ *www.christmastreeshops.com*) sell a wide variety of household goods at bargain prices. There are other locations in Falmouth, Hyannis, West Yarmouth, West Dennis, and Orleans.

SANDWICH

★ A well-preserved New England village, Sandwich wears its history proudly, despite having become increasingly suburban over the past few decades. The oldest town on Cape Cod, Sandwich was established in 1637 by some of the Plymouth Pilgrims and incorporated on March 6, 1638. Driving through town past the white-column town hall, the gristmill on Shawme Pond, and the 18th- and 19th-century homes that line the streets is like driving back in time—you may feel as if you should be holding a horse's reins rather than a car's steering wheel.

When you reach Main Street, park the car and get out for a stroll. Look at old houses on Main Street, stop at a museum or two, and work your way to the delightful Shawme Pond. Unlike other Cape towns, whose deepwater ports opened the doors to prosperity in the whaling days, Sandwich was an industrial town for much of the 19th century. It produced vividly colored glass, called Sandwich glass, which is now sought by collectors. The Boston and Sandwich Glass Company's factory here produced the glass from 1825 until 1888, when competition with glassmakers in the Midwest—and finally a union strike—closed it. While you walk, look for etched Sandwich glass from the old factory on the front doors. There probably aren't two identical glass panels in town.

GETTING HERE AND AROUND

Sandwich, 3 mi east of Sagamore Bridge, is accessed along Route 6A and Route 130. Driving east on Route 6A east brings you to the Sagamore and Bourne bridges; going west will take you all the way to Orleans. Route 130 heads southwest to Falmouth. The center of town is easily explored on foot, but a car is needed to reach nearby attractions.

ESSENTIALS

Visitor Information Sandwich Chamber of Commerce (⊠ *502 Rte. 130, Sandwich Center* ☎ *508/833–9755* ⊕ *www.sandwichchamber.com*).

EXPLORING

TOP ATTRACTIONS

Cape Cod Canal Visitor Center. Run by the U.S. Army Corps of Engineers, the Cape Cod Canal Visitor Center's interactive exhibits and video presentations reveal the canal's history, operation, and flora and fauna. Among the special ranger-led programs are guided hikes, bike trips, evening lectures, and junior ranger programs. The visitor center is located opposite the Coast Guard station, near Joe's Fish Market. ⊠ *60 Ed Moffitt Dr., Sandwich Center* ☎ *508/833–9678* ⊕ *www.nae.usace. army.mil/recreati/ccc/ccchome.htm* 🖾 *Free* ☉ *Mid-May–mid-Oct., call for hrs.*

☾ **Heritage Museums and Gardens.** These 100 beautifully landscaped acres
FodorśChoice overlooking the upper end of Shawme Pond are one of the region's top
★ draws. Paths crisscross the grounds, which include gardens planted with hostas, heather, herbs, and fruit trees. Rhododendrons are in full glory from mid-May through mid-June, and daylilies reach their peak from mid-July through early August. In 1967, pharmaceuticals magnate Josiah K. Lilly III purchased the estate and turned it into a nonprofit museum. A highlight is the Shaker Round Barn, which showcases classic and historic cars—including a 1919 Pierce-Arrow, a 1915 Milburn Light Electric, and a 1911 Stanley Steamer, and a 1930 yellow-and-green Duesenberg built for movie star Gary Cooper. The history museum houses a semipermanent exhibit called "A Bird in the Hand," as well as seasonal exhibitions. The art museum has an extraordinary collection of New England folk art, including paintings, weather vanes, Nantucket baskets, and scrimshaw. Both adults and children can enjoy riding on a Coney Island–style carousel dating from the early 20th century. Other features include Hidden Hollow, an outdoor activity center for families with children.

A shuttle bus—equipped with a wheelchair lift and space to stow baby strollers—transports visitors on certain days. In summer, concerts are held in the gardens, often on Wednesday or Saturday evening or Sunday afternoon. The center of the complex is about ¾ mi on foot from the in-town end of Shawme Pond. ⊠ *67 Grove St., Sandwich Center* ☎ *508/888–3300* ⊕ *www.heritagemuseumsandgardens.org* 🖾 *$12* ☉ *Apr.–Nov., daily 10–5.*

Sandwich Boardwalk. For a view of the bay, you can walk to Town Neck Beach on the Sandwich Boardwalk, built over a salt marsh, creek, and low dunes. After Hurricane Bob destroyed the previous boardwalk in 1991, locals donated planks to rebuild it. Some are inscribed with a donor's name; others have jokes (GET OFF OUR BOARD) and words of widsom (SIMPLIFY/THOREAU). The long sweep of Cape Cod Bay stretches out around the beach at the end of the walk, where a platform provides fine views, especially at sunset. You can look out toward Sandy Neck, Wellfleet, and Provincetown or toward the white cliffs beyond Sagamore. Near this mostly rocky beach are dunes covered with rugosa roses, which have a delicious fragrance; this is a good place for birding. The creeks running through the salt marsh make for great canoeing. From the town center it's about a mile to the boardwalk; cross Route 6A on Jarves Street, and at its end turn left, then right, and continue to the boardwalk parking lot. ⊠ *End of Jarves St., Sandwich Center.*

Sandwich Glass Museum. With its more than 10,000 square feet of exhibits, the Sandwich Glass Museum has information about the history of the shimmering glass that was manufactured here more than a century

2

ago. There is a diorama showing how the factory looked in its heyday, an "ingredient room" showcasing a wide spectrum of glass colors along with the minerals added to the sand to obtain them, and an outstanding collection of blown and pressed glass in many shapes and hues. Large lamps, vases, and pitchers are impressive, as are the hundreds of candlesticks and small saucers on display. Daily glassblowing demonstrations are daily on the hour between 10 and 3. The extensive, ornate gift shop sells some handsome reproductions, including some made by local and national artisans. ⊠ *129 Main St., Sandwich Center* ☎ *508/888–0251* ⊕ *www.sandwichglassmuseum.org* ✎ *$5* ☉ *Apr.–Dec., daily 9:30–4; Feb. and Mar., Wed.–Sun. 9:30–4.*

Ⓒ **Thornton W. Burgess Museum.** This delightful museum is dedicated to the

Fodor'sChoice Sandwich native whose tales of Peter Cottontail, Reddy Fox, and a host

★ of other creatures have been part of children's bedtimes for decades. Thornton Burgess (1874–1965), an avid conservationist, made his characters behave true to their species to educate children as he entertained them. Storytelling sessions, often including live animals, take place in July and August. In the Discovery Room, kids can use their imaginations in the prop-filled classroom. On display are some of Burgess's 170 books (although children are welcome here, the exhibits are of the don't-touch variety). The small gift shop carries puppets, books, and dinnerware decorated with Burgess characters. ⊠ *4 Water St., Sandwich Center* ☎ *508/888–4668* ⊕ *www.thorntonburgess.org* ✎ *$2* ☉ *May–Oct., Mon.–Sat. 10–4.*

WORTH NOTING

Benjamin Nye Homestead and Museum. Hailing from the 17th century, the Benjamin Nye Homestead and Museum was once the home of one of the country's first gristmills. Although the mill is long gone, the scenic views are still present, as are the many original details within the home's modest walls. ⊠ *85 Old County Rd., East Sandwich* ☎ *508/888–4213* ⊕ *www.nyefamily.org* ✎ *$3* ☉ *Mid-June–mid-Oct., Tues.–Sat. noon–4:30.*

Dexter Gristmill. Where Shawme Pond drains over its dam, a little wooden bridge leads over a watercourse to this waterwheel-powered mill built in 1654. In season the miller demonstrates the grinding process, talks about the mill's operation, and sells its ground corn. ⊠ *Water and Grove Sts., Sandwich Center* ☎ *508/888–4910 Sandwich Town Hall* ✎ *$3; $5 includes admission to Hoxie House* ☉ *June–early Oct., Mon.–Sat. 10–5.*

OFF THE
BEATEN
PATH

Green Briar Nature Center and Jam Kitchen. Owned and operated by the Thornton Burgess Society, this nature center is a solid symbol of the old Cape. You pass a wildflower garden on your way in, and the Smiling Pool sparkles out back. Birds flit about the grounds, and great smells waft from vintage stoves in the kitchen, where you can watch as jams and pickles are made according to century-old recipes. The Briar Patch Conservation Area behind the building has nature trails—take a walk and visit the real live animals that inspired Peter Cottontail, Grandfather Frog, and other beloved characters. ⊠ *6 Discovery Hill Rd., off Rte. 6A, East Sandwich* ☎ *508/888–6870* ⊕ *www.thorntonburgess.org* ✎ *$2 suggested donation* ☉ *Apr.–Dec., Mon.–Sat. 10–4, Sun. 1–4; Jan.–Mar., Tues.–Sat. 10–4.*

Hoxie House. This remarkable old saltbox is virtually unaltered since it was built in 1675. Although occupied until the 1950s, the house was never modernized with electricity or plumbing. Furnishings reflect daily life in the colonial period, with some pieces on loan from Boston's Museum of Fine Arts. Highlights are diamond-shaped lead-glass windows and a collection of antique textile machines. ⊠ *18 Water St., Sandwich Center* ☎ *508/888–1173* *$3; $5 includes admission to Dexter Gristmill* ۞ *Late May–mid-June, Sat. 10–5, Sun. 1–5; mid-June–mid-Oct., Mon.–Sat. 10–5, Sun. 1–5.*

Old Town Cemetery. Across from Hoxie House is this classic, undulating New England graveyard. You can stop in for a peaceful moment and trace the genealogy of old Sandwich. On Thursday in July and August, you can hear tales during narrated walking tours about the cemetery's more-illustrious inhabitants; call the Sandwich Glass Museum for additional information. ⊠ *Grove St., Sandwich Center* *Free.*

☉ **Sandwich Fish Hatchery.** One of the oldest fish hatcheries in the country, this facility holds more than 200,000 brook, brown, and rainbow trout at various stages of development; they are raised to stock the state's ponds. The mesh over the raceways keeps kingfishers and herons from snagging a free lunch. You can buy feed for 25¢ and watch the fish jump for it. ⊠ *164 Rte. 6A, Sandwich Center* ☎ *508/888–0008* *Free* ۞ *Daily 9–3.*

☉ **Shawme Pond.** A lovely place for a stroll, this park is a favorite with children. The ducks and swans love to be fed, though posted signs warn you not to indulge them. Across the way—a perfect backdrop for this setting—stands the spired, white 1848 First Church of Christ, inspired by a design by British architect Christopher Wren. ⊠ *Water and Grove Sts., Sandwich Center.*

Wing Fort House. The Wing Fort House was built in 1641 and can boast the distinction of being the "oldest house in New England owned and occupied continuously by the same family for over three centuries." The interior reveals changing tastes in decor and architecture over the centuries. ⊠ *69 Springhill Rd., East Sandwich* ☎ *508/833–1540* ⊕ *www.wingfamily.org* *$3* ۞ *Mid-June–late Sept., Tues.–Sat. 10–4.*

WHERE TO EAT

$ ✕ **Bee-Hive Tavern.** This informal, friendly colonial-style tavern hasn't
AMERICAN been here since Revolutionary times (it opened in the early '90s), but the cozy dark-wood booths and wide-board floors look the part. The kitchen turns out solid fare, such as burgers and steaks, freshly caught fish, and lobster. Dinner-size salads are also available, and breads and desserts are made on the premise. Reservations aren't officially taken, but you can call ahead to make the wait a little easier. ⊠ *406 Rte. 6A, East Sandwich* ☎ *508/833–1184* ⊕ *www.thebeehivetavern.com* ⊟ *MC, V.*

$ ✕ **Hemisphere.** The most striking feature here is the supreme vista: via a
AMERICAN generous array of windows, the sun sets over Cape Cod Bay while all manner of boats prepare to make their passage through the Cape Cod Canal. For both lunch and dinner, the menu covers vast ground with everything from fried seafood favorites to the more sophisticated. Try

the apple-and-Brie-stuffed chicken breast with a light amaretto cream sauce. Grab a table on the outdoor deck for a real seaside experience. A full bar makes waiting for a table fairly painless (reservations are available only for parties of five or more). ⊠ *98 Town Neck Rd., Sandwich Center* ☎ *508/888–6166* ⊕ *www.hemispherecapecod.com* ▤ *AE, MC, V* ⊘ *Closed Nov.–Mar.*

$ ✕ **Marshland Restaurant and Bakery.** Sandwich's version of down-home
AMERICAN is this homey coffee shop tucked into a parking lot. For breakfast try "Boardwalk Eggs," which are two poached eggs on an English muffin with Canadian bacon and cheddar cheese. The lunch specials—a grilled chicken club sandwich, a Cobb salad, a turkey Reuben—are the best choices midday. For dinner the prime rib does not disappoint. ⊠ *109 Rte. 6A, Sandwich Center* ☎ *508/888–9824* ⊕ *www. marshlandrestaurant.com* ▤ *AE, MC, V.*

$ ✕ **Seafood Sam's.** Fried seafood reigns supreme at Sam's, across from the
SEAFOOD Coast Guard station and a stone's throw from the Cape Cod Canal. Order from the counter, take a number, and sit in an airy dining room where the munch of fried clams accompanies the sound of lobsters being cracked open. Sam's also has branches in Harwichport, Falmouth, and South Yarmouth. ⊠ *6 Coast Guard Rd., Sandwich Center* ☎ *508/888–4629* ⊕ *www.seafoodsams.com* ▤ *D, MC, V* ⊘ *Closed early Nov.–early Mar.*

WHERE TO STAY

$$ ⬚ **1750 Inn at Sandwich Center.** Across from the Sandwich Glass Museum,
★ this 18th-century house with fine colonial and Victorian furnishings is listed on the National Register of Historic Places. In addition to such decorative flourishes as ornate fireplaces, rooms contain high-thread-count linens, fluffy robes, and Gilchrist & Soames bath amenities. A gazebo on a nearby hill houses a secluded spa where you can arrange a massage. A hearty breakfast is served in the keeping room, which contains a fireplace and an antique table that seats 10. Gracious hosts Jan and Charlie Preus know a lot about the region and have created a warm and inviting inn that's appealing whether you seek quiet seclusion or the opportunity to mingle with fellow guests. **Pros:** easy access to town center; intimate and friendly atmosphere. **Cons:** some steep; narrow stairs. ⊠ *118 Tupper Rd., Sandwich Center* ☎ *508/888–6958 or 800/249–6949* ⊕ *www.innatsandwich.com* ➵ *5 rooms* ⌂ *In-room: a/c, no phone, DVD (some), Wi-Fi. In-hotel: no kids under 12* ▤ *MC, V* ⊘ *Closed Jan.–Mar.* ⊚| *BP.*

$$$ ⬚ **Belfry Inne & Bistro.** This one-of-a-kind inn comprises a 1901 former
Fodor's Choice church, an ornate wood-frame 1882 Victorian, and an 1827 Federal-
★ style house clustered on a main campus. Room themes in each building nod to their respective histories—the Painted Lady's charmingly appointed rooms, for example, are named after former inhabitants. The luxurious rooms in the Abbey, named for the six days of creation, have whirlpool tubs and gas fireplaces, and are set along a corridor overlooking the restaurant below. (If it's available, splurge on the Tuesday room—the incredible stained-glass "compass" window will take your breath away.) The Bistro serves dazzling, globally inspired dishes

such as black grouper roasted with tamarind-yogurt sauce in a striking setting. The Painted Lady restaurant serves innovative renditions of home-style American favorites, including a delicious baked mac-and-cheese. **Pros:** great in-town location; bright, beautiful, and spacious rooms. **Cons:** some steep stairs. ⊠ *8 Jarves St., Sandwich Center* ☎ *508/888–8550 or 800/844–4542* ⊕ *www.belfryinn.com* ⟳ *20 rooms* ⚘ *In-room: a/c, Wi-Fi (some). In-hotel: 2 restaurants, bar* ⊟ *AE, D, DC, MC, V* ⊚ *BP.*

$$$ ⊡ **Dan'l Webster Inn and Spa.** Built on the site of a 17th-century inn, the Dan'l Webster is a contemporary hotel within the heart of Sandwich's historic downtown. Rooms are decked out in high-end colonial-inspired cherrywood and mahogany furnishings in traditional colors. You might find a hand-painted reproduction armoire in one room, a pencil-post four-poster bed in another; some units have fireplaces, and most have balconies overlooking the nicely manicured gardens. The restaurant serves modern Continental dishes such as lamb dusted with organic cocoa and finished with a chèvre cream sauce. A casual tavern serves pizzas, burgers, and salads. The spa offers a full slate of massage, facial, and beauty treatments. **Pros:** ideal in-town location; tasteful setting. **Cons:** very popular with bus tours. ⊠ *149 Main St., Sandwich Center* ☎ *508/888–3622 or 800/444–3566* ⊕ *www.danlwebsterinn.com* ⟳ *35 rooms, 13 suites* ⚘ *In-room: a/c, Wi-Fi. In-hotel: 2 restaurants, room service, pool, spa* ⊟ *AE, D, DC, MC, V.*

$ ⊡ **Earl of Sandwich Motel.** Single-story Tudor-style buildings form a U around a duck pond and wooded lawn set with lawn chairs. Rooms, attractively if simply furnished, are nicely sized with large windows and dark pine headboards and doors. Many rooms have canopy beds. A Continental plan is offered from late May to October. **Pros:** countryside setting with picnic areas; reasonable rates. **Cons:** bathrooms are a little outdated; some rooms feel crowded. ⊠ *378 Rte. 6A, East Sandwich* ☎ *508/888–1415 or 800/442–3275* ⊕ *www.earlofsandwich.com* ⟳ *24 rooms* ⚘ *In-room: a/c, refrigerator, Wi-Fi. In-hotel: pool* ⊟ *AE, D, DC, MC, V* ⊙ *Closed Dec.–Mar.* ⊚ *CP.*

$$$–$$$$ ⊡ **Isaiah Jones Homestead Bed & Breakfast.** Innkeepers Don and Kather-
★   ine Sanderson know how to give their guests extraordinary service in an equally stellar setting. Their venerable Victorian is all graceful lines and high ceilings, adorned with authentic period antiques and moody stained glass. Despite intricate wall coverings, sweeping velvet drapes, and canopy beds, the spacious rooms are uncluttered and welcoming. Recline in the comfortable parlor with afternoon cordials or peruse the DVD library for an in-room movie. You'll want to rest up after a three-course breakfast that might include a special house omelet with fresh herbs. The two suites in the adjacent carriage house have a simpler, cottage style. **Pros:** easy walk to town center; beautiful grounds. **Cons:** some steep stairs. ⊠ *165 Main St., Sandwich Center* ☎ *508/888–9115 or 800/526–1625* ⊕ *www.isaiahjones.com* ⟳ *5 rooms, 2 suites* ⚘ *In-room: no phone, a/c, DVD, Wi-Fi. In-hotel: bicycles, no kids under 12* ⊟ *AE, D, MC, V* ⊚ *BP.*

$ ⊡ **Sandy Neck Motel.** Like the roadside country motels of old, this white-shingled motel with cheery blue shutters offers simple and convenient lodging for a reasonable price. Standard rooms are outfitted with white bedspreads and matching wicker furniture. The expansive grounds are dotted with barbecue grills, picnic tables, and Adirondack chairs, set back a bit off Route 6A. The efficiency is a good bet for families on a budget (or who just like to make their own meals) with a full-size kitchen and two bedrooms. The entrance to Sandy Neck Beach is about 1 mi away; for those in search of the entertainment and vacation glitz of Hyannis, it's a mere 15-minute drive. **Pros:** quiet setting; reasonable rates; close to beach. **Cons:** not for those looking for an in-town location. ⊠ *669 Rte. 6A, East Sandwich* ☎ *508/362–3992 or 800/564–3992* ⊕ *www.sandyneck.com* ⇆ *11 rooms, 1 efficiency* ⚹ *In-room: a/c, refrigerator, Wi-Fi* ⊟ *AE, MC, V* ⊘ *Closed Nov.–Apr.*

¢ ⚹ **Shawme-Crowell State Forest.** Less than a mile from the Cape Cod Canal, this 742-acre state forest is a good base for local biking and hiking, and campers get free day use of Scusset Beach. Open-air campfires are allowed at the wooded tent and RV (no hookups) campsites. Heated bathroom and shower facilities are a blessing on chilly mornings. The campground is generally open year-round, but if you're planning a winter trip, call to confirm before visiting. **Pros:** heated bathroom and shower facilities. **Cons:** beach is on the other side of the Cape Cod Canal. ⊠ *Rte. 130, Sandwich Center* ☎ *508/888–0351, 877/422–6762 reservations* ⊕ *www.reserveamerica.com* ⇆ *285 sites* ⚹ *fFlush toilets, drinking water, showers* ⊟ *MC, V.*

NIGHTLIFE AND THE ARTS

THE ARTS

Town-band concerts (⊠ *Bandstand, Henry T. Wing Elementary School, Rte. 130 and Beale Ave., Sandwich Center* ☎ *508/888–5144*) are held Thursday evening from July through late August starting at 7:30.

NIGHTLIFE

Bobby Byrne's Pub (⊠ *65 Rte. 6A, Sandwich Center* ☎ *508/888–6088*), with other locations in Hyannis and Mashpee, is a comfortable pub, with a jukebox and a good menu.

British Beer Company (⊠ *46 Rte. 6A, Sandwich Center* ☎ *508/833–9590* ⊕ *www.britishbeer.com*), with other locations in Cedarville, Falmouth, Hyannis, and Plymouth, has a traditional British "public house" atmosphere with a great menu that includes fish, ribs, and pizza. Sunday evenings feature karaoke; a variety of bands play Thursday through Saturday nights.

BEACHES, SPORTS, AND THE OUTDOORS

BEACHES

East Sandwich Beach lies behind the grass-covered dunes beyond a row of gray-shingle beach cottages. It's a long stretch of sand, but nearby parking is very limited (and restricted to residents between 8 AM and 4 PM in season). From Route 6A follow Ploughed Neck Road to North Shore Road. ⊠ *North Shore Rd., East Sandwich.*

Town Neck Beach is a long, dune-backed bay beach with a mix of sand and pebbles. You need a resident parking sticker to leave your car in the large parking area between 8 AM and 4 PM in season. There are restrooms and a snack bar. ⊠ *Town Neck Rd., Sandwich Center.*

GOLF

Holly Ridge Golf Club (⊠ *121 Country Club Rd., Sandwich Center* ☎ *508/428–5577* ⊕ *www.hollyridgegolf.com*) has an 18-hole, par-54 course that's good for all levels of golfers.

Sandwich Hollows Golf Club (⊠ *1 Round Hill Rd., East Sandwich* ☎ *508/888–3384* ⊕ *www.sandwichhollows.com*) has an 18-hole, par-71 course that's open to the public.

SHOPPING

★ The **Brown Jug** (⊠ *155 Main St., Sandwich Center* ☎ *508/888–4669* ⊕ *www.thebrownjug.com*) is a tantalizing food and wine shop in a cozy brown-shingle house in the center of Sandwich—the perfect place to pick up delicious picnic supplies. You'll find cheeses, chocolate, and all sorts of hard-to-find imported foods; you can also order tasty sandwiches to go or enjoy lunch on the patio.

The **Giving Tree** (⊠ *550 Rte. 6A, East Sandwich* ☎ *508/888–5446 or 888/246–3551* ⊕ *www.givingtreejewelry.com*) sells jewelry and metal sculpture. The shop is open Memorial Day through Christmas.

Joe's Lobster Mart (⊠ *Cape Cod Canal, Sandwich Center* ☎ *508/888–2971*), opposite Seafood Sam's and the Coast Guard station, sells fresh-from-the-tank lobsters. Call ahead, and they'll boil your crustaceans to order—a great idea for an easy dinner at your cottage or hotel or for a picnic overlooking the canal. Joe's also sells fresh fish.

Sandwich Auction House (⊠ *15 Tupper Rd., Sandwich Center* ☎ *508/888–1926* ⊕ *www.sandwichauction.com*) is a fun place to spend a Wednesday night (Saturday in the off-season); come after 2 PM to preview the items for sale. This local institution has sales three to four times a month. In addition, specialty sales every six to eight weeks feature upscale antiques received during that period. Sales are also held for antique and modern rugs.

Fodor's Choice
★ **Titcomb's Bookshop** (⊠ *432 Rte. 6A, East Sandwich* ☎ *508/888–2331* ⊕ *www.titcombsbookshop.com*) stocks used, rare, and new books, including a large collection of Cape and nautical titles and Americana, as well as an extensive selection of children's books.

FALMOUTH

Falmouth, the Cape's second-largest town, was settled in 1660 by Congregationalists from Barnstable who had been ostracized by their church and deprived of voting privileges and other civil rights for sympathizing with the Quakers (then the victims of severe repression). The town was incorporated in 1686 and named for Falmouth, England. The Falmouth area, sprawling over 44 square mi, consists of eight villages: Falmouth, North Falmouth, West Falmouth, Hatchville, Teaticket, East Falmouth,

DRIVING SCENIC ROUTE 6A

Route 6A heads east from Sandwich, passing through the oldest settlements on the Cape. Part of the Old King's Highway historic district, the route is protected from development. Classic inns and enticing antiques shops alternate with traditional gray-shingle homes on this tree-lined road, and the woods periodically give way to broad vistas across the marshes.

In autumn the foliage along the way is bright; maples with their feet wet in ponds and marshes put on a good display. Along Route 6A just east of Sandwich Center, you can stop to watch cranberries being harvested in flooded bogs.

If you're heading down-Cape and you have plenty of time, this is a lovely route to take. And if you do wish to take the faster but less-interesting U.S. 6 as your primary route through the region, it's easy to hop off here and there and travel certain stretches of parallel Route 6A. Barnstable, Dennis, and Brewster offer plenty to explore.

Waquoit, and Woods Hole. Each has a different character, from Falmouth's colonial center to the ferry port of Woods Hole to quiet East Falmouth and Waquoit.

FALMOUTH AND WOODS HOLE

15 mi south of Bourne Bridge, 20 mi south of Sandwich.

Falmouth's lovely Village Green is listed on the National Register of Historic Places. It served as a militia training field in the 18th century and a grazing ground for horses in the early 19th century. Also on the green is the 1856 Congregational Church, built on the timbers of its 1796 predecessor, with a bell made by Paul Revere. The bell's cheery inscription reads THE LIVING TO THE CHURCH I CALL, AND TO THE GRAVE I SUMMON ALL. South of the town center is Nantucket Sound, where you'll find several often-crowded beaches popular with families. To the east, the Falmouth Heights neighborhood mixes inns, B&Bs, and private homes nestled close together on residential streets leading to the sea. Bustling Grand Avenue, the main drag in Falmouth Heights, hugs the shore and the beach. Parks and ponds dot the town; one of the nicest, Grews Pond in Goodwill Park, is north of the town center—it's a lovely site for a picnic on a summer afternoon.

The village of Woods Hole dangles from the Cape's southwestern tip. As a major departure point for ferries to Martha's Vineyard, it draws crowds of through-traffic in season. Because Woods Hole is home to four international research centers, each summer the one-street village overflows with thousands of scientists and graduate students who come from around the globe to participate in study programs or to work on independent research projects. A handful of waterside cafés along Water Street compete for the distinction of having the most bicycles stacked up at the door.

GETTING HERE AND AROUND

The Cape Cod Regional Transit Authority operates the SeaLine from Hyannis to Woods Hole, connecting Centerville, Osterville, Mashpee, Falmouth Center, and Woods Hole. Parking in Woods Hole, with its small number of metered spaces, can be nearly impossible. If you're coming from Falmouth to wander around Woods Hole, consider riding a bicycle or taking public transportation.

ESSENTIALS

Visitor Information Falmouth Chamber of Commerce (⊠ *20 Academy La., Falmouth* ☎ *508/548–8500 or 800/526–8532* ⊕ *www.falmouthchamber.com*).

EXPLORING

TOP ATTRACTIONS

Falmouth Museums on the Green. This cluster of museums represents life in colonial Cape Cod. The 1790 **Julia Wood House** retains wonderful architectural details—a widow's walk, wide-plank floors, leaded-glass windows, and a colonial kitchen with a huge hearth. Antique embroideries, baby shoes and clothes, toys and dolls, portraits, furniture, and the trappings of an authentically equipped doctor's office, all from the house's onetime owner, fill the premises. Out back, a barn displays antique farm implements, a 19th-century horse-drawn sleigh, and other interesting items. Next door, the smaller **Conant House**, a 1730–60 half Cape (an asymmetrical 1½-story building), holds changing exhibitions including military memorabilia, whaling items, scrimshaw, sailors' valentines, and a genealogical- and historical-research library. One collection includes books, portraits, and other items relating to Katharine Lee Bates, the native daughter who wrote "America the Beautiful."

Guides give tours of the museums at 11, and the adjacent formal garden with a gazebo and flagstone paths is a great place to relax afterward. Free demonstrations of colonial skills are offered on Friday in July and August. You might get a chance to dip a candle, churn butter, weave a basket, or learn some sea chanteys. ⊠ *Village Green, 55 Palmer Ave., Falmouth Center* ☎ *508/548–4857* ⊕ *www.falmouthhistoricalsociety. org* 🎟 *Free* ☉ *Mid–May–mid-Oct., Tues.–Fri. 10–4, Sat. 10–1; mid-Oct.–mid- May, Tues. and Thurs. 10–4, Sat. 10–1.*

QUICK BITES For a region that eagerly fought for independence from Mother England, there are many places in Cape Cod to enjoy the oh-so-British pastime of having a spot of tea. **Molly's Tea Room** (⊠ *227 Main St., Falmouth Center* ☎ *508/457–1666*), in the center of Falmouth, has dozens of flavors to choose from, as well as a selection of sandwiches, salads, soups, and quiches, should you find yourself a bit hungry as well. Non–tea drinkers can partake in the wine or beer offerings.

National Marine Fisheries Service Aquarium. This impressive facility displays 16 large tanks and many more smaller ones filled with regional fish and shellfish. The rooms are small, but they are crammed with stuff to see. Magnifying glasses and a dissecting scope help you examine marine life. Several hands-on pools hold banded lobsters, crabs, snails, starfish, and other creatures. The stars of the show are two

Fodor's Choice
★

harbor seals, on view in the outdoor pool near the entrance; watch their feedings weekdays at 11 and 4. ⊠ *Albatross and Water Sts., Woods Hole* ☎ *508/495–2267* ⊕ *www.nefsc.nmfs.gov/nefsc/aquarium* ⊠ *Free* ☉ *Tues.–Sat. 11–4.*

Nobska Light. This imposing lighthouse has spectacular views from its base of the nearby Elizabeth Islands and of Martha's Vineyard, across Vineyard Sound. The 42-foot cast-iron tower, lined with brick, was built in 1876 with a stationary light. It shines red to indicate danger-ous waters or white for safe passage. Since the light was automated in 1985, the adjacent keeper's quarters have been the headquarters of the Coast Guard group commander—a fitting passing of the torch from one safeguarder of ships to another. The interior is open to the public only sporadically. ⊠ *Church St., Woods Hole* ⊕ *www.lighthouse.cc/nobska.*

Woods Hole Oceanographic Institution Ocean Science Exhibit Center. You can learn about the Woods Hole Oceanographic Institution at this small center with exhibits on its various projects. This is a great way to see some of the research vessels, including a full-scale mock-up of the sub-mersible *Alvin.* If you'd prefer to see the actual institution, hour-long walking tours are offered weekdays at 10:30 and 1:30 in July and August. Tours begin at 93 Water Street and are free, but reservations are required. ⊠ *15 School St., Woods Hole* ☎ *508/289–2663 for exhibit center, 508/289–2252 for walking tours* ⊕ *www.whoi.edu/visitus* ⊠ *$2* ☉ *Call for hrs.*

WORTH NOTING

Charles D. and Margaret K. Spohr Gardens. These privately owned gardens on Oyster Pond are a pretty, peaceful place. The springtime explosion of more than 700,000 daffodils gives way in turn to the tulips, azaleas, magnolias, flowering crab apples, rhododendrons, lilies, and climbing hydrangeas in summer. A collection of old millstones, bronze church bells, and ships' anchors decorates the landscape. ⊠ *45 Fells Rd., off Oyster Pond Rd., Falmouth* ☎ *508/548–0623* ⊕ *www.spohrgardens. org* ⊠ *Free* ☉ *Daily 8–8.*

Episcopal Church of the Messiah. This 1888 stone church has a conical steeple and a small medicinal-herb garden in the shape of a Celtic cross. The garden, enclosed by a holly hedge, has a bench for medita-tion. Inscriptions on either side of the carved gate read ENTER IN HOPE and DEPART IN PEACE. ⊠ *13 Church St., Woods Hole* ☎ *508/548–2145* ⊠ *Free* ☉ *Daily sunrise–sunset.*

Leary Family Amusement Center. Video-game rooms and candlepin bowl-ing make this a great place to take the kids on a rainy day. It's open daily 10 to 10. ⊠ *23 Town Hall Sq., off Rte. 28, Falmouth Center* ☎ *508/540–4877.*

Marine Biological Laboratory–Woods Hole Oceanographic Institution Library. This is one of the best collections of biological, ecological, and oceano-graphic literature in the world. The library has access to more than 200 computer databases and subscribes to more than 5,000 scientific journals in 40 languages, with complete collections of most. The Rare Books Room contains photographs, monographs, and prints, as well as journal collections that date from 1665.

Unless you are a scientific researcher, the only way you can get to see the library is by taking the hour-long tours offered weekdays at 1 and 2 from late June to late August. The tours, led by retired scientists, include an introductory slide show as well as stops at the library and the marine resources center. ⊠ *7 Marine Biological Laboratory St., off Water St., Woods Hole* ☎ *508/289–7423 for library, 508/289–7623 for tours* ⊕ *www.mbl.edu.*

QUICK BITES

Pie in the Sky (⊠ *10 Water St., Woods Hole* ☎ *508/540–5475*), a small bakery with indoor and outdoor seating, sells scratch-made cookies, pastries, and sandwiches along with all-organic, fair-trade coffee roasted in small batches by Pie in the Sky owner Eric Gura. The Oreo-cookie bars are truly decadent. It's a short walk from the ferry terminal, and a good bet for breakfast.

Woods Hole Historical Museum. This three-building complex houses a model of the town as it looked in the 1890s. One room is filled with elegant ladies' clothing from the late 1800s. The archives hold old ships' logs, postcards, newspaper articles, maps, diaries, and photographs; more than 200 tapes of oral history provided by local residents; and a 100-volume library on maritime history. Free guided walking tours of the village depart from the museum Tuesday at 4 in July and August. ⊠ *573 Woods Hole Rd., Woods Hole* ☎ *508/548–7270* ⊕ *www.woodsholemuseum.org* ⊠ *Free* ⊙ *Mid-June–mid-Oct., Tues.–Sat. 10–4.*

WHERE TO EAT

¢ ✕ **Betsy's Diner.** A classic American treasure, Betsy's is a shiny, happy,
AMERICAN busy place with a reassuring pink-neon sign urging you to EAT HEAVY. The generous dining room, gleaming counter, and stools and booths by the big windows are done in pretty pastel mauve-and-cream tones. Memorabilia and neon grace the walls. Pancakes, waffles, and omelets are served all day, and typical dinner options include meat loaf and mashed potatoes, knockwurst and sauerkraut, and charbroiled pork chops. ⊠ *457 Main St., Falmouth Center* ☎ *508/540–0060* ⊠ *Reservations not accepted* ⊟ *AE, D, MC, V* ⊙ *No dinner Sun.*

$ ✕ **Captain Kidd.** The stately bar, festive atmosphere, and a small number
AMERICAN of cozy tables that cluster around a woodstove and overlook Eel Pond make this a year-round favorite for locals. Baked scrod, broiled scallops, lemon-herb roasted chicken, and mussels in a light tomato broth are a few of the favorites. In the bar area, a lighter and less-expensive menu is offered, including pizzas, steaks, pastas, fish-and-chips, and

fried seafood platters. ⊠ *77 Water St., Woods Hole* ☎ *508/548–8563* ⊕ *www.thecaptainkidd.com* ⊟ *AE, MC, V.*

$$ × **Chapoquoit Grill.** Comfortable and bustling, this unassuming local AMERICAN favorite has an Italian slant, starting with creative pastas and wood-★ fired pizzas. The long list of daily specials might include wood-grilled duck with orange-molasses glaze or sirloin with a tamarind-mango glaze. A fireplace and coral-color walls make the front room intimate, and the larger rear dining room seems vaguely tropical (with a palm tree in the middle). Half portions of many entrées are available for those with smaller appetites. Expect daunting waits on summer weekends. ⊠ *410 W. Falmouth Hwy., West Falmouth* ☎ *508/540–7794* ⊕ *www.,chapoquoitgrill.com* ⩜ *Reservations not accepted* ⊟ *MC, V* ⊘ *No lunch.*

$ × **The Clam Shack.** Fried clams top the menu at this basic seafood joint AMERICAN right on Falmouth Harbor. The clams are crisp and fresh; the meaty lobster roll and the fish-and-chips platter are good choices, too. Place your order at the counter and then take your tray to the picnic tables on the roof deck for the best views. More tables are on the dock in back, or you can squeeze into the tiny dining room. Just don't plan on a late night here—the Shack closes most evenings around 8. ⊠ *227 Clinton Ave., Falmouth Harbor* ☎ *508/540–7758* ⊟ *No credit cards* ⊘ *Closed early Sept.–late May.*

$$$ × **Glass Onion.** This classy yet comfortable dinner-only spot has cre-AMERICAN ated a buzz among diners who appreciate that everything from the yeasty rosemary bread to the fresh mint ice cream is made in house, sourced whenever possible from local providers. Candlelight reflects off sage-green walls and the original 1926 street-front windows. A handsome coffered ceiling and heavy mirrors create a sophisticated, clubby atmosphere. Favorites on the constantly changing menu include lobster strudel with mascarpone and lobster butter sauce, and seafood risotto with cod and little neck clams in a chowder broth. Leave room for the sumptuous desserts, such as the chocolate terrine with raspberry-thyme sorbet. ⊠ *37 N. Main St., Falmouth Center* ☎ *508/540--3730* ⊕ *www. theglassoniondining.com* ⩜ *Reservations not accepted* ⊟ *AE, D, MC, V* ⊘ *Closed Sun. No lunch.*

$$ × **La Cucina Sul Mare.** Northern Italian and Mediterranean cooking is the ITALIAN specialty at this classy, popular place. The staff is friendly and the setting Fodor's Choice is both intimate and festive, if a bit crowded. Calamari, warm green ★ salad with goat cheese and cranberries, a classic lemon chicken sautéed with shallots and capers, and a variety of specials—including plenty of local fresh fish—adorn the menu. The *zuppa de pesce,* a medley of seafood sautéed in olive oil and garlic and finished in a white-wine, herb-and-tomato broth, is a specialty. Make sure to come hungry—the portions here are huge—and expect a long wait during prime hours in season (there is also a call-ahead wait list). ⊠ *237 Main St., Falmouth Center* ☎ *508/548–5600* ⩜ *Reservations not accepted* ⊟ *AE, D, MC, V.*

$$$ × **Landfall.** Request a window table overlooking the water at this classic SEAFOOD seafood spot, where lobster pots, buoys, and other nautical parapher-nalia hang from the ceilings. Lobster, fried clams, and baked scrod lead off the menu of traditional seafood fare. Though the kids will need

their restaurant manners, it's still family friendly, and the children's all-you-can-eat specials are a great value. ⊠ *2 Luscombe Ave., Woods Hole* ☎ *508/548–1758* ⊕ *www.woodshole.com/landfall* ▤ *AE, MC, V* ⊘ *Closed Dec.–Mar.*

¢ ✕ **Maryellen's Portuguese Bakery.** It's easy to drive right past this no-frills spot hidden behind a Dairy Queen. Take a seat at the counter or at one of the few tables, and then order up breakfast with a Portuguese twist. Try the savory Portuguese omelet, filled with spicy *linguica* (sausage), parsley, onions, and cheese, or the French toast made with Portuguese bread. The lunch menu starts with BLTs and burgers but quickly moves on to kale soup and marinated pork. ⊠ *829 Main St., near Falmouth Heights Rd., Falmouth* ☎ *508/540–9696* ▤ *No credit cards* ⊘ *No dinner.*

PORTUGUESE

$$ ✕ **Quarterdeck.** Part bar, part restaurant—but all Cape Cod—this spot is across the street from Falmouth's town hall, so the lunch talk tends to focus on local politics. The stained glass is not authentic, but the huge whaling harpoons certainly are. Low ceilings and rough-hewn beams seem a good match for the menu, which includes hearty sandwiches such as Reubens and grilled chorizo at lunch and specials at night. The swordfish kebab, skewered with mushrooms, onions, and green peppers and served over jasmine rice, is especially good. ⊠ *164 Main St., Falmouth Center* ☎ *508/548–9900* ▤ *AE, D, DC, MC, V.*

AMERICAN

$$$ ✕ **The RoöBar.** Sleek and sassy, the RoöBar brings a distinctly urban hipness to Falmouth. The bar is a popular watering hole, and the menu—grilled shrimp with edamame puree, barbecued chicken pizza, Gorgonzola-crusted filet mignon—draws its inspiration from many cultures. There's also a terrific wine list. ⊠ *285 Main St., Falmouth Center* ☎ *508/548–8600* ⊕ *www.theroobar.com* ▤ *AE, MC, V* ⊘ *No lunch.*

ECLECTIC
★

$$ ✕ **Shuckers World Famous Raw Bar and Cafe.** Some of the harborside tables at this casual nautical-theme restaurant are so close to the dock that you almost feel as if you're sitting in the bobbing sailboats. The menu ranges from chicken marsala to roasted vegetable ravioli to lobster ravioli, but it's best to stick with the grilled fish and other simple seafood dishes. The "world-famous" lobster boil—a boiled lobster, steamed clams and mussels, and an ear of corn—is justifiably popular. ⊠ *91A Water St., Woods Hole* ☎ *508/540–3850* ⊕ *www.woodshole.com/shuckers* ▤ *AE, D, MC, V* ⊘ *Closed Nov.–Apr., and Mon.–Thurs. mid-May–late May and early Sept.–mid-Oct.*

SEAFOOD

WHERE TO STAY

$$ ▦ **Beach Rose Inn.** This rambling 1863 farmhouse sits on more than an acre of peaceful landscape, slightly off the beaten trail but within close distance of local amenities. The outdoor fire pit is a great place to spend cooler evenings, or you can relax in the hot tub. The rooms—some in the main inn, some in the adjacent carriage house—are simply furnished with quilts, Cape Cod art, and a mix of antiques and reproductions. The Falmouth Suite has an airy, private sunporch. All rooms have private baths, some with whirlpool tubs. In addition to breakfast, light lunch and dinner items, beer and wine are available for purchase at the inn's Bike Rack bar, on a lovely patio overlooking the Shining Sea Bikeway. **Pros:** idyllic setting; on bike path. **Cons:** must drive to beaches,

restaurants, and other attractions. ⊠ *17 Chase Rd., off Rte. 28A, West Falmouth* ☎ *508/540–5706 or 800/498–5706* ⊕ *www.thebeachroseinn. com* ↩ *7 rooms, 1 suite, 1 cottage* ⚬ *In-room: a/c, no phone, kitchen (some), no TV (some), refrigerator (some), Wi-Fi. In-hotel: some pets allowed, no kids under 12* ⊟ *MC, V* ⦿∣*BP.*

$$–$$$ ⚿ **The Captain's Manor Inn.** With its deep, landscaped yard and wrought-
★ iron fence, this elegant inn with a wraparound porch resembles a private estate. The imposing 1849 Italianate house has an upscale style. An expansive and grand foyer welcomes guests to the inn. A full breakfast is served in the formal dining room with original 1849 black marble fireplace, or outside on the veranda overlooking the gardens and gazebo. Although the inn is steps from the town center, you can lounge in the greenery and feel a world away. **Pros:** walk to town center; elegant setting. **Cons:** long stairway to second-floor rooms. ⊠ *27 W. Main St., Falmouth Center* ☎ *508/548–3786* ⊕ *www.captainsmanorinn.com* ↩ *8 rooms* ⚬ *In-room: a/c, Wi-Fi. In-hotel: no kids under 12* ⊟ *D, MC, V* ⦿∣*BP.*

$$ ⚿ **Capt. Tom Lawrence House.** A lawn shaded by old maple trees sur-
rounds this pretty white house, which is steps from downtown yet set back from the street enough to feel secluded. Built in 1861 for a whaling captain, the intimate B&B has romantic rooms with antique and painted furniture, luxurious linens, country wallpaper, and thick carpeting. An efficiency apartment is bright, spacious, and suitable for families, with a fully equipped eat-in kitchen. Breakfast and afternoon snacks are served near the fireplace in the common room. The owners are extremely friendly and helpful. **Pros:** easy walk to town center; great breakfasts. **Cons:** steep, curving staircase; some rooms may feel a little tight. ⊠ *75 Locust St., Falmouth Center* ☎ *508/548–9178* ⊕ *www. captaintomlawrence.com* ↩ *6 rooms, 1 efficiency* ⚬ *In-room: a/c, no phone, refrigerator, Wi-Fi. In-hotel: no kids under 5* ⊟ *AE, MC, V* ⊙ *Closed Jan.* ⦿∣*BP.*

$$$ ⚿ **Chapoquoit Inn.** Four-poster beds, designer bed coverings, and gar-
den views fill the rooms at this cozy B&B in a 1739 former Quaker homestead surrounded by woodland and flower beds. Owners Kim and Tim McIntyre (she's a former marketing exec, he's a landscape designer) have furnished their inn with antiques and other family heirlooms. In the sunny breakfast room, which opens to the deck, you might find lemon pancakes or crème brûlée French toast. Chapoquoit Beach is a short walk away. **Pros:** beach chairs and towels available; nearby public tennis courts. **Cons:** not an in-town location; a bit run-down. ⊠ *495 W. Falmouth Hwy., West Falmouth* ☎ *508/540–7232 or 800/842–8994* ⊕ *www.chapoquoit.com* ↩ *5 rooms* ⚬ *In-room: no phone, no TV (some). In-hotel: bicycles, Wi-Fi hotspot, no kids under 12* ⊟ *AE, MC, V* ⦿∣*BP.*

$$–$$$ ⚿ **Coonamessett Inn.** At this delightful old-Cape-style inn, five buildings
of one- and two-bedroom suites ring a landscaped lawn that leads to a scenic wooded area. Rooms are casually decorated with bleached wood or pine paneling and New England antiques or reproductions. A large collection of Cape artist Ralph Cahoon's work appears throughout the inn. In the main dining room, a few contemporary flourishes

enhance the traditional menu; you can still find rack of lamb and baked-stuffed lobster, but you might also see cumin-scented scallops with Israeli couscous. Lighter fare is served in the cozy Eli's Lounge ($). **Pros:** lush grounds; high marks in romantic-dining setting. **Cons:** weddings are a constant here. ⊠ *311 Gifford St., at Jones Rd., Falmouth* ☎ *508/548–2300* ⊕ *www.capecodrestaurants.org/coonamessett* ⇱ *28 suites, 1 cottage* ⚒ *In-room: a/c. In-hotel: restaurant, bar* ⊟ *AE, D, MC, V* ⦿ *CP.*

$$$ ⬚ **Holiday Inn.** This chain hotel is a dependable option for families. A
☾   tried-and-true comfort formula has been applied here: large rooms with contemporary furnishings open onto a large pool area surrounded by patio furniture and greenery. K.C. Steak & Seafood serves breakfast and dinner year-round. You'll find Cape Cod specialties as well as huge quantities of beef—it's an unexpectedly good restaurant despite its setting inside a chain property. The hotel is adjacent to a pond and is close to Falmouth Center. **Pros:** big-name dependability; distractions for the kids. **Cons:** lack of regional character. ⊠ *291 Jones Rd., Falmouth Center* ☎ *508/540–2000 or 800/465–4329* ⊕ *www.holidayinn.com/falmth/capecod* ⇱ *93 rooms, 5 suites* ⚒ *In-room: Wi-Fi. In-hotel: restaurant, room service, pool, gym* ⊟ *AE, D, DC, MC, V.*

$$ ⬚ **The Inn at Siders Lane.** Housed in a contemporary Federal reproduction building nearly indistinguishable from its authentic neighbors, this elegant B&B blends traditional New England hospitality and 19th-century style with modern amenities. Just steps from downtown's bustle, the inn feels private and intimate on its quiet corner by the Village Green. The two upstairs guest rooms are spacious and tastefully appointed with graceful furnishings in pale neutral tones. The downstairs room is smaller but has a big bathroom with a claw-foot tub. Hosts Jim and Maureen Trodden serve a superb hot breakfast, and you can join them again in the afternoon for tea and fresh-baked cookies. **Pros:** easy walk to town; intimate setting; privacy. **Cons:** some stairs. ⊠ *51 W. Main St., Falmouth Center* ☎ *508/495–4359* ⊕ *www.innatsiderslane.com* ⇱ *3 rooms* ⚒ *In-room: a/c. In-hotel: no kids under 10* ⊟ *MC, V* ⦿ *BP.*

$$$$ ⬚ **Inn on the Sound.** At this understated but stylish inn, perched on a
Fodor's Choice   bluff overlooking Vineyard Sound, the living room and most of the
★   guest rooms face the water. All contain unfussy, contemporary furnishings such as natural oak tables, unbleached cottons, ample shelf space, and ceiling fans; four have private decks. Common areas include an art-laden living room with a boulder fireplace, oversize windows, and modern white couches; a bistrolike breakfast room; and a porch with more stunning water views. **Pros:** grand water views; elegant setting. **Cons:** not an in-town location. ⊠ *313 Grand Ave., Falmouth Heights* ☎ *508/457–9666 or 800/564–9668* ⊕ *www.innonthesound.com* ⇱ *10 rooms* ⚒ *In-room: a/c, Wi-Fi. In-hotel: beachfront, no kids under 10* ⊟ *MC, V* ⦿ *BP.*

$$ ⬚ **Palmer House Inn.** This turn-of-the-20th-century Queen Anne home stands on a tree-lined street, just a short stroll from Falmouth's Village Green. The Victorian interior of Falmouth's largest B&B is pretty if slightly over the top, with heavy period furniture, endless lace, and ornate stained-glass windows—many rooms have fireplaces. One good bet is the third-floor Tower Room, which has a view across the treetops. The large rooms in the 1910 carriage house are airier, with more-tailored appointments, and four newer rooms, all with whirlpool baths, are less ornate. There's a two-bedroom suite in a separate cottage (where young children are permitted). A candlelight breakfast is served, and afternoon refreshments are available. **Pros:** ideal, walk-to-town location; elegant breakfast. **Cons:** with all the Victorian flourish, the smallish rooms can feel a bit overdone; most rooms (one is ADA compliant) are accessed via steep stairs (especially third-floor rooms). ⊠ *81 Palmer Ave., Falmouth Center* ☎ *508/548–1230 or 800/472–2632* ⊕ *www.palmerhouseinn.com* ⇥ *16 rooms, 1 cottage* ⟲ *In-room: a/c. In-hotel: bicycles* ▤ *AE, D, MC, V* ⦿⧠ *BP.*

$$$$ ⊞ **Sea Crest Beach Hotel.** Location and amenities are strong draws at this
ℭ   modern hotel, whose eight buildings sprawl along one end of beautiful Old Silver Beach. You'll enjoy some 700 feet of frontage right along the sand. Renovated at the end of 2010, rooms are done in crisp, clean beach colors. Many rooms have ocean views, and some have gas fireplaces. The poolside restaurant is a good bet for a quick burger or sandwich if you don't want to stray far from the beach; it's easily accessible to nonguests. **Pros:** a kids' paradise; beachfront location. **Cons:** less-than-quiet surroundings; can feel crowded. ⊠ *350 Quaker Rd., North Falmouth* ☎ *508/540–9400 or 800/225–3110* ⊕ *www.seacrest-resort. com* ⇥ *258 rooms, 8 suites* ⟲ *In-room: a/c, refrigerator, Wi-Fi. In-hotel: 2 restaurants, room service, bar, pools, gym, beachfront, water sports* ▤ *AE, D, DC, MC, V.*

$$$ ⊞ **Woods Hole Inn.** Originally built in 1878, this eco-friendly inn sits smack-dab in the quaint village center, just steps from a variety of shops and eateries. Done up in beach colors by a Los Angeles set designer, the rooms have thoughtful touches like docking stations for your iPod. Breakfast chef Sara Dillon wakes up sleepyheads with maple crème brûlée French toast, roasted tomato and asparagus tartlette, and her signature secret-recipe granola. **Pros:** free parking; central location; steps from Martha's Vineyard ferry. **Cons:** some street noise. ⊠ *28 Water St., Woods Hole* ☎ *508/495–0248* ⊕ *www.woodsholeinn.com* ⇥ *8 rooms, 2 suites* ⟲ *In-room: a/c, no phone, DVD, Internet, Wi-Fi. In-hotel: Internet terminal, Wi-Fi hotspot, parking (free), some pets allowed, no kids under 6* ▤ *D, MC, V* ⦿⧠ *BP.*

$$ ⊞ **Woods Hole Passage.** A century-old carriage house and barn have
★   been converted into a romantic showcase. The large rose-hue common room radiates comfort with its lace curtains and overstuffed furniture. One guest room (the smallest) is in the main house; the others are in the restored barn, where the upstairs rooms have soaring ceilings. Gregarious and helpful owner Deb Pruitt sells Martha's Vineyard ferry tickets at cost, so you can avoid long lines at the dock. You can enjoy a delicious breakfast on the lovely patio; early risers can request "breakfast-in-a-bag" to take on the road. Kids are accepted, by prior arrangement. A member of the Green Hotel Association, the inn encourages guests to leave their cars in the lot as much as possible; the town trolley runs right by the inn. **Pros:** beautiful gardens; historic structure; extremely helpful innkeeper. **Cons:** not an in-town location; some steep stairs.

✉ *186 Woods Hole Rd., Woods Hole* ☎ *508/548–9575 or 800/790–8976* ⊕ *www.woodsholepassage.com* ⇱ *5 rooms* ⅙ *In-room: no phone, no TV, Wi-Fi. In-hotel: bicycles* ⊟ *AE, MC, V* ❍❘ *BP.*

NIGHTLIFE AND THE ARTS

THE ARTS

The **Cape Cod Theatre Project** (☎ *508/457–4242* ⊕ *www.capecod-theatreproject.org*) helps develop new American plays through a series of staged readings. Each July the project presents three or four readings, which are followed by audience discussion with the playwright. Productions have included works by Gloucester Stage Company director Israel Horovitz and by Pulitzer Prize winners Lanford Wilson and Paula Vogel. (Readings are not recommended for those under 16 years of age.) Performances take place at **Falmouth Academy** (✉ *7 Highfield Dr., off Depot Ave., Falmouth Center*).

The **College Light Opera Company** (✉ *Highfield Theatre, off Depot Ave., Falmouth Center* ☎ *508/548–0668* ⊕ *www.collegelightopera.com*) presents nine musicals or operettas for one week each, the results of a summer program involving music and theater majors from colleges around the country. The company consists of more than 30 singers and an 18-piece orchestra. Be forewarned: the quality can vary from show to show.

Performing at the same venue as the College Light Opera Company, the **Falmouth Theatre Guild** (✉ *Highfield Theatre, 58 Highfield Dr., Falmouth Center* ☎ *508/548–0400* ⊕ *www.falmouththeatreguild.org*) is a first-rate community theater that presents four plays—a mix of musicals and dramas—from fall through spring.

Falmouth's summer **town-band concerts** (✉ *Falmouth Music and Arts Pavillon, Scranton Ave., Falmouth Center* ☎ *508/548–8500 or 800/526–8532*) are held in Marina Park on Thursday evening starting at 7.

The **Woods Hole Folk Music Society** (✉ *Community Hall, 68 Water St., Woods Hole* ☎ *508/540–0320* ⊕ *www.arts-cape.com/whfolkmusic*) presents professional and local folk and blues in a smoke- and alcohol-free environment, with refreshments available during intermission. Concerts by nationally known performers take place the first and third Sunday of the month from October to May.

Woods Hole Theater Company (✉ *Community Hall, 68 Water St., Woods Hole* ☎ *508/540–6525* ⊕ *www.woodsholetheater.org*), the community's resident theater group since 1974, presents several productions each year, generally between late spring and early fall.

NIGHTLIFE

Liam Maguire's (✉ *281 Rte. 28, Falmouth Center* ☎ *508/548–0285*) is a festive, authentic Irish pub with nightly Irish and other acoustic music and dependable pub fare.

Nimrod Inn (✉ *100 Dillingham Ave., Falmouth Center* ☎ *508/540–4132*) presents jazz and contemporary music at least six nights a week year-round. The Nimrod is also a great spot for late-night dining.

Sea Crest Beach Hotel (✉ *350 Quaker Rd., North Falmouth* ☎ *508/540–9400*) has a summer and holiday-weekend schedule of nightly entertainment on the outdoor terrace, including dancing to country, Top 40, reggae, and jazz bands and a big-band DJ.

BEACHES, SPORTS, AND THE OUTDOORS

BASEBALL

The **Falmouth Commodores** (✉ *790 Rte. 28, Falmouth Center* ☎ *508/432–6909* ⊕ *www.falcommodores.org*) of the collegiate Cape Cod Baseball League play their home games at Guv Fuller Field from mid-June to mid-August. Players and coaches lead youth baseball clinics in June and July.

BEACHES

Many town beaches require a parking sticker, or are pay-as-you-go. Weekly nonresident stickers cost $60; two weeks cost $70, three weeks cost $80, and four weeks cost $90. If you're staying at a local lodging establishment, there is the discounted rate of $10 per day. <R>Parking stickers can be obtained at the **Falmouth Town Hall** (✉ *59 Town Hall Sq., Falmouth Center* ☎ *508/548–7611* ⊕ *www.falmouthmass.us*).

Chapoquoit Beach (✉ *Chapoquoit Rd., West Falmouth*), a narrow stretch of white sand, lines a peninsula that juts dramatically into the bay. Resident parking stickers are required at the beach lot in season, but the surrounding roads are popular with bicyclists. The beach has lifeguards and portable toilets.

Falmouth Heights Beach (✉ *Grand Ave., Falmouth*) is an often-crowded arc of sand on Nantucket Sound, backed by a row of inns and B&Bs. The beach has lifeguards in summer and portable toilets. There's a small strip of metered parking on Grand Avenue between Walden Avenue and Crescent Park Avenue.

Grews Pond (✉ *Goodwill Park, Falmouth*), a pretty tree-lined freshwater pond with a sandy beach and swimming area with lifeguard, is popular with local families. You'll find several sites for picnicking, along with restrooms and a volleyball net; there's also a playground nearby. You can enter the park from Route 28 just north of Jones Road or from Gifford Street opposite St. Joseph's Cemetery. Parking is free.

Megansett Beach (✉ *County Rd., North Falmouth*), hidden in a residential neighborhood, is a small, family-friendly location. Weathered gray-shingle homes line the cove, and boats moored at the adjacent yacht club bob in the bay. The beach has lifeguards and a portable toilet but no other services. Resident parking stickers are required at the beach lot in season.

★ **Old Silver Beach** (✉ *Off Quaker Rd., North Falmouth*) is a long, beautiful crescent of soft white sand bordered by the Sea Crest Beach Resort at one end. It's especially good for small children because a sandbar keeps it shallow at the southern end and creates tidal pools full of crabs and minnows. The beach has lifeguards, restrooms, showers, and a snack bar. There's a $20 fee for parking in summer.

Family-friendly **Surf Drive Beach** (✉ *Surf Dr., Falmouth*) faces Nantucket Sound, with views out toward the Vineyard. The beach has restrooms and showers as well as lifeguards. Public parking is available; in summer the daily parking fee is $10.

Wood Neck Beach (✉ *Wood Neck Rd., West Falmouth*), in the Sippewisset area, is a sandy bayside beach backed by grass-covered dunes. At high tide the beach is very narrow, but sandbars and shallow tidal pools make this a good place for children when the tide is out. Resident parking stickers are required in season.

BICYCLING

Fodor'sChoice
★
The wonderful **Shining Sea Bikeway** is an 11-mi paved bike path through four of Falmouth's villages, running from Woods Hole to North Falmouth. It follows the shore of Buzzards Bay, providing water views and dips into oak and pine woods; a detour onto Church Street takes you to Nobska Light. A brochure is available at the trailheads. If you're going to Martha's Vineyard with your bike, you can park your car in one of Falmouth's Steamship Authority lots and ride the Shining Sea Bikeway to the ferry. The free shuttle buses between the Falmouth lots and the Woods Hole ferry docks also have bike carriers.

Corner Cycle (✉ *115 Palmer Ave., Falmouth* ☎ *508/540–4195*) rents bikes (including tandems and children's bikes) by the hour, day, or week. It also rents Burley trailers for carrying small children and does on-site repairs. The shop is two blocks from the Shining Sea Bikeway. **Holiday Cycles** (✉ *465 Grand Ave., Falmouth Heights* ☎ *508/540–3549*) has surrey, tandem, and other unusual bikes.

FISHING

Freshwater ponds are good for perch, pickerel, trout, and more; you can obtain the required license (along with rental gear) at tackle shops, such as **Eastman's Sport & Tackle** (✉ *783 Rte. 28, Falmouth Center* ☎ *508/548–6900* ⊕ *www.eastmanstackle.com*).

Patriot Party Boats (✉ *227 Clinton Ave., Falmouth Center* ☎ *508/548–2626 or 800/734–0088* ⊕ *www.patriotpartyboats.com*) has deep-sea fishing from party or charter boats. Advance bookings are recommended, particularly for weekend trips.

HORSEBACK RIDING

Haland Stables (✉ *878 Rte. 28A, West Falmouth* ☎ *508/540–2552*) offers lessons and trail rides by reservation Monday through Saturday.

ICE SKATING

Skaters take to the ice at the **Falmouth Ice Arena** (✉ *9 Skating La., off Palmer Ave., Falmouth Center* ☎ *508/548–7080* ⊕ *www.falmouth-icearena.com*) fall through spring. You can rent skates from the pro shop.

TENNIS AND RACQUETBALL

The huge **Falmouth Sports Center** (✉ *33 Highfield Dr., Falmouth Center* ☎ *508/548–7433*) has three outdoor and six indoor tennis courts and two racquetball courts, as well as steam rooms and saunas, a full health club, and physical-therapist services. Day and short-term rates are available.

SHOPPING

★ **Bean & Cod** (✉ *140 Rte. 28, Falmouth Center* ☎ *508/548–8840*), a specialty food shop, sells cheeses, breads, and picnic fixings, along with pastas, coffees and teas, and unusual condiments. The store also packs and ships gift baskets.

Eight Cousins Books (✉ *189 Rte. 28, Falmouth Center* ☎ *508/548–5548* ⊕ *www.eightcousins.com*) is the place to find reading material for toddlers through young adults, plus a handpicked selection of current titles for adults. In addition to comprehensive sections on oceans and marine life, Native American peoples, and other Cape topics, the well-stocked shop carries CDs, and games.

Half Shell Company (✉ *49 N. Main St., Falmouth Center* ☎ *508/388–7689* ⊕ *www.halfshellco.com*) started with a handcrafted soy-based candle with a lead-free wick. Today, in addition to an array of candles made on the attractive premises, handmade soaps and pillows join the carefully edited collection of sea-inspired, reasonably priced gifts.

Handworks (✉ *68 Water St., Woods Hole* ☎ *508/540–5291*), tucked in the back of the Community Hall building next to the drawbridge, is a cooperative arts-and-crafts gallery showcasing the work of local artists.

Howlingbird (✉ *91 Palmer Ave., Falmouth Center* ☎ *508/540–3787*) stocks detailed hand-silk-screened marine-themed T-shirts and sweatshirts, plus cards and silk-screened hats and handbags.

Maxwell & Co. (✉ *200 Main St., Falmouth Center* ☎ *508/540–8752* ⊕ *www.maxwellandco.com*) has traditional men's and women's clothing with flair from European and American designers, handmade French shoes and boots, and leather goods and accessories.

Rosie Cheeks (✉ *233 Rte. 28, Falmouth Center* ☎ *508/548–4572*), whose name was inspired by the owner's daughter, specializes in creative women's clothing and jewelry, with a particularly nice selection of hand-knit sweaters. They also have a branch at Mashpee Commons.

EAST FALMOUTH AND WAQUOIT

4 mi northeast of Falmouth, 13 mi south of Bourne Bridge.

East Falmouth and Waquoit sit on narrow fingers of land that poke out toward Nantucket Sound, so water is never far away. Here you'll find quiet inlets and marshy bays rather than the crashing surf of the open ocean. Residential neighborhoods, with both seasonal and year-round homes, often end in dirt lanes that lead to the water. Menauhant Beach, the area's nicest stretch of sand, sits on a thin sliver of land with the sound on one side and a grassy cove on the other. Inland, the land is more rural, with a number of farms (and farm stands) still operating.

GETTING HERE AND AROUND

Route 28 is the main road through these parts, though you may notice it is also referred to as East Falmouth Highway, Waquoit Highway, and Falmouth Road as you continue eastward. Several major thoroughfares meet up with Route 28, including Route 151, which heads westward toward North Falmouth, and Route 130, which heads toward

Cotuit to the east or Sandwich to the northwest.

EXPLORING

Ashumet Holly Wildlife Sanctuary. True to its name, this park has more than 1,000 holly trees and shrubs composed of 65 American, Asian, and European varieties. Like Heritage Museums and Gardens in Sandwich, this 49-acre tract of woodland, shady groves, and meadows crisscrossed by hiking trails was purchased and donated by Josiah K. Lilly III to preserve local land.

Grassy Pond, a rare coastal plain pond, is home to numerous turtles and frogs, and in summer dozens of nesting pairs of swallows live in the open rafters of the barn. Trail maps cost $1, and interpretive panels are located along the trails. ⊠ *286 Ashumet Rd., East Falmouth* ☎ *508/362–1426* ⊕ *www.massaudubon.org* ⊠ *$3* ⊙ *Trails daily sunrise–sunset.*

Cape Cod Winery. Rows and rows of grapevines—8,000 in all—line the fields of Kristina and Antonio Lazzari's vineyard. It now produces seven wines; the Nobska red won a bronze medal at the International Eastern Wine Competition. ⊠ *681 Sandwich Rd., East Falmouth* ☎ *508/457–5592* ⊕ *www.capecodwinery.com* ⊙ *July and Aug., tastings Thurs.–Sun. 11–4; late May, June, and Sept.–late Dec., tastings weekends 11–4.*

☽ **Waquoit Bay National Estuarine Research Reserve.** This state park is one of 27 research reserves in the country. It encompasses 3,000 acres of estuary, woodlands, salt marshes, and barrier beach, making it a good site for walking, kayaking, fishing, and birding. The visitor center includes displays about the area. An interactive exhibit, outside on the lawn, lets kids trace the path of a raindrop through its journey from cloud to land to river. In July and August there are nature programs for families, including an outdoor lecture series on Tuesday evenings.

South Cape Beach is part of the reserve; you can lie out on the sand or join one of the interpretive walks. **Flat Pond Trail** runs through several different habitats, including fresh- and saltwater marshes. You can reach **Washburn Island** on your own by boat, or by joining a Saturday-morning tours. It offers 330 acres of pine barrens and trails, swimming, and 10 wilderness campsites (an advance reservation and permit are required). ⊠ *149 Rte. 28, 3 mi west of Mashpee rotary, Waquoit* ☎ *508/457–0495* ⊕ *www.waquoitbayreserve.org* ⊙ *Visitor center late June–early Sept., Mon.–Sat. 10–4; late May–late June, weekdays 10–4.*

WHERE TO EAT

¢ ✕ **Moonakis Café.** Breakfast gets high marks at this humble roadside
AMERICAN diner. You'll find all the standards and then some—eggs, pancakes, fruit salad—all nicely done. The chunky hash browns are fried with just the right amount of onions, and if the omelet with roasted tomatoes, olives, and goat cheese is on the menu, it's an excellent choice. Also

recommended (if you're not on a diet) are the decadent Belgian waffles buried under strawberries, bananas, and whipped cream. Lunch is burgers, sandwiches, and salads at rock-bottom prices. ⊠ *460 Waquoit Hwy., Waquoit* ☎ *508/457–9630* ▭ *No credit cards* ⊙ *No dinner. No lunch Sun.*

WHERE TO STAY

$$–$$$ Ⓣ **Admiralty Inn & Suites.** This large roadside motel has several types of ℭ rooms and suites, and its child-friendly facilities make it a good bet for families. Some rooms have whirlpool tubs in the bedroom. Town-house suites have soaring cathedral ceilings with skylights, king-size beds, and living rooms with sofa beds. **Pros:** good spot for exploring the area; activities for kids. **Cons:** some rooms a bit stale and outdated. ⊠ *51 Teaticket Hwy., East Falmouth* ☎ *508/548–4240 or 800/341–5700* ⊕ *www.theadmiraltyinn.com* ⇗ *70 rooms, 28 suites* ☪ *In-room: a/c, refrigerator, Wi-Fi. In-hotel: pools* ▭ *AE, D, DC, MC, V* ⏐◎⏐ *CP.*

$$$ Ⓣ **Cape Wind Waterfront Resort.** If you're traveling with children who ℭ need space to run, this gray-shingle motel on 5 acres is a dependable option. The rooms face a broad green lawn that slopes down to the bay; it's a great place to launch your canoe or kayak, or head out in one of the motel's paddleboats. The rooms are decidedly basic, with standard furnishings that are being continually updated and refreshed. All have refrigerators and coffeemakers, and some have microwaves; others have kitchenettes. The motel is in a quiet residential neighborhood. **Pros:** beautiful grounds; access to water; heated pool. **Cons:** lots of families may put off couples. ⊠ *34 Maravista Ext., East Falmouth* ☎ *508/548–3400 or 800/267–3401* ⊕ *www.capewind.com* ⇗ *31 rooms* ☪ *In-room: a/c, kitchen (some), refrigerator, Wi-Fi. In-hotel: pool, water sports, some pets allowed* ▭ *D, MC, V.*

$$$ Ⓣ **Green Harbor Waterfront Lodging.** Although the modest rooms here are ℭ clean and adequate, it's the friendly summer camp–like feel that makes this attractive compound great for families. There are old-fashioned lawn swings, a heated swimming pool, umbrella-topped picnic tables, and barbecue grills, but the main attraction is the waterfront. It's not open ocean here but a peaceful tree-lined inlet, with rowboats and paddleboats free for guests' use. (If you've got your own boat, you can launch it here and keep it at the dock.) All of the no-frills rooms in the 1960s-vintage motel have microwaves, small refrigerators, and coffeemakers; others have kitchenettes. It's down a quiet lane off Route 28. **Pros:** great for active families; right on the water. **Cons:** can be noisy; rooms could use some updating. ⊠ *134 Acapesket Rd., East Falmouth* ☎ *508/548–4747 or 800/548–5556* ⊕ *www.gogreenharbor.com* ⇗ *34 rooms, 1 cottage* ☪ *In-room: a/c, kitchen (some), refrigerator, Wi-Fi. In-hotel: pools, beachfront, water sports, laundry facilities, some pets allowed (fee)* ▭ *AE, D, DC, MC, V* ⊙ *Closed Nov.–Apr.*

BEACHES, SPORTS, AND THE OUTDOORS

Menauhant Beach (⊠ *Menauhant Rd., East Falmouth*) is a long, narrow stretch of sand with a pond in a quiet residential neighborhood. Its slightly more-secluded location means it can be a bit less crowded than the beaches near Falmouth Center. The beach has lifeguards, restrooms, outdoor showers, and a small snack bar. Public parking is $10.

SHOPPING

☺ **Coonamessett Farm.** For an $8 membership you can pick your own straw-
★ berries, lettuce, herbs, rhubarb, and other fruits and vegetables, as well as tour the greenhouses and fields, learn about hydroponic-growing systems, and visit the animals. A small café serves soups, sandwiches, and salads; on Friday night in summer don't miss the dinners with live music. The farm also rents canoes for use on the adjacent Coonamessett Pond. ✉ *277 Hatchville Rd., East Falmouth* ☎ *508/563–2560* ⊕ *www. coonamessettfarm.com* ☉ *Call for hrs.*

Tony Andrews Farm and Produce Stand. This local favorite has pick-your-own strawberries (June), peas and beans (June and July), herbs (July and August), and tomatoes (August), as well as other produce from the region. The farm schedules hayrides in fall, and a haunted house is set up in October. You can pick your own pumpkins in fall and choose your Christmas tree in December. ✉ *394 Old Meeting House Rd., East Falmouth* ☎ *508/548–4717* ⊕ *www.tonyandrewsfarmstand. com* ☉ *June–Oct., call for hrs.*

MASHPEE

Mashpee is one of two Massachusetts towns with both municipally governed– and Native American–governed areas (the other town is Aquinnah, formerly known as Gay Head, on Martha's Vineyard). Today several residential-resort communities have developed in the Mashpee area; the largest, the Country Club of New Seabury, has one of the best golf courses on the Cape. Mashpee has also become a popular shopping and dining destination. Yet away from the stores, the town retains a more rural character, with wooded roads, inland ponds, and reminders of the area's original settlers.

In 1660 the Reverend Richard Bourne, a missionary, gave a 16-square-mi parcel of land to the Wampanoags (consider the irony—an outsider "giving" Native people their own land). Known as the Mashpee Plantation and governed by two local sachems, it was the first Native American reservation in the United States. In 1974 the Mashpee Wampanoag Tribal Council was formed to continue its government with a chief, a supreme sachem, a medicine man, and clan mothers. More than 600 residents are descended from the original Wampanoags, and some continue to observe their ancient traditions.

GETTING HERE AND AROUND

Mashpee, 7 mi east of East Falmouth and 10 mi south of Sandwich, doesn't have a distinct town center; rather it is spread out amid the busy byways of Route 28 and Route 130. The Cape Cod Regional Transit Authority operates SeaLine buses along Route 28, connecting Mashpee with Falmouth Center and Woods Hole.

Powwow, Wampanoag Style

Dancers and drummers re-creating ancient rhythms, and vivid deer-skin costumes decorated with colorful beads and bold plumage are a far cry from the fried clams, shingled saltboxes, and antiques shops that typify Cape Cod, yet they represent the very essence of a culture that has made this area home for thousands of years. It was the Wampanoag tribe who peacefully greeted, assisted, and befriended the Pilgrims who came ashore in 1620. And although their presence is often overlooked amid the luxury resorts and golf courses that dominate the town of Mashpee, the tribe continues to embrace and celebrate their ancestors' way of life.

The Mashpee Wampanoag Powwow, held every year since 1924, is a lively showcase of the tribe's traditions. Open to the public, the early July powwow is a large gathering of local Wampanoags and numerous tribes from throughout the Northeast; some even travel here from the western states. Tents and tables fill the tribal grounds, selling everything from Native American foods to jewelry and T-shirts. A series of intricately costumed dancing and drumming contests takes place during the three-day festival, along with one of the most dramatic events—the fireball ceremony. This ancient healing ritual involves Wampanoag males in what looks a little bit like soccer—except the ball is on fire.

The Mashpee Wampanoag tribal grounds are in Mashpee, off Great Neck Road. For more information, contact the **Mashpee Wampanoag Tribal Council** (☎ 508/477–0208 ⊕ www.mashpeewampanoagtribe. com).

ESSENTIALS

Visitor Information Mashpee Chamber of Commerce (✉ *520 Main St.* ☎ *508/477–0792, 800/423–6274 outside Massachusetts* ⊕ *www. mashpeechamber.com*).

EXPLORING

☼ **Cape Cod Children's Museum.** In a cavernous former church building, the Cape Cod Children's Museum welcomes kids with interactive play, science exhibits, a 30-foot pirate play ship, a planetarium, and other playtime activities. The museum is best suited for preschoolers and children in the early elementary grades. ✉ *577 Great Neck Rd. S* ☎ *508/539–8788* ⊕ *www.visitccm.org* ▨ *$6* ⊙ *Memorial Day–Labor Day, Mon.–Sat. 10–5, Sun. noon–5; Labor Day–Memorial Day, Tues.–Thurs. 10–3, Fri. and Sat. 10–5, Sun. noon–5.*

Mashpee River Woodlands. Perfect for bird-watching, fishing, or canoeing, the Mashpee River Woodlands occupy 391 acres along the Mashpee River. More than 8 mi of trails meander through the marshlands and pine forests. Park on Quinaquisset Avenue, River Road, or Mashpee Neck Road (where there's a public landing for canoe access).

Old Indian Burial Ground. On Meeting House Road, this 18th-century cemetery has headstones typical of the period, intricately carved with scenes and symbols and inscribed with witty sayings.

WHERE TO EAT

$ ✕ **Bleu.** Chef Frederic Feufeu, a native of the Loire Valley, brings the flavors of France to this urbane restaurant in the pseudo-quaint Mashpee Commons Mall. From bistro classics to haute cuisine and sophisticated lunch sandwiches to decadent desserts, the flavors are astounding. Seasonal specialties include roasted filet mignon with poached foie gras, fingerling potatoes, candied shallots, and bordelaise sauce. Shrimp tempura with miso mustard sauce and Asian slaw is one of the tempting lighter and less-expensive dishes served in the natty bar. There's also a jazz brunch on Sunday, from Labor Day to Memorial Day. ⊠ *10 Market St.* ☎ *508/539–7907* ⊟ *AE, D, MC, V.*

FRENCH

Fodor's Choice

★

$$$ ✕ **Popponesset Inn.** The surroundings, more so than the lobster rolls, burgers, grilled swordfish, steaks, and other straightforward offerings, are exceptional here. The site is a gem, with old Cape Cod saltbox houses nearby, lovely Nantucket Sound in the background, and perfect light in the evening. The restaurant has a lounge called Poppy's and comprises several small dining rooms, all overlooking the water through glass walls. Sit outside, either under the tent or at one of the umbrella tables. ⊠ *Country Club of New Seabury, 95 Shore Dr.* ☎ *508/477–1100* ⊟ *AE, MC, V* ☉ *Closed mid-Oct.–late Apr., and Mon.–Thurs. Sept. and Oct. No lunch.*

AMERICAN

$ ✕ **The Raw Bar.** At this funky little seafood joint you can pull up a bar stool and chow down on giant lobster rolls, littlenecks, cherrystones, oysters, steamers, and peel-your-own shrimp, all easily washed down with a local brew or a rum punch. Despite a few picnic tables out back, the scene here is more "bar" than "seafood shack." There's live music some nights, too, at the Marketplace. ⊠ *Popponesset Marketplace* ☎ *508/539–4858* ⊕ *www.therawbar.com* ⊟ *AE, D, MC, V* ☉ *Closed late Oct.–early Apr.*

SEAFOOD

$$ ✕ **Siena.** A boisterous, high-ceilinged space at Mashpee Commons, this modern Italian restaurant warms the hearts of patrons with its genuinely friendly service and well-crafted Tuscan cuisine. You might start with the exceptional buffalo mozzarella salad before moving on to pan-seared scallops over pasta. Try one of the several fine brick-oven pizzas, especially one with crispy bacon, Gorgonzola, caramelized onions, candied walnuts, and mozzarella. Drunken lemon cake makes for a magnificent ending. In warm weather, you can dine on the ample patio. ⊠ *11A Steeple St.* ☎ *508/477–5929 or 877/477–5929* ⊕ *www. siena.us* ⊟ *AE, D, MC, V.*

ITALIAN

★

WHERE TO STAY

$$$$ ⓣ **Alexander Hamilton House.** Surrounded by trees with a private beach on serene Ashumet Pond, this small guesthouse is ideal for those looking to be close to nature. With just two suites, each with a private entrance, you may feel you have this lovely place all to yourself. The

upstairs Carriage Suite is a large, one-room space, complete with a two-person whirlpool tub, wood-burning fireplace, and several sitting areas. Downstairs is the Family Suite, which is more akin to a very large apartment with two bedrooms (sleeps up to six), a living room/dining room, and a huge screened-in porch. A Continental breakfast is provided in your room; each comes equipped with a stocked refrigerator, toaster, microwave, and coffeemaker. Gracious innkeepers Barbara and Steve welcome dogs of all sizes—and the surrounding area is a dog's paradise. Kayaks, canoes, and a paddleboat are ready for your use. Single travelers get even better pricing, Monday through Thursday. **Pros:** spacious, well-appointed rooms; peaceful, natural setting; close to nature preserve. **Cons:** not an in-town location; may feel a little remote for some. ⊠ *9 Horseshoe Bend Way* ☎ *508/419–1584* ⊕ *www.alexanderhamiltonhousecapecod.com* ⥲ *2 suites* ⌂ *In-room: a/c, no phone, refrigerator, DVD, Wi-Fi. In-hotel: beachfront, some pets allowed* ⊟ *AE, D, MC, V* ¶◯¶ *CP.*

NIGHTLIFE AND THE ARTS

Bobby Byrne's Pub (⊠ *Mashpee Commons, Rtes. 28 and 151* ☎ *508/477–0600*) is a comfortable pub with an outdoor café, a jukebox, and reliable pub fare.

BEACHES, SPORTS, AND THE OUTDOORS

BEACHES

Attaquin Park Beach (⊠ *End of Lake Ave. off Rte. 130, near Great Neck Rd.*) is a pretty, sandy place with a spectacular view of the interconnecting Mashpee and Wakeby ponds, the Cape's largest freshwater expanse. It's popular for swimming, fishing, and boating, but resident parking stickers are required in season.

South Cape Beach (⊠ *Great Oak Rd.*) is a 2½-mi-long state and town beach on warm Nantucket and Vineyard sounds, accessible via Great Neck Road south from the Mashpee rotary. You can walk to get a bit of privacy on this beach, which is wide, sandy, and pebbly in parts, with low dunes and marshland. The only services are portable toilets, although lifeguards are on duty in season. A hiking trail loops through marsh areas and ponds, linking it to the Waquoit Bay National Estuarine Research Reserve. Resident parking stickers are required for the town-beach parking section, but anybody may park at the state-beach section for $7 per day in season.

GOLF

Quashnet Valley Country Club (⊠ *309 Old Barnstable Rd.* ☎ *508/477–4412*) has a beautiful course in an area of cranberry bogs, the Quashnet River, ponds, and mature trees. It's a 6,601-yard, par-72 championship layout.

HIKING AND WALKING

The 4 mi of walking trails at 135-acre **Lowell Holly Reservation** (⊠ *S. Sandwich Rd. off Rte. 130* ☎ *508/679–2115* ⊕ *www.thetrustees.org*), administered by the Trustees of Reservations, wind through American beeches, hollies, white pines, and rhododendrons on a peninsula between Mashpee and Wakeby ponds. The reservation has picnic tables and a little swimming beach. A small free parking area is open year-round, and an additional parking lot opens from late May to early September ($6). You can also launch a boat from the landing ($6 per day).

In summer the **Mashpee Conservation Commission** (☎ *508/539–1400*) has information about free naturalist-led guided walks of Mashpee's woods and conservation areas. Family nature walks, animal scavenger hunts, and "pond scoops" to explore aquatic life are a few of the activities offered for kids and their parents; sunrise walks on South Cape Beach and natural-history tours of the Lowell Holly Reservation are also on the program.

SHOPPING

Mashpee Commons (✉ *Junction of Rtes. 28 and 151* ☎ *508/477–5400* ⊕ *www.mashpeecommons.com*) has about 80 upscale stores, including restaurants, art galleries, and a mix of local boutiques and national chains, in an attractive village square. There's also a movie theater and free outdoor entertainment in summer. **M. Brann & Co.** (☎ *508/477–0299*), a creative home-and-gift shop, carries everything from funky refrigerator magnets and unusual candlesticks to handcrafted glassware, one-of-a-kind lamps, mirrors, and furniture, with many works by New England artists. **Soft As a Grape** (☎ *508/477–5331*), a sporty men's and women's clothier, has several branches around the Cape. **Cape Cod Toys** (☎ *508/477–2221*) is crammed full of anything the children might possibly need, including beach toys, board games, and science projects.

Popponesset Marketplace (✉ *Off Great Neck Rd. S, New Seabury ⊹ 2½ mi south of Rte. 28 from Mashpee rotary* ☎ *508/477–9111* ⊕ *www. popponessetmarketplace.com*), open from late spring to early fall, has 20 shops (boutique clothing, home furnishings), eating places (a raw bar, pizza, ribs, ice cream), miniature golf, and weekend entertainment (bands, fashion or puppet shows, sing-alongs).

The Mid Cape

WORD OF MOUTH

"There are so many different villages in the town of Dennis that it gets confusing. My favorite set of directions is that when you are in West Dennis, if you go due north you end up in South Dennis. The villages are close to each other. Beaches on the north shore of Dennis are all good and similar. Dennis village does have a center with a town common and some shops. Dennis village and East Dennis are on the north shore of Cape Cod Bay. The beaches of the north shore villages have good swimming and a large expanse of sand flats for walking at low tide."

—Nikki

Updated
by Laura V.
Scheel

More a colloquialism than a proper name, the designation "Mid Cape" refers to central Cape Cod, the most heavily populated—and touristed—part of the peninsula. Like a fat deli sandwich with all the meat in the middle, this area of Cape Cod is stuffed to the gills with attractions, shopping, and all manner of entertainment, and it will leave you feeling either uncomfortably full or blissfully sated.

To the north lies tranquil Cape Cod Bay, laced with wide beaches, inlets, creeks, and marshes. The tides on the bay are dramatic—at dead low some beaches double in size as tidal flats stretch out for hundreds to thousands of feet. The calmer waters on the bay side make these beaches particularly suitable for kids, and when the tide is out, they can explore and play in the tidal pools left behind.

The main thoroughfare through the north side of the Mid Cape is Route 6A, a scenic section that dates from 1684, making it one of the first major roads constructed on Cape Cod. Alternately called Old King's Highway, Main Street, and Hallet Street, the road winds through the villages of West Barnstable, Barnstable, Cummaquid, Yarmouth Port, and Dennis, with north-side harbors and beaches just a short drive from village centers. A residential and commercial mix, Route 6A is lined with antique captains' mansions and farmhouses that are now private homes, bed-and-breakfasts, art galleries, restaurants, and antiques shops. Protected by a historical society, colors and architecture along the road are kept to the standards set by early settlers.

On the south side of the Mid Cape, sunbathers flock to the expansive beaches along Nantucket Sound. The main thoroughfare here is the busy and overdeveloped Route 28, which passes through Centerville, Osterville, Hyannis, West and South Yarmouth, and Dennisport. This stretch is particularly unpleasant and tawdry between West Yarmouth and Dennisport, where it's lined with strip motels, clam shacks, miniature-golf courses, ice-cream parlors, and tacky T-shirt outlets. A draw for families in its 1960s heyday, the area hasn't seen much renovation since. However, if you stray from the congestion of Route 28, the serenity of soft sand and quiet back roads awaits. It's hard to get too lost on the Cape—you can't go far off the main roads without hitting water—so poking around is worth the risk.

Between routes 6A and 28 is the "mid" of the Mid Cape, a mostly residential area with some historic sections, a few quiet freshwater ponds, and the bustling commercial sections of Hyannis. Nearby are tony Osterville and Hyannis Port, a well-groomed enclave and site of the Kennedy compound.

TOP REASONS TO GO

Exploring by bike: Bike along the scenic 25-mi Cape Cod Rail Trail, which begins in South Dennis and ends in South Wellfleet. There are plenty of stops along the way for ice cream, refreshing swims, nature watching, and impromptu picnics.

Making beautiful music: Impressive acts take to the stage for summer-time performances at the Cape Cod Melody Tent in Hyannis and the Cape Playhouse in Dennis. Find other live music at a many restaurants in Hyannis.

Taking a dip in the ponds: The area has a number of freshwater kettle

ponds, created by receding glaciers eons ago. Pond beaches are usually not crowded and appeal to those who like cooling off in gentle water without the salt and sand.

Shopping for special items: There's a bounty of shopping at the boutiques, crafts shops, bookstores, antiques centers, and galleries along beautiful Route 6A.

Enjoying the sunset: The gentle surf and long stretches of sand at Sandy Neck Beach, along the north side of Barnstable Harbor, make it ideal for sunset viewing. This is one of the Cape's loveliest beaches.

ORIENTATION AND PLANNING

GETTING ORIENTED

The Mid Cape includes the towns of Barnstable, Yarmouth, and Dennis, each divided into smaller townships and villages. The town of Barnstable, for example, consists of Barnstable Village, West Barnstable, Cotuit, Marstons Mills, Osterville, Centerville, and Hyannis, with the smaller quasi villages (distinguished by their separate postal codes) of Craigville, Cummaquid, Hyannis Port, West Hyannis Port, and Wianno. Yarmouth contains Yarmouth Port, along the north shore, and the mid and south villages of West Yarmouth and South Yarmouth. The town of Dennis's villages are easy to remember: Dennis, West Dennis, South Dennis, East Dennis, and Dennisport. Route 6A winds along the north shore through tree-shaded scenic towns and village centers, and Route 28 dips south through some of the more overdeveloped parts of the Cape. Generally speaking, if you want to avoid malls, heavy traffic, and cheesy motels, stay away from Route 28 from Falmouth to Chatham.

Barnstable, Hyannis, and Environs. Like a houseful of independently minded siblings, villages within Barnstable are widely different. The dignified village of Barnstable sits along historic Route 6A. West Barnstable, Cotuit, Osterville, Hyannis Port, Cummaquid, and Wianno are filled with art galleries and fine shops. Hyannis thrives on endless amusements.

Yarmouth. Along Route 6A and branching off onto many quiet lanes leading to the bay, Yarmouth Port is all grand architecture, fine art, and antiques. The sister towns of West Yarmouth and South Yarmouth are on the south side, right in the midst of the animated, highly commercial offerings along Route 28.

Dennis. Like Yarmouth, Dennis has multiple personalities. Dennis Village and East Dennis are quiet and historic, while Dennisport, West Dennis, and South Dennis have their share of lively entertainments.

PLANNING

WHEN TO GO

In summer the Mid Cape bustles with tourists. But from Columbus Day weekend through April the area is a peaceful collection of towns and villages, with beaches for strolling, trails for walking and biking, and a wealth of shopping and entertainment. Although the year-round population has ballooned in the last decade, the off-season is still a laid-back and welcome time to catch the best of the Cape minus the crowds. Fall sees bursts of color in the easily accessed forests and marshes; winter brings a slower pace of life and a holiday spirit that locals love to celebrate with Christmas strolls featuring tours of shops, B&Bs, and old homes. Spring is also quiet, as the Mid Cape awakens to blooming trees, warmer days, reopened B&Bs, newly landscaped golf courses, and flower festivals. Boats come out of hibernation—Hyannis Whale Watcher Cruises, for instance, starts its program in May.

PLANNING YOUR TIME

The Mid Cape makes a great base for exploring the region, as day trips to the Outer Cape are perfectly feasible from here. Hyannis has everything you could want, whether it's beachfront lodging, diversions for the kids, or being able to leave your car in the lot and walk to restaurants, shopping, and attractions. Since ferries to Nantucket and Martha's Vineyard depart from Hyannis, it provides very easy access to the islands.

If you prefer a quieter setting, head to the smaller towns. Driving the narrow and tree-shaded Old King's Highway (Route 6A) is an adventure in itself, and can take days depending on your penchant for antiques shops, nature trails, art galleries, and beautiful beaches.

GETTING HERE AND AROUND

BOAT AND FERRY TRAVEL

Ferries to Nantucket and Martha's Vineyard leave from Hyannis year-round. *For details, see* ⇨ *Boat and Ferry Travel in Travel Smart Cape Cod in the back of this book.*

BUS TRAVEL

Hyannis is the Cape's transit hub and is served by a number of bus routes, including the local Hyannis Villager and the Barnstable Villager lines. Buses also link Hyannis with Orleans, Woods Hole, Provincetown, Plymouth, downtown Boston, and Logan airport, as well as various towns on each route. *For more information, see* ⇨ *Bus Travel in Travel Smart Cape Cod in the back of this book.*

Bus Depots Hyannis Transportation Center (⊠ *215 Iyanough Rd., Hyannis* ☎ *508/775–8504* ⊕ *www.capecodtransit.org*). **Plymouth & Brockton Street Railway Terminals** (⊠ *South Station Bus Terminal, 700 Atlantic Ave., Boston* ☎ *508/746–0378*).

The Mid Cape

Cape Cod Bay

Sandy Neck

Barnstable Harbor

Corporation Beach

Chapin Beach

Sandy Neck Beach

West Barnstable

Sandy Neck Rd.

6A

149

149

Marstons Mills

South County Rd.

TO COTUIT

28

Osterville

Centerville

TO DOWSES BEACH

Craigville Beach

Wequaquet Lake

Shoot Flying hill Rd.

Cape Cod Community College

BARNSTABLE

132

Barnstable Municipal Airport

Barnstable Village

Cummaquid

Keveney Bridge

Mill Pond

Hathaway's Pond

Yarmouth Port

Willow St.

Dennis Pond

Bass Hole Boardwalk

Dennis Village

6A

Center St.

Yarmouth

Union St.

6

Cape Playhouse

Scargo Tower

134

Scargo Lake

Scargo Hill Rd.

Old Bass River Rd.

Follins Pond

Flax Pond

Station Ave.

YARMOUTH

Higgins Crowell Rd.

Buck Island Rd.

Yarmouth Boardwalk

Swan Pond

South Yarmouth

Winslow Gray Rd.

28

West Yarmouth

Yarmouth Rd.

W. Main St.

Hyannis
see detail map

Hyannis Port

Kalmus Park Beach

Lewis Bay

Seagull Beach

Parker's River Beach

South Dennis

Bass River

DENNIS

West Dennis

West Dennis Beach

Lower County Rd.

28

Dennisport

TO HARWICH

Great Western Rd.

Swan Pond

6

Setucket Rd.

Clough Rd.

Stony Brook Rd.

Upper Mill Pond

Seymour Pond

Tubman Rd.

0   2 miles

0   2 kilometers

CAR TRAVEL

Expect Route 28 to be anything but relaxing in summer, especially on weekends. This corridor is crawling with drivers looking for that lost turn, the best miniature-golf place, or the next bargain. Route 6A is much calmer, with drivers paying more attention to the scenery than to the speed limit. Try to be patient.

TAXI TRAVEL

There are taxi stands at the Hyannis airport, the Hyannis bus station, the ferry terminals, and the Capetown Mall, across the street from the Cape Cod Mall. In Hyannis, call Checker Taxi for pickups. Cape Coach Taxi will pick you up and has a stand at the airport. Cape Taxi is often waiting at the airport; otherwise call for trips anywhere in Barnstable. Town Taxi serves the Hyannis area.

Taxi Companies **Cape Coach Taxi** (☎ 508/790–8008). **Cape Taxi** (☎ 508/790–0222). **Checker Taxi** (☎ 508/771–8294). **Town Taxi** (☎ 508/771–5555).

RESTAURANTS

The Mid Cape is chock-full of eateries, ranging from sedate, high-end haute cuisine houses such as Hyannis's Paddock, the Regatta of Cotuit, and Dennis's Red Pheasant to such family-friendly places as the Red Cottage in Dennis. Expect good fun and great eats at the area's dozens of clam shacks and other super-casual restaurants along Route 28 in Yarmouth and Dennis. If you simply want lots of choices, head to Barnstable and its villages, particularly Hyannis, where a stroll down Main Street will bring you to a dozen fine restaurants ranging from lunch joints to Thai, Italian, Cajun, and upscale American dining establishments.

HOTELS

On the northern (bay) side, Route 6A from Barnstable to Dennis has dozens of B&Bs, many in the elegant former homes of sea captains. In contrast, Route 28 on the south side has row after row of lodgings, from tacky roadside motels to medium-range family hotels, with larger seaside resorts along the side roads on Nantucket Sound. Main Street, Hyannis, is lined with motels, and several inns and B&Bs perch on side streets leading to Hyannis Harbor and Lewis Bay.

WHAT IT COSTS				
	¢	$	$$	$$$	$$$$
Restaurants	under $10	$10–$16	$17–$22	$23–$30	over $30
Hotels	under $90	$90–$140	$141–$200	$201–$260	Over $260

Restaurant prices are per person for a main course at dinner. Hotel prices are for a standard double room, excluding 5.7% sales tax (more in some counties) and up to an additional 6% tourist tax.

CONDO AND HOUSE RENTALS

Mid-Cape Rentals offers properties throughout the villages of Dennis, Yarmouth, and Harwich. Peter McDowell Associates offers a wide selection of properties for rent by the week, month, or season; the company also rents larger homes for family reunions and other gatherings.

Most places are in Dennis. Waterfront Rentals covers Bourne to Truro, listing everything from condos to estates.

Local Agents Mid-Cape Rentals (✉ 592 Rte. 28, West Dennis ☎ 888/394–6588 ⊕ www.midcaperentals.com). **Peter McDowell Associates** (✉ 585 Rte. 6A, Dennis ☎ 508/385–9114 or 888/385–9114 ⊕ www.rentcapecodproperties. com). **Waterfront Rentals** (✉ 20 Pilgrim Rd., West Yarmouth ☎ 508/778–1818 ⊕ www.waterfrontrentalsinc.com).

TOURS

Cape Cod Scenic Tours takes Mid Cape visitors on four- or six-hour tours to such destinations as Chatham, Eastham, Wellfleet, and Provincetown. The van picks you up at your Mid Cape lodging in Hyannis, Dennis, or Harwich. Hit the rails from Hyannis for scenic rides with the Cape Cod Central Railroad. Trips leave from the Hyannis Depot. Cape Cod Soaring Adventures offers glider flights and lessons out of Marstons Mills.

Information Cape Cod Central Railroad (✉ 252 Main St., Hyannis ☎ 508/771–3800 ⊕ www.capetrain.com). **Cape Cod Scenic Tours** (☎ 508/394–2221 ⊕ www.capecodscenictours.com). **Cape Cod Soaring Adventures** (☎ 508/420–4201 ⊕ www.capecodsoaring.com).

VISITOR INFORMATION

The Cape Cod Chamber of Commerce is open year-round, Monday through Saturday 9 to 5 and Sunday 10 to 4.

Information Cape Cod Chamber of Commerce (✉ Shoot Flying Hill Rd. off U.S. 6 and U.S. 132, Hyannis 02601 ☎ 508/362–3225 ⊕ www.capecodchamber.org).

BARNSTABLE, HYANNIS, AND ENVIRONS

With nearly 50,000 year-round residents, Barnstable is the largest town on the Cape, extending from the bay to the sea and comprising several prominent villages, including Centerville, Cotuit, and Osterville. The village of Barnstable itself rests on the bay side and still retains much of the small-town, historic nature that has existed since the 17th century.

The community of Hyannis feels like its own distinct municipality, but is actually a village within the town of Barnstable. As the commercial center of the area, Hyannis constitutes what folks around here call "the big city." There's a large downtown with plenty in the way of shopping, restaurants, and amusements.

BARNSTABLE

11 mi east of Sandwich, 4 mi north of Hyannis.

Barnstable is the second-oldest town on the Cape—it was founded in 1639, two years after Sandwich. You can sense its history in Barnstable Village, on and near Main Street (Route 6A), a lovely area of large old homes dominated by the Barnstable County Superior Courthouse. In the Village Hall is the Barnstable Comedy Club, one of the oldest community theater groups in the country. Just north of the village are the marshes and beaches of Cape Cod Bay, including beautiful Sandy Neck

Beach, as well as busy Barnstable Harbor. The Cape Cod Conservatory of Music and Arts and Cape Cod Community College are also in the vicinity.

GETTING HERE AND AROUND

Most people drive to Barnstable via Route 6 or Route 6A. The Cape Cod Regional Transit Authority operates the Barnstable Villager, a small bus that travels from Barnstable to Hyannis. Service is daily from late June through Labor Day; buses run about every hour.

ESSENTIALS

Transportation Contact **Cape Cod Regional Transit Authority** (✉ *215 Iyannough Rd., Hyannis* ☎ *800/352-7155* ⊕ *www.capecodtransit.org*).

EXPLORING

Coast Guard Heritage Museum. Housed in the old Trayser Building, this museum is continually evolving and expanding. The structure itself is on the National Register of Historic Places, and the museum is filled with all things related to this seafaring branch of the U.S. military. Artifacts and displays also highlight early lifesaving and lighthouse histories, and a small shop sells related books and items. Elsewhere on the grounds are a blacksmith shop and the circa 1690 jail, with two cells bearing former inmates' graffiti. ✉ *3353 Rte. 6A* ☎ *508/362-8521* ⊕ *www.coastguardheritagemuseum.org* ◱ *$5* ⊗ *Mid-May–mid-Oct., Tues.–Sat. 10–3.*

Olde Colonial Courthouse. Built in 1772 as the colony's second court-house, the Olde Colonial Courthouse is the home of **Tales of Cape Cod** (✉ *3018 Rte. 6A* ☎ *508/362-8927* ⊕ *www.talesofcapecod.org*). The historical society holds a weekly slide-illustrated lecture on Tuesday in July and August, plus special events in the shoulder seasons: in May there's a lecture during Maritime Week, and in June there's one during Heritage Week. In September, a "mystery" bus trip takes visitors to areas of historic interest.

Sturgis Library. Established in 1863, Sturgis Library is in a 1644 building listed on the National Register of Historic Places. Its holdings date from the 17th century and include hundreds of maps and land charts, the definitive collection of Cape Cod genealogical material, and an extensive maritime history collection. ✉ *3090 Rte. 6A* ☎ *508/362-6636* ⊕ *www.sturgislibrary.org* ⊗ *Mon. and Wed.–Fri. 10–5; Tues. 1–8; Sat. 10–4.*

W.B. Nickerson Cape Cod History Archives. These archives at Cape Cod Community College has the largest collection of Cape Cod information, including books, records, ships' logs, oral-history tapes, photographs, and films. It also has materials on the neighboring islands of Martha's Vineyard and Nantucket. ✉ *2240 Iyanough Rd., off Rte. 132, West Barnstable* ☎ *508/362-2131* ⊕ *www.capecod.edu/web/nickerson* ⊗ *Mon., Wed., and Fri. 8:30–4.*

WHERE TO EAT

$$ ✕ **Barnstable Restaurant & Tavern.** This handsome old building right in
AMERICAN the village center across from the courthouse, holds both a formal restaurant and a more relaxed tavern. Fresh seafood dishes and the chef's

rich pasta dishes are local favorites. Lighter lunch fare includes the much heralded Tavern Burger—topped with smoked bacon, caramelized onions, roasted mushrooms, and cheddar cheese—as well as salads and sandwiches. Look for live music on the patio Friday evening. ⊠ *3176 Rte. 6A* ☎ *508/362–2355* ⊕ *www.barnstablerestaurant.com* ⊟ *AE, MC, V.*

$$$ ✕ **Dolphin Restaurant.** For the scoop on local politics, eavesdrop at the
AMERICAN Dolphin. A popular spot among local political figures, for decades this has been the place in town where opinions clash and deals are cut. The dark, inviting interior has a colonial feel. Lunch favorites include the shrimp-and-crab melt, rib-eye steak, and fish-and-chips. Dinner consists of a straightforward, well-prepared roster of traditional steaks, chops, and seafood grills and sautéed meals. The small but welcoming bar is a good spot to chow down if you're dining solo. ⊠ *3250 Rte. 6A* ☎ *508/362–6610* ⊕ *www.dolphinrestaurantcapecod.com* ⊟ *AE, MC, V* ⊘ *No lunch Sun.*

$$$ ✕ **Mattakeese Wharf.** Propped above the tides on sturdy wooden pilings,
SEAFOOD this weathered old building looks as if it's been here forever. Views of passing boats are visible from every seat in the house; the best get the benefit of golden sunsets beyond. Aside from the splendid location, seafood is the big draw at this nautical-themed spot, which is often packed with locals and visitors alike. House favorites include the giant lobster rolls and the pasta with sautéed seafood. Many prefer the expansive bar, where you can enjoy a cold beer and a bowl of local steamers. Sunday brunch is popular. ⊠ *273 Millway Rd., Barnstable Harbor* ☎ *508/362–4511* ⊕ *www.mattakeese.com* ⊟ *D, MC, V* ⊘ *Closed Nov.–Apr.*

$ ✕ **Osterville Fish Too.** This combination seafood market/casual restau-
SEAFOOD rant sits on Barnstable Harbor, giving it access to the freshest seafood
★ around. It's tiny, with a fistful of outside picnic tables on a wooden deck and limited parking, but the fried clams and fish sandwiches are worth the inevitable wait. Arrive hungry and try the fat onion rings or the prodigious seafood platters (piled high with sole, shrimp, scallops, and clams). ⊠ *275 Mill Way* ☎ *508/362–2295* ⊟ *MC, V* ⊘ *Closed mid-Oct.–Apr.*

WHERE TO STAY

$$–$$$ 🖫 **Acworth Inn.** This 1860 house 2 mi east of Barnstable Village has four large rooms and a spacious two-room suite. Rooms are decorated with soft pastels, lacy designer linens, and tasteful hand-painted furniture. The suite, with modern furnishings, also has a fireplace, and a whirlpool tub. Breakfast includes granola, fresh muffins or homemade coffee cake, fruit, yogurt, and an entrée that might use herbs from the inn's gardens. There are chairs and an inviting hammock in the shaded backyard. **Pros:** intimate setting; good spot for exploring nearby towns. **Cons:** some rooms have tiny stall showers; steep stairs. ⊠ *4352 Rte. 6A, Cummaquid* 🕮 *Box 256, Cummaquid 02637* ☎ *508/362–3330* ⊕ *www.acworthinn.com* ↪ *4 rooms, 1 suite* ☖ *In-room: a/c, no phone, refrigerator (some), DVD (some), no TV (some), Wi-Fi. In-hotel: no kids under 12* ⊟ *AE, D, MC, V* ⎮◯⎮ *BP.*

$$–$$$ 🖫 **Ashley Manor.** Set behind hedges and a wide lawn, this B&B is a short drive from the village center. The 1699 inn has preserved its antique wide-board floors and has open-hearth fireplaces (one with a beehive oven) in the living room, the dining room, and the keeping room. The rooms are toasty, too—all but one have working fireplaces, and the suites have whirlpool tubs. Antique and country furnishings, Oriental rugs, and glimmers of brass and crystal create an elegant feel. Breakfast is served on the backyard terrace or in the formal dining room. **Pros:** near Barnstable Village; spacious; working fireplaces; in-room spa treatments. **Cons:** very steep stairs. ⊠ *3660 Rte. 6A* ☏ *508/362–8044 or 888/535–2246* ⊕ *www.ashleymanor.net* ↩*2 rooms, 4 suites* ⚲ *In-room: a/c, DVD, refrigerator, Wi-Fi. In-hotel: tennis court, no kids under 14* ▭ *AE, D, MC, V* ⦿| *BP.*

$$ ★ **Beechwood Inn.** Debbie and Ken Traugot's yellow-and-pale-green 1853 Queen Anne house has gingerbread trim and is wrapped by a wide porch with wicker furniture and a glider swing. Named for the property's two magnificent and aged beech trees (one grand weeping, the other copper), the inn emphasizes its Victorian splendor. Although the parlor is pure mahogany-and-red-velvet Victorian, guest rooms (all with queen- or king-size beds) have antiques in lighter Victorian styles; several have fireplaces, and one has a bay view. Bathrooms have pedestal sinks and antique lighting fixtures. Breakfast is served in the dining room, which has a pressed-tin ceiling, a fireplace, and lace-covered tables. **Pros:** afternoon tea; seven beaches within a 5-mi radius. **Cons:** narrow, curved stairs. ⊠ *2839 Rte. 6A* ☏ *508/362–6618 or 800/609–6618* ⊕ *www.beechwoodinn.com* ↩*6 rooms* ⚲ *In-room: a/c, DVD, no phone, refrigerator, Wi-Fi. In-hotel: no kids under 12* ▭ *AE, D, MC, V* ⦿| *BP.*

$$$–$$$$ **The Highpointe Inn.** Debbie and Rich Howard's intimate haven is nes-
Fodor'sChoice tled high on a hill overlooking dunes, the Great Salt Marsh, and the
★ Bay at Sandy Neck. Although it's just minutes from historic Route 6A, the light and airy B&B transports you to a dreamlike getaway, offering casual luxury at its best. Each of the inn's three rooms inspires serenity with comforting colors, decor, and magical views. Breakfast offers a choice of five hot entrées and may include Rich's famed French toast and Debbie's homemade goodies. **Pros:** in-room spa services; serene and private setting. **Cons:** not an antique home. ⊠ *70 High St., West Barnstable* ☏ *508/362–4441 or 888/362–4441* ⊕ *www.thehighpointeinn.com* ↩*3 rooms, 1 suite* ⚲ *In-room: a/c, no phone, refrigerator, DVD, Wi-Fi. In-hotel: no kids under 12* ▭ *AE, D, MC, V* ⦿| *BP.*

$$–$$$ **Honeysuckle Hill.** Innkeepers Freddy and Ruth Riley provide plenty of
Fodor'sChoice little touches here: fresh flowers in every room, a guest fridge stocked
★ with beverages (including wine and beer), beach chairs with umbrellas (perfect for nearby Sandy Neck Beach), and an always-full cookie jar. Additional indulgences include the self-serve liquor and cordial trays in the parlor. Guests are often seen carrying their evening cocktails to the gazebo for a game of cards. The airy, country-style guest rooms in this 1810 Queen Anne–style cottage have lots of white wicker, checked curtains, and pastel-painted floors. The spacious second-floor Wisteria Room overlooking the lush yard is a particularly comfortable retreat, and the screened-in porch is a peaceful place to sip early-morning coffee. **Pros:** gracious and generous innkeepers; lush gardens on the grounds;

tasteful, large rooms; very short drive to Sandy Neck Beach. **Cons:** most rooms are accessed via steep stairs. ⊠ *591 Rte. 6A, West Barnstable* 🕾 *508/362–8418 or 866/444–5522* ⊕ *www.honeysucklehill.com* ⇄ *4 rooms, 1 suite* 🜄 *In-room: a/c, DVD (some), no phone, Wi-Fi. In-hotel: bicycles, no kids under 12* ⊟ *AE, MC, V* ⦾ *BP.*

$$–$$$ ⊡ **Lamb and Lion Inn.** Lamb and Lion occupies a 1740 farmhouse and barn, as well as several additions, with rooms and suites gathered around a courtyard and large swimming pool. Inside, some rooms are summery, with blue-and-white-stripe wallpaper and wicker chairs, whereas others are more staid, furnished with antiques and dark woods. The Innkeeper's Pride Suite has a fireplace and Jacuzzi tub that opens to a private deck; the rustic Barn-Stable, in the original barn, has three sleeping lofts that can accommodate six. If you're up for exploring, the innkeepers have designed several themed driving tours. Fodors. com reader Frankie156 said the innkeepers "were so friendly and help-ful, making our first visit to the Cape and informative and fun-filled experience." **Pros:** convenient location; island ferry drop-offs. **Cons:** not an antique-home experience. ⊠ *2504 Rte. 6A* 🕾 *508/362–6823 or 800/909–6923* ⊕ *www.lambandlion.com* ⇄ *4 rooms, 6 suites* 🜄 *In-room: a/c, kitchen (some), DVD, Wi-Fi. In-hotel: pool, some pets allowed (fee), no kids under 10 (in summer)* ⊟ *MC, V* ⦾ *CP.*

NIGHTLIFE

The **Barnstable Comedy Club** (⊠ *Village Hall, Rte. 6A* 🕾 *508/362–6333* ⊕ *www.barnstablecomedyclub.com*), the Cape's oldest amateur the-ater group, gives much-praised musical and dramatic performances throughout the year. Folks who appeared here before they made it big include Geena Davis, Frances McDormand, and Kurt Vonnegut, a past president of the BCC.

BEACHES, SPORTS, AND THE OUTDOORS

BEACHES AND PONDS

Sandy Neck Beach stretches some 6 mi across a peninsula that ends at **Sandy Neck Light.** The beach is one of the Cape's most beautiful—dunes, sand, and sea spread endlessly east, west, and north. The marsh used to be harvested for salt hay; now it's a haven for birds, which are out and about in the greatest numbers in morning and evening. The lighthouse, standing a few feet from the eroding shoreline at the tip of the neck, has been out of commission since 1952. It was built in 1857 to replace an 1827 light, and it used to run on acetylene gas. The main beach at Sandy Neck has lifeguards, a snack bar, restrooms, and show-ers. As you travel east along Route 6A from Sandwich, Sandy Neck Road is just *before* the Barnstable line, although the beach itself is in West Barnstable. ⊠ *Sandy Neck Rd., West Barnstable* ⦿ *Daily 8* AM*–9* PM*, but staffed only until 5* PM.

Hathaway's Pond (⊠ *Off Phinney's La.*) is a freshwater pond with a beach, restrooms, and a lifeguard (in season).

FISHING

Aquarius Charters (✉ *Barnstable Harbor* ☎ *508/362–9617* ⊕ *www. aquariussportfishing.com*) supplies all gear on its 35-foot boat and offers four-, six-, and eight-hour trips for up to six people to catch bass, blues, tuna, and shark. Reservations are recommended.

WHALE-WATCHING

On **Hyannis Whale Watcher Cruises** out of Barnstable Harbor, a naturalist narrator comments on whale sightings and the natural history of Cape Cod Bay. Trips last about four hours, and there are concessions on board. In July and August you can cruise at sunset, too; go for a real treat and sign on for a clambake cruise that includes a traditional dinner of steamed lobster, corn on the cob, steamers, linguica, potatoes, onions, and Bailey's bread pudding. Prices for adults are about $65; reservations are recommended. ✉ *Millway Marina off Phinney's La.* ☎ *508/362– 6088 or 888/942–5392* ⊕ *www.whales.net* ⊠ *$45* ⊘ *May–Oct.*

SHOPPING

Heading through the villages of Barnstable along Route 6A, you'll find no shortage of intriguing art galleries and rustic antiques shops.

Columbia Trading Company (✉ *1022 Rte. 6A, West Barnstable* ☎ *508/362– 1500* ⊕ *www.columbiatrading.com*) specializes in all things nautical, including rare and out-of-print books, ship models, marine art and antiques, charts, maps, and nautical instruments.

West Barnstable Tables (✉ *2454 Rte. 149, West Barnstable* ☎ *508/362– 2676* ⊕ *www.westbarnstabletables.com*) has exquisite handcrafted tables, chairs, chests, and other furniture made from the finest woods.

CENTERVILLE

7 mi southwest of Barnstable Village, 4 mi west of Hyannis.

Centerville was once a busy seafaring village, its history evident in the 50 or so shipbuilders' and sea captains' houses along its quiet, tree-shaded streets. Offering the pleasures of sheltered ocean beaches on Nantucket Sound, such as **Craigville Beach,** and of freshwater swimming in Lake Wequaquet, it has been a popular vacation area since the mid-19th century. Shoot Flying Hill Road, named by Native Americans, is the highest point of land on the Cape, with panoramic views of Plymouth and Provincetown to the north and Falmouth and Hyannis to the south.

GETTING HERE AND AROUND

To drive to the center of town from Route 28, head toward Craigville Beach on Old Stage Road.

EXPLORING

1856 Country Store. This old-time store sells penny candy, except that these days each candy costs at least 25 pennies. The store also carries newspapers, coffee, crafts, jams, and all kinds of gadgets and toys. You can sip your coffee—and take a political stance—by choosing a wooden bench out front: one is marked DEMOCRAT, and the other REPUBLICAN. ✉ *555 Main St.* ☎ *508/775–1856* ⊕ *www.1856countrystore.com.*

Centerville Historical Society Museum. In a 19th-century house, this museum has furnished period rooms, Sandwich glass, miniature carvings of birds by Anthony Elmer Crowell, models of ships, marine artifacts, military uniforms and artifacts, antique tools, perfume bottles (dating from 1760 to 1920), historic costumes and quilts, and a research library. Each summer there are special costume exhibits or other shows. ✉ *513 Main St.* ☎ *508/775–0331* ⊕ *www.centervillehistoricalmuseum. org* 🎟 *$6* ⊙ *May–mid-Dec., Tues.–Sat. noon–4.*

QUICK BITES

Sample a variety of creamy homemade flavors at **Four Seas Ice Cream** (✉ **360 S. Main St.** ☎ **508/775–1394** ⊕ **www.fourseasicecream.com**), a tradition for generations of summer visitors. The kitchen also turns out short-order lunch and dinner fare. It's open from late May to mid-September until 10 PM.

WHERE TO STAY

$$ 🏨 **Centerville Corners Motor Lodge.** One of the few Mid Cape motels that's not on a traffic-choked, crassly developed road, this attractive redbrick and shingled motor lodge is in the heart of peaceful Centerville Village. Although the rooms are a bit dull and the furnishings are dated, you can't beat the location. Golf packages are available. **Pros:** near Craigville Beach; affordable rates. **Cons:** most rooms overlook parking lot. ✉ *1338 Craigville Beach Rd.* ☎ *508/775–7223 or 800/242–1137* ⊕ *www.centervillecorners.com* 🛏 *48 rooms* ⚴ *In-room: a/c, kitchen (some), refrigerator, Wi-Fi (some). In-hotel: pool, some pets allowed (fee), Wi-Fi hotspot* ⊟ *AE, D, MC, V* ⊙ *Closed Nov.–Apr.* ⊚ *CP.*

BEACHES, SPORTS, AND THE OUTDOORS

Craigville Beach (✉ *Craigville Beach Rd.*) is a long, wide strand that is extremely popular with the collegiate crowd. The beach has lifeguards, showers, and restrooms, and there's food nearby.

COTUIT AND OSTERVILLE

7 mi west of Centerville.

Cotuit is a charming little community formed around seven homesteads belonging to the family of 18th-century trader Winslow Crocker. Much of the town lies along and just south of Route 28, east of Mashpee, and its center is not much more than a crossroads with a post office, an old-time coffee shop, a pizza parlor, and a general store, which all seem unchanged since the 1940s. Large waterfront estates line sections of Main Street and Ocean View Drive, where small coves hide the uncrowded Loop Beach and Ropes Beach.

About 5 mi east of Cotuit, Osterville is lined with elegant waterfront houses, some of which are large "cottages" built in the 19th century when the area became popular with the moneyed set. Despite its haute homes, the village of Osterville retains the small-town charm that permeates the Cape; its Main Street and Wianno Avenue area has a collection of trendy boutiques and jewelry shops mixed with a library, a post office, and country stores. You'll find that most beaches in the village, including the impressive **Dowses Beach,** are restricted to residents-only parking. The village's festivals of Daff O'ville Day (late April) and Christmas Stroll (mid-December) are heavily attended.

GETTING HERE AND AROUND

Most people drive here via Route 28. It's best to get to the beach by bike, because traffic is light and parking is for residents only.

EXPLORING

Cahoon Museum of American Art. In a 1775 Georgian colonial farmhouse that was once a tavern and an overnight way station for travelers on the Hyannis–Sandwich stagecoach line, this museum has a permanent collection of American primitive paintings by Ralph and Martha Cahoon, along with other artists from the 19th century to the present. ⊠ *4676 Rte. 28, Cotuit* ☎ *508/428–7581* ⊕ *www.cahoonmuseum.org* ☜ *$5* ⊗ *Feb.–Dec., Tues.–Sat. 10–4, Sun. 1–4.*

Osterville Historical Museum. In an 1824 sea captain's house, this museum has antiques, dolls, and exhibits on Osterville's history. Two wooden-boat museums—each showcasing various sailing vessels—and the late-18th-century Cammett House are also on the lovely, rambling 2-acre property. Special events include a large outdoor antiques show in mid-August and a weekly summer farmers' market. ⊠ *155 W. Bay Rd., Osterville* ☎ *508/428–5861* ⊕ *www.ostervillemuseum.org* ☜ *$5* ⊗ *Early June–mid-Sept., Thurs.–Sat. 10–2.*

Santuit-Cotuit Historical Society Museum. The first motor-driven firefighting apparatus on Cape Cod, a 1916 Model T chemical-fire engine, is on display here. Look for blooming 19th-centure herbs and flowers in the authentically reproduced kitchen garden. ⊠ *1148 Main St., Cotuit* ☎ *508/428–0461* ⊕ *www.cotuithistoricalsociety.org* ☜ *Free* ⊗ *Memorial Day–Labor Day, weekends 1–4.*

WHERE TO EAT

$$$
NEW AMERICAN

✕ Five Bays Bistro. With its stylish feel and creative menu, this contemporary bistro wouldn't be out of place in Boston or Manhattan. Dishes such as vegetable wontons or tuna with coconut milk draw inspiration from the East, whereas others—perhaps a linguine, duck, and artichoke appetizer or an entrée of seared halibut with shallot risotto—have a more Mediterranean flavor. The lobster macaroni and cheese brings this comfort food to new heights. Sit at the bar for generous and creative cocktails and a lighter menu. ⊠ *825 Main St., Osterville* ☎ *508/420–5559* ⊕ *www.fivebaysbistro.com* ⊟ *AE, D, MC, V* ⊗ *No lunch.*

$$$$
AMERICAN
Fodor's Choice
★

✕ Regatta of Cotuit. It's worth driving out of your way to this refined restaurant in a handsomely restored cinnamon-hue stagecoach inn filled with wood, brass, and Oriental rugs. Chef-owner Weldon Fizell turns out wonderfully inventive versions of classic regional American fare, such as lobster roasted with shallots and brandy. The signature fillet of North Dakota buffalo tenderloin is prepared differently each night. The cozy tap room has its own bar menu (a bit more modestly priced), offering such treats as macadamia-encrusted scallops with lo mein salad. Try tackling the half-pound Tap Burger with blue cheese, grilled Vidalia onion, and barbecue sauce. There's also an assortment of colorful cocktails (prickly-pear margaritas, appletinis); in warmer months there's a nice view from the outdoor terrace. ⊠ *4631 Rte. 28,*

Cotuit ☎ *508/428–5715* ⊕ *www.regattaofcotuit.com* ⚲ *Reservations essential* ▭ *AE, MC, V* ⊙ *Closed Mon. No lunch.*

¢ ✕ **Sweet Tomatoes.** Don't be put off by the prosaic setting of this small

PIZZA pizza place. Sweet Tomatoes serves absolutely tantalizing pizza made with whole-wheat dough, plus a slew of calzones, panini sandwiches, grinders, and wraps, all with fresh, creative ingredients. Top picks among the pies include the Dirty Bomb, with shaved steak, portobello mushrooms, onions, peppers, mozzarella, and red sauce; and the tangy white three-cheese with mozzarella, ricotta, Asiago, and garlic (try ordering it with anchovies for a little extra kick). The Mediterranean salad makes for a delicious starter. ⊠ *770 Main St., Osterville* ☎ *508/420–1717* ⊕ *www.sweettomatoescapecod.com* ▭ *MC, V.*

$$ ✕ **Wimpy's.** No, this is not a fast-food hamburger joint—it's a Cape

SEAFOOD standby with an extensive menu that favors Italian food and lots of fish, from swordfish to salmon. There's also a good dose of meat entrées, pasta, and chicken. Wimpy's loyal clientele fills a big family dining room, a sunny atrium, and a dark traditional tavern that has cozy booths and a fine old bar. Opt for the more-inventive specials, such as tortilla-crusted salmon topped in a caper sauce, or try a simple prime rib (when available). You can get takeout here, too. Sunday brunch is filled with traditional offerings such as Belgian waffles, crepes, and eggs Benedict prepared six different ways. ⊠ *752 Main St., Osterville* ☎ *508/428–6300* ⊕ *www.wimpysseafoodcafe.com* ▭ *AE, DC, MC, V* ⊙ *No lunch Sun.*

SPORTS AND THE OUTDOORS

The **Cotuit Kettleers** of the collegiate Cape Cod Baseball League play home games at **Lowell Park** (⊠ *10 Lowell Ave., 2 mi south of Rte. 28, Cotuit* ☎ *508/428–3358* ⊕ *www.kettleers.org*) from mid-June to mid-August. The team also puts on youth and advanced baseball clinics in summer.

SHOPPING

★ **Oak & Ivory** (⊠ *1112 Main St., Osterville* ☎ *508/428–9425* ⊕ *www.oakandivory.com*) specializes in Nantucket lightship baskets made on the premises, as well as gold miniature baskets and scrimshaw. China, gold jewelry, and other gifts round out the selection.

The **Sow's Ear Antique Company** (⊠ *4698 Falmouth Rd. [Rte. 28], Cotuit* ☎ *508/428–4931* ⊕ *www.sowsearantiqueco.com*), in a late-1600s house next to the Cahoon Museum, specializes in folk art—dolls, ship models, wood carvings, antique quilts, and paintings.

HYANNIS

4 mi south of Barnstable Village, 11 mi east of Mashpee

Hyannis was named for the Native American sachem Iyanno, who sold the area for 20 pounds and two pairs of pants. Perhaps he would have sold it for far more had there been any indication that Hyannis would become known as the "home port of Cape Cod" or that the Kennedys would pitch so many tents here. Hyannis is effectively the transportation center of the Cape: it's near the airport, and ferries depart here for

Nantucket and (in season) Martha's Vineyard. The busy roads feeding into the town are lined with a few of the same big-box stores you'd find anywhere.

A bustling year-round hub of activity, Hyannis has the Cape's largest concentration of businesses, shops, malls, hotels and motels, restaurants, and entertainment venues. Main Street is lined with used-book and gift shops, jewelers, clothing stores, summer-wear and T-shirt shops, and ice-cream and candy stores. The street can have a somewhat forlorn, down-at-the-heels feeling, as the malls outside downtown have taken their toll on business, but there are plenty of good-fun and fancy eateries here.

Perhaps best known for its association with the Kennedy clan, the Hyannis area was also a vacation site for President Ulysses S. Grant in 1874 and later for President Grover Cleveland. Today Hyannis is making an effort to preserve its historical connection with the sea. By 1840 more than 200 shipmasters had established homes in the Hyannis–Hyannis Port area. Aselton Park (at the intersection of South and Ocean streets) and the Village Green on Main Street are the sites of events celebrating this history, and Aselton Park marks the starting point of the scenic Walkway to the Sea, which extends to the dock area.

GETTING HERE AND AROUND

Three parallel streets run through the heart of town. Busy, shop-filled Main Street runs one-way from east to west; South Street runs from west to east; and North Street is open to two-way traffic. The airport rotary connects with heavily trafficked routes 132 and 28 and with U.S. 6. Off Ocean Street and Sea Street lie several excellent beaches, including Kalmus Park Beach, renowned for its stiff winds and hordes of windsurfers, and the smaller Veterans Park Beach, next to the Kennedy Memorial.

Getting around downtown Hyannis in your car can be a frustrating chore—it's best to leave your vehicle in a lot and venture out on foot. The downtown area is walkable, though if you're doing a lot of shopping you should take advantage of the free Hyannis Trolley that runs from late June to Labor Day.

ESSENTIALS

Transportation Contact Hyannis Trolley (✉ 215 Iyannough Rd. ☎ 800/352–7155 ⊕ www.capecodrta.org).

Visitor Information Hyannis Chamber of Commerce (✉ 397 Main St. ☎ 508/775–2201 ⊕ www.hyannis.com).

EXPLORING

TOP ATTRACTIONS

John F. Kennedy Hyannis Museum. In Main Street's Old Town Hall, this museum explores JFK's Cape years (1934–63) through enlarged and annotated photographs culled from the archives of the JFK Library near Boston, as well as a seven-minute video narrated by Walter Cronkite. Also on-site is the **Cape Cod Baseball League Hall of Fame and Museum,** housed in several rooms in the basement of the JFK museum (which is appropriately referred to as "The Dugout"). Plaques of Hall

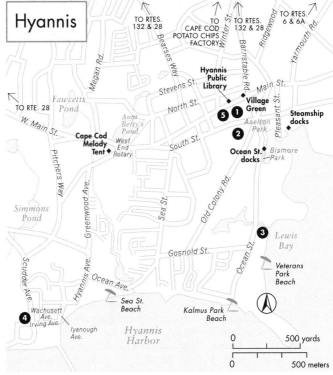

of Famers, autographed items from former players who went on to play professional ball, and other Cape League memorabilia are on view; several films about the league and baseball itself are played continuously. ⊠ *397 Main St.* ☎ *508/790–3077* ⊕ *www.jfkhyannismuseum.org* 🖾 *$5; $8 for joint admission with baseball museum* ☉ *Mid-Apr.–Memorial Day, Mon.–Sat. 10–4, Sun. noon–4; Memorial Day–Oct., Mon.–Sat. 9–5, Sun. noon–5; Nov. and Dec., Thurs.–Sat. 10–4, Sun. noon–4.*

WORTH NOTING

OFF THE
BEATEN
PATH

Cape Cod Potato Chips Factory. There's a standing invitation on the back of the bag: come for a free tour of the factory and get free samples of the crunchy all-natural chips hand-cooked in kettles in small batches. ⊠ *100 Breed's Hill Rd., off Rte. 132* ☎ *508/775–3358* ⊕ *www.capecodchips. com* ☉ *Weekdays 9–5.*

John F. Kennedy Memorial. Beyond the bustling docks where ferries, harbor-tour boats, and deep-sea fishing vessels come and go, you'll find the quiet esplanade. JFK loved to sail these waters, and in 1966 the people of Barnstable erected a plaque and fountain pool here in his memory. Adjacent to the memorial is **Veterans Park,** with a beach, a tree-shaded picnic and barbecue area, and a playground. ⊠ *Ocean St. south of Channel Point, Hyannis Harbor.*

Kennedy Compound. Hyannis Port became a hot spot for Americans during the Kennedy presidency, when the Kennedy Compound became the summer White House. The days of hordes of Secret Service agents and swarms of tourists trampling down the bushes are gone, and the area is once again a community of quietly posh estates—though the Kennedy mystique is such that tourists still seek it out. The best way to get a glimpse of the compound is from the water on one of the many harbor tours or cruises.

Joseph P. and Rose Kennedy bought their house here—the largest one, closest to the water—in 1929 as a healthful place to summer with their soon-to-be-nine kids. (Son Ted bought the house before his mother's death in 1995.) Sons Jack and Bobby bought neighboring houses in the 1950s. Jack's is the one at the corner of Scudder and Irving, with the 6-foot-high stockade fence on two sides. Bobby's is next to it, with a white fieldstone chimney. Ted bought a home on Squaw Island, a private island connected to the area by a causeway at the end of Scudder Avenue. It now belongs to his ex-wife, Joan.

The compound is relatively self-sufficient in terms of entertainment: Rose Kennedy's former abode (with 14 rooms and nine baths) has a movie theater, a private beach, a boat dock, a swimming pool, a tennis court, and a sports field that was the scene of the famous Kennedy touch-football matches. Maria Shriver, Caroline Kennedy Schlossberg, and other family members have had their wedding receptions here. In the summer of 1999 family members waited at the compound, with local and international media lining the streets, for confirmation of John F. Kennedy Jr.'s death in a plane crash off Martha's Vineyard. He and his wife, Carolyn Bessette Kennedy, were flying her sister Lauren Bessette to the Vineyard before continuing on to a cousin's wedding in Hyannis; all three were killed.

A year after Senator Edward Kennedy's death in 2009, there was still no official word as to the future of the compound. There has been some speculation that the late senator's home may become a museum. ⊠ *Ocean St. south of Channel Point, Hyannis Port.*

☾ **Ryan Family Amusement.** Perfect for a rainy day, this park is replete with bowling lanes, video-game rooms, and that old seaside favorite, Skee-Ball. ⊠ *441 Main St., Downtown* ☎ *508/775–3411* ⊕ *www.ryanfamily. com* ☾ *Daily; hrs vary.*

St. Francis Xavier Church. This is where Rose Kennedy and her family worshipped during their summers on the Cape; the pew that John F. Kennedy used regularly is marked with a plaque. Docent-led tours are conducted weekdays, from 9 to 11 and 1:30 to 3:30, from mid-May through October. Mass is given in English, Spanish, and Portuguese. ⊠ *347 South St.* ☎ *508/771–7200* ⊕ *stfrancishyannis.homestead.com.*

WHERE TO EAT

$$ ✕ **Baxter's Boathouse.** Since fried seafood is a Cape staple, you may want
SEAFOOD to pay homage to one of the best Fry-o-lators around. Right on Hyannis Harbor, it's been a favorite of boaters and bathers alike since 1957. The picnic tables outside, some set up on an old floating ferry, allow you to catch some rays while enjoying lobster, fish-and-chips, or something

CLOSE UP

The New Face of Hyannis

More than 1 million people travel to Hyannis each year—but many are merely passing *through* the town on their way to its ferry docks and boats to the outlying islands. For decades, townsfolk wished that these travelers would spend a little bit of time—and money—in Hyannis, but there wasn't much to entice them to stay.

But today, changes are afoot. In a move to become more family-friendly, sophisticated, and appealing, Hyannis has been revitalizing its downtown and waterfront areas. One pleasant improvement is the "Walkway to the Sea," a wave-pattern brick path that winds from Main Street at the Village Green all the way down to Bismore Park at Hyannis Harbor. Along the way are colorful art installations of lobster buoys, complete with educational

information about the fishing industry. The Village Green itself is now host to a weekly farmers' market, free movie showings, and band concerts in summer.

As part of the "Harbor Your Arts" initiative, a series of wood "shanties" now populate Aselton Park along the Walkway to the Sea. Juried artists and artisans rent the sheds as both work space and selling arenas for their products. There's also a seasonal stage, where free musical and theatrical performances are held in summer.

The entire downtown corridor is abuzz with building restorations, improvements, expansions, creative landscaping, new sidewalks, and spruced-up storefronts. You may just want to linger before catching your ferry.

---

from the raw bar. If the weather's not on your side, there's indoor seating overlooking the harbor. A passageway off the dining room leads to Baxter's Boat House Club, a slightly more upscale space that has the same menu. ⊠ *177 Pleasant St., Hyannis Harbor* ☎ *508/775–4490* ⊕ *www.baxterscapecod.com* ⊕ *Reservations not accepted* ▤ *AE, DC, MC, V* ⊗ *Closed mid-Oct.–Apr. and weekdays early Sept.–mid-Oct.*

$$ ╳ **Brazilian Grill.** The Cape has a large Brazilian population, and you
BRAZILIAN can find many of these residents, plus plenty of satisfied visitors, at
Fodor'sChoice this all-you-can-eat *churrascaria* (Brazilian barbecue). Be prepared for
★ some serious feasting: this experience is not for light eaters or vegetarians. Waiters circulate through the dining room offering more than a dozen grilled meats—beef, pork, chicken, sausage, even quail—on long swordlike skewers. You can help yourself to a buffet of salads and side dishes, including *farofa* (a couscouslike dish made of manioc [also known as cassava or yuca]), plantains, rice, and beans. The atmosphere is often loud and jovial. For dessert, the homemade flan is the best anywhere. Dine on the redbrick patio in warm weather. ⊠ *680 Main St.* ☎ *508/771–0109* ⊕ *www.braziliangrill-capecod.com* ▤ *AE, D, DC, MC, V.*

$$ ╳ **Colombo's.** With its sleek leather-backed booths, walls painted tawny
ITALIAN hues, and warm wood floors, Colombo's has added simple sophistication to Main Street. For lunch, the menu covers the ground from simple wraps and sandwiches to more-substantial choices like veal saltimbocca and chicken Parmesan. Dinner favorites include scallops sautéed in a

vodka marinara with prosciutto, and Tuscan-style braised short ribs. It's a lively spot with a late-night menu and live music several summer nights a week on the ample brick patio. ⊠ *544 Main St.* ☎ *508/790–5700* ⊕ *www.colomboscafe.com* ⊟ *AE, D, MC, V.*

$$ ✕ **Fazio's Trattoria.** Set in an old Italian-bakery building, swank but
ITALIAN affordable Fazio's looks like the trattoria it is, with wood floors, high
★ ceilings, and a deli case full of fresh pasta, breads, and cheeses. There's also an espresso and cappuccino bar. Chef Tom Fazio's menu leans on fresh ingredients and herbed pastas, such as basil fettuccine with shrimp, lemon, and plum tomatoes. All ravioli, pastas, and breads are homemade, and the brick-oven pizzas are delicious. Take home some fresh cannoli for dessert. ⊠ *294 Main St.* ☎ *508/775–9400* ⊕ *www. fazio.net* ⊟ *AE, MC, V* ⊗ *No lunch Sun.*

$$ ✕ **Misaki.** Tucked away on quiet West Main Street, frantically popular
JAPANESE Misaki serves authentic Japanese food in an intimate space with tables arranged closely together. The menu has a diverse array of traditional Japanese dishes, such as vegetable tempura, yaki soba, and chicken or beef teriyaki, but the sushi and sashimi—prepared by an experienced master sushi chef—are the real stars here. Try the tuna rolls, which are delectably soft and silky. Two traditional Japanese "sitting booths" are available by reservation. ⊠ *379 W. Main St.* ☎ *508/771–3771* ⊕ *www. misakisushi.com* ⊟ *AE, MC, V.*

$$$ ✕ **Naked Oyster.** In a favored location on Main Street, this restaurant
ECLECTIC is known, not surprisingly, for its oysters. With its own oyster farm in
Fodor'sChoice nearby Barnstable, the kitchen—and diners—benefit from near-daily
★ deliveries of the succulent bivalves. Well over 1,000 oysters are eaten here on an average summer weekend. You'll always find close to two dozen raw and "dressed" oyster dishes (such as barbecue oysters on the half shell with blue cheese, caramelized onions, and bacon) plus a nice range of salads and appetizers. The oyster stew is also out of this world. Exposed brick walls inside and a few street-side tables outside make dining a pleasure. ⊠ *410 Main St.* ☎ *508/778–6500* ⊕ *www.nakedoyster. com* ⊟ *AE, D, MC, V.*

$$$ ✕ **The Paddock.** The Paddock is synonymous with tried-and-true formal
CONTINENTAL dining on the Cape. Sumptuous upholstery in the main dining room
★ and old-style wicker on the breezy summer porch create authentic Victorian ambience. The menu is traditional yet subtly innovative, and fresh ingredients are combined in novel ways: Chatham scrod comes with caramelized onions, roasted peppers, artichokes, and a basil-lemon beurre blanc. The steak au poivre, with several varieties of crushed peppercorns, is masterful; the fire-roasted salmon is stuffed with lobster, goat cheese, and mushrooms, topped with avocado-compound butter. ⊠ *20 Scudder Ave.* ☎ *508/775–7677* ⊕ *www.paddockcapecod.com* ⊟ *AE, DC, MC, V* ⊗ *Closed mid-Nov.–Mar.*

$$$ ✕ **Roadhouse Café.** Candlelight flickers off the white-linen tablecloths
ECLECTIC and dark-wood wainscoting at the Roadhouse Café, a smart choice
★ for a night out. Popular dishes include the "lobster martini" appetizer with a half lobster, seaweed salad, avocado puree, and fresh mango. For dinner, many rave about the spicy Caribbean stew. In the more casual bistro and the mahogany bar, you can order from a separate menu,

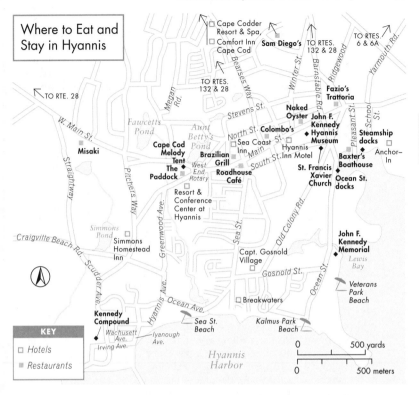

Where to Eat and Stay in Hyannis

KEY

□ Hotels

■ Restaurants

which includes thin-crust pizza as well as burgers and lighter fare. Listen to excellent straight-ahead jazz on Monday night year-round in the bistro. There's also a piano bar on Friday and Saturday. ⊠ *488 South St.* ☎ *508/775–2386* ⊕ *www.roadhousecafe.com* ⚭ *Reservations essential* ▭ *AE, D, MC, V* ☉ *No lunch.*

$　✕ **Sam Diego's.** The bar has a busy social scene, and the menu has satisfy-

MEXICAN　ing—if predictable—Tex-Mex burritos, enchiladas, and fajitas. Crispy deep-fried ice cream served in a giant goblet is a house favorite; the margaritas, which come in several flavors, are another crowd-pleaser. The prop-shop furnishings may be a little cheesy—sombreros, Aztec birds, and the like—but the place is fun, friendly, and popular with families. Fodors.com reader Brewsterskip advises: "Don't fill up on the great free salsa and chips because you need room for a good meal." Weekday lunch options include an all-you-can-eat chili-and-taco bar, and dinner is served nightly until midnight. ⊠ *950 Rte. 132* ☎ *508/771–8816* ⊕ *www.samdiegos.com* ▭ *AE, D, MC, V.*

WHERE TO STAY

$$$–$$$$　▥ **Anchor-In.** Most rooms at this small-scale motel on the north end of ★ Hyannis Harbor have harbor views and small balconies overlooking the water. Its simple street-side appearance belies its spacious accommodations and extensive grounds. Rooms are up-to-date, with down comforters, terry robes, and flat-screen televisions. Some rooms have refrigerators, and the deluxe rooms have wraparound porches. Lisa and Skip Simpson deliver the warm, personal service of a small B&B. The Continental breakfast is a real treat, served in the Lewis Bay Library with its extraordinary views. **Pros:** easy walk to downtown; great harbor views. **Cons:** second-floor rooms accessed via stairs. ⊠ *1 South St.* ☎ *508/775–0357* ⊕ *www.anchorin.com* ↩ *42 rooms* ⚄ *In-room: a/c, refrigerator (some), DVD (some), Wi-Fi. In-hotel: pool* ▤ *AE, D, MC, V* ⵀⵔ*CP.*

$$$–$$$$ ⬚ **Breakwaters.** These privately owned, weathered gray-shingle cottages rent by the week in summer (or nightly in spring and fall). It's a relaxed place, set on a quiet dead-end lane. Cottages are divided into one-, two-, and three-bedroom units and offer all the comforts of home. Each unit has one or two full baths; a kitchen with microwave, coffeemaker, refrigerator, toaster, and stove; and a deck or patio with a grill and picnic table. Most have water views. An in-ground heated pool is less than 200 feet from the town beach on Nantucket Sound. **Pros:** excellent waterfront location; ideal for families. **Cons:** hard to reserve unless you're staying for a week. ⊠ *432 Sea St.* ☎ *508/775–6831* ⊕ *www.thebreakwaters.com* ↩ *19 cottages* ⚄ *In-room: no a/c, kitchen. In-hotel: pool, beachfront, Wi-Fi hotspot* ▤ *No credit cards* ⊘ *Closed mid-Oct.–Apr.*

$$$–$$$$ ⬚ **Cape Codder Resort & Spa.** Don't let the kids spy the indoor wave
ⵁ pool here—a fantasy of waves, waterfalls, and waterslides—or you'll never get out to see anything else on the Cape. Although it's set on an unattractive stretch of Route 132, this sprawling, family-friendly compound has quite a few amenities, including an excellent spa. Rooms range from basic to more elaborate—the Cape Codder rooms are more upscale than the "deluxe" ones. The best rooms face the inner courtyard, overlooking the lawn or the "beach" (a stretch of sand that's used for seasonal clambakes). The suites are huge; several have spiral staircases that lead up to a sleeping loft. **Pros:** many amenities for kids; close to downtown. **Cons:** not the place for peaceful poolside contemplation. ⊠ *1225 Iyanough Rd.* ☎ *508/771–3000 or 888/297–2200* ⊕ *www.capecodderresort.com* ↩ *252 rooms, 8 suites* ⚄ *In-room: a/c, Wi-Fi. In-hotel: 2 restaurants, room service, bar, tennis court, gym, spa* ▤ *AE, D, DC, MC, V.*

$$$–$$$$ ⬚ **Capt. Gosnold Village.** An easy walk from Kalmus Beach and town, this
ⵁ peaceful, low-key colony of motel rooms and pink-shutter cottages is
★ ideal for families. Kids can ride their bikes around the quiet street, and the pool is fenced in and watched over by a lifeguard. In some rooms, walls are attractively paneled with painted pine; floors are carpeted, and simple furnishings are colonial or modern. All cottages have decks and gas grills and receive maid service. Choose from efficiency units or one- to three-bedroom cottages. **Pros:** a good bet for families; short walk to nearby beaches. **Cons:** no air-conditioning; no water views. ⊠ *230 Gosnold St.* ☎ *508/775–9111* ⊕ *www.captaingosnold.com* ↩ *23 units* ⚄ *In-room: no a/c, kitchen (some), Wi-Fi. In-hotel: pool* ▤ *MC, V* ⊘ *Closed Nov.–mid-Apr.*

$$–$$$ Comfort Inn Cape Cod. All the rooms at this mid-range chain motel have white-oak-veneer furnishings and include one king-size or two double beds, a table and chairs or a desk and chair, and a wardrobe. Some king rooms have sofa beds. The quietest rooms are on the top floor, facing the pond and woods; all have free HBO and Nintendo, and pets are allowed. Although the location is fairly convenient to U.S. 6, the Comfort Inn is a few miles north of downtown Hyannis up traffic-choked Route 132—it is quiet and set well back from the road, though. Pros: good package deals; not far from downtown. Cons: on a heavily trafficked road; no views. ⊠ *1470 Rte. 132* ☎ *508/771–4804* ⊕ *www. comfortinn-hyannis.com* ⇆ *103 rooms, 1 suite* ⚐ *In-room: a/c, refrigerator (some), Wi-Fi. In-hotel: pool, gym, some pets allowed* ⊟ *AE, D, MC, V* ⊚| *CP.*

$–$$ Hyannis Inn Motel. The main building of this second-oldest motel in Hyannis, a modest two-story spread, served as press headquarters during JFK's presidential campaign. Today, it's right in the heart of the downtown shopping and retail action. The main building's immaculate rooms have double, queen-size, or king-size beds; some have whirl-pool tubs. Other deluxe rooms in a separate wing out back are larger, sunnier, and quieter (they don't face Main Street) and have queen-or king-size beds. The restaurant serves breakfast only. Pros: in the thick of downtown; spacious rooms; nice outside sundecks for relaxing. Cons: not a beachfront spot. ⊠ *473 Main St.* ☎ *508/775–0255 or 800/922–8993* ⊕ *www.hyannisinn.com* ⇆ *77 rooms* ⚐ *In-room: a/c, refrigerator (some), Wi-Fi. In-hotel: restaurant, bar, pool* ⊟ *AE, D, MC, V* ⊗ *Closed Nov.–Mar.*

$$$–$$$$ Resort & Conference Center at Hyannis. Sparklingly new and sleek, contemporary-style rooms have granite counters in the bathrooms and tasteful neutral color schemes. Rooms face either the golf course or the nicely maintained courtyard. Deluxe rooms and suites with separate sitting areas are also available, though all rooms are generously sized and have their own private balcony or patio. Dining options range from casual pub-style to more-formal dinners, or alfresco under the cabana tent by the pool. Guests have complimentary access to the on-site Atlantis Sports Club. Pros: many amenities; easy access to downtown. Cons: no Cape feel. ⊠ *35 Scudder Ave.* ☎ *508/862–6920 or 866/828–8259* ⊕ *www.capecodresortandconference.com* ⇆ *232 rooms* ⚐ *In-room: a/c, refrigerator, Wi-Fi. In-hotel: 4 restaurants, room service (summer months), bars, golf course, pools, gym, spa* ⊟ *AE, D, DC, MC, V.*

$ SeaCoast Inn. After a top-to-bottom renovation, the rooms at this centrally located hotel sparkle. Between downtown and the harbor, the inn is recognizable by its abundantly blooming window boxes. Most rooms are equipped with kitchenettes; in addition, you have complimentary use of a washer and dryer, beach chairs, and umbrellas. Ask about discount ferry and whale-watch tickets. Pros: rooms are big and immaculate; reasonable rates; walk to beaches, downtown, and ferries. Cons: not a pretty location; no great views. ⊠ *33 Ocean St.* ☎ *508/775–3828* ⊕ *www.seacoast.capecod.com* ⇆ *26 rooms* ⚐ *In-room: a/c, kitchen (some), refrigerator, Wi-Fi. In-hotel: Internet terminal, parking (free)* ⊟ *AE, D, MC, V* ⊗ *Closed Nov.–Apr.* ⊚| *CP.*

$$–$$$ ⛺ **Simmons Homestead Inn.** At this 1820 former sea captain's estate, each room in the main house or the detached barn is named for an animal and decorated (somewhat excessively) accordingly. This offbeat and casual inn has rooms with antique, wicker, or canopied four-poster beds topped with brightly colored quilts; some have fireplaces, and some, such as the large, cheery Bird Room, have private decks. You can borrow 10-speed mountain bikes, and Simmons Pond is a short jaunt on the property's trail. Gregarious innkeeper Bill Putman encourages you to return each evening for a wine-and-socializing hour. He'll also be happy to show you his collection of nearly 60 vintage cars or his roughly 500 vintages of single-malt Scotch. About three dozen friendly cats roam about the property. **Pros:** good place for people with pets; lots of socializing. **Cons:** if you're not an animal lover, steer clear. ⊠ *288 Scudder Ave., Hyannis Port* ☎ *508/778–4999* ⊕ *www.simmonshomesteadinn. com* ⬏ *12 rooms, 2 suites* ⚐ *In-room: a/c, no phone, no TV. In-hotel: bicycles, some pets allowed (fee)* ⊟ *AE, D, MC, V* ⭕️ *BP.*

NIGHTLIFE AND THE ARTS

THE ARTS

The **Boston Pops Esplanade Orchestra** (☎ *508/362–0066* ⊕ *www. artsfoundationcapecod.org*) wows the crowd with its annual Pops by the Sea concert, held in August at the Hyannis Village Green. Each year a celebrity guest conductor strikes up the band for a few selected numbers; past baton bouncers have included Rachel Ray, Joan Kennedy, Mike Wallace, Art Buchwald, Maya Angelou, and Sebastian Junger.

In 1950 actress Gertrude Lawrence and her husband, producer-manager Richard Aldrich, opened the **Cape Cod Melody Tent** (⊠ *21 W. Main St.* ☎ *508/775–5630* ⊕ *www.melodytent.com*) to showcase Broadway musicals and concerts. Today it's the Cape's top venue for pop concerts and comedy shows. Performers who have played here, in the round, include the Indigo Girls; Lyle Lovett; Tony Bennett; Bill Cosby; and Crosby, Stills & Nash. The Tent also holds an 11 AM Wednesday children's theater series in July and August.

The 90-member **Cape Cod Symphony Orchestra**, under talented and passionate conductor Jung-Ho Pak, gives regular classical and children's concerts with guest artists September through May. Performances are held at the Barnstable Performing Arts Center at **Barnstable High School** (⊠ *744 W. Main St.* ☎ *508/362–1111* ⊕ *www.capesymphony.org*).

Harbor Your Arts (☎ *508/862–4990* ⊕ *www.hyartsdistrict.com*) is a great program of visual and performing arts sponsored by the town of Hyannis. Early evenings in July and August come alive with various free musical programs. All events take place at Aselton Memorial Park, at the intersection of South and Ocean streets.

NIGHTLIFE

Hyannis is Barnstable's nightlife hub, with more than a dozen popular bars and taverns, most of them along Main Street in the heart of downtown. Elsewhere in this otherwise lightly developed town, bars and clubs are few and far between.

The British Beer Company (⊠ *412 Main St.* ☎ *508/771–1776* ⊕ *www. britishbeer.com*) has a hearty selection of beers, from stouts to pilsners;

most nights there's also live entertainment—usually local rock bands. The BBC also has branches on the Cape in Sandwich and Falmouth.

Bud's Country Lounge (✉ *3 Bearses Way* ☎ *508/771–2505*) has pool tables and live music, dancing, and karaoke year-round.

Club 477/Mallory Dock (✉ *477 Yarmouth Rd.* ☎ *508/771–7511*), in the old Hyannis train station, is the Cape's only gay club outside Provincetown. There's a piano bar on the lower level and a dance bar on the upper floor with music almost as hot as the crowd.

The Comedy Lounge (✉ *Radisson Hotel Hyannis, Rte. 28* ☎ *877/548–3237* ⊕ *www.comedylounge.com*), despite its location in a ubiquitous chain hotel, pulls in top comedy acts from throughout the Northeast. Shows are held Friday and Saturday night June to September; only on Friday otherwise.

The Island Merchant (✉ *302 Main St.* ☎ *508/771–1337* ⊕ *www.the-islandmerchant.com*) showcases a fine range of acoustic, blues, open jazz jams, and rock. There's even a dinner music series. The food is pretty tasty, too; look for some good island-influenced items like the West Indian pumpkin bisque, and jerk chicken.

BEACHES, SPORTS, AND THE OUTDOORS

BASEBALL

The **Hyannis Harbor Hawks** (☎ *508/420–0962* ⊕ *www.harborhawks.org*) of the collegiate Cape Cod Baseball League play home games at **McKeon Park** (✉ *High School Rd.*) from mid-June to mid-August. Interested 5- to 17-year-olds can sign up with the Youth Baseball Academy.

BEACHES

Kalmus Park Beach, at the south end of Ocean Street in Hyannis, is a fine, wide sandy beach with an area set aside for windsurfers and a sheltered area that's good for kids. It has a snack bar, restrooms, showers, and lifeguards.

Veterans Park Beach, next to the John F. Kennedy Memorial on Ocean Street, has a small beach that's especially good for kids; it's sheltered from waves and fairly shallow. There are picnic tables, barbecue facilities, showers, and restrooms.

BOATING

Eastern Mountain Sports (✉ *1513 Rte. 132* ☎ *508/362–8690*) rents kayaks and camping gear.

The catboat **Eventide** (✉ *Ocean St. Dock* ☎ *508/775–0222 or 800/308–1837* ⊕ *www.catboat.com*) sails in Hyannis Harbor and out into Nantucket Sound on several one- and two-hour cruises; options include a nature tour and a sunset cruise.

Hy-Line (✉ *Ocean St. Dock* ☎ *508/790–0696* ⊕ *www.hy-linecruises.com*) offers cruises on reproductions of old-time Maine coastal steamers. The one-hour tours of Hyannis Harbor and Lewis Bay include a view of the Kennedy compound and other points of interest.

FISHING

Helen H Deep Sea Fishing (✉ *137 Pleasant St.* ☎ *508/790–0660* ⊕ *www.helen-h.com*) has a fleet of several sturdy vessels in search of everything from fluke to tuna. There's also a seal-watching cruise.

GOLF

Hyannis Golf Course (⊠ *Rte. 132* ☎ *508/362–2606* ⊕ *www.town.barnstable.ma.us/hyannisgolfclub*) is an 18-hole, par-71 public golf course that is open year-round.

Twin Brooks (⊠ *Resort and Conference Center at Hyannis, 35 Scudder Ave.* ☎ *508/862–6980* ⊕ *www.twinbrooksgolf.net*) is a beautifully landscaped, challenging 18-hole, par-3 public course. You may bump into some famous faces; many performers from the Cape Cod Melody Tent tee off here while they're in town.

SHOPPING

Main Street in downtown Hyannis has gradually been gentrified in recent years and has become one of the top shopping destinations on the Cape, buzzing with several art galleries and antiques shops, numerous clothiers, and a slew of other, mostly independent, boutiques and gift emporia. You'll also find quite a few restaurants along this walkable stretch, including several cafés that are nice for a cup of coffee or a light snack. Heading through the villages of Barnstable along Route 6A, you'll find no shortage of intriguing art galleries and rustic antiques shops.

Cape Cod Mall (⊠ *Between Rtes. 132 and 28* ☎ *508/771–0200* ⊕ *www.capecodmall.com*), the Cape's largest, has 120 mid- to upper-end mostly chain shops, including department stores such as Macy's and Sears.

Christmas Tree Shops (⊠ *655 Iyanough Rd.* ☎ *508/778–5521* ⊕ *www.christmastreeshops.com*), a Cape mainstay, are a bargain shoppers' haven. Take home Cape souvenirs at a great discount along with just about anything you might need—or not need—to decorate your home.

The handsome flagship **Puritan of Cape Cod** (⊠ *408 Main St.* ☎ *508/775–2400* ⊕ *www.puritancapecod.com*) store carries upscale clothing brands, from North Face to Eileen Fisher and Ralph Lauren; they also sell outdoor gear. Service is great here, and they also have several other stores around the Cape.

YARMOUTH

Once known as Mattacheese, or "the planting lands," the town of Yarmouth was settled in 1639 by farmers from the Plymouth Bay Colony. It consists of three villages of interest to travelers: Yarmouth Port, West Yarmouth, and South Yarmouth. Yarmouth Port, on scenic Route 6A near Cape Cod Bay on the Cape's north shore, is serene; West Yarmouth and South Yarmouth, near Route 28, have plenty of commercial bustle from strip malls to mini-golf.

YARMOUTH PORT

3 mi east of Barnstable Village, 43 mi west of Provincetown.

The town's northernmost village of Yarmouth Port wasn't established as a distinct village until 1829. By then the Cape had begun a thriving maritime industry, and men turned to the sea to make their fortunes. Many impressive sea captains' houses—some now B&Bs and museums—still line enchanting Route 6A and nearby side streets, and Yarmouth Port has some real old-time stores in town. A mile's drive north of Route 6A is the small but lovely Gray's Beach, where a boardwalk at Bass Hole stretches hundreds of feet over the wide marsh and the Callery-Darling conservation land trails loop through forest and marshland.

GETTING HERE AND AROUND
Route 6A is the main route to Yarmouth Port, and there are lovely streets heading north toward the water and through hidden residential areas filled with beautiful old homes.

EXPLORING
TOP ATTRACTIONS

Bass Hole Boardwalk. One of Yarmouth Port's most beautiful areas is Bass Hole, which stretches from Homer's Dock Road to the salt marsh. Bass Hole Boardwalk extends over a marshy creek; amid the salt marshes, vegetated wetlands, and upland woods. Gray's Beach is a little crescent of sand with still water good for kids—but don't go beyond the roped-in swimming area, the only section where the current isn't strong. At the end of the boardwalk, benches provide a place to relax and look out over abundant marsh life and, across the creek, the beautiful, sandy shores of Dennis's Chapin Beach. At low tide you can walk out on the flats for almost a mile. ⊠ *Center St. near Gray's Beach parking lot.*

Captain Bangs Hallet House. Built in 1840 onto an existing 1740 house for a sea captain in the China trade, this Greek Revival building has a hitching post out front and a weeping beech in back. The house and its contents typify a 19th-century sea captain's home, with pieces of pewter, china, nautical equipment, antique toys, and clothing on display. The kitchen has an original 1740 brick beehive oven and butter churns. Tour guides relate salty sea captains' stories from the 19th century. ⊠ *11 Strawberry La., off Rte. 6A* ☎ *508/362–3021* ⊕ *www.hsoy.org* 🔄 *$3* ⊗ *June–mid-Oct., Thurs.–Sun. 1–4; tours at 1, 2, and 3.*

Edward Gorey House Museum. Explore the eccentric illustrations and off-beat humor of the late acclaimed artist. The regularly changing exhibitions, arranged in the downstairs rooms of Gorey's former home, include drawings of his oddball characters and reveal the mysterious psyche of the sometimes dark but always playful illustrator. ⊠ *8 Strawberry La.* ☎ *508/362–3909* ⊕ *www.edwardgoreyhouse.org* 🔄 *$5* ⊗ *Mid-Apr.–June, Thurs.–Sat. 11–4, Sun. noon–4; July–early Oct., Wed.–Sat. 11–4, Sun. noon–4; mid-Oct.–late Dec., Fri. and Sat. 11–4, Sun. noon–4.*

Hallet's. For a peek into the past, make a stop at this country drugstore preserved as it was in 1889 when it was opened by Thacher Hallet, the current owner's grandfather. Hallet served not only as druggist but also as postmaster and justice of the peace. Sit at a swivel stool at the all-marble soda fountain and order the secret-recipe ice-cream soda. ⊠ *139 Rte. 6A* ☎ *508/362–3362* ⊗ *Apr.–mid-Nov.; call for hrs.*

Thacher Taylor Hallet Museum. Above Hallet's Store, this museum displays photographs and memorabilia of Yarmouth Port and the Hallet family. ⊠ *139 Rte. 6A* ☎ *508/362–3362* 🔄 *Free* ⊗ *Apr.–mid-Nov.; call for hrs.*

Winslow Crocker House. This elegantly symmetrical two-story Georgian from 1780 has 12-over-12 small-pane windows and rich paneling in every room. Crocker was a well-to-do trader and land speculator; after his death, his two sons built a wall dividing the house in half. The structure was moved here from West Barnstable in 1936 by Mary Thacher, who donated it—along with her collection of 17th- to 19th-century furniture, pewter, hooked rugs, and ceramics—to Historic New England. ⊠ *250 Rte. 6A* ☎ *617/227–3956* ⊕ *www.historicnewengland.org* 🖾 *$5* ☉ *June–mid-Oct., 2nd and 4th Sat. of month, tours at 11, noon, 1, 2, 3, and 4.*

WORTH NOTING

Botanical Trails of the Historical Society of Old Yarmouth. This park consists of 50 acres of oak and pine woods and a pond, accented by blueberries, lady's slippers, Indian pipes, rhododendrons, and hollies. Stone markers and arrows point out the 2 mi of trails; you'll find trail maps in the gatehouse mailbox. Just beyond the historical society's trails, you can find **Kelley Chapel**, built in 1873 by a father for his daughter, who was grieving over the death of her child. An iron woodstove and a pump organ dominate the simple interior. ⊠ *Off Rte. 6A* 🖾 *50¢* ☉ *Gatehouse July and Aug., daily 1–4. Trails during daylight hrs year-round.*

Taylor-Bray Farm. Purchased in 1640 and established as a prosperous farm in the late 1700s, this farm is listed on the National Register of Historic Places. It hosts special events, such as an annual sheep shearing, a fall festival, and a crafts fair. The public is welcome to take advantage of the farm's picnic tables, walking trails, and great views of the tidal marsh year-round from dawn to dusk. ⊠ *Bray Farm Rd.* ☎ *508/385–9407* ⊕ *www.taylorbrayfarm.org.*

WHERE TO EAT

$$
JAPANESE
Fodor'sChoice
★

✕**Inaho.** Yuji Watanabe, chef-owner of the Cape's best Japanese restaurant, makes early-morning journeys to Boston's fish markets to shop for the freshest local catch. His selection of sushi and sashimi is vast and artful, and vegetable and seafood tempura come out of the kitchen fluffy and light. If you're a teriyaki lover, you can't do any better than the chicken's beautiful blend of sweet and sour. One remarkable element of the restaurant is its artful lighting: small pinpoint lights on the food accentuate the presentation in a dramatic way. Can't decide what to order? For $100 and up per person, the chef designs a varied and generous tasting menu. The serene and simple Japanese garden out back has a traditional koi pond. ⊠ *157 Main St.* ☎ *508/362–5522* ⊕ *www. inahocapecod.com* ▭ *MC, V* ☉ *Closed Sun.*

$$$
NEW AMERICAN

✕**Lyric.** Everything seems aglow within this charming 18th-century building. Chef Melissa Allen has created an intriguing menu that utilizes a great deal of locally grown and harvested produce, seafood, and meats. A liberal and inventive use of spices ensures that nothing here is commonplace. Appetizers range from escargot to duck meatballs to lamb turnovers with a cilantro mint chili sauce. For dinner, try the chili-rubbed tenderloin with braised fennel. The atmosphere is soothing and sophisticated, and an attractive bar makes waiting for a table a pleasant respite. ⊠ *43 Rte. 6A* ☎ *774/330–0000* ⊕ *www.lyriccapecod. com* ▭ *MC, V* ☉ *No lunch.*

$$$ ✕**Old Yarmouth Inn Restaurant & Tavern.** Established in 1696, this inn—the
AMERICAN oldest on Cape Cod—is still satisfying guests with fine food and drink. It
comprises a main dining room, which is bright and airy, and two smaller
and more intimate ones, plus the wood-paneled Tavern, which has a
full bar and serves more-casual fare. Colonial-style wallpaper, exposed
paneling, and thoughtful renovation have made this old beauty a favor-
ite choice for elegant weddings. Fresh ingredients are a priority, so the
menu changes seasonally; the wide range of meat, poultry, seafood,
and pasta dishes infused with clever combinations of familiar flavors
offers something for just about everyone. The Sunday brunch buffet is
popular. ⊠ *223 Rte. 6A* ☎ *508/362–9962* ⊕ *www.oldyarmouthinn.com*
▤ *AE, D, MC, V* ☽ *No lunch Sun. or Mon.*

¢ ✕**The Optimist Café.** From the outside, this bold Gothic Victorian looks
BRITISH like something out of a Brothers Grimm tale, with its steeply pitched
roof, turrets, elaborate gingerbread trim, and deep rose-and-green paint
job. Inside, vibrant yellow walls help convey the café's mission to "turn
a frown upside down." Chances are you'll be delighted with the great
selection for breakfast (served all day) and lunch, featuring traditional
English fare like the Ploughman's Lunch. Other British Isles favorites
include several curries, smoked fish options, scones, and crumpets. Roy-
alty or no, you're bound to be most pleased with the afternoon tea. Go
all out with The Majesty: scones with clotted cream and preserves, a
selection of finger sandwiches and desserts, a pot of tea, and a flute of
champagne. ⊠ *134 Rte. 6A* ☎ *508/362–1024* ⊕ *www.optimistcafe.com*
▤ *AE, D, MC, V* ☽ *No dinner.*

WHERE TO STAY

$$$–$$$$ ▤**The Inn at Cape Cod.** A stately Greek Revival building with imposing
★ columns, the inn has one of the most dramatic facades of any house on
the Cape; it sits near the Botanical Trails and has its own fine gardens,
patios, and tree-shaded lawns. On the first floor, the Sears Room, with
a mahogany king-size four-poster bed and antique furnishings, is a tra-
ditional Victorian chamber. Upstairs, the stately Plantation Suite, with
an Italian armoire and cherry writing desk, opens to a private balcony.
Some rooms, particularly the Bronte Room, are on the small side, but
don't feel cramped because of lots of natural light and views of the gar-
dens. **Pros:** elegant lodging; close to attractions. **Cons:** no water views or
direct beach access; some steep stairs. ⊠ *4 Summer St.* ☎ *508/375–0590*
or 800/850–7301 ⊕ *www.innatcapecod.com* ⇆ *7 rooms, 2 suites* ⚄ *In-
room: a/c, DVD, no phone, Wi-Fi hotspot* ▤ *AE, MC, V* ⏻⌖ *BP.*

$$–$$$ ▤**Liberty Hill Inn.** Smartly but traditionally furnished common areas—
Fodor'sChoice including the high-ceiling parlor, the formal dining room, and the wrap-
★ around porch—are a major draw to this dignified 1825 Greek Revival
house. Guest rooms in both the main building and the carriage house
are filled with a mix of Old World romantic charm and modern ame-
nities; each is uniquely decorated, and some have whirlpool tubs and
fireplaces for those chilly evenings. Breakfast might include blueberry
French toast or a frittata, and afternoon tea is also available. If you're
traveling with children under 5, please make advanced arrangements
with the innkeepers. **Pros:** tasteful surroundings; beautiful grounds.
Cons: some steep stairs; some bathrooms have only small shower stalls;

not a waterfront location. ⊠ *77 Rte. 6A* ☎ *508/362–3976* ⊕ *www. libertyhillinn.com* ⇶ *8 rooms, 1 suite* ఛ *In-room: a/c, DVD, Wi-Fi. In-hotel: Internet terminal* ⊟ *AE, D, MC, V* ⑩ *BP.*

NIGHTLIFE AND THE ARTS

Oliver's (⊠ *6 Bray Farm Rd., off Rte. 6A* ☎ *508/362–6062*) has live music in a variety of genres in its Planck's Tavern on weekends year-round.

BEACHES, SPORTS, AND THE OUTDOORS

BEACHES

Parking at Yarmouth beaches for nonresidents is $15 daily Memorial Day through Labor Day. Weekly stickers are also available for $70 and can be purchased right at most beach booths.

Dennis Pond (⊠ *Off Summer St.*) is a freshwater pond with a sandy beach, and restrooms. In season, a resident parking sticker is required.

SHOPPING

Design Works (⊠ *159 Rte. 6A* ☎ *508/362–9698*) specializes in home furnishings, from luxurious linens, bath products, and antique furniture (especially Scandinavian) to high-end women's accessories, baby items, and glassware. If it's furniture you're after, ask to make an appointment to tour their large warehouse in nearby Hyannis.

Parnassus Book Service (⊠ *220 Rte. 6A* ☎ *508/362–6420*), occupying a three-story 1840 former general store, has a huge selection of old and new books—Cape Cod, maritime, Americana, antiquarian, and others—and is a great place to browse. Its bookstall, outside on the building's side, is open 24 hours a day and works on the honor system—tally up your purchases and leave the money in the mail slot. Parnassus also carries Robert Bateman's nature prints.

Peach Tree Designs (⊠ *173 Rte. 6A* ☎ *508/362–8317*) carries home furnishings and decorative accessories; some are from local craftspeople, all are beautifully made.

WEST YARMOUTH

4 mi south of Yarmouth Port, 2 mi east of Hyannis.

The commercial hub (and the major road through West Yarmouth) is, for better or worse, Route 28—the part of the Cape people love to hate. As you pass through the area—probably very slowly in summer traffic—it's one motel, strip mall, nightclub, and miniature-golf course after another. In 1989, as *Cape Cod Life* magazine put it, "the town [began] to plant 350 trees in hopes that eventually the trees' leaves, like the fig leaf of Biblical lore, [would] cover the shame of unkempt overdevelopment."

Yelverton Crowe settled the village of West Yarmouth in 1643 after acquiring the land from a Native American sachem. The deal they struck was that Crowe could have as much land as he could traverse in an hour in exchange for an "ox-chain, a copper kettle, and a few trinkets." The first settlers were farmers; when Central Wharf near Mill Creek was built in the 1830s, the town turned to more-commercial ventures as it became headquarters for the growing packet service that ferried passengers from the Cape to Boston.

GETTING HERE AND AROUND

West Yarmouth lies in the midst of busy Route 28, between Hyannis and South Yarmouth. If you want to avoid this road entirely, a sensible option is to take speedy U.S. 6 to the exit nearest what you want to

visit and then cut south across the interior. If you must travel the Route 28 area, take Buck Island Road, which runs north of and parallel to much of the busy route in West and South Yarmouth.

ESSENTIALS

Visitor Information **Yarmouth Chamber of Commerce** (⊠ *425 Rte. 28* ☎ *508/778–1008 or 800/732–1008* ⊕ *www.yarmouthcapecod.com*).

EXPLORING

Baxter Grist Mill. Listed on the National Register of Historic Places, this 1710 structure is the only mill on Cape Cod powered by an inside water turbine; the others use either wind or paddle wheels. The mill was converted to the indoor metal turbine in 1860 because of the pond's low water level and the damage done to the wooden paddle wheel by winter freezes. The original metal turbine is displayed on the grounds. A videotape tells the mill's history. There are no scheduled hours or tours, but feel free to walk around the grounds. ⊠ *Rte. 28 across from Baxter Ave.* ☎ *508/362–3021* ⊕ *www.hsoy.org/historic/baxtermill.htm*.

Yarmouth Boardwalk. This unique and lovely walking trail stretches through swamp and marsh and leads to the edge of pretty Swan Pond, which is ringed with woods. To get here, take Winslow Gray Road northeast from Route 28, turn right on Meadowbrook Lane, and take it to the end. ⊠ *Off Meadowbrook La.*

Ⓒ **ZooQuarium.** This entertaining, educational, and occasionally hokey stop for kids has sea-lion shows, a petting zoo with native wildlife, a touch-friendly tidal pool, wandering peacocks, aquariums, and educational programs, plus pony rides in summer. The Children's Discovery Center presents changing exhibits such as *What's the Buzz on Bees* and *What's for Lunch* (for which kids can prepare meals for animals). You can pack a lunch and sit in the picnic area. ⊠ *674 Rte. 28* ☎ *508/775–8883* ⊕ *www.zooquariumcapecod.net* 🖾 *$11.75* Ⓢ *Mid-May–mid-Sept., daily 9:30–5; mid-Sept.–Nov., Wed.–Mon. 9:30–4; Dec.–Jan., week-ends 9:30–4; late Feb.–mid-May, Wed.–Mon. 9:30–4.*

QUICK BITES

Jerry's Seafood and Dairy Freeze (⊠ *654 Rte. 28* ☎ *508/775–9752*), open year-round, serves fried clams and onion rings, along with thick frappés (milk shakes), frozen yogurt, and soft-serve ice cream at good prices.

WHERE TO EAT

¢ ✕ **Keltic Kitchen.** If you like to start your day with a substantial meal, stop
CAFÉ in at this friendly café for a traditional Irish breakfast—eggs, sausage,
★ rashers (bacon), black-and-white pudding, home fries or beans, tomato,
and brown bread or scones. The potato pancakes with sour cream and
scallions are also tasty, as are the more "American" options, including
French toast and omelets. At midday, you can still get breakfast, or
choose from an assortment of sandwiches that might include corned
beef or burgers. Just don't come by too late—the kitchen closes around
2 PM. ✉ *415 Rte. 28* ☎ *508/771–4835* ▱ *AE, MC, V* ☉ *No dinner.*

$$$ ✕ **Yarmouth House Restaurant.** This festive, family-owned, green-shingle
AMERICAN restaurant has built a devoted local following over the years. The menu
has classic Italian dishes such as chicken Parmesan and veal marsala,
as well as traditional grilled steaks and plenty of fresh seafood dishes.
Try the filet mignon à la Neptune (topped with lobster meat and hol-
landaise sauce), and accompany your meal with a selection from their
long list of beers, wines, and specialty cocktails. Early-bird specials,
Sunday specials, and a kids' menu are available. "We tried the Sunday
'early bird' specials and were very pleased with the food and service,"
says Fodors.com reader Brewsterskip. ✉ *335 Rte. 28* ☎ *508/771–5454*
⊕ *www.yarmouthhouse.com* ▱ *AE, D, MC, V.*

WHERE TO STAY

$$–$$$ ⊡ **Bayside Resort.** A bit more upscale than most of the properties along
★ Route 28, the Bayside overlooks pristine salt marshes and, beyond
them, Lewis Bay. Although it's not right on the water, there is a small
beach and a large outdoor pool with a café (there's also an indoor
pool). Rooms have contemporary light-wood furnishings, and several
have cathedral ceilings, whirlpool tubs, and views toward the bay.
Many members of the staff have worked here for years, which helps to
explain the resort's family-friendly vibe. The Bayside Resort also offers
a number of package deals related to everything from golf to day trips
to Martha's Vineyard and Nantucket. **Pros:** ideal for families with chil-
dren; close to attractions of busy Route 28. **Cons:** no swimming; not for
those seeking intimate surroundings. ✉ *225 Rte. 28* ☎ *508/775–5669
or 800/243–1114* ⊕ *www.baysideresort.com* ⇥ *128 rooms* ♿ *In-room:
a/c, refrigerator, Wi-Fi. In-hotel: bar, pools, gym, beachfront* ▱ *AE, D,
MC, V* �🍴 *CP.*

$$–$$$ ⊡ **Cape Point Hotel.** Families flock to this sensibly priced miniresort, tak-
ing advantage of the many amenities and the fact that kids are nearly
always certain to find plenty of other playmates here, especially in sum-
mer. Rooms contain simple but updated modern furniture. The poolside
Cabana Grill serves lunch in July and August. After one overnight visit
here, you're eligible to receive the Cape Point's unbelievably low-price
off-season specials. The hotel puts together some great golf packages
with a number of local clubs. **Pros:** great for families with kids; reason-
able and attractive golf package deals. **Cons:** not for those looking for a
quiet retreat; no beachfront or water views. ✉ *476 Rte. 28* ☎ *508/778–
1500* ⊕ *www.capepointhotel.com* ⇥ *116 rooms* ♿ *In-room: a/c, DVD,
Wi-Fi. In-hotel: restaurant, bar, pools, gym* ▱ *AE, D, MC, V.*

$$ ⊡ **Inn at Lewis Bay.** Affordable and beautiful, this 1920s Dutch Colonial
★ overlooks Lewis Bay, a short walk from the beach. Innkeepers Bob and
Tanya Liberman have many years of New England B&B ownership, so
you're in good hands. Elaborate quilts top the antique or canopy beds
and adorn the walls in the country-style rooms. Each room has a name
and a theme; Whale Watch, with its distinctive navys and maroons, is
one of two rooms with water views. Electric fireplaces have been added
to all rooms, just one of the many thoughtful additions you'll find.
Bountiful breakfasts are served in the dining room or on the spacious
front porch, which is also a pleasant place for afternoon tea. **Pros:** one
block to beach; friendly B&B feel; peaceful surroundings. **Cons:** some
rooms up a set of stairs. ⊠ *57 Maine Ave.* ☎ *508/771–3433* ⊕ *www.
innatlewisbay.com* ⟳ *6 rooms* ⚘ *In-room: a/c, no phone, Wi-Fi. In-
hotel: no kids under 6* ⊟ *AE, D, MC, V* ⏐◎⏐ *BP.*

$–$$ ⊡ **Mariner Motor Lodge.** Although crowded Route 28 is more commercial than serene, it's also home to several value-packed hotels. The
Mariner is a good family lodging and a bargain. Although the rooms
are standard-issue motel—think basic furnishings such as floral bedcovers and carpets that can take a direct hit from a spilled soft drink—
the outdoor pool is heated and large, and a heated indoor pool, with
an oversize whirlpool hot tub, is great for rainy days. Also on-site
are a miniature-golf course, picnic area with BBQ grills, and vending
machines for snacks. Kids stay free, and weekday rates are reduced.
Pros: ideal for those traveling with children; great golf packages; reasonable rates; close to attractions and restaurants. **Cons:** not for a quiet
retreat; no beachfront or water views. ⊠ *573 Rte. 28* ☎ *508/771–7887
or 800/445–4050* ⊕ *www.mariner-capecod.com* ⟳ *100 rooms* ⚘ *In-
room: a/c, safe, refrigerator. In-hotel: restaurant, pools, Wi-Fi hotspot*
⊟ *AE, D, MC, V.*

NIGHTLIFE AND THE ARTS
Cape Cod Irish Village (⊠ *512 Rte. 28* ☎ *508/771–0100*) has dancing
to two- or three-piece bands performing traditional and popular Irish
music year-round. The crowd is mostly couples and people over 35.

BEACHES, SPORTS, AND THE OUTDOORS
BEACHES
Parking at Yarmouth beaches for nonresidents is $15 daily Memorial
Day through Labor Day. Weekly stickers are also available for $70 and
can be purchased right at most beach booths.

Seagull Beach (⊠ *Seagull Rd. off South Sea Ave.*), a long, wide beach
along Nantucket Sound, has restrooms, showers, and a seasonal concession stand.

BOATING
Great Marsh Kayak Tours (⊠ *Rte. 28* ☎ *508/775–6447* ⊕ *www.great-
marshkayaktours.com*) offers a range of great excursions along the
water, from fly-fishing trips to sunset jaunts—you can also customize
your own itinerary.

FISHING
Truman's (⊠ *608 Rte. 28* ☎ *508/771–3470*) can supply you with a
required freshwater license and rental gear.

SOUTH YARMOUTH

12 mi east of Hyannis, 4 mi south of Yarmouth Port.

A few miles east of West Yarmouth, you'll reach its similarly exuberant sister village, South Yarmouth. Here you can find charter boats, a river cruise, and boat and kayak rentals, plus seafood restaurants and markets. For a good indication of what the town looked like in the late 19th century, take a drive down Pleasant Street and the Main Street section south of Route 28 to view old homes in the Federal and Greek Revival styles. This section along Bass River was once home to the village's elite businessmen, bankers, and sea merchants. Adding to the pastoral aura of the area is the Judah Baker Windmill; the grounds here are pretty and peaceful.

GETTING HERE AND AROUND

Like West Yarmouth, South Yarmouth has a stretch of blight and overdevelopment on Route 28, but it also has some nice beaches that are good for families. Avoid Route 28 if you aim to get anywhere quickly.

EXPLORING

Pirate's Cove. This is the most elaborate of the Cape's many miniature-golf setups, with a hill, a waterfall, a stream, and the 18-hole Blackbeard's Challenge course. ☒ *728 Rte. 28* ☎ *508/394–6200* ⊕ *www. piratescove.net* ☽ *July and Aug., daily 10–10; late Apr.–June, Sept., and Oct., most days 10–7.*

Quaker Meeting House. South Yarmouth was once known as Quaker Village for the large numbers of Quakers who settled the area in the 1770s after a smallpox epidemic wiped out the local Native American population. The 1809 meetinghouse is still open for worship. Two separate entrance doors and the partition down the center were meant to divide the sexes. The adjacent cemetery has simple markers with no epitaphs, an expression of the Friends' belief that all are equal in God's eyes. Behind the cemetery is a circa-1830 one-room Quaker schoolhouse. ☒ *58 N. Main St.* ☎ *508/398–3773* ☽ *Meeting for worship Sun. at 10.*

Ryan Family Amusements. For rainy-day fun, this place offers video-game rooms, Skee-Ball, and bowling. A snack bar serves pizza, sandwiches, and beer and wine. ☒ *1067 Rte. 28* ☎ *508/394–5644* ⊕ *www. ryanfamily.com* ☽ *Daily; hrs vary.*

WHERE TO EAT

$ — MEDITERRANEAN — ✗ **Ardeo.** Despite its unpromising location in a shopping plaza, this smart-casual Mediterranean bistro has built a local following for its pizzas, pastas, salads, panini sandwiches, and Middle Eastern fare. Some may find the food more Americanized than authentic, but it's tasty nonetheless. There's something for everyone here—you could bring the kids, or your grandparents, or a group of pals, and it's a good choice for vegetarians, too. ☒ *23V Whites Path* ☎ *508/760–1500* ⊕ *www. ardeocapecod.com* ⊟ *AE, D, MC, V.*

$$ — SEAFOOD — ✗ **The Skipper.** This classic Cape restaurant has been around since 1936. Sit downstairs in the nautical-themed main room or upstairs on the outside deck, which has terrific views of nearby Nantucket Sound. The kitchen turns out an appealing mix of fish and shellfish dishes, plus a handful of Italian specialties and landlubber options (such as pan-seared chicken and prime rib au jus). Try the scrod with artichoke hearts, asparagus, sun-dried tomatoes, and wild mushrooms. ✉ *152 S. Shore Dr.* ☎ *508/394–7406* ⊕ *www. skipper-restaurant.com* ⚠ *Reservations not accepted* ▤ *AE, D, MC, V* ⊘ *Closed Nov.–mid-Apr.*

> **LAY OF THE LAND**
>
> Locals sometimes refer to South Yarmouth as Bass River, after the river that separates the village from West Dennis.

3

WHERE TO STAY

$$–$$$ 🏠 **Capt. Farris House.** Steps from the Bass River Bridge and a short spin
Fodor'sChoice away from congested Route 28 sits this imposing 1845 Greek Revival
★ home. Thoughtful amenities abound, from the plush bathrobes, beach supplies, and fresh flowers in each room to a selection of complimentary cordials. The large rooms and suites have either antique or canopied beds, plush comforters, fancy drapes, and deep tile baths (all but one with a whirlpool tub). Some have fireplaces and sundecks. Breakfast is served in the formal dining room or the greenhouse-style interior courtyard and might include quiche with pumpkin-pecan scones or buttermilk oatmeal pancakes. Baked goods and coffee are available after hours. **Pros:** beautiful grounds; ideal location for exploring Mid Cape area; close to area restaurants and attractions. **Cons:** no elevator; not an in-town or on-beach location. ✉ *308 Old Main St., Bass River Village* ☎ *508/760–2818* ⊕ *www.captainfarris.com* ⛱ *6 rooms, 4 suites* ⚬ *In-room: a/c, Wi-Fi. In-hotel: no kids under 14* ▤ *AE, D, MC, V* ⊘ *Closed Jan.* ⦿| *BP.*

$$–$$$ 🏠 **Clarion Inn.** This well-cared-for motor lodge (completely renovated in 2009) in downtown South Yarmouth ranks above the others in town because of its great staff, a lovely outdoor pool with attractive grounds and patio furniture, and large guest rooms with clean and updated fixtures and furnishings—many have balconies or patios overlooking the pool and courtyard. Plus, it's right by the Cape Cod Creamery ice-cream shop. The dining room serves lunch by the pool during the summer season. **Pros:** easy access to Route 28; reasonable prices; two pools. **Cons:** not for a quiet romantic getaway. ✉ *1199 Rte. 28* ☎ *508/394–7600* ⊕ *www.clarioncapecod.com* ⛱ *114 rooms* ⚬ *In-room: a/c, refrigerator, DVD, Wi-Fi. In-hotel: pools, gym* ▤ *AE, D, MC, V* ⦿| *CP.*

$$–$$$ 🏠 **Ocean Mist.** This three-story, motel-style resort sits on its own private (if tiny) beach on Nantucket Sound. The rooms have generic modern furnishings, cable TV, and either wet bars (with sink and refrigerator) or fully stocked kitchenettes. The duplex loft suites are a step above, with cathedral ceilings, sitting areas with pullout sofas, skylights, and one or two private balconies overlooking the water; more than half the rooms here have water views. **Pros:** beachfront location; a good bet for those with children. **Cons:** not for those looking for a quiet ocean-side retreat. ✉ *97 S. Shore Dr.* ☎ *508/398–2633* ⊕ *www.capecodoceanresorts.com* ⛱ *32 rooms, 31 suites* ⚬ *In-room: a/c, kitchen (some), refrigerator. In-hotel: pool, beachfront, laundry facilities, Wi-Fi hotspot* ▤ *AE, D, MC, V* ⊘ *Closed mid-Oct.–mid-Apr.*

$$–$$$ ⛾ **Seaside Cottages.** Right on Nantucket Sound, this 5-acre village of Cape-style cottages (studios and one- or two-bedroom units) has a view of scalloped beaches in both directions. Seaside was built in the 1940s, and the furnishings vary from cottage to cottage, since each is individually owned. All have kitchens or kitchenettes, and many have wood-burning fireplaces. The oceanfront cottages, right off a strip of grass set with lounge and Adirondack chairs, have the best views. Rentals are by the week in summer; cottages can be rented by the night in late spring and fall. **Pros:** great beachfront location; daily housekeeping; spacious grounds. **Cons:** cottages are very close together; nightly reservations hard to come by. ⊠ *135 S. Shore Dr.* ☏ *508/398–2533* ⊕ *www.seasidecapecod.com* ⇨ *44 cottages* ঙ *In-room: no a/c, no phone, kitchen (some). In-hotel: beachfront, Wi-Fi hotspot* ☰ MC, V ⊘ *Closed mid-Oct.–Apr.*

BEACHES, SPORTS, AND THE OUTDOORS

BASEBALL

The **Yarmouth-Dennis Red Sox** of the collegiate Cape Cod Baseball League play home games at Dennis-Yarmouth High School's **Red Wilson Field** (⊠ *Station Ave.* ☏ *508/394–9387* ⊕ *www.ydredsox.org*) from mid-June to mid-August. Baseball clinics for girls and boys age 5 and up run throughout the season.

BEACHES

Parking at Yarmouth beaches for nonresidents is $15 daily Memorial Day through Labor Day. Weekly stickers are also available for $70 and can be purchased right at most beach booths.

Flax Pond (⊠ *N. Main St. between High Bank and Great Western Rds.*) has freshwater swimming, a lifeguard, and ducks. There's a pine-shaded picnic area with grills, as well as volleyball and basketball courts and plenty of parking.

Parker's River Beach (⊠ *South Shore Dr.*), a flat stretch of sand on warm Nantucket Sound, is perfect for families. It has a lifeguard, a concession stand, a gazebo and picnic area, a playground, outdoor showers, and restrooms.

GOLF

Blue Rock Golf Course (⊠ *Off Great Western Rd.* ☏ *508/398–9295*) is a highly regarded, easy-to-walk 18-hole, par-3, 3,000-yard public course crossed by a pond. The pro shop rents clubs; reservations are mandatory in season.

HEALTH AND FITNESS CLUBS

Mid Cape Racquet Club (⊠ *193 White's Path* ☏ *508/394–3511* ⊕ *www. midcaperacquet.com*) has one racquetball, one squash, and nine indoor tennis courts; indoor basketball; a sauna, steam room, and whirlpools; massage services; and a free-weight and cardiovascular room—plus day care. Daily rates are available.

SHOPPING

Wild Birds Unlimited (✉ *1198 Rte. 28* ☎ *508/760–1996*) sells all things bird related, from bird-watching tools to feeders, seed, and suet. You'll also find bird- and nature-themed gifts, garden accents, T-shirts, birdbaths, and all sorts of avian treasures.

DENNIS

Like Yarmouth, Dennis has a split personality. The town's southern villages, such as Dennis Port and West Dennis, tend to be heavily developed and commercialized and are more popular with families, whereas the northern section, anchored by historic Dennis Village, is peaceful and dignified, with countless old homes and inns lining Route 6A.

DENNIS VILLAGE

4 mi east of Yarmouth Port.

The backstreets of Dennis Village still retain the colonial charm of its seafaring days. The town, which was incorporated in 1793, was named for the Reverend Josiah Dennis. There were 379 sea captains living here when fishing, salt making, and shipbuilding were the main industries, and the elegant houses they constructed—now museums and B&Bs—still line the streets. In 1816, resident Henry Hall discovered that adding sand to his cranberry fields' soil improved the size of his harvest and the quality of the fruit. The following decades saw cranberry farming and tourism become the Cape's main commercial enterprises. Dennis has a number of conservation areas and nature trails and numerous freshwater ponds for swimming. The village center has antiques shops, general stores, a post office, and ice-cream shops. There's also a village green with a bandstand, the site of occasional summer concerts.

GETTING HERE AND AROUND

Route 6A is also known as Main Street as it passes through Dennis Village.

EXPLORING

Cape Cod Museum of Art. This museum on the grounds of the Cape Playhouse has a permanent collection of more than 850 works by Cape-associated artists. Important pieces include a portrait of a fisherman's wife by Charles Hawthorne, the father of the Provincetown art colony; a 1924 portrait of a Portuguese fisherman's daughter by William Paxton, one of the first artists to summer in Provincetown; a collection of wood-block prints by Varujan Boghosian, a member of Provincetown's Long Point Gallery cooperative; an oil sketch by Karl Knaths, who painted in Provincetown from 1919 until his death in 1971; and works by abstract expressionist Hans Hoffman and many of his students. ✉ *60 Hope La.* ☎ *508/385–4477* ⊕ *www.ccmoa.org* 🏷 *$8* ⊗ *Mon.–Wed., Fri., and Sat. 10–5; Thurs. 10–8; Sun. noon–5. Closed Mon. mid-Oct–late May.*

Indulge in sumptuous baked goods at the **Underground Bakery** (✉ *780 Rte. 6A* ☎ *508/385–4700*), just behind the Dennis Post Office near the Cape Playhouse and the Cape Cod Museum of Art. Get a heavenly breakfast of soft scrambled eggs with prosciutto, Parmesan, and truffle oil, or a tasty homemade scone, then wash it all down with a cappuccino or latte made from fair-trade coffee. All breads are made on-site, as is the crisp biscotti.

Josiah Dennis Manse. This saltbox house was built in 1736 for the Reverend Josiah Dennis. Inside, the home reflects life in the Reverend Dennis's day. A child's room includes antique furniture and toys, the keeping room has a fireplace and cooking utensils, and the attic exhibits spinning and weaving equipment. Throughout you'll see china, pewter, and portraits of sea captains. The Maritime Wing has ship models, paintings, and nautical artifacts. On the grounds is a 1770 one-room schoolhouse, furnished with wood-and-wrought-iron desks and chairs. Events throughout summer include guided cemetery walking tours, an old-fashioned pie sale, a Victorian tea party, and open houses with costumed interpreters plying old-time 19th-century home skills. As of this writing, this site was being renovated; it is expected to be open again in 2011. ✉ *77 Nobscussett Rd., at Whig St.* ☎ *508/385–3528* ⊕ *www. dennishistsoc.org* ✎ *Free* ◷ *Late June–Sept., Tues. 10–noon, Thurs. 2–4.*

Scargo Tower. On a clear day, you'll have unbeatable views of Scargo Lake, Dennis Village's scattered houses below, Cape Cod Bay, and distant Provincetown from the top of this tower. A wooden tower built on this site in 1874 was one of the Cape's first tourist attractions; visitors would pay 5¢ to climb to the top for the views. That tower burned down, and the present all-stone 30-foot tower was built in 1901 to replace it. Winding stairs bring you to the top; don't forget to read the unsightly, but amusing, graffiti on the way up. Expect crowds at sunrise and sunset. ✉ *Scargo Hill Rd. off Rte. 6A or Old Bass River Rd.* ✎ *Free* ◷ *Daily sunrise–sunset.*

Dip into homemade ice cream and frozen yogurt at the **Ice Cream Smuggler** (✉ *716 Rte. 6A* ☎ *508/385–5307* ⊕ *www.icecreamsmuggler.com*), across the street from the town green and cemetery. The ginger ice cream is a specialty, but order the triple hot-fudge sundae for the ultimate decadence.

WHERE TO EAT

$
SEAFOOD
Fodor's Choice
★

✕ Cap'n Frosty's. A great stop after the beach, this is where locals go to get their fried seafood. This modest joint has a regular menu that includes ice cream, a small specials board, and a counter where you order and take a number written on a french-fries box. The staff is young and hardworking, pumping out fresh fried clams and fish-and-chips on paper plates. All frying is done in 100% canola oil, and rice pilaf is offered as a substitute for fries. There's seating inside as well as outside on a shady brick patio. ✉ *219 Rte. 6A* ☎ *508/385–8548* ⊕ *www.captainfrosty.com* ✎ *Reservations not accepted* ▭ *MC, V* ◷ *Closed early Sept.–Mar.*

$$ **✕Gina's by the Sea.** Some places are less than the sum of their parts;
ITALIAN Gina's is more. This funky old building is tucked into a sand dune, so
★ that the aroma of fine northern Italian cooking blends with a fresh
breeze off the bay. The dining room is tasteful, cozy, and especially won-
derful in fall when the fireplace is blazing. Blackboard specials could
include angel-hair pasta or linguine with clams. If you don't want a long
wait, come early or late. An enthusiastic staff rounds out the experi-
ence. ⊠ *134 Taunton Ave.* ☎ *508/385–3213* ⊕ *www.ginasbythesea.com*
⚐ *Reservations not accepted* ⊟ *AE, MC, V* ☾ *Closed Dec.–Mar. and
Mon.–Wed.*

¢ **✕Grumpy's Restaurant.** This airy diner consistently packs its tables and
AMERICAN counter space year-round, and for good reason. From baked goods to
waffles and eggs done any way you like them, Grumpy's jump-starts
your day with generous portions for breakfast and lunch. Get here
early to avoid a line that often curls out the door. ⊠ *1408 Rte. 6A*
☎ *508/385–2911* ⊕ *wwwgrumpyscapecod.com* ⚐ *Reservations not
accepted* ⊟ *MC, V* ☾ *No dinner.*

$$$ **✕Red Pheasant.** This is one of the Cape's best cozy country restau-
AMERICAN rants, with a consistently good kitchen where creative American food
Fodor's Choice is prepared with elaborate sauces and herb combinations. For instance,
★ organic chicken is served with an intense preserved-lemon and fresh
thyme sauce, and exquisitely grilled veal chops come with a dense red
wine–and–portobello mushroom sauce. In fall, look for the specialty
game dishes, including venison and quail. Try to reserve a table in the
more intimate Garden Room. The expansive wine list is excellent. A
nice Sunday brunch is served from mid-October to June. "Don't miss
the opportunity to try this place," says Fodors.com reader ciaotebaldi.
⊠ *905 Rte. 6A* ☎ *508/385–2133* ⊕ *www.redpheasantinn.com* ⚐ *Reservations essential* ⊟ *AE, D, MC, V* ☾ *No lunch.*

$$$ **✕Scargo Café.** With the Cape Playhouse right across the street, this
AMERICAN upscale contemporary American restaurant is a favorite before- and
after-show haunt. There's plenty of seafood on the eclectic menu, which
includes seafood strudel with crab, shrimp, and scallops baked in a
pastry crust and topped with Newburg sauce. Carnivores will take
delight in dishes like pan-seared pork medallions, rack of lamb, and
tenderloin à la chevre. Lighter meals include a ginger shrimp salad and
an Asian-style fish sandwich served with seaweed salad. Save room
for their signature grape-nut custard. ⊠ *799 Rte. 6A* ☎ *508/385–8200*
⊕ *www.scargocafe.com* ⊟ *AE, D, MC, V.*

WHERE TO STAY

$–$$ **▥Isaiah Hall B&B Inn.** Lilacs and pink roses trail along the white-picket
Fodor's Choice fence outside this 1857 Greek Revival farmhouse on a quiet residential
★ road near the bay. Innkeepers Jerry and Judy Neal set the scene for a
romantic getaway with guest rooms that have country antiques, floral-
print wallpapers, and homey touches, such as quilts and Priscilla curtains. In the attached carriage house, rooms have three walls stenciled
white and one paneled with knotty pine, and some have small balconies
overlooking a wooded lawn with gardens, grape arbors, and berry
bushes. The Isaiah Hall Suite, with king bed and fireplace, can connect with another room to create a good-size two-bedroom/two-bath

3

unit. **Pros:** beautiful grounds; near beaches and attractions. **Cons:** some very steep steps; some rooms are on the small side. ⊠ *152 Whig St., Box 1007, Dennis Village* ☎ *508/385–9928* ⊕ *www.isaiahhallinn.com* ⤴ *10 rooms, 2 suites* ⚲ *In-room: DVD, Wi-Fi. In-hotel: no kids under 7* ⊟ *AE, D, MC, V* ⎢◯⎢ *BP.*

$$–$$$ ◲ **Scargo Manor.** This 1895 sea captain's home has a prime location on Scargo Lake, with a private beach and dock. Inside, a collection of art and antiques are at home amid the Victorian furnishings. There's plenty of room to spread out on the big screened porch, in the sitting room or more formal living room, or in the cozy third-floor reading room. If you want a lake view, choose the cozy all-blue Hydrangea Room, with a pineapple-top four-poster bed and a skylight overhead. For more space, the Captain Howe's Suite has a king-size canopy bed, plus a separate sitting room with a working fireplace. **Pros:** lakefront location; water views; historic lodging. **Cons:** some steep stairs; some rooms have small shower stalls. ⊠ *909 Rte. 6A* ☎ *508/385–5534* ⊕ *www.scargomanor.com* ⤴ *5 rooms, 2 suites* ⚲ *In-room: a/c, no phone, refrigerator (some), Wi-Fi. In-hotel: beachfront, bicycles, no kids under 5* ⊟ *D, MC, V* ⎢◯⎢ *BP.*

NIGHTLIFE AND THE ARTS
THE ARTS

Part of the Cape Playhouse Center for the Arts, the **Cape Cinema** offers independent and art films that are a refreshing change from standard mall fare. The building's exterior is in the style of the Congregational church in Centerville. Inside, a 6,400-square-foot mural of heavenly skies—designed by Massachusetts artist Rockwell Kent, who also designed the gold-sunburst curtain—covers the ceiling. ⊠ *35 Hope La.* ☎ *508/385–2503* ⊕ *www.capecinema.com.*

⟳
Fodor'sChoice
★

For Broadway-style dramas, comedies, and musicals, as well as kids' plays, you can attend a production at the **Cape Playhouse,** the oldest professional summer theater in the country. In 1927 Raymond Moore, who had been working with a theatrical troupe in Provincetown, bought an 1838 former Unitarian meetinghouse and converted it into a theater. The original pews still serve as seats. The opening performance was *The Guardsman,* starring Basil Rathbone. Other stars who performed here in the early days—some in their professional stage debuts—include Bette Davis (who first worked here as an usher), Gregory Peck, Lana Turner, Ginger Rogers, Humphrey Bogart, Tallulah Bankhead, and Henry Fonda, who appeared with his then-unknown 20-year-old daughter, Jane. Behind-the-scene tours are also given in season; call for a schedule. The playhouse offers children's theater on Friday morning during July and August. Also on the 26-acre property, now known as the Cape Playhouse Center for the Arts, are a restaurant, the **Cape Cod Museum of Art,** and the **Cape Cinema.** ⊠ *820 Rte. 6A* ☎ *508/385–3911 or 877/385–3911* ⊕ *www.capeplayhouse.com* ⊙ *Call for tour schedule.*

The Screening Room (⊠ *60 Hope La.* ☎ *508/385–2503*), at the Cape Cod Museum of Art, shows avant-garde, classic, art, and independent films throughout the year. Call for a schedule.

NIGHTLIFE

Harvest Gallery Wine Bar (⊠ *776 Main St.* ☎ *508/385–2444* ⊕ *www. harvestgallerywinebar.com*) is right at home near the Cape Cod Museum of Art, Cape Cod Cinema, and the Cape Playhouse. There's an extensive wine list; a good variety of hors d'oeuvres, salads, and desserts; eclectic artwork; and live music. They're closed Tuesday.

Lost Dog Pub (⊠ *1374 Rte. 134* ☎ *508/385–6177* ⊕ *www.lostdogpub. biz*) offers basic pub eats and a relaxed social atmosphere; it's a popular place for locals and visitors to grab a beer after a long day. There's live music at least once a week.

BEACHES, SPORTS, AND THE OUTDOORS

BEACHES

Parking at all Dennis beaches is $20 a day for nonresidents.

Chapin Beach (⊠ *Chapin Beach Rd.*) is a lovely dune-backed bay beach with long tidal flats—you can walk really far out at low tide. It has no lifeguards or services.

Corporation Beach (⊠ *Corporation Rd.*) has lifeguards, showers, restrooms, and a food stand. Once a packet landing owned by a corporation of the townsfolk, the beautiful crescent of white sand backed by low dunes now serves a decidedly noncorporate purpose as a public beach.

Mayflower Beach (⊠ *Dunes Rd. off Bayview Rd.*) reveals hundreds of feet of tidal flats at low tide. The beach has restrooms, showers, lifeguards, and a food stand.

For freshwater swimming, **Scargo Lake** (⊠ *Scargo Hill Rd.*) has two beaches with restrooms, playgrounds, and a picnic area. The sandy-bottom lake is shallow along the shore, which is good for kids. It's surrounded by woods and is stocked for fishing.

FISHING

Sesuit Harbor, on the bay side of Dennis off Route 6A, is busy with fishing and pleasure boats; several are available for fishing charters. **Hannah C. Charters** (⊠ *Sesuit Harbor, East Dennis* ☎ *508/385–8150* ⊕ *www. hannahccharters.com*) runs half- or full-day trips in search of stripers and bluefish with up to six people.

The **Prime Rate** (⊠ *Sesuit Harbor, East Dennis* ☎ *508/385–4626* ⊕ *www. primeratesportfishing.com*) makes four-, five-, and six-hour fishing excursions.

SHOPPING

Antiques Center of Cape Cod (⊠ *243 Rte. 6A, Dennis Village* ☎ *508/385–6400* ⊕ *www.antiquecenterofcapecod.com*) is a large and busy market populated by more than 160 dealers offering furniture, artwork, jewelry, china, clocks, books, antique dolls, and other collectibles.

The Barn & Co. (⊠ *574 Rte. 6A, Dennis Village* ☎ *508/385–2100* ⊕ *www. barnandco.com*) has a varied selection of cards, jewelry—much of it made by local artisans—as well as candles, housewares, and unusual clocks.

Emily's Beach Barn (⊠ *708 Rte. 6A, Dennis Village* ☎ *508/385–8328* ⊕ *www.emilysbeachbarn.com*) has fashionable women's beachwear, from bathing suits and wraps to sun hats and summer dresses and tops.

★ **Robert C. Eldred Co.** (⊠ *1483 Rte. 6A, East Dennis* ☎ *508/385–3116* ⊕ *www.eldreds.com*) holds more than two dozen auctions per year, dealing in Americana; estate jewelry; top-quality antiques; marine, Asian, American, and European art; tools; and dolls.

Ross Coppelman, Goldsmith (⊠ *1439 Rte. 6A, East Dennis* ☎ *508/385– 7900* ⊕ *www.rosscoppelman.com*) sells original jewelry in high-karat gold, semiprecious gemstones, and other materials (customized wedding bands are a specialty). The pieces are designed by Coppelman, a self-taught goldsmith who has been honing his craft for more than 30 years.

Fodor's Choice **Scargo Pottery** (⊠ *30 Dr. Lord's Rd. S, off Rte. 6A, Dennis Village*
★   ☎ *508/385–3894* ⊕ *www.scargopottery.com*) is in a pine forest, where potter Harry Holl's unusual wares—such as his signature castle birdhouses—sit on tree stumps and hang from branches. Inside are the workshop and kiln, plus work by Holl's four daughters.

WEST DENNIS AND DENNISPORT

1 mi east of South Yarmouth.

The Mid Cape's last southern village is Dennisport, a prime summer-resort area, with gray-shingle cottages, summer homes and condominiums, and lots of white-picket fences covered with rambling roses. The Union Wharf Packing Company operated here in the 1850s, and sailmakers and ship chandlers lined the shore. Sunbathers now pack the sands where sea clams once laid primary claim.

In another one of those tricks of Cape geography, the village of West Dennis is actually south of South Dennis, on the east side of the Bass River. Dennisport is farther east, near the Harwich town line.

GETTING HERE AND AROUND

If you're driving between West Dennis and Harwich, Lower County Road is a more scenic alternative to overdeveloped Route 28. It gives you occasional glimpses of the sea between the cottages and beachfront hotels.

ESSENTIALS

Visitor Information Dennis Chamber of Commerce (⊠ *238 Swan River Rd., West Dennis* ☎ *508/398–3568 or 800/243–9920* ⊕ *www.dennischamber.com*).

EXPLORING

West Dennis Beach. This is one of the best beaches on the south shore. A breakwater was started here in 1837 in an effort to protect the mouth of Bass River, but was abandoned when a sandbar formed on the shore side. It's a long, wide, and popular sandy beach, stretching for 1½ mi, with marshland and the Bass River across from it. Popular with windsurfers, the beach also has bathhouses, lifeguards, a playground, concessions, and parking for 1,000 cars. ⊠ *Lighthouse Rd. off Lower County Rd., West Dennis.*

QUICK BITES

Set in a rustic mid-19th-century barn decorated with a working nickelodeon, the **Sundae School Ice Cream Parlor** (⊠ *387 Lower County Rd., Dennisport* ☎ *508/394–9122*), open mid-April through mid-October, serves great homemade ice cream, frozen yogurt, and old-fashioned sarsaparilla and cream soda from an antique marble soda fountain. Don't be intimidated by summer crowds. You'll be greeted by parking attendants with flashlights guiding you to a parking space, as well as young people scooping ice cream at lightning speed.

WHERE TO EAT

$ ╳ **Clancy's.** A local landmark on the bucolic Swan River, Clancy's is AMERICAN popular—the parking lot is often jammed by 5 PM, so expect a substantial wait during peak hours in season. This is an enormous operation, with long family tables, round tables, booths, a deck overlooking the river, and two bars. On the seemingly endless menu are several variations of nachos, salads, and chili. Clancy's likes to be creative with the names of its dishes, so you can find items such as steak Lucifer (sirloin topped with lobster, asparagus, and béarnaise sauce) and a Sunday-brunch menu with the likes of crab, steak, or eggs Benedict. ⊠ *8 Upper County Rd., Dennisport* ☎ *508/394–6661* ⊕ *www.clancysrestaurant. com* ⌲ *Reservations not accepted* ▭ *AE, DC, MC, V.*

$ ╳ **Kream 'N Kone.** The Kream 'N Kone has been going strong since 1953: SEAFOOD order up some fried clams and a shake or a soda, get a number, wait five minutes, and sit down to some of the best fast food anywhere. Fried food will overflow your paper plate onto a plastic tray, but it's so good that what you thought you'd never be able to finish somehow vanishes. The onion rings in particular are a knockout. At times the prices seem surprisingly high, but the quality and quantity of what you get are well worth the splurge. Sit on the outdoor patio for views of Swan River. *961 Rte. 28, West Dennis* ☎ *508/394–0808* ⊕ *www.kreamnkone.com* ▭ *D, MC, V* ☉ *Closed Nov.–Jan.*

$$$ ╳ **Ocean House.** Overlooking Nantucket Sound, this noisy but superb NEW AMERICAN restaurant has views to match the spectacular food and service. For din-**Fodor's**Choice ner, try sake-roasted Alaskan butter fish with smoked corn potato puree, ★ followed by vanilla-bean crème brûlée. Chef Anthony Silvestri changes the menu seasonally. There are plenty of decadent options to choose from. Half plates are available for many entrées, ideal for smaller appetites or sharing. "This is the perfect place for a fancy, special night out if you have $$$$ to spend," says Fodors.com reader Lippylulu. ⊠ *End of Depot St., Dennisport* ⌂ *Box 9, Dennisport 02639* ☎ *508/394–0700* ⊕ *www.oceanhouserestaurant.com* ⌲ *Reservations essential* ▭ *AE, D, MC, V* ☉ *Closed Mon. and Jan. and Feb. No lunch.*

$$$ ╳ **The Oyster Company.** Surprise, surprise: oysters are the big stars at this SEAFOOD popular, lively restaurant. The owners have their own oyster farm out in Dennis waters, and oysters from other towns are also well represented—as are clams—and can be had a variety of ways (though raw on the half shell is the best way to enjoy these super-fresh bivalves). Seafood dominates the menu, from salmon to a great cioppino, with lobster, shrimp, mussels, and littlenecks in a lobster saffron broth. There's also some hearty land fare, from organic beef and duck to lamb. A roster of fancy martinis are nearly as popular as the oysters. It's a fun place all around, with great food and a boisterous atmosphere. ⊠ *202 Depot St., Dennisport* ☎ *508/398–4600* ⊕ *www.theoystercompany.com* ▭ *AE, MC, V* ☉ *No lunch.*

¢   ✕**Red Cottage.** Up Old Bass River Road ½ mi north of the town hall,
AMERICAN   the Red Cottage is indeed a red cottage and serves breakfast and lunch
year-round. Locals pack this place even in the off-season, and you can
expect a wait in summer. The cottage is a no-frills, friendly place with
food that runs the gamut from decadent stuffed French toast specials
to a list of health-conscious offerings with egg whites, "lite" cheese,
and turkey bacon. The grill is in plain view; if you want to watch your
meal being cooked, the swivel stools at the counter have the best angle.
The breakfasts are better than the lunches, but both are no-nonsense
and just plain reliably good. ⊠ *36 Old Bass River Rd., South Dennis*
☎ *508/394–2923* ⊕ *www.redcottagerestaurant.net* ⌕ *Reservations not
accepted* ⊟ *No credit cards* ⊘ *No dinner. No lunch Sun.*

$$ ✕**Swan River Seafood.** From the right table you can have a beautiful
SEAFOOD   view of the Swan River marsh and Nantucket Sound beyond at this
informal little eatery, which turns out great fresh fish in both traditional
and creative preparations. Besides the usual fried and broiled choices,
try the spicy cioppino or the seafood strudel. There's also a takeout
window and a fish market. Listen to live music on Saturday evening.
⊠ *5 Lower County Rd., Dennisport* ☎ *508/394–4466* ⊟ *AE, MC, V*
⊘ *Closed mid-Sept.–late May. No lunch weekdays late May–mid-June.*

WHERE TO STAY

$$$–$$$$ ⊡ **The Corsair and Cross Rip.** These motels, built side by side, offer clean
and crisp rooms, many with captivating beach views. Rooms in the
main motel buildings range from smaller "value" units with one queen
bed to pricier deluxe accommodations with kitchenettes and sitting
areas, plus a few spacious condo-style suites. Three large three- and
four-bedroom vacation houses are also available for rent; they can sleep
up to 12 and are fully equipped with luxurious amenities. Decor in the
motel buildings is more basic, but between the oceanfront location
(there are three private beaches) and the extensive facilities, you prob-
ably won't be spending much time in your room. **Pros:** right on the
beach; plenty of activities; great for families. **Cons:** not for those seeking
a quiet retreat. ⊠ *33 and 41 Chase Ave., Dennisport* ☎ *508/398–2279
or 800/889–8037* ⊕ *www.corsaircrossrip.com* ⌕ *49 rooms, 7 suites*
⌂ *In-room: DVD (some), kitchen (some), refrigerator, Wi-Fi. In-hotel:
pools, beachfront, laundry facilities* ⊟ *AE, D, MC, V* ⊘ *Closed late
Oct.–Mar.*

$$ ⊡ **English Garden Bed & Breakfast.** Anita and Joe Sangiolo—she's a former
actress and he's a retired engineer—have turned their 1922 home into
a comfortable B&B. The eight rooms are done in a cheerful country
style, with quilts, four-poster or iron beds, and pine armoires; four
rooms have ocean views. The adjacent carriage house has two modern
suites, each with a bedroom, separate living area with gas fireplace, in-
room laundry, and kitchenette—these are available on a weekly basis.
Beach chairs and towels are provided (the house is a block from the
sand), and Joe has put together a meticulously detailed notebook of
things to do. **Pros:** walk to beach; quiet area; many ocean-view rooms.
Cons: not an in-town location; some stairs. ⊠ *32 Inman Rd., Dennisport* ☎ *508/398–2915 or 888/788–1908* ⊕ *www.anenglishgardenbb.
com* ⌕ *9 rooms, 2 suites* ⌂ *In-room: a/c, DVD (some), kitchen (some),*

no phone. In-hotel: Wi-Fi hotspot, no kids under 10 (except in suites) ⊟ *D, MC, V* ¹⊙¹ *BP.*

$$ ⛫ **The Garlands.** Old Wharf Road in Dennisport is lined with strip motels and cottage colonies, but few places provide comfort and views to match this bi-level motel-style complex. Each unit has a fully equipped kitchen, private sundeck or patio, and daily maid service. The ocean-front VIP suites, simply named A and B (two bedrooms) and C and D (one bedroom), are the best picks here—the nearly floor-to-ceiling windows offer unobstructed water views; at high tide you're almost in the surf. **Pros:** beachfront location. **Cons:** not in town. ✉ *117 Old Wharf Rd., Dennisport* ☎ *508/398–6987* ⊕ *www.thegarlandscapecod.com* ↪ *20 suites* ⚂ *In-room: no a/c, DVD (some), kitchen, Wi-Fi. In-hotel: beachfront, no kids under 5* ⊟ *AE, MC, V* ⊘ *Closed mid-Oct.–mid-Apr.*

$$$–$$$$ ⛫ **Lighthouse Inn.** On a small private beach adjacent to West Dennis Beach, this venerable Cape resort has been in family hands since 1938. The main inn was built around a still-operational 1855 lighthouse. Along a landscaped lawn are 23 individual one- to three-bedroom shingled cottages and five larger buildings with multiple guest rooms. Cottages have decks, fireplaces, two double (or one double and one king-size) beds, and sitting areas (but no kitchens). In the main inn are five guest rooms, a living room, a library, and a waterfront restaurant serving New England fare. **Pros:** good beachfront location; tons of activities kids. **Cons:** not for those seeking a quiet getaway. ✉ *1 Lighthouse Rd., West Dennis* ☎ *508/398–2244* ⊕ *www.lighthouseinn. com* ↪ *40 rooms, 23 cottages* ⚂ *In-room: a/c, refrigerator, safe, Wi-Fi. In-hotel: restaurant, room service, bar, tennis court, pool, beachfront, children's programs (ages 3–12)* ⊟ *MC, V* ⊘ *Closed mid-Oct.–mid-May* ¹⊙¹ *BP, MAP.*

NIGHTLIFE

Improper Bostonian (✉ *Rte. 28, Dennisport* ☎ *508/394–7416*), open only in summer, has a mix of live music and DJ-spun dance tunes several nights a week and attracts a young crowd.

The **Sand Bar** (✉ *Lighthouse Rd., West Dennis* ☎ *508/398–7586*) presents the boogie-woogie piano playing of local legend Rock King on Saturday night, who's been tickling the ivories—and people's funny bones—since the 1960s. There's also live entertainment on Friday.

In season, you can dance to a DJ and live bands at **Sundancer's** (✉ *116 Rte. 28, West Dennis* ☎ *508/394–1600*). Various sporting events flash from multiple televisions. It's closed December and January.

SPORTS AND THE OUTDOORS
BICYCLING

You can pick up the 25-mi Cape Cod Rail Trail at several points along its path. In fact, riding the entire trail in one day doesn't do justice to its sights and side trips (though it certainly can be done). Many cyclists, especially those with small kids, prefer the piecemeal method because they can relax and enjoy the sights—and not turn their legs into jelly.

The ride in Dennis starts as a flat, straight spin through a small pine forest—a good warm-up exercise. Your first road crossing is at busy Great Western Road, one of the town's major thoroughfares, after which you'll pass Sand Pond and Flax Pond in Harwich. The Dennis part of the trail is short, but it's worth starting here for the ample parking at the trail's entrance and for the several bike-rental places that set up shop on Route 134.

A guidebook published by the Dennis Chamber of Commerce includes bike tours and maps. You can rent bikes from a number of places along the Cape Cod Rail Trail.

Barbara's Bike Shop (⊠ *430 Rte. 134, South Dennis* ☎ *508/760–4723* ⊕ *www.barbsbikeshop.com*) is at the rail trail entrance.

BOATING

Cape Cod Waterways (⊠ *16 Rte. 28, Dennisport* ☎ *508/398–0080* ⊕ *www.capecodwaterways.com*) rents canoes, kayaks, and electric paddleboats for leisurely travel on the Swan River.

SHOPPING

Cape Cod Shoe Mart (⊠ *271 Rte. 28, Dennisport* ☎ *508/398–6000*) has such brand names as Capezio, Dexter, Clark, Esprit, Nike, Reebok, L. A. Gear, and Rockport.

Dick & Ellie's Flea Market (⊠ *Theophilus Smith Rd. off Rte. 134, next to Patriot Square Plaza, South Dennis* ☎ *508/394–6131* ⊕ *www.capecodoutdoormarket.com*) has vendors selling clothing, jewelry, handbags, crafts, plants, and even lobsters, in a large outdoor market. It's open Thursday through Monday from late June to Labor Day, weekends through Columbus Day.

The Lower Cape

WORD OF MOUTH

Eastham is very convenient, not just for the beaches, although the beaches are superb, but because it is so central to several other towns that typify Cape Cod. Provincetown, Chatham, and Hyannis are all 20–30 minutes away. Keep in mind that the Cape Cod National Seashore has preserved about half of the Outer Cape land (from Eastham to Provincetown) and prevented the commercialization of the shore. If you like long walks on deserted stretches of pristine beach with dunes at your back and nothing but sea and sand, then base your selves where you have easy access to the National Seashore.

—yellowbyrd

Updated
by Laura V.
Scheel

Speckled with still-active cranberry bogs, sturdy trees, and pastures, the Lower Cape exudes a peaceful residential aura. It's blessed with large tracts set aside for conservation, so you won't find roadways cluttered with minigolf complexes, trampolines, or bumper boats. (They are close by if you happen to have kids in tow, however.) Although an influx of year-round residents has transformed much of the Upper Cape into a commuter's haven, the Lower Cape still has a quiet sense of history and simple purpose.

Rich in history and Cape flavor, Brewster and Harwich stand opposite each other in the area just shy of the Cape's elbow. Harwich, farther inland, has antique homes, rambling old burial grounds, and a modest town center with shops, restaurants, museums, churches, and public parks. Brewster is similarly historic; examples of Victorian, Greek Revival, and colonial architecture abound, most meticulously preserved. Many homes have been converted to welcoming guesthouses and bed-and-breakfasts, whereas others are privately owned.

The traditional, elegant town of Chatham perches dramatically at the end of the peninsular elbow. It's here that the Atlantic begins to wet the shores of the Cape, sometimes with frightening strength. Chatham has shown its vulnerability to the forces of nature over the years, as little by little the town's shores have succumbed to the insatiable sea.

North of Chatham is Orleans, supply center of the Lower and Outer Capes, replete with large grocery chains and shopping plazas. The famed Nauset Beach is here, its dune-backed shores crammed with sun-seeking revelers in summer. Orleans also has a rich history—you just have to leave the maze of industry to find it. Continuing north, you can reach Eastham, a town often overlooked because of its position on busy U.S. 6. It, too, is perfectly charming, if you know where to look.

South of Chatham, the Monomoy National Wildlife Refuge is a twin-island bird sanctuary. Here dozens of species of birds are free to feed, nest, and expand their numbers without human meddling. Recreation seekers should head straight to Nickerson State Park in Brewster to frolic in freshwater ponds or enjoy a serene bike ride under the shade of stately white pine, oak, and maple trees. In Eastham, where the Cape Cod National Seashore officially begins, the Salt Pond Visitor Center has a wealth of area information, educational programs, and guided tours.

TOP REASONS TO GO

Exploring the Cape Cod National Seashore. You can start at the Salt Pond Visitor Center in Esatham for an orientation to the seashore's beaches, marshes, forest, wildlife, and historic structures. Don't miss Coast Guard and Nauset Light beaches.

Walking in Cape Cod Bay at low tide. Brewster's glory is Cape Cod Bay, and dozens of beaches (public and private) expand by acres at low tide. Treasure hunters can stroll the sands, keeping an eye out for shells left behind by the retreating waters.

Taking in summer theater. Harwich Junior Theatre stages performances year-round and offers children's classes in summer. Community theater dominates the scene in Orleans and Chatham. In Brewster, the professional Cape Cod Repertory Theatre stages productions indoors and under the stars

Seeing a collegiate ball game. Cheer on the teams of the Cape Cod Baseball League, made up of the nation's top college players. Bring a blanket, chair, and even a picnic for the free games. Harwich, Chatham, Brewster, and Orleans all have their own teams that play from mid-June through early August.

Checking out local art and crafts. Galleries and studios in Chatham and Brewster showcase local and national artists. Orleans has excellent galleries, as well as a weekly outdoor art show. Eastham and Harwich hold outdoor arts-and-crafts shows; Harwich's biggie is the Professional Arts and Crafts Festival in July and August.

ORIENTATION AND PLANNING

GETTING ORIENTED

The towns of Brewster, Harwich, Chatham, Orleans, and Eastham make up the Lower Cape. Of these, only Brewster and Orleans touch Route 6A. Harwich, Chatham, and Orleans span Route 28—but have no fear. Although the road is known for traffic, Route 28's congestion eases as the road winds toward the Lower Cape. Eastham sits along U.S. 6, which is the fastest way to get to all the towns—but if you're concerned about the journey as well as the destination, it's worthwhile to amble along Route 28 or 6A. Along the way, picturesque harbors, scenic side roads, and the towns' main streets, antiques stores, romantic inns, and colonial homes dot the landscape. Follow Route 28 into Chatham and make your way to the Chatham Lighthouse for breathtaking views of Nantucket Sound.

Brewster. Here you'll find an incredible number of beautifully preserved historic homes. Brewster's Cape Cod Bay beaches are famous for the expanse of sand revealed at low tide, as well as the striking sunsets. Visitors love the small-town feel, complete with plenty of unique shopping in specialty stores (no chains here) and antiques shops.

Harwich. Harwich has two personalities. The peaceful and more rural half is in Harwich, which has much history to share in its old cemeteries and museums. The fun-loving side with plenty of attractions to keep the kids happy is in Harwich Port, on Nantucket Sound.

Chatham. With a long Main Street filled with shops and restaurants, downtown Chatham is best explored on foot. You'll see grand houses at every turn, all meticulously kept with impressive gardens. Head to Chatham Light to see the untamed ocean, or ride a bike along back roads to see calm harbors.

Orleans. The commercial center of the lower Cape, Orleans retains its small-town feel. Rock Harbor, on Cape Cod Bay, is perfect for sunset watching. Nauset Beach is a major draw. Don't miss the lovely village of East Orleans, where you can launch a boat on Pleasant Bay.

Eastham. The Cape Cod National Seashore has a large visitor center here, as well as two beaches that make Eastham a popular spot. There is no distinct downtown, but the best attractions are its abundance of nature areas and beaches.

PLANNING

WHEN TO GO

Although the crowds of summer are testament to the appeal of the Lower Cape and its spectacular beaches, outdoor pursuits, crafts and art shows, concerts, and special events, the region is becoming a popular year-round destination. Because of its ocean-side climate, spring and fall are simply lesser shades of full-blown summer. Seasonal businesses reopen in late May and early June, but lodging rates remain less pricey than during the high season, and the agonies of summertime traffic, long waits at restaurants, and parking restrictions at area beaches can be avoided. September, October, and even November are the same. The waters usually remain warm enough to swim well into October, and many shops attempt to rid their stocks of merchandise by having generous sales.

You won't get the expected splendors of New England foliage on the Lower Cape, because the landscape changes are subtle. Swaying salt-marsh grasses turn golden, cranberry bogs explode into ruby-red quilts, and the ocean relaxes into a deep, deep blue. The light becomes softer and its patterns more dramatic on both land and sea. In the towns of Harwich, Brewster, and Orleans, where the soil is substantial enough to support mighty oaks and maples, the colors of autumn do peer through. A drive along Route 6A under the canopy of changing leaves is just as breathtaking as a summer jaunt past blooming gardens.

PLANNING YOUR TIME

If you're here for the beaches and other natural pursuits, you could easily spend a week in the area. Cape Cod National Seashore has spectacular beaches for swimming (even if the water is a tad chilly), and its wealth of walking trails, bike paths, and guided kayak tours could keep you busy for days. Eastham is closest to the park, but any of the nearby towns are also good options. Traffic is a consideration, though.

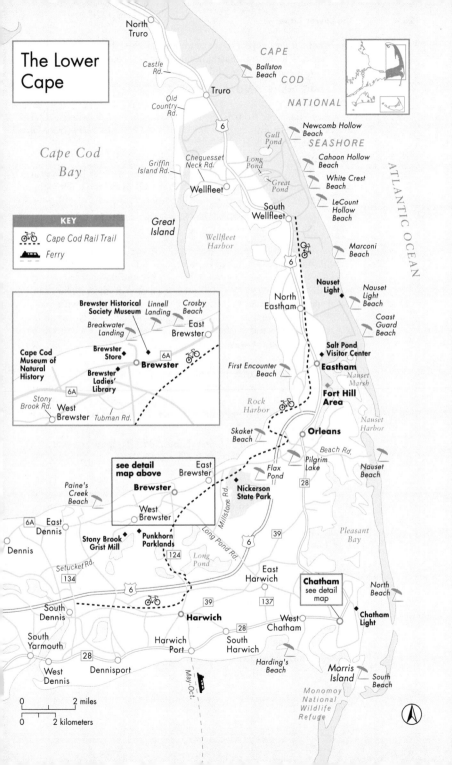

The Lower Cape

Cape Cod Bay

CAPE COD NATIONAL SEASHORE

ATLANTIC OCEAN

North Truro

Castle Rd.

Truro

Old Country Rd.

Ballston Beach

Gull Pond

Newcomb Hollow Beach

Cahoon Hollow Beach

White Crest Beach

LeCount Hollow Beach

Griffin Island Rd.

Chequesset Neck Rd.

Long Pond

Great Pond

Wellfleet

South Wellfleet

Great Island

Wellfleet Harbor

Marconi Beach

Nauset Light

Nauset Light Beach

Coast Guard Beach

North Eastham

Salt Pond Visitor Center

Eastham

Nauset Marsh

KEY

Cape Cod Rail Trail

Ferry

Brewster Historical Society Museum

Linnell Landing

Crosby Beach

Breakwater Landing

East Brewster

Cape Cod Museum of Natural History

Brewster Store

Brewster

6A

Brewster Ladies' Library

6A

Stony Brook Rd.

West Brewster

Tubman Rd.

First Encounter Beach

Fort Hill Area

Rock Harbor

Nauset Harbor

Skaket Beach

Orleans

Beach Rd.

Nauset Beach

see detail map above

East Brewster

Brewster

West Brewster

Flax Pond

Pilgrim Lake

28

Paine's Creek Beach

Nickerson State Park

Pleasant Bay

6A

East Dennis

Stony Brook Grist Mill

Punkhorn Parklands

Millstone Rd.

Long Pond Rd.

Dennis

124

Long Pond

6

39

134

Setucket Rd.

East Harwich

Chatham see detail map

North Beach

South Dennis

6

39

137

West Chatham

Chatham Light

South Yarmouth

Harwich

28

South Harwich

Morris Island

South Beach

28

West Dennis

Dennisport

Harwich Port

May–Oct.

Harding's Beach

Monomoy National Wildlife Refuge

0   2 miles

0   2 kilometers

On a summer day, expect to spend about 30 to 40 minutes driving from Brewster or Chatham to Eastham. For shopping, theater, and nightlife Orleans or Chatham are excellent choices.

GETTING HERE AND AROUND

BOAT TRAVEL

In season, the ferry from Harwich to Nantucket is a less-hectic alternative to the Hyannis crowd. *For details* ⇨ *Boat and Ferry Travel in Travel Smart Cape Cod.*

BUS TRAVEL

Run by the Cape Cod Regional Transit Authority, the Flex bus has year-round service running from Harwich Port to Provincetown with stops in Brewster, Orleans, Eastham, Wellfleet, and Truro.

Bus Companies **The Flex** (☎ *800/352-7155* ⊕ *www.capecodrta.org*).

CAR TRAVEL

Unless you're staying put in one place, you need a car to explore the Cape. On rainy days you can expect major roadways to be filled with folks looking for something to do. Route 28 from Chatham to Harwich Port will be a challenge, as will Route 6 from Orleans through Eastham. Local maps will reveal the secondary roads connecting towns; you'll discover a lot more and not feel so stymied by the crowds. Route 6A is a beautiful ride and is often taken at a slower pace since there is so much to see along the way.

TAXI TRAVEL

Based in Orleans, Chatham, Wellfleet, and Provincetown, Cape Cab is really more of a car service, with various vehicles available depending on the number of people traveling. The company serves local airports, including those in Boston and Providence. Eldredge Taxi in Chatham is another option.

Taxi Companies **Cape Cab** (✉ *Orleans* ☎ *508/240-1500* ⊕ *www.capecabtaxi. com*). **Eldredge Taxi** (✉ *Chatham* ☎ *508/945-0068*).

RESTAURANTS

Each town has its own batch of treasured and traditional restaurants, and all will be crowded in summer. A significant number of restaurants close their doors once the crowds thin in October—including the beloved fried-seafood shacks—but plenty remain open throughout the year. Fresh seafood is a major staple.

If you are celebrating a milestone or hoping to delight someone special, Brewster's Chillingsworth impresses with French-country elegance. The Chatham Bars Inn recalls an era of gentle tranquillity. If you're undecided, a stroll down Chatham's Main Street will tempt your palate. The restaurants in Orleans, Brewster, Harwich, and Eastham are spread out through the towns, but top restaurants such as the Brewster Fish House are worth finding.

All towns have banished smoking from restaurants and bars; smokers can retreat for a break outdoors.

HOTELS

Money made in early maritime fortunes helped build exquisite homes, many of which are now unique and lovely inns. Chatham is blessed with dozens of these aged beauties, most with all the modern conveniences. B&Bs and intimate guesthouses are the primary lodging choices, but even larger hotels such as Chatham Bars Inn and the Chatham Wayside Inn capture the charm of Old Cape Cod. Expect fewer hotel and motel options on this part of the Cape. However, there are a few roadside or waterfront hotels outside the town centers. These complexes, which usually welcome families with small children, can be a bit softer on the wallet.

Brewster is essentially a B&B kind of town, offering lodging in former sea captains' homes. The full-service Ocean Edge Resort is also here, though. Harwich and Orleans have a mixture of both family-friendly hotel complexes and lovingly restored inns. Eastham has quite a few large-scale hotels along U.S. 6, including a Sheraton. Don't expect to find bargains here during the high season.

Other options include camping or weekly cottage rentals—all towns have the Cape's trademark cottage colonies. Note that in summer these must be secured well in advance, usually through a local real-estate agent or online.

WHAT IT COSTS					
	¢	$	$$	$$$	$$$$
Restaurants	under $10	$10–$16	$17–$22	$23–$30	over $30
Hotels	under $90	$90–$140	$141–$200	$201–$260	Over $260

Restaurant prices are per person for a main course at dinner. Hotel prices are for a standard double room, excluding 5.7% sales tax (more in some counties) and up to an additional 6% tourist tax.

CONDO AND HOUSE RENTALS

At the Cape Rentals lists vacation rentals in Brewster, Harwich, Chatham, Orleans, and Eastham. Cape Cod Rentals covers vacation homes in the Brewster community of Ocean Edge, as well as throughout the towns of Dennis, Harwich, Brewster, Chatham, Orleans, Eastham, Wellfleet, and Truro. Commonwealth Associates can assist in finding vacation rentals in the Harwiches, including waterfront properties. Great Locations Inc. specializes in vacation rentals in Brewster, Dennis, and Orleans.

Local Agents At the Cape Rentals (✉ Orleans ☎ 508/255–0136 ⊕ www.atthecaperentals.com). **Cape Cod Rentals** (✉ Brewster ☎ 508/896–4606 ⊕ www.capecodrentals.com). **Commonwealth Associates** (✉ Harwich Port ☎ 508/432–2618 ⊕ www.commonwealthrealestate.com). **Great Locations** (✉ Brewster ☎ 508/896–2090 or 800/626–9984 ⊕ www.greatcapevacations.com).

BREWSTER

Brewster calls itself the Sea Captains' Town, honoring its rich heritage as a seafaring community. Historic Route 6A, the Old King's Highway, winds through its center; it's also known as Main Street. This road, the old stagecoach route, was once nearly the only one at this end of the Cape, and residents and legislators alike are determined to keep it well preserved. Homes and businesses must adhere to historic detail: there are no neon signs, no strip malls—only the gentle facades of a graceful era.

Brewster's location on Cape Cod Bay makes it a perfect place to learn about the region's ecology. The Cape Cod Museum of Natural History is here, and the area is rich in conservation lands, state parks, forests, freshwater ponds, and brackish marshes. When the tide is low in Cape Cod Bay, you can stroll the beaches and explore tidal pools up to 2 mi from the shore on the Brewster flats. When it's high tide, the water is relatively warm and very calm for swimming. Both Nickerson State Park and the Punkhorn Parklands have thousands of acres through which to wander.

Named for Plymouth leader William Brewster, the area was settled in 1659 but was not incorporated as a separate town until 1803. In the early 1800s, Brewster was the terminus of a packet cargo service from Boston. In 1849 Henry David Thoreau wrote that "this town has more mates and masters of vessels than any other town in the country." Many mansions built for sea captains remain, and quite a few have been turned into handsome B&Bs (though in recent years, more than a few of these have reverted to private homes). In the 18th and 19th centuries, the bay side of Brewster was the site of a major salt-making industry. Of the 450 saltworks operating on the Cape in the 1830s, more than 60 were here.

GETTING HERE AND AROUND

Brewster—6 mi north of Chatham and 5 mi west of Orleans—is spread along Route 6A. Take it slow through the town limits, not just in honor of the speed limit, but to appreciate the abundant display of grand old homes, fanciful rose arbors, antiques shops, and countless historic details that make this one of the region's prettiest towns.

ESSENTIALS

Visitor Information Brewster Chamber of Commerce (⊠ *2198 Rte. 6A* ☎ *508/896–3500* ⊕ *www.brewstercapecod.org*).

EXPLORING

TOP ATTRACTIONS

Brewster Store. Built in 1852 as a church, this local landmark is a typical New England general store with such essentials as the daily papers, penny candy, and benches out front for conversation. Out back, the Brewster Scoop serves ice cream mid-June to early September. Upstairs, memorabilia from antique toys to World War II bond posters is displayed. Downstairs there's a working antique nickelodeon; locals warm

CAPE COD RAIL TRAIL

The Cape's top bike route, the 25-mi Cape Cod Rail Trail, follows the paved right-of-way of the old Penn Central Railroad from South Dennis to South Wellfleet. You can also pick up the trail in Harwich, Brewster, Orleans, or Eastham.

Nickerson State Park, in Brewster, has 8 mi of its own forested trails, some with access to the rail trail. From the Salt Pond Visitor Center in Eastham, take a jaunt off the rail trail and follow meandering paths leading to Nauset Beach, Coast Guard Beach, and beautiful Nauset Marsh.

Another option is a spin on the Old Colony Rail Trail, beginning in Harwich center from the Cape Cod Rail Trail, 8 mi to downtown Chatham. Cyclists in Chatham can follow the little green signs that denote the Chatham Bike Route, which runs beside the ocean, past all the stunningly majestic homes that dominate the waterfront. Use caution, though, as the roadway is shared with cars.

themselves by the old coal stove in the colder months. ⊠ *1935 Rte. 6A* ☎ *508/896–3744* ⊕ *www.brewsterstore.com*

🖙 **Cape Cod Museum of Natural History.** A short drive west from the heart of Brewster, this spacious museum and its pristine grounds include a shop, a natural-history library, and exhibits such as a working beehive and a pond- and sea-life room with live specimens. Walking trails wind through 80 acres of forest, marshland, and ponds, all rich in birds and other wildlife. The exhibit hall upstairs has a wall display of aerial photographs documenting the process by which the famous Chatham sandbar was split in two. In summer there are guided field walks, nature programs, and art classes for preschoolers through ninth graders. ⊠ *869 Rte. 6A, West Brewster* ☎ *508/896–3867* ⊕ *www.ccmnh.org* 🖙 *$8* ☉ *Oct.–Dec. and Feb.–Mar., Wed.–Sun. noon–4; Apr. and May, Wed.–Sun. 10–4; June–Sept., daily 9:30–4.*

Fodor'sChoice ★

🖙 **Drummer Boy Park.** The expansive grounds include a great playground and open spaces for dogs to run or for impromptu picnics with views of the bay. Craft fairs, antique shows, and other happenings, including Sunday town band concerts, take place here throughout summer. ⊠ *Rte. 6A, West Brewster* ☎ *No phone.*

Harris-Black House. On the grounds of the Higgins Farm Windmill in Drummer Boy Park, this one-room home dates to 1795. Today, the restored building is partially furnished and is dominated by a brick hearth and original woodwork. ⊠ *Drummer Boy Park, Off Rte. 6A, West Brewster* ☎ *508/896–9521* ⊕ *www.brewsterhistoricalsociety.org* 🖙 *Free* ☉ *July–Sept., Thurs.–Sat. 1–4.*

Higgins Farm Windmill. Windmills used to be prominent in Cape Cod towns; the Brewster area once had four. This octagonal mill shingled in weathered pine with a roof like an upturned boat was moved here in 1974. The millstones are original. At night the mill is often spotlighted, which makes for quite a sight. ⊠ *Off Rte. 6A, Drummer Boy Park, just west of the Cape Cod Museum of Natural History, West Brewster*

☎ *508/896–9521* ⊕ *www.brewsterhistoricalsociety.org* ⊙ *July–Sept., Thurs.–Sat. 1–4.*

☺ **Nickerson State Park.** These 1,961 acres were once part of a vast estate belonging to Roland C. Nickerson, son of Samuel Nickerson, a Chatham native who founded the First National Bank of Chicago. Roland and his wife, Addie, lavishly entertained such visitors as President Grover Cleveland at their private beach and hunting lodge in English country-house style, with coachmen dressed in tails and top hats and a bugler announcing carriages entering the front gates. The grand stone mansion built in 1908 is now part of the Ocean Edge resort. In 1934 Addie donated the land for the state park in memory of Roland and their son, who died during the 1918 flu epidemic.

The park consists of acres of oak, pitch pine, hemlock, and spruce forest speckled with seven freshwater kettle ponds formed by glaciers. Some ponds are stocked with trout for fishing. You can swim canoe, sail, and kayak along 8 mi of paved trails that have access to the Cape Cod Rail Trail. Bird-watchers seek out the thrushes, wrens, warblers, woodpeckers, finches, larks, cormorants, great blue herons, hawks, owls, ospreys, and other species. Red foxes and white-tailed deer are occasionally spotted in the woods. Both tent and RV camping are popular here, and nature programs are offered in season. ✉ *3488 Rte. 6A, East Brewster* ☎ *508/896–3491* ⊕ *www.mass.gov/dcr* 💲 *Free* ⊙ *Daily dawn–dusk.*

> **QUICK BITES**
>
> If you need a quick break, **Hopkins House Gift and Bakery** (✉ *2727 Rte. 6A, East Brewster* ☎ *508/896–9337*) is the perfect pit stop. Wash down a chewy hermit cookie, baked with molasses and raisins, with some strong, hot coffee. A home-furnishings shop attached to the bakery might tempt you to stretch your legs a while longer.

WORTH NOTING

Brewster Historical Society Museum. In an 1830s house, this museum has a sea captain's room with paintings and artifacts, an 1890 barbershop, a child's room with antique toys and clothing, a room of women's gowns and accessories, and other exhibits on local history and architecture. Out back, a ¼-mi nature trail over dunes leads to the bay. ✉ *3171 Rte. 6A, East Brewster* ☎ *508/896–9521* ⊕ *www.brewsterhistoricalsociety. org* 💲 *Free* ⊙ *July and Aug., Thurs.–Sat. 1–4.*

> **QUICK BITES**
>
> More than the sublime truffles, the **Chocolate Peddler** (✉ *2628 Rte. 6A, East Brewster* ☎ *774/263–2751* ⊕ *www.chefpaulstruffles.com*) is a multi-sensory experience. The place is decorated with tapestries, Oriental rugs, African art, and Victorian couches, which set the stage for an astounding 59 varieties of chocolates. Each has a flavor as intense and distinct as their namesakes, thanks to Chef Paul's infusion techniques and creativity.

Brewster Ladies' Library. This restored Victorian building with a more modern addition are painted in eye-catching hues of deep cranberry and creamy yellow. The library is host to a full schedule of regular events for all ages, including book discussion groups, lectures, readings, and craft programs for children. ⊠ *1822 Rte. 6A* ☎ *508/896–3913* ⊕ *www. brewsterladieslibrary.org* ⊠ *Free* ⊗ *Tues. and Thurs. 10–8; Wed., Fri., and Sat. 10–5.*

First Parish Church. Known as the Church of the Sea Captains, this handsome house of worship (Unitarian Universalist) is full of pews marked with the names of famous Brewster seamen. Out back is an old graveyard where militiamen, clergy, farmers, and sea captains rest side by side. The church is the site of a summer musical program, which includes the ever-popular Tanglewood marionette show, Tuesday through Thursday mornings at 9:30. ⊠ *1969 Rte. 6A* ☎ *508/896–5577.*

QUICK BITES

Looking for a little south-of-the-border zing? Then stop in at El Guapo's Taqueria (⊠ **239 Underpass Rd. near Cape Cod Rail Trail crossing, South Brewster** ☎ **508/896–3338** ⊕ **www.elguapostaqueria.com**) for a quick lunch or dinner. It's mostly a take-out place (there are a few tiny tables inside, several picnic tables outside) where you can choose from basic but tasty Mexican standards like tacos—the fish tacos are especially good—quesadillas, generous burritos, enchiladas, and fajitas.

Punkhorn Parklands. For a lovely hike or run through the local wilds, try the freshwater kettle-hole ponds and 45 mi of scenic trails meandering through these 800 acres of meadows, marshes, and pine forests. ⊠ *End of Run Hill Rd. off Stony Brook Rd., West Brewster* ☎ *508/896–3701* ⊕ *www.town.brewster.ma.us* ⊠ *Free* ⊗ *Trails daily dawn–dusk.*

Stony Brook Grist Mill. A short drive from Route 6A is this restored, operating 19th-century fulling mill (a mill that shrinks and thickens cloth), now also a museum. The old mill's waterwheel slowly turns in a small, tree-lined brook. Inside, exhibits include old mill equipment and looms; you can watch cornmeal being stone-ground and get a lesson in weaving on a 100-year-old loom. Out back, across wooden bridges, a bench has a view of the pond and of the sluices leading into the mill area.

Early each spring, in April and early May, Stony Brook's **Herring Run** boils with alewives (herring) making their way to spawning waters; it's an amazing sight. The fish swim in from Cape Cod Bay up Paine's Creek to Stony Brook and the ponds beyond it. The herring run, a rushing stream across the street from the mill, consists of ladders that help the fish climb the rocky waters. Seagulls swarm in and pluck herring from the run into midair. Farther down the path to the stream, there's an ivy-covered stone wishing well and a wooden bridge with a bench. ⊠ *Stony Brook Rd., West Brewster Off Rte. 6A* ☎ *No phone* ⊠ *Donations accepted* ⊗ *June–Aug., Sat. 10–2.*

WHERE TO EAT

$$$
ECLECTIC
★

✗ **Bramble Inn.** Inside an inviting 1860s white house in Brewster's historic village center, this romantic property presents well-crafted, globally inspired contemporary fare in five dining rooms with floral wallpaper or wood-paneled walls, hung with gilt-framed mirrors and watercolor and oil paintings (much of the artwork is for sale). During the warmer months, dine on a patio amid fragrant flower beds. The menu changes often but always includes the assorted seafood curry—the house favorite—which combines lobster, shrimp, scallops, and cod in a light curry sauce with grilled banana, toasted coconut, sliced almonds, and house chutney. If you'd rather graze, opt for the Bramble Bites—choose from risottos, skillet roasted mussels, salmon Niçoise, and the like—served in the bar as well as the garden patios. ⊠ *2019 Rte. 6A, East Brewster* 🕾 *508/896–7644* ⊕ *www.brambleinn.com* ⊟ *AE, D, MC, V* ⊘ *Closed Mon. No lunch. Call for Jan. and early Feb. hrs.*

$$$ ✕**Brewster Fish House.** Humble on the outside yet vibrant and flavorful
SEAFOOD within, the Fish House has carved a niche for itself. There is nothing ordinary about the menu here: the sweet perfection of just-off-the-boat scallops is enhanced by oyster mushrooms, pancetta, and a chive béarnaise. Look for other favorites like pan-seared Long Island duck. For lunch, the fried oyster po'boy sandwich is a real treat. Locals are known to drive from all points of the Cape to this lovably rickety restaurant for the super-fresh fish. It can be noisy and it's always crowded in summer, but it's worth the wait. The wine list includes a flavorful selection of by-the-glass offerings. Note: The lack of booster seats and high chairs signals that this is not the place to bring small children. ⊠ *2208 Rte. 6A, Brewster* 🕾 *508/896–7867* ⊕ *brewsterfish.com* ⌲ *Reservations not accepted* ⊟ *MC, V.*

$$ ✕**Brewster Inn and Chowder House.** The consistently good food at this
AMERICAN long-standing Cape institution continues to live up to its great reputation among locals. Home cooking in the traditional New England style is the rule; you'll find no fancy or fussy fusion recipes here—just comfort food. Look for simple but tasty meat and seafood standards, and don't miss the rich and full-bodied New England clam chowder. The service is friendly, the prices are kind, and you won't leave hungry. The restaurant serves lunch and dinner daily year-round. ⊠ *1993 Rte. 6A* 🕾 *508/896–7771* ⊟ *MC, V.*

$$$$ ✕**Chillingsworth.** One of the crown jewels of Cape restaurants, Chilling-
FRENCH sworth combines formal presentation with an excellent French menu
Fodor'sChoice and a diverse wine cellar to create a memorable dining experience.
★ Super-rich risotto, roast lobster, and grilled Angus sirloin are favorites. Dinner in the main dining rooms is prix-fixe and includes seven courses—appetizer, soup, salad, sorbet, entrée, "amusements," and dessert, plus coffee or tea. Less-expensive à la carte options for lunch, dinner, and Sunday brunch are served in the more casual, patio-style Bistro. There are also a few guest rooms here for overnighting. ⊠ *2449 Rte. 6A, East Brewster* 🕾 *508/896–3640* ⊕ *www.chillingsworth.com* ⊟ *AE, DC, MC, V* ⊘ *Closed Thanksgiving–mid-May.*

$$ ✕**JT's Seafood.** Fresh and ample portions of fried seafood take center
AMERICAN stage at this casual joint, which is very popular with families. Pick from several seafood platters, or gnaw on baby back ribs or burgers if you need a break from the fruits of the sea. Several items, including corn dogs, grilled cheese (lunch only), and peanut butter and jelly, are good kid-friendly choices. Place your order at the counter and sit inside or out. Leave your mark by sticking a pin in your town's name on the big map by the order counter. Takeout is also available. ⊠ *2689 Rte. 6A* 🕾 *508/896–3355* ⊕ *www.jt-seafood.com* ⌲ *Reservations not accepted* ⊟ *MC, V* ⊘ *Closed mid-Oct.–mid-Apr.*

$ ✕ **Laurino's Tavern.** There's something timeless about this noisy pizza
AMERICAN joint and American eatery with warm wood paneling, generous booth-style seating, and red-and-white-checked tablecloths, plus a big patio and a playground for kids. Meatball grinders, steak-and-cheese sandwiches, and specialty pizzas are mainstays. Try a buffalo-chicken pizza, topped with wing sauce and cheddar cheese, with a blue cheese dipping sauce. Lasagna, shrimp scampi, and mussels marinara are popular choices. A play area out back is ideal for unleashing the kids before, during, or after dinner. The long, friendly bar is a great place to sit with a buddy over a beer and a big plate of Macho Nachos. In summer live music serenades the late-night crowd. ⊠ *3668 Rte. 6A, East Brewster* ☎ *508/896–6135* ⌔ *Reservations not accepted* ☐ *AE, MC, V.*

$$$ ✕ **Peddler's Restaurant.** The husband-and-wife team Alain and Beth have
FRENCH been quietly serving French bistro fare to a loyal (and tight-lipped) crowd of very satisfied locals. A lack of advertising and generous word-of-mouth following have kept this lovely little spot somewhat shrouded in mystique; and wisteria vines—which cover the building so entirely that it's hard to find the front door—help keep the place a secret. Inside, about a dozen tables dressed in white linen are illuminated by the glow of candles and dangling white lights, setting the stage for a meal that should be savored slowly. French-born Alain uses his native culinary training to prepare a host of pâtés, escargots, flounder meuniére, and the house favorite, duck à l'orange with a Grand Marnier sauce. The menu changes daily; it's handwritten on a blackboard on a side wall. Finish with the homemade pistachio ice cream with chocolate ganache. ⊠ *67 Thad Ellis Rd., East Brewster* ☎ *508/896–9300* ⊕ *www.peddlersrestaurant.com* ⌔ *Reservations not accepted* ☐ *AE* ☯ *Closed Sun. and Mon. in Aug, Sun.–Wed. Sept.–July. No lunch.*

WHERE TO STAY

$$$–$$$$ ▦ **Brewster By the Sea Inn & Spa.** Weather permitting, a three-course
★ breakfast is served on the patio overlooking a swimming pool and 2 acres of landscaped gardens at this restored, beautifully decorated 1846 farmhouse on historic Route 6A. A fireplace is the focal point in one guest room, and another has a king-size canopy bed and sliders that open onto a private deck. Three more guest rooms, furnished with authentic and reproduction antiques, fireplaces, and hot tubs, are in an adjacent carriage house. The setting and amenities make for an ideal getaway: think fireside massages or lazy poolside lounging. **Pros:** intimate lodging; ideal for relaxation. **Cons:** not an in-town or beach-side location; not for those traveling with children. ⊠ *716 Rte. 6A* ☎ *508/896–3910 or 800/892–3910* ⊕ *www.brewsterbythesea.com* ⇱ *6 rooms, 2 suites* ⌔ *In-room: a/c, DVD, refrigerator (some), Wi-Fi. In-hotel: pool, spa, no kids under 16* ☐ *AE, D, MC, V* ⎢◯⎮ *BP.*

$$ ▦ **Candleberry Inn.** This 1790s Georgian mansion sits along scenic Main Street (Route 6A) and was once the home of writer Horatio Alger. The sun-filled rooms are unfussy but elegant, with Oriental rugs, wide-plank floors, original woodwork, and tall windows with the original wavy glass. Several have working fireplaces, and two particularly cozy units—the Seabreeze and Treetops rooms—have pitched ceilings and access to a deck overlooking the leafy grounds and fragrant gardens. The Seacroft Suite has French doors leading to a large sitting area. Gracious innkeepers Stuart and Charlotte Fyfe serve a delicious full breakfast out by the garden in summer and in a cozy dining room during the cooler months. **Pros:** in the heart of Brewster; historic lodging; spacious gardens and grounds. **Cons:** many rooms accessed via steep stairs; some rooms are on the smaller size because of the home's age. ⊠ *1882 Rte. 6A* 🖀 *508/896–3300 or 800/573–4769* ⊕ *www.candleberryinn.com* 📨 *6 rooms, 1 suite* ⚓ *In-room: a/c, DVD (some), Wi-Fi. In-hotel: no kids under 10* ⊟ *AE, D, DC, MC, V* ⏀ *BP.*

$$ 🛏 **Isaiah Clark House.** This former 18th-century sea captain's residence, just west of the town proper, retains its wide-plank flooring and low, sloping ceilings and has a varied selection of antiques. The original inhabitants have left their mark all over the house, from the scrawled signature of 13-year-old son Jeremiah in a closet to the framed historic documents and photographs on the walls to the namesake of each of the rooms (all Clark family women). Most rooms have queen-size four-poster or canopy beds, braided rugs, and fireplaces. The extensive gardens yield some of the fruit used in the homemade pies, muffins, and breads that are served at breakfast. **Pros:** beautifully maintained; historic lodging; near beaches. **Cons:** not for those traveling with younger children. ⊠ *1187 Rte. 6A* 🖀 *508/896–2223 or 800/822–4001* ⊕ *www. isaiahclark.com* 📨 *7 rooms* ⚓ *In-room: a/c, no phone, Wi-Fi. In-hotel: no kids under 13* ⊟ *AE, MC, V* ☺ *Closed mid-Nov.–mid-Apr.* ⏀ *BP*

$$$$ 🛏 **Ocean Edge.** One of the Cape's few full-service resorts, Ocean Edge is
★   a luxury community straddling both sides of Route 6A—it borders Cape Cod Bay on the west, and its champion 18-hole golf course is on the east side. Accommodations range from hotel rooms in the conference center to one- to three-bedroom condominiums in the woods and two- to three-bedroom beachfront villas. Condominiums have full kitchens and washer-dryers; some units have fireplaces, and many have ocean views. All rooms and condos have balconies or patios. Clambakes, concerts, and tournaments take place throughout summer. **Pros:** great for golfers; many rooms have water views; full-service resort. **Cons:** not an intimate lodging experience. ⊠ *2907 Rte. 6A* 🖀 *508/896–9000 or 800/343–6074* ⊕ *www.oceanedge.com* 📨 *292 condominium units, 90 rooms* ⚓ *In-room: a/c, kitchen (some), Wi-Fi. In-hotel: 4 restaurants, room service, bar, spa, tennis courts, pools, gym, beachfront, bicycles, children's programs (ages 4–12), laundry facilities* ⊟ *AE, D, DC, MC, V.*

$-$$ 🛏 **Old Sea Pines Inn.** With its white-column portico and wraparound
Fodor's Choice   veranda overlooking a broad lawn, Old Sea Pines, which housed a
★   "charm and personality" school in the early 1900s, resembles a vintage summer estate. Climb the sweeping staircase to guest rooms decorated with reproduction wallpaper, antiques, and framed old photographs. Some are quite large; others have fireplaces. One of the more popular rooms has a sitting area in an enclosed sunporch. Rooms in a newer building are simple, with bright, white modern baths and cast-iron queen-size beds. The inn also holds a Sunday-night Broadway musical dinner revue from mid-June through mid-September. **Pros:** not far from town; beautiful grounds; reasonable rates. **Cons:** some rooms

have shared baths; steep stairway to upper floors. ⊠ *2553 Rte. 6A* ☎ *508/896–6114* ⊕ *www.oldseapinesinn.com* ⇨ *24 rooms, 19 with bath; 5 suites* ⚴ *In-room: no phone, no TV (some), Wi-Fi. In-hotel: no kids under 8 (except for family suites)* ⊟ *AE, D, MC, V* ⊘ *Closed Jan.–Mar.* ℉⚬❙ *BP.*

¢ ⚠**Nickerson State Park.** Shaded by a canopy of white pine, hemlock, and spruce, Nickerson State Park is a nature lover's haven. Encompassing close to 2,000 acres of wooded landscape teeming with wildlife, the park is the Cape's largest and most popular camping site. While away a summer afternoon trout fishing, walking, biking on 8 mi of paved trails (which connect to the Cape Cod Rail Trail), canoeing, sailing, kayaking, or bird-watching; there are four ponds for swimming, plus ocean beaches nearby. Reservations can be made by phone or online at ⊕ *www.ReserveAmerica.com.* ⚴ *Flush toilets, dump station, drinking water, showers, fire grates, grills, picnic tables, public telephone, general store, play area, ranger station, swimming (ponds)* ⇨ *420 sites, some yurts* ⊠ *3488 Rte. 6A* ☎ *508/896–3491, 877/422–6762 reservations* ⊕ *www.mass.gov/dcr* ⊟ *No credit cards.*

NIGHTLIFE AND THE ARTS

The **Cape Cod Repertory Theatre Co.** (⊠ *3299 Rte. 6A, East Brewster* ☎ *508/896–1888* ⊕ *www.caperep.org*) performs several impressive productions, from original works to classics, in its indoor Arts and Crafts–style theater way back in the woods. The season runs from May to November. Mesmerizing entertainment for children, in the form of lively outdoor (and often interactive) theater, is provided here, too. One-hour puppet shows and age-appropriate productions are given Monday through Wednesday mornings at 10 from late June through August. The theater is just west of Nickerson State Park.

Sunday evenings by the bay are filled with the sounds of the **town-band concerts** (⊠ *Rte. 6A, West Brewster*), held in the gazebo on the grounds of Drummer Boy Park. Bring your beach chairs, blankets, and a picnic for a lovely evening outing. The park is about ½ mi west of the Cape Cod Museum of Natural History, on the western side of Brewster.

The **Woodshed** (⊠ *1993 Main St.* ☎ *508/896–7771*), the rustic bar at the Brewster Inn, is a good place to soak up local color and listen to pop duos or bands that perform nightly. It's open from May through October.

BEACHES, SPORTS, AND THE OUTDOORS

BASEBALL

The **Brewster Whitecaps** (☎ *508/385–5073* ⊕ *www.brewsterwhitecaps.com*) of the collegiate Cape Cod Baseball League play home games at **Stony Brook School** (⊠ *384 Underpass Rd.*) from mid-June to mid-August.

BEACHES

Flax Pond (✉ *3488 Rte. 6A, East Brewster* ☎ *508/896–3491*) in Nickerson State Park, surrounded by pines, has picnic areas, a bathhouse, and water-sports rentals.

Brewster's **bay beaches** all have access to the coastal flats—a vast expanse of smooth sand and eel grass beds—that make for very interesting tidal-pool exploration. During particularly low tides, you can walk nearly a mile before reaching water. Eponymous roads to each beach branch off Route 6A; there's limited parking. All of the bay beaches require a daily, weekly, or seasonal parking pass (which for nonresidents cost $15, $50, and $125, respectively); these can be purchased at the town hall (☎ *508/896–4511*). **Breakwater Landing** is one of the most popular beaches in town and has an ample parking area. **Linnell Landing** has a small lot and tends to fill up quickly. A favorite among the toddler crowd and the sunset seekers, **Paine's Creek** also lacks a large lot, but if you get there early enough, you can find a spot. Harder to find down a dead-end street but worth it, **Robbin's Hill** is known for its intriguing tidal pools. Farther east off Route 6A is **Crosby Beach,** ideal for beach walkers—you can trek straightway to Orleans if you so desire.

BICYCLING

The **Cape Cod Rail Trail** has many access points in Brewster, among them Long Pond Road, Underpass Road, and Nickerson State Park.

Near Nickerson State Park, **Barb's Bike Shop** (✉ *Rte. 6A* ☎ *508/896–7231* ⊕ *www.barbsbikeshop.com*) is ideally located for rides along the Cape Cod Rail Trail; rentals include kid-friendly gear.

Brewster Bike (✉ *442 Underpass Rd.* ☎ *508/896–8149* ⊕ *www.brewsterbike.com*) carries a large selection of bikes for rent.

The **Rail Trail Bike and Kayak** (✉ *302 Underpass Rd.* ☎ *508/896–8200* ⊕ *www.railtrailbikeshop.com*) rents bikes, including children's bikes, and in-line skates. Parking is free, and there's a picnic area with easy access to the rail trail.

FISHING

Many of Brewster's freshwater ponds are good for catching perch, pickerel, and other fish; five ponds are well stocked with trout. Especially good for fishing is Cliff Pond in Nickerson State Park. You'll need a **fishing license**, available from most bait and tackle shops. To get your fishing license online, visit the Massachusetts Department of Fish and Game Web site at ⊕ *www.sport.state.ma.us.*

GOLF

The **Captain's Golf Course** (✉ *1000 Freeman's Way, east of Rte. 6* ☎ *508/896–1716 or 877/843–9081* ⊕ *www.captainsgolfcourse.com*) is an excellent public facility with two fine 18-hole courses—*Golf Digest* has named it one of the leading public courses in the nation. Ask about specials, including one for players under 17.

HORSEBACK RIDING

Emerald Hollow Farm (✉ *235 Run Hill Rd.* ☎ *508/685–6811* ⊕ *www.emeraldhollowfarm.com*) leads gentle rides for ages 7 and up through the wooded Punkhorn Parklands.

WATER SPORTS

Jack's Boat Rentals (⌧ *Flax Pond, Nickerson State Park, Rte. 6A, East Brewster* ☎ *508/896–8556* ⊕ *www.jacksboatrental.com*) rents canoes, kayaks, Seacycles, Sunfish, pedal boats, and sailboards.

SHOPPING

B. D. Hutchinson (⌧ *1274 Long Pond Rd., South Brewster* ☎ *508/896–6395*), a watch and clock maker, sells antique and collectible watches, clocks, and music boxes.

★ **Brewster Book Store** (⌧ *2648 Rte. 6A, East Brewster* ☎ *508/896–6543 or 800/823–6543* ⊕ *www.brewsterbookstore.com*) prides itself on being a special Cape bookstore. It's filled to the rafters with all manner of books by local and international authors and has an extensive fiction selection and kids section. A full schedule of author signings and children's story times continues year-round.

Clayton's Clay Works (⌧ *3820 Rte. 6A, East Brewster* ☎ *508/255–4937* ⊕ *www.claytonsclayworks.com*) is housed in a light-filled barn/studio; inside you'll see the artist's signature clay fish pieces, as well as pots, urns, planters, and vases. The fish are colored in vivid phosphorescent hues and double as platters or unusual wall art.

Countryside Antiques (⌧ *2052 Rte. 6A* ☎ *508/896–1444*) specializes in European and Asian antique furniture, home-accent pieces, china, and silver.

HandCraft House (⌧ *3996 Rte. 6A, East Brewster* ☎ *508/240–1412* ⊕ *www.handcrafthousegallery.com*) has "handmade in the USA" art for the home and garden, wood sculptures, handblown glass, stoneware, watercolors, and jewelry.

Kings Way Books and Antiques (⌧ *774 Rte. 6A, West Brewster* ☎ *508/896–3639*) sells out-of-print and rare books—they have a large medieval section—plus small antiques, china, glass, silver, coins, and linens.

Lemon Tree Village (⌧ *1069 Rte. 6A*) is a cheery complex filled with many unusual stores. You can find garden statuary, top-of-the-line cooking implements, locally made arts and crafts, pottery, birding supplies, clothing, gifts, jewelry, and toys. There's even a café next door if all that shopping makes you hungry.

Open from Memorial Day through Labor Day, the **Satucket Farm Stand** (⌧ *76 Harwich Rd.* ☎ *508/896–5540* ⊕ *www.satucketfarm.com*) is a real old-fashioned farm stand and bakery. There is lots of local produce as well as some homemade baked goods and other treats.

The **Spectrum** (⌧ *369 Rte. 6A, West Brewster* ☎ *508/385–3322* ⊕ *www. spectrumamerica.com*) carries a great selection of imaginative American arts and crafts, including pottery, stained glass, and art glass.

★ **Sydenstricker Galleries** (⌧ *490 Rte. 6A, West Brewster* ☎ *508/385–3272* ⊕ *www.sydenstricker.com*) stocks glassware handcrafted by a unique process, which you can watch while you're in the shop.

HARWICH

Like other townships on the Cape, Harwich is actually a cluster of several small villages. Harwich and Harwich Port are the commercial centers, and although the two have very different natures, both have graceful old architecture and rich histories. Harwich Port is the more bustling of the two: brimming with shops, calm-water beaches facing the waters of Nantucket Sound, restaurants, and hotel complexes, it packs all manner of entertainment and frivolity along its roadways. Harwich is more relaxed; its commerce is more centered, and its outlying areas are graced with greenery, large shade trees, and historic homesteads. The Harwich Historical Society has a strong presence here, maintaining exhibits and artifacts significant to the town's past.

Three naturally sheltered harbors on Nantucket Sound make the town, like its English namesake, popular with boaters. You'll find dozens of elegant sailboats and elaborate yachts in Harwich's harbors, plus plenty of charter-fishing boats. Each year in August the town pays celebratory homage to its large boating population with a grand regatta, Sails Around the Cape.

Beaches are plentiful in Harwich, and nearly all rest on the warm and mild waters of Nantucket Sound. Freshwater ponds, ideal for swimming as well as small-scale canoeing and kayaking, also speckle the area. Several conservation areas have miles of secluded walking trails, many alongside vivid cranberry bogs.

Originally known as Setucket, Harwich separated from Brewster in 1694 and was renamed for the famous English seaport. Historically, the villages of Harwich were marked by their generous number of churches and the styles of worship they practiced—small villages often sprang up around these centers of faith. The Cape's famous cranberry industry took off in Harwich in 1844, when Alvin Cahoon was its principal grower. You'll still find cranberry bogs throughout Harwich.

GETTING HERE AND AROUND

The center of Harwich, 6 mi south of Brewster, is easily accessed off Exit 10 of U.S. Route 6. It sits right at the crossroads of several roads that branch off to various towns. Route 39, which doubles as Main Street, leads to Orleans. Bank Street, next to the Brooks Free Library, is the most direct route to Harwich Port.

ESSENTIALS

Visitor Information **Harwich Chamber of Commerce** (⊠ *1 Schoolhouse Rd. and Rte. 28, Harwich Port* ☎ *508/432–1600 or 800/442–7942* ⊕ *www. harwichcc.com*).

EXPLORING

☾ **Brooks Park.** Just off Route 39, this pretty park is a good place to stretch your legs. It has a playground, picnic tables, a ball field, tennis courts, and a bandstand where summer concerts are held. Local musician perform on Monday, while the town band entertains on Tuesday. ⊠ *Oak St.*

🖑 **Bud's Go-Karts.** For children who have spent too much time in the car watching you drive, a spin behind the wheel of one of 20 top-of-the-line go-karts may be just the thing. ⊠ *9 Sisson Rd., off Rte. 28, Harwich Port* 🕾 *508/432–4964* ☉ *June–early Sept., Mon.–Sat. 9 AM–10 PM, Sun. 10 AM–10 PM.*

🖑 **Grand Slam Entertainment.** Softball- and baseball-batting cages and pitching machines, including one with fastballs up to 80 MPH, are the draw here. There's also a Wiffle-ball machine for younger kids, plus a bumper-boat pool and a video-arcade room. ⊠ *322 Main St. (Rte. 28), Harwich Port* 🕾 *508/430–1155* ⊕ *www.capecodbumperboats* ☉ *Apr., May, and Sept.–mid-Oct., Mon.–Sat. 11–7, Sun. 11–9; June–Aug., daily 9 AM–10 PM.*

Harwich Historical Society. Once the home of a private school offering the first high school–level curriculum in Harwich, this pillared 1844 Greek Revival building houses a large photo-history collection and exhibits on artist Charles Cahoon (grandson of cranberry grower Alvin), the socio-technological history of cranberry culture, and shoe making, the museum has antique clothing and textiles, china and glass, fans, and toys. There's also an extensive genealogical collection for researchers (open year-round by appointment). On the grounds is a powder house used to store gunpowder during the Revolutionary War, as well as a restored 1872 outhouse that could spur your appreciation for indoor plumbing. On the schedule throughout the season are historic lectures, children's programs, and special events such as the annual Civil War reenactment. ⊠ *80 Parallel St.* 🕾 *508/432–8089* ⊕ *www. harwichhistoricalsociety.org* 🕮 *Donations accepted* ☉ *Late June–mid-Oct., Thurs.–Sat. 1–4.*

🖑 **Trampoline Center.** A dozen trampolines are set up at ground level over pits for added safety. ⊠ *296 Main St. (Rte. 28), West Harwich* 🕾 *508/432–8717* ☉ *Apr.–mid-June, weekends, hrs vary widely, call ahead; mid-June–early Sept., daily 9 AM–10 PM.*

WHERE TO EAT

$ ✕ **400 East.** This big, dark restaurant buzzing with conversation is in a
AMERICAN nondescript shopping plaza. The menu includes teriyaki chicken, prime rib, lobster ravioli, burgers, and baked scrod, but also has excellent pizza, with toppings such as wild mushrooms, blue cheese, and chicken sausage. Eating at the busy, U-shaped bar is a good alternative to waiting for a table. Drop by in late afternoon for half-price appetizers. ⊠ *1421 Orleans Rd. (Rte. 39)* 🕾 *508/432–1800* ▤ *AE, D, MC, V.*

$$ ✕ **Brax Landing.** In this local stalwart perched alongside busy Saquatucket
SEAFOOD Harbor, you can get a menu tip-off as you pass by tanks full of lobsters in the corridor leading to the dining room. The restaurant sprawls around a big bar that serves specialty drinks such as the Banzai (frozen piña colada with a float of dark rum). The broiled scallops and the herb-crusted Chatham scrod are favorites, both served simply and well. And if you've been after the ultimate lobster roll—and never thought you could get full on it—sample the one at Brax Landing, bursting with the meat of a 1¼-pound lobster. There's also a notable children's menu, and

Sunday brunch is an institution. ✉ *705 Main St. (Rte. 28 at Saquatucket Harbor), Harwich Port* ☎ *508/432–5515* ⊕ *www.braxlanding.com* ⏴ *Reservations not accepted* ═ *AE, DC, MC, V* ⊘ *Restaurant closed Jan. and Feb.; bar open year-round.*

$$$ ✗ **Buca's Tuscan Roadhouse.** This romantic roadhouse near the Chatham
ITALIAN border, adorned with tiny white lights, wine bottles, and warm-hued
★ walls, might just transport you to Italy—and if it doesn't, the food will. From the baby arugula, goat cheese, pancetta, and pistachio salad to veal with red wine, balsamic butter, sun-dried cherries, and roasted tomatoes, this is mouthwatering Italian fare taken far beyond traditional home cooking. Save room for the signature three-tiered chocolate cake with a coconut-chocolate sauce. ✉ *4 Depot Rd.* ☎ *508/432–6900* ⊕ *www.bucasroadhouse.com* ═ *AE, MC, V* ⊘ *No lunch.*

$$$ ✗ **Cape Sea Grille.** Sitting primly inside a dashing Gothic Victorian house
AMERICAN on a side street off hectic Route 28, this gem with distant sea views
Fodor'sChoice cultivates a refined ambience with fresh flowers, white linens, and a
★ vibrant, welcoming atmosphere. Chef-owner Douglas Ramler relies on the freshest ingredients. Specialties from the seasonally changing menu may include pan-seared lobster with pancetta, potatoes, grilled asparagus, and a Calvados-saffron reduction, or grilled Atlantic halibut with smoked bacon, fennel, and basil tart. In spring and fall, try the very popular three-course dinner for $25. There's also a generous wine, martini, and drink list. ✉ *31 Sea St., Harwich Port* ☎ *508/432–4745* ⊕ *capeseagrille.com* ═ *AE, D, MC, V* ⊘ *Closed Mon.–Wed. Columbus Day–early Dec. and mid-Dec.–early Apr. No lunch.*

$$ ✗ **Ember.** Not your average pie joint, this place has given pizza a funky,
PIZZA sophisticated upgrade. There are nearly 20 types from which to choose, or you can build your own. One favorite is dressed with Granny Smith apples, andouille sausage, spinach, and a blend of five cheeses. There are also some great salads, including one that combines baby arugula, peanuts, grilled peaches, and goat cheese. Creamsicle-color walls, chic lighting, and black leather booths give the place a contemporary look. You dine in full view of the massive stone oven, where specialty pizzas are coal fired. The bar area is loud and jovial; there's an ample wine list and beer selection, but no liquor. ✉ *600 Rte. 28, Harwich Port* *508/430–0407* ⊕ *www.emberpizza.com* ═ *AE, MC, V* ⊘ *No lunch.*

$$$ ✗ **L'Alouette Bistro.** Owners Alan and Gretchen Champney serve authen-
FRENCH tic French food in this unassuming gray-shingle house. Look for traditional and contemporary selections such as butter-poached lobster with a saffron-vanilla sauce; pistachio-crusted roast rack of lamb; and spicy seafood bouillabaisse with clams, mussels, shrimp, and scallops. Desserts here are a particular delight, especially the light and not-too-sweet tarte tatin. There's also a superb wine list. ✉ *787 Main St. (Rte. 28), Harwich Port* ☎ *508/430–0405* ⊕ *www.lalouettebistro.com* ═ *AE, DC, MC, V* ⊘ *Closed Mon. in Nov.–Apr. No lunch.*

$$$ ✗ **The Port.** An urbane and homey storefront café in downtown Har-
SEAFOOD wich Port, the kitchen focuses on fairly traditional American fare, espe-
★ cially seafood, but with some inventive interpretations. You might, for instance, sample pistachio-crusted halibut with baby spinach and lemongrass rice, finished with an orange beurre blanc; or the sautéed

scallops with a Sambuca cream sauce, shaved fennel, candied walnuts, and sun-dried cranberries. The local mussels sautéed in garlic,
white wine, and butter make for a nice starter, or choose from a variety of local oysters from the raw bar. There's also an extensive, well-
chosen wine list. ⊠ *541 Main St. (Rte. 28)* ☎ *508/430–5410* ⊕ *www.*
theportrestaurant.com ⊟ *AE, MC, V* ☉ *Closed Dec.–Apr. No lunch.*

WHERE TO STAY

$–$$ 🛏 **Bluefish Bed & Breakfast.** The rooms in this 1846 yellow Victorian
are indeed comfortable, but don't sleep in and miss the extraordinary
breakfasts prepared by Tim O'Brien, who owns the inn with his wife,
Lori. You might awaken to the aroma of sweet bananas Foster French
toast; whatever is on the menu, expect that many of the ingredients
will have been freshly picked at the nearby community garden. Rooms
have the high ceilings typical of Victorians, with large windows letting
in light filtered through the surrounding trees; each room is furnished
with a mix of antiques and casual pieces. In the common area you'll
find a book exchange, a good movie selection, and a peaceful backyard patio to pass the time. **Pros:** relaxed atmosphere; reasonable rates;
walk to town center. **Cons:** suite bathrooms located outside room; some
steep stairs. ⊠ *102 Parallel St.* ☎ *508/430–9995* ⊕ *www.bluefishbnb.*
com 📑 *1 room, 2 suites* ⚴ *In-room: a/c, no phone, refrigerator, DVD,*
Wi-Fi ⊟ *MC, V* ☉ *Closed Nov.–mid-Apr.* 🍽 *BP.*

$$$$ 🛏 **Dunscroft by-the-Sea.** This charming, luxurious beach house sits a half
★ block from Nantucket Sound and within walking distance of several restaurants, yet it's on a peaceful street away from the crowds. The rooms
have many romantic amenities, including king- and queen-size canopy
and four-poster beds, whirlpool tubs, luxury linens, cotton robes, and
working fireplaces in some rooms. The cottage suite has a living room
with a fireplace, kitchenette, and Jacuzzi. In the common gathering
room you'll find a baby grand piano and extensive library. Innkeeper
Alyce's full breakfasts are fantastic (she makes killer French toast). **Pros:**
walk to beach; quiet setting; grand breakfasts. **Cons:** some steep stairs;
no water views. ⊠ *24 Pilgrim Rd., Harwich Port* ☎ *508/432–0810 or*
800/432–4345 ⊕ *www.dunscroftbythesea.com* 📑 *8 rooms, 1 cottage*
⚴ *In-room: a/c, DVD, kitchen (some), no phone, Wi-Fi. In-hotel: no*
kids under 14 ⊟ *AE, MC, V* 🍽 *BP.*

$$$$ 🛏 **Wequassett Inn Resort & Golf Club.** Twenty Cape-style cottages and an
Fodor's Choice attractive hotel make up this traditionally elegant resort by the sea. Set
★ on 22 acres of shaded landscape partially surrounded by Pleasant Bay,
the Wequassett is an informally upscale resort. An attentive staff, evening entertainment, fun in the sun, and golf at the exclusive Cape Cod
National Golf Club are just a few of the benefits you can count on at
Wequassett. Chef Bill Brodsky's creative globally inspired cuisine graces
the menus of the three restaurants—the star being the sophisticated 28
Atlantic, one of the top destination restaurants on the Cape. After a
day at the beach or on the links, retire to your spacious room and relax
amid fresh pine furniture, floral bedcovers or handmade quilts, and
overflowing window boxes. **Pros:** waterfront setting; activities and programs for all ages; babysitting services. **Cons:** rates are very steep; not

an in-town location. ✉ *2173 Orleans Rd. (Rte. 28)* ☎ *508/432–5400 or 800/225–7125* ⊕ *www.wequassett.com* 🗘 *115 rooms, 7 suites* ⚹ *In-room: a/c. In-hotel: 3 restaurants, room service, bar, tennis courts, pool, gym, water sports, children's programs (ages 4–12)* ⊟ *AE, D, DC, MC, V* ☽ *Closed Nov.–Mar.* ☉|*FAP.*

$$$$ ⊞ **Winstead Inn and Beach Resort.** Comprising two distinct properties, the
★   Winstead Inn and Beach Resort offer a two-for-one Cape Cod experience. Harking back to an earlier era, the airy, attractive Beach Resort sits on a private beach overlooking Nantucket Sound. You can gaze at the sweep of coast and surrounding grasslands while enjoying a generous Continental breakfast from rockers and umbrella tables on the deck and wraparound porches. At the other end of the spectrum, the Winstead Inn sits along a quiet street on the edge of downtown. Greenery surrounds this Gothic Victorian house, and many of the rooms have a view of the heated, saltwater outdoor pool, a real oasis with potted palms, fountains, and flowers. **Pros:** most rooms have water views; spacious, elegant rooms. **Cons:** numerous stairs; not for those on a budget. ✉ *114 Parallel St.* ✉ *4 Braddock La., Harwich Port* ☎ *508/432–4444 or 800/870–4405* ⊕ *www.winsteadinn.com* 🗘 *18 rooms, 4 suites* ⚹ *In-room: a/c, Wi-Fi. In-hotel: pool* ⊟ *D, MC, V* ☽ *Closed Nov.–Easter* ☉| *CP.*

NIGHTLIFE AND THE ARTS

THE ARTS
Harwich Junior Theatre (✉ *105 Division St., West Harwich* ☎ *508/432–2002* ⊕ *www.hjtcapecod.org*) gives theater classes for kids year-round and presents 12 family-oriented productions.

NIGHTLIFE
The **Hot Stove Saloon** (✉ *551 Main St. [Rte. 28], Harwich Port* ☎ *508/432–9911* ⊕ *www.hotstovesaloon.com*) is a convivial spot for tasty pub fare and a wide selection of beers and cocktails. The baseball-themed tavern also airs sporting events on TV.

Irish Pub (✉ *126 Main St. [Rte. 28], West Harwich* ☎ *508/432–8808* ⊕ *www.capecodsirishpub.com*) has dancing to bands—playing Irish, American, and dance music—as well as sing-alongs, pool, darts, and sports TV.

Jake Rooney's (✉ *119 Brooks Rd., off Rte. 28, Harwich Port* ☎ *508/430–1100* ⊕ *www.jakerooneys.com*) is a comfortable watering hole. Live entertainment three nights a week make it a fun place to hang out with friends.

Wequassett Inn Resort & Golf Club (✉ *173 Orleans Rd. [Rte. 28], Pleasant Bay* ☎ *508/432–5400*) has live jazz at 8 on Tuesday and Wednesday evening from July through Labor Day. Best of all, it's free.

BEACHES, SPORTS, AND THE OUTDOORS

BASEBALL

The **Harwich Mariners** (⊠ *Harwich High School, Oak St.* ☎ *508/432–2000* ⊕ *www.harwichmariners.org*) of the collegiate Cape Cod Baseball League, play home games at Whitehouse Field on Oak Street from mid-June through mid-August.

BEACHES

Harwich has 21 beaches, more than any other Cape town, though not all are accessible by car. Parking lots are available at Bank Street, Atlantic Avenue, Earle Road, and Red River beaches. Most of the ocean beaches are on Nantucket Sound, where the water is a bit calmer and warmer. Freshwater pond beaches are also abundant.

Nonresident beach parking stickers, sold at the **Harwich Community Center** (⊠ *100 Oak St.* ☎ *508/432–7638*), cost $55 for one week, and $125 for the season, which runs from June through Labor Day. Ask for the free map of the town's beaches when you get your sticker.

BICYCLING

The **Bike Depot** (⊠ *500 Depot St.* ☎ *508/430–4375*) has rentals, including some antique bikes. It's in North Harwich, right off the bike trail.

BOATING

Whether you're in the mood to sail under the moonlight, hire a private charter, or learn to navigate yourself, **Cape Sail** (⊠ *337 Saquatucket Harbor, off Rte. 28, Harwich Port* ☎ *508/896–2730* ⊕ *www.capesail.com*) can accommodate any whim.

Nauti Jane's (⊠ *Off Rte. 28 at Wequassett Inn, East Harwich* ☎ *508/430–6893* ⊕ *www.nautijanesboatrentals.com*) has Day Sailers, powerboats, paddleboards, or peaceful kayaks for rent.

FISHING

Sign up for casting lessons (fly-fishing is the specialty), take a guided fishing charter, or just talk shop with the folks at **Fishing the Cape** (*Harwich Commons, 120 Rte. 137* ☎ *508/432–1200* ⊕ *www.fishingthecape.com*).

Take a six-hour trip with **Fishtale Sportfishing** (⊠ *Saquatucket Harbor, Harwich Port* ☎ *508/432–3783* ⊕ *www.fishtalesportfishing.com*) to look for bluefish, striped bass, and tuna.

The **Yankee** (⊠ *Saquatucket Harbor, Harwich Port* ☎ *508/432–2520* ⊕ *www.capecodtravel.com/yankeefishing*) invites passengers in search of fluke, scup, sea bass, and tautog aboard the 65-foot party boat. Two trips depart daily Monday through Saturday in season; there's also one on Sunday. Reservations are recommended.

GOLF

Cranberry Valley Golf Course (⊠ *183 Oak St.* ☎ *508/430–5234* ⊕ *www.cranberrygolfcourse.com*) has a championship layout of 18 well-groomed holes surrounded by cranberry bogs.

Harwich Port Golf Club (⊠ *51 South St., Harwich Port* ☎ *508/432–0250* ⊕ *www.harwichportgolf.com*) has a 9-hole course that's great for beginners.

SHOPPING

820 Main Gallery (⊠ *820 Main St., Harwich Port* ☎ *508/430–7622*) sells original works in oil, acrylics, watercolors, and photography, as well as limited-edition prints by established local artists. The gallery specializes in regional land- and seascapes.

Cape Cod Braided Rug Co. (⊠ *537 Rte. 28, Harwich Port* ☎ *508/432– 3133*) makes braided rugs in all colors, styles, and sizes.

★ **Cape Cod Lavender Farm** (⊠ *Corner of Rte. 124 and Weston Woods Rd., off U.S. 6, Exit 10* ☎ *508/432–8397* ⊕ *www.capecodlavenderfarm. com*) consists of some 14,000 lavender plants, making it one of the largest such farms on the East Coast. Harvesttime (best for visits) is usually around late June and July, when you'll see acres and acres of stunning purple waves. The farm sells soaps and bath salts, candles, potpourri, marmalade, lemonade, and many other lavender-infused goods. Keep your eyes peeled for their sign (on the right) as you're driving south on Route 124—it's easy to miss.

Cedar Spring Herb Farm (⊠ *159 Long Pond Dr.* ☎ *508/430–4372* ⊕ *www. cedarspringherbfarm.com*) spreads out over 7 acres of walking trails, picnic areas, and fragrant, lush herb gardens. The emphasis here is on health, both of the spiritual and physical sort. There is a full schedule of lectures, classes, and events. The farm is open from May to November.

The **Potted Geranium** (⊠ *188 Main St., West Harwich* ☎ *508/432–1114*) stocks country-inspired home-related gifts, including colorful wind flags, handcrafted items, and wind chimes.

CHATHAM

Low-key, well-heeled Chatham feels like a sliver of Nantucket that's floated over to the Cape. It's neatly groomed and blue-blooded yet artsy, prim but eccentric, straight-arrow but with loads of personality. Originally populated by Native Americans, Chatham came into the hands of white settlers from Plymouth in 1656, when William Nickerson traded a boat for the 17 square mi of land that make up the town. In 1712 the area separated from Eastham and was incorporated as a town; the surnames of the Pilgrims who first settled here still dominate the census list. Although Chatham was originally a farming community, the sea finally lured townspeople to turn to fishing for their livelihood, and the industry has held strong to this day.

At the bent elbow of the Cape, with water nearly surrounding it, Chatham has all the charm of a quietly posh seaside resort, with plenty of shops but none of the crass commercialism that plagues some other towns on the Cape. And it's charming: the town has gray-shingle houses with tidy awnings and cheerful flower gardens, an attractive Main Street with crafts and antiques stores alongside dapper cafés, and a five-and-dime. It's a traditional town (said to have more registered Republican voters than any other town on Cape Cod), where elegant summer cottages share the view with stately homes rich in Yankee architectural detail. In fact, this tiny town by the sea is where you'll find some of the finest examples of bow-roof houses in the country. Chatham's nowhere near as kitschy as Provincetown, but it's not overly quaint, either—it's casual and fun, in a refined New England way.

Because of its location at the elbow, Chatham is not a town you just pass through—it's a destination in itself. During summer months, the town bursts into bloom as hydrangeas blossom in shades of cobalt blue, indigo, and deep violet. And although it can get crowded in high season—and even on weekends during shoulder seasons—Chatham remains a true New England village.

> ### ROUGH NEIGHBORHOOD
>
> Chatham's position on the confluence of Nantucket Sound and the Atlantic Ocean makes the town especially vulnerable to the destructive wrath of stormy seas. Many a home and beachfront have been lost to the tumultuous waters. But like any stalwart New England character, Chatham will continue to hold on to its fortunes, its past, and its future.

GETTING HERE AND AROUND

Route 28 is the main road leading to Chatham, though at the beginning of downtown there is a rotary that abruptly sweeps the road northward on its way to Orleans; continue straight toward Main Street and all its shops and restaurants.

ESSENTIALS

Visitor Information Chatham Chamber of Commerce (✉ *533 Main St., Chatham* ☎ *508/945–5199 or 800/715–5567* ⊕ *www.chathaminfo.com*).

EXPLORING

TOP ATTRACTIONS

★ **Atwood House Museum.** Built by sea captain Joseph C. Atwood in 1752, this museum has a gambrel roof, variable-width floor planks, fireplaces, an old kitchen with a wide hearth and a beehive oven, and some antique dolls and toys. The New Gallery displays portraits of local sea captains. The Joseph C. Lincoln Room has the manuscripts, first editions, and mementos of the Chatham writer, and there is an antique-tool room in the basement. The 1974 Durand Wing has collections of seashells from around the world and threaded Sandwich glass, as well as Parian-ware figures, unglazed porcelain vases, figurines, and busts. In a remodeled freight shed are the stunning and provocative murals (1932–45) by Alice Stallknecht Wight portraying religious scenes in Chatham settings. On the grounds are an herb garden, the old turret and lens from the Chatham Light, and a simple camp house rescued from eroding North Beach. ✉ *347 Stage Harbor Rd., West Chatham* ☎ *508/945–2493* ⊕ *www.chathamhistoricalsociety.org* ✆ *$5* ☉ *Mid-June–Oct., Tues.–Sat. 1–4; July and Aug., Tues.–Sat. 10–4.*

★ **Chatham Light.** The view from this lighthouse—of the harbor, the sandbars, and the ocean beyond—justifies the crowds. The lighthouse is especially dramatic on a foggy night, as the beacon's light pierces the mist. Coin-operated telescopes allow a close look at the famous

"Chatham Break," the result of a fierce 1987 nor'easter that blasted a channel through a barrier beach just off the coast. The U.S. Coast Guard auxiliary, which supervises the lighthouse, offers free tours April through October on most Wednesdays. The lighthouse is also open on three special occasions during the year: Seafest, an annual tribute to the maritime industry held in mid-October; mid-May's Cape Cod Maritime Week; and June's Cape Heritage Week; otherwise, this working lighthouse is off-limits. There is free but limited parking in front of the lighthouse facing the beach: the 30-minute time limit is closely monitored. ⊠ *Main St. near Bridge St., West Chatham.*

Fish Pier. When Chatham's fishing fleet returns, sometime between noon and 2 PM daily, this pier bustles with activity. The unloading of the boats is a big local event, drawing crowds who watch it all from an observation deck. From their fishing grounds 3 to 100 mi offshore, fishermen bring in haddock, cod, flounder, lobster, halibut, and pollack, which are packed in ice and shipped to New York and Boston or sold at the fish market here. Also here is *The Provider,* a monument to the town's fishing industry, showing a hand pulling a fish-filled net from the sea. If you can be patient with the long lines coming out of the tiny Chatham Pier Fish Market, they serve up some of the finest lobster rolls (loads of meat) and fish sandwiches. ⊠ *Shore Rd. and Barcliff Ave., North Chatham.*

Fodor's Choice
★
Monomoy National Wildlife Refuge. This 2,500-acre preserve includes the Monomoy Islands, a fragile 9-mi-long barrier-beach area south of Chatham. Monomoy's North and South islands were created when a storm divided the former Monomoy Island in 1978. A haven for bird-watchers, the refuge is an important stop along the North Atlantic Flyway for migratory waterfowl and shorebirds—peak migration times are May and late July. It also provides nesting and resting grounds for 285 species, including gulls—great black-backed, herring, and laughing—and several tern species. White-tailed deer wander the islands, and harbor and gray seals frequent the shores in winter. The only structure on the islands is the **South Monomoy Lighthouse,** built in 1849.

Monomoy is a quiet, peaceful place of sand and beach grass, tidal flats, dunes, marshes, freshwater ponds, thickets of bayberry and beach plum, and a few pines. Because the refuge harbors several endangered species, activities are limited. Certain areas are fenced off to protect nesting areas of terns and the threatened piping plover. In season, the **Rip Ryder** (☎ *508/945–5450* ⊕ *www.monomoyislandferry.com*) leads for bird- or seal-watching tours. **Monomoy Island Excursions** (☎ *508/430–7772* ⊕ *www.monomoyislandexcursions.com*) offers seal and seabird tours and boat trips out around Monomoy Island on a 43-foot high-speed catamaran. **Outermost Adventures** (☎ *508/945–5858* ⊕ *www.outermostharbor.com*) provides water-taxi services to Monomoy Island and offers fishing, birding, and seal-watching cruises.

Monomoy National Wildlife Refuge Headquarters. On the misleadingly named Morris Island (it's connected to the mainland) is a visitor center and bookstore where you can pick up pamphlets on the birds, wildlife, and flora and fauna found on the Monomoy Islands. A ¾-mi

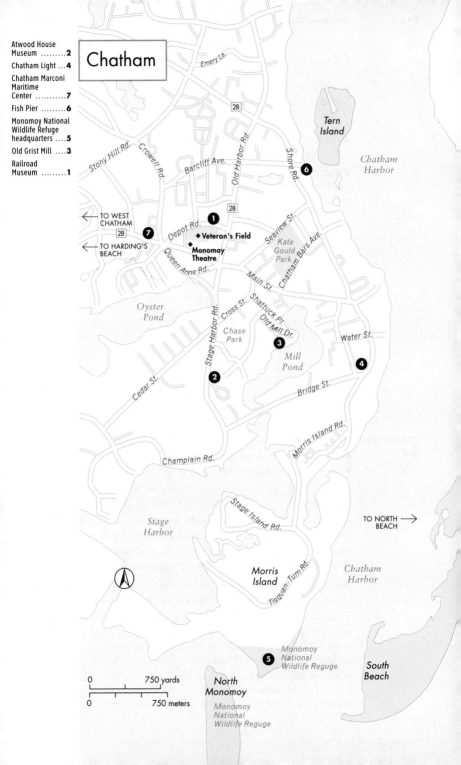

Chatham

Emery La.

28

Tern
Island

Chatham
Harbor

Stony Hill Rd.

Crowell Rd.

Barcliff Ave.

Old Harbor Rd.

Shore Rd.

6

28

TO WEST
CHATHAM

28

7

Depot Rd.

1

♦ Veteran's Field

♦ Monomoy
Theatre

Seaview St.

Kate
Gould
Park

Chatham Bars Ave.

TO HARDING'S
BEACH

Queen Anne Rd.

Oyster
Pond

Main St.

Stage Harbor Rd.

Cross St.

Shattuck Pl.

Chase
Park

Old Mill Dr.

3

Water St.

Mill
Pond

4

Cedar St.

2

Bridge St.

Morris Island Rd.

Champlain Rd.

Stage
Harbor

Stage Island Rd.

TO NORTH
BEACH →

Morris
Island

Tisquan-Tum Rd.

Chatham
Harbor

5

Monomoy
National
Wildlife Reguge

South
Beach

North
Monomoy

0   750 yards

0   750 meters

Monomoy
National
Wildlife Reguge

interpretive walking trail around Morris Island, closed at high tide, gives a good view of the refuge and the surrounding waters. ⊠ *Off Morris Island Rd., Morris Island* ☎ *508/945–0594* ⊕ *www.fws.gov/ northeast/monomoy* 🎫 *Free* ⊘ *Mon.—Sat., 8–4; call for winter hrs.*

🔄 **Railroad Museum.** In a restored 1887 depot, this museum include a walk-through 1910 New York Central caboose, old photographs, equipment, thousands of train models, and a diorama of the 1915 Chatham rail yards. ⊠ *153 Depot Rd., West Chatham* ☎ *No phone* 🎫 *Free* ⊘ *Mid-June–mid-Sept., Tues.–Sat. 10–4.*

WORTH NOTING

Chatham Glass Company. Known for their artful contemporary treatment of blown glass, Jim Holmes and Deborah Doane create everything from candleholders to vases in a vast spectrum of colors. You can watch them perform the fascinating process of glassblowing. ⊠ *758 Main St.* ☎ *508/945–5547* ⊕ *www.chathamglass.com* 🎫 *Free* ⊘ *Late May–early Sept., Mon.–Sat. 10–5; early Sept.–late May, daily 10–5.*

Chatham Marconi Maritime Center. This interesting museum sits on the original site of Guglielmo Marconi's Chatham Station Center, which overlooks Ryder Cove. The museum occupies a handsome brick build-ing from 1914 and focuses on the history of 20th-century wireless operators, beginning with Marconi. ⊠ *847 Rte. 28, North Chatham* ☎ *508/945–8889* ⊕ *www.chathammarconi.org* 🎫 *$3* ⊘ *Late June–early Sept., Tues.–Sat. 10–4, Sun. 1–4.*

Eldredge Public Library. This library has a special genealogy department (open Tuesday, Thursday, and Saturday 1—5) as well as story times for kids, book-discussion groups, and special programs and lectures. ⊠ *564 Main St.* ☎ *508/945–5170* ⊕ *www.eldredgelibrary.org* 🎫 *Free* ⊘ *Mon., Wed., Fri., and Sat. 10–5; Tues. and Thurs. 1–9.*

▌QUICK
BITES

If you're looking for a fat and fancy sandwich, a morning bagel, or an after-noon cappuccino pick-me-up, stop in at the Chatham Village Cafe (⊠ 400 Main St. ☎ 508/945–2525). Eat inside at one of the few tables for some good street-side people-watching, or head over to the Village Green for an impromptu picnic. Head to Buffy's (⊠ 456 Main St. ☎ 508/945–5990) for Chatham's finest (and only homemade) ice cream. You can nosh on your cone at one of the tables set along the lawn outside. Don't overlook the fresh-squeezed lime rickeys and tangy smoothies. Carmine's (⊠ 595 Main St. ☎ 508/945–5300) serves great New York–style pizza (by the slice or the pie). There are just a handful of tables inside this storefront eatery, also an excellent source for grinders and mouthwatering gelato.

Mill Pond. A lovely place to stop for a picnic, Mill Pond has fishing from the 19th-century wooden drawbridge. You'll often see bullrakers at work, plying the pond's muddy bottom with 20-foot rakes in search of shellfish. ⊠ *Bridge St. off Main St.*

Old Grist Mill. One of a number of windmills still on the Cape, the Old Grist Mill was built in 1797 by Colonel Benjamin Godfrey for grind-ing corn. How practical the mill actually was is a matter of debate:

for it to work properly, a wind speed of at least 20 MPH was necessary, but winds more than 25 MPH required the miller to reef the sails or to quit grinding altogether. The mill was moved to its present location in 1956. ⊠ *Old Mill Dr. near Mill Pond* ☏ *No phone* 🖅 *Free* ☉ *July and Aug., weekdays 10–3.*

Stage Harbor. Sheltered by Morris Island, Stage Harbor is where Samuel de Champlain anchored in 1606. The street on its north side is, not surprisingly, called Champlain Road. A skirmish here between Europeans and Native Americans marked the first bloodshed in New England between native people and colonial settlers. ⊠ *Stage Harbor Rd.*

WHERE TO EAT

$$ ✕ **Campari's Bistro.** It's just a short drive north of downtown, toward
ITALIAN Pleasant Bay, to reach this reliable spot known for good regional Italian fare. The softly lighted dining room has large and comfy booths and wood paneling. You can also dine in the more casual tavern, which has a children's menu. Nice starters include lemon-poached shrimp wrapped in prosciutto, and crab cakes with creole mustard aioli. Seafood Florentine and veal-and-spinach-stuffed cannelloni rank among the better entrées, but the wood-fired thin-crust pizzas steal the show here. ⊠ *323 Orleans Rd. (Rte. 28), North Chatham* ☏ *508/945–9123* ⊕ *www.camparis.com* ▤ *AE, D, DC, MC, V* ☉ *No lunch.*

$$ ✕ **Chatham Squire.** You can't go wrong by ordering anything local from
SEAFOOD the long list of tried-and-true American standbys. The fish is as fresh and good as you get on Cape Cod, and the kitchen continues to innovate while still remaining true to its Cape roots. The calamari is always tender, the New England smoked-fish plate is delicious, and the clam chowder is a must. Expect a long wait in season, in which case you can visit the bar and pick up on the local gossip. A Fodors.com reader advises, "Go early, as this terrific place fills up fast on the weekends." ⊠ *487 Main St.* ☏ *508/945–0945* ⊕ *www.thesquire.com* ⌕ *Reservations not accepted* ▤ *AE, D, MC, V.*

$$$ ✕ **Del Mar Bar & Bistro.** This restaurant's stylish, art deco interior is far,
ECLECTIC far away from its former life as a Friendly's franchise. The fanciful cocktails, intriguing menu, and daily blackboard specials make this a popular Chatham spot. The thin-crust pizzas—try balsamic fig puree and prosciutto with goat cheese and toasted almonds—come piping hot out of the ever-glowing wood-fired oven. Other dishes get a subtle and pleasing smokiness from the fire, including the Wellfleet oysters Rockefeller, and the roasted Chatham cod topped with basil and pine nut pesto. Try the grilled New Zealand rack of lamb marinated in Moroccan spices with eggplant fries and minted yogurt. ⊠ *907 Rte. 28* ☏ *508/945–9988* ⊕ *www.delmarbistro.com* ⌕ *Reservations not accepted* ▤ *D, MC, V* ☉ *No lunch.*

$$$ ✕ **Impudent Oyster.** A cozy, festive tavern with an unfailingly cheerful
SEAFOOD staff and superb but reasonably priced seafood, this always-packed res-
★ taurant sits inside a dapper house just off Main Street. It's a great place for a romantic meal or dinner with the kids, and the menu offers light burgers and sandwiches as well as more-substantial fare. The mussels

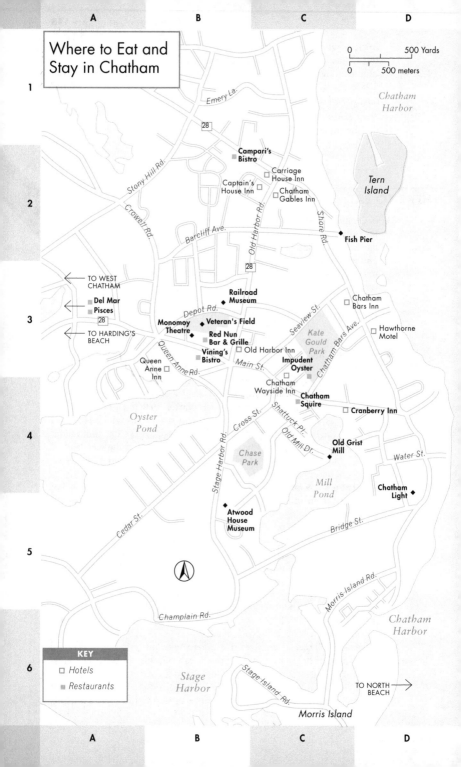

Where to Eat and Stay in Chatham

A   **B**   **C**   **D**

0   500 Yards

0   500 meters

Chatham Harbor

Emery La.

28

Tern Island

Stony Hill Rd.

Crowell Rd.

Campari's Bistro

Carriage House Inn

Captain's House Inn

Chatham Gables Inn

Old Harbor Rd.

Shore Rd.

Barcliff Ave.

Fish Pier

28

TO WEST CHATHAM

Del Mar

Pisces

28

TO HARDING'S BEACH

Depot Rd.

Railroad Museum

Monomoy Theatre

Veteran's Field

Red Nun Bar & Grille

Old Harbor Inn

Vining's Bistro

Queen Anne Rd.

Queen Anne Inn

Main St.

Seaview St.

Kate Gould Park

Impudent Oyster

Chatham Bars Inn

Chatham Bars Ave.

Hawthorne Motel

Chatham Wayside Inn

Chatham Squire

Cranberry Inn

Stage Harbor Rd.

Cross St.

Shattuck Pl.

Old Mill Dr.

Chase Park

Old Grist Mill

Water St.

Mill Pond

Chatham Light

Atwood House Museum

Bridge St.

Cedar St.

Champlain Rd.

Morris Island Rd.

Chatham Harbor

KEY

☐ *Hotels*

▪ *Restaurants*

Stage Harbor

Stage Island Rd.

TO NORTH BEACH →

Morris Island

A   **B**   **C**   **D**

1

2

3

4

5

6

with white-wine sauce is a local favorite. The dining room is split-level, with a bar in back. There's not a ton of seating, so reserve on weekends. ⊠ *15 Chatham Bars Ave.* ☎ *508/945–3545* ▤ *AE, MC, V.*

$$$
SEAFOOD
Fodor's Choice
★

✕**Pisces.** An intimate dining room inside a simple yellow house, Pisces serves coastal-inspired fare. If it swims in local waters, you can probably sample it here. A rich chowder of lobster, white truffle oil, and corn is a terrific way to start your meal. Move on to Mediterranean-style fisherman's stew in saffron-lobster broth, or local cod with lemon-caper aioli. Complement your dinner with a selection from the extensive wine list, which offers more than 20 vintages by the glass. ⊠ *2653 Main St., South Chatham* ☎ *508/432–4600* ⊕ *www.piscesofchatham.com* ▤ *D, MC, V* ⊗ *Closed mid-Oct.–Mar. No lunch.*

$
AMERICAN

✕**Red Nun Bar & Grille.** It's easy to find this vibrant red restaurant as you're heading toward Harwich Port. Inside this diminutive and friendly pub you'll find nothing fancy—just a few tried-and-true favorites like New England clam chowder, stuffed quahogs, basic salads, a great half-pound burger, and hefty, hot sandwiches. For something a little different, try the fish tacos, made with local cod. For dinner selections, check out the mixed grill, which changes daily. Blackboard specials for lunch and dinner are numerous and varied, the food is satisfying, and the prices are reasonable. ⊠ *746 Main St.* ☎ *508/348–0469* ⊕ *www.rednun.com* ▤ *AE, D, MC, V.*

$$$
ECLECTIC

✕**Vining's Bistro.** An exceptionally inventive menu and a determination not to rest on its laurels make this restaurant a standout. The wood grill infuses many dishes with a distinctive flavor heightened further by the chef's use of zesty rubs and spices from all over the globe. The Thai-style crab cakes come with a sharp chili-cucumber vinaigrette, and pan-seared sea scallops are served with apple bacon, mixed mushrooms, and caramelized red-onion confit. The restaurant is upstairs at the Gallery Building, and many windows look out on the art below. Despite the casual atmosphere, this is not a place to bring the kids. ⊠ *595 Main St.* ☎ *508/945–5033* ⌦ *Reservations not accepted* ▤ *AE, MC, V* ⊗ *Closed Jan.–mid-Apr.*

WHERE TO STAY

$$$–$$$$
★

▦**Captain's House Inn.** A Victorian tile ceiling, wide-board floors, and elaborate moldings and wainscoting are just part of what makes Jill and James Meyer's inn one of the Cape's most popular. Each room has its own personality; some are quite large, and all have fireplaces. The Hiram Harding Room, in the bow-roof Captain's Cottage, has 200-year-old hand-hewn ceiling beams, a wall of raised walnut paneling, and a large, central working fireplace. Suites in the former stables are spacious and have hot tubs, fireplaces, TV–DVDs, mini-refrigerators, and private patios or balconies. A young staff of European hospitality students serves an over-the-top full breakfast each morning and high tea in the afternoon. The herb and flower gardens and neatly trimmed lawns are stunning. **Pros:** elegant lodging in authentic historic setting; beautiful grounds ideal for croquet (accoutrements provided); pampered service. **Cons:** many rooms accessed via steep stairs; not an in-town or beach-front location. ⊠ *369 Old Harbor Rd.* ☎ *508/945–0127 or 800/315–*

0728   ⊕ *www.captainshouseinn.*
com ⊏⊅ *12 rooms, 4 suites* ⌂ *In-*
room: a/c, DVD, refrigerator
(some), DVD, Wi-Fi. In-hotel:
pool, gym, laundry service, no kids
under 10 ☐ *AE, D, MC, V* ⊺◎⎮ *BP.*

WORD OF MOUTH

"Chatham Bars Inn is one of my favorite hotels in the world. The main dining room is like a trip back in time: imagine yourself as a first class passenger on an Atlantic crossing in 1910. and the food is very good too." —seafox

$$$–$$$$ 🖼 **Carriage House Inn.** Innkeepers
   ★   Paula and Tim Miller have brought
a sense of fresh, beach-resort ele-
gance to this aged inn just outside
Chatham's town center. Rooms
throughout the inn are a blend of contemporary with a distinct Cape
Cod feel; walls are painted in soothing hues of cream, soft blues, and
greens, and each is blessedly uncluttered with unnecessary frills. The
former stables contain three larger and more secluded rooms with high-
pitched ceilings, fireplaces, and French or sliding-glass doors leading
to private outdoor areas. Paula brings her extensive spa experience
to the mix; you can indulge in an array of luxury treatments in the
privacy of your room. Each morning a delicious full breakfast begins
the day, which might include Tim's special blueberry French toast with
strawberry salsa. The beach is a mile away. **Pros:** beautifully appointed,
spacious rooms; added decadence of in-house spa services; ample and
well-maintained grounds; romantic and intimate setting. **Cons:** near a
busy intersection though still quiet; long walk to town; no water views
or beachfront. ⊠ *407 Old Harbor Rd.* ☎ *508/945–4688 or 800/355–*
8868 ⊕ *www.thecarriagehouseinn.com* ⊏⊅ *6 rooms* ⌂ *In-room: a/c, no*
phone, DVD, Wi-Fi (some). In-hotel: Wi-Fi hotspot, no kids under 10
☐ *MC, V* ⊘ *Closed Mar.* ⊺◎⎮ *BP.*

$$$$ 🖼 **Chatham Bars Inn.** Overlooking Pleasant Bay from atop a windswept
   ★   bluff, Chatham Bars Inn is a grande-dame hotel that has long been one
of the Cape's most coveted retreats. The ground-floor lobby gives way
to the formal restaurant on one side and a porch-fronted lounge on
the other. Elegant guest rooms in the resort's main inn, and multiple
buildings and cottages spread far and wide are filled with hand-painted
furnishings by local artists and colorful fabrics depicting sunny seaside
scenes. Adding to the well-heeled flavor of the inn is an additional
massive spa complex, complete with a 4,000-square-foot hydrother-
apy pool. If you'd like to be as close as possible to this pampering
palace, you can stay in one of the lavishly appointed suites within the
new space. **Pros:** serene ocean views; well-appointed rooms; plenty of
activities for all ages. **Cons:** not an in-town location; rates are fairly
steep. ⊠ *297 Shore Rd.* ☎ *508/945–0096 or 800/527–4884* ⊕ *www.*
chathambarsinn.com ⊏⊅ *149 rooms, 68 suites* ⌂ *In-room: DVD, Wi-Fi.*
In-hotel: 4 restaurants, bar, tennis courts, pools, gym, spa, beachfront,
children's programs (ages 4–14) ☐ *AE, D, MC, V.*

$$$–$$$$ 🖼 **Chatham Gables Inn.** Released from the excessive trappings of decades
Fodor'sChoice   of overzealous decoration, this 1839 former sea captain's home now
   ★   shines in all its original glory. New owners Brian Dougherty and Nick
Robert embarked on a full-scale renovation; now revealed is the simple
beauty of 19th-century craftsmanship in gleaming wide-plank floors,

and graceful molding and wainscoting. Original old maps dating from the home's era are framed in the dining room, and aside from the addition of carefully chosen antiques and artwork, the inn is refreshingly uncluttered. White Matouk luxury linens make up every bed, while designer fabrics add color on upholstered chairs, headboards, and pillows; several rooms have working fireplaces and private entrances. Eager and gracious hosts, Brian and Nick are very knowledgeable and on hand to make dinner reservations, schedule an in-room massage, or help you best plan your visit. Bountiful breakfasts are served on the enclosed porch. This inn is truly the embodiment of understated elegance. **Pros:** exquisite historic lodging; 10-minute walk to town and beach; exceptional service. **Cons:** not a waterfront location; not for those traveling with small children. ⊠ *364 Old Harbor Rd.* ☎ *508/945–5859* ⊕ *www.chathamgablesinn.com* ⊅ *7 rooms* ⌂ *In-room: a/c, no phone, DVD (on request), Wi-Fi. In-hotel: Wi-Fi hotspot, no kids under 10* ⊟ *D, DC, MC, V* ⍣ *BP.*

$$$$ 🖵**Chatham Wayside Inn.** Once a stop on a turn-of-the-20th-century stagecoach route, this venerable inn is still an oasis for weary travelers. Everything is crisp and colorful here, from the floral comforters and wallpapers to freshly painted walls and bright carpeting. Some rooms have balconies, fireplaces, and hot tubs. With a great location smack-dab in the center of town, you may not have to leave your room to hear the sounds of the weekly town-band concerts. The restaurant serves reliable contemporary American fare and a very good Sunday brunch. Guests staying in the spring and fall seasons can enjoy a complimentary Continental breakfast with their room rate. **Pros:** right in the center of town; many amenities and services; spacious and efficient rooms. **Cons:** not for those seeking authentic historic lodging—more of an upscale feel than an old inn; no water views or beachfront. ⊠ *512 Main St.* ☎ *508/945–5550 or 800/242–8426* ⊕ *www.waysideinn.com* ⊅ *56 rooms* ⌂ *In-room: a/c, DVD, Wi-Fi. In-hotel: restaurant, pool, gym* ⊟ *D, MC, V* ⍣ *Closed Jan.*

$$$–$$$$ 🖵**Cranberry Inn.** This grand 1830s inn is a short walk east of the commercial span of Main Street, near the heart of downtown—but it has a protected marsh in its backyard. Billed as the oldest continuously operating lodging establishment in Chatham, the inn is filled with antique and reproduction furniture, plus handmade quilts, braided rugs, and other homey touches. The 18 rooms and suites come in a wide variety of shapes and sizes, some of them accommodating as many as six guests. Several rooms have fireplaces, wet bars, and private balconies. Breakfast, which is also available to the public by reservation, is served in a lovely dining room that doubles as the setting for an informal afternoon tea with delicious sweets and treats. An intimate pub with a wood-burning fireplace has a full liquor license and is open to the public. On hot days you can cool off on the great big north-facing veranda overlooking Main Street. **Pros:** fine location and an easy walk to town center; spacious rooms, many with fireplaces for chilly nights; gym privileges at local club (fee). **Cons:** no water views or beachfront; not for those traveling with young children. ⊠ *359 Main St.* ☎ *508/945–9232 or 800/332–4667* ⊕ *www.cranberryinn.com*

15 rooms, 3 suites ⚿ *In-room: Wi-Fi. In-hotel: bar, no kids under 12* ⊟ *AE, D, MC, V* ⦶ *BP.*

$$$–$$$$ ⊡ **Hawthorne Motel.** Beyond the Hawthorne Motel's modest roadside
★ appearance extends a private beach overlooking Pleasant Bay, the
Atlantic, and Chatham Harbor. Nearly all the rooms have stunning
water views. Choose from spotless, no-nonsense, simply decorated
motel rooms or kitchenette efficiency units with small refrigerators,
two heating plates, and a countertop-sink work area. There's also a
two-bedroom cottage (rented by the week in season) with full kitchen
and a separate living-dining room, plus amenities such as a DVD player
and an outdoor grill. Down at the beach is a fire pit with plenty of wood
on hand. You'll find fresh-brewed coffee and complimentary morn-
ing newspapers in the lobby. **Pros:** supreme waterfront location (most
rooms have direct views); easy access to nearby attractions and activi-
ties; pretty reasonable for the area. **Cons:** rooms are pretty standard
motel fare though clean and comfortable; a 10- to 15-minute walk to
town center. ⊠ *196 Shore Rd.* ☎ *508/945–0372* ⊕ *www.thehawthorne.
com* *16 rooms, 10 efficiencies, 1 cottage* ⚿ *In-room: a/c, kitchen
(some), refrigerator, Wi-Fi. In-hotel: Wi-Fi hotspot* ⊟ *AE, MC, V*
⦸ *Closed mid-Oct.–mid-May.*

$$$–$$$$ ⊡ **Old Harbor Inn.** Congenial, thoughtful hosts Ray and Judith Braz
run this cheery B&B set inside a 1930s colonial-revival house a few
steps from Main Street and downtown shopping. You'll receive plenty
of extras and treats, from in-room snack baskets and extensive com-
plimentary bath products to hair dryers and fluffy robes. Most rooms
feel distinctly Victorian in flavor—the cozy yet spacious Port Fortune
room has exposed beams, pitched ceilings, white wicker furniture, and
Laura Ashley linens. If it's luxury you're after, book the Stage Harbor
Suite, which has a two-person Jacuzzi and separate shower. Relax out
back on the deck or in the verdant, shaded garden. **Pros:** quick walk
to center of town; well-appointed rooms; plenty of amenities. **Cons:**
not a beachfront location. ⊠ *22 Old Harbor Rd.* ☎ *508/945–4434 or
800/942–4434* ⊕ *www.chathamoldharborinn.com* *9 rooms, 1 suite*
⚿ *In-room: a/c, DVD, no phone, refrigerator, Wi-Fi. In-hotel: gym,
Wi-Fi hotspot, no kids under 12* ⊟ *MC, V* ⦶ *BP.*

$$$–$$$$ ⊡ **Queen Anne Inn.** Built in 1840 as a wedding present for the daughter
★ of a famous clipper-ship captain, the Queen Anne first opened as an
inn in 1874. Some of the large guest rooms have hand-painted murals,
working fireplaces, balconies, and hot tubs. Lingering and lounging are
encouraged—around the large heated outdoor pool, at the tables on
the veranda, in front of the fireplace in the sitting room, or in the plush
parlor. A licensed massage therapist is on hand, should you wish to
indulge in a treatment. The Eldredge Room (closed January–April, no
lunch) offers dishes like seared Chatham cod on parsnip puree. Unlike
many historic inns, this one is very welcoming to traveling families.
Pros: spacious rooms; historic setting. **Cons:** long walk to the town
center; some steep stairs. ⊠ *70 Queen Anne Rd.* ☎ *508/945–0394 or
800/545–4667* ⊕ *www.queenanneinn.com* *33 rooms* ⚿ *In-room: a/c,
Wi-Fi (some). In-hotel: restaurant, bar, gym, pool, spa, Wi-Fi hotspot*
⊟ *AE, D, MC, V* ⦸ *Closed Jan.–Mar.*

NIGHTLIFE AND THE ARTS

THE ARTS

Chatham Drama Guild (⊠ *134 Crowell Rd.* ☎ *508/945–0510* ⊕ *www. chathamdramaguild.org*) stages productions year-round, including musicals, comedies, and dramas.

The **Creative Arts Center** (⊠ *154 Crowell Rd.* ☎ *508/945–3583* ⊕ *www. capecodcreativearts.org*) thrives year-round with classes, changing gallery exhibitions, demonstrations, lectures, and other activities.

From late June to early September, the **Guild of Chatham Painters** presents an outdoor art gallery on Thursday and Friday from 9:30 to 5 on the lawn of the First Congregational Church. ⊠ *650 Main St.* ⊕ *www. guildofchathampainters.com.*

The **Monomoy Theatre** (⊠ *776 Main St.* ☎ *508/945–1589* ⊕ *www. monomoytheatre.org*) stages summer productions—thrillers, musicals, classics, and modern drama—by the Ohio University Players.

Chatham's summer **town-band concerts** (⊠ *Kate Gould Park, Main St.* ☎ *508/945–5199*) begin at 8 PM on Friday and draw thousands of onlookers. As many as 500 fox-trot on the roped-off dance floor, and there are special dances for children and sing-alongs for all.

NIGHTLIFE

Chatham Squire (⊠ *487 Main St.* ☎ *508/945–0945*), with four bars—including a raw bar—is a rollicking year-round local hangout, drawing a young crowd to the bar side and a mixed crowd of locals to the restaurant. There's live entertainment on weekends.

BEACHES, SPORTS, AND THE OUTDOORS

BASEBALL

The **Cape Cod Baseball League**, begun in 1885, is an invitational league of college players that counts Carlton Fisk, Ron Darling, Mo Vaughn, Nomar Garciaparra, and the late Thurman Munson as alumni. Considered the country's best summer league, it's scouted by every major-league team. The 10 teams of the Cape Cod Baseball League play a 44-game season from mid-June to mid-August; games held at all 10 fields are free. The **Chatham Anglers** (⊠ *Veterans' Field, Main and Depot Sts. by rotary* ☎ *508/996–5004* ⊕ *www.chathamas.com*) baseball games are great free entertainment by college players in the Cape Cod Baseball League.

BEACHES

Beachcomber (⊠ *Crowell Rd.* ☎ *508/945–5265* ⊕ *www.sealwatch.com*) runs a fleet of bright yellow boats for beach shuttles to North Beach from the Fish Pier (off Shore Road), seal-watching trips, and sunset cruises. A free old-fashioned trolley (it's green) runs from the satellite parking lot (also free) on Crowell Road, at the Chatham Boat Company.

Outermost Harbor Marine (⊠ *Morris Island Rd., Morris Island* ☎ *508/945– 2030* ⊕ *www.outermostharbor.com*) runs boats to South Beach or Monomoy Island; rides cost $20.

The Cape Cod Baseball League

At the Baseball Hall of Fame in Cooperstown, New York, you can find a poster announcing a showdown between archrivals Sandwich and Barnstable. The date? July 4, 1885. In the more than a century since that day, the Cape's ball-playing tradition has continued unabated. To see a game on the Cape today is to come into contact with baseball's roots—you'll remember why you love the sport.

GREAT COLLEGE PLAYERS

As they have since the 1950s, top-ranked college baseball players from around the country descend on the Cape when school lets out, just in time to begin the season in mid-June. Each player joins one of the league's 10 teams, each based in a different town: the Bourne Braves, Wareham Gatemen, Falmouth Commodores, Cotuit Kettleers, Hyannis Mets, Dennis-Yarmouth Red Sox, Harwich Mariners, Brewster Whitecaps, Chatham Athletics (A's), and Orleans Cardinals.

Players lodge with local families and work day jobs cutting lawns, painting houses, or giving baseball clinics in town parks. In the evening, though, their lives are given over to baseball.

The Cape League's motto is "Where the Stars of Tomorrow Shine Tonight." By latest count, one of every eight active major-league ballplayers spent a summer in the Cape League on the way up. You could build an all-star roster with names such as Nomar Garciaparra, Frank Thomas, Jeff Bagwell, Todd Helton, and Barry Zito.

To enshrine these heroes past, the Cape League inducted the first members into its Hall of Fame at the Heritage Museums & Gardens in

Sandwich in January 2001. Among the 12 players honored were Thurman Munson, Mike Flanagan, Jeff Reardon, Mo Vaughn, and Frank Thomas.

FUN BALLPARKS

Yet as good as the baseball is—you'll often see major-league scouts at a game—another great reason to come out to the ballpark is . . . the ballpark. Chatham's Veterans Field is the Cape's Monster Park at Candlestick Point: much like the San Francisco park, fog tends to engulf the games here. Orleans's Eldredge Park is a local favorite—immaculate, cozy, and comfortable. Some parks have bleachers; in others, it's up to you to bring your own chair or blanket and stretch out behind a dugout or baseline. Children are free to roam and can even try for foul balls—which they are, however, asked to return because, after all, balls don't grow on trees. When hunger hits, the ice-cream truck and hot-dog stand are never far away.

THE SCHEDULE

Games start at either 5 or 7 PM, depending on whether the field has lights; occasionally there are afternoon games. Each team plays 44 games in a season, so finding one is rarely a problem (⊕ *www.capecodbaseball.org* has information). And, best of all, they're always free. The Cape's baseball scene is so American, the ambience so relaxed and refreshing, it's tempting to invoke the old *Field of Dreams* analogy. But the league needs no Hollywood comparison. This is the real thing.

—Seth Rolbein

Cockle Cove Beach (⊠ *Cockle Cove Rd. off Rte. 28, South Chatham*) is a favorite with families because of its gentle waves and the warmer waters of Nantucket Sound. It's a good, large beach for strolling and exploring. There are lifeguards and restrooms. Nonresident parking fees are in effect *(see above)*.

Harding's Beach (⊠ *Harding's Beach Rd. off Barn Hill Rd., West Chatham*), west of Chatham center, is open to the public and charges daily parking fees to nonresidents in season. Lifeguards are stationed here in summer. This beach can get crowded, so plan to arrive early or late. Nonresident parking fees at Chatham beaches are $15 daily, $60 weekly, and $125 seasonally.

Ridgevale Beach (⊠ *Ridgevale Rd. off Rte. 28, West Chatham*) is very popular in summer; there are lifeguards, a snack bar, boat rentals, and restrooms. Nonresident parking fees are in effect *(see above)*.

BICYCLING

All manner of bikes are available for rent at **Chatham Cycle** (⊠ *193 Depot Rd.* ☎ *508/945–8981* ⊕ *www.brewsterbike.com*).

BOATING

Monomoy Sail & Cycle (⊠ *275 Orleans Rd., North Chatham* ☎ *508/945–0811*) rents sailboards and kayaks. You'll need your own roof rack; this location is not on the water.

Nauti Jane's (⊠ *Ridgevale Beach at Ridgevale Rd.* ☎ *508/432–4339*) has Sunfish and kayaks for rent.

Rip Ryder (☎ *508/237–0420* ⊕ *www.monomoyislandferry.com*) boat tours offers naturalist-led trips that leave from the Monomoy National Wildlife Refuge area to view birds and seals and explore the rich and ever-changing habitat of the North and South Monomoy Island areas.

FLYING

For some dramatic sightseeing in a three-passenger plane, contact **Cape Aerial Tours** (⊠ *240 George Ryder Rd.* ☎ *508/945–2363* ⊕ *www.chathamairport.com*), which flies out of Chatham Municipal Airport.

GOLF

Chatham Seaside Links (⊠ *209 Seaview St.* ☎ *508/945–4774*), a 9-hole course, is good for beginners.

SURFING

The Lower and Outer Cape beaches, including North Beach in Chatham, are the best on the peninsula for surfing, which is tops when there's a storm offshore. Chatham does not have any surf shops, but you'll find them in nearby Orleans.

TENNIS

Chatham Bars Inn (⊠ *297 Shore Rd.* ☎ *508/945–0096 Ext. 6759*) offers three waterfront all-weather tennis courts, which are open to the public by reservation for $35 an hour. You can also take lessons and visit the pro shop.

SHOPPING

Main Street is a busy shopping area with a diverse range of merchandise, from the pocketbook-friendly to the pricier and more upscale. Here you'll find galleries, crafts, clothing stores, bookstores, and a few good antiques shops.

★ **Chatham Jam and Jelly Shop** (✉ *10 Vineyard Ave., at Rte. 28, West Chatham* ☎ *508/945–3052* ⊕ *www.chathamjamandjellyshop.com*) sells delicious concoctions like rose-petal jelly, apple-lavender chutney, and beach-plum jam, as well as all the old standbys. All preserves are made on-site in small batches, and about 75 of the 120-plus varieties are available for sampling (which is encouraged).

The **Crooked Fence** (✉ *593 Main St.* ☎ *508/945–4622* ⊕ *www. crookedfence.com*), tucked inconspicuously behind Dunkin' Donuts, stocks eclectic, well-chosen home furnishings and gifts, such as cast-iron planters, Nantucket baskets, wind chimes, imported Tuscan tableware, and models of vintage planes and boats.

The **East Wind Silver Co.** (✉ *878 Main St.* ☎ *508/945–8935* ⊕ *www. eastwindsilver.com*) specializes in artful silver jewelry but also sells watercolor paintings, pottery, fountains, and Tiffany-style lighting.

Maps of Antiquity (✉ *1409 Main St.* ☎ *508/945–1660* ⊕ *www. mapsofantiquity.com*) sells original and reproduction maps of Cape Cod, New England, and other parts of the world. Some date to the 1700s. Above the shop in this restored 18th-century home are several guest rooms and suites for rent ($95–$165).

Marion's Pie Shop (✉ *2022 Main St., West Chatham* ☎ *508/432–9439* ⊕ *www.marionspieshopofchatham.com*) sells homemade and home-style fruit breads, pastries, prepared foods such as lasagna, Boston baked beans, and chowder base, and, of course, pies, both savory and sweet.

S. Wilder & Co. (✉ *309 Orleans Rd., North Chatham* ☎ *877/794–5337* ⊕ *www.capecodlanterns.com*), also known as Cape Cod Lanterns, displays old-style colonial crafts. Handcrafted brass and copper lanterns are made here.

Tale of the Cod (✉ *450 Main St., Chatham* ☎ *508/945–0347* ⊕ *www. taleofthecod.com*) has a wide selection of Chatham-related gifts for the home or individual, including painted furniture; specialty dolls; and Chatham-themed rugs, throws, and glass.

Yankee Ingenuity (✉ *525 Main St.* ☎ *508/945–1288* ⊕ *www.yankee-ingenuity.com*) stocks a varied selection of unique jewelry and lamps and a wide assortment of unusual, beautiful trinkets at reasonable (especially for Chatham) prices. The name doesn't mean the items are all from New England, however.

Yellow Umbrella Books (✉ *501 Main St.* ☎ *508/945–0144* ⊕ *www. yellowumbrellabooks.net*) has an excellent selection of new books, many about Cape Cod, as well as used books.

EN ROUTE

North of Chatham and on the way to Orleans, you'll encounter perhaps the most beautiful stretch of Route 28, the road that's so blighted by overdevelopment in Harwich, Dennis, and Yarmouth. Along here, the narrow road twists and turns alongside the western shoreline of rippling **Pleasant Bay**. Turn east onto any number of peaceful country roads, and you'll end up near the water and within view of Nauset Spit and Pleasant Bay's several islands. This is excellent biking and jogging territory— but keep in mind that Route 28 is fairly narrow along this span, with a tiny shoulder, so keep your eye out for oncoming traffic.

> **WORD OF MOUTH**
>
> "Inner vs. outer beaches—water temperature! The water on the Cape Cod Bay side will be much warmer, usually, especially if the tide is coming in over sand heated by the sun during the day—wading and swimming toward the end of the afternoon if the tide is high then will be lovely. Do keep an eye on how fast the tide rises, though, if you've walked way out at low tide." —Cyanna

ORLEANS

Today Orleans is part quiet seaside village and part bustling center with strip malls. The commercial hub of the region, Orleans is one of the more steadily populated areas, year-round, of the Lower Cape. Yet the town retains a fervent commitment to preserving its past, and residents, in support of local mom-and-pop shops, maintain an active refusal policy of many big-time corporations.

Orleans has a long heritage in fishing and seafaring, and many beautifully preserved homes remain from the colonial era. Many are found in the small village of East Orleans, home of the town's Historical Society and Museum. In other areas of town, such as down by Rock Harbor, more modestly grand homes stand near the water's edge.

As you head north, Orleans is the first Cape town to touch both Cape Cod Bay and the Atlantic Ocean. Nauset Beach, on the Atlantic, is enormously popular. Backed by towering dunes dotted with sea grass and colorful *rosa Rugosa,* this beach could be the starting point for a long but beautiful trek clear to the very tip of the Cape. Skaket Beach, just south of Rock Harbor, is the main bay-side beach and affords both scenic views and calm, warm waters for swimming.

Named for Louis-Philippe de Bourbon, *duc d'Orléans* (duke of Orléans), who reputedly visited the area during his exile from France in the 1790s, Orleans was incorporated as a town in 1797. Historically, it has the distinction of being the only place in the continental United States to have received enemy fire during either world war. In July 1918 a German submarine fired on commercial barges off the coast. Four were sunk, and one shell is reported to have fallen on American soil.

GETTING HERE AND AROUND

Downtown Orleans, 8 mi north of Chatham, is a kind of extended triangle made by Route 28, Route 6A, and Main Street. Main Street crosses Route 28 as it makes its way east toward the lovely enclave of East Orleans and Nauset Beach. Heading west, Main Street blends into Rock Harbor Road, which makes its journey all the way to Cape Cod Bay.

ESSENTIALS

Visitor Information **Orleans Chamber of Commerce** (✉ *Eldredge Pkwy. off Rte. 6A* ☎ *508/255–1386 or 800/856–1386* ⊕ *www.capecod-orleans.com*).

EXPLORING

TOP ATTRACTIONS

French Cable Station Museum. This was the stateside landing point for the 3,000-mi-long transatlantic cable that originated in Brittany. Another cable laid between Orleans and New York City completed the France–New York link, and many important messages were communicated through the station. During World War I, when it was an essential connection between army headquarters in Washington and the American Expeditionary Force in France, the station was under guard by the marines. By 1959 telephone service had rendered the station obsolete, and it closed—but the equipment is still in place. ✉ *41 S. Orleans Rd.* ☎ *508/240–1735* ⊕ *www.frenchcablestationmuseum.org* ⊠ *Free* ☉ *June and Sept., Fri.–Sun. 1–4; July and Aug., Thurs.–Sat. 1–4.*

Meeting House Museum. Home of the Orleans Historical Society, this museum hosts changing exhibits about the town's history as well as a permanent collection of photos, deeds, diaries, and genealogical information. Local historians lead near weekly guided walks in local cemeteries, along Main Street, or down at Rock Harbor. ✉ *3 River Rd.* ☎ *508/240–1329* ⊕ *www.orleanshistoricalsociety.org* ⊠ *Free* ☉ *July and Aug., Thurs.–Sat. 10–1.*

Rock Harbor. A walk along Rock Harbor Road leads to the bay-side Rock Harbor, site of a War of 1812 skirmish in which the Orleans militia kept a British warship from docking. In the 19th century Orleans had an active saltworks, and a flourishing packet service between Rock Harbor and Boston developed. Today the former packet landing is the base of charter-fishing and party boats in season, as well as of a small commercial fishing fleet. Sunsets over the harbor are spectacular. Parking is free here; it's a great place to watch the boats go by and do some limited swimming and sunbathing.

WORTH NOTING

Church of the Transfiguration. The Community of Jesus, a religious group whose members come from a variety of Christian traditions, owns a large chunk of the Rock Harbor area. Their dramatic cathedral showcases the work of local and international artisans, and reflects the community's dedication to the arts. Inside there's an organ with thousands of pipes, authentic frescoes depicting biblical scenes, colorful stained-glass windows, and gorgeous, intricate mosaic work mixing religious themes with images of local flora and fauna. ⊠ *Rock Harbor Rd. across from Rock Harbor* ☎ *508/255–1094* ⊕ *www.churchofthe transfiguration.org* ⊠ *Free* ⊘ *Tours Tues., Fri., and Sat. at 3.*

QUICK BITES
The **Cottage St. Bakery** (⊠ *5 Cottage St.* ☎ *508/255–2821*) prepares delicious artisanal breads, pastries, cakes, and sweets, as well as healthful breakfast and lunch fare, from homemade granola to hefty sandwiches.

Jonathan Young Windmill. A pretty if somewhat incongruous sight on the busy highway, this windmill is a landmark from the days of salt making in Orleans, when it would pump saltwater into shallow vaults for evaporation. A program explaining the history and operation of the mill demonstrates the old millstone and grinding process. ⊠ *Rte. 6A and Town Cove* ⊘ *July and Aug., daily 11–4; June and Sept., weekends 11–4.*

QUICK BITES
Grab baked treats, chocolates of all varieties, and any number of coffee concoctions at **the Chocolate Sparrow** (⊠ *5 Old Colony Way* ☎ *508/240–2230*), right by the Cape Cod Rail Trail. The adjacent Ice Cream at the Sparrow serves tasty hard and soft ice cream. It's a very popular local hangout with free Wi-Fi.

Snow Library. This local landmark has been in operation since around 1876; today there are kids' story hours and numerous lecture and music programs offered year-round. ⊠ *Main St. and Rte. 28* ☎ *508/240–3760* ⊕ *www.snowlibrary.org.*

QUICK BITES
For a quick fix for your sweet tooth, or something more substantial like a cup of homemade soup, grilled panini, or other great sandwiches, head to **Cape Cup** (⊠ *54 Main St.* ☎ *508/255–1989*). It's also a great spot for a hot blast of espresso when you need a jolt or a breakfast treat. There's free Wi-Fi, except during the lunch rush.

WHERE TO EAT

$$$
MEDITERRANEAN
Fodor's Choice
★
✕**Abba.** Abba serves inspired pan-Mediterranean cuisine in an elegant and intimate setting. Chef and co-owner Erez Pinhas skillfully combines Middle Eastern, Asian, and southern European flavors in such dishes as herb-crusted rack of venison with shiitake risotto and asparagus in port sauce, and grilled tuna with vegetable nori roll tempura in a balsamic miso-and-mustard sauce. Cushy pillows on the banquettes and soft candlelight flickering from Moroccan glass votives add a touch of opulence. A Fodors.com member gives Abba a perfect score, saying, "Everything is prepared with care and creativity." Reservations are suggested. ⊠ *89 Old Colony Way* ☎ *508/255–8144* ⊕ *www.abbarestaurant.com* ⊟ *AE, D, MC, V* ⊘ *No lunch.*

Rotary 101

The English cheerfully call them "roundabouts," and although that lighthearted moniker might sound like it describes a fun (albeit slightly nauseating) carnival ride, rotaries are serious business. Uninitiated drivers are often so confused upon entering one that they either ignore all rules of the road or freeze up completely. Both reactions will likely cause horns to blare and the fists and fingers of your fellow motorists to come out in full force.

Follow a few simple rules, and you'll be swinging around traffic circles like a local. The most important thing to remember is that drivers who are already in the rotary have the right of way: those entering must yield to the traffic in the rotary. This means that if you're approaching the rotary, you must wait until there is enough space for you to enter—you can't just hit the gas and hope for the best. Because if you do, you probably just caused a fellow motorist to commit another cardinal sin: stopping while in the rotary. Either that, or he just hit you.

Using a rotary is actually a very simple concept. Now that you know the rules, you may even grow to appreciate their exquisite logic (at the very least, you'll see fewer unfriendly hand gestures).   —Laura V. Scheel

$$$
CONTINENTAL

✕ **Academy Ocean Grill.** Academy Ocean Grill occupies a stately shingle house surrounded by gardens—in warm weather, you can dine on the patio amid the flowers and greenery. It's a nice place for a relaxed and elegant luncheon; do try the tasty crab melt. Top dishes include chunky crab cakes; haddock broiled with oregano, Romano cheese, and seasoned bread crumbs; and traditional veal saltimbocca. An exceptional wine list rounds out the offerings. There's also a Sunday brunch. ⊠ *2 Academy Pl., off Rte. 28* ☎ *508/240–1585* ⊕ *www.academyoceangrille. com* ⊟ *AE, D, MC, V* ☉ *Closed Mon and mid-Jan.–early Apr.*

$$$
ECLECTIC

✕ **The Beacon Room.** Adorned with crisp linens, frilly curtains, and wood furnishings, this homey cottage bistro serves up a nice mix of seafood and meats enhanced with sophisticated and inventive flavors. Start with the Gorgonzola, sun-dried cranberry, and walnut salad, then move on to pan-seared scallops with Parmesan risotto or pecan-crusted venison with a sauce of red zinfandel and pan drippings. In warmer months, dinner on the garden patio is particularly urbane. An ambitious wine list complements the fine selection. There is a call-ahead waiting list for busy summer nights. ⊠ *23 West Rd.* ☎ *508/255–2211* ⚔ *Reservations not accepted* ⊟ *MC, V.*

$$$
CONTINENTAL
★

✕ **Captain Linnell House.** Sea captain Eben Linnell built this stunning mansion in 1840, basing its design on a neoclassical villa he'd once visited in the south of France. Linnell's masterpiece now contains one of the Cape's most esteemed formal restaurants, a longtime favorite for celebrating special occasions. A competent and polite staff serves Continental cuisine, which is consistently superb. The kitchen tends to stick with tried-and-true classics, such as herb-and-mustard-crusted rack of lamb with a pinot-noir reduction, and grilled Black Angus steak au poivre with a zinfandel-peppercorn sauce. ⊠ *137 Skaket Beach Rd.*

☎ *508/255–3400* ⊕ *www.linnell.com* ⊟ *AE, MC, V* ⊗ *Closed Mon. No lunch.*

$ ✕ **Land Ho!** Tried-and-true tavern fare is the rule at Orleans's flagship
AMERICAN local restaurant. The scene is usually fun and boisterous; dozens of
★ homemade wooden signs hang from the rafters above the red-checked
tablecloths. The burgers and the sea-clam pie are both excellent, and
the blackboard specials change daily. This is a good place for a rainy-
day lunch. On weekend nights, it livens up even more with the music
of local bands. ✉ *38 Cove Rd.* ☎ *508/255–5165* ⊕ *www.land-ho.com*
⚑ *Reservations not accepted* ⊟ *AE, MC, V.*

$$$ ✕ **Mahoney's Atlantic Bar and Grill.** Chef-owner Ted Mahoney cooked for
ECLECTIC years at one of Provincetown's busiest restaurants before opening this
★ always-hopping downtown spot that serves commendable dinner fare
and draws big crowds for cocktails and appetizers. The menu empha-
sizes seafood, with such favorites as tuna sashimi, scallops, and a classic
bouillabaisse brimming with shrimp, scallops, squid, haddock, little-
necks, and mussels in an herbed saffron broth, served over pasta. There
are a few good vegetarian options as well, and several good steak, lamb,
and chicken dishes. The bar is long and comfortable, and is a good spot
to dine if there are no tables available. ✉ *28 Main St.* ☎ *508/255–5505*
⊕ *www.mahoneysatlantic.com* ⊟ *AE, MC, V.*

$$$ ✕ **Nauset Beach Club.** Locals have long favored this upscale but casual
ITALIAN trattoria on the road leading out to Nauset Beach. The kitchen produces
★ seasonally inspired northern Italian food, with an emphasis on locally
harvested seafood and produce. Choose from a fixed-price option
(offered nightly starting at about $25 for three courses), or the à la
carte menu, which includes favorites like a panko-crusted Berkshire
pork cutlet, and seared veal rib chop and potato gnocchi with mushrooms. Known for its extensive wine list (it has won several awards), the
restaurant creates themed dinners with wine pairings. ✉ *222 Main St.,
East Orleans* ☎ *508/255–8547* ⊕ *www.nausetbeachclub.com* ⊟ *AE, D,
DC, MC, V* ⊗ *No lunch.*

$$ ✕ **Saltwater Grille.** This popular local spot serves delicious pan pizzas
ECLECTIC with inventive toppings (apples, linguica sausage, and pine nuts, to
name a few). You'll find grilled meats and seafood aplenty here, as well
as a good selection of pastas and salads. Inside, it's a bit like eating in
your favorite bright beach house. "Loads of great food choices and
a wonderful bar," says one Fodors.com reader. ✉ *20 S. Orleans Rd.
(Rte. 28)* ☎ *508/255–5149* ⚑ *Reservations not accepted* ⊟ *AE, MC,
V* ⊗ *No lunch.*

$ ✕ **Sir Cricket's Fish and Chips.** For a beautifully turned-out fish sandwich,
SEAFOOD pull into this hole-in-the-wall attached to Nauset Fish & Lobster Pool.
Built mainly for takeout, this no-frills fish joint does have three or four
tiny tables and a soda machine. Try the fresh oyster roll or go for a
full fisherman's platter. As you eat, check out the chair seats—each is
an exquisitely rendered mini-mural of Orleans history or a personal-
ity painted by legendary local artist Dan Joy. ✉ *39 Cranberry Hwy.*
☎ *508/255–4453* ⚑ *Reservations not accepted* ⊟ *No credit cards.*

WHERE TO STAY

$–$$ 🏠 **Cove Motel.** Consisting of two main buildings overlooking Orleans
★   Town Cove, this tidy but prosaic year-round motel has large rooms,
most with decks or patios overlooking the water. Furnishings are undistinguished but updated and pleasant, and rooms have tasteful, neutral
color schemes. Some units have fireplaces and kitchens, and two-room
suites can comfortably accommodate four guests. An attractive picnic
area overlooks the heated pool. **Pros:** many water-view rooms; right on
Town Cove; easy walk to town. **Cons:** on semi-busy road; not for those
looking for historic lodgings. ⊠ *13 S. Orleans Rd.* ☎ *508/255–1203
or 800/343–2233* ⊕ *www.thecoveorleans.com* ⤳ *37 rooms, 10 suites*
⚐ *In-room: a/c, kitchen (some), refrigerator, DVD. In-hotel: pool, Wi-Fi
hotspot* ▤ *AE, D, MC, V.*

$$$–$$$$ 🏠 **A Little Inn on Pleasant Bay.** Run by sisters Sandra Zeller and Pamela
Fodor's Choice   Adam and Sandra's husband, Bernd Zeller—all of whom have exten-
★   sive corporate and hospitality backgrounds—this gorgeously decorated
inn occupies a 1798 building on a bluff beside a cranberry bog, across
Route 28 from the bay for which it's named. The main house has four
rooms, and two adjoining nearby buildings contain another five rooms.
Many of the accommodations look clear out to the bay, and others face
the lush gardens. The Mercury room has French doors leading out to
a private garden patio, and the spacious Wianno room is warmed by
a fireplace and has a lovely sitting area. The breakfast buffet includes
a dazzling variety of fresh fruits, baked goods, smoked fish, cold cuts,
fine cheeses, yogurts, cereals, and other treats. Walk across the street to
a small private beach with its own dock. **Pros:** great water views; abun-
dant buffet breakfast; spacious, modern baths. **Cons:** not an in-town
location. ⊠ *654 S. Orleans Rd., South Orleans* ☎ *508/255–0780 or
888/332–3351* ⊕ *www.alittleinnonpleasantbay.com* ⤳ *9 rooms* ⚐ *In-
room: a/c, no phone, no TV, Wi-Fi. In-hotel: no kids under 10* ▤ *AE,
MC, V* ⎥○⎢ *CP* ☾ *Closed mid-Oct.–Apr.*

$–$$ 🏠 **Nauset House Inn.** You could easily spend a day trying out all the
★   places to relax in this early-19th-century farmhouse. There's a parlor
with comfortable chairs and a large fireplace, an orchard set with picnic tables, and a lush conservatory with a weeping cherry tree in its
center. Rooms in both the main building and the adjacent Carriage
House have stenciled walls, quilts, and unusual antique pieces, as well
as hand-painted furniture, stained glass, and prints done by one of the
owners. The beach is ½ mi away (they'll set you up with beach chairs
and towels). In early evening, wine and snacks are served to guests
in the main house. **Pros:** authentic historic lodging; walk to excellent
beach. **Cons:** many rooms share a bath; some steep stairways. ⊠ *143
Beach Rd., Box 774, East Orleans* ☎ *508/255–2195 or 800/771–5508*
⊕ *www.nausethouseinn.com* ⤳ *14 rooms, 8 with bath* ⚐ *In-room: no
a/c, no phone, no TV, Wi-Fi. In-hotel: no kids under 12* ▤ *D, MC, V*
☾ *Closed Nov.–mid-Apr.* ⎥○⎢ *BP.*

$$$–$$$$ 🏠 **Orleans Inn.** This bustling inn and restaurant, housed in an 1875 sea
captain's mansion, is run with warmth and enthusiasm by the Maas
family. The imposing, turreted structure has two distinct faces: one is
turned toward a busy intersection and a large shopping plaza, whereas

the other looks longingly over tranquil Town Cove. Rooms here are simply but charmingly appointed with classic wood furniture and floral quilts on the beds; the larger waterfront suites have sitting areas, fireplaces, and great views of the harbor. Common areas include a kitchenette and a sitting room with a large TV. The restaurant, which uses some creative ingredients in its traditional standbys, serves large portions of fish-and-chips, grilled sirloin, and grilled salmon with orange-honey glaze. On Friday evenings the tavern is filled with the sounds of live traditional Irish music, played by local musicians. **Pros:** great waterfront location; outdoor dining; many amenities. **Cons:** some rooms face busy intersection; some steep stairs. ⊠ *3 Old County Rd.* ☎ *508/255–2222 or 800/863–3039* ⊕ *www.orleansinn.com* ⤢ *8 rooms, 3 suites* ⟁ *In-room: a/c, refrigerator, DVD, Wi-Fi. In-hotel: restaurant, bar* ⊟ *AE, MC, V* ⦿*CP.*

$$–$$$ 🖼 **Ship's Knees Inn.** With a generous nod to its name and it's 19th-century heritage, this inn is full of nautical and historic touches: seaside artwork and furnishings, steeply pitched roof lines, wide-board floors, antiques, and a good deal of painted furniture (even the room refrigerators are disguised as old-time safes). Sleep with your windows open and you'll likely hear the waves of nearby Nauset Beach, a five-minute walk from the inn. (The two upstairs rooms that share a bath happen to be the only ones that have views of the ocean, and are priced significantly lower.) Have morning repast inside the homey pine-paneled breakfast room, or outdoors on the stone patio. **Pros:** short walk to beach; beautifully maintained property, knowledgeable innkeepers. **Cons:** not an in-town location; some steep stairs. ⊠ *186 Beach Rd.* ☎ *508/255–1312* ⊕ *www. shipskneesinn.com* ⤢ *16 rooms, 1 apartment* ⟁ *In-room: a/c, no phone, refrigerator, Wi-Fi. In-hotel: pool, no kids under 12* ⊟ *D, MC, V* ⦿*CP.*

$–$$ 🖼 **Skaket Beach Motel.** Rooms in this convenient-to-everything inland motel overlooking a busy intersection are well sized and nicely renovated; a handful of suites have kitchens and two or three bedrooms. A large, fully equipped apartment can sleep up to five. Outdoor facilities include horseshoes, a heated pool, and grills. **Pros:** tasty homemade blueberry muffins in the morning; good amenities. **Cons:** faces busy intersection; pool area can be loud. ⊠ *203 Cranberry Hwy.* ☎ *508/255– 1020 or 800/835–0298* ⊕ *www.skaketbeachmotel.com* ⤢ *42 rooms, 2 suites, 1 apartment* ⟁ *In-room: kitchen (some), refrigerator, Wi-Fi. In-hotel: pool, laundry facilities, Wi-Fi hotspot* ⊟ *AE, D, MC, V* ⦿ *Closed late Nov.–late-Mar.* ⦿*CP.*

NIGHTLIFE AND THE ARTS

The **Academy Playhouse** (⊠ *120 Main St.* ☎ *508/255–1963* ⊕ *www. apacape.org*), one of the oldest community theaters on the Cape, stages 12 or 13 productions year-round, including original works.

Lost Dog Pub (⊠ *63 Rte. 6A, at Rte. 28* ☎ *508/240–3647*) has live local bands twice a week in summer and occasionally on weekends the rest of the year.

CLAMMING EXCURSIONS TWO WAYS

Cape Codders have been clamming for generations, and their iconic mollusks are a celebrated part of the culture here.

GOING CLAMMING

Commercial shellfishing on the Cape is one of America's oldest industries, and locals aren't the only ones clamoring for shellfishing licenses these days. Some of the Cape's more "clambitious" visitors also want to get in on the hunt for these scrumptious fruits of the sea. But it's not as easy as just hitting the shore with your rake and basket. Shellfishing is regulated by the state, and each town has its own regulations regarding license costs, clam size and quantity, and the areas and days shellfishing is permitted. If you're ready to try recreational clamming, put on your clamdiggers, grab your rake and basket, and head to the local town hall to get your license and any other necessary information. You can also take a class, like the ones offered by **Barnstable's Association for**

Recreational Shellfishing (⊕ *www. shellfishing.org*) and **Eastham's Salt Pond Visitor Center** (⊕ *www. easthamchamber.com/activities.cfm*), or check in with the local shellfish warden to find out about any organized clamming excursions.

EATING AT CLAM SHACKS

We all know that the best thing about clams is not wading around and looking for them in the wet sand; it's eating them. Classic clam shacks are known for their bountiful baskets of crispy fried clams, which, according to Cape Codders, should always be ordered "whole"—that is, with the bellies. Fried clams are never the only item on the menu. Typical fare also includes clam chowder, lobster rolls, fried fish, scallops, shrimp, coleslaw, fries, potato salad, and other non-seafood items. The quintessential experience usually involves ordering at one window, picking up at another, and eating at a picnic table—hopefully one with a beach or harbor view.

BEACHES, SPORTS, AND THE OUTDOORS

BASEBALL

The **Orleans Firebirds** (⊠ *Rte. 28 at Eldredge Pkwy.* ☎ *508/255–0793* ⊕ *www.orleansfirebirds.com*) of the collegiate Cape Cod Baseball League play home games at Eldredge Park from mid-June to mid-August.

BEACHES

The town-managed **Nauset Beach** (⊠ *Beach Rd., Nauset Heights* ☎ *508/240–3780*)—not to be confused with Nauset Light Beach on the National Seashore—is a 10-mi sweep of sandy ocean beach with low dunes and large waves good for bodysurfing or board surfing. The beach has lifeguards, restrooms, showers, and a food concession. Despite its size, the massive parking lot often fills up when the sun is strong; arrive quite early or in the late afternoon if you want to claim a spot. The beach is open to off-road vehicles with a special permit. Daily parking fees are $15.

Freshwater seekers can access **Pilgrim Lake** (⊠ *Pilgrim Lake Rd. off Monument Rd. and Rte. 28, South Orleans*).

Skaket Beach (⊠ *Skaket Beach Rd.* ☎ *508/240–3775*) on Cape Cod Bay is a sandy stretch with calm, warm water good for children. There are restrooms, lifeguards, and a snack bar. Daily parking fees are the same as at Nauset Beach. The parking lot fills up fast on hot August days; try to arrive before 11 or after 2. The many tide pools make this a favorite spot for families. Sunsets here draw a good crowd.

BIKING

For bike rentals just across the way from the Cape Cod Rail Trail, head to **Orleans Cycle** (⊠ *26 Main St.* ☎ *508/255–9115*).

Idle Times Bike Shop (⊠ *29 Main St.* ☎ *508/240–1122*) is close to the Cape Cod Rail Trail.

BOATING

Arey's Pond Boat Yard (⊠ *43 Arey's La., off Rte. 28, South Orleans* ☎ *508/255–0994* ⊕ *www.areyspondboatyard.com*) has a sailing school with individual and group lessons. They also rent sailboats.

★ **Dick Hilmer's Explore Cape Cod** (☎ *508/240–1211* ⊕ *www.explorecapecod. com*) has an experienced, knowledgeable, and jovial crew that leads half-day kayak tours of Nauset Marsh and Pleasant Bay. Paddle among the seals, look for osprey, and enjoy the spectacular scenery.

FISHING

Many of Orleans's freshwater ponds offer good fishing for perch, pickerel, trout, and more. The required fishing license, along with rental gear, is available at the **Goose Hummock Shop** (⊠ *15 Rte. 6A* ☎ *508/255–0455* ⊕ *www.goose.com*), which also rents kayaks and gives kayaking lessons and tours.

Rock Harbor Charter Boat Service (⊠ *Rock Harbor* ☎ *508/255–9757* ⊕ *www.rockharborcharters.com*) goes for bass and blues in the bay from spring through fall. Walk-ons and charters are both available.

HEALTH AND FITNESS CLUBS

Fitness Revolution (⊠ *5B Namskaket Rd.* ☎ *508/247–8100* ⊕ *www. fitrevs.com*) is a no-frills gym with ample equipment, a room for various classes, and very reasonable rates.

Willy's Gym (⊠ *21 Old Colony Way* ☎ *508/255–6826* ⊕ *www.willysgym. com*) is one of the Cape's top fitness facilities, with state-of-the-art cardio and weight-training equipment and a studio for yoga, aerobics, and dance classes. Daily, weekly, and monthly passes are available.

SPAS

Heaven Scent You (⊠ *13 Cove Rd.* ☎ *508/240–2508*) offers massage, spa services, and beauty treatments—everything you need for some relaxation and rejuvenation.

SURFING

The Lower and Outer Cape beaches, including Nauset Beach in Orleans, are the best spots for surfing, especially when there's a storm offshore. For a surf report—water temperature, weather, surf, tanning factor— call ☎ *508/240–2229*.

Nauset Surf Shop (⊠ *Jeremiah Sq., Rte. 6A at rotary* ☎ *508/255–4742*) rents surf-, body-, skim-, and wake boards as well as wet suits.

Pump House Surf Co. (✉ *9 Rte. 6A* ☎ *508/240–2226*) rents wet suits and surfboards, and sells boards and gear.

SHOPPING

Orleans's Main Street, between Route 6A and Route 28, is lined with a good number of specialty shops. It's a great area for browsing or taking a break on a park bench.

Baseball Shop (✉ *26 Main St.* ☎ *508/240–1063*) sells licensed products relating to baseball and other sports—new and collectible cards (and nonsports cards) as well as hats, clothing, and videos.

Bird Watcher's General Store (✉ *36 Rte. 6A* ☎ *508/255–6974*) stocks nearly everything avian but the birds themselves: feeders, paintings, houses, books, binoculars, calls, bird-themed apparel, and more.

Karol Richardson (✉ *47 Main St.* ☎ *508/255–3944*) sells fine contemporary clothing, plus silk wraps and scarves, hats, shoes, handbags, and handcrafted jewelry. You'll usually pay more for the quality goods here, but bargains can be found at the shop's off-season warehouse sales.

Kemp Pottery (✉ *9 Cranberry Hwy.* ☎ *508/255–5853*) features the often whimsical works of a father-and-son team—including functional and decorative stoneware and porcelain—often with natural and fantastical themes. They also have fountains, garden sculpture, pottery sinks, and stained glass.

Main Street Books (✉ *46 Main St.* ☎ *508/255–3343*) is tiny but packed full with thoughtful choices in fiction, poetry, nonfiction, and children's books. Browsing is a fine art here, with a helpful staff to offer recommendations. The shop is housed in a 19th-century building with a welcoming front porch.

Oceana (✉ *1 Main St. Sq.* ☎ *508/240–1414*) has a beautiful selection of nautical-themed home accents, gifts, and jewelry, as well as colorful hooked rugs made by Cape artist Claire Murray.

The **Orleans Farmers' Market** (✉ *Old Colony Way* ☎ *508/255–0951*) is the place to go for local delicacies such as fresh produce, flowers, and homemade goodies. It's open 8 AM to noon Saturday morning throughout summer. Be forewarned—early birds get the best selection, and things tend to disappear quickly.

Village Farm Market (✉ *199 Main St., East Orleans* ☎ *508/255–1949*) sells local produce, fresh sandwiches and roll-ups, salads (salad bar or prepared varieties), homemade soup, ice cream, fresh-baked breads, and other supplies for a great picnic. There's also a full-service butcher counter and fish market. A wide assortment of flowers, both dried and fresh, are sold, adding great color to the beautiful, beamed old-style barn.

ART AND CRAFTS GALLERIES

The **Addison Art Gallery** (✉ *43 S. Orleans Rd.* ☎ *508/255–6200*), in four rooms of a brick-red Cape house, represents more than two dozen regional artists. Peruse the collection of contemporary works, many of which were inspired by life on Cape Cod. The sculpture garden in the side yard is a perfect complement to the tasteful gallery. Receptions, where you can often meet the week's featured artist, are held year-round from 5 to 7 on Saturday night.

Gallery 31 (⊠ *31 Main St.* ☎ *508/247–9469*) is a partnership of nearly one dozen local artists, representing a wide range of mediums and styles.

Left Bank Gallery (⊠ *8 Cove Rd.* ☎ *508/247–9172*) carries an eclectic mix of handcrafted jewelry, fine art by both local and national artists, hand-painted furniture, pottery, and handmade clothing.

On Tuesday in July and August, **Nauset Painters** (⊠ *Depot Sq. at Old Colony Way* ☎ *No phone*) presents outdoor juried art shows.

At various times in June, July, and August, the **Orleans Professional Arts and Crafts Association** (⊠ *Rte. 28* ☎ *508/385–8689*) sponsors a giant outdoor show on the grounds of the Nauset Middle School featuring the works of more than 100 artists and craftspeople.

★ **Tree's Place** (⊠ *Rte. 6A at Rte. 28* ☎ *508/255–1330*), one of the Cape's best and most original shops, has a collection of handcrafted kaleidoscopes, as well as art glass, hand-painted porcelain and pottery, handblown stemware, jewelry, imported ceramic tiles, and fine art. Tree's displays the work of New England artists, including Robert Vickery, Don Stone, and Elizabeth Mumford (whose popular folk art is bordered in mottos and poetic phrases). Champagne openings are held on Saturday night in summer.

EASTHAM

Often overlooked on the speedy drive up toward Provincetown on U.S. 6, Eastham is a town full of hidden treasures. Unlike other towns on the Cape, it has no official town center; the highway bisects Eastham, and the town is spread out on both Cape Cod Bay and the Atlantic. Amid the gas stations, convenience stores, restaurants, and large motel complexes, Eastham's wealth of natural beauty takes a little exploring to find.

One such gem is the National Seashore, which officially begins here and comprises thousands of acres of wooded areas, salt marshes, and wild, open-ocean beaches. The Salt Pond Visitor Center just off U.S. 6 is one of Cape Cod National Seashore's main centers, host to numerous nature and history programs and lectures; it also maintains a paved bike path. Nearby is the much-beloved Nauset Light, the red-and-white-stripe lighthouse saved from imminent destruction when it was moved from its perilous perch atop eroding cliffs. The Fort Hill area is another pretty spot, with lots of walking trails and a stately old mansion called the Penniman House.

It was here in 1620 that an exploring band of *Mayflower* passengers met the Nauset tribe on a bay-side beach, which they then named First Encounter Beach. The meeting was peaceful, but the Pilgrims moved on to Plymouth anyway. Nearly a quarter century later, they returned to settle the area, which they originally called by its Native American name, Nawsett. Eastham was incorporated as a town on June 7, 1651.

Like many other Cape towns, Eastham started as a farming community and later turned to the sea and to salt making for its livelihood; at one time there were more than 50 saltworks in town. A less-typical industry that once flourished here was asparagus growing; from the late 1800s through the 1920s, Eastham was known as the asparagus capital of the United States. The runner-up crop, Eastham turnips, are still the pride of many a harvest table.

GETTING HERE AND AROUND

Eastham's main drag is busy Route 6, which gives visitors no feel for the town's natural beauty. It's hard to get lost in Eastham, about 3 mi north of Orleans. You're never a few miles from the road ending at a beach. Take the time to meander about and see what's off the highway on both the bay and ocean sides.

ESSENTIALS

Visitor Information **Eastham Chamber of Commerce** (✉ *U.S. 6 at Fort Hill Rd.* ☎ *508/240-7211* ⊕ *www.easthamchamber.com).*

EXPLORING

TOP ATTRACTIONS

Cape Cod National Seashore. The region's most expansive national treasure, Cape Cod National Seashore was established in 1961 by President John F. Kennedy, for whom Cape Cod was home and haven. The 27,000-acre park, extending from Chatham to Provincetown, protects 30 mi of superb beaches; great rolling dunes; swamps, marshes, and wetlands; and pitch-pine and scrub-oak forest. Self-guided nature trails, as well as biking and horse trails, lace through these landscapes. Hiking trails lead to a red-maple swamp, **Nauset Marsh,** and to **Salt Pond,** in which breeding shellfish are suspended from floating "nurseries." Their offspring will later be used to seed the flats. Also in the seashore is the Buttonbush Trail, a nature path for people with vision impairments. A hike or bike ride to Coast Guard Beach leads to a turnout looking out over marsh and sea. A section of the cliff here was washed away in 1990, revealing the remains of a prehistoric dwelling.

Fodor's Choice ★

The first visitor center of the Cape Cod National Seashore (the other is in Provincetown), **Salt Pond Visitor Center** offers guided walks, boat tours, demonstrations, and lectures from mid-April through Thanksgiving, as well as evening beach walks, campfire talks, and other programs in summer. The center includes a museum with displays on whaling and the old saltworks, as well as early Cape Cod artifacts including scrimshaw, the journal that Mrs. Penniman kept while on a whaling voyage with her husband, and some of the Pennimans' possessions, such as their tea service and the captain's top hat. An air-conditioned auditorium shows films on geology, sea rescues, whaling, Henry David Thoreau, and Guglielmo Marconi. ✉ *Doane Rd. off U.S. 6* ☎ *508/255-3421* ⊕ *www.nps.gov/caco* ✆ *Visitor center free* ☉ *Daily 9–4:30 (hrs extended slightly in summer).*

Captain Edward Penniman House. This French Second Empire–style home was built in 1868 for a whaling captain. The impressive exterior is

BEST NATIONAL SEASHORE ACTIVITIES

HIT THE BEACH

There's no question that the Cape Cod National Seashore's beaches are the main attractions for sunbathers, swimmers, and surfers. It's not at all uncommon for the parking lots to fill up by 11 AM on hot sunny days. Arrive early to find your spot on the sand, or venture out on some of the less traveled trails to find solitude in the high season.

TAKE A WALK

Walking the marked trails, beaches, and wooded fire roads is an excellent way to truly experience the diverse natural splendor within the park. There are 11 self-guided trails that begin at various points, leading through shaded swamps, alongside marshes, and through meadows, forest, and dunes. Most of the terrain is flat and sometimes sandy.

RIDE A BIKE

Three well-maintained bicycle trails run through parts of the park. In Eastham, the short Nauset Trail heads from the Salt Pond Visitor Center through the woods and out to Coast Guard Beach. Truro's Head off the Meadow Trail edges a large salt meadow, an ideal place for birding. The most physically demanding—and most dramatic—of the park's bike trails is the Province Lands Trail, more than 7 mi of steep hills and hairpin curves through forest and sand dunes. Mountain bikers can make their own trails on the miles of fire roads.

SEE THE SIGHTS

Several historic homes and sites are open for touring; there are also a few notable overlooks easily accessible by car. Climb the steep steps of lighthouses in Eastham and Truro or see rescue reenactments at the Old Harbor Life-Saving Station in Provincetown. Scenic overlooks include Eastham's exquisite Fort Hill area; Wellfleet's Marconi Station Site, where the first transatlantic wireless message was sent in 1903; Truro's Pilgrim Heights; and Provincetown's scenic 2-mi Race Point Road.

TOUR WITH A RANGER

From mid-April through Thanksgiving there is a full schedule of mostly free ranger-guided activities. Combining history, folklore, science, and nature, rangers take visitors right to the source, whether for a full-moon hike in the dunes, a campfire on the beach, a paddling trip, or a photography workshop.

notable for its mansard roof; its cupola, which once commanded a dramatic view of bay and sea; and its whale-jawbone entrance gate. The interior is open for guided tours or for browsing through changing exhibits. Call ahead to find out when tours are available. ⊠ *Fort Hill Rd., Fort Hill area* ☎ *508/255–3421* 🎫 *Free* ☉ *Weekdays 1–4.*

Coast Guard and Nauset Light beaches. Under the domain of the National Seashore, roads and bicycle trails lead to this unbroken 30-mi stretch of barrier beach—the "Cape Cod Beach" of Thoreau's 1865 classic, *Cape Cod.* You can still walk its length, as Thoreau did, though the Atlantic continues to claim more of the Cape's eastern shore every year. The site of the famous beach cottage of Henry Beston's 1928 book, *The Outermost House,* is to the south, near the end of Nauset Spit. Designated as a literary landmark in 1964, the cottage was destroyed in the Great

Blizzard of 1978. Coast Guard Beach has no parking lot of its own, so park at Salt Pond Visitor Center or at the lot on Doane Road and take the free shuttle to the beach. ⊠ *Off Ocean View Dr.* ☎ *508/255–3421* ⊕ *www.nps.gov/caco.*

Eastham Windmill. A smock mill built in Plymouth in the early 1680s, it was moved to this site in 1793. The mill was restored by local shipwreck historian William Quinn and friends. It's the oldest surviving windmill on the Cape. Each September, just after Labor Day, Eastham celebrates its history and the change of the season with the annual Windmill Weekend, an event with a full roster of activities for all ages. ⊠ *U.S. 6 at Samoset Rd.* ▣ *Free* ⊙ *July and Aug., Mon.–Sat. 10–5, Sun. 1–5.*

First Encounter Beach. A great spot for watching sunsets over Cape Cod Bay, First Encounter Beach is rich in history. Near the parking lot, a bronze marker commemorates the first encounter between local Native Americans and passengers from the *Mayflower,* led by Captain Myles Standish, who explored the entire area for five weeks in 1620 before moving on to Plymouth. The remains of a navy target ship retired after 25 years of battering now rest on a sandbar about 1 mi out; it can only be spotted at low tide. ⊠ *End of Samoset Rd. off U.S. 6.*

★ **Fort Hill Area.** The road to the Cape Cod National Seashore's Fort Hill Area ends at a parking area with a lovely view of old farmland traced with stone fences that rolls gently down to **Nauset Marsh**. The marsh winds around brilliant green grasses and makes its way to the ocean beyond; it is one of the more dramatic views on the Cape. Appreciated by bird-watchers and nature photographers, the 1-mi **Red Maple Swamp Trail** winds through the area, branching into two separate paths, one of which eventually turns into a boardwalk that meanders through wetlands. The other path leads directly to Skiff Hill, an overlook with benches and informative plaques that quote Samuel de Champlain's account of the area from when he moored off Nauset Marsh in 1605. Also on Skiff Hill is Indian Rock, a large boulder moved to the hill from the marsh below. Once used by the local Nauset tribe as a sharpening stone, the rock is cut with deep grooves and smoothed in circles where ax heads were whetted. Trails are open from dawn to dusk. ⊠ *Fort Hill Rd. off U.S. 6.*

Nauset Light. Moved 350 feet back from its perch at cliff's edge in 1996, this much-photographed red-and-white lighthouse tops the bluff where the Three Sisters Lighthouses once stood; the Sisters themselves can be seen in a little landlocked park surrounded by trees, reached by paved walkways off Nauset Light Beach's parking lot. How the lighthouses got there is a long story. In 1838 three brick lighthouses were built 150 feet apart on the bluffs in Eastham overlooking a particularly dangerous area of shoals (shifting underwater sandbars). In 1892, after the eroding cliff dropped the towers into the ocean, they were replaced with three wooden towers. In 1918 two were moved away, as was the third in 1923. Eventually the National Park Service acquired the Three Sisters and brought them together in the inland park, where they would be safe. Lectures on and guided walks to the lighthouses are conducted Sunday from early May through October, as well as Wednesday in

July and August. ⊠ *Ocean View Dr. and Cable Rd.* ☎ *508/240–2612* ⊕ *www.nausetlight.org.*

WORTH NOTING

Swift-Daley House. Frozen in time, this 1741 home was once owned by Gustavus Swift, founder of the Swift meatpacking company. Inside the full Cape with bow roof you can find beautiful pumpkin-pine woodwork and wide-board floors, a ship's-cabin staircase that, like the bow roof, was built by ships' carpenters, and fireplaces in every downstairs room. The colonial-era furnishings include an old cannonball rope bed, tools, a melodeon (similar to an accordion), and a ceremonial quilt decorated with beads and coins. Among the antique clothing is a stunning 1850 wedding dress. ⊠ *U.S. 6* ☎ *No phone* ⊕ *www.easthamhistorical. org* 🖙 *Free* ☉ *July and Aug., weekdays 10–1.*

4

WHERE TO EAT

There are several good delis and a few bars that serve food, but Eastham is not a restaurant town. A few dining spots have seen great turnover in the past few years, making the scene even more tenuous. With plenty of places to choose from in nearby Orleans and Wellfleet, diners in Eastham still have many good options.

$$
SEAFOOD
✕ **Arnold's Lobster & Clam Bar.** You can't miss this hot spot on the side of Route 6: look for the riot of colorful flowers lining the road and the patient folks waiting in long lines in the parking lot. That crowd is testament to the freshness and flavors that come out of this busy kitchen for lunch, dinner, and takeout, putting forth everything from grilled burgers to 3-pound lobsters. Unusual for a clam shack like this is the full bar, offering beer, wine, mixed drinks, and the house specialty, margaritas. There's ice cream and an artfully designed miniature-golf course to keep the kids happy. ⊠ *3580 State Hwy. (U.S. 6)* ☎ *508/255–2575* ⊕ *www. arnoldsrestaurant.com* ▭ *No credit cards* ☉ *Closed Nov.–Apr.*

$
ITALIAN
✕ **Fairway Restaurant and Pizzeria.** The friendly family-run Fairway specializes in Italian comfort food and pizzas. Attached to the Hole in One Donut Shop (very popular among locals for early-morning coffee and exceptional donuts and muffins), the Fairway puts a jar of crayons on every paper-covered table and sells its own brand of root beer. Entrées come with salad and homemade rolls. Try the eggplant Parmesan, fettuccine and meatballs, or a well-stuffed calzone. The pizzas are hearty, not the thin-crust variety but the kind that really fills you up. ⊠ *4295 U.S. 6* ☎ *508/255–3893* 🥄 *Reservations not accepted* ▭ *AE, D, DC, MC, V* ☉ *No lunch.*

$
SEAFOOD
✕ **The Friendly Fisherman.** Not just another roadside lobster shack with buoys and nets for decoration, this place is serious about its fresh seafood. It's both a great place to pick up ingredients to cook at home—there's a fish and produce market on-site—and a good bet for dining out on such favorites as fish-and-chips, fried scallops, and lobster. The market also sells homemade pies, breads, soups, stews, and pasta. ⊠ *U.S. 6, North Eastham* ☎ *508/255–6770 or 508/255–3009* ▭ *AE, MC, V* ☉ *Closed Nov.–Apr.*

FISH FRIES AND CHURCH SUPPERS

For some very good eats, try two of Eastham's institutions. It's a good way to get some true local flavor, in more ways than one. The Friday-night fish fry at the **Orleans-Eastham Elks Lodge** (✉ *McKoy Rd., North Eastham* ☎ *508/255–4258*) has been faithfully filling the halls for decades. The fish is fresh, the portions are generous, and the price is well below what you would pay at a restaurant. You can even order spirits, wine, and beer. Drop by early, as it runs from 5:30 to 7:30 PM.

At **Eastham United Methodist Church** (✉ *3200 Rte. 6* ☎ *508/255–8774* ⊙ *Late June–late Aug. 5:30–7*), the Thursday night Chowder Supper has been a summer tradition for nearly 50 years.

Dinner, which runs from 5:30 to 7 between late June and August, includes a hearty bowl of clam chowder, salad, a beverage, and cranberry dessert.

WHERE TO STAY

$–$$ 🚗 **Cove Bluffs Motel.** This old-fashioned haven for nature lovers and families is nestled among the trees and within walking distance of Orleans Town Cove and several nature trails. Settle into a standard motel room or choose a more self-sufficient getaway in studio or two-bedroom housekeeping units with stoves, refrigerators, and microwaves. Grounds include basketball courts, shuffleboard, swing sets, grills, and swinging hammocks in the shade. Kayakers and canoeists will love the close proximity to the water. **Pros:** peaceful setting; ideal for those traveling with children; reasonable rates. **Cons:** not an in-town location. ✉ *25 Seaview Rd.* ☎ *508/240–1616* ⊕ *www.covebluffs.com* 🛏 *5 rooms, 8 housekeeping units* ⚂ *In-room: a/c, Wi-Fi. In-hotel: pool, laundry facilities* ▤ *MC, V* ⊙ *Closed Nov.–late Apr.*

$$$–$$$$ 🚗 **Fort Hill Bed and Breakfast.** Gordon and Jean Avery run this enchanting
Fodor's Choice   B&B in an 1864 Greek Revival farmhouse nestled in the tranquil Fort
★   Hill area (it is the only lodging within the National Seashore). The location is perfect—minutes off busy Route 6, but steps away from quiet, secluded trails that wind through cedar forests, fields crisscrossed by old stone fences, and a red-maple swamp. Two very large and cozy suites in the main house, tastefully decorated with period pieces and antiques, share a living room with fireplace. The crown jewel, however, is the light and airy Nantucket Cottage, with stone floors, a gas fireplace, and a classic white-and-blue Cape Cod bedroom loft. Breakfasts are superb, with offerings like oven-poached pears in sweet cream. **Pros:** pastoral setting; close to nature trails; private and elegant lodging. **Cons:** not an in-town location. ✉ *75 Fort Hill Rd.* ☎ *508/240–2870* ⊕ *www.forthillbedandbreakfast.com* 🛏 *2 suites, 1 cottage* ⚂ *In-room: a/c, no phone, kitchen (some), DVD (some), Wi-Fi. In-hotel: no kids under 18* ▤ *No credit cards* ⋈ *BP.*

$$$–$$$$ 🚗 **Four Points Sheraton.** This reliable if ordinary midrange chain hotel is within a mile of the entrance to the National Seashore. Rooms have views of the tropical indoor pool (with lush plants, pirate-themed bar,

and resident live parrot), the parking lot, or the woods. Outside rooms are a little bigger and brighter and have mini-refrigerators. Several different themed packages are available. **Pros:** good location; great for those with kids. **Cons:** no water views or beachfront; standard chain-hotel fare. ⊠ *3800 U.S. 6* ☎ *508/255–5000* ⊕ *www.capecodfourpoints. com* ↩ *107 rooms, 2 suites* ⅍ *In-room: a/c, refrigerator, Wi-Fi. In-hotel: restaurant, room service, bar, tennis courts, pools, gym* ⊟ *AE, D, DC, MC, V.*

¢ 🏨 **Hostelling International–Mid Cape.** On 3 wooded acres near the Cape Cod Rail Trail and a 15-minute walk from the bay, this hostel has cabins that sleep six to eight each; two can be used as family cabins. It has a common area and a kitchen, and there are a number of guest programs. Linens are provided (no sleeping bags); bring your own towels. Keep in mind that all guests must provide photo identification upon check-in (a valid driver's license or passport). **Pros:** perfect for those on limited budget; quiet location near bike trail and bay beaches. **Cons:** no privacy. ⊠ *75 Goody Hallet Dr.* ☎ *508/255–2785* ⊕ *www.capecod.hiusa. org* ↩ *8 cabins* ⅍ *In-room: no a/c, kitchen, no TV. In-hotel: Internet terminal* ⊟ *MC, V* ⊗ *Closed mid-Sept.–mid-May.*

$$–$$$ 🏨 **Inn at the Oaks.** If it weren't for this three-story inn's vivid-yellow paint job, it would be lost among the trees, even though it's right along U.S. 6. Victorian touches at this 19th-century refuge include graceful high ceilings and intricate interior wood molding. Each room has antiques, brass beds, and soft down comforters, plus a few modern amenities such as DVD players; some have claw-foot tubs, which are great to slide into after a day at the beach. Whale-watching, biking, and "adventure" packages are available. The inn is very child-friendly, with both indoor and outdoor play areas. **Pros:** good bet for those traveling with kids; on-site massages. **Cons:** on busy U.S. 6. ⊠ *3085 County Rd.* ☎ *508/255–1886* ⊕ *www.innattheoaks.com* ↩ *6 rooms, 4 suites* ⅍ *In-room: a/c, DVD, refrigerator (some), Wi-Fi. In-hotel: some pets allowed (fee)* ⊟ *AE, D, MC, V* ⎟◎⎟ *BP.*

$–$$ 🏨 **Ocean Park Inn.** Rooms at this property are clean, simple, and straightforward. There are larger family units available—one with a fireplace—but most rooms are for double occupancy, with full- or queen-size beds. You are welcome to use the amenities, including the pools and tennis courts, of the Four Points Sheraton. **Pros:** lots of special packages; good bet for those traveling with kids; close to bike trail and area beaches. **Cons:** no water views or beachfront. ⊠ *3900 U.S. 6* ☎ *508/255–1132 or 800/862–5550* ⊕ *www.capecodopi.com* ↩ *54 rooms, 1 suite* ⅍ *In-room: a/c, refrigerator, Wi-Fi. In-hotel: laundry facilities, some pets allowed (fee)* ⊟ *AE, D, DC, MC, V* ⊗ *Closed Nov.–Mar.*

$$$–$$$$ 🏨 **Penny House Inn & Spa.** Tucked behind a wave of privet hedge, this ★ rambling gray-shingle inn's spacious rooms are furnished with antiques, collectibles, and wicker. The luxurious accommodations are cozy rather than stuffy; many are romantic, with whirlpool tubs, fireplaces, or both. Take a dip in the saltwater pool, or indulge in a massage, facial, or mud wrap in the on-site spa room. Common areas include a great room with lots of windows and a selection of videos, a combination sunroom-library, and a garden patio with umbrella tables. A full homemade

breakfast starts the day, and afternoon tea is available. **Pros:** private and secluded, ideal for a romantic getaway; full range of spa services. **Cons:** off busy U.S. 6; no water views or beachfront. ⊠ *4885 County Rd. (U.S. 6)* ☎ *508/255–6632 or 800/554–1751* ⊕ *www.pennyhouseinn. com* ↵ *10 rooms, 3 suites* ⚒ *In-room: a/c, refrigerator (some), DVD, Wi-Fi. In-hotel: pool, spa, no kids under 8* ☐ *AE, D, MC, V* ⦿ *BP.*

$$$–$$$$

Fodor's Choice

★

▣ **Whalewalk Inn & Spa.** This 1830 whaling master's home is on 3 landscaped acres. Wide-board pine floors, fireplaces, and 19th-century country antiques provide historical appeal. Rooms in the main inn have four-poster queen- or king-size beds and antique or reproduction furniture. Suites with fully equipped kitchens are in the converted barn and guesthouse. A secluded saltbox cottage has a fireplace, kitchen, and private patio. Deluxe rooms in the carriage house have fireplaces, hot tubs, and private patios or balconies. The property also has an opulent state-of-the-art spa, complete with a small resistance pool and fitness center. Breakfast is served in the cheerful sunroom or on the garden patio. **Pros:** beautiful grounds; elegantly appointed rooms; decadent spa treatments. **Cons:** no water views or beachfront. ⊠ *220 Bridge Rd.* ☎ *508/255–0617 or 800/440–1281* ⊕ *www.whalewalkinn.com* ↵ *11 rooms, 6 suites* ⚒ *In-room: kitchen (some), no phone, refrigerator (some), DVD, Wi-Fi. In-hotel: pool, gym, spa, no kids under 12* ☐ *D, MC, V* ⊘ *Closed Jan.–Mar.* ⦿ *BP.*

⚠ **Atlantic Oaks Campground.** This campground in a pine-and-oak forest is less than 1 mi north of the Salt Pond Visitor Center and minutes from Cape Cod National Seashore. Primarily an RV camp (year-round hookups are available), it offers limited tenting as well. You can rent bikes, and there's direct access to the Cape Cod Rail Trail. Reservations are essential during peak season. ⚒ *Flush toilets, full hookups, drinking water, guest laundry, showers, fire grates, grills, picnic tables, electricity, public telephone, general store, play area, swimming (pond and ocean), Wi-Fi hotspot* ↵ *99 RV sites, 12 tent sites* ⊠ *3700 U.S. 6* ☎ *508/255–1437 or 800/332–2267* ⊕ *www.atlanticoaks.com* ☐ *D, MC, V* ⊘ *Closed Nov.–Apr.*

NIGHTLIFE AND THE ARTS

The **Cape Cod National Seashore** (☎ *508/255–3421*) sponsors summer-evening programs, such as slide shows, sunset beach walks, concerts by local groups or military bands, and campfire sing-alongs.

The **Eastham Painters Guild** holds outdoor art shows every Thursday, Friday, and holiday weekends from 9 to 5, July through mid-September, at the Schoolhouse Museum. It's next to Salt Pond Visitor Center. ⊠ *U.S. 6.*

Monday and Wednesday evenings in July and August are filled with the sounds of **Concerts on the Green;** local acts perform everything from folk to reggae starting at 6:30 PM. ⊠ *Eastham Village Green, U.S. 6.*

BEACHES, SPORTS, AND THE OUTDOORS

BEACHES

★ **Coast Guard Beach** (⊠ *Off Ocean View Dr.*), part of the National Seashore, is a long beach backed by low grass and heathland. A handsome former Coast Guard station is also here, though it's not open to the public. The beach has no parking lot of its own, so park at the Salt Pond Visitor Center or at the lot up Doane Road from the center and take the free shuttle to the beach. At high tide the size of the beach shrinks considerably, so watch your blanket. There are showers here, and lifeguards are posted between June and August. There's a daily charge of $15 for cars for the seashore beaches, or you can buy an annual pass for $45.

> ### WORD OF MOUTH
>
> "Sunset at First Encounter Beach…pick a night where sunset is around low tide. There will be beautiful views, many families (but not crowded) and you can walk out/play in the tide pools quite a ways out. Try to arrive 1–2 hours before sunset—there's no parking charge after 5 PM. It's magical." —tmagyari

On the bay side of the Outer Cape, **First Encounter Beach** (⊠ *End of Samoset Rd.*) is open to the public and charges daily parking fees of $15 to nonresidents in season. It's a popular sunset spot. Parking fees or passes also apply to several other bay beaches and ponds, both saltwater and freshwater.

Fodor'sChoice **Nauset Light Beach** (⊠ *Off Ocean View Dr.*), adjacent to Coast Guard
★ Beach, continues the National Seashore landscape of long, sandy beach backed by tall dunes, grass, and heathland. It has showers and lifeguards in summer, but as with other National Seashore beaches, there's no food concession. Nauset charges $15 daily per car, but you can buy an annual pass for $45. Parking here fills up very quickly in summer; plan to arrive early or you may have to go elsewhere.

BICYCLING

The **Idle Times Bike Shop** (⊠ *4550 U.S. 6, at Brackett Rd.* ☎ *508/255–8281* ⊕ *www.idletimesbikes.com*) provides bikes of all sizes and types and is right near the Cape Cod Rail Trail.

Across from Salt Pond Visitor Center, the **Little Capistrano Bike Shop** (⊠ *Salt Pond Rd.* ☎ *508/255–6515* ⊕ *www.capecodbike.com*) has plenty of bikes and trailers available for rent and is between the Cape Cod Rail Trail and the National Seashore Bike Trail.

Nauset Trail, maintained by the Cape Cod National Seashore, stretches 1½ mi from Salt Pond Visitor Center through groves of apple and locust trees to Coast Guard Beach.

BOATING

Castaways Marine (⊠ *4655 Rte. 6* ☎ *508/255–7751* ⊕ *www.castaways-marine.com*) rents canoes, kayaks, surfboards, several different kinds of boats. Also for sale is all manner of beach paraphernalia—you can't possibly miss all that colorful plastic from the road.

HEALTH AND FITNESS CLUBS

Willy's Gym (⊠ *4730 U.S. 6, North Eastham* ☎ *508/255–6370* or *508/255–6826* ⊕ *www.willysgym.com*) is the astounding 100,000-square-foot branch of the original Willy's in Orleans. Kids will love Play World, a massive indoor playground. Other facilities include an Olympic-size pool, a rock-climbing wall, and indoor and outdoor tennis courts. After your workout, relax in the hot tub, steam room, or sauna, or book a massage or skin-care treatment at Kembali Spa.

SHOPPING

On your way to a day at the beach, a long bike ride, or a hike in the National Seashore? Bring some sandwiches along and pack an easy picnic. Build your own sub at **Nauset Market** (⊠ *5030 U.S. 6* ☎ *508/255–4879*). There are plenty of other snacks and beverages on hand to fill your knapsack.

Sam's Deli (⊠ *100 Brackett Rd.* ☎ *508/255–9340*) has giant sandwiches, a large variety of prepared salads, and some of the best chocolate chip cookies around. For a take-home barbecue, there is an excellent butcher counter.

The Outer Cape

WORD OF MOUTH

"I am back just today from a week's stay in Truro. I spent a lot of time in the area around Race Point Beach in Provincetown. The park services offer a lot of activities at all of their beaches—I did a walk and a hike where the ranger described how you can walk 40 miles and still be within the federal park system. These beaches would include Marconi, Race Point and Herring Cove. I also read too late that you can do kayaking and canoeing through the Park service for reasonable prices."

—Jackie

By Andrew Collins
Updated by Laura V. Scheel

As you drive through the Outer Cape, the topography flattens out, the vegetation grows sparser and more coniferous, and the sea approaches as the land narrows. Much of the region is undeveloped, protected by the sprawling Cape Cod National Seashore. The three towns that make up this region—Wellfleet, Truro, and Provincetown—each have a very distinct sense of spirit and character.

Technically part of the Lower Cape, the Outer Cape is nonetheless its own entity, forming the wrist and fist of Cape Cod. Long, straight, dune-backed beaches appear to go on forever; inland, trails wind through wind-stunted forests of scrub pine, beech, and oak. Many locals and visitors will tell you that this is where "the real Cape" begins.

Wellfleet is a sleepy town in the off-season, but it comes to life in summer. Home to a large community of artists, Wellfleet has an abundance of galleries and studios, as well as upscale shops and restaurants and an active harbor. Truro is for those in search of peace and quiet. With an expanse of high dunes, salt marshes, pine forests, and winding back roads, Truro is the least-populated, least-developed town on the entire Cape.

The promise of solitude has long drawn artists and writers to the Outer Cape. Provincetown has two faces—a quiet little fishing village in winter and a party town in summer. Those in search of fun, including many gay and lesbian folks, come for the rugged beaches, photogenic streets lined with historic homes, zany nightlife, shops selling everything from antiques to zoot suits, and the galleries, readings, and classes that carry on Provincetown's rich history as an artist colony.

ORIENTATION AND PLANNING

GETTING ORIENTED

Making your way around narrow Outer Cape, you really have one key option for getting around: driving along U.S. 6. There are some less congested but slower and indirect roads between the area's two least-developed communities, Wellfleet and Truro. In Wellfleet, many businesses and attractions are strung along U.S. 6, but there's also a compact downtown with art galleries, cafés, and boutiques that's ideal for strolling. Truro has just the tiniest commercial district, and its few attractions are best reached by car, as they're somewhat far apart. In Provincetown, on the other hand, a car—especially in summer—can actually be a hindrance. This is a walkable town with two main thoroughfares, Commercial and Bradford streets. Provincetown also has some excellent beaches, which are a short drive or bike ride from downtown.

TOP REASONS TO GO

Exploring the beaches: Cape Cod National Seashore has serious surf and sand dunes so tall that they block the late-afternoon sun. The beaches are also contiguous, so you can walk from Eastham to Provincetown if you've got the stamina.

Browsing art galleries: Wellfleet's town center has nearly two dozen art galleries representing local and national artists, and Provincetown is at least its match. The works aren't limited to kitschy seaside scenes—you can also find abstract works and interesting crafts.

Watching for whales: Several species of whales frequent the area from April to mid-October. These massive creatures to swim so close to whale-watching boats that you can often look them in the eye. Boats depart from Provincetown's harbor.

Strolling Commercial Street: One continuous parade, Commercial Street is Provincetown's best place to see and be seen. Day-trippers, drag queens, and couples of all kinds fill the street day and night. Keep an eye out for a Cher impersonator riding a scooter.

Wellfleet and South Wellfleet. Spread out along both sides of U.S. 6, Wellfleet also has a densely clustered downtown of shops, galleries, and restaurants. Wellfleet is known for its stunning beaches, both bayside and on the ocean, and its lively arts culture. South Wellfleet, extending from the Eastham border, is a mostly residential area with no commercial hub.

Truro and North Truro. Although it lacks an obvious downtown area, Truro has strong appeal for its dramatic shoreline, immense dunes, and great natural beauty. There's less commercialism here than in other Outer Cape towns, though plenty of giant homes can be found off the main roads, many overlooking Cape Cod Bay. North Truro blends into Provincetown's outermost reaches.

Provincetown. Commercial Street is where the action is. You'll find drag shows, dance clubs, outdoor dining, and pure frivolity, along with all kinds of shops and art galleries. But plenty of peace can be had in the town's outer reaches. Head out to the Provincelands for hiking and biking, or the beach for some sun and sand. The town is popular with gay and lesbian travelers, although it draws a wide selection of visitors.

PLANNING

WHEN TO GO

Prime time on the Outer Cape—when everything is open—is from Memorial Day to around Columbus Day; July and August are by far the most crowded times. The shoulder seasons of late May and June, and after Labor Day, have become more and more popular with childless travelers who aren't locked into a school schedule. Rates are lower during these times, and restaurants and shops are still open. If the weather has been generous, swimming is still a pleasant possibility.

Wellfleet pretty much seals itself up after OysterFest, held the weekend after Columbus Day; most galleries and restaurants close, leaving just a handful of year-round businesses. But you'll have the entire outside world to explore, now free of thousands of others trying to do the same thing. Ocean climates keep winters milder than on the mainland. It's quiet—beautifully so—and distractions and pleasures take on a more basic flavor.

Provincetown clears out as well, but not as fully as Wellfleet. Various theme weekends throughout the year have boosted tourism in the off-season, and there are always readings, films, and places to eat. The off-season is truly a time to discover the essence of the place, see its changing natural beauty, and experience a more restful and relaxed pace.

PLANNING YOUR TIME

One reason that the Outer Cape is so popular is that few other areas can so thoroughly combine natural splendor with sophisticated cultural offerings. Wellfleet and Provincetown, the region's largest communities, are equally good choices for your base of operations. Wellfleet's small-town feel is decidedly less frenetic than that of Provincetown. On the other hand, Provincetown has the best selections of bars and clubs. You could also easily spend a full day or two just walking around Provincetown's downtown and checking out the dozens and dozens of shops, galleries, and restaurants. Truro is downright sleepy in comparison, though not dull.

GETTING HERE AND AROUND

BOAT AND FERRY TRAVEL

In season, ferries run from Provincetown to Boston and Plymouth. *For more information, see ⇨ Boat and Ferry Travel in Travel Smart Cape Cod in the back of this book.*

BUS TRAVEL

The Plymouth & Brockton Street Railway provides bus service to Provincetown from downtown Boston or Logan Airport, with stops en route. *For more information, see ⇨ Bus Travel in Travel Smart Cape Cod in the back of this book.*

The Shuttle, run by the Cape Cod Regional Transit Authority, provides a much-needed transportation boost. The route begins at Horton's Camping Resort in Truro and continues to Provincetown along Route 6A; it stops wherever a passenger or roadside flagger dictates. Once in Provincetown, the shuttle continues up Bradford Street, with alternating trips to Herring Cove Beach and Pilgrim Park as well as summertime service up to Provincetown Airport and Race Point Beach. It runs every 30 minutes and is outfitted to carry bicycles. The service is popular and reasonably priced ($2 for a single fare, $6 for a day pass), and the only trouble seems to be finding parking on the Truro end (plans are in the works to find alternative parking areas). The shuttle runs throughout the day from late May until mid-October, with more-limited service during the off-season.

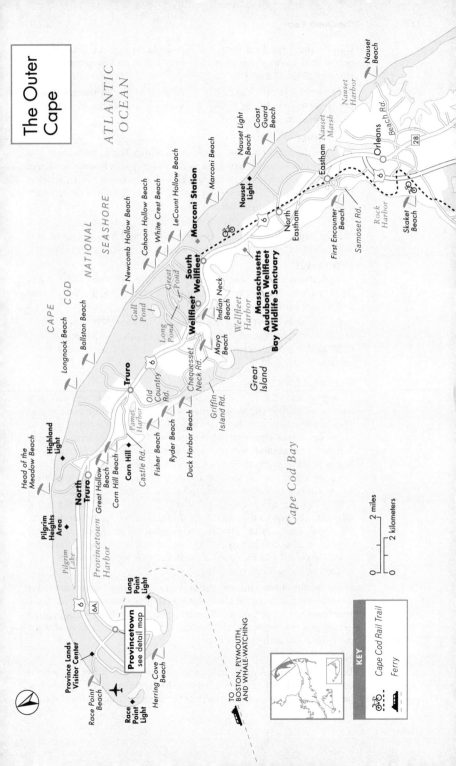

The Outer Cape

ATLANTIC OCEAN

CAPE COD NATIONAL SEASHORE

Nauset Beach

Nauset Beach

Nauset Harbor

Nauset Marsh

Coast Guard Beach

Nauset Light Beach

Nauset Light

Marconi Beach

Marconi Station

LeCount Hollow Beach

White Crest Beach

Cahoon Hollow Beach

Newcomb Hollow Beach

South Wellfleet

Wellfleet

Indian Neck Beach

Wellfleet Harbor

Massachusetts Audubon Wellfleet Bay Wildlife Sanctuary

Mayo Beach

Great Pond

Gull Pond

Long Pond

Chequesset Neck Rd.

Griffin Island Rd.

Great Island

Eastham

North Eastham

First Encounter Beach

Samoset Rd.

Rock Harbor

Skaket Beach

Orleans

Beach Rd.

28

6

Cape Cod Bay

Ballston Beach

Truro

Old Country Rd.

Pamet Harbor

Duck Harbor Beach

Ryder Beach

Fisher Beach

Castle Rd.

Corn Hill

Corn Hill Beach

Great Hollow Beach

North Truro

Longnook Beach

Highland Light

Head of the Meadow Beach

Pilgrim Heights Area

Pilgrim Lake

Provincetown Harbor

Long Point Light

Province Lands Visitor Center

Race Point Beach

Race Point Light

Herring Cove Beach

Provincetown see detail map

6

6A

TO BOSTON, PLYMOUTH, AND WHALE-WATCHING

KEY

Cape Cod Rail Trail

Ferry

0   2 miles
0   2 kilometers

Run by the Cape Cod Regional Transit Authority, the Flex bus has year-round service running from Harwich Port to Provincetown that stops in Wellfleet and Truro.

Bus Lines Flex (☏ *800/352–7155* ⊕ *www.capecodrta.org*). **Plymouth & Brockton Street Railway** (☏ *508/746–0378* ⊕ *www.p-b.com*). **Shuttle** (☏ *800/352–7155* ⊕ *www.capecodtransit.org*).

CAR TRAVEL

U.S. 6 is the only road from Wellfleet to North Truro; from there you can enter Provincetown via U.S. 6 or the slower-paced Route 6A. Expect backups when you're approaching Wellfleet, because the road goes from two lanes to one. The slowdown usually lasts through Wellfleet, then eases up by the time you reach Truro.

In summer, heavy traffic is common Saturday, when weekly rentals change hands. It's a similar story on Friday and Sunday afternoons when weekenders are making their way to and from the Outer Cape.

TAXI TRAVEL

Cape Cab operates throughout the Outer Cape. Mercedes Cab offers local and long-distance service in vintage Mercedes sedans. Jody's Taxi and Queen Cab are good options in Provincetown.

Taxi Companies Cape Cab (✉ *Provincetown* ☏ *508/487–2222*). **Jody's Taxi** (✉ *Provincetown* ☏ *508/487–0265*). **Mercedes Cab** (✉ *Provincetown* ☏ *508/487–3333* ⊕ *www.mercedescab.com*). **Queen Cab** (✉ *Provincetown* ☏ *508/487–5500*).

RESTAURANTS

Dining on the Outer Cape means everything from humble fried-clam shacks to candlelit elegance. Many restaurants have withstood the tests of time and fashion and have developed loyal followings that keep their doors open year after year. Menus frequently highlight local seafood. Wellfleet's restaurants, although not inexpensive, cater as much to families as to adult sophisticates and typically have menus offering a wide range of items, from less-expensive burgers and fried-seafood platters to creatively prepared steaks and fish grills. Truro has just a handful of restaurants spread out along the byways. Provincetown opens a world of great variation to the eager diner. Alongside snazzy, hip restaurants, all aglow with candles, crystal, and fine linens, are an equal number of lively and boisterous cafés. Many have outdoor seating, providing good views of the town's constant action. Smoking is banned inside all of the town's bars and restaurants.

In the height of the summer season, you may have to wait a while for a table—even if you have a reservation. To make matters worse, in the past few years Cape Cod has been experiencing a labor shortage; good help is at a premium, and this has caused some restaurants to shorten their season or reduce their hours.

HOTELS

Lodging options on the Outer Cape are diverse. Wellfleet has several cozy inns and bed-and-breakfasts in the center of town, with a few larger motels on busy U.S. 6. Despite the strict building codes, there are a surprising number of large (though not imposing) hotel complexes and cottage colonies spread out along Cape Cod Bay in North Truro. These places may be crowded, but they're also right on the sand, with commanding views of sunsets and the Provincetown skyline.

Provincetown's lodging scene has changed dramatically in recent years, as a number of old guesthouses and inns have been sold and converted to private homes. Those that remain have mostly transformed themselves from modest, affordable lodgings to sophisticated—and quite pricey—fine inns. With the shrinkage in available rooms, it's become even harder to find a room during the summer months. Minimum stays of at least three nights are often the norm during the peak season and holiday times, and sometimes there's a week minimum in July and August. That being said, more and more Provincetown properties have begun staying open for most or even all of the year—if you don't feel a need to visit during the busiest time of year, consider the quieter, yet still wonderfully atmospheric, off months. May, June, September, and October are especially nice, as most of the town's restaurants and shops are still open then, but hotel rates are lower and rooms easier to find.

WHAT IT COSTS					
	¢	$	$$	$$$	$$$$
Restaurants	under $10	$10–$16	$17–$22	$23–$30	over $30
Hotels	under $90	$90–$140	$141–$200	$201–$260	over $260

Restaurant prices are per person for a main course at dinner. Hotel prices are for a standard double room, excluding 5.7% sales tax (more in some counties) and up to an additional 6% tourist tax.

CONDO AND HOUSE RENTALS

Cape Cod Realty lists rentals for Wellfleet; Atlantic Bay Real Estate specializes in Provincetown, Truro, and Wellfleet. Kinlin Grover Vacation Rentals lists available apartments and houses on the Outer Cape.

Local Agents Atlantic Bay Real Estate (✉ *Provincetown* ☎ *508/487–2430* ⊕ *www.atlanticbayre.com*). **Cape Cod Realty** (✉ *Wellfleet* ☎ *508/349–2245* ⊕ *www.capecodrealty.net*). **Kinlin Grover Vacation Rentals** (✉ *Wellfleet* ☎ *508/349–9000* ⊕ *www.vacationcapecod.com*).

VISITOR INFORMATION

The Provincetown Chamber of Commerce is open from March until New Year's Day and has the only staffed visitor center in town, just off Commercial Street near MacMillan Wharf. The Provincetown Business Guild specializes in gay tourism and is open year-round to offer answers over the phone or send out its directory—but it has no visitor center. The Truro Chamber of Commerce and Wellfleet Chamber are open daily from late May through early September, and on weekends from mid-April through late May and from early September through mid-October.

WELLFLEET AND SOUTH WELLFLEET

Still famous for its world-renowned and succulent namesake oysters and for having been a colonial whaling and cod-fishing port, Wellfleet is today a tranquil community; many artists and writers call it home. Less than 2 mi wide, it's one of the most attractively developed Cape resort towns, with a number of fine restaurants, historic houses, art galleries, and a good old Main Street in the village proper. The South Wellfleet section of town extends to the North Eastham border and has a wonderful Audubon nature sanctuary and a drive-in theater that doubles on weekends as a flea market. There's no village center here, just a handful of motels, restaurants, and businesses along busy U.S. 6.

Historic buildings that once housed oyster and fish-drying shacks or stately residences now contain upscale art galleries, designer-clothing stores, and restaurants. Wellfleet's small-town nature still somehow accommodates the demands of a major tourist industry; the year-round population of around 2,800 residents explodes to more than 18,000 people in July and August.

Tourism isn't the only industry, though. Fishing boats still head out from the harbor daily in search of scallops, cod, and other fish. Shellfishing accounts for a major portion of the town's economy. Whaling played a role in the 18th and 19th centuries; a raucous whaling tavern once thrived out on the now-sunken Billingsgate Island. Dozens of world-traveling sea captains found their way to Wellfleet as well, the effect evident in many of the grand old houses that line the narrow streets of town. The Wellfleet Historical Society is a fine stop for those who wish to see the town as it was in its early days.

Natural splendor, as well as history and sophisticated artistic culture, accounts for Wellfleet's popularity. The beaches are spectacular, with their towering sand dunes, bracing surf, and miles of unfettered expanse. Seemingly endless wooded paths in the domain of the National Seashore make for terrific walking and hiking trails, and the sheltered waters of the tidal Herring River and Wellfleet Harbor are a favorite destination for canoeists, kayakers, windsurfers, and sailors.

GETTING HERE AND AROUND

Like many Cape Cod towns, Wellfleet is spread out on either side of U.S. 6. Wellfleet Village is on the bay side, about 3 mi north of the entrance to Marconi Beach. Main Street makes its way past several businesses. A left turn will take you toward the harbor along Commercial Street, which is full of shops and galleries. The downtown center of Wellfleet is quite compact, so it's best to leave your car in one of the public parking areas and take off on foot.

For a scenic loop through a classic Cape landscape near Wellfleet's Atlantic beaches—with scrub and pines on the left, heathland meeting cliffs and ocean below on the right—take LeCount Hollow Road just north of the Marconi Station turnoff. All the beaches on this strip rest at the bottom of a tall grass-covered dune, which lends dramatic character to this outermost shore.

ESSENTIALS
Visitor Information **Wellfleet** (⊠ *U.S. 6, near the post office South Wellfleet*
☎ *508/349–2510* ⊕ *www.wellfleetchamber.com*).

EXPLORING

TOP ATTRACTIONS

Great Island. Chequessett Neck Road makes for a pretty 2½-mi drive from the harbor to the bay past Sunset Hill—a great place to catch one. At the end, on the left, is a parking lot and wooded picnic area from which nature trails lead off to Great Island, perfect for beachcombers and solitude seekers. The "island" is actually a peninsula connected by a sand spit built by tidal action. More than 7 mi of trails wind along the inner marshes and the water—these are the most difficult paths on the seashore because they're mostly in soft sand. In the 17th century, a tavern and shore whaling lookout towers stood here. By 1800 the hardwood forest that had covered the island had been cut down for use in the building of ships and homes. The pitch pines and other growth you see today were introduced in the 1830s to keep the soil from washing into the sea. To the right of the Great Island lot, a road leads to **Griffin Island,** which has its own walking trail. ⊠ *Chequessett Neck Rd., Greater Wellfleet.*

★ **Marconi Station.** On the Atlantic side of the Cape is the site of the first transatlantic wireless station erected on the U.S. mainland. It was from here that Italian radio and wireless-telegraphy pioneer Guglielmo Marconi sent the first American wireless message to Europe—"most cordial greetings and good wishes" from President Theodore Roosevelt to King Edward VII of England—on January 18, 1903. An outdoor shelter contains a model of the original station, of which only fragments remain as a result of cliff erosion. Underneath a roofed structure at Marconi Station is a mock-up of the spark-gap transmitter Marconi used. There's a lookout deck that offers a vantage point of both the Atlantic and Cape Cod Bay. Off the parking lot, a 1½-mi trail and boardwalk lead through the **Atlantic White Cedar Swamp,** one of the most beautiful trails on the seashore; free maps and guides are available at the trailhead. **Marconi Beach,** south of the Marconi Station on Marconi Beach Road, is one of the National Seashore's lovely ocean beaches. ⊠ *Marconi Site Rd., South Wellfleet* ☎ *508/349–3785* ⊕ *www.nps.gov/caco* ⊠ *Free* ☉ *Daily dawn–dusk.*

QUICK BITES

The **PB Boulangerie Bistro** (⊠ *15 LeCount Hollow Rd., South Wellfleet* ☎ *508/349–1600* ⊕ *www.pbboulangeriebistro.com*) has caused a serious sensation in this seaside town. Painted a vivid shade of coral, this former clam shack has found new life selling just-baked breads and succulent pastries. By early morning—even in off-season—the line snakes down the ramp and into the parking lot. Look for brioche with dark chocolate and pastry cream, *pain aux fromage* (cheese bread), and numerous other knee-weakening choices. There's outdoor and indoor seating for breakfast and dinner.

Massachusetts Audubon Wellfleet Bay Wildlife Sanctuary. This 1,100-acre reserve is home to more than 250 species of birds. The jewel of the Massachusetts Audubon Society, the sanctuary is a superb place for walking, birding, and watching the sun set over the salt marsh and bay. The **Esther Underwood Johnson Nature Center** contains two

Fodor's Choice
★

WORD OF MOUTH

"Wellfleet is famous (at least from *New Yorker* cartoons) for the number of NY psychiatrists vacationing there. It may be the better choice if you have episodes of drama in your life."   —Ackislander

700-gallon aquariums that offer an up-close look at marine life common to the Cape's tidal flats and marshlands. From the center you can hike five short nature trails, including a fascinating Boardwalk Trail that leads over a salt marsh to a small beach—or you can wander through the Butterfly Garden. The Audubon Society is host to naturalist-led wildlife tours around the Cape, including trips to the Monomoy Islands, year-round. The sanctuary also has camps for children in July and August and weeklong field schools for adults. ⊠ *291 U.S. 6, South Wellfleet* ☎ *508/349–2615* ⊕ *www.massaudubon.org/wellfleetbay* ⊠ *$5* ☉ *Trails daily 8 AM–dusk; nature center late May–mid-Oct., daily 8:30– 5; mid-Oct.–late May, Tues.–Sun. 8:30–5.*

Uncle Tim's Bridge. A good stroll around town would take in Commercial and Main streets, ending perhaps at this bridge. The short walk across this arching landmark—with its beautiful, much-photographed view over marshland and a tidal creek—leads to a small wooded island. ⊠ *E. Commercial St., Downtown Wellfleet.*

Wellfleet Historical Society Museum. For a glimpse into Wellfleet's past, this diminutive museum exhibits furniture, paintings, shipwreck salvage, needlework, navigation equipment, early photographs, Native American artifacts, and clothing. Short guided walks around the center of town are given Tuesday and Friday mornings at 10:15 in July and August for $3. ⊠ *266 Main St., Downtown Wellfleet* ☎ *508/349–9157* ⊕ *www.wellfleethistoricalsociety.com* ⊠ *Free* ☉ *Late June–early Sept., Wed., Thurs., and Sat. 1–4, Tues. and Fri. 10–4.*

QUICK BITES

Box Lunch (⊠ *50 Briar La., Downtown Wellfleet* ☎ *508/349–2178* ⊕ *www. boxlunch.com*) is a popular chain, but this is the original location. It serves hot and cold roll-up sandwiches, a style it claims to have invented and perfected. A wide variety of fillings are available for breakfast, lunch, or early dinner. This tiny place gets ferociously busy in the summer season—call your order in ahead of time.

WORTH NOTING

First Congregational Church. This courtly 1850 Greek Revival building is said to have the only town clock in the world that strikes on ship's bells. The church's interior is lovely, with pale blue walls, a brass chandelier hanging from an enormous gilt ceiling rosette, subtly colored stained-glass windows, and pews curved to form an amphitheater facing the altar and the 738-pipe Hook and Hastings tracker-action organ, dating from 1873. To the right is a Tiffany-style window depicting a clipper ship. Concerts are given in July and August on Sunday at 7:30 PM. ⊠ *200 Main St., Downtown Wellfleet* ☎ *508/349–6877.*

WHERE TO EAT

$$ ✕ **Bookstore and Restaurant.** This quirky place, with views of Wellfleet
AMERICAN Harbor and Great Island, serves consistently tasty—if predictable—fare. It's attached to a funky vintage bookstore close to the town docks, and there's outdoor seating. The kitchen serves American classics, from grilled filet mignon and vegetable penne primavera to fresh seafood (the shellfish comes right from Wellfleet Harbor), including a first-rate oyster stew. The adjoining Bombshelter sports bar is a diverting spot to watch a game on TV; this basement tavern is packed to the rafters in summer. ⊠ *50 Kendrick Ave., Wellfleet Harbor* ☎ *508/349–3154* ⊕ *www.wellfleetoyster.com* ⚑ *Reservations not accepted* ⊟ *AE, D, MC, V* ⊗ *Closed Jan.–mid-Feb.*

$$ ✕ **Finely JP's.** Chef John Pontius consistently turns out wonderful, afford-
AMERICAN able food full of the best Mediterranean and local influences and ingre-dients at his beloved restaurant along U.S. 6. Housed in a handsome Arts and Crafts–inspired structure, this spot has long been a local favor-ite. Appetizers are especially good, among them oysters baked in a white wine–cream sauce and jerk-spiced duck salad with a raspberry vinai-grette. The Wellfleet paella and the roast duck with cranberry-orange sauce draw rave reviews. Early birds can take advantage of the very reasonable three-course prix-fixe menu for $22. Off-season hours vary, so call ahead. ⊠ *554 U.S. 6, South Wellfleet* ☎ *508/349–7500* ⊕ *www. finelyjps.com* ⚑ *Reservations not accepted* ⊟ *D, MC, V* ⊗ *Closed some nights during off-season. No lunch.*

$ ✕ **Flying Fish.** Set inside a handsome little Cape-style house with wood
AMERICAN floors and a simple dining room, this downtown café serves a wide range of foods for breakfast, lunch, and dinner—spinach-feta pizzas, Greek salads, curried-chicken-salad sandwiches, hummus platters, ice cream, smoothies, and a full range of coffees and pastries. It's perfect for a full sit-down meal (inside or on the brick patio) or a quick bite on the go. Don't forget to check out the selection of fresh-baked pas-tries. ⊠ *28 Briar La., Downtown Wellfleet* ☎ *508/349–7292* ⊕ *www. flyingfishwellfleet.com* ⊟ *MC, V* ⊗ *Closed mid-Oct.–Apr.*

$$ ✕ **Lighthouse.** A line snakes out the door of this simple wood-frame
AMERICAN house on summer mornings for classic bacon-and-egg breakfasts and tasty blueberry pancakes. Try a plate of steamers and a beer for lunch and perhaps chowder, cod fritters, lemon-butter scallops, and another beer for dinner—but keep in mind that it's as much about the value and the people-watching here as the food itself. Mexican fare, mar-garitas, and Dos Equis beer are served on Thursday. Downstairs you can order coffees, gelato, and lighter fare from the Lighthouse To-Go Shoppe. ⊠ *Main St., Downtown Wellfleet* ☎ *508/349–3681* ⊕ *www. mainstreetlighthouse.com* ⚑ *Reservations not accepted* ⊟ *D, MC, V.*

5

$ ✕ **Mac's Seafood.** Right at Wellfleet Harbor, this ambitious little spot has
SEAFOOD some of the freshest seafood around. There's not a whole lot of seating
★ here—some inside and some outside on picnic tables—but when you've
got a succulent mouthful of raw oyster or fried scallop, who cares? You
can always sit along the pier and soak up the great water views while
you chow down. This place serves a vast variety of seafood, plus sushi,
Mexican fare (grilled-scallop burritos), linguica sausage sandwiches,
and raw-bar items. There's also a selection of smoked fish, pâtés, lobster, and fish you can take home to grill yourself. Mac's also has **Mac's
Shack** (⊠ 91 Commercial St. ☎ 508/349–6333 ☯ Closed Mon. and mid-
Oct.–mid-May), a funky sit-down BYOB restaurant in a rambling mid-
19th-century barn overlooking Duck Creek, with a lobster boat on the
roof. ⊠ Wellfleet Town Pier, Wellfleet Harbor ☎ 508/349–0404 ⊕ www.
macsseafood.com ▤ MC, V ☯ Closed mid-Sept.–late May.

$ ✕ **Moby Dick's.** A meal at this good-natured, rough-hewn fish shack with
SEAFOOD a hyper-nautical theme is an absolute Cape Cod tradition for some
people. There's a giant blackboard menu (order up front, and food is
brought to you); a big, breezy screened-in porch in which to eat; and
red-checked tablecloths. Go for the Nantucket Bucket—a pound of
whole-belly Monomoy steamers, a pound of native mussels, and corn
on the cob served in a bucket. Also consider the rich and creamy lobster
bisque or the complete lobster-in-the-rough dinner. Bring your own liba-
tions, and if you need to kill time, stop inside Moby's Cargo, the bustling gift shop next door. ⊠ U.S. 6, Greater Wellfleet ☎ 508/349–9795
⊕ www.mobydicksrestaurant.com ⚑ Reservations not accepted ▤ AE,
MC, V ☯ Closed mid-Oct.–Apr. ⊮ BYOB.

$ ✕ **PJ's.** There's always a good-size but fast-moving line here, waiting for
SEAFOOD a heap of steamers or a creamy soft-serve cone. At PJ's you place your
order and take a number. Food is served in utilitarian style: Styrofoam
soup bowls, paper plates, plastic forks. The lobster-and-corn chowder
doesn't have much lobster in it, so stick to the traditional clam chowder.
Fried calamari and clam or oyster plates are generous and fresh. Try
the dense, spicy stuffed clams and a pile of crispy onion rings. ⊠ U.S. 6,
Greater Wellfleet ☎ 508/349–2126 ⚑ Reservations not accepted ▤ MC,
V ☯ Closed Nov.–mid-Apr.

$$ ✕ **Russ & Marie's Marconi Beach Restaurant.** The nondescript interior of
SOUTHERN this cavernous restaurant may not inspire you, but once you pull up
and smell the enticing aroma of barbecue from the smoker in front,
it's hard to resist the temptation to step inside for a meal. Drop in for
a lighter dish, such as a pulled-pork sandwich or a few littlenecks and
oysters from the raw bar, or savor a more substantial meal, perhaps a
platter of smoked barbecue ribs, a grilled porterhouse steak, or fish-
and-chips. It's all pretty tasty, but the barbecue stands out—you could
order most of the other items on the menu at any nearby steak-and-
seafood joint. ⊠ 545 U.S. 6, South Wellfleet ☎ 508/349–6025 ⊕ www.
marconibeachrestaurant.net ▤ MC, V ☯ Closed mid-Oct.–early Apr.

$$ ✕ **Van Rensselaer's.** This casual family seafood restaurant across from
SEAFOOD Marconi Station—not too far from the Eastham town line—stands out
for its nice mix of traditional standbys (baked-stuffed lobster, prime
rib) and more-creative offerings. You might start with coconut tempura

shrimp with an orange-ginger sauce or steamed littleneck clams with lemongrass-ginger-soy butter. Favorite main dishes include potato-crusted salmon with lobster-butter, and cranberry-orange duck with sweet-potato puree. Smaller portion meals are available from a bistro menu. The restaurant also an all-you-can-eat Sunday buffet. ⊠ *U.S. 6, South Wellfleet* ☎ *508/349–2127* ⊕ *www.vanrensselaers.com* ▤ *AE, D, DC, MC, V* ⊗ *Closed Nov.–mid-Apr. No lunch.*

$$$

AMERICAN

Fodor'sChoice

★

✕ **Wicked Oyster.** In a rambling, gray clapboard house, the Wicked Oyster serves up the most-innovative fare in Wellfleet. Try the roasted lamb loin wrapped in prosciutto with baked polenta, or the pan-roasted catch of the day with littleneck clams, leeks, bacon, and fingerling potatoes. Oyster stew and the open-face burger (with blue-cheese aioli and applewood-smoked bacon) are among the top lunch dishes. Breakfast is a favorite here—try the smoked-salmon Benedict. There's also an outstanding wine list. ⊠ *50 Main St., Downtown Wellfleet* ☎ *508/349–3455* ⊕ *www.thewickedo.com* ▤ *AE, D, MC, V* ⊗ *Closed Wed.*

$$

SEAFOOD

★

✕ **Winslow's Tavern.** This 1805 Federal-style captain's house contains five dining rooms; try for a table on the porch overlooking the center of town. The kitchen specializes in bistro-inspired seafood, mostly with American and Mediterranean preparations. Bacon-wrapped scallops with mango chutney and grilled lobster with sweet-corn relish rank among the better dishes. Head to the cozy lounge upstairs for live music Thursday through Sunday night in July and August. It's filled with plush sofas and tables lit by flickering candles. ⊠ *316 Main St., Downtown Wellfleet* ☎ *508/349–6450* ⊕ *www.winslowstavern.com* ⚠ *Reservations not accepted* ▤ *AE, MC, V* ⊗ *Closed mid-Oct.–mid-May.*

WHERE TO STAY

$$$$

★

⊡ **Aunt Sukie's Bayside Bed & Breakfast.** Hosts Sue and Dan Hamar treat you like you're actual guests in their home, a part-contemporary, part-antique inn with three rooms and multiple decks. It's set on the marsh grass fronting Wellfleet Harbor and Cape Cod Bay, along a quiet residential stretch of road near Power's Landing. The birds, the water, and the stunning bay views will probably be enough to keep you content in the shade of trees with a pair of binoculars. Rooms are welcoming, with flowered quilts and private decks, and the two upstairs beds grant vistas of the water without a lift of the head. The room in the antique portion of the home has a gas fireplace, a brick patio, and a grand claw-foot tub. **Pros:** overlooking Cape Cod Bay; private and quiet; pretty grounds. **Cons:** a little too far to walk to dining and shopping. ⊠ *525 Chequessett Neck Rd., Greater Wellfleet* ☎ *508/349–2804 or 800/420–9999* ⊕ *www.auntsukies.com* ⇱ *2 rooms, 1 suite* ⚙ *In-room: no a/c, refrigerator, no phone, no TV, Wi-Fi. In-hotel: beachfront, no kids under 8* ▤ *MC, V* ⊗ *Closed Oct.–mid-June* ⦿ *CP.*

$$–$$$

⊡ **Even'tide.** Long a summer favorite, this motel is set back off the main road, surrounded by 5 acres of trees and lawns; it has direct access to the Cape Cod Rail Trail. A central attraction is the 60-foot indoor pool (although Wellfleet's beaches are also close by). Rooms have simple modern furnishings; choose from doubles, two-room family suites, and efficiencies with kitchens. Cottages speckled about the property are available for stays of a week or longer. The staff is friendly and enthusiastic. **Pros:** short drive or bike ride from beach; suites are a bargain for families. **Cons:** need a car to get downtown; motel-style rooms. ⊠ *650 U.S. 6, South Wellfleet* ☎ *508/349–3410 or 800/368–0007* ⊕ *www.eventidemotel.com* ⊲ *31 units, 10 cottages* ♿ *In-room: a/c, kitchen (some), refrigerator, Wi-Fi. In-hotel: pool, laundry facilities, Wi-Fi hotspot* ☞ *1- or 2-wk minimum for cottages in summer* ⊟ *MC, V* ☉ *Closed Nov.–Apr.*

¢–$ ⊡ **Holden Inn.** If you're watching your budget and can deal with modest basics and rather drab furnishings, try this no-frills place on a tree-shaded street just outside the town center but within walking distance of several galleries and restaurants. Rooms are simply decorated with Grandma's house–type wallpapers, ruffled sheer or country-style curtains, and antiques such as brass-and-white-iron or spindle beds or marble-top tables. Private baths with old porcelain sinks are available in the adjacent 1840 and 1890 buildings. The lodge has shared baths, an outdoor shower, and a large screened-in porch with a lovely view of the bay and Great Island, far below. The main house has a common room and a screened front porch with rockers and a bay view through the trees. **Pros:** rock-bottom prices; walking distance to shopping. **Cons:** old-fashioned feel; many units share a bath. ⊠ *140 Commercial St., Downtown Wellfleet* ☎ *508/349–3450* ⊕ *www.theholdeninn.com* ⊲ *21 rooms, 12 with bath; 3 suites* ♿ *In-room: a/c (some), no phone, no TV* ⊟ *No credit cards* ☉ *Closed Nov.–Apr.*

$–$$ ⊡ **Inn at Duck Creeke.** Set on 5 wooded acres by a pond, a creek, and a salt marsh, this old inn consists of a circa-1815 main building and two other houses from the same era. Rooms in the main inn (except rustic third-floor rooms) and in the Saltworks house have a simple charm but could use some upgrading. Typical furnishings include claw-foot tubs, country antiques, lace curtains, chenille spreads, and rag rugs on hardwood floors. The two-room Carriage House is cabinlike, with rough barn-board and plaster walls. There's full-service dining with live jazz at the Tavern Room. **Pros:** very low rates; walking distance to downtown. **Cons:** some units share a bath; long walk to harbor or ocean. ⊠ *70 Main St., Downtown Wellfleet* ☎ *508/349–9333* ⊕ *www.innatduckcreeke. com* ⊲ *27 rooms, 19 with bath* ♿ *In-room: a/c (some), no phone, no TV, Wi-Fi (some). In-hotel: restaurant, Wi-Fi hotspot* ⊟ *AE, D, MC, V* ☉ *Closed mid-Oct.–late Apr.* ⦿ *CP.*

$–$$ ⊡ **Southfleet Motor Inn.** Geared toward active families, this carefully maintained motor inn is directly across from the entrance to the National Seashore at Marconi Station for easy access to ocean beaches. Bring your bikes to cruise the 25-mi Cape Cod Rail Trail. Rooms, which have utilitarian furnishings and an assortment of beds, can sleep up to five people. Indoor and outdoor pools and game room keep the kids busy and happy. **Pros:** short drive or bike ride from beach; lots of activities for kids; reasonable rates. **Cons:** on busy road; need a car to get downtown; motel-style rooms. ⊠ *U.S. 6, South Wellfleet* ☎ *508/349–3580 or 800/334–3715* ⊕ *www.southfleetmotorinn.com* ⊲ *33 rooms*

⚲ *In-room: a/c, refrigerator, Wi-Fi. In-hotel: pools, bicycles, laundry facilities, Internet terminal* ⊟ *AE, MC, V* ⊘ *Closed mid-Oct.–late Apr.*

$$–$$$
Fodor's Choice
★

🏨 **Stone Lion Inn.** B&Bs are places to feel welcome, at ease, and taken care of. All of these requirements are met at the Stone Lion Inn, a gracious mansard-roof Victorian just outside the town center and a short walk away from both the harbor and the village. Rooms have queen beds, ceiling fans to encourage the breezes, hardwood floors, and a mix of antiques and contemporary pieces that balance the house's 19th-century heritage with today's decorating sensibilities. Relax amid the gardens, in the outdoor shower, or in the pretty common room. New Yorkers may recognize the subtle Brooklyn theme—nostalgic, yet happily devoid of frenzy. **Pros:** short walk to shopping; stylish yet unpretentious decor; friendly owners. **Cons:** need a car to get to beach; not for younger kids. ⊠ *130 Commercial St., Downtown Wellfleet* ☎ *508/349–9565* ⊕ *www.stonelioncapecod.com* ⤳ *3 rooms, 1 apartment, 1 cottage* ⚲ *In-room: a/c, no phone (some), kitchen (some), refrigerator, no TV (some), Wi-Fi. In-hotel: no kids under 10* ⊟ *MC, V* ⊙︎ *BP.*

$$$–$$$$
★

🏨 **Surf Side Cottages.** Most of the units here are scattered on either side of Ocean View Drive, and a few additional cottages are nearby. Accommodations range from units in a piney grove to well-equipped ocean-side cottages. The cottages are a few minutes' walk from the town beach, a beautiful wide strand of sand, dunes, and surf. Though most of the exteriors are retro-cool Floridian, with pastel shingles and flat roofs, cottage interiors are Cape-style, including knotty-pine paneling. All units have phones, wood-burning fireplaces, screened porches, kitchens, and grills. Some have roof decks with an ocean view and outdoor showers. **Pros:** steps from the ocean; ideal for longer holidays; architecturally interesting compound. **Cons:** could stand some updating; not within walking distance of shops or restaurants. ⊠ *Ocean View Dr.* ⌂ *Box 937, South Wellfleet 02663* ☎ *508/349–3959* ⊕ *www.surfsidecottages. com* ⤳ *25 cottages* ⚲ *In-room: no a/c, kitchen, no TV. In-hotel: some pets allowed (fee)* ⌖ *1- to 2-wk minimum in summer* ⊟ *No credit cards* ⊙ *Closed Nov.–Mar.*

$$–$$$

🏨 **Wellfleet Motel & Lodge.** A mile from Marconi Beach, this clean and tasteful highway-side complex sits on 12 wooded acres. Rooms in the single-story motel aren't fancy but are renovated regularly; those in the two-story lodge are bright and spacious, with king- or queen-size beds and balconies or patios. The property offers direct access to the Cape Cod Rail Trail as well as indoor and outdoor pools; barbecue grills are available in a garden picnic area. **Pros:** short drive or bike ride to beach; on bike trail. **Cons:** need a car to get downtown; motel-style rooms. ⊠ *146 U.S. 6, South Wellfleet 02663* ☎ *508/349–3535 or 800/852–2900* ⊕ *www.wellfleetmotel.com* ⤳ *57 rooms, 8 suites* ⚲ *In-room: a/c, refrigerator, Wi-Fi. In-hotel: restaurant, bar, pools* ⊟ *AE, DC, MC, V* ⊙ *Closed Dec.–Mar.*

5

NIGHTLIFE AND THE ARTS

THE ARTS

During July and August the **First Congregational Church** (✉ *200 Main St., Downtown Wellfleet* ☎ *508/349–6877*) trades the serenity of worship for Sunday evening concerts. The music begins at 7:30 PM and could include opera, blues, jazz, or chamber music.

The drive-in movie is alive and well on Cape Cod at the **Wellfleet Drive-In Theater** (✉ *51 U.S. 6, South Wellfleet* ☎ *508/349–7176* ⊕ *www.wellfleetcinemas.com*), which is right by the Eastham town line. Regulars spend the night in style: chairs, blankets, and picnic baskets. Films start at dusk nightly from May to September, and there's also a standard indoor cinema with four screens, a miniature-golf course, and a bar and grill. A summer evening here is a classic Cape experience for many families.

★   The well-regarded **Wellfleet Harbor Actors Theater** (✉ *Kendrick St., Wellfleet Harbor* ☎ *508/349–9428* ⊕ *www.what.org*) has two venues: a first-rate 200-seat theater and the original 90-seat auditorium. WHAT continues its tradition, since 1985, of showing provocative, often edgy, world premieres of American plays, satires, farces, and black comedies in its mid-May to late-November season. In July and August there are productions aimed for kids, held under a white tent.

NIGHTLIFE

★   **Beachcomber** (✉ *1120 Cahoon Hollow Rd., Greater Wellfleet* ☎ *508/349–6055*) is big with the college crowd. Near Cahoon Hollow Beach, it offers dancing nightly in summer. You can order appetizers, salads, burgers, seafood, and barbecue indoors or at tables by the beachfront bar. There's also a raw bar.

In the venerable Inn at Duck Creeke, the **Tavern Room** (✉ *70 Main St., Downtown Wellfleet* ☎ *508/349–7369*), set in an 1800s building with a beam ceiling, a fireplace, and a bar covered in nautical charts, has live entertainment—anything from jazz and pop to country and Latin ensembles. Munchies are served alongside a menu of traditional and Caribbean dishes.

BEACHES, SPORTS, AND THE OUTDOORS

BEACHES

PUBLIC BEACHES

Extensive storm-induced erosion has made the cliffs to most of Wellfleet's ocean beaches quite steep—so be prepared for a taxing trek up and down the dune slope. Only the Cape Cod National Seashore beach at Marconi has steps; some have handrails to aid in the descent.

Cahoon Hollow Beach (✉ *Ocean View Dr., Greater Wellfleet*) has lifeguards, restrooms, and a restaurant and music club on the sand. This beach tends to attract younger and slightly rowdier crowds; it's a big Sunday-afternoon party place. There are daily parking fees of $15 for nonresidents in season only; parking is free for those with beach stickers. Space is limited, though the Beachcomber restaurant has paid parking.

Fodor's Choice ★ **Marconi Beach** (✉ *Off U.S. 6, South Wellfleet*), part of the Cape Cod National Seashore, charges $15 for daily parking. You can buy a yearly pass for $45. There are lifeguards, restrooms, and outdoor showers from late June through early September, which is the only period when admission fees are collected. A very long and steep series of stairs lead down to the beach.

Mayo Beach (✉ *Commercial St., Wellfleet Harbor*) is free, but swimming here is pleasant only around high tide—once the water recedes, it's all mud and sharp shells.

White Crest Beach (✉ *Ocean View Dr., Greater Wellfleet*) is a prime surfer hangout where the dudes often spend more time waiting for waves than actually riding them. Lifeguards are on duty daily 9 AM to 5 PM from July through Labor Day weekend. If you're up to the challenge, join one of the spontaneous volleyball games that frequently pop up. There are daily parking fees of $15 for nonresidents in season only; parking is free for those with beach stickers.

RESTRICTED BEACHES

Resident or temporary resident parking stickers are required for access to Wellfleet beaches in season only, from the last week of June through Labor Day. To get a three-day ($35), weekly ($70), or season ($225) pass, visit the Beach Sticker Booth on the town pier with your car registration in hand and a proof-of-stay form, available from rental agencies and hotels. For the rest of the year anyone can visit the beaches for free. Note that people arriving on foot or by bicycle, or after 5 PM, can visit the beaches at any time; the sticker is for parking only.

For information about restricted beaches, call the **Wellfleet Beach Sticker Office** (☎ *508/349–9818*).

🐧 **Duck Harbor Beach** (✉ *End of Chequessett Neck Rd., Greater Wellfleet*) seems like it's nearly at the end of the world. Its shores are on the warm waters of Cape Cod Bay, and there's plenty of room to wander and find your own private space. You can look out to Provincetown across the bay, but the finest view by far is the nightly sunset.

Indian Neck Beach (✉ *Pilgrim Spring Rd., Wellfleet Harbor*) is on the bay side, fronting Wellfleet Harbor, and is thus affected by the tides. Low tide reveals plenty of beach but less water—you'll have to walk way out before your hips get wet. It's a good spot to watch the comings and goings of fishing boats from Wellfleet Pier. With its shallow and calm waters, warmer temperatures, and ample opportunity for treasure hunting at low tide, it's also a great beach for families—just keep an eye out for plenty of foot-slicing oyster shells.

★ **LeCount Hollow Beach** (✉ *Ocean View Dr., South Wellfleet*) is the beach closest to U.S. 6 in South Wellfleet, along the meandering Ocean View Drive. The dunes are steep here, so be prepared to carry all beach belongings down (and up) the sandy slope.

Newcomb Hollow Beach (✉ *Ocean View Dr., Greater Wellfleet*) is the northernmost beach on the Wellfleet strip, closest to Truro. If you keep your eyes on the horizon, it's not at all uncommon to see the distant spout of a passing whale. This beach is also a popular nighttime fishing spot.

The **Wellfleet Ponds**, nestled in the woods between U.S. 6 and the ocean, were formed by glaciers and are fed by underground springs. Mild temperatures and clear, clean waters make swimming here pleasant for the whole family, a refreshing change from the bracing salty surf of the Atlantic. The ponds are also perfect for canoeing, sailing, or kayaking (boats are available from Jack's Boat Rental). A Wellfleet beach sticker is required to visit these fragile ecosystems in season (the sticker is only for cars, though—anyone can walk or ride a bike over to the ponds). Motorized boats are not allowed.

BICYCLING

The Cape Cod Rail Trail ends at the South Wellfleet post office. Other scenic routes for bicyclists include winding, tree-lined Old County Road, just outside Wellfleet center at the end of West Main Street. Ambitious riders can bike all the way to Truro on this often-bumpy road, but be sure to watch for vehicular traffic around the tight curves. Ocean View Drive, on the ocean side, winds through miles of wooded areas; there are several ponds along the route that are perfect for taking a quick dip. The Wellfleet Chamber of Commerce publishes a pamphlet called "Bicycling in Wellfleet."

Idle Times Bike Shop (⊠ *U.S. 6 just west of Cahoon Hollow Rd., Greater Wellfleet* ☎ *508/349–9161* ⊕ *www.idletimesbikes.com*) opens Memorial Day and rents bikes, trailer bikes (a tandem bike with a backseat for children who are big enough to pedal), and trailer attachments for the smaller passengers. The shop also handles repairs and sells parts and assorted accessories. Depending on the crowds and weather, it usually remains open until Columbus Day, but there's a branch in Eastham open year-round.

Little Capistrano Bike Shop (⊠ *1446 U.S. 6, South Wellfleet* ☎ *508/349–2363* ⊕ *www.capecodbike.com*) has a branch at the Cape Cod Rail Trail's terminus in South Wellfleet. It's open weekends from the end of May through mid-June and mid-September to mid-October, and daily from mid-June to early September.

BOATING

Jack's Boat Rental (⊠ *Gull Pond south of U.S. 6, Greater Wellfleet* ☎ *508/349–9808 or 508/349–7553* ⊕ *www.jacksboatrental.com*) has canoes, kayaks, Sunfish, pedal boats, surfboards, boogie boards, and sailboards. Guided kayak tours are also available.

Wellfleet Marine Corp (⊠ *25 Holbrook Ave., Wellfleet Harbor* ☎ *508/349–6417* ⊕ *www.wellfleetmarine.com*) rents sailboats and motorboats in various sizes by the hour or the day.

FISHING

Commercial Street leads to Wellfleet Pier, busy with fishing boats, sailboats, yachts, charters, and party boats. At the twice-daily low tides, you can dig on the tidal flats for oysters, clams, and quahogs.

You can climb aboard the charter boat **Jac's Mate** (⊠ *Wellfleet Pier, Wellfleet Harbor* ☎ *508/255–2978* ⊕ *home.comcast.net/~jacsmate*) for fishing expeditions in search of bass and blues.

The **Naviator** (⊠ *Wellfleet Pier, Wellfleet Harbor* ☎ *508/349–6003* ⊕ *www.naviator.com*) operates fishing trips on a walk-on basis from spring through fall. Rods, reels, and bait are included.

GOLF

Chequessett Yacht Country Club (⊠ *680 Chequessett Neck Rd., Greater Wellfleet* ☎ *508/349–3704* ⊕ *www.cycc.net*) has a 9-hole golf course. There are two sets of tees, so you can play 18 holes by repeating the course. Lessons are available.

SKATEBOARDING

The state-of-the-art Skateboard Park down at **Baker's Field** (⊠ *Kendrick Ave., Wellfleet Harbor*) was professionally designed for tricks and safety; it's manned by local teens. There's also a large playground for the little ones.

SURFING

Atlantic-coast Marconi and White Crest beaches are the best for surfing. Surfboard rentals can be arranged at Jack's Boat Rental.

Fun Seekers (☎ *508/349–1429* ⊕ *www.funseekers.org*) gives surf lessons, as well as pointers on windsurfing and kiteboarding.

Sickday Surf Shop (⊠ *361 Main St., Downtown Wellfleet* ☎ *508/214–4158* ⊕ *www.sickdaysurfandskate.com*) has rentals, lessons, and a shop full of surfer-approved clothing.

SHOPPING

ART GALLERIES

Andre Pottery (⊠ *5 Commercial St., Downtown Wellfleet* ☎ *508/349–2299* ⊕ *www.andrepottery.com*) specializes in handmade bowls, vases, and pitchers, mostly in greens, blues, and grays, the shades of the sea and shore.

Blue Heron Gallery (⊠ *20 Bank St., Downtown Wellfleet* ☎ *508/349–6724* ⊕ *www.blueheronfineart.com*) is one of the Cape's best galleries, with contemporary works—including Cape scenes, jewelry, sculpture, and pottery—by regional and nationally recognized artists.

★ **Brophy's Fine Art** (⊠ *313 Main St., Downtown Wellfleet* ☎ *508/349–6479* ⊕ *www.brophysfineart.com*), one of the few year-round shops in Wellfleet, carries a nice selection of pottery, jewelry, and landscape paintings by several prominent New England artists as well as the beautiful stained-glass works of owner Thomas Brophy.

Cove Gallery (⊠ *15 Commercial St., Downtown Wellfleet* ☎ *508/349–2530* ⊕ *www.covegallery.com*) displays the works of John Grillo, Tomie dePaola, and Leonard Baskin, among others. The gallery hosts Saturday-night artist receptions in July and August.

★ **Frying Pan Gallery** (✉ *250 Commercial St., Wellfleet Harbor* ☎ *508/349–0011* ⊕ *www.fryingpangallery.com*) has given new life to a very old oyster shack down by the harbor. Founder Steve Swain creates extraordinary fish sculptures and objects out of steel. Local painters like Paul Suggs and Jennifer Morgan capture Wellfleet's artistic spirit.

★ **Kendall Art Gallery** (✉ *40 Main St., Downtown Wellfleet* ☎ *508/349–2482* ⊕ *www.kendallartgallery.com*) carries eclectic modern works, including Harry Marinsky's bronzes in the sculpture garden, photography by Walter Baron and Alan Hoelzle, watercolors by Walter Dorrell, and contemporary art by several prominent Chinese artists.

Left Bank Gallery (✉ *25 Commercial St., Downtown Wellfleet* ☎ *508/349–9451* ⊕ *www.leftbankgallery.com*) displays the larger works of local and national artists and sells fine crafts in the back room facing Duck Creek.

Nicholas Harrison Gallery (✉ *25 Bank St., Downtown Wellfleet* ☎ *508/349–7799* ⊕ *www.thenicholasharrisongallery.com*) has made a name for itself in the area of lovely and unusual American crafts, including beautiful lamps, resin-and-silver jewelry, and hand-painted cabinets. Owners Mark and Laura Evangelista are also accomplished potters, and you'll see their vibrant ceramic works here as well.

SPECIALTY STORES

Abiyoyo (✉ *286 Main St., Downtown Wellfleet* ☎ *508/349–3422*) has a full line of Wellfleet T-shirts and sweatshirts, along with shoes, children's clothing, and bath and beauty products.

Chocolate Sparrow (✉ *326 Main St., Downtown Wellfleet* ☎ *508/349–1333*) makes nine types of fudge, luscious hand-dipped chocolates, and a wide array of decadent baked goods and sweets. It's open May through early September.

Eccentricity (✉ *354 Main St., Downtown Wellfleet* ☎ *508/349–7554*) keeps Main Street offbeat. One of the most interesting stores on the Cape, it sells African carved-wood sculptures, odd Mexican items, and trinkets made from recycled materials.

Hatch's Fish Market (✉ *310 Main St., Downtown Wellfleet* ☎ *508/349–2810*) brightens up the town hall parking lot with the vivid hues of fresh vegetables, fruits, and flowers. Arranged artfully in baskets, there are nearly 50 different varieties of produce, as well as homemade pesto, salsa, and cheese. The fish market sells the catch of the day and shellfish from nearby Indian Neck. Fill your basket from late May to mid-September.

★ **Herridge Books** (✉ *140 Main St., Downtown Wellfleet* ☎ *508/349–1323*) is the perfect store for a town that has been host to so many writers. Its dignified literary fiction, art and architecture, literary biography and letters, mystery, Americana, sports, and other sections are full of used books in very nice condition. Herridge also carries new editions on the Cape and its history.

Jules Besch Stationers (✉ *15 Bank St., Downtown Wellfleet* ☎ *508/349–1231*) has extraordinary cards, fine stationery, journals, papers, and pens. Proprietor Michael Tuck's warm and welcoming nature is as beautiful as his products.

Karol Richardson (⊠ *11 W. Main St., Downtown Wellfleet* ☎ *508/349–6378* ⊕ *www.karolrichardson.com*) fashions women's wear in luxurious fabrics and sells interesting shoes, hats, and jewelry.

Secret Garden (⊠ *Main St., Downtown Wellfleet* ☎ *508/349–1444*) doesn't waste any precious space—the walls are covered from floor to ceiling with whimsical folk-art pieces, handbags, clothing, shoes, and decorative accessories. There are good buys on sterling silver jewelry.

Wellfleet Marine (⊠ *25 Holbrook Ave., Downtown Wellfleet* ☎ *508/349–6417* ⊕ *www.wellfleetmarine.com*) sells ocean-themed jewelry, toys, and more. Mermaid and pirate lovers will find plenty of goodies here.

Wellfleet Marketplace (⊠ *295 Main St., Downtown Wellfleet* ☎ *508/349–3156*) is *the* place to pick up gourmet foods in town. In addition to the meat and seafood counters, you'll also find great deli treats, beer and wine, organic produce, and other tasty foods.

FLEA MARKET

Fodor'sChoice
★

The giant **Wellfleet Flea Market** (⊠ *51 U.S. 6, South Wellfleet* ☎ *508/349–0541* ⊕ *www.wellfleetcinemas.com/flea_market*) sets up shop in the parking lot of the Wellfleet Drive-In Theater mid-April through June and September and October, weekends and Monday holidays 8 to 4; July and August, Monday holidays, Wednesday and Thursday, and weekends 8 to 4. You'll find antiques, sweat socks, old advertising posters, books, Beanie Babies, Guatemalan sweaters, plants, trinkets, and plenty more among the 300 vendors. On Monday and Tuesday in July and August the vendors make way for large arts-and-crafts shows. A snack bar and playground keep fatigue at bay.

EN
ROUTE

If you're in the mood for a quiet, lovely ride winding through what the Cape might have looked like before Europeans arrived, follow **Old County Road** from Wellfleet to Truro on the bay side. It's bumpy and beautiful, with a stream or two along the way. So cycle on it, or drive slowly, or just stop and walk to take in the nature around you.

TRURO AND NORTH TRURO

Today Truro is a town of high dunes, estuaries, and rivers fringed by grasses, rolling moors, and houses sheltered in tiny valleys. It's a popular retreat for artists, writers, politicos, and numerous vacationing psychoanalysts. Edward Hopper summered here from 1930 to 1967, finding the Cape light ideal for his austere brand of realism. One of the largest towns on the Cape in terms of land area—almost 43 square mi—it's also the smallest in population, with about 1,400 year-round residents. Truro is also the Cape's narrowest town, and from a high perch you can see the Atlantic Ocean on one side and Cape Cod Bay on the other.

If you thought neighboring Wellfleet's downtown was small, wait until you see—or don't see—Truro's. It consists of a post office, a town hall, and a shop or two—you'll know it by the sign that says DOWNTOWN

TRURO at a little plaza entrance. Truro also has a library, a firehouse, and a police station, but that's about all. The North Truro section contains most of the town's accommodations, either along U.S. 6 or fronting the bay along Route 6A, just south of the Provincetown border. Many people who live or vacation in Truro choose it for its easygoing, quiet personality and lack of development—and its proximity to the excitement and commerce of Provincetown.

Settled in 1697, Truro has had several names during its long history. It was originally called Pamet after the local Native Americans, but in 1705 the name was changed to Dangerfield in response to all the sailing mishaps off its shores. "Truroe" was the final choice, named for a Cornish town that homesick settlers thought it resembled; the final "e" was eventually dropped. The town relied on the sea for its income—whaling, shipbuilding, and cod fishing were the main industries.

GETTING HERE AND AROUND

Truro sits near the end of Cape Cod, 2 mi north of Wellfleet and 7 mi southeast of Provincetown. U.S. 6 is the way most people reach Truro, though the real beauty of the town lies farther afield on back roads that lead to either Cape Cod Bay or the Atlantic. The Cape is fairly narrow here, so you will never find yourself hopelessly lost.

The Provincetown/NorthTruro Shuttle, run by the Cape Cod Regional Transit Authority, provides a much-needed transportation boost. Running along Route 6A, it stops wherever a passenger requests. It runs every 30 minutes and can carry bicycles.

ESSENTIALS

Cape Cod Regional Transit Authority (☏ 800/352–7155 ⊕ *www. capecodtransit.org*). **Truro** (✉ *U.S. 6 at Head of the Meadow Rd.* ☏ *508/487–1288* ⊕ *www.trurochamberofcommerce.com*).

EXPLORING

TOP ATTRACTIONS

Highland House Museum. Built in 1907 as a summer hotel, this appealingly low-key museum of local life and history has 17th-century firearms, mementos of shipwrecks and an exhibit on the U.S. Lifesaving Service, early fishing and whaling gear, ship models, a pirate's chest, and scrimshaw. One room exhibits wood carvings, paintings, blown glass, and ship models by Courtney Allen, artist and founder of the Truro Historical Society. Another shows a room furnished for guests. There's also a weekly lecture series from late June through late September. ✉ *6 Lighthouse Rd., off S. Highland Rd., North Truro* ☏ *508/487–3397* ⊕ *www.trurohistorical.org* 🖃 *$5; $7 includes admission to Highland Light* ⊘ *Late May–Sept., Mon.–Sat. 10–4:30, Sun. 1–4:30.*

Highland Light. Truly a breathtaking sight, this is the Cape's oldest lighthouse. The first light on this site, powered by 24 whale-oil lamps, began warning ships of Truro's treacherous sandbars in 1797—the dreaded Peaked Hills Bars, to the north, had claimed hundreds of ships. The current light, a 66-foot tower built in 1857, is powered by two 1,000-

Edward Hopper and Truro

The Outer Cape has inspired thousands of acclaimed artists, but perhaps none is more closely associated with its serene yet romantic landscape than Edward Hopper, the esteemed realist painter who lived in Truro for most of the last four decades of his life. Quiet Truro, with its peaceful, sandy lanes, suited the introspective Hopper perfectly.

Hopper, born in Nyack, New York, in 1882, enjoyed little commercial or critical success before middle age. Early in his career, he worked as a commercial illustrator to support himself while living in New York City's Greenwich Village. It was during the 1920s, after his marriage to Josephine Nivison, that Hopper achieved marked success as both an oil painter and watercolorist and became known for his starkly realistic scenes, often depicting public places filled with people, such as his most iconic work, *Nighthawks*.

Edward and Josephine first summered in Truro in 1930, and a few years later they designed their own Truro home. Much of Hopper's work conveyed the emptiness and alienation of big-city life, and although his Cape paintings were similar in their simplicity, they nevertheless offered a slightly more hopeful vision, if for no other reason than their tendency to focus more on the region's sensuous luminosity than strictly on lonely or bored people.

Most famously, Hopper's Truro work captured the undulating auburn hills along Pamet Road in his 1930 work *Corn Hill (Truro, Cape Cod)*. Other notable paintings that portray the Outer Cape include *Cape Cod Evening* (1939), *Route 6 Eastham* (1941), *Martha McKeen of Wellfleet* (1944), and *Cape Cod Morning* (1950).

—Andrew Collins

watt bulbs reflected by a huge Fresnel lens; its beacon is visible for more than 20 mi.

One of four active lighthouses on the Outer Cape, Highland Light has the distinction of being listed in the National Register of Historic Places. Henry David Thoreau used it as a stopover in his travels across the Cape's backside (as the Atlantic side is called). Twenty-five-minute tours of the lighthouse are given daily in summer. Especially grand are the special full-moon tours. ⊠ *S. Highland Rd., North Truro* ☎ *508/487–3397* ⊕ *www.capecodlight.org* ▨ *$5; $7 includes admission to Highland House Museum* ◷ *Mid-May–mid-Oct., daily 10–5:30.*

⟲ **Pamet Harbor.** For a few hours of exploring, take the children to this protected bay. At low tide you can walk out on the flats and discover the creatures of the salt marsh. A nearby plaque identifies plants and animals and describes the area's ecological importance. It's also a busy launching site for boats of all kinds, a favorite spot for kayakers, and a fine place for sunset watching. ⊠ *Depot Rd., Truro.*

QUICK BITES

Jams (⊠ *12 Truro Center Rd., Truro* ☎ *508/349–1616*) has fixings for a great picnic lunch: sandwiches, fresh produce, bottles of wine, and sweet treats.

EROSION ON CAPE COD

Forged by massive moving glaciers more than 20,000 years ago, Cape Cod's landscape is still in perpetual motion, continually shaped by the powerful forces of sand, wind, and water.

The Cape's land is slowly giving way to rising ocean levels and erosion, losing an average of nearly 4 feet of outer beach per year. Many a home or structure has succumbed to the unrelenting ocean over the years; some—like Truro's Highland Light and Eastham's Nauset Light—have been moved to safety. Eventually Cape Cod will likely be lost to the sea, though not for thousands of years.

You'll see many signs on beaches and trails asking walkers to keep off the dunes. Take heed, for much of the fragile landscape of the outer Cape is held together by its dune formations and the vegetation that grows within them.

Unless you like getting your knees knocked, don't bother sitting at the bench outside.

Pilgrim Heights. Part of Cape Cod National Seashore, Pilgrim Heights has a short trail that leads to the spring where members of a Pilgrim exploring party stopped to refill their casks, tasting their first New England water in the process. Walking through this still-wild area of oak, pitch pine, bayberry, blueberry, beach plum, and azalea gives you a taste of what it was like for these voyagers in search of a new home. "Being thus passed the vast ocean." William Bradford wrote in *Of Plimoth Plantation*, "they had no friends to welcome them, no inns to entertain them or refresh their weather-beaten bodies; no houses, or much less towns to repair to, to seek for succour."

From an overlook you can see the bluffs of High Head, where glaciers pushed a mass of earth before melting and receding. ⊠ *Off U.S. 6, North Truro.*

★ **Truro Vineyards of Cape Cod Winery.** Owned and run by the Roberts family since 2007, this vineyard has greatly stepped up production, and has begun experimenting with some new vintages. At the moment, the vineyard makes a commendable cabernet franc, chardonnay, zinfandel, sauvignon blanc, vignoles, and several notable blends. It also makes a red table wine that's flavored with cranberries and known for its unusual bottle, shaped like a lighthouse (along with two other "lighthouse" varieties). Free daily tours are given at 1 and 3 Memorial Day to Columbus Day. Sign up for the very popular Wednesday-evening wine and music series from late June to late August. ⊠ *Rte. 6A, North Truro* ☎ *508/487–6200* ⊕ *www.trurovineyardsofcapecod.com* ☑ *Free* ⊙ *Apr. and Dec., Fri. and Sat. 11–5, Sun. noon–5; May–Nov., Mon.– Sat. 11–5, Sun. noon–5.*

WORTH NOTING

Corn Hill. Near the beach of the same name, Co
memorates the finding of a buried cache of
and the *Mayflower* crew. They took it to Plyn
returning later to pay the Native American
⊠ *Corn Hill Rd., Truro.*

WHERE TO EAT

$$$ ✕ **Adrian's.** Adrian Cyr's restaurant crowns a ...g
AMERICAN grim Lake and all of Provincetown; his cooking also hits great neights.
Cayenne-crusted salmon with maple-mustard sauce is just one of the
well-prepared dishes here. Tuscan salad is also a hit, with tomatoes,
olives, fresh basil, plenty of garlic, and balsamic vinegar. The small
plates menu is a great way to sample lots of flavors for a very reason-
able price. The outdoor deck overflows at the popular breakfasts and
brunches, served every day in season and weekends in spring and fall—
try the cranberry pancakes with orange butter. ⊠ *Outer Reach Hotel,
535 U.S. 6, North Truro* ☎ *508/487–4360* ⊕ *www.adriansrestaurant.
com* ⊟ *AE, MC, V* ☉ *Closed late Sept.–mid-May and Mon.–Wed. spring
and fall. No lunch.*

$$ ✕ **Babe's Mediterranean Bistro.** It looks like a modest roadhouse from the
MEDITERRANEAN outside, but this rambling, casual space in North Truro serves quite
★ authentic and sophisticated Middle Eastern, North African, and Spanish
fare. It's run by chef-owner Peter Thrasher, who whips up such memorable dishes as Istanbul-style farfalle pasta with slow-braised lamb and
garlic yogurt, and Aegean-style meatballs studded with figs, pistachios,
and bell peppers, tossed with a spicy tomato-yogurt sauce; Moroccan tagines are another specialty. Be sure to start your meal with the
meze sampler. ⊠ *69 Rte. 6A, North Truro* ☎ *508/487–9955* ⊕ *www.
babesmedbistro.com* ⊟ *MC, V* ☉ *Closed mid-Oct.–mid-May. No lunch.*

$$$ ✕ **Blackfish.** Opened by talented chef Eric Jansen (originally behind Well-
AMERICAN fleet's celebrated Wicked Oyster), this favorite local spot sits inside a
★ rambling old blacksmith shop. Fans of fresh and creative food convene
here to sample rustic Italian fare using local ingredients. Consider the
rare-tuna Bolognese-style, or a savory rabbit ragout over pappardelle
pasta. The intimate, old-fashioned space is cozy and romantic—but it
can get a little hot on summer nights. ⊠ *17 Truro Center Rd., Truro*
☎ *508/349–3399* ⊟ *AE, MC, V* ☉ *Closed late Oct.–mid-May. No lunch.*

$$$ ✕ **Terra Luna.** An insider's favorite for fresh and inventive bistro fare with
ECLECTIC an Italian slant, Terra Luna has an intimate art-filled dining room with
Fodor'sChoice lace curtains, beam ceilings, and simple wooden tables. The food is styl-
★ ish, with sophisticated sauces for both fish and meat dishes. The littleneck clams with sausage, fennel, garlic, and tomatoes is a house favorite,
and the grilled duck breast with rhubarb-fennel chutney is an excellent
alternative to the usual fish. For dessert, don't miss the unusual black-
berry polenta custard, or a more traditional chocolate-silk cake with
caramel sauce. ⊠ *104 Rte. 6A, North Truro* ☎ *508/487–1019* ⊕ *www.
theterraluna.com* ⊟ *AE, MC, V* ☉ *Closed Nov.–early May. No lunch.*

Whitman House. What began as a modest pancake house has been transformed by the Rice family into a vast—if touristy—restaurant, but pewter plates, candlelight, and rustic wood accents make the place feel comfortably tavernlike. Predictable seafood, steaks, and surf-and-turf combos (consider the crabmeat casserole with petite filet mignon) keep the menu uncomplicated and the portions ample. Lunch and lighter dinner fare are served daily in the Bass Tavern. If you have to wait for a table, browse in the adjacent Amish quilt shop. ⊠ *Off U.S. 6 at Great Hollow Rd., North Truro* ☎ *508/487–1740* ⊕ *www.whitmanhouse.com* ⊟ *AE, D, DC, MC, V* ☺ *Closed Jan.–Mar.*

WHERE TO STAY

$–$$ **Cape View Motel.** The true appeal of this tan-clapboard roadside motel is its noble perch on a westward bluff, looking out over Cape Cod Bay sunsets and the distant lights of Provincetown. Deluxe rooms have private balconies, as well as fully equipped kitchenettes and a king bed or two doubles. The style inside can't compete with the vistas outside, but the rooms are clean, simple, reasonably priced, and a 10-minute drive from Provincetown. Free coffee and doughnuts are provided in the morning. **Pros:** inexpensive rooms; nice harbor views. **Cons:** few restaurants or shops nearby; feels a bit dated. ⊠ *Junction of U.S. 6 and Rte. 6A, North Truro* ☎ *508/487–0363 or 800/224–3232* ⊕ *www.capeviewmotel.com* ⇄ *32 rooms* ⌂ *In-room: a/c, kitchen (some), refrigerator, Wi-Fi. In-hotel: pool* ⊟ *AE, D, MC, V* ☺ *Closed mid-Oct.–mid-Apr.*

$$–$$$ **Crow's Nest Resort.** Amid the mostly run-of-the-mill motels and cottage compounds along Route 6A, this beautifully modernized all-suites beachfront property stands head and shoulders above the rest. Given the prime location, friendly service, and top-notch facilities and furnishings, this is one of the Outer Cape's best values for families and friends traveling together. Ground-floor units front an attractive wooden deck overlooking the bay, and upstairs units have private balconies with similar views. You can choose from studio, two-bedroom, and three-bedroom units, and all have full kitchens, fireplaces, whirlpool tubs, and washers and dryers, making them perfect for longer stays. The resort also rents three attractive beachfront bungalows, about ½ mi away. **Pros:** tasteful and contemporary furnishings; fantastic water views. **Cons:** a long walk to dining and shopping; no pool. ⊠ *496 Rte. 6A, North Truro* ☎ *508/487–9031 or 800/499–9799* ⊕ *www.caperesort.com* ⇄ *21 suites, 3 cottages* ⌂ *In-room: a/c, kitchen, DVD, Wi-Fi. In-hotel: beachfront* ⊟ *AE, MC, V* ☺ *Closed late Nov.–early Apr.*

Fodor's Choice ★

$$ ⊞ **East Harbour.** The views here are grand, reaching out to the lights of Provincetown. It's the proximity to the beach that attracts most people, however. Motel units are furnished with simple wood furniture, but are larger than most in the area. Cottages, rented by the week, are fully stocked with all amenities. The grounds are spacious, with plenty of deck chairs, gas grills, umbrellas, and even a gazebo. **Pros:** great location; reasonable rates; not far from Provincetown. **Cons:** no pool; not right on the beach. ⊠ *618 Rte. 6A, North Truro* ☎ *508/487–0505* ⊕ *www.eastharbour.com* ⤴ *9 rooms, 7 cottages, 1 apartment* ♿ *In-room: a/c, kitchen (some), refrigerator, DVD (some), Wi-Fi. In-hotel: beachfront, laundry facilities, Internet terminal* ⊟ *AE, D, MC, V* ⊘ *Closed late Oct.–mid-Apr.*

$–$$ ⊞ **Horizons Beach Resort.** You'll discover a wide range of accommodations at this nicely-cared-for compound fronting a stunning 480-foot stretch of beach, including spacious waterfront efficiencies, dune-facing studios, and private bungalows with separate sitting areas, kitchenettes, and—in some cases—fireplaces. Rates vary greatly according to view and proximity to the water, but you're also relatively close to the beach as well as the resort's swimming pool. A professional, thoughtful staff, spotless rooms, and casual, contemporary furnishings make this a highly popular getaway among the several properties on North Truro's Route 6A. **Pros:** view of the beach and harbor; beautifully maintained. **Cons:** a long walk to Provincetown; pricey if you want a water-view unit. ⊠ *190 Rte. 6A, North Truro* ☎ *508/487–0042 or 800/782–0742* ⊕ *www.horizonsbeach.com* ⤴ *77 rooms, 3 bungalows* ♿ *In-room: a/c, kitchen, DVD, refrigerator, Wi-Fi. In-hotel: pool, beachfront* ⊟ *MC, V* ⊘ *Closed mid-Oct.–mid-May.*

$ ⊞ **Hostelling International–Truro.** In a former Coast Guard station right on the dunes, this handsome hostel has kitchen facilities, a common area, and naturalist-led programs—not to mention panoramic views of the ocean and dunes. It's also right by the ½-mi-long Cranberry Bog Trail, which takes you by a refurbished cranberry bog and an old bog house. The dorm rooms are single-sex, and there are no curfews or lockouts—just come and go as you like. A limited number of private rooms are available. **Pros:** cheapest rooms on Outer Cape; fantastic beachside location. **Cons:** mostly dorm-style rooms; shared bathrooms. ⊠ *N. Pamet Rd., Box 402, Truro* ☎ *508/349–3889 or 888/901–2086* ⊕ *www.capecod.hiusa.org* ⤴ *42 beds, 2 private rooms* ⊟ *MC, V* ⊘ *Closed early Sept.–mid- June.*

$–$$ ⊞ **Top Mast Resort.** This North Truro beach motel complex, which sits
�) on 52 acres, has been family-owned and operated for nearly 40 years.
★ The staff's warm and sincere attention has much to do with that distinction. Recent improvements to the crisp and spotless rooms include new kitchens, tile floors, and carpeting. A restaurant serves traditional American fare, and there's a pool, tennis court, playground, gym, and a whirlpool tub. Most rooms are on the beach and have semiprivate decks, but there are some significantly cheaper units in a building across the road. Two cottages are available on a weekly basis. **Pros:** great views; lots of diversions for kids. **Cons:** a long walk to Provincetown; not ideal if you're seeking seclusion. ⊠ *217 Rte. 6A, North Truro 02652*

5

☏ *508/487–1189* ⊕ *www.topmastresort.com* ⇌ *70 rooms, 2 cottages* ⚹ *In-room: no a/c, kitchen (some), refrigerator, no phone, Wi-Fi. In-hotel: restaurant, bar, tennis courts, pool, gym, beachfront* ▭ *MC, V* ⊙ *Closed late Oct.–early May.*

THE ARTS

★ From mid-June through late September, the **Payomet Performing Arts Center of Truro** (⊠ *29 Old Dewline Rd., North Truro* ☏ *508/487–5400* ⊕ *www.ppactruro.org*) presents a wide range of concerts, plays, films, and music inside a big tent at Cape Cod National Seashore. Past performers have included the Cape Cod Opera, Patty Larkin, and the Shakespeare on the Cape troupe. There's also a kids' summer stage, featuring children's entertainment.

BEACHES, SPORTS, AND THE OUTDOORS

BEACHES

Parking at a number of Truro's town beaches is reserved for residents and renters in season, although anyone can walk or bicycle in. Truro has several accessible beaches stretched along Cape Cod Bay. All are beautiful and ideal for long, lazy days of watching boats go by and taking in views of Provincetown in the distance. On the ocean side, a few spectacular beaches are marked by massive dunes and bracing surf. Ask at the **beach office** (⊠ *36 Rte. 6A, North Truro* ☏ *508/487–6983*) about obtaining a seasonal sticker.

Ballston Beach (⊠ *Pamet Rd., Truro*) lies on the ocean side at the end of the winding, residential Pamet Road, backed by the golden hills that artist Edward Hopper made famous in his Truro paintings. Parking is reserved for residents and renters in season, although anyone can walk or bicycle in.

Fodor's Choice ★ **Coast Guard Beach** (⊠ *Coast Guard Rd., North Truro*) sits just down the road from Highland Light on the ocean side. Parking is for residents and renters with stickers only, although anyone can walk or bicycle in to enjoy this pristine swath of golden sand that stretches for miles in either direction and sees relatively few crowds—even in the heart of summer. Keep in mind that the parking area is small and tends to fill quickly.

Corn Hill Beach (⊠ *Corn Hill Rd., Truro*), on the bay, has beautiful views of Provincetown. The waters are generally calm and warm, typical of bay beaches. There are restrooms on-site. Parking requires a Truro beach sticker or a $15 daily fee.

Cold Storage Beach (⊠ *Pond Rd. off Rte. 6A, North Truro*) is just as popular with anglers looking for passing blues and stripers as it is with sunseekers and swimmers. A Truro beach sticker is required for parking.

Just off one of Truro's backcountry roads, **Fisher Road Beach** (⊠ *Fisher Rd., Truro*) has a smaller parking area, so it's usually quiet. A Truro beach sticker is required for parking.

To get to **Great Hollow Beach** (⊠ *Great Hollow Rd. off U.S. 6, North Truro*) you must be ready to scale some moderate stairs from the parking lot to the sands below. A Truro beach sticker is required for parking.

Head of the Meadow Beach (⊠ *Meadow Rd. off U.S. 6, North Truro*) in North Truro, part of the Cape Cod National Seashore, is often less crowded than other beaches in the area. The dunes here are not high, and there may be a sandbar at low tide. There are basic restroom facilities available in summer and no showers. The daily parking fee is $15 in season (late June–early September); you can also purchase a season pass ($45) that is good for all National Seashore locations.

A not-so-secret favorite of nude sunbathers, ocean-side **Longnook Beach** (⊠ *Long Nook Rd., North Truro*) shares the sense of wildness and isolation synonymous with Truro's outer reaches. Truro beach stickers are required for parking.

Ryder Beach (⊠ *Ryder Beach Rd., off Old County Rd., Truro*) rests just below a rise in the small dunes. A Truro beach sticker is required for parking at this bay beach.

BIKING

The **Head of the Meadow Trail** provides 2 mi of easy cycling between dunes and salt marshes from High Head Road, off Route 6A in North Truro, to the Head of the Meadow Beach parking lot.

GOLF

★ The **Highland Golf Links** (⊠ *Lighthouse Rd., North Truro* ☎ *508/487–9201* ⊕ *www.truro-ma.gov/html_pages/facilities/golf*), a 9-hole, par-35 course on a cliff overlooking the Atlantic and Highland Light, is unique for its resemblance to Scottish links.

SHOPPING

Atlantic Spice Co. (⊠ *U.S. 6 at Rte. 6A, North Truro* ☎ *508/487–6100* ⊕ *www.atlanticspice.com*) has bulk spices, teas, and potpourris, as well as herbs, pastas, nuts, dried flowers, soaps, sauces, and kitchenware items.

Jobi Pottery (⊠ *3 Depot Rd., Truro* ☎ *508/349–2303* ⊕ *www.jobipottery.com*) has been making one-of-a-kind pieces (mugs, bowls, vases, plates, and more) on the Cape since the 1950s. Owner Susan Kurtzman adds her own distinctive designs to the mix.

Whitman House Quilt Shop (⊠ *County Rd. just off U.S. 6, North Truro* ☎ *508/487–3204* ⊕ *www.whitmanhousequilts.com*) sells Amish quilts and other country items.

PROVINCETOWN

The Cape's smallest town in area and its second smallest in year-round population, Provincetown is a place of liberating creativity, startling originality, and substantial diversity. Like so much of Cape Cod, it's also a town that's become progressively—and rather dramatically—more upscale and sophisticated in recent years. A number of the casual—if cheesy—T-shirt and souvenir shops that once lined the town's main drag, Commercial Street, have given way to first-rate art galleries and upscale boutiques. Many of the town's funky B&Bs and inns, which once felt more like glorified boardinghouses than proper accommodations, have been sold as private homes or transformed into fabulous, upscale hideaways with cushy amenities.

With the change has come at least a mild concern that Provincetown may become too upscale and cosmopolitan for its own good—but so far there's little evidence that this lovably eccentric, individualistic place will ever become any less free-spirited. A strong sense of community spirit and civic pride remains. In the busy downtown, Portuguese-American fishermen mix with painters, poets, writers, whale-watching families, cruise-ship passengers on brief stopovers, and gay and lesbian residents and visitors. In summer Commercial Street is packed with sightseers and shoppers hunting for treasures in the overwhelming number of galleries and crafts shops. At night raucous music and people spill out of bars, drag shows, and sing-along lounges galore. It's a fun, crazy place, with the extra dimension of the fishing fleet unloading their catch at MacMillan Wharf, in the center of the action.

The town's 8 square mi are also rich in history. The fist at the very tip of the Cape, Provincetown has shores that curve protectively around a natural harbor, perfect for sailors from any epoch to anchor. Historical records suggest that Thorvald, brother of Viking Leif Erikson, came ashore here in AD 1004 to repair the keel of his boat and consequently named the area Kjalarness, or Cape of the Keel. Bartholomew Gosnold came to Provincetown in 1602 and named the area Cape Cod after the abundant codfish he found in the local waters.

GETTING HERE AND AROUND

You're at the end of the line here, which means driving to Provincetown in the height of summer often means slogging through slow traffic. No matter, there are plenty of pretty vistas on the way along U.S. 6 and Route 6A. Once in town, leave the car in the outer reaches and spend the day on foot.

The Provincetown/North Truro Shuttle, run by the Cape Cod Regional Transit Authority, provides a much-needed seasonal transportation boost. Once in Provincetown, the shuttle heads up Bradford Street, with alternating trips to Herring Cove Beach and Pilgrim Park.

ESSENTIALS

Visitor Information **Cape Cod Regional Transit Authority** (☎ 800/352–7155 wwww.capecodtransit.org). **Provincetown** (✉ 307 Commercial St., Downtown Center ☎ 508/487–3424 ⊕ www.ptownchamber.com).

EXPLORING

Provincetown's main thoroughfare, Commercial Street, stretches 3 mi from end to end. In season, driving from one end to the other can seem to take forever, so wear comfortable shoes and get ready to walk. Check out the many architectural styles (Greek Revival, Victorian, Second Empire, and Gothic, to name a few) used in the design of the impressive houses for wealthy sea captains and merchants.

Be on the lookout for blue plaques fastened to housefronts explaining their historical significance—practically the entire town has been designated part of the Provincetown Historic District. The Historical Society puts out a series of walking-tour pamphlets—available for about $1 each at many shops in town as well as at the chamber of commerce visitor center—with maps and information on the history of many buildings.

The center of town is where the crowds and most of the touristy shops are. The quiet East End is mostly residential, with an increasing number of nationally renowned galleries; the similarly quiet West End has a number of small inns with neat lawns and elaborate gardens.

TOP ATTRACTIONS

Expedition *Whydah* Sea Lab and Learning Center. On MacMillan Wharf, this museum is a home for artifacts recovered from the pirate ship *Whydah,* which sank off the coast of Wellfleet in 1717. The tiny museum is entertaining and educational, with one display on the restoration and conservation processes and another on the untold story of the 18th-century pirating life. The curators hope to eventually collect all the recovered pieces; some are on loan to other museums across the country. ⊠ *16 MacMillan Wharf, Downtown Center* ☏ *508/487–8899* ⊕ *www.whydah.org* ☏ *$10* ⊙ *Mid-June–early Sept., daily 10–8; mid-May–mid-June and early Sept.–mid-Oct., daily 10–5.*

Fine Arts Work Center. A nonprofit organization founded in 1968, the FAWC sponsors 10 writers and 10 artists from October through May each year, providing them with a place to live and work. A summer program has open-enrollment workshops in both writing and the visual arts. The buildings in the complex around the center were formerly Day's Lumber Yard Studios, built above a lumberyard by a patron of the arts to provide poor artists with cheap accommodations. Robert Motherwell, Hans Hoffmann, and Helen Frankenthaler have been among the studios' roster of residents over the years. ⊠ *24 Pearl St., East End* ☏ *508/487–9960* ⊕ *www.fawc.org* ☏ *Free, $5 for special events* ⊙ *Weekdays 9–5.*

MacMillan Wharf. This one of five remaining wharves of the original 54 that once jutted into the bay. The wharf serves as the base for whale-watch boats, fishing charters, high-speed ferries, and party boats. ⊠ *Off Commercial St., Downtown Center.*

QUICK BITES

The **Provincetown Fudge Factory** (⊠ *210 Commercial St., Downtown Center* ☏ *508/487–2850* ⊕ *www.ptownfudge.com*), across from the post office, makes silky peanut-butter cups, chocolates, saltwater taffy, yard-long licorice whips, custom-flavor frozen yogurt, and the creamiest fudge on the Cape—and will ship sweet goodies to you, too.

★ **Pilgrim Monument.** This grandiose edifice, which seems somewhat out of proportion to the rest of the town, commemorates the Pilgrims' first landing in the New World and their signing of the Mayflower Compact before they set off from Provincetown Harbor to explore the mainland. The tower was erected of granite shipped from Maine, according to a design modeled on a tower in Siena, Italy. President Theodore

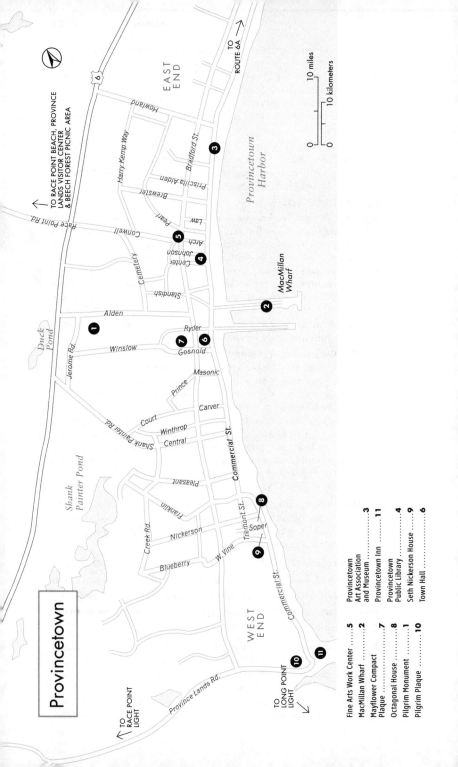

Provincetown

TO RACE POINT BEACH, PROVINCE
LANDS VISITOR CENTER
& BEECH FOREST PICNIC AREA

TO RACE POINT, PROVINCE
LANDS VISITOR CENTER

TO
RACE POINT
LIGHT

TO
LONG POINT
LIGHT

TO
ROUTE 6A

EAST END

WEST END

Provincetown Harbor

MacMillan Wharf

Duck Pond

Shank Painter Pond

Race Point Rd.

Shank Painter Rd.

Jerome Rd.

Creek Rd.

Province Lands Rd.

Commercial St.

Commercial St.

Bradford St.

Howland

Harry Kemp Way

Priscilla Alden

Brewster

Pearl

Law

Conwell

Arch

Center

Johnson

Cemetery

Standish

Alden

Winslow

Gosnold

Ryder

Masonic

Prince

Carver

Court

Winthrop

Central

Pleasant

Franklin

Nickerson

Blueberry

W. Vine

Tremont St.

Soper

0   10 miles

0   10 kilometers

Fine Arts Work Center **5**
MacMillan Wharf **2**
Mayflower Compact
Plaque **7**
Octagonal House **8**
Pilgrim Monument **1**
Pilgrim Plaque **10**

Provincetown
Art Association
and Museum **3**
Provincetown Inn **11**
Provincetown
Public Library **4**
Seth Nickerson House **9**
Town Hall **6**

Cape Cod's Pirate Ship Whydah

Amid the gently swaying dune grasses and beneath the waves of the Atlantic waft the whispers of a legend. It's a classic tale with all the key ingredients—true love, pirate treasure, and a storm-wrought tragedy—and for nearly three centuries it has inspired fanciful embellishments and lustful searching. Though she was wrecked in a treacherous storm back in April 1717, the pirate ship *Whydah* still has the power to captivate.

PIRATE SAM BELLAMY

As with any great legend, there are several conflicting versions of the *Whydah* tale. Many say the story began with an innocent love, when a dark, ambitious sailor named Sam Bellamy met the beautiful Maria Hallett in Wellfleet. From their brief acquaintance blossomed love, grand promises, and a child (the latter unknown to the wayward Bellamy), and the sailor gave his word that he would return, armed with riches.

He set off for England in hopes of finding fortune in shipping, but he soon realized that piracy was far more lucrative. Black Sam Bellamy, as he became known, and his men were wildly successful, taking over dozens of ships. On a pirating jaunt in the Caribbean, Bellamy and his men captured a beauty—a slave ship loaded with gold and silver. Wealthy beyond their dreams, the men headed north with Bellamy at the helm of this exciting vessel, called the *Whydah*.

MARIA HALLETT'S STORY

While the sailors grew rich and famous, young Maria Hallett was banished by her family because of her pregnancy. She fled to a small cabin in Eastham, awaiting the birth of her child and the return of her lover. She had a son, but he died in infancy, and the discovery of the dead child landed Maria in jail. Reputations were made swiftly in those days: it wasn't long before the townspeople decided Maria was a witch who had made an unholy pact with the devil. She suffered in isolation as Bellamy made his way back to Wellfleet.

THE SHIP'S WRECK AND REMAINS

Mariners have long feared the dangerous shoals, sandbars, and temperamental weather of the waters off Cape Cod. On the night of April 26, 1717, a sudden fierce storm interrupted Bellamy's homecoming, and the once sleek and swift *Whydah* was no match for the fury of the sea. Blasted by wave and wind, she met her demise in the form of a sturdy sandbar—nearly all hands were lost, and the ship lay broken, exposed to the tides.

In 1984 modern-day pirate Barry Clifford and his crew uncovered some of the *Whydah*'s remains, but the promise of grand treasure has yet to be fulfilled. In Provincetown, at the Expedition Whydah museum, you can see some artifacts from this ship and other historic wrecks.

And what of poor Maria? Some say her ghost still wanders among the dunes, wailing and cursing all sailors. Listen closely on a foggy and ominous evening, and decide for yourself.

—by Laura V. Scheel

PROVINCETOWN'S HISTORY

The Pilgrims remain Provincetown's most famous visitors. On Monday, November 21, 1620, the *Mayflower* dropped anchor in Provincetown Harbor after a difficult 63-day voyage from England. While in the harbor the passengers signed the Mayflower Compact, the first document to declare a democratic form of government in America. One of the first things the Pilgrims did was come ashore to wash their clothes, thus beginning the ages-old New England tradition of Monday washday. They lingered for five weeks before moving on to Plymouth. Plaques and parks throughout town commemorate the landing.

BUSY SEAPORT

Incorporated as a town in 1727, Provincetown was for many decades a bustling seaport, with fishing and whaling as its major industries. In the late 19th century, groups of Portuguese fishermen and whalers began to settle here, lending their expertise and culture to an already cosmopolitan town. Fishing is still an important source of income for many Provincetown locals, but now the town ranks among the world's leading whale-watching—rather than whale-hunting—outposts.

ART SCHOOLS AND THEATERS

Artists began coming here in the late 1890s to take advantage of the unusual Cape Cod light—in fact,

Provincetown is the nation's oldest continuous art colony. Poets, writers, and actors have also been part of the art scene. Eugene O'Neill's first plays were written and produced here, and the Fine Arts Work Center continues to have in its ranks important writers.

During the early 1900s, Provincetown became known as Greenwich Village North. Artists from New York and Europe discovered the town's unspoiled beauty, special light, lively community, and colorful Portuguese flavor. By 1916, with five art schools flourishing here, painters' easels were nearly as common as shells on the beach.

This bohemian community, along with the availability of inexpensive summer lodgings, attracted young rebels and writers as well, including John Reed (*Ten Days That Shook the World*) and Mary Heaton Vorse (*Footnote to Folly*), who in 1915 began the Cape's first significant theater group, the Provincetown Players. The young, then unknown Eugene O'Neill joined them in 1916, when his *Bound East for Cardiff* premiered in a tiny wharf-side East End fish house. After 1916 the Players moved on to New York. Their theater, at present-day 571 Commercial Street, is long gone, but a model of it and the old Lewis Wharf on which it stood is on display at the Pilgrim Monument.

Roosevelt laid the cornerstone in 1907, and President Howard Taft attended the 1910 dedication. Climb the 116 steps and 60 short ramps of the 252-foot-high tower for a stunning and dramatic panoramic view—dunes on one side, harbor on the other, and the entire bay side of Cape Cod beyond. On an exceptionally clear day you can see the Boston skyline.

At the tower's base is a museum with exhibits on whaling, shipwrecks, and scrimshaw; a diorama of the *Mayflower*; and another of a glass factory. Guided walking tours are given each Wednesday and Friday in July and August; the $10 fee includes admission to the museum. ⊠ *High Pole Hill Rd., Downtown Center* ☎ *508/487–1310* ⊕ *www.pilgrim-monument.org* ⬛ *$7* ⊙ *Early Apr.–June, Sept., and Oct., daily 9–5; July and Aug., daily 9–7; Nov., weekends 9–5.*

WORD OF MOUTH

"We are not beach people, but we rented bikes and rode on the 8+ miles of trails in that area [Province Lands]. It was lots of fun, with great scenery. The trails have a bit of uphill and downhill, and occasional sharp turns. You can ride the bike all the way out to Race Point Beach and Herring Cove."   —yk

Province Lands. This area, stretch from High Head in Truro to the tip of Provincetown, is scattered with ponds, cranberry bogs, and scrub. More than 7 mi of bike and walking trails lace through forests of stunted pines, beech, and oak and across desertlike expanses of rolling dunes. At the visitor center you'll find short films on local geology and exhibits on the life of the dunes and the shore. You can also pick up information on guided walks, birding trips, lectures, and other programs, as well as on the Province Lands' pristine beaches, Race Point and Herring Cove, and walking, biking, and horse trails. Don't miss the awe-inspiring panoramic view of the dunes and the surrounding ocean from the observation deck. ⚠ **This terrain provides optimal conditions for the deer tick, which can cause Lyme disease, so use extra caution.** ⊠ *Race Point Rd. east of U.S. 6, Greater Provincetown* ☎ *508/487–1256* ⊕ *www.nps.gov/caco* ⬛ *Free* ⊙ *Early May–late Oct., daily 9–5.*

Fodor'sChoice ★ **Provincetown Art Association and Museum.** Founded in 1914 to collect and show the works of artists with Provincetown connections, this facility has a 1,650-piece permanent collection, displayed in changing exhibits that mix up-and-comers with established 20th-century figures, including Milton Avery, Philip Evergood, William Gropper, Charles Hawthorne, Robert Motherwell, Claes Oldenburg, Man Ray, John Singer Sargent, Andy Warhol, and Agnes Weinrich. A stunning, contemporary wing has greatly expanded the exhibit space. The museum store carries books of local interest, including works by or about area artists and authors, as well as posters, crafts, cards, and gift items. Art classes (one day and longer) offer the opportunity to study under such talents as Hilda Neily, Franny Golden, and Doug Ritter. ⊠ *460 Commercial St., East End* ☎ *508/487–1750* ⊕ *www.paam.org* ⬛ *$7* ⊙ *Late May–Sept., Mon.–Thurs. 11–8, Fri. 11–10, weekends 11–5; Oct.–late May, Thurs.–Sun. noon–5.*

QUICK BITES

Wired Puppy (⊠ *379 Commercial St., Downtown Center* ☎ *508/487–0017*) is a slick but comfy café serving outstanding organic coffees and teas and plus a nice variety of cookies, brownies, and treats. There's free Wi-Fi, too.

Purple Feather (✉ *334 Commercial St., Downtown Center* ☎ *508/487–9100*) comes in handy when you're craving superb handmade chocolates, decadent cakes, and house-made gelato and sorbets.

WORTH NOTING

Beech Forest. A beautiful spot to stop for lunch before biking to the beach, this picnic area in the National Seashore borders a small pond covered with water lilies. The adjacent bike trails lead to Herring Cove and Race Point, beautiful beaches that area part of the National Seashore. ✉ *Race Point Rd. east of U.S. 6, Greater Provincetown.*

Mayflower Compact Plaque. In a little park behind Town Hall, this plaque, carved in bas-relief by sculptor Cyrus Dalin, depicts the historic signing. ✉ *Bradford St., Downtown Center.*

Octagonal House. Built in 1850, this eight-sided house is an interesting piece of Provincetown architecture in the West End. The private home is not open to the public. ✉ *74 Commercial St., West End.*

Old Harbor Station. Not far from the present Coast Guard Station, this historic structure was rescued from an eroding beach and towed here by barge from Chatham in 1977. It's reached by a boardwalk across the sand, and plaques along the way tell about the lifesaving service and the whales seen offshore. Inside are displays of such equipment as Lyle guns, which shot rescue lines out to ships in distress when seas were violent, and breeches buoys, in which passengers were hauled across those lines to safety. In summer there are reenactments of this old-fashioned lifesaving procedure at 6:30 on Thursday night. ✉ *Race Point Beach at end of Race Point Rd., Greater Provincetown* ☎ *508/487–1256* 🖼 *Free; Thurs. night $3* ☉ *July and Aug., daily 3–5.*

Pilgrim Plaque. Set into a boulder at the center of a little park, the Pilgrim Plaque commemorates the first footfall of the Pilgrims onto Cape soil—Provincetown's humble equivalent to Plymouth Rock. ✉ *West end of Commercial St., West End.*

Provincetown Inn. Here you can see a series of 19 murals, painted in the 1930s from old postcards, depicting life in the 19th-century town. The inn still operates as a hotel; the murals are in the lobby and hallways. ✉ *1 Commercial St., West End* ☎ *508/487–9500.*

ⓒ ★ **Provincetown Public Library.** Occupying a beautifully restored and redesigned church, this library has a steeple you can see from all over the Outer Cape. You can also check out *The Rose Dorothea*, a half-scale replica of an early 1900s fishing schooner that was built by some 15 Provincetown fishermen and woodworkers as a tribute to the town's rich nautical heritage. The 62-foot-long boat has ingeniously been built into the library's second floor. Architecturally, this is one of the town's most striking and distinctive buildings, but it's also a great cultural resource, hosting children's storytelling on Wednesday and Saturday mornings, educational workshops, and other community events. There's also a children's room with computers, books, and educational resources. ✉ *356 Commercial St., Downtown Center* ☎ *508/487–7094* ⊕ *www.ptownlib.com* 🖼 *Free* ☉ *Mon. and Fri. 10–5, Tues. and Thurs. noon–8, Wed. 10–8, Sat. 10–2, Sun. 1–5.*

Seth Nickerson House. The oldest building in town, dating from 1746, this Cape-style structure is still a private home. It was built by a ship's carpenter, with massive pegged, hand-hewn oak beams and wide-board floors. Modern renovations have somewhat obscured the glimpse into centuries past that it once provided, but it's still impressive. ⊠ *72 Commercial St., West End.*

Town Hall. Paintings donated to the town over the years—including Provincetown scenes by Charles Hawthorne and WPA–era murals by Ross Moffett—are displayed here. The art collection here is significant and impressive; and now has a fitting and extravagant home thanks to a $6 million renovation of this mid-19th century beauty. After years of neglect, it truly is a sight to behold. ⊠ *260 Commercial St., Downtown Center* ☎ *508/487–7000* ☉ *Weekdays 8–5.*

> **GHOST SHIP**
>
> During the American Revolution, Provincetown Harbor was controlled by the British, who used it as a port from which to sail to Boston and launch attacks on colonial and French vessels. In November 1778, the 64-gun British frigate *Somerset* ran aground and was wrecked off Provincetown's Race Point. Every 60 years or so, the shifting sands uncover its remains.

WHERE TO EAT

Use the coordinate (✛ B2) at the end of each listing to locate a site on the Where to Eat in Provincetown map.

$$$
AMERICAN
✕ **Bayside Betsy's.** Named for the feisty chef and co-owner, this campy, infectiously fun bar-and-grill serves a mix of homespun American favorites and slightly more contemporary dishes, such as lobster tortellini, seafood wontons with orange-horseradish sauce, and classic steamed mussels in white wine with garlic, shallots, and tomatoes. Nightly specials often reflect the luck of local fishermen. You might try pan-seared scallops with chorizo tossed with fettuccine. You can expect reliable food for breakfast (try the banana-walnut pancakes), lunch, and dinner year-round, but the real draws are the colorful people-watching, good-natured attitude, and nice views of Provincetown Harbor. ⊠ *177 Commercial St., West End* ☎ *508/487–6566* ⊕ *www.baysidebetsys.com* ▭ *AE, D, MC, V* ☉ *Closed Mon.–Wed. Nov.–May* ✛ *C3.*

$$$
AMERICAN
Fodor's Choice
★
✕ **Bistro at Crowne Pointe.** Set inside the snazzy Crowne Pointe Inn, this intimate, casually handsome restaurant occupies the parlor and sunroom of a grand sea captain's mansion. The kitchen serves finely crafted, healthful, modern American food, such as wakame-crusted tuna sashimi with a spicy blood orange–mango-wasabi drizzle, followed by smoky-seared duck breast with sautéed-carrot coulis and Asian vegetables, and prosciutto-wrapped pork tenderloin with a thyme-caramelized-onion-and-wild-mushroom sauce. A Fodors.com reader "fell in love with the intimate bar and dining area and were warmly welcomed by the staff." ⊠ *82 Bradford St., Downtown Center* ☎ *508/487–2365* ⊕ *www.provincetown-restaurant.com* ⚟ *Reservations essential* ▭ *AE, D, MC, V* ☉ *No lunch* ✛ *B3.*

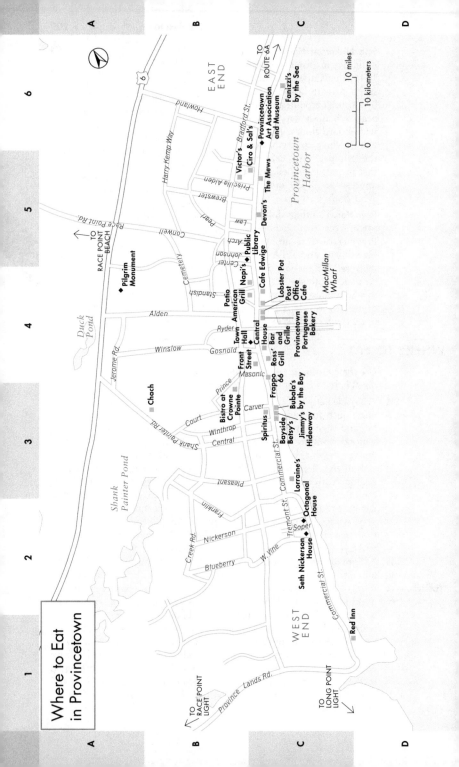

Where to Eat in Provincetown

EAST END

WEST END

Shank Painter Pond

Duck Pond

Provincetown Harbor

TO
RACE POINT LIGHT

TO
ROUTE 6A

TO
RACE POINT
BEACH

TO
LONG POINT
LIGHT

TO
RACE POINT
BEACH

Province Lands Rd.

Race Point Rd.

Shank Painter Rd.

Jerome Rd.

Creek Rd.

Nickerson

Blueberry

W. Vine

Franklin

Pleasant

Tremont St.

Commercial St.

Commercial St.

Soper

Bradford St.

Howland

Harry Kemp Way

Priscilla Alden

Brewster

Pearl

Conwell

Law

Cemetery

Standish

Center

Johnson

Alden

Winslow

Gosnold

Ryder

Masonic

Prince

Court

Carver

Winthrop

Central

Pilgrim
Monument

Patio
American
Grill

Napi's

Cafe Edwige

Public
Library

Victor's

Ciro & Sal's

The Mews

Devon's

Provincetown
Art Association
and Museum

Fanizzi's
by the Sea

Lobster Pot

Post
Office
Cafe

MacMillan
Wharf

Town
Hall

Central
House

Bar
and
Grille

Provincetown
Portuguese
Bakery

Front
Street

Ross'
Grill

Frappo
66

Bubala's
by the Bay

Jimmy's
Hideaway

Bistro at
Crowne
Pointe

Chach

Spiritus

Bayside
Betsy's

Lorraine's

Octagonal
House

Seth Nickerson
House

Red Inn

0   10 miles

0   10 kilometers

$$$ ✕ **Bubala's by the Bay.** Look for the bright yellow building adorned on
SEAFOOD top with campy carved birds. The kitchen rarely stops, serving breakfast, lunch, and dinner; it's known for seafood bought directly off local boats, although the food here is less impressive than the views and the festive setting, with outdoor seats overlooking Commercial Street and indoor seating facing the bay. Lobster salad, seafood cassoulet with white beans and chorizo, and grilled venison rack with currant, sage, and shiitake demi-glace are reliable options. The U-shaped bar picks up into the evening. It's one of the few Commercial Street restaurants with off-street parking. ✉ *183 Commercial St., West End* ☎ *508/487–0773* ⊕ *www. bubalas.com* ▭ *AE, D, MC, V* ⊗ *Closed late Oct.–late Apr.* ✛ *C3.*

$$$ ✕ **Cafe Edwige.** A longtime East End restaurant set rather discreetly up
AMERICAN a flight of stairs, Cafe Edwige consists of an intimate dining room with
★ varnished-wood floors and dim lighting, and a casual side patio with tile tables and billowing drapes. Start things off at the bar with one of their signature white-ginger cosmos, and perhaps the tuna-avocado tartare appetizer with sweet-chili vinaigrette and wasabi cream, which has long been a staple here. Popular entrées from the contemporary menu include the Brazilian seafood *moqueca* (halibut, shrimp, scallops, coconut milk, and palm oil simmered with basmati rice) and braised short rib with jalepeño potatoes. For a superb breakfast, consider the omelet with portobello mushrooms and Brie. ✉ *333 Commercial St., Downtown Center* ☎ *508/487–4020* ⊕ *www.edwigeatnight.com* ▭ *MC, V* ⊗ *Closed Oct.–Apr., Mon.–Thurs. May–mid-June, and Wed.* ✛ *C4.*

$$$ ✕ **Central House Bar and Grille.** At the Crown & Anchor, Central House
AMERICAN serves commendable contemporary American fare, such as halibut cassoulet with white beans, chorizo, and chard, and pan-seared scallops with celery root and cider risotto. Several lighter options are offered, too, including three kinds of mac-and-cheese. For breakfast, you might try the lobster Benedict or French toast topped with Vermont syrup, sweet butter, and powdered sugar. Apart from the good food, this is one of the best venues in town for socializing and observing the assorted merrymakers who frequent the resort's many bars. ✉ *247 Commercial St., Downtown Center* ☎ *508/487–1430* ⊕ *www.onlyatthecrown.com* ▭ *AE, D, MC, V* ⊗ *Closed Wed. off-season* ✛ *C4.*

¢ ✕ **Chach.** A cute, airy, and contemporary clapboard restaurant out on
CAFÉ Shank Painter Road toward the beach, Chach is a big hit with locals. It's a sweet little place serving creative omelets (try one with green chili, cheddar, and sour cream), vanilla custard French toast with Vermont maple syrup, fried chicken salad with buttermilk dressing, and falafel sandwiches with cucumber-mint sauce. Fresh ingredients and artful presentation make this a winner. Closing time is 3 PM. ✉ *73 Shank Painter Rd., Greater Provincetown* ☎ *508/487–1530* ▭ *MC, V* ⊗ *No dinner* ✛ *B3.*

$$$ ✕ **Ciro & Sal's.** Tucked inside a cozy house down an alley behind Com-
ITALIAN mercial Street, this longtime local favorite offers a low-key, romantic alternative to some of the town's busier restaurants. The most memorable tables are inside a cozy brick wine cellar. The rest fill a pair of art-filled dining rooms; one is warmed by a huge fireplace. You can also relax with a cocktail on the garden patio. The restaurant is justly

known for its fresh pastas and bountiful antipasto selections. Favorite entrées include calamari sautéed with anchovies, lemon, garlic, and cream; and chicken livers sautéed with prosciutto, marsala wine, and sage. ⊠ *4 Kiley Ct., East End* ☎ *508/487–6444* ⊕ *www.ciroandsals.com* ▭ *AE, D, MC, V* ☉ *Closed Jan. No lunch* ✛ *C5.*

$$$

AMERICAN

Fodor's Choice

★

✕ **Devon's.** This unassuming, tiny white cottage—with a dining room that seats just 37 lucky patrons—serves some of the best food in town. Specialties from the oft-changing menu might include herb-roasted halibut with spicy lentils and bacon, or seared duck with red-onion marmalade. Another plus is the great little wine list. Be sure to save some room for knockout dessert selections like blackberry mousse over ginger-lemon polenta cake with wild-berry coulis. Devon's also serves up a terrific breakfast each day until 1 PM, where you might sample truffle cheese–and–baby spinach omelets with rosemary home fries. ⊠ *401½ Commercial St., East End* ☎ *508/487–4773* ⊕ *www.devons. org* ⌆ *Reservations essential* ▭ *MC, V* ☉ *Closed Wed. and Nov.–mid-May* ✛ *C5.*

$$

ECLECTIC

★

✕ **Fanizzi's by the Sea.** A dependable, year-round East Ender that sits directly over the bay and offers fine water views, Fanizzi's presents a varied menu strong on well-prepared comfort food (including a memorable chicken potpie and juicy burgers), but often with a few creative twists. The baked cod is served with a tangy coating of almonds and mustard, and the hearty roasted half chicken is glazed with fresh garlic, lemon juice, rosemary, and thyme. You can order burgers and substantive dinner salads, including a fine salmon Caesar. The dining room, lined with large windows, is softly lighted and casual. A Fodors.com reader says Fannizzi's has "one of the best water views in town." ⊠ *539 Commercial St., East End* ☎ *508/487–1964* ⊕ *www.fanizzisrestaurant. com* ▭ *AE, D, DC, MC, V* ✛ *C6.*

$

ECLECTIC

★

✕ **Frappo 66.** Adjoining the Provincetown Art House Theatre, this eatery presents fresh and imaginative contemporary American fare in a low-cost, no-hassle setting. You can explore the prepared foods on display at the counter or order à la carte from a menu, mixing and matching main courses and sides as you wish, and then choose your own seat in the sunny dining room or on the patio overlooking Commercial Street (or order to go). Service is quick, and prices are low. The menu changes daily but might feature pork vindaloo, tomato-and-mint couscous, tuna-avocado tartare, fried oysters over baby spinach, sweet-pea-falafel sandwiches, warm flourless chocolate torte—the menu is seemingly endless. ⊠ *214 Commercial St., Downtown Center* ☎ *508/487–9066* ⊕ *www. frappo66.com* ▭ *MC, V* ✛ *C4.*

$$$

MEDITERRANEAN

★

✕ **Front Street.** Front Street is very elegant and quite romantic, if not as revered by locals as it used to be (in part because several noteworthy competitors have opened in recent years). Here classic Italian cooking is linked to offerings from Greece, southern France, and even North Africa. There's a nightly char-grilled fish special: match salmon, halibut, or tuna with a Latin, Berber, or Cajun spice rub; lemon-caper butter; or a ginger-soy-wasabi glaze. Other stellar dishes include sage-and-butternut risotto with crisped baby spinach, and truffled wild-mushroom bisque. The wine list is also a winner. ⊠ *230 Commercial St.,*

Downtown Center ☎ *508/487–9715* ⊕ *www.frontstreetrestaurant.com* ⌂ *Reservations essential* ▤ *AE, D, MC, V* ☯ *Closed Jan.–mid-May and Mon. and Tues. No lunch* ✛ *C4.*

$$$ ✕**Jimmy's Hideaway.** Down a set of stairs from Commerical Street, this
AMERICAN spot is a cool, dark oasis. Rich wood, stained glass, and low lighting makes the place very welcoming. Diners rave about appetizers like the beef Wellington and the grilled oysters. The menu includes plenty of seafood options, including Portuguese cod, pan seared and topped with linguica, kale, kidney beans, and roasted tomatoes—a tasty nod to the area's heritage. A small but lower-priced tavern menu includes burgers, fish, and pasta. ⊠ *179 Commercial St., West End* ☎ *508/487–1011* ⊕ *www.jimmyshideaway.com* ▤ *MC, V* ☯ *Closed mid-Feb.–mid-Apr.* ✛ *C3.*

$$$ ✕**Lobster Pot.** Provincetown's Lobster Pot is fit to do battle with all
SEAFOOD the lobster shanties anywhere (and everywhere) else on the Cape—it's often jammed with tourists, but that's truly a reflection of the generally high quality. The hardworking kitchen turns out classic New England cooking: lobsters, generous and filling seafood platters (try the seafood Pico with a half lobster, shrimp, littlenecks, mussels, calamari, and fish over pasta with tomatoes, rose wine, onions, and garlic), and some of the best chowder around. The upstairs deck overlooking the harbor is a great spot for lunch. There's also a take-out lobster market and bakery on the premises. "It gets very busy but the wait was not long and the service was excellent," says a Fodors.com reader. ⊠ *321 Commercial St., Downtown Center* ☎ *508/487–0842* ⊕ *www.ptownlobsterpot.com* ⌂ *Reservations not accepted* ▤ *AE, D, DC, MC, V* ☯ *Closed Jan.* ✛ *C4.*

$$$ ✕**Lorraine's.** In a cozy cottage toward the West End, Lorraine's has an
LATIN AMERICAN intimate feel, but the nouvelle Latin American–inspired menu is as good
★ as ever. An appetizer of blackened seafood tostadas with black bean-and-corn relish packs a punch, and the tender, slow-cooked pork carnitas are a revelation. Also wonderful is a mesquite-grilled rack of lamb with roasted-garlic chipotle demi-glace. The bar draws a loyal, lively crowd and is famous for its long list of premium tequilas. A tantalizing brunch is served in summer—consider the chorizo with scrambled eggs, tortillas, and beans. ⊠ *133 Commercial St., West End* ☎ *508/487–6074* ▤ *MC, V* ☯ *Closed Mon.–Wed. Nov.–Mar. No lunch* ✛ *C3.*

$$$ ✕**The Mews.** This perennial favorite with magnificent harbor views
AMERICAN focuses on seafood and grilled meats with a cross-cultural flair. Some
Fodor's Choice popular entrées include roasted vegetable and polenta lasagna with a
★ tomato-olive sauce, and Vietnamese shaking beef wok sautéed with scallions and red onions and a lime–black pepper dipping sauce. A piano bar upstairs serves lunch (weekdays in summer) and dinner from a light, less-expensive café menu. The view of the bay from the bar is nearly perfect, and the gentle lighting makes this a romantic spot to have a drink. The restaurant claims its vodka bar is New England's largest, with some 285 varieties. ⊠ *429 Commercial St., East End* ☎ *508/487–1500* ⊕ *www.mews.com* ▤ *AE, D, DC, MC, V* ☯ *Closed Jan. No lunch weekdays off-season or Sat. mid-Oct.–late May* ✛ *C5.*

$$ ✕**Napi's.** A steady favorite for its lively ambience and dependable Medi-
ECLECTIC terranean fare, Napi's presents a long and varied menu. The food and

the interior share a penchant for unusual, striking juxtapositions—a classical sculpture in front of an abstract canvas, for instance. On the gustatory front, look for sharp combinations such as Thai chicken and shrimp, cod amandine, and Brazilian-style shrimp. Asparagus ravioli is just one of several very nice vegetarian dishes. ✉ *7 Freeman St., Downtown Center* ☎ *508/487–1145* ⊕ *www.napis-restaurant.com* ☲ *AE, D, MC, V* ⊘ *No lunch May–Sept.* ⊹ *C4.*

$$$ ✕ **Patio American Grill.** One of Provincetown's favorite see-and-be-seen
AMERICAN spots for colorful cocktails (guava mojitos, mixed-berry caipirinhas), this hip restaurant in the center of town comprises a huge shaded patio overlooking Commercial Street, plus a more intimate indoor lounge and dining area. Although the drinks pack plenty of punch, don't overlook chef Todd Schiller's top-notch seafood-intensive cuisine, such as yellowfin tartar with a lime vinaigrette, ginger-sesame lobster stir-fried with fresh veggies over jasmine rice, or the jalapeño-marinated hanger steak. ✉ *328 Commercial St., Downtown Center* ☎ *508/487–4003* ⊕ *www. ptownpatio.com* ☲ *AE, MC, V* ⊘ *Closed mid-Oct.–mid-May* ⊹ *C4.*

$$ ✕ **Post Office Cafe.** A dapper yet casual bistro beneath Provincetown's
AMERICAN favorite cabaret bar, the Post Office serves food most nights until 1 AM, making it one of the area's best options for late-night snacking. The kitchen turns out a mix of substantial but straightforward American entrées, such as scallops Alfredo, along with lighter pub favorites. Sandwiches are a specialty; consider the grilled yellowfin tuna and greens on focaccia, or the grilled portobello mushroom with artichokes, sun-dried tomatoes, roasted red peppers, feta cheese, and mixed greens on a pita. The place becomes increasingly festive—even a little raucous—the later it gets. ✉ *303 Commercial St., Downtown Center* ☎ *508/487–3892* ☲ *AE, D, MC, V* ⊘ *Closed Jan. and Feb.* ⊹ *C4.*

¢ ✕ **Provincetown Portuguese Bakery.** This town standby makes fresh Por-
PORTUGUESE tuguese breads and pastries and serves breakfast and lunch all day from March to October. Although it may be difficult to choose among the sweet splendor, favorite pastries include *malassadas,* a sweet fried dough, lemon custard, and the more unusual *trutas,* with rich, sweet potato filling. Another excellent bet is the traditional Portuguese kale soup, with cabbage, potatoes, ham, and linguica. It's open until 11 PM in summer. ✉ *299 Commercial St., Downtown Center* ☎ *508/487–1803* ☲ *D, MC, V* ⊘ *Closed Nov.–Feb. No dinner* ⊹ *C4.*

$$$$ ✕ **Red Inn.** Inside the striking red house on P-town's West End that's also
AMERICAN an enchanting B&B, the Red Inn is perhaps even better known as one of the Outer Cape's most romantic dining destinations—the views are simply stunning. The remarkable setting aside, the inventive contemporary fare as well as the service can be hit-or-miss, especially given the lofty prices. You might start off with the Kobe beef mini-burgers seared rare with rémoulade sauce before moving on to chili-rubbed pork chops with a tomatillo salsa. Breakfast and lunch are also served. ✉ *15 Commercial St., West End* ☎ *508/487–7334* ⊕ *www.theredinn. com* ☲ *AE, MC, V* ⊹ *C1.*

$$$ ✕ **Ross' Grill.** Likening itself to a French bistro with American tastes,
AMERICAN the kitchen here is modest but busy, preparing everything from scratch,
★ including its signature hand-cut, double-dipped french fries. Local fish

and shellfish dominate the menu; a favorite is the shellfish risotto with clams, scallops, mussels, shrimp, and squid. Portions are generous—you'll get eight meaty racks of baby New Zealand lamb with an herb crust—and prices are reasonable. Choose from 75 wines by the glass. The location is grand: up on the second floor of the Whaler's Wharf complex, views of Provincetown Harbor are unlimited. ⊠ *237 Commercial St., Downtown Center* ☎ *508/487–8878* ⊕ *www.rossgrillptown. com* ☰ *MC, V* ⊗ *No lunch Mon. and Thurs. Closed Tues., Wed., and Jan.–mid-Apr.* ✛ *C4.*

¢ ✕**Spiritus.** The local bars close at 1 AM, at which point this pizza joint–
PIZZA coffee stand becomes the town's epicenter. It's the ultimate place to see and be seen, pizza slice in hand and witty banter at the ready. In the morning, the same counter serves restorative coffee and croissants as well as Häagen-Dazs ice cream. ⊠ *190 Commercial St., West End* ☎ *508/487–2808* ⊕ *www.spirituspizza.com* ☰ *No credit cards* ⊗ *Closed Nov.–Apr.* ✛ *C3.*

$ ✕**Victor's.** This modern, light-filled restaurant on the western end of
AMERICAN Bradford Street became an instant hit, thanks to chef Mike Fennelly's affordable, well-prepared small plates and a slew of colorful cocktails (consider the Bellini fling, with champagne, strawberry puree, and strawberry schnapps). Among the deftly prepared nibbles, be sure to try the baked oysters with pancetta and Korean barbecue sauce, the seafood cakes with corn salsa and guacamole, and the braised short ribs with quinoa, tomatoes, and a sweet but savory port sauce. The afternoon raw bar happy hour is a great deal. For a real treat and taste of Provincetown, get a table for the drag brunch, taking place every Sunday from Memorial Day through Labor Day. ⊠ *175 Bradford St. Ext., West End* ☎ *508/487–1777* ⊕ *www.victorsptown.com* ☰ *AE, MC, V* ⊗ *Closed Jan.–Mar. No lunch* ✛ *B5.*

WHERE TO STAY

Use the coordinate (✛ B2) at the end of each listing to locate a site on the Where to Stay in Provincetown map.

$$–$$$ ⊡ **Admiral's Landing.** Painted a cheery shade of lemon chiffon with sea-blue shutters, this 19th-century Greek Revival is just as warm and colorful on the inside. The walls are filled with paintings by local artists. The uncluttered rooms are generously sized and done up in a cottage style, and many have hardwood floors and wicker furniture. Five of the rooms have gas fireplaces for cool evenings; there's also an outdoor hot tub. Innkeepers Audrey and Robyn have added many thoughtful touches, from the chocolates on the pillows to free ferry or airport transfers. **Pros:** close to downtown action; gracious innkeepers; fresh and lovely decor. **Cons:** on busy road; bathrooms are small. ⊠ *158 Bradford St., Downtown Center* ☎ *508/487–9665 or 800/934–0925* ⊕ *www. admiralslanding.com* ⇗ *8 rooms* ♿ *In-room: a/c, kitchen (some), refrigerator, DVD, Wi-Fi. In-hotel: Internet terminal, parking (free)* ☰ *AE, D, MC, V* ⦿| *CP* ✛ *B5.*

$$–$$$ ⊡ **Ampersand Guesthouse.** Helpful, low-key owners Robert Vetrick and Ken Janson (the latter an architect) run this peaceful West End inn that

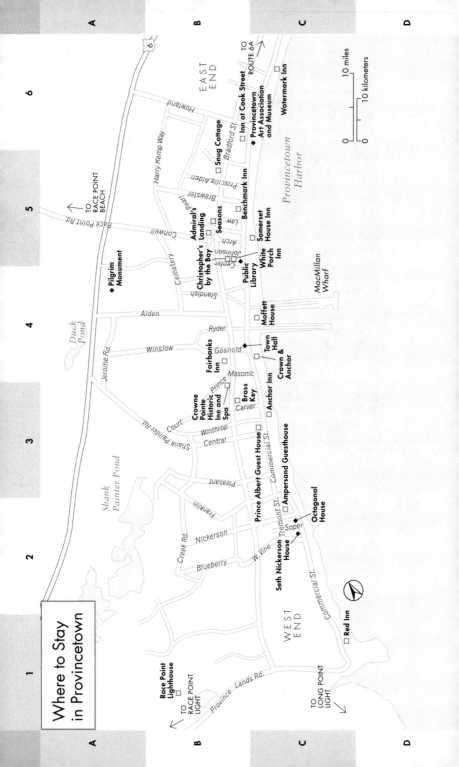

Where to Stay in Provincetown

TO ROUTE 6A

EAST END

Watermark Inn
Inn at Cook Street
Provincetown Art Association and Museum
Snug Cottage
Priscilla Alden
Benchmark Inn
Admiral's Landing
Seasons
Somerset House Inn
Christopher's by the Bay
White Porch Inn
Public Library
Pilgrim Monument
Moffett House
Fairbanks Inn
Town Hall
Crown & Anchor
Crowne Pointe Historic Inn and Spa
Brass Key
Anchor Inn
Prince Albert Guest House
Ampersand Guesthouse
Octagonal House
Seth Nickerson House
Soper
Red Inn

WEST END

TO LONG POINT LIGHT

TO RACE POINT BEACH

Race Point Lighthouse
TO RACE POINT LIGHT

Province Lands Rd.

Provincetown Harbor

MacMillan Wharf

Duck Pond

Shank Painter Pond

Harry Kemp Way
Howland
Bradford St.
Brewster
Conwell
Cemetery
Alden
Standish
Arch
Johnson
Center
Ryder
Winslow
Gosnold
Masonic
Prince
Carver
Winthrop
Central
Pleasant
Franklin
Nickerson
Blueberry
Creek Rd.
Jerome Rd.
Shank Painter Rd.
Court
Commercial St.
Tremont St.
W. Vine
Commercial St.
Law
Race Point Rd.

0   10 miles
0   10 kilometers

feels far from the din of Commercial Street but is actually just a short walk away. This natty mid-19th-century Greek Revival guesthouse contains nine eclectically furnished rooms, many with high-pitched ceilings, fireplaces, and tall windows—furnishings tend toward simple, understated, and elegant. For more seclusion, book the studio apartment in the neighboring carriage house, which also has a kitchen. Guests relax in the leafy yard with pretty gardens, or out on the sundeck on the second floor, with views of the harbor a couple of blocks away. Robert bakes fresh muffins each morning for breakfast. **Pros:** peaceful and charming location; stylish and well-chosen decor; great value. **Cons:** longish walk to businesses; some steep stairs. ✉ *6 Cottage St., West End* ☎ *508/487–0959* 🌐 *www.ampersandguesthouse.com* *9 rooms, 1 apartment* *In-room: a/c, kitchen (some), refrigerator (some), DVD, Wi-Fi. In-hotel: no kids under 15* *AE, MC, V* *CP* *C2.*

$$$–$$$$ ★ **Anchor Inn.** This regal, turreted beach house in the heart of Provincetown enjoys a wonderful location just steps from bars, shops, and restaurants. It has unobstructed water views from most rooms (rooms without water views cost a fraction of the price). White-picket porches and balconies envelope the inn's dapper shingle exterior. You won't find frill and excess here—the airy rooms are done in a palette of whites and tans, with tasteful wicker furniture and, in many cases, four-poster beds and fireplaces. Four cottage units have private entrances, and the three most romantic accommodations occupy the turret. There's a substantial Continental-breakfast buffet in the morning. **Pros:** unobstructed water views; near the action; sleek and luxurious style. **Cons:** among the highest rates in town; significant minimum-stay requirements in summer. ✉ *175 Commercial St., Downtown Center* ☎ *508/487–0432 or 800/858–2657* 🌐 *www.anchorinnbeachhouse.com* *25 rooms* *In-room: a/c, DVD, refrigerator, Wi-Fi. In-hotel: no kids under 18, parking (paid)* *AE, MC, V* *Closed Jan.–mid-Apr.* *CP* *C3.*

$$$$ **Benchmark Inn.** Set on a quiet, narrow street just a block from downtown, this is an inn of simple, refined luxury. Rooms are painted in soothing neutral tones, floors are bare wood, and fresh flowers are placed atop every stainless-steel wet bar; the bathrooms have marble tile and hair dryers. All rooms have private entrances and outdoor seating areas, and fireplaces; most have skylights and private balconies with rooftop and water views. When you're ready to turn in, indulge in the nightly turndown service. The management is environmentally conscious, using mostly "green" products and practices. **Pros:** large rooms; immaculate and luxurious. **Cons:** among the highest rates in town; no water views from many rooms; significant minimum-stay requirements in summer. ✉ *6 Dyer St., East End* ☎ *508/487–7440 or 888/487–7440* 🌐 *www.benchmarkinn.com* *7 rooms* *In-room: a/c, refrigerator, DVD, Wi-Fi. In-hotel: laundry service, parking (free), no kids under 12, some pets allowed (fee)* *AE, MC, V* *Closed Jan.–late Feb.* *CP* *B5.*

$$$$ Fodor's Choice ★ **Brass Key.** One of the Cape's most luxurious small resorts, this meticulously kept year-round getaway was purchased by the talented owners of the Crowne Pointe Inn in 2008 and has undergone extensive improvements, including the addition of spa treatment rooms, an

elegant outdoor (covered) wedding space, and a hip martini bar. The resort comprises a beautifully restored main house—originally an 1828 sea captain's home—and several other carefully groomed buildings and cottages. Rooms mix antiques with such modern amenities as Bose stereos. Deluxe rooms come with gas fireplaces and whirlpool baths or French doors opening onto wrought-iron balconies. A widow's-walk sundeck has a panoramic view of Cape Cod Bay. Complimentary cocktails are served in the courtyard; in winter, wine is served before a roaring fire in the common room. As is true of many of Provincetown's smaller hotels, the Brass Key draws a largely gay clientele, especially in summer. **Pros:** ultraposh rooms; beautiful and secluded grounds; pool. **Cons:** among the highest rates in town; some noisy rooms; significant minimum-stay requirements in summer. ✉ *67 Bradford St., Downtown Center* ☎ *508/487–9005 or 800/842–9858* ⊕ *www.brasskey.com* ↘ *43 rooms* ⚲ *In-room: a/c, safe, DVD, Wi-Fi. In-hotel: bar, pool, spa, no kids under 18, some pets allowed (fee), parking (free)* ▤ *D, MC, V* ⏀ *CP* ✛ *B3.*

$$–$$$
Fodor's Choice
★

Christopher's by the Bay. The rooms in this elegant but reasonably priced art-inspired inn are named after the greats—Rembrandt, Picasso, Monet, Van Gogh—and are warmly appointed with brass beds and rich fabrics. Several of these tall-windowed rooms have partial views of the bay, and all receive plenty of light. The building is a graceful old Victorian surrounded by carefully maintained gardens and brick patios. Rooms on the upper floors are compact and share bathrooms, but they're also very low priced. Set back from the bustle, it's just a quick walk from the center of town. Helpful owners Jim Rizzo and Dave McGlothlin often throw guest barbecues on Sunday. A Fodors. com reader says, "I travel to Provincetown often and look forward to Christopher's being my home away from home." **Pros:** excellent value; steps from shopping and dining; friendly and professional service. **Cons:** some rooms share a bath; third-floor rooms are a climb. ✉ *8 Johnson St., Downtown Center* ☎ *508/487–9263 or 877/487–9263* ⊕ *www. christophersbythebay.com* ↘ *10 rooms, 5 with bath* ⚲ *In-room: a/c, refrigerator, Wi-Fi. In-hotel: some pets allowed (fee), no kids under 16* ▤ *AE, MC, V* ⏀ *BP* ✛ *B5.*

$$$–$$$$
Crown & Anchor. If you're looking to eat, sleep, and live amid the pulsing entertainment center of Provincetown, this is the place. Upstairs from the daily clamor of drag shows and discos are 18 rooms handsomely adorned with Oriental rugs and deep cranberry hues. Deluxe rooms have two-person whirlpool tubs, fireplaces, and private balconies facing Provincetown Harbor. Complimentary Continental breakfast is served, but why not take advantage of the choice room service and simply stay in bed? There's a dependable restaurant, Central House, as well. A highly professional staff with a great attitude holds everything together. **Pros:** many bars and dining options on-site; great location; some rooms have harbor views. **Cons:** noise from bars and clubs carries to many rooms; contemporary vibe. ✉ *247 Commercial St., Downtown Center* ☎ *508/487–1430* ⊕ *www.onlyatthecrown.com* ↘ *18 rooms* ⚲ *In-room: a/c, DVD (some), kitchen (some), refrigera-*

tor (some), Wi-Fi. In-hotel: restaurants, bars, pool, beachfront ⊟ AE, D, MC, V ☉ Closed early Dec.–late Dec. ⓄI CP ⊹ C4.

$$$–$$$$ 🔲 **Crowne Pointe Historic Inn and Spa.** Created meticulously from six dif-
Fodor'sChoice ferent buildings, this inn has not left a single detail unattended. Own-
★ ers Tom Walter and David Sanford skillfully mix luxury and comfort. Period furniture and antiques fill the common areas and rooms; a queen-size bed is the smallest you'll find, dressed in 300-thread-count linens, with treats on the pillow for nightly turndown service. Penthouse suites have two floors of living space with a full kitchen, and many rooms have private balconies with water or town views. The grounds are accented with brick pathways, flowers, and trees. Start the day with a full, hot breakfast, then graze on freshly baked treats and wine and cheese in the afternoon—there's also an excellent restaurant, the Bistro at Crowne Pointe. In the handsome, full-service Shui Spa, you might opt for sooth-ing treatments. **Pros:** great on-site amenities; posh and luxurious room decor; professional and well-trained staff. **Cons:** among the highest rates in town; significant minimum-stay requirements in summer; contempo-rary vibe. ✉ 82 Bradford St., Downtown Center 🕾 508/487–6767 or 877/276–9631 ⊕ www.crownepointe.com ⮠ 37 rooms, 3 suites ⚭ In-room: a/c, kitchen (some), refrigerator, DVD, Wi-Fi. In-hotel: pool, spa, laundry service, Wi-Fi hotspot, no kids under 16, some pets allowed (fee), parking (free) ⊟ AE, D, MC, V ⓄI BP ⊹ B3.

$$–$$$ 🔲 **Fairbanks Inn.** This meticulously restored colonial inn a block from Commercial Street includes the 1776 main house and auxiliary buildings. Guest rooms have four-poster or canopy beds, Oriental rugs on wide-board floors, and antique furnishings; some have fireplaces or kitchens. Many original touches remain here, from the 18th-century wallpaper to artifacts from the inn's first residents. The baths are on the small side, but they help preserve the colonial integrity of the home. The garden and the wicker-filled sunporch are good places for afternoon cocktails or breakfast—which you can also enjoy inside before the warm glow of the fireplace on cold days. **Pros:** central location; nice variety of rooms; rich with historic character. **Cons:** some rooms get a bit of noise. ✉ 90 Bradford St., Downtown Center 🕾 508/487–0386 or 800/324–7265 ⊕ www.fairbanksinn.com ⮠ 13 rooms, 11 with bath ⚭ In-room: a/c, no phone, kitchen (some), refrigerator (some), DVD, Wi-Fi. In-hotel: Internet terminal, parking (free) ⊟ AE, MC, V ⓄI CP ⊹ B4.

$$$–$$$$ 🔲 **Inn at Cook Street.** Connecticut transplants and enthusiastic innkeepers
★ Lisa Feistel and Doreen Birdsell have done an admirable job decorating the 1836 Greek Revival where author Michael Cunningham penned *Home at the End of the World*. The sophisticated rooms have high-thread-count linens, flat-screen TVs, and well-placed reading lights; two have decks, three have fireplaces, and three have private entrances. Continental breakfast includes organic cappuccino, herbal teas, fruit and breads, and a hot entrée such as pancakes or omelets. Guests can relax in a hammock out back amid the fragrant gardens or walk a block to the galleries along Commercial Street. **Pros:** top-notch staff and ser-vice; steps from shopping and dining; elegant yet unfussy furnishings. **Cons:** some rooms get a bit of noise; no water views. ✉ 7 Cook St., East End 🕾 508/487–3894 or 888/266–5655 ⊕ www.innatcookstreet.

5

com ⌇ *5 rooms, 2 suites, 2 cottages* ⚒ *In-room: a/c, kitchen (some), refrigerator, DVD, Wi-Fi. In-hotel: no kids under 16, parking (free)* ⊟ *MC, V* ⓘⓞ︎ *BP* ✛ *B6.*

$–$$ 🏠 **Moffett House.** This simple, affordable, handsomely refurbished Cape-style B&B lies down a charming, narrow alley that runs between Commercial and Bradford streets. There are 10 cheerfully furnished rooms, most of them with shared baths (some of these have unbelievably low rates), and all have top-notch linens and country quilts, and 20-inch flat-screen TVs; some rooms have pitched ceilings with rustic beams. You are free to use the common kitchen and a computer in the lobby, and may also borrow the inn's Trek mountain bikes at no charge. It's a friendly option that's ideal for budget travelers. **Pros:** great value; good location; free mountain bikes. **Cons:** most rooms have shared bath; no optimal views. ⊠ *296A Commercial St., Downtown Center* ☎ *508/487–6615 or 800/990–8865* ⊕ *www.moffetthouse.com* ⌇ *10 rooms, 3 with bath* ⚒ *In-room: a/c, refrigerator, DVD, Wi-Fi. In-hotel: bicycles, parking (paid), some pets allowed (fee)* ⊟ *MC, V* ⓘⓞ︎ *CP* ✛ *C4.*

$$$–$$$$ 🏠 **Prince Albert Guest House.** This establishment is made up of two historic sea captains' homes built in the latter half of the 19th century. These stately Victorians are only a short walk from the center of town and sit across the street from Provincetown Bay. Some rooms are done up with antique furnishings and four-poster beds. Most rooms have water views; some have private decks. There is an outdoor hot tub, and several rooms have private decks. **Pros:** handsome buildings; some pets allowed; central location. **Cons:** significant minimum-stay requirements in summer. ⊠ *164–166 Commercial St., West End* ☎ *508/487–1850 or 800/400–2278* ⊕ *www.princealbertguesthouse.com* ⌇ *17 rooms, 2 suites* ⚒ *In-room: a/c, refrigerator, DVD, Wi-Fi. In-hotel: Internet terminal, some pets allowed (fee), parking (free)* ⊟ *AE, D, MC, V* ⓘⓞ︎ *CP* ✛ *C3.*

$$ 🏠 **Race Point Lighthouse.** One of the most unusual lodging opportunities on the Cape, the restored 1840 keeper's house at the stunning Race Point Lighthouse has three sparsely furnished guest rooms with lace curtains, braided rugs, and simple wooden chests and tables—pillows and blankets are provided, but you'll need to bring your own linens, towels, drinking water, and food. You don't stay here because it's cushy, but rather to enjoy the seclusion and romance of staying at an authentic, working lighthouse with a pristine beach just outside the window. Opportunities to see whales, dolphins, and migratory birds abound, both from the grounds and from the house itself. A gift shop on premises sells scrimshaw, sweatshirts, baseball caps, and other keepsakes. The maximum stay is four nights. **Pros:** distinctive lodging; truly secluded setting. **Cons:** very limited amenities; books up fast; extremely isolated. ⊠ *Race Point Rd., Greater Provincetown* ☎ *508/487–9930* ⊕ *www. racepointlighthouse.net* ⌇ *3 rooms* ⚒ *In-room: no a/c, no phone, refrigerator, no TV* ⊟ *No credit cards* ☽ *Closed mid-Oct.–Apr.* ✛ *B1.*

$$$ 🏠 **Red Inn.** A rambling red 1915 house that once was host to Franklin and Eleanor Roosevelt, this small, luxurious inn has been completely refurbished after several years of neglect. Most of the airy rooms afford bay views, and all are fitted with big plush beds with high-thread-count linens, goose-down comforters, and pillow-top mattresses. The

Cape Light Room contains a decorative fireplace with an ornate hand-painted fresco, and the secluded Chauffer's Cottage has a living room with a soaring vaulted ceiling and a sundeck with far-reaching water views. The restaurant offers some of the best bay views in town. **Pros:** charmed and peaceful setting; close to beach; ultraposh rooms. **Cons:** among the highest rates in town; far from most dining and nightlife; not geared to children. ⊠ *15 Commercial St., West End* ☎ *508/487–7334 or 866/473–3466* ⊕ *www.theredinn.com* ⇆ *4 rooms, 2 suites, 2 cottages* ⚐ *In-room: a/c (some), refrigerator (some), Wi-Fi. In-hotel: restaurant, room service, parking (free), no kids under 18* ⊟ *AE, MC, V* ⑩ *CP* ⊹ *C1.*

$$ ⬚ **Seasons.** This petite 1860s cream-color Victorian with a Dutch-style gambrel roof is an outstanding value. Owners John Mirthes and Rick Reynolds run a relaxed ship, freely offering guests advice on local restaurants and lending out chairs, towels, and cooler bags for the beach. Rick is a professional chef and prepares exceptional breakfasts replete with filling hot entrées, such as pumpkin pancakes with maple-poached pears, which can render lunch unnecessary. Rooms contain mostly classic Victorian pieces, wallpapers, and fabrics—it's a little old-fashioned, especially compared with all the flashier and more social guesthouses in town, and that's a big reason many guests here come back year after year. **Pros:** friendly and first-rate staff; easy walk to shops and restaurants; free ferry pickup. **Cons:** some rooms get a bit of noise; some steep stairs. ⊠ *160 Bradford St., Downtown Center* ☎ *508/487–2283 or 800/563–0113* ⊕ *www.provincetownseasons.com* ⇆ *5 rooms* ⚐ *In-room: a/c, no phone, refrigerator (some), DVD, Wi-Fi. In-hotel: parking (free)* ⊟ *D, MC, V* ⑩ *BP* ⊹ *B5.*

$$$ ⬚ **Snug Cottage.** Noted for its extensive floral gardens and enviable perch atop one of the larger bluffs in town, this convivial Arts and Crafts–style inn dates to 1825 and is decked in smashing English country antiques and fabrics. The very spacious rooms have distinctly British names (Victoria Suite, Royal Scot); most have sitting areas, and many have wood-burning fireplaces and private outdoor entrances. The Churchill Suite has 10 big windows overlooking the flowers and bushes outside, and the York Suite has a partial view of Cape Cod Bay. Nightly turndown service and plush robes in each room lend a touch of elegance. **Pros:** steps from dining and shopping; stunning grounds. **Cons:** rooms close to Bradford Street can get a bit of noise; a bit of a walk from West End businesses; the top suites don't come cheaply. ⊠ *178 Bradford St., East End* ☎ *508/487–1616 or 800/432–2334* ⊕ *www.snugcottage.com* ⇆ *3 rooms, 5 suites* ⚐ *In-room: a/c, kitchen (some), DVD, Wi-Fi. In-hotel: no kids under 7, parking (free)* ⊟ *AE, D, MC, V* ⑩ *BP* ⊹ *B5.*

$$–$$$ ⬚ **Somerset House Inn.** Competent and helpful owners run this cheer-★ ful property known for its hip, whimsical decor and superb personal service. From the outside, the inn looks like a classic 1830s Provincetown house, but inside it's a cozy den of mod sofas and cool colors. A communal computer is equipped with high-speed wireless, and you'll find reams of magazines throughout the common areas. The sleekly furnished rooms are compact but charming. The third-floor units, with pitched ceilings, are especially romantic; some have fireplaces. Somerset

House serves one of the better breakfasts in town and also has an extensive afternoon wine-and-cheese social. **Pros:** top-notch service; steps from shopping and dining. **Cons:** some units quite small; third-floor rooms require some stair climbing. ☒ *378 Commercial St., Downtown Center* ☎ *508/487–0383 or 800/575–1850* ⊕ *www.somersethouseinn. com* ⤴ *12 rooms* ⟁ *In-room: a/c, refrigerator, DVD, Wi-Fi. In hotel: no kids under 12, parking (free)* ⊟ *AE, MC, V* ⦿ *BP* ⚓ *C5.*

$$$–$$$$ ⊡ **Watermark Inn.** A modern all-suites inn facing the bay at the very east end of Commercial Street, the Watermark has enormous accommodations with separate living-dining rooms, making it a favorite for longer stays (weekly or daily rates are available in summer; rates are daily the rest of the year). Although these airy suites with tall windows feel more like rental condos than hotel rooms, they do come with fine linens and daily maid service. Four suites on the top level have private sundecks and panoramic water views; two less-expensive ground-floor units overlook a courtyard. **Pros:** close to shopping and dining; plenty of privacy; great water views. **Cons:** long walk to many businesses; some rooms have no water view. ☒ *603 Commercial St., East End* ☎ *508/487–0165* ⊕ *www.watermark-inn.com* ⤴ *10 suites* ⟁ *In-room: no a/c, refrigerator, DVD, kitchen, Wi-Fi. In-hotel: beachfront, parking (free)* ⊟ *AE, MC, V* ⚓ *C6.*

$$–$$$ ⊡ **White Porch Inn.** What had been a decrepit, almost dodgy, old-school
★   Provincetown guesthouse just several years ago has been transformed it into a light-filled B&B. Seven of the nine rooms, all of which are named for Cape Cod lighthouses, have gas fireplaces, and three have whirlpool tubs. White, tan, and chocolate color schemes, bead-board walls, and pedestal stinks in the bathrooms (some of these have radiant-floor heating) impart a crisp, clean, modern-beach-house flair. Opt for one of the carriage-house rooms for more seclusion—you can always mingle with your fellow guests and gracious hosts on the inn's eponymous white porch while enjoying selections from the bounteous breakfast buffet. **Pros:** steps from shopping and dining; enthusiastic and friendly staff. **Cons:** most rooms lack a water view. ☒ *7 Johnson St., Downtown Center* ☎ *508/364–2549 or 866/922–0333* ⊕ *www.whiteporchinn.com* ⤴ *9 rooms* ⟁ *In-room: a/c, refrigerator (some), DVD, Wi-Fi. In-hotel: no kids under 16, parking (paid)* ⊟ *D, MC, V* ⦿ *CP* ⚓ *B5.*

NIGHTLIFE AND THE ARTS

THE ARTS

The annual **Provincetown International Film Festival** (☎ *508/487–3456* ⊕ *www.ptownfilmfest.com*) has become so popular that most of the screenings sell out. Aside from a full schedule of independent films, there are guest appearances by such notables as director John Waters, Lily Tomlin, and Christine Vachon. The festival hits town in mid-June.

The **Provincetown Theater Company** (☒ *238 Bradford St., Downtown Center* ☎ *508/487–9793* ⊕ *www.provincetowntheater.com*) hosts a wide variety of performances throughout the year, especially during the summer high season, including classic and modern drama as well as works by local authors.

CLOSE UP

Provincetown: Gay Summer Playground

America's original gay resort, Provincetown developed as an artists' colony at the turn of the 20th century. In 1899 a young artist and entrepreneur named Charles Hawthorne founded the Cape Cod School of Art. Within 20 years, a half dozen art schools opened; the Provincetown Art Association staged its first exhibitions; and the Provincetown Players, a small band of modernist theater folk, began to produce plays on a small wharf in the town's East End.

After a year in Provincetown the Players moved to New York City's Greenwich Village, where gay culture was already thriving. This kinship helped spur Provincetown's early flourishing as a gay community. Tourism became a significant revenue source, and local homes began letting rooms to the hundreds of writers, painters, and other creative spirits drawn to the town's thriving arts community.

Over the next few decades, many innovative writers and artists spent time in Provincetown, including several openly gay luminaries such as Truman Capote and Tennessee Williams. The town became identified increasingly for its willingness to flout convention, and by the 1960s it was a haven for anyone whose artistic leaning, political platform, or sexual persuasion was subject to persecution elsewhere in America. This hotbed of counterculture naturally nurtured one of the country's most significant gay communities.

Today Provincetown is as appealing to artists as it is to gay and lesbian—as well as straight—tourists. The awareness brought by the AIDS crisis and, most recently, Massachusetts's becoming the first state to legalize same-sex marriage has turned the town into the most visibly gay vacation community in America.

—by Andrew Collins

NIGHTLIFE

★ **Atlantic House** (✉ *4 Masonic Pl., Downtown Center* ☎ *508/487–3821* ⊕ *www.ahouse.com*), the grandfather of the gay nightlife scene, is the only gay bar open year-round. It has several lounge areas and an outdoor patio.

The Boatslip (✉ *161 Commercial St., West End* ☎ *508/487–1669* ⊕ *www.boatslipresort.com*) holds a gay and lesbian late-afternoon tea dance daily in summer and on weekends in spring and fall on the outdoor pool deck. The club has indoor and outdoor dance floors. There's ballroom dancing here, in addition to two-stepping Thursday through Sunday nights.

★ The gay-oriented **Crown & Anchor** (✉ *247 Commercial St., Downtown Center* ☎ *508/487–1430* ⊕ *www.onlyatthecrown.com*) has plenty of action—perhaps the most in town—with the Wave video bar, the Vault leather bar, several stages, and a giant disco called Paramount. Seven nightly shows in summer range from cabaret to comedy.

The Governor Bradford (✉ *312 Commercial St., Downtown Center* ☎ *508/487–9618*) is perhaps better known as a sometimes-rowdy pool and dance hall. In the afternoon you can play chess or backgammon at the tables by the window. After 8 PM, the place revs up with live music or a DJ spinning everything from hip-hop to disco.

Pied Bar (✉ *193A Commercial St., Downtown Center* ☎ *508/487–1527* ⊕ *www.piedbar.com*) draws hordes of gay men to its post–tea dance gathering at 6:30 every evening in July and August and weekends during the shoulder seasons. Later in the evening, the crowd is mostly (though not exclusively) women. The club has a deck overlooking the harbor, a small dance floor with a good sound system, and two bars.

The **Post Office Cabaret** (✉ *303 Commercial St., Downtown Center* ☎ *508/487–0006*) has long been a dishy and lively spot for piano cabaret, musical comedy, and drag performances. The upstairs lounge draws some of the top talents in the region, and downstairs an excellent restaurant serves dependable American bistro fare until 1 AM most nights.

The **Squealing Pig** (✉ *335 Commercial St., Downtown Center* ☎ *508/ 487–5804* ⊕ *www.squealingpigptown.com*) has DJs presenting rock, hip-hop, reggae, and house; they also show late-night movies on Monday. There's never a cover charge, and the kitchen turns out super-tasty bar chow, from burgers to fish-and-chips.

Vixen (✉ *336 Commercial St., Downtown Center* ☎ *508/487–6424* ⊕ *www.ptownvixen.com*), a lively women's club, gets packed with dancers. On most nights, before the dance crowd sets in, there are both national and local women entertainers. There are also a couple of pool tables in the front room.

BEACHES, SPORTS, AND THE OUTDOORS

BEACHES

The entire stretch of Commercial Street is backed by the waters of Provincetown Harbor, and most hotels have private beaches. Farther into town there are plenty of places to settle on the sand and take a refreshing dip—just be mindful of the busy boat traffic.

Herring Cove Beach is relatively calm and warm for a National Seashore beach, but it's not as pretty as some because its parking lot isn't hidden behind dunes. However, the lot to the right of the bathhouse is a great place to watch the sunset. There's a hot-dog stand, as well as showers and restrooms. Lifeguards are on duty in season. From late June through early September, parking costs $15 per day, or $45 for a yearly pass to all National Seashore beaches.

For a day of fairly private beachcombing and great views, you can walk across the stone jetty at low tide to **Long Point**, a sand spit south of town with two lighthouses and two Civil War bunkers—called Fort Useless and Fort Ridiculous because they were hardly needed. It's a 2-mi walk across soft sand—beware of poison ivy and deer ticks if you stray from the path.

Fodor's Choice ★ **Race Point Beach** (✉ *Race Point Rd., east of U.S. 6, Greater Provincetown*), one of the Cape Cod National Seashore beaches in Provincetown, has a wide swath of sand stretching far off into the distance around the point and Coast Guard station. Behind the beach is pure duneland, and bike trails lead off the parking lot. Because of its position on a point facing north, the beach gets sun all day long (east-coast beaches get fullest sun early in the day). Parking is available, there are showers and restrooms, and lifeguards are stationed in season. From late June through early September, parking costs $15 per day, or $45 for a yearly pass good at all National Seashore beaches.

BICYCLING

The **Beech Forest bike trail** (⊠ *Off Race Point Rd. east of U.S. 6, Greater Provincetown*) in the National Seashore offers an especially nice ride through a shady forest to Bennett Pond.

The **Province Lands Trail** is a 5¼-mi loop off the Beech Forest parking lot on Race Point Road, with spurs to Herring Cove and Race Point beaches and to Bennett Pond. The paths wind up and down hills amid dunes, marshes, woods, and ponds, affording spectacular views. More than 7 mi of bike trails lace through the dunes, cranberry bogs, and scrub pine of the National Seashore, with many access points, including Herring Cove and Race Point.

Gale Force Bikes (⊠ *144 Bradford St. Ext., West End* ☎ *508/487–4849* ⊕ *www.galeforcebikes.com*) stocks a wide variety of bikes for sale and for rent; it's also a good source for parts and repairs. There's also a deli on-site.

P'town Bikes (⊠ *42 Bradford St., Downtown Center* ☎ *508/487–8735* ⊕ *www.ptownbikes.com*) has Trek and Mongoose mountain bikes at good rates, and you can reserve online. The shop also provides free locks and maps.

BOATING AND KAYAKING

Bay Lady II (⊠ *MacMillan Wharf, Downtown Center* ☎ *508/487–9308* ⊕ *www.sailcapecod.com*), a beautiful 73-foot sailing vessel, heads out for two-hour cruises three times daily. You're welcome to bring your own spirits and snacks for this scenic and peaceful sail.

Flyer's Boat Rental (⊠ *131A Commercial St., West End* ☎ *508/487–0898* ⊕ *www.flyersrentals.com*) has kayaks, surf bikes, Sunfish, Hobies, Force 5s, Lightnings, powerboats, and rowboats. Flyer's will also shuttle you to Long Point.

Venture Athletics Kayak Shop (⊠ *237 Commercial St., Downtown Center* ☎ *508/487–9442*) rents kayaks and equipment and offers guided kayak tours.

FISHING

You can go after fluke, bluefish, and striped bass on a walk-on basis from spring through fall with **Cee Jay Fishing Parties** (⊠ *MacMillan Wharf, Downtown Center* ☎ *508/487–4330* ⊕ *www.ceejayfishingparties.com*).

5

PARASAILING

Provincetown Parasail (⊠ *MacMillan Wharf, Downtown Center* ☎ *508/ 487–8359* ⊕ *www.provincetownparasail.com*) offers high-flying parasailing adventures, which take you some 300 feet above town and Cape Cod Bay.

SPAS

Jonathan Williams Salon & Spa (⊠ *139A Bradford St., Downtown Center* ☎ *508/487–0422* ⊕ *www.jonathanwilliamssalonandspa.com*) offers a wide range of spa treatments, including skin treatments, hair care, pedicures, and aromatherapy.

At the posh Crowne Pointe Historic Inn, the intimate and fabulous **Shui Spa** (⊠ *82 Bradford St., Downtown Center* ☎ *508/487–6767* ⊕ *www. crownepointe.com*) pampers guests with everything from hot stone massage to sweet-sugar body scrubs to grape wine–peel facials.

TENNIS

Herring Cove Tennis Club (⊠ *21 Bradford St. Ext., West End* ☎ *508/487– 9512* ⊕ *www.bissellstennis.com*) has five clay courts and offers lessons.

Provincetown Tennis Club (⊠ *288 Bradford St. Ext., East End* ☎ *508/487– 9574* ⊕ *www.provincetowntennis.com*) has five clay and two hard courts open to nonmembers; you can also take lessons with the resident tennis pro.

TOURS

Fodor's Choice ★ **Art's Dune Tours** (⊠ *Commercial and Standish Sts., Downtown Center* ☎ *508/487–1950* ⊕ *www.artsdunetours.com*) has been taking eager passengers into the dunes of Province Lands since 1946. Bumpy but controlled rides transport you through sometimes surreal sandy vistas peppered with beach grass and along shoreline patrolled by seagulls and sandpipers. Tours are filled with lively tales, including the fascinating history of the exclusive (and reclusive) dune shacks (18 still stand today). These one-hour tours are offered several times daily; especially intriguing are the sunset and moonlight tours. Rides coupled with clambakes or barbecues are popular; call for availability and pricing.

★ **P-town Pedicab** (☎ *508/487–0660* ⊕ *www.ptownpedicabs.com*) provides highly enjoyable town tours in vehicles you won't find in too many places around the country. A guide pedals you and up to two more guests around town in an open-air, three-wheel chariotlike cab, pointing out local sights and offering an unusual perspective on this already unusual town.

Provincetown Trolley (☎ *508/487–9483* ⊕ *www.provincetowntrolley.com*) offers 40-minute narrated tours of Provincetown, which leave from outside town hall every 30 minutes daily 10 to 4, and every hour daily 5 to 7 PM. The ride takes you through downtown, out to the Pilgrim Monument, and by the beaches; the fare is $11.

Harbor tours on the **Viking Princess** (⊠ *MacMillan Wharf, Downtown Center* ☎ *508/487–7323* ⊕ *www.capecodecotours.com*) are given in mornings throughout summer. These narrated excursions tell stories of shipwrecks and pirate raids and pass by Civil War forts and the Long

Provincetown's Dune Shacks

Provincetown's rich artistic legacy continues to manifest itself in the dozens of galleries along Commercial Street and through countless resident writers and painters. But out along the seashore, along a 3-mi stretch of sand extending from about Race Point to High Head (in Truro), you can see a more unusual remnant of the town's artistic past—the dune shacks.

FROM SEAMEN TO ARTISTS

These small, austere structures were built by the Life Saving Service in the 19th century to house seamen. Sometime around the 1920s, long after the dune shacks ceased housing lifesaving personnel, many of the community's creative or eccentric spirits began using them as retreats and hideaways. Probably the most famous of these was playwright Eugene O'Neill, who purchased one and spent many summers there with his wife, Agnes Boulton. O'Neill penned *Anna Christie* (1920) and *The Hairy Ape* (1921) while living in his shack, and in doing so gave the whole collection of dune shacks something of an arty cachet.

Other Provincetown artists soon followed O'Neill, including the self-proclaimed "poet of the dunes," Harry Kemp, who wrote many a verse about the seashore's stark, desolate splendor. Author Hazel Hawthorne-Werner wrote *The Salt House*, a memoir tracing her time amid the dunes, in 1929. It's said that this book helped get the shacks, along with the entire dunes district, onto the National Register of Historic Places in 1988, helping to preserve them for years to come. In later years, Jack Kerouac, e. e. cummings, Norman Mailer, and Jackson Pollack also lived in these primitive structures.

VISITING THE SHACKS

The dune shacks haven't been modernized much—none has electricity, running water, or toilets. You stay in them for a chance to be with nature and perhaps commune with the spirits of artists who have gone before you.

The dune shacks are now all set along the part of the Cape Cod National Seashore that is known as the Province Lands. The park owns most of the Provincetown dune shacks, though a few are managed by nonprofit groups aimed at preserving them and their legacy. Some of these organizations, such as the Peaked Hills Bars Trust and the Provincetown Community Compact, allow visitors to stay in the dune shacks through a variety of arrangements. Both groups run an artist-in-residence program—artists can apply for short stays in some of the shacks during the summer season. Only a handful of applicants are admitted each year.

If you're not an artist, you can enter a lottery for the opportunity to lease one of the shacks for a week in spring or fall. If you're interested in applying to spend time in a dune shack or you'd like to join one of the nonprofit organizations that sponsors them, contact **Dune Shacks** (🏠 *Box 1705, Provincetown 02657* 📠 *508/487–3635*).

If you're simply interested in exploring the terrain and seeing the shacks, you can either book a tour with **Art's Dune Tours** (📠 *508/487–1950 or 800/894–1951* ⊕ *www.artsdunetours. com*) or park behind the Cape Inn, on Snail Road just off U.S. 6, where a 3-mi trail winds through the dunes and past many of the dune shacks.

—by Andrew Collins

WHALE-WATCHING TRIP TIPS

Cameras have replaced harpoons in the waters north of Cape Cod. While you can learn about New England's whaling history and perhaps see whales in the distance from shore, a whale-watching excursion is the best way to connect with these magnificent creatures—who may be just as curious about you as you are about them.

Once relentlessly hunted around the world by New Englanders, whales today are celebrated as intelligent, friendly, and curious creatures. Whales are still important to the region's economy and culture, but now in the form of ecotourism. Easily accessible from several ports in Massachusetts, the 842-square-mi Stellwagen Bank National Marine Sanctuary attracts finback, humpback, minke, and right whales who feed and frolic here twice a year during their migration. The same conditions that made the Stellwagen Bank area of the mouth of Massachusetts Bay a good hunting ground make it a good viewing area. Temperature, currents, and nutrients combine to produce plankton, krill, and fish to feed marine mammals.

When to Go: Tours operate April through October; May through September are the most active months in the Stellwagen Bank area.

Ports of Departure: Boats leave from Barnstable and Provincetown on Cape Cod, heading to the Stellwagen area. Book tours at least a day ahead.

Cost: Around $40. Check company Web sites and freebie tourist magazines for coupons.

What to Expect: All companies abide by guidelines so as not to harass whales. Tours last 3 to 4 hours and almost always encounter whales; if not, vouchers are often given for another tour. Passengers are encouraged to watch the horizon for water spouts, which indicate a surfaced whale clearing its blowhole to breathe air. Upon spotting an animal, the boat slows and approaches the whale to a safe distance; often, whales will approach an idling boat and even swim underneath it.

What to Bring: Plastic bags protect binoculars and cameras from damp spray. Most boats have a concession stand, but pack bottled water and snacks. Kids (and adults) will appreciate games or other items to pass the time in between whale sightings.

What to Wear: Wear rubber-soled footwear for slick decks. A waterproof outer layer and layers of clothing will help in varied conditions, as will sunscreen, sunglasses, and a hat that can be secured. Most boats have cabins where you can warm up and get out of the wind.

Comforting Advice: Seat cushions like those used at sporting events may be appreciated. Take motion-sickness medication before setting out. Ginger candy and acupressure wristbands can also help. If you feel queasy, get some fresh air and focus your eyes on a stable feature on the shore or horizon.

Photo Hints: Use a fast shutter speed, or sport mode, to avoid blurry photographs. Most whales will be a distance from the boat; have a telephoto lens ready. To avoid shutter delay on your point-and-shoot camera, lock the focus at infinity so you don't miss that breaching whale shot.

THE CAPE'S WHALES

One of the joys of Cape Cod is spotting whales swimming in and around the feeding grounds at Stellwagen Bank, about 6 mi off the tip of Provincetown. Here's what you might see.

Atlantic white-sided dolphin. Although they're not whales, dolphins are a familiar sight on whale-watching trips. These playful marine mammals can grow to 7 feet. Note the distinct yellow-to-white patches on their sides. Highly social, dolphins group in pods of up to 60 and hunt fish and squid. They may play in the boat's bow waves.

Minke whale. Named for a Norwegian whaler, this smallest of baleen whales grows to 30 feet and 10 tons. It is a solitary creature, streamlined compared to other whales, and has a curved dorsal fin on its back.

Humpback whale. These 40-ton baleen whales are known for their acrobatics and communicative songs. Curious animals, they often approach boats. By blowing bubbles, humpbacks entrap krill and fish for food. They put on an amazing show when they breach.

North Atlantic right whale. Called the "right" whales to hunt, this species travels close to shore and is the rarest of all whales—there are only around 300. Note the callosities (rough skin) on their large heads.

Finback whale. The second-largest animal on Earth (after the blue whale, which is rarely seen here), these baleen whales can weigh 50 tons and eat 4,000 lbs of food a day. Look for the distinctive dorsal fin near their fluke (tail).

Point Lighthouse. There are also sunset cruises, "critter cruises" with onboard naturalists, and kids-oriented "pirate fun cruises."

WHALE-WATCHING

Many people also come aboard not just for whales but for birding, especially during spring and fall migration. You can see gannets, shearwaters, and storm petrels, among many others. Several boats take you out to sea (and bring you back) with morning, afternoon, or sunset trips lasting from three to four hours.

The municipal parking area by the harbor in Provincetown fills up by noon in summer; consider taking a morning boat to avoid crowds and the hottest sun. Although April may be cold, it's one of the better months for spotting whales, which at that time have just migrated north after mating and are very hungry. Good food is, after all, what brings the whales to this part of the Atlantic.

Dolphin Fleet tours are accompanied by scientists from the Center for Coastal Studies in Provincetown, who provide commentary while collecting data on the whale population they've been monitoring for years. They know many of the whales by name and will tell you about their habits and histories. Reservations are required. ⊠ *MacMillan Wharf, Downtown Center* ☎ *508/240–3636 or 800/826–9300* ⊕ *www. whalewatch.com* ✉ *$39* ☉ *Tours mid-Apr.–Oct.*

SHOPPING

ART GALLERIES

★ **Albert Merola Gallery** (✉ *424 Commercial St., East End* ☎ *508/487–4424* ⊕ *www.universalfineobjects.com*) focuses on 20th-century and contemporary master prints and Picasso ceramics. The gallery showcases artists from in and around Provincetown, Boston, and New York, including James Balla, Richard Baker, and iconic gay filmmaker and arbiter of bad taste John Waters.

Berta Walker Gallery (✉ *208 Bradford St., East End* ☎ *508/487–6411* ⊕ *www.bertawalker.com*) specializes in Provincetown-affiliated artists, including Selina Trieff and Nancy Whorf, and such Provincetown legends as Ross Moffett, Charles Hawthorne, Hans Hofmann, and Karl Knaths.

Charles-Baltivik Gallery (✉ *432 Commercial St., East End* ☎ *508/487–3611* ⊕ *www.cbgallery.net*) features several leading contemporary artists and has a small sculpture garden.

The **DNA Gallery** (✉ *288 Bradford St., East End* ☎ *508/487–7700* ⊕ *www.dnagallery.com*) represents artists working in various mediums, including many emerging talents.

Ernden Fine Art Gallery (✉ *397 Commercial St., Downtown Center* ☎ *508/487–6700* ⊕ *www.erndengallery.com*) is one of the more recent additions to the emerging local art scene, showing works by an impressive range of both newer and established painters and photographers.

★ **Gallery Voyeur** (✉ *444 Commercial St., East End* ☎ *508/487–3678* ⊕ *www.voy-art.com*) shows artist-owner Johniene Papandreas's provocative, larger-than-life portraits, which are inspired by classical and Romantic artists of the past.

Hilda Neily Art Gallery (✉ *398 Commercial St., Downtown Center* ☎ *508/ 487–6300* ⊕ *www.hildaneilygallery.com*) is named for its featured artist, who was once a student of impressionist painter Henry Hensche.

Fodor's Choice ★ **Julie Heller Gallery** (✉ *2 Gosnold St., Downtown Center* ☎ *508/487–2169* ⊕ *www.juliehellergallery.com*) has contemporary artists as well as some Provincetown icons. The gallery has works from the Sol Wilson and Milton Avery estates, as well as from such greats as Robert Motherwell, Agnes Weinrich, and Blanche Lazzell.

Rice/Polak Gallery (✉ *430 Commercial St., East End* ☎ *508/487–1052* ⊕ *www.ricepolakgallery.com*) stocks a remarkably comprehensive and eclectic variety of contemporary works, from paintings and pastels to photography and sculpture.

★ The **Schoolhouse Galleries** (✉ *494 Commercial St., East End* ☎ *508/487–4800* ⊕ *www.schoolhouseprovincetown.com*), in an 1844 former school, shows the works of more than 25 local and national artists and photographers.

Simie Maryles Gallery (✉ *435 Commercial St., East End* ☎ *508/487–7878* ⊕ *www.simiemaryles.com*) represents about 15 contemporary artists, most of whom work in traditional styles. Oil paintings, glasswork, ceramics, and metal sculpture are among the strong suits here.

The **William-Scott Gallery** (✉ *439 Commercial St., East End* ☎ *508/487–4040* ⊕ *www.williamscottgallery.com*) primarily shows contemporary works such as John Dowd's reflective, realistic Cape 'scapes.

SPECIALTY STORES

Farland Provisions (✉ *150 Bradford St., Downtown Center* ☎ *508/487–0045*) proffers all kinds of fine foods and snacks, including excellent deli sandwiches.

Forbidden Fruit (✉ *173 Commercial St., West End* ☎ *508/487–9800*) is a one-stop shop for all irreverent and offbeat gifts, from strange costumes to erotic trinkets to Gothic tchotchkes.

ID (✉ *220A Commercial St., Downtown Center* ☎ *508/487–4300*) stocks a wonderful array of cool clocks, watches, offbeat jewelry, and belt buckles.

Impulse (✉ *188 Commercial St., Downtown Center* ☎ *508/487–1154*) has contemporary American crafts, original paintings, jewelry, and an extraordinary kaleidoscope collection.

Kidstuff (✉ *381 Commercial St., Downtown Center* ☎ *508/487–0714*) carries unusual, colorful children's wear.

★ **Marine Specialties** (✉ *235 Commercial St., Downtown Center* ☎ *508/487–1730*) is full of treasures, knickknacks, and clothing. Here you can purchase some very reasonably priced casual- and military-style clothing, as well as seashells, marine supplies, stained-glass lamps, candles, rubber sharks (you get the idea), and prints of old advertisements.

Moda Fina (✉ *349 Commercial St., Downtown Center* ☎ *508/487–6632*) displays an eclectic selection of women's fashions, shoes, and jewelry—everything from flowing linen or silk evening wear to funky and casual pieces. Unique Mexican crafts are also for sale.

Now Voyager Bookstore (✉ *357 Commercial St., Downtown Center* ☎ *508/487–0848*) is a first-rate independent bookstore with an emphasis on lesbian and gay titles; the store hosts prominent authors throughout the year (especially in summer) and has a small art gallery.

Provincetown Antique Market (✉ *131 Commercial St., West End* ☎ *508/487–1115*) has one of the town's better selections of vintage lighting, jewelry, costumes, toys, textiles, and furnishings.

The Shell Shop (✉ *276 Commercial St., Downtown Center* ☎ *508/487–1763* ⊕ *www.theshellshop.com*) has been selling seashells—as well as coral, sponges, and other treasures from the deep—since 1957. The inventory comes from over 50 countries around the world.

Silk & Feathers (✉ *377 Commercial St., Downtown Center* ☎ *508/487–2057*) carries an assortment of fine lingerie, women's clothing, and jewelry.

Tim's Used Books (✉ *242 Commercial St., Downtown Center* ☎ *508/487–0005*) is packed with volumes of volumes—rooms of used-but-in-good-shape books, including some rare and out-of-print texts.

★ **Utilities** (✉ *393 Commercial St., Downtown Center* ☎ *508/487–6800*) supplies customers with some of the coolest kitchen and bathroom gadgetry and decorative pieces around.

Wa (✉ *220 Commercial St., Downtown Center* ☎ *508/487–6355*) is an oasis of peace and Zen-like tranquillity. Unusual- and Japanese-inspired items include fountains, home-accent pieces, and framed (and sometimes frightening) tropical insects.

West End Trading Co. (✉ *137 Commercial St., West End* ☎ *508/487–2327*) sells folk art, as well as a wide selection of boat and architectural salvage, nautical objects, and furniture.

Womencrafts (✉ *376 Commercial St., Downtown Center* ☎ *508/487–2501* ⊕ *www.womencrafts.com*) has a varied and unusual selection of jewelry, pottery, mosaics, and other fine craft item, all made by women around the United States and Canada.

Martha's Vineyard

WORD OF MOUTH

"Walk through Oak Bluffs and make sure to walk through the Martha's Vineyard Camp Meeting Association—300+ small, gingerbread-style cottages that are mostly summer houses with an open-air tabernacle in the center and a beautiful old Methodist church. Check out the Flying Horses Carousel where kids and adults ride and try to catch the brass ring for a free ride. Take the MVTA bus to Edgartown for a completely different atmosphere and architectural style. Quintessential New England with old whaling captains houses. Quite a few art galleries, too. You will not find a traffic light, no Starbucks, MacDonald's or Walmart on the island."

—mvisle

Updated
by Laura V.
Scheel

From Memorial Day through Labor Day, Martha's Vineyard quickens into a vibrant, star-studded place. Edgartown floods with people who come to wander narrow streets flanked with elegant boutiques, stately whaling captains' homes, and charming inns. The busy main port, Vineyard Haven, welcomes day-trippers fresh off ferries and private yachts to browse in its own array of shops. Oak Bluffs, where pizza and ice-cream emporiums reign supreme, attracts diverse crowds with its boardwalk-town air and nightspots that cater to high-spirited, carefree youth.

The island of Martha's Vineyard is far less developed than Cape Cod—thanks to a few local conservation organizations—yet more cosmopolitan than neighboring Nantucket. Summer regulars have included a host of celebrities over the years, among them the Obama family, William Styron, Art Buchwald, Walter Cronkite, Beverly Sills, Patricia Neal, Spike Lee, and Diane Sawyer. Former president Bill Clinton and his wife, Senator Hillary Clinton, are frequent visitors. Concerts, theater, dance performances, and lecture series draw top talent to the island; a county agricultural fair, weekly farmers' markets, and miles of walking trails provide earthier pleasures.

Most people know the Vineyard's summer persona, but in many ways its other self has even more appeal, for the off-season island is a place of peace and simple beauty. Drivers traversing country lanes find time to linger over pastoral and ocean vistas without being pushed along by a throng of other cars. In nature reserves, the voices of summer are gone, leaving only the sounds of birdsong and the crackle of leaves underfoot. Private beaches open to the public, and the water sparkles under crisp, blue skies. Locals are at their convivial best off-season. After the craziness of their short moneymaking months, they reestablish contact with friends and take up pastimes temporarily crowded out by work. The result for visitors—besides the extra dose of friendliness—is that cultural, educational, and recreational events continue year-round.

ORIENTATION AND PLANNING

GETTING ORIENTED

The island is roughly triangular, with maximum distances of about 20 mi east to west and 10 mi north to south. The west end of the Vineyard, known as Up-Island—from the nautical expression of going "up" in degrees of longitude as you sail west—is more rural and wild than the eastern Down-Island end, comprising Vineyard Haven, Oak Bluffs, and Edgartown.

TOP REASONS TO GO

Walking the beaches: On the Vineyard's south shore, the 18 mi stretching eastward from the Aquinnah Cliffs are said to be among the longest white-sand beaches from Georgia to Maine. The protected beaches on the Nantucket and Vineyard sounds are perfect for families.

Reveling in 19th-century architecture: The Vineyard has an extraordinary amount of beautifully preserved antique homes. In Oak Bluffs, the Campground Cottages are works of art and whimsy. Edgartown's grand captain's homes reflect the sensibilities of the 19th-century whaling era.

Experiencing the Aquinnah Cliffs: Atop the cliffs, nature reveals itself at its most dramatic. You'll be stunned by sunsets, hear the waves crashing on the rocks below; feel the mist of an oncoming fog, and take in the ever-present dance of the wind.

Communing with nature: The island's nature reserves and conservation areas are crisscrossed by well-marked trails through varied terrains. At the trailheads of most you'll find small parking areas and bulletin boards with maps and directions. The Felix Neck Wildlife Sanctuary, Wasque Reservation, and Mytoi are three good places to start.

Hooking a big one: Some of the island's most zealous fishing is done by amateurs—the striped bass and bluefish derby in fall is serious business. Several outfits operate deep-sea fishing trips if you want to catch your own.

Vineyard Haven (Tisbury). One of the island's busiest towns, Vineyard Haven sees ferry traffic all year long. A fairly compact downtown area keeps most shopping and dining options within easy reach.

Oak Bluffs. Once a Methodist campground, Oak Bluffs is a little less refined than the other towns. It has a vibrant vacation vibe, with lots of nightlife, dining, and shopping.

Edgartown. Dominated by the impeccably kept homes of 19th-century sea captains, Edgartown has a sense of sophistication. There's great history here, and several museums tell the story.

Chappaquiddick Island. Take the tiny ferry from Edgartown to explore Chappaquiddick Island's vast nature preserves. It's a favorite place for bird-watchers and anglers.

West Tisbury. There's beautiful farm country out this way, and the 1859 Grange Hall is still the center of action. During the warmer months, don't miss the bountiful West Tisbury Farmers' Market.

Chilmark. The beaches here, best reached by bike, are spectacular. Quiet Chilmark is mostly residential, lacking any large downtown center.

Menemsha. An active fishing harbor, Menemsha is known for its splendid sunsets. There are a few shops and galleries, and a couple of excellent take-out spots for the freshest of seafood.

Aquinnah. Known until recently as Gay Head, Aquinnah is famous for its grand and dramatic red clay cliffs, as well as the resident lighthouse.

PLANNING

WHEN TO GO

Summer is the most popular season on the Vineyard, the time when everyone is here and everything is open and happening. With weather perfect for all kinds of activities, the island hosts special events from the Martha's Vineyard Agricultural Fair to the Edgartown Regatta. Another busy season, fall brings cool weather, harvest celebrations, and fishing derbies. Tivoli Day, an end-of-summer/start-of-fall celebration, includes a street fair in downtown Oak Bluffs. The island does tend to curl up for winter, when many shops and restaurants close. However, during the weeks surrounding the Hanukkah-Christmas-New Year's holidays, the Vineyard puts bells on for all kinds of special events and celebrations, most notably in Edgartown and Vineyard Haven. Spring sees the island awaken from its slumber in a burst of garden and house tours as islanders warm up for the busy season.

PLANNING YOUR TIME

It's nearly impossible to see everything in Martha's Vineyard in just one day. If you're short on time, consider a narrated island tour. If you're traveling without a car and want to have easy access to restaurants, shopping, and entertainment, it's best to base yourself in Edgartown, Oak Bluffs, or Vineyard Haven. Depending on your interests, you could easily spend several hours or even an entire day exploring each town.

GETTING HERE AND AROUND

AIR TRAVEL

⇨ *Air Travel in Essentials in Travel Smart Cape Cod in the back of this book.*

BIKE TRAVEL

Martha's Vineyard offers superb terrain for biking—you can pick up a map that shows the island's many dedicated bike paths from the chamber of commerce. Several shops throughout the island rent bicycles, many of them close to the ferry terminals; many will even deliver your bike rental to your lodging establishment.

Bike Rentals Anderson's Bike Rental (✉ *Circuit Ave. Exit, Oak Bluffs* ☎ *508/693-9346*). **Edgartown Bicycles** (✉ *212 Upper Main St., Edgartown* ☎ *508/627-9008* ⊕ *www.edgartownbicycles.com*). **Martha's Bike Rentals** (✉ *4 Lagoon Pond Rd., Vineyard Haven* ☎ *508/693-6593* ⊕ *www.marthasvineyardbikes.com*). **R. W. Cutler Bike Rentals** (✉ *1 Main St., Edgartown* ☎ *508/627-4052*).

BOAT AND FERRY TRAVEL

⇨ *Boat and Ferry Travel in Travel Smart Cape Cod in the back of this book.*

BUS TRAVEL

The big buses of the Martha's Vineyard Transit Authority (VTA) provide regular service to all six towns on the island, with frequent stops in peak season and very limited service in winter. The fare is $1 per town, including the town of departure. One-day ($7), three-day ($15), one-week ($25), and one-month ($40) passes are available. The VTA also has two free in-town shuttle-bus routes, one in Edgartown and one in Vineyard Haven.

Bus Information **Martha's Vineyard Transit Authority** (*VTA* ☎ *508/693–9940* ⊕ *www.vineyardtransit.com*).

CAR TRAVEL

Traffic can be a challenge on Martha's Vineyard, especially in season, but driving can be worth the hassle if you really want to see the whole island and travel freely between towns. Bringing a car over on the ferry in summer, however, requires reservations far in advance, costs almost double what it does in the off-season, and necessitates standing in long lines—it's sometimes easier and more economical to rent a car once you're on the island, and then only for the days when you plan to explore. Where you stay and what you plan on seeing can greatly influence your transportation plans; discuss the different options for getting around Martha's Vineyard with your innkeeper or hotel staff as soon as you've booked a room.

TAXI TRAVEL

Taxis meet all scheduled ferries and flights, and there are taxi stands by the Flying Horses Carousel in Oak Bluffs, at the foot of Main Street in Edgartown, and by the steamship office in Vineyard Haven. Fares range from $6 within a town to $35 to $42 one-way from Vineyard Haven to Aquinnah.

Taxi Information **AdamCab** (☎ *508/627–4462 or 800/281–4462* ⊕ *www.adamcab.com*). **All Island Taxi** (☎ *508/693–2929 or 800/693–8294* ⊕ *www.allislandtaximv.com*). **Atlantic Cab** (☎ *508/693–7110 or 877/477–8294*). **Mario's** (☎ *508/693–8399*).

RESTAURANTS

From fried fish at roadside stands to boiled lobster and foie gras at fancy French restaurants and a growing array of international influences—Thai, Brazilian, Japanese, Mexican, to name just a few—the Vineyard serves an amazing variety of culinary choices.

The majority of eating establishments, both take-out and sit-down, are concentrated in the three Down-Island towns of Vineyard Haven, Oak Bluffs, and Edgartown. As you travel Up-Island—to West Tisbury, Chilmark, and Aquinnah—choices dwindle, especially when it comes to sit-down dinners. Sadly, Vineyard diners—all-American institutions where you can get an honest, no-frills meal at reasonable prices—are a dying breed. Luckily, you can pick up sandwiches, pastries, and other to-go specialties at a number of places around the island, and with good planning you can eat well on a modest budget and splurge for an elegant dinner.

Most restaurants are open on weekends starting in late spring, and by Memorial Day weekend most are serving daily. Although the season

Martha's Vineyard

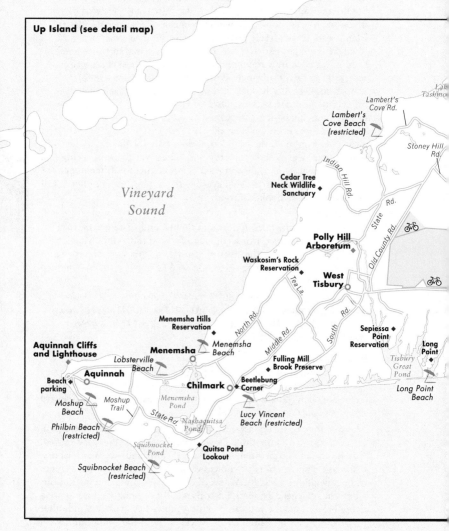

Up Island (see detail map)

*Vineyard
Sound*

Lambert's
Cove Beach
(restricted)

*Lambert's
Cove Rd.*

*Lak
Tashmo*

*Stoney Hill
Rd.*

Cedar Tree
Neck Wildlife
Sanctuary

Indian Hill Rd.

State Rd.

Old County Rd.

**Polly Hill
Arboretum**

Waskosim's Rock
Reservation

**West
Tisbury**

Tea L.a.

North Rd.

Middle Rd.

South Rd.

Menemsha Hills
Reservation

*Menemsha
Beach*

Sepiessa
Point
Reservation

**Long
Point**

*Tisbury
Great
Pond*

**Aquinnah Cliffs
and Lighthouse**

*Lobsterville
Beach*

Menemsha

Fulling Mill
Brook Preserve

Long Point
Beach

Beach
parking

Aquinnah

*Moshup
Trail*

Chilmark

*Menemsha
Pond*

Beetlebung
Corner

Moshup
Beach

State Rd.

*Nashaquitsa
Pond*

Lucy Vincent
Beach (restricted)

Philbin Beach
(restricted)

*Squibnocket
Pond*

**Quitsa Pond
Lookout**

Squibnocket Beach
(restricted)

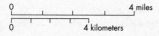

0				4 miles

0			4 kilometers

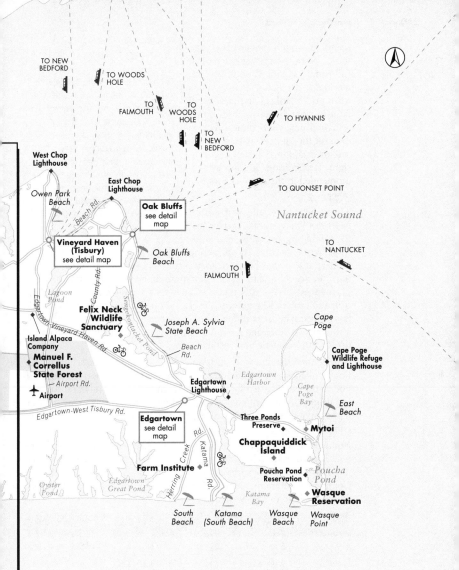

TO NEW
BEDFORD

TO WOODS
HOLE

TO
FALMOUTH

TO
WOODS
HOLE

TO
NEW
BEDFORD

TO HYANNIS

TO QUONSET POINT

TO
FALMOUTH

TO
NANTUCKET

West Chop
Lighthouse

*Owen Park
Beach*

East Chop
Lighthouse

Oak Bluffs
see detail
map

Nantucket Sound

**Vineyard Haven
(Tisbury)**
see detail map

*Oak Bluffs
Beach*

*Lagoon
Pond*

**Felix Neck
Wildlife
Sanctuary**

*Joseph A. Sylvia
State Beach*

*Cape
Poge*

**Island Alpaca
Company**

*Beach
Rd.*

**Cape Poge
Wildlife Refuge
and Lighthouse**

**Manuel F.
Correllus
State Forest**

Airport Rd.

Airport

*Edgartown
Harbor*

*Cape
Poge
Bay*

*East
Beach*

**Edgartown
Lighthouse**

Edgartown-West Tisbury Rd.

Edgartown
see detail
map

Herring Creek Rd.

Katama Rd.

**Three Ponds
Preserve**

Mytoi

**Chappaquiddick
Island**

Farm Institute

**Poucha Pond
Reservation**

*Poucha
Pond*

**Wasque
Reservation**

*Oyster
Pond*

*Edgartown
Great Pond*

*Katama
Bay*

*South
Beach*

Katama
(South Beach)

*Wasque
Beach*

*Wasque
Point*

A T L A N T I C   O C E A N

KEY

Bike Trail

Ferry

seems to stretch longer each year, most restaurants remain open full-time through Columbus Day weekend, then only on weekends through Thanksgiving (a small handful of die-hard restaurants remain open year-round). Dress, even for the upscale spots, is casual; a man in a sports jacket is a rare sight. Reservations are highly recommended in the summer months.

HOTELS

The variety of lodging options on Martha's Vineyard ranges from historic whaling captains' mansions filled with antiques to sprawling modern oceanfront hotels to cozy cottages in the woods. When choosing your accommodations, keep in mind that each town has a different personality: Oak Bluffs tends to cater to a younger, active, nightlife-oriented crowd; Edgartown is more subdued and dignified. Chilmark has beautiful beaches and miles of conservation lands, but not much of a downtown shopping area. Vineyard Haven provides a nice balance of downtown bustle and rustic charm.

Bear in mind that many of the island's bed-and-breakfasts, set in vintage homes filled with art and antiques, have age restrictions—call ahead if you're traveling with a family. And remember that in July and August, the height of the summer season, minimum stays of as many as four nights may be required. If you're planning to visit for a week or more, consider renting a house.

Make reservations for summer stays as far in advance as possible; late winter is not too early. Rates in season are very high but can fall by as much as 50% in the off-season. The Martha's Vineyard Chamber of Commerce maintains a listing of availability in the peak tourist season, from mid-June to mid-September.

WHAT IT COSTS				
	¢	$	$$	$$$	$$$$
Restaurants	under $10	$10–$16	$17–$22	$23–$30	over $30
Hotels	under $90	$90–$140	$141–$200	$201–$260	over $260

Restaurant prices are per person for a main course at dinner. Hotel prices are for a standard double room, excluding 5.7% sales tax (more in some counties) and up to an additional 6% tourist tax.

TOURS

Liz Villard's Vineyard History Tours leads walking tours of Edgartown's "history, architecture, ghosts, and gossip," including a stop at the Vincent House. Tours are run from April through December; call for times. Liz and her guides also lead similar tours of Oak Bluffs and

Vineyard Haven. Walks last a little more than an hour. Local author Holly Nadler also leads her own Vineyard Ghosts Walking Tours by lantern light; in Oak Bluffs, Edgartown, and Vineyard Haven. Martha's Vineyard Sightseeing runs 2½-hour tours covering the entire island. For a thrilling tour in an open biplane, sign up with Classic Aviators for a variety of island tours; the sunset trip is especially spectacular.

Contacts Classic Aviators (☎ *508/627-7677* ⊕ *www.biplanemv.com*). **Martha's Vineyard Sightseeing** (☎ *508/627-8687* ⊕ *www.mvtour.com*). **Vineyard Ghosts Walking Tours** (☎ *508/627-9445*). **Vineyard History Tours** (☎ *508/627-8619*).

VISITOR INFORMATION

The Martha's Vineyard Chamber of Commerce is two blocks from the Vineyard Haven ferry. The chamber information booth by the Vineyard Haven steamship terminal is open late May to the last weekend in June, Friday through Sunday 8 to 8; July through early September, daily 8 to 8; and early September through mid-October, Friday through Sunday 8:30 to 5:30. The chamber itself is open weekdays 9 to 5. There are also town information kiosks on Circuit Avenue in Oak Bluffs and on Church Street in Edgartown.

Tourist Information Martha's Vineyard Chamber of Commerce (✉ *34 Beach Rd., Vineyard Haven 02568* ☎ *508/693-4486 or 800/505-4815* ⊕ *www.mvy.com*).

VINEYARD HAVEN

Most people call this town Vineyard Haven because of the name of the port where ferries arrive, but its official name is Tisbury. Not as high-toned as Edgartown or as honky-tonk as Oak Bluffs, Vineyard Haven blends the past and the present with a touch of the bohemian. Visitors arriving here step off the ferry right into the bustle of the harbor, a block from the shops and restaurants of Main Street.

GETTING HERE AND AROUND

Vineyard Haven sees ferry traffic year-round, so this port town is always active. If you're traveling without a car, you can get around by taxi or the white buses run by Martha's Vineyard Transit Authority. Bike, scooter, and car rentals are also possibilities. Much of the downtown area is easily explored on foot, and a good number of the lodgings are within reach. Vineyard Haven is 3.5 mi west of Oak Bluffs.

EXPLORING

Association Hall. This stately, neoclassic 1844 building houses the town hall and the Katharine Cornell Memorial Theatre. The walls of the theater on the second floor are painted with murals depicting whaling expeditions and a Native American gathering, and the ceiling resembles a blue sky with seagulls overhead. Island artist Stan Murphy painted the murals on the occasion of the town's tercentenary in 1971. ✉ *51 Spring St.* ☎ *508/696–4200.*

QUICK BITES

The delicious breads, pastries, and quick-lunch items at **Black Dog Bakery** (⊠ *11 Water St.* ☎ *508/693–4786*) are simply not to be missed—it's a popular stop for good reason.

West Chop Lighthouse. One of two lighthouses that mark the opening to the harbor, the 52-foot white-and-black West Chop Lighthouse was built of brick in 1838 to replace an 1817 wood building. It's been moved back from the edge of the eroding bluff twice. ⊠ *W. Chop Rd.*

DROUGHT'S OVER

Vineyard voters approved beer and wine sales at restaurants in Vineyard Haven in 2010. The experiment was a big success, and the BYOB heyday was officially ended. Vineyard Haven's nearly 200 years of drought has now been properly "moistened" or "dampened," as locals like to say.

WHERE TO EAT

$
AMERICAN
★

✕ **ArtCliff Diner.** This vintage diner has been a year-round breakfast and lunch meeting place for locals since 1943. Owner-chef Gina Stanley, who was on call to make desserts for Blair House when she lived in Washington, D.C., serves anything but ordinary diner fare. She whips up pecan pancakes with real rum raisins for breakfast, and crepes with chèvre, arugula, or almost anything you ask for at lunch. There's a small porch with additional seating, but expect long waits at breakfast. ⊠ *39 Beach Rd.* ☎ *508/693–1224* ▤ *MC, V* ☉ *Closed Wed. No dinner.*

¢
CAFÉ

✕ **Beetlebung Coffee House.** This cozy coffeehouse is within easy walking distance of the ferry terminal and downtown shops and restaurants. A hip crowd convenes here for the great sandwiches (try the Taos panini, with flame-roasted New Mexico green chilies, turkey, and cheddar), designer-coffee drinks, and delicious desserts. The breakfast "eggwich," with Black Forest ham, poached egg, and Vermont cheddar, is a treat. There's an attractive side patio that's perfect on a warm afternoon. A Fodors.com reader calls it "a good local hangout to relax for an hour or two with a book or a laptop." ⊠ *32 Beach St.* ☎ *508/696–7122* ▤ *MC, V.*

$$$
AMERICAN

✕ **Black Dog Tavern.** This island landmark—more popular with tourists than locals—lies just steps from the ferry terminal in Vineyard Haven. In July and August, the wait for breakfast (with an expansive omelet assortment) can be as much as an hour. Why? Partly because the ambience inside—roaring fireplace, dark-wood walls, maritime memorabilia, and a grand view of the water—makes everyone feel so at home. The menu is heavy on local fish, chowders, and chops. ⊠ *20 Beach St. Ext.* ☎ *508/693–9223* ⌑ *Reservations not accepted* ▤ *AE, D, MC, V.*

$$$
AMERICAN

✕ **Blue Canoe Waterfront Grill.** With its front-row view of Vineyard Harbor, this spot lets you enjoy passing boats and nightly sunsets. It's not just the scenery that draws folks here for lunch, dinner, and Sunday brunch. Chef Nick Wilson, like many on the island, is a strong advocate for using local ingredients, whether they be from the sea or the land. Start with the large and meaty crab cakes, then try the catch of the day served with wild-mushroom gnocchi and a butter-sage sauce.

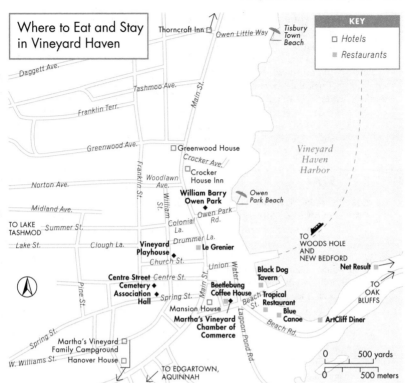

Where to Eat and Stay in Vineyard Haven

KEY
□ Hotels
■ Restaurants

There's a nice selection of salads and sandwiches for lunch; the goat-cheese spinach salad is a favorite. A slightly different brunch option is the chicken and waffles served with chipotle-maple syrup. ⊠ *52 Beach Rd.* ☎ *508/693–3332* ⊕ *www.bluecanoegrill.com* ⊟ *MC, V* ☉ *Closed Nov.–Apr.*

\$\$\$\$ ✕ **Le Grenier.** Owner-chef Jean Dupon has been serving classic French
FRENCH   food since the late 1970s above the M. V. Bagel Authority at the upper end of Vineyard Haven's downtown. All this time, he's been consistently loyal to the French standards: frogs' legs, sweetbreads, lobster flambéed with calvados, chicken livers Provençale, and tournedos are among the entrées. Quail, venison, and duck are more unusual offerings. The decor is almost backyard casual, with a string of lightbulbs, hand-painted floral designs, and souvenir wine-bottle corks lining the walls. ⊠ *Upper Main St.* ☎ *508/693–4906* ⊕ *www.legrenierrestaurant. com* ⊟ *AE, MC, V* ☉ *No lunch.*

\$ ✕ **Net Result.** It may not have quite the ambience of the fish markets in
SEAFOOD   Menemsha, but this simple take-out market and restaurant in a shop-
★   ping center just outside downtown Vineyard Haven serves some of the best food around, including superb sublime lobster bisque, hefty scallop and oyster platters, steamed lobsters, grilled swordfish sandwiches, and crab salad. Net Result also has a sushi counter: the Martha's Vineyard roll—packed with tuna, salmon, yellowtail, and avocado—is a

local favorite. You can dine at picnic tables outside and view Vineyard Haven's harbor across the busy road. "Have some shrimp cocktail and hang out with the lobsters while you wait for your food," says a Fodors. com reader. ⊠ *Tisbury Marketplace, 79 Beach Rd.* ☎ *508/693–6071* ⊕ *www.mvseafood.com* ⊟ *MC, V.*

$$ ✕ **Tropical Restaurant.** The house specialty at this roadside restaurant is
BRAZILIAN *rodizio,* a Brazilian style of barbecue where slow-roasted meats—in this case beef, chicken, sausage, pork, and lamb—are carved table-side and served continuously throughout your meal. Along with rice and beans, side dishes include collard greens and yucca. ⊠ *13 Beach St.* ☎ *508/696–0715* ⊟ *MC, V.*

WHERE TO STAY

$$$–$$$$ ▢ **Crocker House Inn.** This 1890 farmhouse-style inn is tucked into a quiet
★ lane off Main Street, minutes from the ferries and Owen Park Beach. The rooms are decorated casually with understated flair—pastel-painted walls, softly upholstered wing chairs, and white-wicker nightstands. Each contains a small, wall-mounted "honor bar," with a disposable camera, suntan lotion, and other useful sundries. Three rooms have soothing whirlpool tubs, and two have fireplaces. No. 6, with a small porch and a private entrance, has the best view of the harbor. Breakfast is served at a large farmer's table inside the small common room and kitchen area. Jeff and Jynell Kristal are the young, friendly owners, and Jynell also creates whimsically painted glassware, tote bags, and tiles, which are available for sale. **Pros:** great owners; short walk from town; easygoing vibe. **Cons:** you pay a premium for this location; books up quickly in summer. ⊠ *12 Crocker Ave.* ☎ *508/693–1151 or 800/772–0206* ⊕ *www.crockerhouseinn.com* ⮎ *8 rooms* ⚲ *In-room: a/c, no phone, DVD, Wi-Fi. In-hotel: Internet terminal, parking (free), no kids under 12* ⊟ *AE, MC, V* ⦿| *BP.*

$$–$$$ ▢ **Greenwood House.** A low-key B&B on a quiet lane around the corner from Vineyard Haven's public library, the Greenwood House is one of the better values in town. Affable innkeepers Kathy Stinson and Larry Gomez own this homey, three-story Arts and Crafts–style cottage with classic shingle siding and a shaded yard. The rooms are decorated with a mix of antiques and contemporary pieces, including brass and four-poster beds, island artwork, and functional but attractive nightstands and bureaus. It's a 10- to 15-minute walk from the ferry and even closer to many shops and restaurants. **Pros:** easy walk to shops and dining; good value; personal service. **Cons:** no harbor views. ⊠ *40 Greenwood Ave.* ☎ *508/693–6150 or 866/693–6150* ⊕ *www.greenwoodhouse.com* ⮎ *4 rooms* ⚲ *In-room: a/c, no phone, refrigerator, Wi-Fi. In-hotel: Wi-Fi hotspot* ⊟ *AE, MC, V* ⦿| *BP.*

$$$–$$$$ ▢ **Hanover House.** Set on ½ acre of landscaped lawn on a busy road—but within walking distance of the ferry—this three-property, children-friendly inn consists of a classic, home-style B&B, a country inn, and a carriage house. Rooms are decorated with a combination of antiques and reproduction furniture, mostly in the Victorian style, and each has individual flair: in one, an antique sewing machine serves as the

TV stand. The two carriage-house suites have private decks or patios, and kitchenettes. **Pros:** good value, 10-minute walk to shops and dining. **Cons:** off busy road, no water or beach views from most units. ⊠ *28 Edgartown Rd.* ☎ *508/693–1066 or 800/696–8633* ⊕ *www. hanoverhouseinn.com* ⤶ *13 rooms, 2 suites* ⚘ *In-room: a/c, kitchen (some), refrigerator (some), Wi-Fi* ⊟ *AE, D, MC, V* ⦿ *BP.*

$$$$ 🏨 **Mansion House.** There has been a hostelry on this Main Street site just above Vineyard Haven Harbor since 1794. Even though the current hotel dates from 2003, it had to be rebuilt on its historical footprint; as a result, rooms are all different in shape and configuration. Apart from the cheerful, summery rooms—some with balconies, gas fireplaces, and soaking tubs—the cupola deck provides a stunning spot for a respite. It affords sweeping views of the harbor, the town, and the lagoon that stretches between Vineyard Haven and Oak Bluffs. The hotel's Zephrus Restaurant serves reliable American fare and is also a nice spot for outside dining. **Pros:** restaurant and spa; steps from shopping and ferry; light-filled rooms. **Cons:** location can be a little noisy; not historic. ⊠ *9 Main St.* ☎ *509/693–2200 or 800/332–4112* ⊕ *www.mvmansionhouse. com* ⤶ *34 rooms, 6 suites* ⚘ *In-room: a/c, refrigerator, Wi-Fi. In-hotel: restaurant, room service, pool, gym, spa* ⊟ *AE, D, MC, V* ⦿ *CP.*

$$$$ 🏨 **Thorncroft Inn.** On 2½ wooded acres about 1 mi from the ferry, this inn's main building, a 1918 Craftsman bungalow, combines fine colonial and richly carved Renaissance Revival antiques with tasteful reproductions to create a somewhat formal environment. Most rooms have working wood-burning fireplaces and canopy beds; three rooms have two-person whirlpool baths, and two have private hot-tub spas. Rooms in the carriage house, set apart from the main house via a breezeway, are more secluded. Popular with honeymooners and those seeking the ultimate in romantic surroundings, look for perks like breakfast in bed and plush robes. **Pros:** antiques galore; lots of privacy. **Cons:** a bit formal and fussy; some rooms are very small. ⊠ *460 Main St.* ☎ *508/693–3333 or 800/332–1236* ⊕ *www.thorncroft.com* ⤶ *13 rooms, 1 cottage* ⚘ *In-room: a/c, refrigerator (some), DVD, Internet, Wi-Fi. In-hotel: no kids under 16* ⊟ *AE, D, DC, MC, V* ⦿ *BP.*

¢–$ ⛺ **Martha's Vineyard Family Campground.** Wooded sites, a ball field, a
★ camp store, bicycle rentals, and electrical and water hookups are among the facilities at this 20-acre campsite a few miles from Vineyard Haven. A step up from tents are 21 rustic one- or two-room cabins, which come with electricity, refrigerators, gas grills, and combinations of double and bunk beds (but bring your own bedding). This is the only campsite on the island, so book early; discounts are available for extended stays. **Pros:** great value; secluded setting; has some private cabins. **Cons:** no dogs allowed; 1½-mi walk from town; books up fast. ⊠ *569 Edgartown Rd., Box 1557* ☎ *508/693–3772* ⊕ *www.campmvfc.com* ⤶ *130 tent sites, 50 RV sites, 21 cabins* ⚘ *flush toilets, dump station, drinking water, showers, fire grates, grills, picnic tables, public telephone* ⊟ *D, MC, V* ⦿ *Closed mid-Oct.–mid-May.*

BIKING MARTHA'S VINEYARD

First the downside: you'll be sharing winding roads with wide trucks and tour buses cruising right by your elbow, inexperienced moped riders, and automobile drivers unfamiliar with the island roads, not to mention other cyclists of various levels of experience. In addition, most roads are bordered by sand—even those that aren't near the beach. The bottom line is this: pay attention at all times. And if ever there was a place to commit to wearing a helmet, this would be it.

That being said, the Vineyard is also a cyclist's paradise, and you don't have to be an experienced rider to enjoy the paths and roads here. The highest elevation is about 300 feet above sea level, and you'll find relatively easy uphill and downhill biking with well-paved bike paths both Down-Island and Up. There are a couple of fun roller-coaster-like dips on the state-forest bike path (watch out for the occasional in-line skater here). Quiet country roads wind up and down gentle hills covered by low-hanging trees that make you feel as though you're riding through a lush green tunnel. The views—across open fields to the Atlantic Ocean, alongside ponds with floating swans, or of sun-flecked meadows where handsome horses graze—will nearly knock you off your bike seat. There is another benefit: you'll be helping environmentalists who would rather see more nonpolluting bikes here than fossil fuel–guzzling vehicles.

Two of the quietest and most scenic roads without paths are North Road, from North Tisbury center all the way to Menemsha; and Middle Road, from its start at Music Street west to Beetlebung Corner, where South Road and Menemsha Cross Road intersect. This ride from Up-Island to the western tip of the island in Aquinnah is challenging—winding and sandy roads with a steep hill or two—but worth the rewards of spectacular views.

NIGHTLIFE AND THE ARTS

The **Vineyard Playhouse** (⊠ *24 Church St.* ☎ *508/696–6300* ⊕ *www. vineyardplayhouse.org*) has a year-round schedule of professional productions. From mid-June through early September, a troupe performs drama, classics, and comedies on the air-conditioned main stage. Summer Shakespeare and other productions take place at the natural amphitheater at Tashmoo Overlook on State Road in Vineyard Haven—bring insect repellent and a blanket or lawn chair. The theater is wheelchair-accessible and provides hearing devices.

BEACHES, SPORTS, AND THE OUTDOORS

Lake Tashmoo Town Beach (⊠ *End of Herring Creek Rd.*) provides swimmers with access to the warm, relatively shallow, brackish lake—or cooler, gentler Vineyard Sound.

Owen Park Beach (⊠ *Off Main St.*), a small, sandy harbor beach, is just steps away from the ferry terminal in Vineyard Haven, making it a great spot to catch some last rays before heading home.

Tisbury Town Beach (⊠ *End of Owen Little Way, off Main St.*) is a public beach next to the Vineyard Haven Yacht Club.

SHOPPING

Beadniks (⊠ *14 Church St.* ☎ *508/693–7650*) has a vast array of beads and supplies from around the world. Jewelry-making classes are popular.

Bramhall & Dunn (⊠ *23 Main St.* ☎ *508/693–6437*) carries crafts, linens, hand-knit sweaters, and fine antique country-pine furniture.

Bunch of Grapes Bookstore (⊠ *44 Main St.* ☎ *508/693–2291*) sells new books and sponsors book signings.

Midnight Farm (⊠ *18 Water-Cromwell La.* ☎ *508/693–1997*) stocks furniture, clothes, shoes, jewelry, linens, dinnerware, books, soaps, candles, garden supplies, snack foods, and, of course, co-owner Carly Simon's books and CDs.

Mix (⊠ *4 Union St.* ☎ *508/693–8240*) has a wonderfully colorful selection of new and vintage clothing, tablecloths, bedspreads, and bags. You'll also find lots of funky accessories.

Nochi (⊠ *29 Main St.* ☎ *508/693–9074* ⊕ *www.nochimv.com*) carries fragrant soaps, plush blankets and bedding, and comfy pajamas and robes.

Fodor's Choice ★ **Rainy Day** (⊠ *66 Main St.* ☎ *508/693–1830*), as the name suggests, carries gifts and amusements that are perfect for one of the island's gloomy rainy days, when you just need a warm, dry diversion. You'll find toys, crafts, cards, soaps, home accessories, gifts, and more.

★ Nationally renowned for their distinctive, hand-sculpted metal weather vanes, **Tuck and Holand** (⊠ *275 State Rd.* ☎ *508/693–3914 or 888/693–3914*) has a studio gallery a 10-minute walk from downtown. Here you can examine Anthony Holand and the late Travis Tuck's otherworldly creations, including copper Martha's Vineyard wall maps, school-of-bluefish chandeliers, and the signature custom weather vanes.

Wind's Up! (⊠ *199 Beach Rd.* ☎ *508/693–4340*) sells swimwear, windsurfing and sailing equipment, boogie boards, and other outdoor gear.

OAK BLUFFS

Circuit Avenue is the bustling center of the Oak Bluffs action, with most of the town's shops, bars, and restaurants. Colorful gingerbread-trimmed guesthouses and food and souvenir joints enliven Oak Bluffs Harbor, once the setting for several grand hotels (the 1879 Wesley Hotel on Lake Avenue is the last remaining one). This small town is more high spirited than haute, more fun than refined.

Oak Bluffs has a fascinating history. Purchased from the Wampanoags in the 1660s, the town was a farming community that did not come into its own until the 1830s, when Methodists began holding summer revivalist meetings in a stand of oaks known as Wesleyan Grove, named for Methodism's founder, John Wesley. As the camp meetings caught on, attendees built small cottages (today's colorful Oak Bluffs

Campground) in place of tents. Then the general population took notice and the area became a popular summer vacation spot. Hotels, a dance hall, a roller-skating rink, and other shops and amusements were built to accommodate summer visitors. Today the Tabernacle of the Martha's Vineyard Camp Meeting Association still holds religious services as well as hosting cultural events, and a small Cottage Museum recalls the community's history.

GETTING HERE AND AROUND
About 3½ mi east of Vineyard Haven, Oak Bluff is the terminal for season ferries. If you have a car, it's best to find a space and leave it while you walk, bike, or take the white buses operated by Martha's Vineyard Transit Authority.

■ TIP→ Look for the yellow tourist information booth at the bottom of Circuit Avenue. It's open from June through mid-October and is staffed with helpful folks from the area.

EXPLORING

East Chop Lighthouse. This lighthouse was built out of cast iron in 1876 to replace an 1828 tower (used as part of a semaphore system of visual signaling between the island and Boston) that burned down. The 40-foot structure stands high atop a 79-foot bluff with spectacular views of Nantucket Sound. ⊠ *E. Chop Dr.* ☎ *508/627–4441* 🖾 *$5* ⊙ *Mid-June–mid-Sept., Sun. 1½ hrs before sunset–½ hr after sunset.*

QUICK BITES

These aren't just any dogs, they're **Dinghy Dogs** (⊠ *Dockside Marketplace, Oak Bluffs Harbor* ☎ *508/693–6900*). The all-beef wieners at this tiny little waterfront stand are billed as "hot dogs for hot dog people." A quarter-pound big dog goes for $5, and it's a real bargain.

☉ **Flying Horses Carousel.** A National Historic Landmark, this is the nation's oldest continuously operating merry-go-round. Handcrafted in 1876 (the horses have real horsehair and glass eyes), the ride gives children a taste of entertainment from a TV-free era. ⊠ *Oak Bluffs Ave.* ☎ *508/693–9481* 🖾 *Rides $1.50* ⊙ *Late May–early Sept., daily 10–10; Easter–late May, weekends 10–5; early Sept.–mid-Oct., weekdays 11–4:30, weekends 10–5.*

Island Alpaca Company. This is a great place to learn about alpacas and the superior wool they produce. There's a self-guided tour ($5) with informative markers along the way that lead to a special viewing area in an exquisite 200-year-old barn. The shop sells yarn and products made from the resident herd, as well as knitting supplies. ⊠ *1 Head of the Pond Rd.* ☎ *508/693–5554* ⊕ *islandalpaca.com.* 🖾 *$5* ⊙ *Daily 11–5.*

★ **Oak Bluffs Campground.** This 34-acre warren of streets is tightly packed with more than 300 gaily painted Carpenter Gothic Victorian cottages with wedding-cake trim; these date mainly to the 1860s and 1870s, when visitors coming for Methodist revivalist services began to lease lots and built houses for summer use. As you wander through this fairy-tale setting, imagine it on a balmy summer evening, lighted by the warm glow of paper lanterns hung from every cottage porch. This describes the scene on Illumination Night at the end of the Camp Meeting season—which is attended these days by some fourth- and fifth-generation cottagers (and newcomers: some houses do change hands, and some are rented). Attendees mark the occasion as they have for more than a century, with lights, song, and open houses for families and friends. Ninety-minute tours of the area are conducted at 10 AM on Tuesday and Thursday in July and August. ✉ *Off Circuit Ave.* ☎ *508/693–0525* ⊕ *www.mvcma.org* 🖼 *Tour $10.*

WHERE TO EAT

$$ ✕ **Coop de Ville.** The waterfront place is tiny—just a few tables and some
SEAFOOD counter seating—but the amount of food that flies out of the kitchen is downright surprising. There are 11 flavors of chicken wings, and the chefs prepare 300 pounds a day at the height of the season. Big hits here include the raw bar and the reasonable seafood specials. Monday is lobster rolls and fries for $12, while Tuesday means steamed lobsters and corn for $15. Especially popular is the deep-fried lobster tail with fries—at $15, it sells out quickly. ✉ *Dockside Marketplace, Oak Bluffs Harbor* ☎ *508/693–3420* ⊕ *www.coopdevillemv.com* ⊟ *MC, V* ⊙ *Closed Nov.–Apr.*

$$$ ✕ **Jimmy Seas.** The irresistible fragrance of sautéed garlic wafting out
ITALIAN these doors beckons lovers of the "stinking rose." Most dishes come in the pan they're cooked in and are among the biggest portions you'll find on the island. Classic red-sauce Italian dishes include *vongole* (whole littleneck clams) marinara and linguine puttanesca. A brightly colored porch and painted ceilings add to the place's charm, although service can be a little uneven. ✉ *32 Kennebec Ave.* ☎ *508/696–8550* ⚑ *Reservations not accepted* ⊟ *MC, V.*

$ ✕ **Linda Jean's.** This is a classic local hangout, a diner that serves food
AMERICAN the way a diner should: with hearty helpings and inexpensive prices.
★ Want breakfast at 6 AM? No problem. Want breakfast at 11:30 AM? No problem. Tired of the gourmet world and want comfortable booths, friendly waitresses, and few frills? No problem. The only problem: you may have to wait—even at 6 AM. ✉ *34 Circuit Ave.* ☎ *508/693–4093* ⚑ *Reservations not accepted* ⊟ *AE, MC, V.*

$$ ✕ **Lookout Tavern.** There are two things about this easygoing Oak Bluffs
SEAFOOD seafood joint that make it stand out. First, its rustic dining room affords direct views of the sea and incoming ferryboats—it's truly the perfect "lookout" if you love watching boats ply the island's waters. Second, it serves usual seafood platters plus first-rate sushi, from the salmon and tuna rolls to more-unusual treats, like the Inkwell Roll, with barbecued eel, cucumber, avocado, crabmeat, and seaweed salad. Highlights from the traditional menu include the snow-crab dinner, fish-and-chips, or the fried scallop plate. ✉ *8 Seaview Ave. Ext.* ☎ *508/696–9844* ⊕ *www.lookouttavern.com* ⊟ *AE, D, DC, MC, V.*

$$$ ✕ **Offshore Ale Company.** The island's first and only microbrewery res-
AMERICAN taurant has become quite popular. There are private wooden booths, a
★ dartboard in the corner, and live music throughout the year (Wednesday-night Irish-music jams are a hoot). Take your own peanuts from a barrel by the door and drop the shells on the floor; then order from

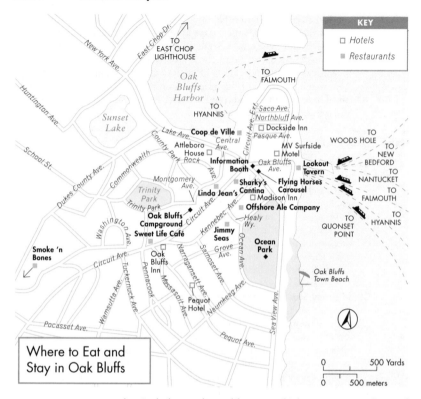

KEY

□ Hotels
■ Restaurants

Where to Eat and
Stay in Oak Bluffs

0   500 Yards

0   500 meters

a menu that includes steaks and burgers, chicken, pasta, gumbo, and fish. However, to truly appreciate the beer, try it with one of the wood-fired brick-oven pizzas. There's a great shaded patio for outdoor dining. ⊠ *30 Kennebec Ave.* ☎ *508/693–2626* ⊕ *www.offshoreale.com* ⌕ *Reservations not accepted* ═ *AE, MC, V* ☉ *No lunch Mon. and Tues. Oct.–May.*

$$ ✕ **Sharky's Cantina.** Sharky's serves tasty—somewhat creative—Mexican
MEXICAN   and Southwestern fare and great drinks, and you may wait awhile to get
★   a table. But once you're in, savor spicy tortilla soup, lobster quesadillas, chicken mole, and gaucho-style skirt steak. There's an extensive margarita list (they're strong here), and for dessert try apple-pie empanadas drizzled with caramel sauce. Limited items from the menu are served until around midnight during the summer season. They have a second location in Edgartown. ⊠ *31 Circuit Ave.* ☎ *508/693–7501* ⊕ *www. sharkyscantina.com* ⌕ *Reservations not accepted* ═ *AE, MC, V.*

$$ ✕ **Smoke 'n Bones.** This is the island's only rib joint, with its own smoker
SOUTHERN   out back and a cord of hickory, apple, oak, and mesquite wood stacked up around the lot. Treats from the smoker include Asian-style dry-rubbed ribs and North Carolina–style pulled pork. The homemade onion rings are addictive. The place has a cookie-cutter, prefab feeling, with all the appropriate touches—neon flames around the kitchen and marble bones for doorknobs. If you're a true rib aficionado, this may

not satisfy you, but on the Vineyard it's an offbeat treat. ⊠ *20 Oakland Ave.* ☎ *508/696–7427* ⊕ *www.smokenbonesmv.com* ⌲ *Reservations not accepted* ▤ *MC, V* ☉ *Closed Nov.–Mar.*

$$$$ ✗ **Sweet Life Café.** Housed in a charming Victorian house, this island

AMERICAN favorite's warm tones, low lighting, and handsome antique furniture

Fodor's Choice will make you feel like you've entered someone's home—but the cook-

★ ing is more sophisticated than home-style. Dishes on the menu are prepared in inventive ways (and change often with the seasons); sautéed halibut is served with sweet-pea risotto, pine nuts, and a marjoram beurre blanc, while the white gazpacho is filled with steamed clams, toasted almonds, sliced red grapes, and paprika oil. The desserts are superb; try the warm chocolate fondant with toasted-almond ice cream. There's outdoor dining by candlelight in a shrub-enclosed garden. ⊠ *63 Upper Circuit Ave., at far end of town* ☎ *508/696–0200* ⊕ *www.sweetlifemv.com* ⌲ *Reservations essential* ▤ *AE, D, MC, V* ☉ *Closed Jan.–Mar.*

WHERE TO STAY

$ ⌂ **Attleboro House.** This guesthouse, part of the Methodist Association Camp Grounds, is across the street from busy Oak Bluffs Harbor. The big 1874 gingerbread Victorian, an inn since its construction, has wraparound verandas on two floors and small, simple rooms with powder-blue walls, lacy white curtains, and a few antiques. Some rooms have sinks. Singles have three-quarter beds, and every room is provided with linen exchange (but no chambermaid service) during a stay. The shared baths are rustic and old but clean. **Pros:** super-affordable; steps from restaurants and shops. **Cons:** shared bathrooms; zero frills. ⊠ *42 Lake Ave., Box 1564* ☎ *508/693–4346* ⇋ *11 rooms with shared bath* ⌂ *In-room: no a/c, no phone, no TV* ▤ *AE, D, MC, V* ☉ *Closed Oct.–May* ⎮◎⎮ *CP.*

$$–$$$ ⌂ **Dockside Inn.** This gingerbread Victorian-style inn sits right by the

☼ dock, steps from the ferry landing and downtown shops, restaurants, and bars. Kids are welcome, and they'll have plenty to do in town and at nearby beaches. Some rooms open onto building-length balconies and have harbor views. **Pros:** close to everything; big porches. **Cons:** on busy street; lots of kids in summer. ⊠ *9 Circuit Ave.* ☎ *508/693–2966 or 800/245–5979* ⊕ *www.vineyardinns.com* ⇋ *17 rooms, 3 suites, 2 apartments* ⌂ *In-room: a/c, refrigerator, DVD (some), kitchen (some), Wi-Fi. In-hotel: Wi-Fi hotspot, some pets allowed (fee)* ▤ *AE, D, MC, V* ☉ *Closed late Oct.–mid-May* ⎮◎⎮ *CP.*

$$–$$$ ⌂ **Madison Inn.** While this stylish little inn doesn't have the high prices of nearby hotels, it does have all the amenities you need. The spacious rooms have high ceilings and are smartly outfitted with quilts and original artwork. Coffee and tea are available all day and night, and there's a complimentary snack basket in each room. There's a pretty brick courtyard for enjoying your morning coffee. Rates are extremely reasonable, and the location is right in town. If you don't mind sharing a bathroom, you can save even more money at the owner's other local lodging; the Nashua House Hotel. **Pros:** excellent rates; walk to everything, sophisticated lodging. **Cons:** no parking. ⊠ *18 Kennebec Ave.* ☎ *508/693–2760 or 800/564–2760* ⊕ *www.madisoninnmv.com*

6

🛏 *14 rooms* ♿ *In-room: a/c, no phone, Wi-Fi. In-hotel: no parking* 🖃 *AE, D, MC, V* ⊘ *Closed Nov.–mid-Apr.*

$$–$$$ 🏨 **Martha's Vineyard Surfside Motel.** These two buildings stand right in the thick of things, steps from restaurants and nightlife, so they tend to get noisy in summer. Rooms are spacious and bright (especially corner units), smartly decorated with carpets, stylish wallpaper, tile floors, and fairly standard but attractive chain-style furnishings that include a table and chairs. Deluxe rooms have water views. Four suites have whirlpool baths, and some are wheelchair-accessible. **Pros:** affordable rates; close to dining and shopping; helpful staff. **Cons:** busy location; lots of kids. 🖃 *70 Oak Bluffs Ave.* ☎ *508/693–2500 or 800/537–3007* ⊕ *www. mvsurfside.com* 🛏 *36 rooms, 5 suites* ♿ *In-room: a/c, refrigerator, Wi-Fi. In-hotel: restaurant, some pets allowed (fee)* 🖃 *AE, D, MC, V.*

$$$–$$$$ 🏨 **Oak Bluffs Inn.** A pink octagonal viewing tower dominates this rosy-hue Victorian B&B with a veranda on Oak Bluffs' main street, a short stroll from the beach. Victorian and country pieces fill the high-ceilinged rooms, all of which have private baths and gauzy white curtains; one has a four-poster bed. One very large room in the carriage house can accommodate two adults and two kids. On the third floor is a newer two-bedroom apartment with a private balcony. **Pros:** steps from shops and restaurants; well-chosen antiques. **Cons:** location can be a little noisy. 🖃 *64 Circuit Ave., at Pequot Ave.* ☎ *508/693–7171 or 800/955–6235* ⊕ *www.oakbluffsinn.com* 🛏 *10 rooms, 1 apartment* ♿ *In-room: a/c, no phone, no TV, Wi-Fi. In-hotel: Internet terminal* 🖃 *AE, MC, V* ⊘ *Closed mid-Nov.–mid– Apr.* ⊠ *CP.*

$$–$$$ 🏨 **Pequot Hotel.** The bustle of downtown Oak Bluffs is a pleasant five-minute walk past Carpenter Gothic houses from this casual cedar-shingle inn on a tree-lined street. The furniture is quirky but comfortable; the old wing has the most atmosphere. In the main section of the building, the first floor has a wide porch with rocking chairs—perfect for enjoying coffee or tea with the cookies that are set out in the afternoon—and a small breakfast room where you help yourself to bagels, muffins, and cereal in the morning. The hotel is one block from the beaches that line Oak Bluffs–Edgartown Road. **Pros:** steps from shops and dining; reasonable rates; charmingly offbeat. **Cons:** some rooms are small. 🖃 *19 Pequot Ave.* ☎ *508/693–5087 or 800/947–8704* ⊕ *www.pequothotel. com* 🛏 *31 rooms, 1 apartment* ♿ *In-room: a/c, no phone. In-hotel: Wi-Fi hotspot* 🖃 *AE, D, MC, V* ⊘ *Closed mid-Oct.–Apr.* ⊠ *CP.*

NIGHTLIFE AND THE ARTS

Dark and crowded, the **Island House** (🖃 *11 Circuit Ave.* ☎ *508/693–4516*) hosts a mixture of rock, blues, and reggae for younger crowds whose ears crave volume.

The **Lampost** (🖃 *6 Circuit Ave.* ☎ *508/696–9352*) is a good, old-fashioned neighborhood bar with a DJ and dancing. Weekly events include a Brazilian night, a Hawaiian night, and a swing night. The bar attracts a young crowd.

VINEYARD BEACH BASICS

The north shore of the island faces Vineyard Sound. The beaches on this side have more gentle waters, and they're also often slightly less chilly. On a clear day you can see across the sound to the chain of Elizabeth Islands, Cape Cod, and sometimes even all the way to New Bedford, Massachusetts.

On the Vineyard's south shore—Atlantic Ocean surf crashes in refreshingly chilly waves; it's a great place for bodysurfing. The more protected beaches on the Nantucket and Vineyard sounds tend to have slightly warmer and calmer waters, perfect for swimmers and for families. A few freshwater beaches at inland ponds provide a change of pace from the salty sea.

Note that public beaches are split between free beaches—such as the Joseph A. Sylvia State Beach, for which no parking fees are required—and several public beaches where parking fees are collected—such as Moshup Beach in Aquinnah. Private beaches are reserved for permanent and summer residents, who must obtain parking or resident stickers from the appropriate town hall.

Fairly new to the Oak Bluffs scene, the **Ocean Club** (⊠ *9 Oak Bluffs Ave.* ☎ *508/696–3000*) has after-dinner entertainment with live music most nights in summer.

The island's only family brewpub, **Offshore Ale** (⊠ *Kennebec Ave.* ☎ *508/693–2626*), hosts live Latin, folk, and blues year-round and serves its own beer and ales and a terrific pub menu. Cozy up to the fireplace with a pint on cool nights.

The **Ritz Café** (⊠ *4 Circuit Ave.* ☎ *508/693–9851*) is a popular year-round bar with a pool table that's removed in summer to make way for dancing. There's an eclectic mix of live performances, including rock, blues, and reggae, from Monday through Saturday in summer and on weekends in the off-season.

BEACHES, SPORTS, AND THE OUTDOORS

BEACH

Joseph A. Sylvia State Beach (⊠ *Between Oak Bluffs and Edgartown, off Beach Rd.*) is a 6-mi-long sandy beach with a view of Cape Cod across Nantucket Sound. Food vendors and calm, warm waters make this a popular spot for families.

FISHING

Dick's Bait & Tackle (⊠ *108 New York Ave.* ☎ *508/693–7669*) rents gear, sells accessories and bait, and keeps a current copy of the fishing regulations.

GOLF

Farm Neck Golf Club (⊠ *1 Farm Neck Way, off County Rd.* ☎ *508/693–3057* ⊕ *www.farmneck.net*), a semiprivate club on marsh-rimmed Sengekontacket Pond, has a driving range and 18 holes in a championship layout.

KAYAKING

Carolyn "Chick" Dowd runs great kayaking tours and offers expert instruction through her company **Island Spirit Sea-Kayak Adventures** (☎ 508/693–9727 ⊕ www.islandsspirit.com). Tours range from day trips around Cape Pogue to evening sunset and champagne trips and full-moon paddles.

SHOPPING

Book Den East (✉ 71 New York Ave. ☎ 508/693–3946) stocks 20,000 out-of-print, antiquarian, and paperback books.

B*tru (✉ 40 Circuit Ave. ☎ 508/693–5222) sells wonderfully stylish, offbeat, funky clothing and accessories.

If you're looking for out-of-the-ordinary, **Craftworks** (✉ 42 Circuit Ave. ☎ 508/693–7463) carries outrageous painted furniture, ceramic figures, stained glass, folk art, and home accessories—all handmade by American artists.

Laughing Bear (✉ 33 Circuit Ave. ☎ 508/693–9342) carries women's clothing made of Balinese or Indian batiks plus jewelry and accessories from around the world.

The **Secret Garden** (✉ 41 Circuit Ave. ☎ 508/693–4759), set in a yellow gingerbread cottage, has a complete line of Shelia collectibles— miniature wooden versions of Camp Ground houses and other island landmarks.

ART GALLERIES

Cousen Rose Gallery (✉ 71 Circuit Ave. ☎ 508/693–6656) displays works by many island artists, including Myrna Morris, John Breckenridge, Marietta Cleasby, Deborah Colter, Lynn Hoefs, Ray Prosser, and Renee Balter. During the summer months, be sure to inquire about children's art classes.

Dragonfly Gallery (✉ Dukes County and Vineyard Aves. ☎ 508/693– 8877) changes shows weekly and holds artist receptions—featuring jazz pianist John Alaimo—every other Saturday in summer from 4 to 7 PM. Check the local papers for a schedule of artists.

EDGARTOWN

Once a well-to-do whaling center, Edgartown remains the Vineyard's toniest town and has preserved great parts of its elegant past. Sea captains' houses from the 18th and 19th centuries, ensconced in well-manicured gardens and lawns, line the streets. You could wander for hours studying the architecture and marveling at the meticulously restored structures. Plenty of shops as well as sights and other activities occupy the crowds who walk the streets in summer. There's a healthy balance of sophistication and small-town local flavor here.

Ever since Thomas Mayhew, Jr., landed here in 1642 as the Vineyard's first governor, the town has served as the county seat. Plenty of settlers inhabited the area, making it the island's first colonial settlement, but the town was not officially named until 1652. First called Great

Harbour, it was renamed for political reasons some 30 years later, after the three-year-old son of the Duke of York.

GETTING HERE AND AROUND

Once you've reached Edgartown, about 5 mi southeast of Oak Bluffs, a car isn't necessary. It's actually a hindrance, as parking can be very tight in summer. The Martha's Vineyard Transit Authority operates a fleet of buses that can get you almost anywhere you want to go. The town runs a well-stocked visitor center on Church Street.

EXPLORING

★ **Martha's Vineyard Historical Society.** To orient yourself before making your way around town, stop by this collection of historic buildings, including the Thomas Cooke House, the Francis Foster Museum, the Captain Francis Pease House, and the Carriage Shed. The museum sells an excellent Edgartown walking-tour booklet full of anecdotes and the history of the people who have lived in the town's houses over the past three centuries; you can purchase the booklet at the entrance gatehouse in summer or at the library in winter. ⊠ *Cooke and School Sts.* ☎ *508/627–4441* ⊕ *www.marthasvineyardhistory.org* ⊠ *$7* ⊘ *Mid-Oct.–mid-June, Mon.–Sat. 10–4; mid-June–mid-Oct., Mon.–Sat. 10–5.*

Edgartown Lighthouse. Surrounded by a public beach, this cast-iron tower was floated by barge from Ipswich, Massachusetts, in 1938. It is still an active navigational aid. Sunset tours are given on Thursday evenings in summer. ⊠ *Off N. Water St.* ☎ *No phone* ⊠ *$5* ⊘ *June–early Sept., 11–6.*

QUICK BITES

If you need a pick-me-up, pop into **Espresso Love** (⊠ *3 S. Water St.* ☎ *508/627–9211*) for a cappuccino and a homemade raspberry scone or blueberry muffin. If you prefer something cold, the staff also makes fruit smoothies. Light lunch fare is served: bagel sandwiches, soups, and delicious pastries and cookies—all homemade, of course.

☾ ★ **Felix Neck Wildlife Sanctuary.** The 350-acre Massachusetts Audubon Society preserve, 3 mi outside Edgartown toward Oak Bluffs and Vineyard Haven, has 4 mi of hiking trails traversing marshland, fields, woods, seashore, and waterfowl and reptile ponds. Naturalist-led events include sunset hikes, stargazing, snake or bird walks, and canoeing. ⊠ *Off Edgartown–Vineyard Haven Rd.* ☎ *508/627–4850* ⊠ *$4* ⊘ *June–Aug., weekdays 8:30–4:30, Sat. 9:30–4:30, Sun. 10–3; Sept.–May, weekdays 9–4, Sat. 10–3, Sun. noon–3. Trails daily sunrise–dusk.*

☾ ★ **Farm Institute.** A beautiful expanse of open fields and working barns, the Farm Institute is a teaching farm with a mission to educate adults and

6

children about sustainable agriculture. There's plenty of produce and livestock to see while taking part in any of the numerous programs offered from early June through October. From June through September, stock up on the farm's bounty of produce, eggs, and meat (when available)—chances are, kids attending the summer program will be staffing the farm stand. ⊠ *14 Aero Ave.* ☎ *508/627–7007* ⊕ *www.farminstitute.org.*

Vincent House Museum. The island's oldest dwelling is this 1672 home. A tour of this weathered-shingle farmhouse takes you along a time line that starts with the sparse furnishings of the 1600s and ends in a Federal-style parlor of the 1800s. ⊠ *Main St.* ☎ *508/627–4440* ⊕ *www. mvpreservation.org/tours.html* ⊡ *$7* ⊙ *May–mid-Oct., Mon.–Sat. 10:30–3.*

WHERE TO EAT

$$$$
FRENCH

✕ **Alchemy Bistro and Bar.** According to the menu, the dictionary meaning of *alchemy* is "a magic power having as its asserted aim the discovery of a panacea and the preparation of the elixir of longevity"—lofty goals for a French-style bistro. This high-class version has elegant gray wainscoting, classic paper-covered white tablecloths, old wooden floors, and an opening cut into the ceiling to reveal the second-floor tables. The only things missing are the patina of age, experience, cigarette smoke—and French working folks' prices—but you can expect quality and imagination. One example is the skillet-roasted pork tenderloin with crispy shallots. The alcohol list, long and complete, includes cognacs, grappas, and beers. On balmy evenings, the half dozen outdoor tables on the candlelit brick patio are highly coveted. ⊠ *71 Main St.* ☎ *508/627–9999* ⊟ *AE, MC, V.*

$$$$
AMERICAN
★

✕ **Atria.** One of the island's more urbane venues, Atria feels like a big-city bistro and cocktail lounge, with a swank dining room, glam crowd, and artful food presentations. Chef Christian Thornton uses eclectic, globally influenced ingredients to come up with such entrées as cracklin' pork shank with collard greens and sour cream–mustard sauce; and grilled lamb T-bones with Tuscan-style white beans, roasted tomatoes, grilled artichokes, and a red-wine reduction. Top starters include steak tartare with crisp shallots, capers, truffle oil, and aged balsamic vinegar; and braised-veal-cheek ravioli with stuffed squash blossoms, shaved Parmesan, and truffle oil. The chocolate-molten cake with cappuccino ice cream is a great finish. ⊠ *137 Main St.* ☎ *508/627–5850* ⊕ *www. atriamv.com* ⊟ *AE, MC, V.*

$$$$
AMERICAN
Fodor'sChoice
★

✕ **Detente.** A dark, intimate wine bar and restaurant with hardwood floors and rich banquette seating, Detente serves more than a dozen wines by the glass as well as numerous half bottles. Even if you're not much of an oenophile, it's worth a trip just for the innovative food, much of it from local farms and seafood purveyors. Try the complex starter of ahi-tuna tartare with toasted pine nuts, vanilla-pear puree, and arugula salad, followed by such choice entrées as roasted venison loin with thyme spaetzle, sautéed Swiss chard, blue cheese, and roasted figs; or lemon-honey–basted halibut with potato au gratin, truffled leek puree, roasted artichokes, and oven-dried tomatoes. ⊠ *Nevin Sq. off*

Water St. ☏ *508/627–8810* ⊕ *www.detentewinebar.com* ▭ *AE, MC, V* ⊘ *Closed Tues. No lunch.*

¢ ✕ **Edgartown Deli.** A no-frills place with a down-home, happy feeling,
AMERICAN this deli has walls and a glass counter plastered with specials written on multicolor paper. Brightly lighted booths fill one side of the room, and customers line up at the counter for orders to go. Breakfast specials, served from 8 until 10:45, include egg, cheese, and linguica (garlicky Portuguese sausage) on a roll. Lunch sandwiches include corned beef and Swiss, roast beef, turkey, pastrami, or steak and cheese. ⊠ *52 Main St.* ☏ *508/627–4789* ⌲ *Reservations not accepted* ▭ *No credit cards* ⊘ *Closed mid-Oct.–Apr. No dinner.*

$$$$ ✕ **l'étoile.** Michael Brisson has been at the helm of this creative French
FRENCH kitchen for about a quarter of a century, yet his dedication to fresh,
★ exquisitely prepared local food remains as fervent as ever. Changing with what's seasonally available, his menu many include sautéed Menemsha fluke served on a saffron risotto cake, or perhaps roasted Long Island duck breast and thigh with a toasted maple-cognac sauce. For lighter fare or an indulgence of fancy martinis, head to the bar with its sleek leather-backed chairs. The restaurant's location, in a former sea captain's home, adds warmth and intimacy to the dining rooms. There's also a terrace for alfresco dining. ⊠ *22 N. Water St.* ☏ *508/627–5187* ⊕ *www.letoile.net* ▭ *MC, V* ⊘ *Closed Tues.–Thurs. mid-Oct.–Apr.*

$$$ ✕ **Lure.** The airy restaurant at Winnetu Oceanside Resort draws plenty
SEAFOOD of discerning diners to sample some of the island's most exquisite and
Fodor's Choice creatively prepared seafood. It's the only dining room with a south-
★ facing water view, and it's a stunning one at that. You won't find a better lobster dish on the island than Lure's tender butter-poached version topped with roasted corn and fava beans and served alongside buttery corn bread. Locally caught fluke with littleneck clams, leeks, smoked bacon, and a rich chowder broth is another star. Finish off with the molten Valhrona chocolate cake with vanilla ice cream and raspberry coulis. If you've got children in tow, you'll appreciate the back dining area, complete with separate play area (you can actually have dinner with the little ones along—without the angry glares from your neighbors). ⊠ *Katama Rd.* ☏ *508/627–3663* ▭ *AE, D, MC, V* ⊘ *No lunch.*

¢ ✕ **Morning Glory Farm.** This farm store is full of incredible goodies, most
AMERICAN made or grown on the premises. Fresh farm greens in the salads and
★ vegetables in the soups; homemade pies, breads, quiches, cookies, and cakes; and a picnic table and grass to enjoy them on make this an ideal place for a simple country lunch. ⊠ *W. Tisbury Rd.* ☏ *508/627–9003* ▭ *MC, V* ⊘ *Closed late Dec.–late May.*

$$$ ✕ **Wharf Pub.** The name may sound generic, and the menu tends toward
AMERICAN the predictable—shrimp scampi, prime rib, burgers, and steaks—but this lively bar and grill earns kudos for its well-prepared food, inviting dining room and pair of bars, and easygoing vibe. Standouts include the grilled flank steak with fries and a horseradish cream sauce, and the Cobb salad with ham and chicken. You can tune in to a game on the TV or mingle with locals. ⊠ *Lower Main St.* ☏ *508/627–9966* ▭ *AE, D, MC, V.*

6

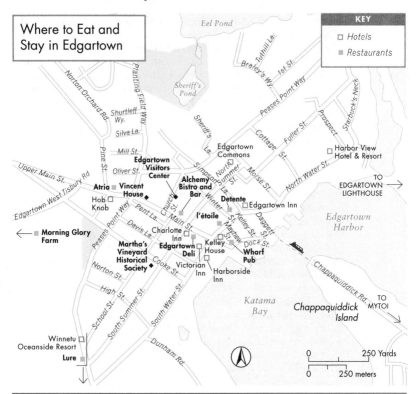

Where to Eat and Stay in Edgartown

WHERE TO STAY

$$$$ 🏨 **Charlotte Inn.** From the moment you walk up to the dark-wood Scot-
★ tish barrister's check-in desk at this regal 1864 inn, you'll be surrounded
by the trappings and customs of a bygone era. Beautiful antique furnishings, objets d'art, and paintings fill the property—the book you pick up
in your room might be an 18th-century edition of Voltaire, and your
bed could be a hand-carved four-poster. All rooms have hair dryers and
robes; rooms in the carriage house have fireplaces and French doors
that open into the brick courtyard as well as private patios. The elegant atmosphere that pervades the property extends to the inn's swank
restaurant, Il Tesoro. **Pros:** over-the-top lavish; quiet yet convenient
location; beautifully landscaped. **Cons:** can feel overly formal; intimi-
dating if you don't adore museum-quality antiques. ⊠ *27 S. Summer
St.* ☎ *508/627–4751 or 800/735–2478* ⊕ *www.charlotteinn.net* ⇆ *23
rooms, 2 suites* ⌂ *In-room: a/c, Wi-Fi. In-hotel: restaurant, no kids
under 14* ⊟ *AE, MC, V.*

$$$–$$$$ 🏨 **Edgartown Commons.** This condominium complex of seven buildings,
which includes an old house and rooms set around a busy pool, is just
a couple of blocks from town. Studios and one- or two-bedroom con-
dos all have full kitchens, and some are very spacious. Each has been
decorated by its individual owner, so the decor varies a bit, though most

all have been recently updated. Definitely family-oriented, the place is abuzz with kids at the pool, playground, and picnic area. **Pros:** sparkling pool; full kitchens; great for families. **Cons:** lacks historical character; lots of kids. ⊠ *20 Pease's Point Way* ☎ *508/627–4671 or 800/439–4671* ⊕ *www.edgartowncommons.com* ⇗ *35 units* ⚭ *In-room: a/c (some), no phone, kitchen, Wi-Fi. In-hotel: pool, laundry facilities, Wi-Fi hotspot* ⊟ *AE, MC, V* ⊗ *Closed mid-Oct.–Apr.*

$$–$$$ 🏨 **Edgartown Inn.** The inside of the former home of whaling captain Thomas Worth still evokes its late-18th-century origins. In fact, its cozy parlor and antique-filled rooms look as if the captain still lives here. The inn was also the spot where Nathaniel Hawthorne wrote much of his *Twice-Told Tales* during a stay. Many an Edgartonian joins inn guests in the paneled dining room or back garden for breakfast in summertime. Some rooms have harbor views. Rooms with shared baths are the best bargain. **Pros:** great value; rich in history; close to shopping and dining. **Cons:** no Internet access. ⊠ *56 N. Water St.* ☎ *508/627–4794* ⊕ *www. edgartowninn.com* ⇗ *17 rooms, 15 with bath* ⚭ *In-room: a/c, no phone. In-hotel: no kids under 8* ⊟ *No credit cards* ⊗ *Closed Nov.–early Apr.*

$$$$
🌀
★ 🏨 **Harbor View Hotel & Resort.** The centerpiece of this historic hotel— looking great after a $80 million overhaul—is a gray-shingle, 1891 Victorian building with wraparound veranda and a gazebo. Accommodations are also in a complex of nearby buildings in a residential neighborhood. The contemporary town houses have cathedral ceilings, decks, kitchens, and large living areas with sofa beds. Rooms in other buildings are laid out like upscale motor-lodge units but have the same fine decor and plush in-room amenities. A beach, good for walking, stretches ¾ mi from the hotel's dock. The extensive children's summer program has a full roster of activities for kids. The hotel is also home to the Water Street restaurant, a worthy spot for a full meal. **Pros:** great harbor views; not far from restaurants. **Cons:** a few blocks from commercial district; steep rates. ⊠ *131 N. Water St.* ☎ *508/627–7000 or 800/225–6005* ⊕ *www.harbor-view.com* ⇗ *88 rooms, 26 suites* ⚭ *In-room: a/c, kitchen (some), refrigerator, Wi-Fi. In-hotel: 2 restaurants, room service, pool, water sports, laundry service, Internet terminal* ⊟ *AE, MC, V.*

$$$–$$$$ 🏨 **Harborside Inn.** Edgartown's only true waterfront accommodation, with boat docks at the end of its nicely landscaped lawn, this large inn provides a central town location, harbor-view decks, and plenty of amenities. Seven two- and three-story buildings sprawl around formal rose beds, brick walkways, a brick patio, and a heated pool. Rooms have colonial-style furnishings, brass beds and lamps, and textured wallpapers. Some units have terraces facing Edgartown Harbor. **Pros:** steps from restaurants and shops; immaculate rooms; lovely gardens. **Cons:** some rooms are quite small; lots of kids in summer. ⊠ *3 S. Water St.* ☎ *508/627–4321* ⊕ *www.theharborsideinn.com* ⇗ *85 rooms, 4 suites* ⚭ *In-room: a/c, refrigerator, Wi-Fi. In-hotel: pool* ⊟ *AE, D, MC, V* ⊗ *Closed mid-Nov.–mid-Apr.*

$$$$
Fodor's Choice
★ 🏨 **Hob Knob.** This 19th-century Gothic Revival boutique hotel blends the amenities and service of a luxury property with the ambience and charm of a small B&B. A short walk from the harbor, it's on the main road into

6

town—but far enough out to avoid crowds. Rooms are gracious and quite large by island standards; the upper floors have dormer windows. Art and antiques help capture the island's rural, seaside charm, and many rooms overlook the spectacular gardens. Fishing trips and charters are available aboard the owner's 27-foot Boston Whaler. Full breakfast—organic and locally gathered—and lavish afternoon tea are included. The front porch, filled with flowers and rocking chairs, is a perfect spot for reading or relaxing. **Pros:** spacious rooms; afternoon tea; removed from crowds. **Cons:** steep rates; not overlooking harbor. ⊠ *128 Main St.* ☎ *508/627–9510 or 800/696–2723* ⊕ *www.hobknob. com* ⊅ *16 rooms, 1 suite* ⚅ *In-room: a/c, refrigerator, DVD, Wi-Fi. In-hotel: gym, spa, bicycles, no kids under 7* ⊟ *AE, MC, V* ⦿| *BP.*

> ## PAGODA TREE
>
> Extending ever up and outward over South Water Street is Edgartown's cherished pagoda tree. Brought home from China in a small flowerpot, this tree was planted by sea captain Thomas Milton in 1837. Believed to be the oldest one of its kind on the continent, the tree towers over the captain's home, braced with cables, its massive limbs reaching out in all directions.

$$$–$$$$ 🖭 **Kelley House.** In the center of town, this sister property of the Harbor View combines services and amenities with a country-inn feel. The 1742 white clapboard main house and the adjacent Garden House are surrounded by pink roses. Large suites in the Chappaquiddick House and the two spacious town houses in the Wheel House have porches (most with harbor views) and living rooms. The Newes from America, a dark and cozy spot with original hand-hewn timbers and ballast-brick walls, serves typical pub victuals and microbrewed beers on tap. **Pros:** lots of historic charm; pretty gardens; some harbor views. **Cons:** on street with lots of pedestrian traffic; pricey rates. ⊠ *23 Kelley St.* ☎ *508/627–7900 or 800/225–6005* ⊕ *www.kelley-house.com* ⊅ *43 rooms, 11 suites* ⚅ *In-room: a/c, kitchen (some), refrigerator, Wi-Fi. In-hotel: restaurant, bar, pool, laundry service* ⊟ *AE, MC, V.*

$$$–$$$$
★ 🖭 **Victorian Inn.** White with the classic black shutters of the town's historic homes and fronted by ornate columns, this appropriately named inn sits a block from the downtown harbor; it was built as the home of 19th-century whaling captain Lafayette Rowley. Today the inn's three floors are done in dark woods and bold floral wallpapers, with rugs over wood floors. Several rooms hold handmade reproduction four-poster beds. A full breakfast, served in season in the brick-patio garden, includes creative muffins and breads. **Pros:** staff is top-notch; close to restaurants. **Cons:** not geared toward families; some very steep stairs. ⊠ *24 S. Water St.* ☎ *508/627–4784* ⊕ *www.thevic.com* ⊅ *14 rooms* ⚅ *In-room: a/c, no phone, no TV, Wi-Fi. In-hotel: some pets allowed (fee), no kids under 8* ⊟ *MC, V* ⊗ *Closed Nov.–Mar.* ⦿| *BP*

$$$$
Fodor'sChoice
★ 🖭 **Winnetu Oceanside Resort.** A departure from most properties on the island, the contemporary Winnetu—styled after the grand multistory resorts of the Gilded Age—has successfully struck a fine balance in that it both encourages families and provides a contemporary seaside-resort experience for couples. This property has units that can sleep

up to 11 guests. All have kitchens and decks or patios with views. Room decor is stylish and modern but casual enough so that kids feel right at home. In addition to lodging in the main inn, there are 65 three- to five-bedroom homes available for rent by the week; it's a great option for large families, and all resort amenities are shared. The resort arranges bicycling and kayaking trips, lighthouse tours, boat excursions to Nantucket Island, and other island activities. A full slate of excellent children's programs is offered late June through early September. **Pros:** outstanding staff; tons of activities; fantastic restaurant. **Cons:** pricey; not an in-town location; lots of kids in summer. ✉ *31 Dunes Rd.* ☎ *866/335–1133 or 508/310–1733* ⊕ *www.winnetu.com* ✈ *52 suites, 65 homes* ♿ *In-room: a/c, kitchen, DVD, Wi-Fi (some). In-hotel: 2 restaurants, room service, tennis courts, pools, gym, spa, children's programs (ages 3–12), laundry facilities, Wi-Fi hotspot* ☰ *MC, V* ⊗ *Closed late Oct.–mid-Apr.*

NIGHTLIFE AND THE ARTS

Atria's **Brick Cellar Bar** (✉ *137 Main St.* ☎ *508/627–5850*) is just out of the central part of town, but that doesn't mean it's empty. It's a bit like a swanky country club den, with leather chairs, a massive brass bar, an extensive Scotch collection, and a working fireplace. Enjoy one of the clever drinks, including the Aunt Katherine Manhattan (Maker's Mark and sweet vermouth, served neat). There's often live music in summer.

Nectar's MV (✉ *Martha's Vineyard Airport, Edgartown–W. Tisbury Rd.* ☎ *508/693–1137* ⊕ *www.nectarsmv.com*) is a great place to listen to live music. If you're hungry, there are some excellent flat-bread pizzas.

The Wharf (✉ *Lower Main St.* ☎ *508/627–9966*) is a great spot for tasty food and a terrific place for cocktails, people-watching, and listening to live rock and pop music.

BEACHES, SPORTS, AND THE OUTDOORS

BEACHES

Bend-in-the-Road Beach (✉ *Beach Rd.*), the town's public beach, is backed by low, grassy dunes and wild roses.

Katama Beach (✉ *Katama Rd.*), also called South Beach, is a 3-mi-long Atlantic beach. There are lifeguards here in season.

Little Beach (✉ *End of Fuller St.*) is a lesser-known beach that looks like a crooked pinkie pointing into Eel Pond; it's a great place for bird-watching (be careful of the fenced-off piping plover breeding grounds in the dunes).

FISHING

Coop's Bait and Tackle (✉ *147 W. Tisbury Rd.* ☎ *508/627–3909*) sells accessories and bait, rents fishing gear, and books fishing charters from a roster of nearly two dozen outfits in the area. Choose from trips in search of bass, blues, and specialty offshore shark and tuna ventures.

SHOPPING ON MARTHA'S VINEYARD

Martha's Vineyard is a shopper's paradise, with unique shops lining picturesque streets and nary a chain store in sight (strict zoning laws make this possible). The three main towns have the largest concentrations of shops: in Vineyard Haven, most of the stores line Main Street; Edgartown's stores are clustered together within a few blocks of the dock, on Main, Summer, and Water streets; and casual clothing and gift shops crowd along Circuit Avenue in Oak Bluffs. At the Aquinnah Cliffs, touristy Native American crafts and souvenirs abound during the season, and cottage industries and the odd shop or gallery appear off the main roads in many locations.

A different, more modest shopping experience unfolds at the West Tisbury Farmers' Market, the largest farmers' market in Massachusetts.

Elsewhere, some of the antiques stores hidden along back roads brim with the interesting and the unusual.

A specialty of the island is wampum—beads made from black, white, or purple shells and fashioned into jewelry sold at the cliffs and elsewhere. Antique and new scrimshaw jewelry, and jewelry incorporating Vineyard and island-specific designs such as lighthouses or bunches of grapes, are also popular. Many island shops carry the ultraexpensive Nantucket lightship baskets, tightly woven creations of wood and rattan that were originally made by sailors but are now valued collectibles made by artisans. A good number of Vineyard shops close for winter, though quite a few in Vineyard Haven and some stores in other locations remain open—call ahead before making a special trip.

SURFING

The Boneyard (⊠ *250 Upper Main St.* ☎ *508/627–7907* ⊕ *www. theboneyardsurfshop.com*) rents surfboards, paddleboards, body boards, and wet suits.

SHOPPING

Claudia (⊠ *51 Main St.* ☎ *508/627–8306*) brings you back to another era with its clever windows, antique display cases, and fabulous French fragrances. You'll find designer, vintage-looking, and fine gold and silver jewelry in a variety of price ranges.

David Le Breton, the owner of **Edgartown Books** (⊠ *44 Main St.* ☎ *508/627–8463*), is a true bibliophile. He carries a large selection of current and island-related titles and will be happy to make a summer reading recommendation.

The **Edgartown Scrimshaw Gallery** (⊠ *43 Main St.* ☎ *508/627–9439*) showcases a large collection of scrimshaw, including some antique pieces.

The **Old Sculpin Gallery** (⊠ *58 Dock St.* ☎ *508/627–4881*) is the Martha's Vineyard Art Association's headquarters. Exhibits of the works of local juried artists change weekly; Sunday evenings are host to opening receptions beginning at 6 PM.

Portobello Road (⊠ *8 Dock St.* ☎ *508/627–4276*) stocks all sorts of unusual items, from vintage prints to reproduction wood signs. It's fun exploring this lofty, barnlike space.

CHAPPAQUIDDICK ISLAND

A sparsely populated area with many nature preserves, Chappaquiddick Island makes for a pleasant day trip or bike ride on a sunny day. It was once connected to Martha's Vineyard by a long sand spit that begins in South Beach in Katama, but then severe storms broke through in 2007. It's a spectacular 2¾-mi walk, or you can take the ferry ($12 round-trip for car and driver and $4 for each additional passenger), which departs about every five minutes from 6:45 AM to midnight daily, June to mid-October, and less frequently from 7 AM to 11:15 PM mid-October to May.

GETTING HERE AND AROUND

The best way to get around Chappaquiddick Island is by bike; bring one over on the ferry and ride the few miles to Cape Pogue Wildlife Refuge. Sign up for a tour with the Trustees of Reservations for an in-depth look at the island's wonders.

ESSENTIALS

Contacts **Trustees of Reservations** (☎ *508/627–3599* ⊕ *www.thetrustees.org*).

EXPLORING

Cape Poge Wildlife Refuge. A conglomeration of habitats where you can swim, walk, fish, or just sit and enjoy the surroundings, the Cape Poge Wildlife Refuge, on the easternmost shore of Chappaquiddick Island, is more than 6 square mi of wilderness. Its dunes, woods, cedar thickets, moors, salt marshes, ponds, tidal flats, and barrier beach serve as an important migration stopover and nesting area for numerous sea- and shorebirds. The **Trustees of Reservations** leads some great tours of the refuge, including canoe and kayak trips, lighthouse, fishing, and natural-history tours. The best way to get to the refuge is as part of a naturalist-led jeep drive. ⊠ *East end of Dike Rd.* ☎ *508/627–3599* ⊕ *www.thetrustees.org.*

Fodor'sChoice **Mytoi.** The Trustees of Reservations' 14-acre preserve is a serene, beau-
★ tifully tended, Japanese-inspired garden with a creek-fed pool spanned by a bridge and rimmed with Japanese maples, azaleas, bamboo, and irises. A boardwalk runs through part of the grounds, where you're apt to see box turtles and hear the sounds of songbirds. There are few more-enchanting spots on the island. Restrooms are available. ⊠ *Dike Rd.2 mi from intersection with Chappaquiddick Rd.* ☎ *508/627–7689* 💷 *Free* ☉ *Daily sunrise–sunset.*

Three Ponds Preserve. The Land Bank's 226-acre Three Ponds Preserve is a popular, scenic picnicking spot. Mown grasses surround a serpentine pond with an island in its center and a woodland backdrop behind—a truly lovely setting. Across the road are fields, woods, and another

pond. It's also a popular spot for
dog walkers. ⊠ *Off Chappaquiddick Rd..*

★ **Wasque Reservation.** The 200-acre
Wasque Reservation (pronounced
wayce-kwee) is mostly a vast
beach. Closing off the south end
of Katama Bay, this is where Chappaquiddick used to connect to the
mainland. You can fish, sunbathe,
take the trail by Swan Pond, walk
to the island's southeasternmost tip

at Wasque Point, or dip into the surf—use caution, as the currents are
strong. Wasque Beach is accessed by a flat boardwalk with benches overlooking the west end of Swan Pond. It's a pretty walk skirting the pond,
with ocean views on one side and poles for osprey nests on the other.
Atop a bluff is a pine-shaded picnic grove with a spectacular, practically
180-degree panorama. ⊠ *At east end of Wasque Rd.* ☎ *508/627–7260*
🚗 *Car and driver $12 round-trip, plus $4 per adult; bike and rider $6*
⊙ *Property 24 hrs. Gatehouse late May–mid-Oct., daily 9–5.*

BEACHES, SPORTS, AND THE OUTDOORS

East Beach, one of the area's best beaches, is accessible by car from Dike
Road. There is a $3 fee to enter the beach.

Wasque Beach, at the Wasque Reservation, is an uncrowded ½-mi sandy
beach with a parking lot and restrooms. The surf and currents are
sometimes strong.

WEST TISBURY

West Tisbury retains its rural appeal and maintains its agricultural
tradition at several active horse and produce farms. The town center
looks very much like a small New England village, complete with a
white-steeple church. Roads out here are lined with open fields, woods,
and incredibly beautiful pastureland surrounded by stone walls. This is
where the true agricultural heart of the island lies, and many an event
takes place at the majestic old Grange Hall.

GETTING HERE AND AROUND
The Martha's Vineyard Transit Authority buses makes stops at West
Tisbury, 8 mi west of Edgartown and 6½ mi south of Vineyard Haven.

EXPLORING

★ **Grange Hall.** Fully restored to its original 1859 simple splendor, this
grand post-and-beam beauty has long been the heart and soul of West
Tisbury. A Martha's Vineyard Preservation Trust Property, it's a popular place for weddings and other events. The lively and bountiful West
Tisbury Farmers' Market is held here on Saturday from mid-June to
mid-October, as well as Wednesday from late June to early September.

The Vineyard Artisans hold summer festivals at the hall on Sunday from mid-June to early October, and on Thursday from July to late August. On Friday from mid-June to August, the Grange Hall is host to a large antiques fair. ✉ *State Rd.* ☎ *508/627–4440* ⊕ *www.mvpreservation.org.*

QUICK BITES

Step back in time with a visit to Alley's General Store (✉ 299 State Rd. ☎ 508/693–0088), a local landmark since 1858. Alley's sells a truly general variety of goods: everything from hammers to housewares and dill pickles to sweet muffins as well as great things you find only in a country store. There's even a post office inside.

Long Point. This 632-acre Trustees of Reservations preserve is bounded on the east by freshwater Homer's Pond, on the west by saltwater Tisbury Great Pond, and on the south by fantastic, mile-long South Beach on the Atlantic Ocean. Long Cove Pond, a sandy freshwater swimming pond, is an ideal spot for bird-watchers. ✉ *Mid-June–mid-Sept., turn left onto unmarked Waldron's Bottom Rd., just west of airport on Edgartown–W. Tisbury Rd.; mid-Sept.–mid-June, take Deep Bottom Rd., 1 mi west of airport* ☎ *508/693–7392* ⊕ *www.thetrustees.org* 🎫 *Mid-June–mid-Sept., $10 per vehicle plus $3 per adult; free rest of yr* ⊙ *Daily 9–6.*

★ **Manuel F. Correllus State Forest.** This a 5,100-acre pine and scrub-oak forest is crisscrossed with hiking trails and circled by a rough bike trail. You'll also find a 2-mi nature trail, a 2-mi par fitness course, and horse trails. The West Tisbury side of the state forest joins with an equally large Edgartown parcel to virtually surround the airport. ✉ *Barnes Rd.* ☎ *508/693–2540* ⊕ *www.mass.gov/dcr* 🎫 *Free* ⊙ *Daily sunrise–sunset.*

★ **Polly Hill Arboretum.** The late horticulturist and part-time Vineyard resident Polly Hill tended some 2,000 species of plants and developed nearly 100 species herself on her old sheep farm in West Tisbury. On-site are azaleas, tree peonies, dogwoods, hollies, lilacs, magnolias, and more. Hill raised them from seeds without the use of a greenhouse, and her patience is the inspiration of the arboretum. Run as a nonprofit center, the arboretum also runs guided tours, a lecture series, and a visitor center and gift shop. ✉ *809 State Rd.* ☎ *508/693–9426* ⊕ *www. pollyhillarboretum.org* 🎫 *$5* ⊙ *Grounds daily sunrise–sunset. Visitor center late May–mid-Oct., daily 9:30–4.*

Sepiessa Point Reservation. A paradise for bird-watchers, Sepiessa Point Reservation consists of 164 acres on splendid Tisbury Great Pond, with expansive pond and ocean views, walking trails around coves and saltwater marshes, bird-watching, horse trails, swimming, and a boat launch. ✉ *New La., which becomes Tiah's Cove Rd.* ☎ *508/627–7141* 🎫 *Free* ⊙ *Daily sunrise–sunset.*

WHERE TO EAT AND STAY

$$$$

AMERICAN

★

✕ **State Road Restaurant.** High ceilings, exposed beams, and a beautiful stone fireplace make for a warm and light-filled meal. There's nothing plain about the breakfasts—try the bacon-cheddar jalapeño grits, served with wilted spinach, roasted shallots, and eggs the way you like them. For lunch try the wood-grilled rainbow trout with local baby greens; as with most of the dishes here, it takes advantage of local and organic products. At night, under the glow of candlelight, order the wood-grilled lamb tenderloin served with roasted tomato risotto, olive tapenade, and curry onion rings. ⊠ *688 State Rd.* ☎ *508/693–8582* ⊕ *www. stateroadmv.com* ⊟ *AE, D, MC, V* ⊘ *Closed mid-Feb.–mid-Apr. and Mon. and Tues. mid-Apr.–late May and mid-Sept.–mid-Feb.*

> **BYOB**
>
> Part of how the Vineyard maintains its charm—and part of what makes it somewhat frustrating as well—is that alcoholic beverages are sold in only four towns: Vineyard Haven, Edgartown, Oak Bluffs, and Aquinnah. At restaurants in the "dry" towns of West Tisbury and Chilmark you can bring your own bottle, but expect to be charged at least $8 for corkage fees.

$$$–$$$$
Fodor's Choice
★

Lambert's Cove Inn. A narrow road winds through pine woods and beside creeper-covered stone walls to this posh, handsomely designed inn surrounded by extraordinary gardens and old stone walls. Genial innkeepers Scott Jones and I. Kell Hicklin have made this 1790 farmhouse inn into an exquisite gem. The richly appointed rooms each have decorative schemes and antiques based on grand East Coast–resort towns, from Key West to Bar Harbor. Those in the outbuildings are airy and a bit more contemporary, some with decks and porches. Guests receive free passes to beautiful and private Lambert's Cove beach. Fireplaces and hardwood floors lend warmth to the stellar contemporary restaurant, where you might dine on braised veal cheeks with sweet corn–English pea risotto. **Pros:** smart and contemporary decor; fantastic restaurant; serene grounds. **Cons:** need a car to explore island; far from the action. ⊠ *Off Lambert's Cove Rd.* ⌖ *R.R. 1, Box 422, Vineyard Haven 02568* ☎ *508/693–2298* ⊕ *www.lambertscoveinn.com* ⇆ *15 rooms* ♿ *In-room: a/c, DVD, refrigerator, Wi-Fi. In-hotel: restaurant, tennis court, pool, Wi-Fi hotspot, no kids under 8* ⊟ *AE, D, MC, V* |⊘| *BP.*

$

Martha's Vineyard International Hostel. The only budget alternative in season, this hostel is one of the country's best. The large, common kitchen, where a free pancake breakfast is served each morning, is outfitted with multiple refrigerators and stoves. The common room has plenty of books, and you'll catch wind of local events on the bulletin board. A limited number of private rooms, also with bunk beds, are available; otherwise, it's dorm-style accommodations. The hostel is near a bike path and about 3 mi from the nearest beach. **Pros:** it's cheap; a fun place to meet backpackers. **Cons:** little privacy. ⊠ *Edgartown–W. Tisbury Rd.* ☎ *508/693–2665* ⊕ *www.capecod.hiusa.org* ⇆ *67 dorm-style beds* ♿ *In-hotel: Wi-Fi hotspot* ⊟ *MC, V* ⊘ *Closed mid-Oct.–mid-Apr.*

BEACHES, SPORTS, AND THE OUTDOORS

Lambert's Cove Beach (⊠ *Lambert's Cove Rd.*), one of the island's prettiest, has fine sand and clear water. The Vineyard Sound Beach has calm waters; it's good for children.

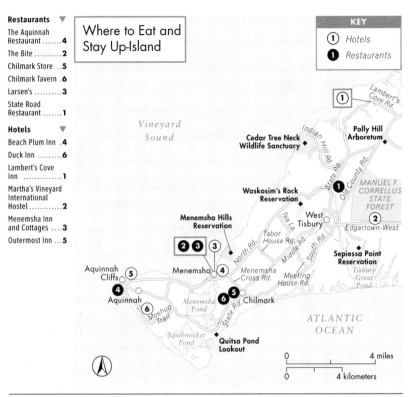

Where to Eat and
Stay Up-Island

KEY
① *Hotels*
❶ *Restaurants*

SHOPPING

The **Granary Gallery at the Red Barn** (✉ *Old County Rd.* ☎ *508/693–0455*) displays early-American furniture and exhibits artworks by island and international artists.

★ **Martha's Vineyard Glassworks** (✉ *683 State Rd.* ☎ *508/693–6026* ⊕ *www.mvglassworks.com*) is a great place to browse for colorful contemporary glass pieces and to watch glassblowers at work in the studio.

CHILMARK

Chilmark is a rural village where ocean-view roads, rustic woodlands, and lack of crowds have drawn chic summer visitors and resulted in stratospheric real-estate prices. Laced with rough roads and winding stone fences that once separated fields and pastures, Chilmark reminds people of what the Vineyard was like in an earlier time, before the developers came.

GETTING HERE AND AROUND

Chilmark, 5½ mi southwest of West Tisbury and 6 mi west of Aquinnah, is served by the big buses of the Martha's Vineyard Transit Authority. The fare is $1 per town, including the town of departure.

WHERE TO EAT

¢ ✕**Chilmark Store.** This local landmark serves pizza, burgers, salads, and
CAFÉ deli sandwiches—it's a solid take-out lunch spot. If you've bicycled into
town, the wooden rockers on the porch may be just the place to take a
break—or find a picnic spot of your own nearby to enjoy a fish burger
or a slice of the pizza of the day. ✉ *7 State Rd.* ☎ *508/645–3655* ⊕ *www.
chilmarkstore.com* ⊟ *D, MC, V* ⊘ *Closed mid-Oct.–Apr.*

$$$$ ✕**Chilmark Tavern.** It's all fresh and crisp inside this homey tavern, with
AMERICAN white linen tablecloths covered in brown butcher paper, and when the
sun sets and the candles are lit, it's a lovely spot for dinner. Arrive at 4
for the daily raw bar happy hour (in summer); another great starter is
the house-made warm ricotta with olive oil, herbs, and grilled bread.
Favorites for dinner include the jumbo prawns with Anson Mills grits,
chorizo, and garlic spinach; or the 16-ounce porcini-rubbed NY sirloin with a cabernet sauce. It's a busy and lively place; regulars have
their own personal liquor lockers for storing their dinner spirits, since
Chilmark is a dry town. A special perk is the free Menemsha Harbor
pickup—come by boat and they'll get you here and back to the pier.
✉ *9 State Rd.* ☎ *508/645–9400* ⊕ *www.chilmarktavern.com* ⊟ *AE, D,
MC, V* ⊘ *Closed mid-Oct.–Apr. and Tues. and Wed. in May and Sept.*

BEACHES, SPORTS, AND THE OUTDOORS

★ A dirt road leads off South Road to beautiful **Lucy Vincent Beach**, which
in summer is open only to Chilmark residents and those staying in town.

Squibnocket Beach (✉ *Off South Rd.*), on the south shore, is a narrow
stretch of boulder-strewn coastline that is part smooth rocks and pebbles, part fine sand. The area has good waves, and it's popular with
surfers. During the season, this beach is restricted to residents and visitors with passes.

SHOPPING

Surrounded by massive stone walls, the grounds of the **Allen Farm Sheep
& Wool Company** (✉ *421 South Rd.* ☎ *508/645–9064*) are a sight to
behold. Once inside the gift shop, you'll swoon over the vibrant selection of handmade sweaters and other items for sale.

★ **Chilmark Chocolates** (✉ *State Rd.* ☎ *508/645–3013*) sells superior chocolates and what might just be the world's finest butter crunch, which you
can sometimes watch being made in the back room.

MENEMSHA

★ Unspoiled by the "progress" of the past few decades, the working port
of Menemsha is a jumble of weathered fishing shacks, fishing and pleasure boats, drying nets, and lobster pots. The village is popular with
cyclists who like to stop for ice cream or chowder.

In 2010, a massive fire completely destroyed a significant stretch of the
pier. There were no injuries, and plans to rebuild were immediately

Martha's Vineyard Facts and Trivia

The year-round population of the island is about 15,000. On any given day in summer, the population increases five-fold, to an estimated 75,000.

Some four decades after the island was charted in 1602, Bay Colony businessman Thomas Mayhew struck a deal with the Crown and purchased Martha's Vineyard, as well as Nantucket and the Elizabeth Islands, for £40.

Jeanne and Hugh Taylor, the latter the brother of recording star James Taylor, operate the Outermost Inn, by the lighthouse in Aquinnah.

Total shoreline: 126 mi. Total land area: 100 square mi.

Martha's Vineyard was formed more than 20,000 years ago as great sheets of ice, as thick as 2 mi, descended from the frigid northern climes into what is now New England, pushing great chunks of earth and rock before them. When the glaciers melted and receded, the island, as well as Nantucket and Cape Cod, remained in their wake.

When residents say they are going "Up-Island," they mean they're heading to the western areas of Aquinnah, Chilmark, Menemsha, and West Tisbury. The designation is based on nautical

terminology, where heading west means going "up" in longitude. "Down-Island" refers to Vineyard Haven, Oak Bluffs, and Edgartown.

During the height of the 19th-century whaling era, it was considered good luck to have an Aquinnah Wampanoag on board. The Wampanoags were renowned as sailors and harpoon-ers. Town residents voted to change the name of Gay Head to Aquinnah in 1997, and the official change was signed into law on May 7, 1998.

The North American continent's last heath hen, an eastern prairie chicken, died in a forest fire on Martha's Vineyard in 1932. A monument to it stands in the State Forest just off the West Tisbury–Edgartown Road.

West Tisbury resident, farmer, and sailor Joshua Slocum became the first man to sail solo around the world. He set out in 1895 in his 36-foot sloop and returned three years later. Ten years later he was lost at sea.

Despite the fact that Great Harbour was renamed Edgartown after the young son of the Duke of York, the unfortunate three-year-old died one month before the name became official.

6

underway. If you visit in 2011, there's a good chance you won't see any signs of damage.

GETTING HERE AND AROUND

Menemsha, 1½ mi northwest of Chilmark, is often busy with folks eager to see the sunset. You can take a Martha's Vineyard Transit Authority bus here; there's frequent service in summer, and more-limited service the rest of the year.

If you're exploring the area by bike, you can get between Menemsha and the Aquinnah Cliffs via the Menemsha Bike Ferry. It's a quick trip across the water ($7 round-trip), but it saves a lot of riding on the busy State Road.

EXPLORING

Menemsha Harbor. Where Menemsha Pond meets Vineyard Sound, this tiny seaside outpost has been an active fishing center for centuries. Well-weathered fishing boats, including some that have been in the same family for generations, tie up at the docks when not out to sea. Spectacular sunsets make this a very popular evening spot. Several fish markets offer the freshest catch of the day. There's also a beach here, with gentle waters that are welcoming to families. If the harbor looks familiar, it might be because several scenes from the movie *Jaws* were filmed here. ⊠ *End of Basin Rd.*

WHERE TO EAT

$ ✕ **The Bite.** Fried everything—clams, fish-and-chips, you name it—is on
SEAFOOD the menu at this simple, roadside shack, where two outdoor picnic tables are the only seating options. Small, medium, and large are the three options: all of them are perfect if you're craving that classic seaside fried lunch. But don't come on a rainy day, unless you want to get wet—the lines here can be long. To beat the crowds, try arriving between traditional mealtimes. The best advice, however, is to be patient and don't arrive too hungry. "Delicious-ness! We were looking for the quintessential roadside seafood shack and found it at the Bite!" declares Fodors.com reader tzimmer. ⊠ *29 Basin Rd.* ☎ *509/645–9239* ⊕ *www. thebitemenemsha.com* ⊟ No credit cards ☉ *Closed Oct.–late May.*

$ ✕ **Larsen's.** Basically a retail fish store, Larsen's has a raw-take-out coun-
SEAFOOD ter and will also boil lobsters for you. Dig into a plate of fresh littlenecks
Fodor's Choice or cherrystones. Oysters are not a bad alternative. There's also seafood
★ chowder and a variety of smoked fish and dips. Bring your own bottle of wine or beer, buy your dinner here, and then set up on the rocks, the docks, or the beach: there's no finer alfresco rustic dining on the island. Larsen's closes at 6 PM weekdays, 7 PM weekends. ⊠ *Dutcher's Dock* ☎ *508/645–2680* ⊟ *MC, V* ⍟ *BYOB* ☉ *Closed mid-Oct.–mid-May.*

WHERE TO STAY

$$$$ ⌂ **Beach Plum Inn.** This mansard-roof inn, sister property of the nearby
★ Menemsha Inn, is surrounded by 7 acres of lavish formal gardens and lush woodland; it sits on a bluff over Menemsha Harbor. The floral-themed rooms—five in the main house and six in cottages—have gorgeous furnishings, and some have whirlpool tubs; in the Daffodil Room, bathed in shades of yellow and blue, you'll find a hand-painted queen bed and a romantic balcony. A vaulted, beamed ceiling rises over the bedroom of the secluded Morning Glory Cottage. You are welcome to use the Menemsha Inn's tennis courts and gym, and passes to nearby Lucy Vincent and Squibnocket beaches are available. As romantic settings go, it's hard to beat the restaurant here, with its knockout harbor views, especially at sunset. **Pros:** gardens will blow you away; superb restaurant. **Cons:** a bit of a drive from any major towns; pricey. ⊠ *North Rd.* ☎ *508/645–9454* ⊕ *www.beachpluminn.com* ⥲ *11 rooms* ⌂ *In-room: a/c, refrigerator. In-hotel: Wi-Fi hotspot* ⊟ *AE, D, MC, V* ☉ *Closed late Oct.–mid-May* ⍾ *CP.*

$$$$ ⊡ **Menemsha Inn and Cottages.** These cottages, owned by the neighboring Beach Plum Inn, overlook Vineyard Sound and Cuttyhunk. They tumble down a hillside behind the main house and vary in privacy and views. You can also stay in the 1989 inn building or the pleasant Carriage House. All rooms have private decks, most with sunset views. Suites include sitting areas, desks, and big tiled baths. A Continental breakfast is served in a solarium-style breakfast room with a deck facing the ocean. Bicycles are available for rent. **Pros:** wonderfully secluded; sunset views from private decks. **Cons:** not for the budget-minded; need a car to explore island from here. ⊠ *North Rd., Box 38* ☎ *508/645–2521* ⊕ *www.menemshainn.com* ⌁ *15 rooms, 11 cottages, one 2-bedroom house* ⟡ *In-room: a/c (some) kitchen (some), refrigerator. In-hotel: tennis court, gym, Wi-Fi hotspot* ⊟ *MC, V* ⊗ *Closed late Oct.–mid-May* ⫣ *CP.*

SPORTS AND THE OUTDOORS

Menemsha Hills Reservation (⊠ *North Rd.*) has 4 mi of some of the most challenging, steep, and breathtaking hiking trails on the island, including a stroll up to Martha's Vineyard's second-highest point and another ramble that descends down through the windswept valley to boulder-strewn Vineyard Sound Beach.

6

AQUINNAH

Aquinnah, called Gay Head until the town voted to change its name in 1997, is an official Native American township. The Wampanoag tribe is the guardian of the 420 acres that constitute the Aquinnah Native American Reservation. Aquinnah (pronounced a-*kwih*-nah) is Wampanoag for "land under the hill." The town is best known for the red-hue Aquinnah Cliffs.

GETTING HERE AND AROUND

This is the end of the world, or so it seems when you're standing on the edge of the cliff looking out over the ocean. Aquinnah, 6½ mi west of Menemsha and 10 mi southwest of West Tisbury, gets lots of traffic, for good reason. You can drive here (and pray for a parking space) or ride the Martha's Vineyard Transit Authority buses, which have frequent service in summer.

EXPLORING

Fodor'sChoice **Aquinnah Cliffs.** A National Historic Landmark, the spectacular Aquin-
★   nah Cliffs are part of the Wampanoag Reservation land. These dramatically striated walls of red clay are the island's major attraction, as evidenced by the tour bus–filled parking lot. Native American crafts and food shops line the short approach to the overlook, from which you can see the Elizabeth Islands to the northeast across Vineyard Sound and Noman's Land Island—a wildlife preserve—3 mi off the Vineyard's southern coast. ⊠ *State Rd.*

Aquinnah Lighthouse. This brick lighthouse is stationed precariously atop the rapidly eroding cliffs. It's open to the public on Friday, Saturday, and

Sunday evenings at sunset, weather permitting. Across from the parking area you'll see the historic **Vanderhoop Homestead,** a handsome 1880s house that's home to the **Aquinnah Cultural Center** (⊠ *Lighthouse Rd.* ☎ *508/645–7900* ⊕ *www.vanderhoophomestead.org* ⊠ *$7* ⊙ *Wed., Fri., and Sat. 11–3*), a museum on Aquinnah's rich history. Displays cover topics such as beadwork, plant identification, and religion. ⊠ *Lighthouse Rd.* ☎ *508/645–2211* ⊠ *$5.*

Quitsa Pond Lookout. This spot has a good view of the adjoining Menemsha and Nashaquitsa ponds, the woods, and the ocean beyond. ⊠ *State Rd.*

WHERE TO EAT AND STAY

$$ ✕ **Aquinnah Restaurant.** At the far end of the row of fast-food take-out
AMERICAN   spots and souvenir shops at the Gay Head Cliffs is this restaurant owned and operated by members of the Vanderhoop and Madison families, native Wampanoags. The view is quite dramatic—especially from the outdoor deck, which is perched hundreds of feet above the open ocean. (Just watch out for bold seagulls, who are not at all afraid to relieve you of your calamari.) The lunch menu includes sandwiches, burgers, and healthful-sounding salads. Dinner entrées include sautéed shrimp, scallops, and lobster with rotini in a chardonnay sauce, and striped bass in a mussel-and-saffron sauce. ⊠ *S27 Aquinnah Circle* ☎ *508/645–3867* ▤ *MC, V* ⊙ *Closed mid-Oct.–mid-Apr.*

$$–$$$ ⊡ **Duck Inn.** The Duck Inn, originally an 18th-century home built by
★   Native American seafarer George Belain, sits on a bucolic 5-acre bluff overlooking the ocean, with the Aquinnah Lighthouse standing sentinel to the north. The eclectic, fun interior blends peach stucco walls, Native American rugs and wall hangings, and wooden ducks. Three upstairs rooms come with balconies; a suite in the stone-wall lower level (cool in summer, warm in winter) has views of the rolling fields. The common room, with a working 1928 Glenwood stove, piano, and fireplace, is the heart of the inn. Massage therapies are available, and the healthful organic breakfast fare includes waffles with strawberries and omelets or chocolate crepes. This inn is very informal—kids and pets are welcome. **Pros:** a good value; totally secluded; ocean views; within walking distance of the beach. **Cons:** a longish drive from town; too quiet for some. ⊠ *10 Duck Pond Way* ☎ *508/645–9018* ⊕ *www.duckinnonmv. com* ⇄ *4 rooms, 1 suite* ⚿ *In-room: no a/c. In-hotel: Wi-Fi hotspot, some pets allowed* ▤ *MC, V* ⋈ *BP.*

$$$$ ⊡ **Outermost Inn.** This rambling, sun-filled inn by the Aquinnah Cliffs
★   stands alone on acres of moorland, a 10-minute walk from the beach. The house is wrapped in windows revealing views of sea and sky in three directions, and there are great views of the Aquinnah Lighthouse from the wide porch and patio. The inn is clean and contemporary, with white walls and polished light-wood floors. The restaurant, open to the public, serves dinner nightly in summer and is all prix-fixe at $70. **Pros:** spectacular setting; wonderful food. **Cons:** far from bigger towns on island; steep rates; not suitable for young kids. ⊠ *81 Lighthouse Rd.* ☎ *508/645–3511* ⊕ *www.outermostinn.com* ⇄ *7 rooms* ⚿ *In-room: no a/c (some), Wi-Fi. In-hotel: restaurant, no kids under 12* ▤ *AE, D, MC, V* ⊙ *Closed mid-Oct.–mid-May* ⋈ *BP.*

Nantucket

WORD OF MOUTH

"In late October, if you stay in town there will be shops and good restaurants—not all but enough—open. Beaches will be chilly, but there are plenty of other things to look at and do. The historical association should still have some museum properties open, and the leaves are likely to still be pretty good. If you are lucky—and I am not kidding—you will get a 24-hour storm. There is nothing cozier in the world than being warm and dry and having a nice drink while it howls outside, knowing that however much you tried, you couldn't get off the island until the weather changes."

—djkbooks

By Sandy
MacDonald

For the first time since its brief golden age as a world-renowned whaling capital in the early 1800s, the tiny island of Nantucket is decidedly on a roll. Modest shingled cottages that might have gone begging for a buyer a few decades ago now fetch millions, and trophy houses in the hinterlands are off the charts. The historic homes of Nantucket Town only rarely change hands, and then at exalted prices. But the well-preserved town and the breezy, wide-openness of the island, with its white-sand beaches and heath-covered moors, still offer elemental pleasures.

The intimate village of Nantucket remains the focal point of island activity, just as it has been since the early 1700s. It consists of a few square blocks of fabulous restaurants, lovingly restored inns, and upscale boutiques and galleries clustered around the waterfront, where the ferries dock.

Beyond the bustle of town, quiet rural roads fan out to scenic points around the island—the charming village of Siasconset (known locally as 'Sconset) is 8 mi to the east, the roiling breakers of Surfside 3 mi to the south, and the peak sunset-viewing vantage point of Madaket 6 mi west. Whatever direction you take, spectacular beaches await.

Essentially Nantucket is *all* beach—a boomerang-shaped sand spit consisting of detritus left by a glacier that receded millennia ago. Off Cape Cod, some 30 mi out to sea, the island measures 3½ by 14 mi at its widest points while encompassing—such are the miracles of inlets and bays—about 80 mi of sandy shoreline, all of it open, as a matter of local pride, to absolutely everyone.

On a day when sun scintillates on sand and the thrumming waves hint at an eternal rhythm, it's hard to imagine that anything could ever go too terribly wrong here. As summer succeeds summer, children will continue to construct their fanciful if foredoomed sand castles and marvel over the odd treasures the tides drag in. Adults will gladly play along, if allowed, remembering their own seemingly endless days of summer and imagining more of the same for their children's children and so on and on.

ORIENTATION AND PLANNING

GETTING ORIENTED

Nantucket is a boomerang-shaped island 26 mi southeast of Hyannis on Cape Cod, or 107 mi southeast of Boston. Its nearest neighbor to the west is the somewhat larger island of Martha's Vineyard; eastward, the

TOP REASONS TO GO

Visiting historic homes: Architecture buffs will have a field day poking about the more than 800 pre-1840 structures that compose the core of Nantucket Town, which has been designated, in its entirety, a National Landmark Historic District.

Relaxing on bountiful beaches: You'd be hard-pressed to find a more accessible, less crowded expanse of sand anywhere on the eastern seaboard. The bay waves couldn't be gentler at Children's Beach, while the ocean side is wild enough for surfing on Cisco Beach.

Biking the island: The best way to tour Nantucket is by bicycle. Some 30 mi of gently rolling bike paths crisscross colorful marshes and lead to all the best beaches. Bring your own bike, or rent right off the boat.

Sailing serenely: If your own yacht happens to be in dry dock, don't hesitate to sign on for a harbor tour with a congenial skipper. You'll find plenty of willing and able guides at Straight Wharf and other docks around the island.

Sampling superb cuisine: You'd swear the chefs of Nantucket were all part of a cabal dedicated to elevating the art of locavore gastronomy. Most summer enclaves are lucky to have a couple of fine restaurants; Nantucket has more than a score.

7

nearest landfall would be the Azores off Portugal. The island has only one town, which also goes by the name of Nantucket. The only other community of note is tiny Siasconset, a cluster of shingled seaside manses and lovingly restored fishing shacks 8 mi west of town. A 3-mi main road directly south of town leads to Surfside Beach, among the island's most popular. Nantucket's small but busy airport is located east of Surfside.

Nantucket Town. As the ferry terminal—from Hyannis and, seasonally, Martha's Vineyard—Nantucket Town is the hub of all activity and the starting point for most visits. At the height of summer, the narrow cobblestone streets are in a constant state of near-gridlock. Town itself is easily walkable, and bikes are available for exploring.

Siasconset and Wauwinet. An allee of green lawns leads to the exclusive summer community of Siasconset (or 'Sconset, as locals say). Tucked away on either side of the village center are warrens of tiny, rose-covered cottages, some of them centuries old. About 5 mi northwest is the even tinier community of Wauwinet, with the country's second-oldest yacht club.

PLANNING

WHEN TO GO

Every July and August, Nantucket's population balloons from about 10,000 to 50,000 or more. Summer is peak season, but autumn is the smart time to visit. Though the ocean is slow to warm up (few people brave the waters in June), it tends to stay warm into fall, so beaching it all the way up to Columbus Day is not out of the question. Hotels rates tend to drop after Labor Day, and they'll stay low—with temporary blips for Christmas Stroll in early December and Daffodil Festival in late April. If you're up for walks alongside blustery surf, winter can be a very atmospheric time to visit.

PLANNING YOUR TIME

Nantucket definitely merits consideration as a day trip—a prospect made easier by the hour-long fast ferries making the crossing from Hyannis. Day-trippers usually take in the architecture and historical sites and browse the boutiques; arrive early enough and there might be enough time for a short van tour of the island. After dining at one of the many delightful restaurants, you can hop a ferry back—or, if you're in no particular hurry, stay at one of the historic inns. Of course, several days or even a week allows you more time to discover the island and sample its many different beaches.

GETTING HERE AND AROUND

BOAT AND FERRY TRAVEL

See ⇨ Boat and Ferry Travel in Travel Smart Cap Cod at the back of this book. Nantucket has first-class marina and mooring amenities for yacht and boat owners.

Marina Contacts Madaket Marine (☎ 508/228–1163 ⊕ www.madaketmarine. com). **Nantucket Boat Basin** (☎ 508/325–1333 or 800/626–2628 ⊕ www. nantucketboatbasin.com). **Nantucket Moorings** (☎ 508/228–4472 ⊕ www. nantucketmoorings.com).

BUS TRAVEL

The Nantucket Regional Transit Authority (NRTA) runs shuttle buses in town and to Madaket, to mid-island areas (including the airport and Surfside Beach), and to 'Sconset. Service is available late May to early October. Each of the routes has its own schedule (you can pick one up at the chamber of commerce, Visitor Services, the NRTA office, or at most any bus stop); service generally begins at 7 AM and ends at 11:30 PM. All shuttle buses have bike racks and lifts. Fares are $1 in town or mid-island; $2 to Madaket, Surfside, the airport, or 'Sconset; seniors pay half fare and children under seven—and pets—ride free. Passes run $7 for 1 day, $12 for 3, $20 for 7, $50 for 30, and $80 for the season, with attendant discounts available. Passes for up to a week can be bought on board; longer-term passes can be purchased at the NRTA office.

Bus Information Nantucket Regional Transit Authority (✉ 3 E. Chestnut St. ☎ 508/228–7025 ⊕ www.shuttlenantucket.com).

CAR TRAVEL

The chamber of commerce strongly discourages bringing cars to Nantucket. They're really not needed—unless you're planning to stay a week or more, and renting far out of town, off the bus routes. The town itself is entirely walkable, and keeping a car there is not practical; the longest you're allowed to park is ½ to 1½ hours at a time ("summer specials"—supplemental police personnel—are right on it, keeping tabs by PDA). The entire island is easily accessible by bike, taxi, or public transportation.

If you're still determined to rent a car while on Nantucket, book early—and expect to spend at least $85 a day during high season. If your car is low-slung, don't attempt the dirt roads. Some are deeply

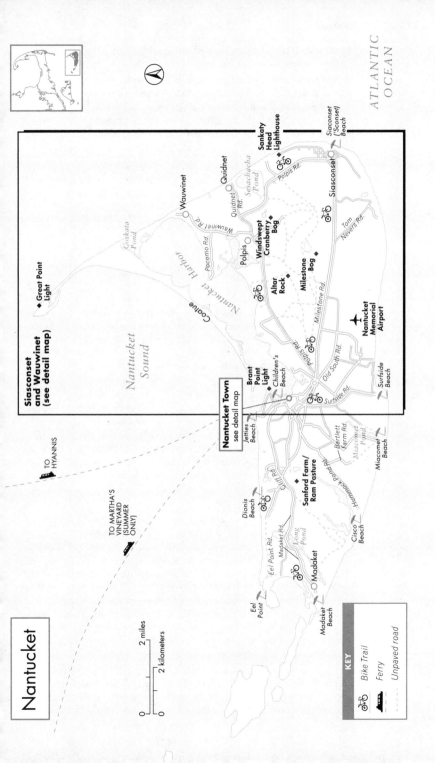

Nantucket

Siasconset and Wauwinet
(see detail map)

Nantucket Town
see detail map

ATLANTIC OCEAN

Nantucket Sound

Nantucket Harbor

Coatue

Great Point Light

Goskata Pond

Wauwinet

Quidnet

Sesachacha Pond

Quidnet Rd.

Polpis

Windswept Cranberry Bog

Altar Rock

Milestone Bog

Siasconset

Siasconset (Sconset) Beach

Sankaty Head Lighthouse

Polpis Rd.

Wauwinet Rd.

Pocomo Rd.

Tom Nevers Rd.

Milestone Rd.

Nantucket Memorial Airport

Polpis Rd.

Old South Rd.

Surfside Rd.

Surfside Beach

Brant Point Light

Children's Beach

Jetties Beach

Dionis Beach

Eel Point

Eel Point Rd.

Madaket Rd.

Long Pond

Madaket

Madaket Beach

Cisco Beach

Sanford Farm/
Ram Pasture

Hummock Pond Rd.

Bartlett Farm Rd.

Miacomet Pond

Miacomet Beach

Gull Rd.

TO HYANNIS

TO MARTHA'S VINEYARD
(SUMMER ONLY)

2 miles

2 kilometers

0

KEY
🚲 Bike Trail
⛴ Ferry
---- Unpaved road

pocked with puddles, and some are virtual sandpits, challenging even to four-wheel-drive vehicles.

Nantucket Agencies Nantucket Island Rent-a-Car (✉ *Nantucket Memorial Airport* ☎ *508/228—9989 or 800/508-9972* ⊕ *www.nantucketislandrentacar. com*). **Nantucket Windmill Auto Rental** (✉ *Nantucket Memorial Airport* ☎ *508/228-1227 or 800/228-1227* ⊕ *www.nantucketautorental.com*). **Young's Bicycle Shop** (✉ *6 Broad St.* ☎ *508/228-1151* ⊕ *www.youngsbicycleshop.com*).

TAXI TRAVEL

Taxis usually wait outside the airport, on Steamboat Wharf, and at the foot of Main Street. Rates are flat fees, based on one person with two bags, 6 AM to 1 AM (another rider adds $2 to the price, and late-night rides incur a $5 surcharge); $7 within town (1½-mi radius); and, from town, $12 to the airport, $21 to 'Sconset, and $23 to Wauwinet. Dogs and bikes cost a little extra.

Nantucket Taxi Companies A1 Taxi (☎ *508/325-3330*). **All Point Taxi** (☎ *508/228-5779*). **Val's Cab Service** (☎ *508/228-9410*).

RESTAURANTS

For such a tiny island, Nantucket is laden with great restaurants—"world class" would not be an exaggeration. Of course, with New York–level sophistication come New York–level prices. And whereas the titans of industry who flock here for a bit of high-rent R&R might not blink at the prospect of a $40 or even $50 entrée, the rest of us may suppress a nervous gulp. Is it worth it? Again and again, in many venues, the answer is yes.

Reservations can be hard to come by in high season, or during popular weekends such as December's Christmas Stroll and the Daffodil Festival in April, so plan and make dinner reservations well ahead. You may still be able to squeeze into a popular establishment at the last minute if you're willing to eat unfashionably early or decadently late. Restaurants tend to drop days from their schedules in the shoulder seasons, so call ahead to check the hours of operation in any month other than July or August.

HOTELS

From small bed-and-breakfasts to the island's few surviving grand hotels, Nantucket knows the value of hospitality. A unique "product" plus good service—as busy as this little island gets—are the deciding factors that keep visitors coming back year after year. The majority of lodgings are in town, convenient to the shops and restaurants. Those seeking quiet might prefer the inns on the periphery of town, a 5- to 10-minute walk from Main Street. The most remote inns, in 'Sconset and Wauwinet, also tend to be among the most expensive. Families with children will probably want to consider the larger, less-formal hotels, since many of the small, historic B&Bs are furnished with antiques.

Nantucket is notoriously expensive, so don't expect to find many bargains in terms of lodging, especially in summer. The best rates can be found in the off-season; however, the spring and fall shoulder seasons are also growing in popularity, and such special-event weekends as the Daffodil Festival in late April and Christmas Stroll in early December command peak-season rates. The only truly "budget" facility you'll find is the youth hostel, which is also the only option for roughing it, since camping is prohibited anywhere on-island.

WHAT IT COSTS					
	¢	$	$$	$$$	$$$$
Restaurants	under $16	$17–$23	$24–$30	$31–$40	over $40
Hotels	under $160	$160–$230	$231–$300	$301–$400	over $400

Restaurant prices are per person for a main course at dinner. Hotel prices are for a standard double room, excluding 9.7% sales tax.

TOURS

No matter what you want to do around Nantucket, be it kayaking, mountain biking, climbing, birding, hiking, snorkeling, or scuba diving, Eco Guides: Strong Wings can customize a small-group tour. Sixth-generation Nantucketer Gail Johnson of Gail's Tours narrates a lively 1½-hour van tour of the island's highlights: the moors, the cranberry bogs, and the lighthouses, in addition to Nantucket Town. The 13-passenger cranberry-red van heads out daily at 10, 1, and 3 in season; pickups at in-town inns can be arranged.

Contacts Eco Guides: Strong Wings (✉ 9 Nobadeer Farm Rd. ☎ 508/228–1769 ⊕ www.strongwings.org). **Gail's Tours** (☎ 508/257-6557 ⊕ www.nantucket.net/tours/gails).

VISITOR INFORMATION

You can stop by the Nantucket Visitor Services and Information Bureau, open weekdays 9 to 6 year-round, to get your bearings, as well as maps, brochures, island information, and advice. The bureau is also a great resource if you need a room at the last minute—they track cancellations daily and might be able to refer you to an inn with newly available rooms. It's in the center of town, within a couple of blocks of both ferry landings, each of which also has an NVS booth in season. The chamber of commerce is another great place to get maps and island information; it's open weekdays 9 to 5, year-round.

Information Nantucket Chamber of Commerce (✉ Zero Main St. ☎ 508/228–1700 ⊕ www.nantucketchamber.org). **Nantucket Visitor Services and Information Bureau** (✉ 25 Federal St. ☎ 508/228-0925 ⊕ www.nantucket-ma.gov).

NANTUCKET TOWN

At the height of its prosperity in the early 19th century, the little town of Nantucket was the foremost whaling port in the world. Shipowners and sea captains built elegant mansions, which today remain remarkably unchanged, thanks to a very strict building code initiated in the 1950s. The entire town of Nantucket is now an official National Historic District encompassing more than 800 pre-1840 structures within 1 square mi.

GETTING HERE AND AROUND

There are only two ways to get to Nantucket Town from the mainland: by airplane, and by ferry from Hyannis or Martha's Vineyard. Although you can bring a car over on the ferries with advance reservations, you'll probably want to save yourself the hassle. If you want to explore the island, take a van tour or rent a car once you are here.

The Nantucket Historical Association's 90-minute Historic Nantucket Walking Tours, offered twice daily in season ($10), provide an overview of the island's history and encompass such sites as Petticoat Row, upper Main Street, and the wharves, churches, and library. The self-guided Black Heritage Trail tour covers nine sites in and around town, including the African Meeting House, the Whaling Museum, and the Atheneum. The trail guide is free from the Friends of the African Meeting House on Nantucket, which also leads a "Walk the Black Heritage Trail" tour by appointment in season.

ESSENTIALS

Tour Information Friends of the African Meeting House on Nantucket (✉ *29 York and Pleasant Sts.* 🕾 *508/228–9833* ⊕ *www.afroammuseum.org*). **Historic Nantucket Walking Tours** (✉ *Whaling Museum, 15 Broad St.* 🕾 *508/325–1894* ⊕ *www.nha.org*).

EXPLORING

TOP ATTRACTIONS

★ **First Congregational Church.** The tower of this church provides the best view of Nantucket—for those willing to climb its 94 steps. Rising 120 feet, the tower is capped by a weather vane depicting a whale catch. Peek in at the church's 1852 trompe l'oeil ceiling. ✉ *62 Centre St.* 🕾 *508/228–0950* ⊕ *www.nantucketfcc.org* 🖾 *Tower tour $5* ☉ *Mid-June–mid-Oct., Mon.–Sat. 10–4; services Sun. 10* AM.

Hadwen House. The pair of magnificent white porticoed Greek Revival mansions on upper Main Street—commonly referred to as the Two Greeks—were built in 1845 and 1846 by wealthy factory owner William Hadwen. No. 94, built as a wedding gift for his adopted niece, was modeled on the Athenian Tower of the Winds, with Corinthian capitals on the entry columns, a domed-stair hall with statuary niches, and an oculus. The Hadwens' own domicile, at No. 96, is now a museum, and its contents reflect how the wealthy of the period lived. Inside, on a guided tour, you'll see such architectural details as the grand circular staircase, fine plasterwork, and carved Italian-marble mantels. ✉ *96 Main St.* 🕾 *508/228–1894* ⊕ *www.nha.org* 🖾 *$6, includes admission to Oldest House* ☉ *Late May–mid-Sept., daily noon–4; mid-Sept.–mid-Oct., Thurs.–Mon. noon–4.*

Main Street. After the Great Fire of 1846 leveled all its wooden buildings, Main Street was widened to prevent future flames from hopping across the street. The cobblestone thoroughfare has a harmonious symmetry: the Pacific Club anchors its foot, and the Pacific National Bank, another redbrick building, squares off the head. The cobblestones were brought to the island as ballast in returning ships and laid to prevent the wheels of carts heavily laden with whale oil from sinking into the dirt. At the center of Lower Main is an old horse trough, today overflowing with flowers. From here the street gently rises; at the bank it narrows to its prefire width and leaves the commercial district for an area of mansions that escaped the blaze.

🐚 ★ **Nantucket Atheneum.** Nantucket's town library is a great white Greek Revival building, with a windowless facade and fluted Ionic columns. Completed in 1847 to replace a

> ### SAVING MONEY
>
> The **Nantucket Historical Association (NHA)** (☎ 508/228–1894 ⊕ www.nha.org) maintains an assortment of venerable properties in town. A $20 pass gets you into all of the association's sites, including the glorious Whaling Museum. A $6 pass excludes the Whaling Museum but includes Hadwen House and Oldest House.

structure lost to the 1846 fire, it's one of the oldest libraries in continuous service in the United States. Astronomer Maria Mitchell was its first librarian. Opening ceremonies included a dedication by Ralph Waldo Emerson, who—along with Daniel Webster, Henry David Thoreau, Frederick Douglass, Lucretia Mott, and John James Audubon—later delivered lectures in the library's second-floor Great Hall. During the 19th century the hall was the center of island culture—a role it fulfills to this day. The adjoining Atheneum Park is a great place to relax for a while, and the spacious Weezie Library for Children hosts readings and activities—a welcome respite for a rainy day. ⊠ 1 India St. ☎ 508/228–1110 ⊕ www.nantucketatheneum. org ☉ Tues. and Thurs. 10–7:30; Wed., Fri., and Sat. 10–5.

🐚
Fodor's Choice
★
Whaling Museum. With exhibits that include a fully rigged whaleboat and a skeleton of a 46-foot sperm whale, this museum—a complex that includes a restored 1846 spermaceti candle factory—is a must-see attraction that offers a crash course in the island's colorful history. Items on display include harpoons and other whale-hunting implements; portraits of whaling captains and their wives (a few of whom went whaling as well); the South Seas curiosities they brought home; a large collection of sailors' crafts, a full-size tryworks once used to process whale oil; and the original 16-foot-high 1850 lens from Sankaty Head Lighthouse. The Children's Discovery Room provides interactive-learning opportunities. Be sure to climb—or take the elevator—up to the observation deck for a view of the harbor. ⊠ 13–15 Broad St. ☎ 508/228–1894 ☞ $15, $20 combination pass includes Hadwen House and Oldest House ☉ Mid-Feb.–mid-Apr., weekends 11–4; mid-Apr.–mid-May and mid-Oct.–mid-Dec., Thurs.–Mon. 11–4; May–mid-Oct., daily 10–5. Closed mid-Dec.–mid-Feb.

WORTH NOTING

African Meeting House. When the island abolished slavery in 1773, Nantucket became a destination for free blacks and escaping slaves. The African Meeting House was built in the 1820s as a schoolhouse, and it functioned as such until 1846, when the island's schools were integrated. A complete restoration has returned the site to its authentic 1880s appearance. ⊠ 29 York St. ☎ 508/228–9833 ⊕ www.afroammuseum. org ☞ $5 ☉ June–Oct., weekdays 11–3, Sat. 11–1, Sun. 1–3.

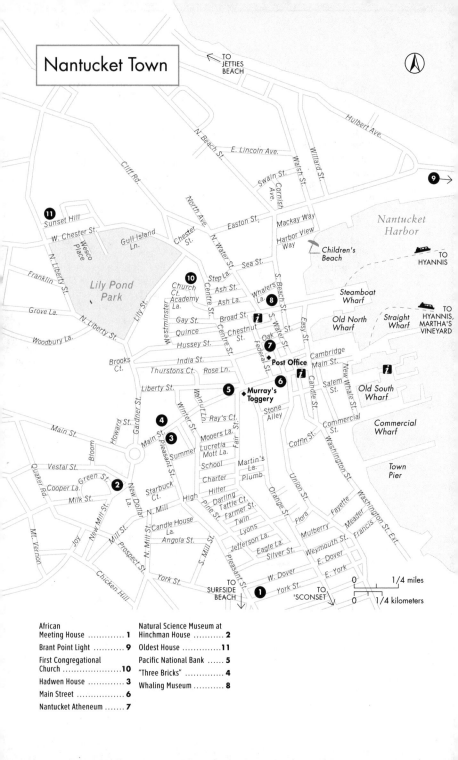

Nantucket Town

TO JETTIES BEACH

TO HYANNIS

Nantucket Harbor

TO HYANNIS, MARTHA'S VINEYARD

Hulbert Ave.

E. Lincoln Ave.

N. Beach St.

Swain St.

Walsh St.

Willard St.

Cornish Ave.

Cliff Rd.

Mackay Way

Harbor View Way

Children's Beach

Easton St.

Chester St.

Gull Island Ln.

N. Water St.

Sea St.

Steamboat Wharf

Wesco Place

W. Chester St.

Sunset Hill

N. Liberty St.

Franklin

Lily Pond Park

Lily St.

Westminster

Church Ct.

Academy La.

Step La.

Ash St.

Ash La.

Whalers La.

S. Beach St.

Easy St.

Old North Wharf

Straight Wharf

Grove La.

Woodbury La.

N. Liberty St.

Gay St.

Quince

Hussey St.

Broad St.

Chestnut St.

Centre St.

Oak St.

S. Water St.

Federal St.

Cambridge

Main St.

New Whale St.

Old South Wharf

Brooks Ct.

India St.

Thurstons Ct.

Rose Ln.

Post Office

Salem St.

Liberty St.

Walnut Ln.

Murray's Toggery

Candle St.

Commercial Wharf

Gardner St.

Winter St.

Ray's Ct.

Fair St.

Stone Alley

Coffin St.

Washington St.

Town Pier

Main St.

Howard

Bloom

Pleasant St.

Main St.

Summer

Mooers La.

Lucretia Mott La.

School

Charter

Martin's La.

Plumb

Union St.

Commercial St.

Vestal St.

Green St.

New Dollar

Starbuck Ct.

High

Hiller

Darling

Tattle Ct.

Pine St.

Farmer St.

Flora

Fayette

Meader

Quaker Rd.

Cooper La.

Milk St.

N. Mill

Candle House La.

Twin

Lyons

Mulberry

Weymouth St.

Francis

Washington St. Ext.

Mt. Vernon

Joy

New Mill St.

Mill St.

Prospect St.

Angola St.

Jefferson La.

Eagle La.

Silver St.

E. Dover

E. York

S. Mill St.

York St.

Pleasant St.

Chicken Hill

TO SURFSIDE BEACH

W. Dover

York St.

TO 'SCONSET

0   1/4 miles

0   1/4 kilometers

WHALING IN NANTUCKET

Nantucket's preeminence as the world's whaling capital (at least until the early 1800s, when New Bedford's deeper harbor took the lead) resulted from a fluke, when, in 1712, Captain Christopher Hussey's crew speared a sperm whale. The waxy spermaceti from the whale's head, it was found, could be used for candles in place of lantern oil produced by the messy, endless task of cooking down whale blubber.

The captains made out like bandits—their grand houses still stand as proof—but the trade went into a downward spiral with the discovery of petroleum in 1836. Here are some key dates in the history of whaling and whales in New England.

Mid-1600s. America enters whaling industry

1690. Nantucket enters whaling industry

1820. *Essex* ship sunk by sperm whale

1840s. American whaling peaked

1851. *Moby-Dick* (based on the story of the *Essex*) published

1927. The last U.S. whaler sails from New Bedford

1970s. Cape Cod whale-watching trips begin

1986. Ban on whaling by the International Whaling Commission

1992. Stellwagen Bank National Marine Sanctuary established

Brant Point Light. The promontory where this 26-foot-tall, white-painted beauty stands offers views of the harbor and town. The point was once the site of the second-oldest lighthouse in the country (1746); the present, much-photographed light was built in 1901. ⊠ *End of Easton St., across footbridge.*

QUICK BITES You can breakfast or lunch inexpensively at the lunch counter at **Nantucket Pharmacy** (⊠ *45 Main St.* ☎ *508/228–0180*). Besides fresh-squeezed juices, the **Juice Bar** (⊠ *12 Broad St.* ☎ *508/228–5799*), open April through mid-October, serves homemade ice cream and frozen yogurt with waffle cones and toppings. Long lines signal that good things come to those who wait.

Natural Science Museum at Hinchman House. Maria Mitchell (1818–89), the first woman to be admitted to the American Academy of Arts and Sciences, studied astronomy at her bank president father's knee. By the time she was in her teens, she was so skilled at adjusting chronometers (an aid to navigation) that whaling captains availed themselves of her services. True to her legacy, this natural history museum takes a hands-on approach. Its intent is to spur wonder while engaging youngsters—and nature-lovers of all ages—to engage on a deeper lever with their surroundings. Any questions you might have as to local flora or fauna can be answered here. The adjoining house where Mitchell grew up, as one of 10 children in a Quaker family that upheld the value of education for both genders, could prove inspirational for the scientists of tomorrow. ⊠ *7 Milk St.* ☎ *508/228–0898* ⊕ *www.mmo.org* 🖼 *$10*

⊘ *June–early Sept., Mon.–Sat. 10–4; mid-Sept.–mid-Oct., weekends 10–4.*

Oldest House. History and architecture buffs should be sure to get a look at this hilltop house, also called the Jethro Coffin House, built in 1686 as a wedding gift for Jethro and Mary Gardner Coffin. The most striking feature of the saltbox is the massive central brick chimney with a brick-horseshoe adornment said to ward away witches. Other highlights are the enormous hearths and diamond-pane leaded-glass windows. Cutaway panels show 17th-century construction techniques. Guides will tell you about the home's history and the interior's sparse furnishings. ⊠ *Sunset Hill (a 10-min walk along Centre St. from Main St.)* ☎ *508/228–1894* ⊕ *www. nha.org* ☞ *$6, includes admission to Hadwen House* ⊘ *Late May–mid-Sept., daily noon–4; mid-Sept.–mid Oct., Thurs.–Mon. noon–4.*

> ### MARIA MITCHELL'S COMET
>
> In 1847 local librarian and amateur astronomer Maria Mitchell discovered a comet, thereby earning worldwide acclaim and a professorship at Vassar College. Established in 1902 by her students and family, the **Maria Mitchell Association** (☎ *508/228-0898* ⊕ *www.mmo.org*) administers several Nantucket Town attractions. A $10 combination admission ticket grants you admission to the Natural Science Museum at Hinchman House, Mitchell's childhood home, and a few other sites.

Pacific National Bank. Like the Pacific Club (a social club that counts whalers' descendants among its members) down the street, the bank, dating to 1818 and still in use today, is a monument to the far-flung voyages of the Nantucket whaling ships it financed. ⊠ *61 Main St.*

Three Bricks. Many of the mansions of the golden age of whaling were built on Upper Main Street. These well-known identical redbrick homes, with columned Greek Revival porches at their front entrances, were built between 1836 and 1838 by whaling merchant Joseph Starbuck for his three sons. They are not open to the public. ⊠ *93–97 Main St.*

WHERE TO EAT

Use the coordinate (✛ B2) at the end of each listing to locate a site on the Where to Eat in Nantucket Town map.

NANTUCKET TOWN

$$ ✕ **American Seasons.** Picture a farmhouse gone sexy: That's the mood—
NEW AMERICAN wholesome yet seductive—at this candlelit hideaway decorated with
Fodor's Choice Rufus Porter–style murals. Chef Michael LaScola works with a half dozen
★ island farms to fashion locavore repasts of surpassing artistry. Highlights of his be-here-now menu include seared day-boat scallops with fried green tomatoes and lemon confit, and oven-roasted guinea hen with sweet corn velouté and foie gras jus. The patio bar draws aficionados eager to sample the rich array, piecemeal. ⊠ *80 Centre St.* ☎ *508/228–7111* ▭ *AE, MC, V* ⊘ *Closed Jan.–mid-Apr. No lunch* ✛ *A2.*

$$ ✕ **Arno's.** Arno's, a brick-walled storefront with a prime location right
AMERICAN on Main Street, presents lush breakfasts (some featuring lobster), hearty

lunches, and fairly ambitious dinners, all with generous portions. (Warning: the salads are meals in themselves.) Owner Chris Morris is an oenophile: hence the growing California influence on the menu (including grilled flatbread pizzas) and a wine bar offering 41 options by the glass or flight. Expect some envious looks—from inside and outside—should you snag the window table, a perfect spot from which to observe the passing parade. ⊠ *41 Main St.* ☎ *508/228–7001* ⊕ *www. arnos.net* ⊟ *AE, MC, V* ⊘ *Closed Jan.–Mar.* ⊹ *B4.*

$$ ╳ **Black-Eyed Susan's.** From a passing glance, you'd never peg this seemingly humble storefront as one of Nantucket's chic eateries—but as the invariable lines attest, it is. The luncheonette setup is offset by improbably fancy glass chandeliers, and hard-core foodies lay claim to the stools to observe chef Jeff Worster's often pyromaniacal "open kitchen." (A note to the heat-averse: it can get toasty inside—you might want to request a patio table.) The dinner menu, which changes every few weeks, ventures boldly around the world: a Massaman pork curry, for instance, might star alongside *ropa vieja* (shredded beef, but the name literally means "old clothes"). Breakfast (served until 1 PM) includes such eye-openers as pancakes fortified with Jarlsberg cheese. ⊠ *10 India St.* ☎ *508/325–0308* ⊟ *No credit cards* ⍾ *BYOB* ⊘ *Closed Dec.–Mar. No dinner Sun. No lunch* ⊹ *B4.*

ECLECTIC
★

$$$ ╳ **The Boarding House.** Beyond the throngs noisily mingling at the bar, you'll encounter a vaulted semisubterranean space reminiscent of a private wine cellar, with leather banquettes circling antique-gold walls. Here, under the watchful eye of star chef-owner Seth Raynor, chef de cuisine Erin Zircher showcases her skill with Mediterranean market cuisine. Comfort is the universal watchword: it's implicit in the house-made cavatelli with braised lamb, grilled lobster with local corn pudding, and the signature dessert, dark-chocolate chocolate-chip cookies served with a pair of mini malted milk shakes. The only discomfort derives from the overresonant noise level. In season, it's best to opt for the sidewalk café. ⊠ *12 Federal St.* ☎ *508/228–9622* ⊕ *www. boardinghouse-pearl.com* ⊟ *AE, MC, V* ⊘ *Closed Jan.–Mar.* ⊹ *B3.*

MEDITERRANEAN

$$$ ╳ **Brant Point Grill.** With its beautiful broad lawn overlooking the harbor, the Brant Point Grill—in-house restaurant for the elegant White Elephant hotel—ventures beyond its à la carte haute–steak house menu with various "Creativities," the best of which is a free-form lobster ravioli in a luscious pool of parsnip puree. Always appealing is the straightforward salmon grilled on a fire cone set up right outside, and the sprightly salads, such as an exemplary white-anchovy Caesar. The desserts (e.g., a trio of mini–whoopie pies) are surefire resolution-destroyers, as is the Sunday brunch, featuring a make-your-own Bloody Mary station. ⊠ *50 Easton St.* ☎ *508/325–1320* ⊕ *www.whiteelephanthotel. com* ⊟ *AE, D, DC, MC, V* ⊘ *Closed early Dec.–late Apr.* ⊹ *D1.*

NEW AMERICAN

$$ ╳ **Brotherhood of Thieves.** No, it's not really an 1840s whaling bar—though the atmospheric basement, which dates all the way back to 1972, presents a more convincing front than the newer, spiffier upper floors, which attract families and friendly singles alike. Upstairs or down, you can dive into the same juicy burgers and signature curly fries, and the entrées—such as peppercorn-crusted swordfish with a

AMERICAN
☼

7

blue cheese potato cake—pack surprising sophistication. In summer, the lines trail down the block; in winter, it's a warm, inviting hideaway. ⊠ *23 Broad St.* ☎ *508/228–2551* ⊕ *www.brotherhoodofthieves.com* ▤ *MC, V* ✛ *B3.*

$$ ✕ **Centre Street Bistro.** Tiny—there are 20 seats indoors, and as many
ECLECTIC out—and perfect, this gem of a bistro is the kind of find that devoted
★ locals wish they could keep to themselves. Chef-owner Tim Pitts's cuisine has proved so reliably winning that popular demand keeps the menu fairly stable: certain signature dishes, such as the warm goat cheese tart and the Black Angus tenderloin with white-truffle oil and polenta crostini are almost always on offer, and prove ample enough to quell the heartiest of appetites. Ruth Pitts's desserts are equally lavish (try the warm chocolate marquise wrapped in phyllo), and the prices are modest for these parts. ⊠ *29 Centre St.* ☎ *508/228–8470* ⊕ *www. nantucketbistro.com* ▤ *MC, V* ⌁ *BYOB* ⊗ *Closed Tues.* ✛ *B3.*

$$$ ✕ **The Club Car.** A longtime favorite among the moneyed set, this boxy
NEW AMERICAN dining room—its adjoining piano bar is an actual railroad car from the dismantled 'Sconset narrow-gauge—has long since shaken shake off its Continental origins and now sings under chef Tom Proch. The Bangkok-style octopus brings a jolt of world-cuisine pizzazz; a salad of paper-thin golden beets is beautifully bolstered by Great Hill blue; and the rack of lamb gets a boost from minted Madeira sauce. ⊠ *1 Main St.* ☎ *508/228–1101* ⊕ *www.theclubcar.com* ▤ *AE, MC, V* ⊗ *Closed mid-Dec.–mid-May* ✛ *C4.*

$$$$ ✕ **Company of the Cauldron.** In this tiny dining room, a sconce-lighted
NEW AMERICAN haven of architectural salvage, chef-owner All Kovalencik issues only
★ one menu per evening (Monday's, priced slightly higher, is lobster-centric). Fans gladly forgo choice when the chef's choice is invariably so dead-on. Rundowns of the weekly roster are available online, and a typically tantalizing lineup might span rosemary-skewered shrimp with Tuscan melon, beef Wellington made with wild mushroom duxelle, and a combo of chocolate ganache and chocolate gelato (don't hold back!). While cherry-picking the menu for recurrent faves, cognoscenti also tend to book on nights when Mary Keller plays her celestial harp. ⊠ *7 India St.* ☎ *508/228–4016* ⊕ *www.companyofthecauldron.com* ⌁ *Reservations essential* ▤ *MC, V* ⊗ *Closed mid-Dec.–late Apr. No lunch* ✛ *B3.*

$$ ✕ **Corazón del Mar.** When Seth and Angela Raynor develop a new culi-
MEXICAN nary passion, they tend to open a new shrine. Complementing the Boarding House (Mediterranean market cuisine) and the Pearl (Asian street food) comes the resplendent Corazón del Mar (literally translated as "Heart of the Sea"). It serves rarefied dishes, the likes of which you'd have a tough time finding in Mexico. Seth combed the country with his surfing buddies for inspiration, and the results span creative tapas, ceviches, and tacos *especiales* (including one packing chili-braised duck leg, sautéed foie gras, and pickled mango salsa). *Platos principales* include crispy pork with a mildly spicy green sauce. It might take all summer to fully explore the options, even with regular visits to the takeout window. ⊠ *S. Water St.* ☎ *508/228–0815* ⊕ *www.corazonnantucket.com* ▤ *AE, MC, V* ⊗ *Closed mid-Oct.–mid-May* ✛ *C3.*

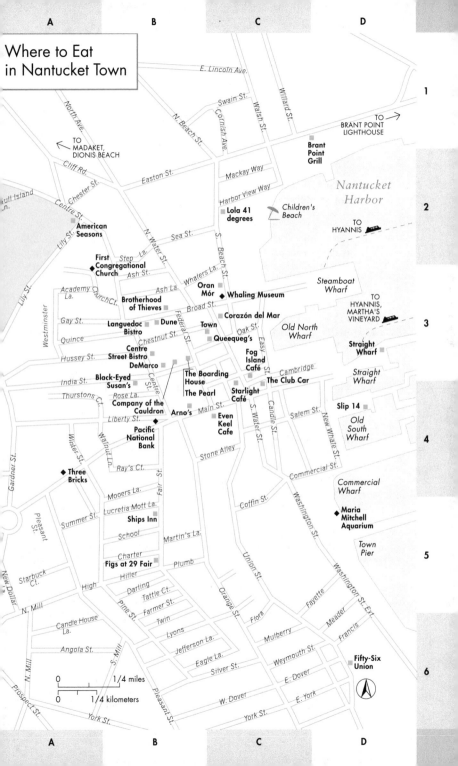

Where to Eat in Nantucket Town

E. Lincoln Ave.

Swain St.

Willard St.

Walsh St.

Cornish Ave.

N. Beach St.

TO BRANT POINT LIGHTHOUSE

TO MADAKET, DIONIS BEACH

North Ave.

Cliff Rd.

Chester St.

Centre St.

Easton St.

Mackay Way

Brant Point Grill

Nantucket Harbor

Harbor View Way

Lola 41 degrees

Children's Beach

TO HYANNIS

American Seasons

Lily St.

Westminster

First Congregational Church

Step La.

Ash St.

N. Water St.

Sea St.

Whalers La.

Beach St.

Academy La.

Church Ct.

Ash La.

Oran Mór

Whaling Museum

Steamboat Wharf

TO HYANNIS, MARTHA'S VINEYARD

Brotherhood of Thieves

Broad St.

Gay St.

Languedoc Bistro

Dune

Corazón del Mar

Quince

Chestnut St.

Federal St.

Town

Queequeg's

Oak St.

Old North Wharf

Straight Wharf

Hussey St.

Centre Street Bistro

DeMarco

Fog Island Café

Cambridge St.

Straight Wharf

India St.

Thurstons Ct.

Black-Eyed Susan's

Rose La.

The Boarding House

The Pearl

Centre St.

The Club Car

Easy St.

Slip 14

Liberty St.

Company of the Cauldron

Arno's

Main St.

Starlight Café

Even Keel Cafe

S. Water St.

Candle St.

Salem St.

New Whale St.

Old South Wharf

Pacific National Bank

Stone Alley

Commercial St.

Commercial Wharf

Three Bricks

Winter St.

Walnut Ln.

Ray's Ct.

Fair St.

Coffin St.

Washington St.

Maria Mitchell Aquarium

Town Pier

Gardner St.

Pleasant St.

Mooers La.

Lucretia Mott La.

Ships Inn

Summer St.

School St.

Martin's La.

Union St.

Washington St. Ext.

5

Starbuck Ct.

Charter St.

Figs at 29 Fair

Plumb La.

Fayette St.

Meader St.

N. Mill St.

High St.

Hiller St.

Darling St.

Tattle Ct.

Farmer St.

Pine St.

Orange St.

Flora St.

Francis St.

New Dollar La.

N. Mill

Candle House La.

Angola St.

Twin St.

Lyons St.

Jefferson La.

Eagle La.

Silver St.

Mulberry St.

Weymouth St.

Fifty-Six Union

Prospect St.

S. Mill St.

Pleasant St.

York St.

W. Dover St.

E. Dover St.

York St.

E. York St.

0   1/4 miles
0   1/4 kilometers

$$ ✕ **DeMarco.** Northern Italian cuisine debuted on-island at this cored-out
ITALIAN   clapboard house in 1980, slightly ahead of the wave. The delights endure:
"badly cut" homemade pasta, for instance, in a sauce of wild mushrooms,
prosciutto, and fresh sage, or luscious lobster cannelloni enrobed in a
corn zabaglione. The time-tested menu must occasionally make way for
a new delight, such as the *gusto de agnello*: lamb two ways (grilled chop,
braised shank), accompanied by pomegranate sauce and saffron cous-
cous. The prevailing aesthetic may be rustic, but the results read as rare
delicacies. ⊠ *9 India St.* ☎ *508/228–1836* ⊕ *www.demarcorestaurant.*
com ⊟ *AE, D, MC, V* ⊘ *Closed Mid-Oct.–late May. No lunch* ✛ *B3.*

$$ ✕ **Dune.** In what is possibly the most restful restaurant setting in town
NEW AMERICAN   (a tucked-away patio outside, sand-tone decor awash in low-key elec-
tronica inside), chef Michael Getter serves well-considered dishes showcasing the local bounty. Entrées range from the delicate seared yellowfin
tuna with panzanella salad to the hearty charred sirloin morsels with
truffle essence and mushroom-smashed Yukon potatoes. For our money,
the ultimate summer dish is the chilled Chatham lobster salad with a
citrus vinaigrette. Come winter, we're coming back for the warm fig
bread-and-butter pudding with toffee sauce. ⊠ *9 India St.* ☎ *508/228–*
5550 ⊕ *www.dunenantucket.com* ⊟ *AE, MC, V* ✛ *B3.*

$ ✕ **Even Keel Cafe.** This former ice-cream parlor, with its tin ceilings and
NEW AMERICAN   pretty backyard patio, is no mere restaurant, but the very heart of
ⓒ   town—the first place to head for a fancy morning coffee or a surprisingly affordable meal. The grilled wild salmon salad with pomegranate
vinaigrette makes for a healthy repast, and the bountiful lobster nachos
invite a communal free-for-all. ⊠ *40 Main St.* ☎ *508/228–1979* ⊕ *www.*
evenkeelcafe.com ⊟ *AE, MC, V* ✛ *B4.*

$$$ ✕ **Fifty-Six Union.** There's a playful spirit at work here, evident from the
NEW AMERICAN   crazily attired mannequin installed at a café table out front. Venture
★   inside and you'll find a city-sophisticated space, with a civilized bar con-
ducive to communal noshing. Inside or out (the lovely garden harbors a
chef's table), Peter Jannelle's cuisine delivers global pizzazz. You'll want
to make a habit of the truffle-Asiago frites, not to mention the mussels
in mild curry broth, and the Javanese spicy fried rice. If this charming
spot were more centrally located (it's about a five-minute walk from
town), you'd have to fight to get in. ⊠ *56 Union St.* ☎ *508/228–6135*
⊕ *www.fiftysixunion.com* ⊟ *AE, MC, V* ⊘ *No lunch* ✛ *D6.*

$$ ✕ **Figs at 29 Fair.** It's a safe bet that you have never chowed down on
MEDITERRANEAN   pizza in a more rarefied setting: a 1709 saltbox retaining its origi-
nal king's wood paneling (so called because the widest trunks were
reserved for the royal navy). Star chef Todd English has built a trans-
continental empire atop his exemplary 'za, and you'll find it here in all
its glory, including the house specialty with prosciutto, Gorgonzola, and
balsamic jam. The thin-crust, ovoid pies tend to outshine the entrées,
though the grilled swordfish (with creamy polenta and lemon-basil vinaigrette) easily holds its own. ⊠ *29 Fair St.* ☎ *508/228–7800* ⊕ *www.*
thesummerhouse.com/29 ⊟ *AE, MC, V* ⊘ *Closed Jan.–mid- May* ✛ *B5.*

¢   ✕ **Fog Island Café.** Cherished year-round for its exceptional breakfasts
AMERICAN   (e.g., pesto scrambled eggs), Fog Island is just as fine a spot for lunch. The
ⓒ   storefront space is cheerily decked out in a fresh country style (echoed

in the friendly service), and chef-owners Mark and Anne Dawson—both Culinary Institute of America grads—seem determined to provide the best possible value to transients and natives alike. ⊠ *7 S. Water St.* ☎ *508/228–1818* ⊕ *www.fogisland.com* ▤ *MC, V* ☯ *No dinner* ✛ *C3.*

$$ ✕ **Languedoc Bistro.** While retaining its Gallic charm and methodology,
FRENCH this lovely auberge-style restaurant, founded in 1975, happily draws on
★ native ingredients. The locally caught wild striped bass, for instance, is accompanied by tempura squash blossoms and carrot beurre blanc. Dining moods are divided into two modes: You can opt for the fairly formal upstairs rooms or the bistro-style conviviality of the cellar. In season, the patio is a lovely place to toy with a salad—or to tackle a decadent, overgenerous dessert, such as a sundae sprinkled with butter crunch. ⊠ *24 Broad St.* ☎ *508/228–2552* ⊕ *www.lelanguedoc.com* ▤ *AE, MC, V* ☯ *Closed Jan.–mid-Apr.* ✛ *B3.*

$$$ ✕ **Lola 41 degrees.** By extending Nantucket's longitude and latitude,
ECLECTIC you'll not only hit on this hit restaurant's name but touch down on
Fodor'sChoice some of the territory that its menu covers. Sushi and sake are special-
★ ties, but so are globe-trotting treats like a chili-fired Spanish shrimp salad, grilled wild salmon with tabbouleh and Greek yogurt sauce, or Maine lobster with morel spaghettini and lemon-chive mascarpone. Everywhere this restaurant ventures is good—especially when it ends up heading south for a killer tres leches cake. The place started out as (and remains) a super-popular watering hole for the chic set. ⊠ *15 S. Beach St.* ☎ *508/325–4001* ⊕ *www.lola41.com* ▤ *AE, MC, V* ☯ *No lunch mid-Apr.–mid-Oct.* ✛ *C2.*

$$$ ✕ **Òran Mór.** Chef-owner Christopher Freeman abandoned the cushy
NEW AMERICAN confines of Topper's at the Wauwinet to strike out on his own at this tasteful little bistro, comprising a trio of butter-yellow rooms accessed via a copper-encased stairway. Though Freeman occasionally errs on the side of nouvelle-cuisine portion control, the innate generosity of a born chef shines through in dishes like crispy Berkshire pork belly with bourbon-caramel glaze, and spiced Peking duck breast with peach-ginger salsa. ⊠ *2 S. Beach St.* ☎ *508/228–8655* ⊕ *www.oranmorbistro. com* ▤ *MC, V* ☯ *Closed Dec.–mid-Apr. No lunch* ✛ *C3.*

$$$ ✕ **The Pearl.** With its white onyx bar illuminated a Curaçao blue and
ASIAN its walls awash in flowing voile, this ultracool space—a sophisticated
★ upstairs cousin to the Boarding House—would seem right at home in South Beach. The cushy white-leather banquettes tucked behind the aquarium are the power seats. Chef-de-cuisine Liam Mackey delivers on executive chef Seth Raynor's enthusiasm for the bold flavors of Asian cuisine, especially in its streetwise guise. You may have a tough time choosing between the beef barbecue with piquant Thai chili-lime sauce and the signature wok-fried lobster—so do yourself a favor and order both. Asian-themed restaurants often disappoint in the dessert round, but not so here. Pace yourself for some esoteric dazzlers such as the mascarpone-and-chèvre cheesecake with cherry syrup and beet sorbet. ⊠ *12 Federal St.* ☎ *508/228–9701* ⊕ *www.boardinghouse-pearl.com* ▤ *AE, MC, V* ☯ *Closed Jan.–Apr. No lunch* ✛ *B3.*

$$ ✕ **Queequeg's.** Though not quite as culinarily refined as some of its com-
NEW AMERICAN parably priced neighbors, this snug little spot—named for an upbeat

Pacific islander in the novel *Moby-Dick*—has the distinction of staying open all day *and* year-round. As options dwindle, its appeal increases. Chef Thomas Walsh, who's also in charge of the adjacent Town, makes a classic haddock chowder and does right by the day's catch. Desserts, an afterthought, are best ignored. ⊠ *6 Oak St.* ☎ *508/325–0992* ⊕ *www.queequegsnantucket.com* ⊟ *AE, MC, V* ⊹ *C3.*

$$$
NEW AMERICAN

✕ **Ships Inn.** Tucked beneath Captain Obed Starbuck's handsome 1831 mansion, this whitewashed hideaway is a cozy candlelit haven where chef Mark Gottwald marries French technique with a California sensibility. If you want to eat healthfully, you can—though the perennial menu faves (grilled Chatham sea scallops with black-truffle hollandaise) tend to the rich end of the spectrum. Don't pass up the specials, as you await the requisite soufflé du jour. Gottwald has a way with lobster: passion-fruit vinaigrette! ⊠ *13 Fair St.* ☎ *508/228–0040* ⊕ *www.shipsinnnantucket.com* ⊟ *AE, D, MC, V* ⊗ *Closed late Oct.–late May. No lunch* ⊹ *B5.*

$$
NEW AMERICAN
★

✕ **Slip 14.** With its picturesque setting at the end of a shell-lined pier flanked by galleries—and bobbing beyond them, yachts—Slip 14 is an ideal spot to while away a summer noon or night. Portions are large, prices fair, presentations festive—and at some point while we were immersed in our mojitos, this popular imbibing spot morphed into an attention-worthy restaurant under the aegis of chef Timothy Thacher-Renshaw. His rioja-braised beef short rib with celery-root purée could not possibly be improved upon; nor could the rhubarb crème brûlée. ⊠ *14 Old South Wharf* ☎ *508/228–2033* ⊕ *www.slip14.com* ⊟ *AE, MC, V* ⊗ *Closed mid-Oct.–mid-May* ⊹ *D4.*

$
AMERICAN
★

✕ **Starlight Café.** This little sidewalk café, spiffed up with cinematic artifacts, is a priceless adjunct to Nantucket's tiny year-round cinema. Not content to offer the best prices in the known Nantucket universe, chef Jeff Weiner stirs in plenty of fun. The perfect topping for five-spiced sashimi tuna? Wasabi-ginger sorbet, of course (prepare to have your mind—and sinuses—blown). And what better way to improve upon a classic crème brûlée than with a surprise cache of "chef's choice" candy? Portions are so generous (especially the massive slab of pepita-encrusted swordfish), you worry for the bistro's bottom line. But wait, there's more: gifted singer-songwriters hold forth in the grapevine-covered arbor. ⊠ *1 N. Union St.* ☎ *508/228–4479* ⊕ *www.starlightnantucket.com* ⊟ *AE, D, MC, V* ⊹ *C3.*

$$$
NEW AMERICAN
Fodor's Choice
★

✕ **Straight Wharf.** This loftlike restaurant with a harborside deck has enjoyed legendary status since the mid-'70s, when chef Marion Morash used to get a helping hand from culinary buddy Julia Child. The young couple now in command—Gabriel Frasca and Amanda Lydon—were fast-rising stars on the Boston restaurant scene, but their approach here is the antithesis of flashy. If anything, they have lent this venerable institution a more-barefoot air, appropriate to the place and season: hurricane lamps lend a soft glow to well-spaced tables lined with butcher paper, and dish towels serve as napkins. Intense champions of local crops and catches, the chefs concoct stellar dishes like island creek oysters with Meyer lemon granita, and line-caught halibut with garlic-chive spaetzle. Their style could be synopsized as simplicity that sings. For a lower-priced preview, explore the menu at the adjoining bar. ⊠ *6 Harbor Sq.* ☎ *508/228–4499* ⊟ *AE, MC, V* ⊗ *Closed mid-Oct.–mid-May* ✢ *D3.*

$$ ✕ **Town.** A sister restaurant to Queequeg's, Town turns toward Asia
ECLECTIC for inspiration. Except for nods to the Southwest (sliders) and Spain (Salamanca salad with cantaloupe and Serrano ham), the menu—like the decor, inside and out—reflects Pacific Rim preferences, from creative sushi to fat noodles in a delicate sake-soy broth to a nicely charred nori-crusted sirloin. This new addition to the dining scene features a few select Indian dishes, including tandoori-spiced lobster—unique on the island so far. ⊠ *4 E. Chestnut St.* ☎ *508/325–8696* ⊕ *www. townnantucket.com* ⊟ *AE, MC, V* ⊗ *No lunch* ✢ *C3.*

OUTSIDE NANTUCKET TOWN

For the location of these restaurants, see the Where to Eat and Stay Outside Nantucket Town map later in the chapter.

¢ ✕ **The Downyflake.** Locals flock to "the Flake" for bountiful breakfasts—
AMERICAN featuring highly prized homemade donuts—and well-priced lunches,
☾ from codfish cakes to burgers. Locals swear that the blueberry pancakes are the best on the island. This spot is easy to find: just look for the giant donut on the facade. ⊠ *18 Sparks Ave.* ☎ *508/228–4533* ⊟ *No credit cards* ⊗ *Closed Feb. and Mar. No dinner.*

$$$$ ✕ **Galley Beach.** A beloved institution since 1958, this cottage on the
NEW AMERICAN Cliffside Beach Club's swath of sand has managed to stay fresh thanks to three generations of congenial restaurateurs. Though chef W. Scott Osif's menu encompasses all sorts of exotic ingredients (miso accompanies the Atlantic halibut, Honshimeji mushrooms the poached lobster), the results tend to be tastefully subdued to suit the crowd; it's rather like country-club cuisine, only with a more elaborate pedigree. Still, the romance-to-price ratio is right—especially if you reserve a table right on the beach, where you can burrow your toes in cool sand. The restaurant, with its gay blue-and-white awning ringed with red geraniums, is perfectly oriented to capture what photographers call "the golden moment" of sunset. ⊠ *54 Jefferson Ave.* ☎ *508/228–9641* ⊕ *www.galleybeach.net* ⊟ *AE, MC, V* ⊗ *Closed mid-Oct.–mid-May.*

$$$ ✕ **SeaGrille.** Though it may lack the flashy profile of other top island
AMERICAN restaurants, this mid-island eatery devoted to all things oceanic deserves
☾ its enduring popularity. The lobster bisque alone, even without the bonus of a dill-flecked pastry bonnet, warrants a following, as does the free-form seafood ravioli and other winning dishes built around house-made pasta. Chef-owner E. J. Harvey is happy to dash off classic fried seafood (his fluffy calamari are state of the art), but he also comes up with creative stunners such as pan-seared salmon with orange salsa and a Parmesan-crusted slab of swordfish. The perfect finale? A light, meringue-topped key lime tart. Off-season, the handsomely appointed dining room is a peaceful haven. ⊠ *45 Sparks Ave.* ☎ *508/325–5700* ⊕ *www.theseagrille.com* ⊟ *AE, MC, V.*

7

WHERE TO STAY

Nantucket has a low profile, so none of the inns or hotels listed has an elevator. Some of the more recently renovated inns have rooms compliant with the Americans with Disabilities Act. Nantucket learned its lesson with the Great Fire of 1846, which is why none of the properties listed permit smoking.

Use the coordinate (✛ B2) at the end of each listing to locate a site on the Where to Stay in Nantucket Town map.

NANTUCKET TOWN

$$$–$$$$ **The Beachside at Nantucket.** Nantucket has only one "motel" in the classic rooms-around-a-pool configuration, and it's a honey—not at all out of place amid its tony neighbors. Located between the town and Jetties Beach (both are within an easy 10-minute walk), the complex ascends to two stories. Rooms—decor is of the cheery wicker-and-florals school—have little terraces separated by whitewashed latticework. Families naturally flock here, but business travelers are equally well served. **Pros:** kids have company; near a safe bay beach; pretty rooms. **Cons:** sounds carry from the pool; not actually beachside. ⊠ *30 N. Beach St.* ☎ *508/228–2241* ⊕ *www.thebeachside.com* ↝ *87 rooms, 3 suites* ⚭ *In-room: a/c, refrigerator, DVD, Internet. In-hotel: pool, gym, some pets allowed* ⊟ *AE, D, DC, MC, V* ⊗ *Closed mid-Oct.–mid-Apr.* ⦿⏐*CP* ✛ *A1.*

$–$$ **Brant Point Inn.** You can't beat the edge-of-town location (Jetties Beach is a 10-minute walk), especially given the modest rates at this cheerful post-and-beam guesthouse. Innkeeper Thea Kaizer grew up in a Nantucket inn; her husband, Peter, leads "catching"—as opposed to just fishing—charters, and he's happy to expedite your haul to the restaurant of your choice. **Pros:** friendly native owners; near town and beaches. **Cons:** on a busy road. ⊠ *6 N. Beach St.* ☎ *508/228–5442* ⊕ *www.brantpointinn.com* ↝ *17 rooms, 2 suites* ⚭ *In-room: a/c (some), kitchen (some)* ⊟ *AE, MC, V* ⦿⏐*CP* ✛ *B2.*

$$$$ **The Cottages & Lofts at the Boat Basin.** Visitors flip out for these weathered-shingle abodes perched on South Wharf amid the yachts—you could reserve a mooring and bring your own boat. Accommodations (including the Woof Cottages, specially kitted out for canine companions) range from studios to three bedrooms. The attractive modern decor adheres to an understated nautical motif: white walls, navy-blue rugs, and polished-pine floors and furniture. All have water views, though they're not always equal—some cottages have picture windows plus a little garden terrace. **Pros:** on the water; marina access; center of town. **Cons:** tourist central; occasional foghorns. ⊠ *New Whale St., Box 1139* ☎ *508/325–1499 or 866/838–9253* ⊕ *www.thecottagesnantucket.com* ↝ *24 cottages, 5 lofts* ⚭ *In-room: kitchen (some), DVD, Wi-Fi. In-hotel: bicycles, some pets allowed* ⊟ *AE, D, DC, MC, V* ⊗ *Closed early Dec.–mid-May* ⦿⏐*BP* ✛ *D4.*

$$$–$$$$ **Jared Coffin House.** The largest house in town when it was built in 1845, this three-story brick manse is still plenty impressive. The antiques-filled parlors are a study in timeless good taste. Rooms vary greatly in terms of size and grandeur (the inn even has some very affordable singles), and all are decorated in a low-key, traditional style. **Pros:**

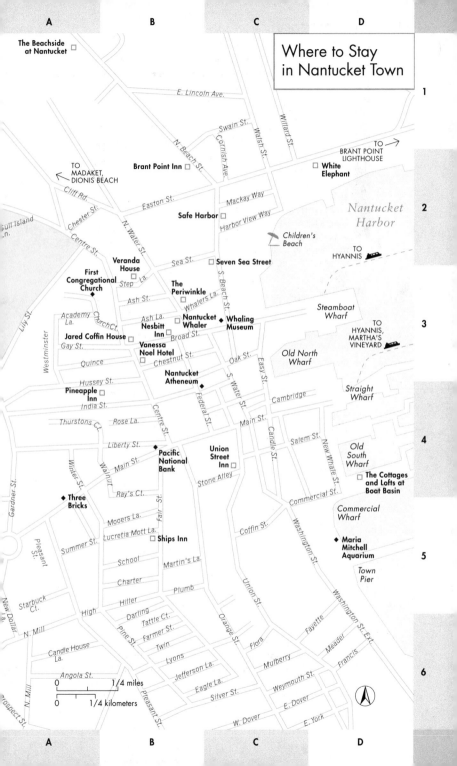

Where to Stay in Nantucket Town

CLOSE UP

Navigating Nantucket's Rental Market

If you're going to be staying for a week or more, you might want to consider renting a cottage or house—an arrangement that gives you a chance to settle in and get a real taste of island living. Many visitors, especially those with children, find renting more relaxing than staying in a hotel or an inn. With your own kitchen, you'll save money by eating in; plus you can enjoy such homey summer pleasures as barbecues. Though decor can vary from chichi to weatherworn, most cottages come equipped with all you'll need to ensure a comfortable stay.

Finding a great cottage or house can be tough, because so many are rented a year or more in advance. The time to start your search is a summer ahead, although you can occasionally find a property as late as spring. Be prepared for sticker shock: prices are about twice what you'd have to pay on Cape Cod. In summer, very rustic (read shabby) rentals start at about $1,500 a week, with waterfront locations commanding a premium.

Information **Country Village Rentals** (✉ *10 Straight Wharf* ☎ *508/228–8840 or 800/599–7368* 🌐 *www.countryvillagere.com*) knows its clientele, who like to flit to sweet spots like Stowe and St. Bart's. **Jordan Real Estate** (✉ *8 Federal St.* ☎ *508/228–4449* 🌐 *www.jordanre.com*) represents a broad range of properties; check the photos lining the storefront windows. The **Maury People** (✉ *37 Main St.* ☎ *508/228–1881* 🌐 *www.maurypeople.com*) boasts the largest rental inventory, including historic and beach homes; service is not only knowledgeable but personable.

knowledgeable concierge; old-money aura. **Cons:** a bit fusty; some tiny rooms; street noise in front. ✉ *29 Broad St., Box 1580* ☎ *508/228–2400* 🌐 *www.jaredcoffinhouse.com* *54 rooms* *In-room: a/c (some), Wi-Fi. In-hotel: restaurant* *AE, D, DC, MC, V* ✥ *B3.*

$$$–$$$$ ★ **Nantucket Whaler.** Let's not mince words: the suites carved out of this 1850 Greek Revival house are gorgeous. Neither Calliope Ligelis nor Randi Ott, the New Yorkers who rescued the place in 1999, had any design experience, but they approached the project as if preparing to welcome friends. Each suite has a private entrance and a kitchen. The spacious bedrooms are lavished with flowers, well-chosen antiques, and plush robes. Couples who have come to explore not so much the island as each other will scarcely have to come up for air. **Pros:** pretty rooms; well appointed; romantic. **Cons:** no common room; the usual in-town noise. ✉ *8 N. Water St., Box 266* ☎ *508/228–6597 or 888/808–6597* 🌐 *www.nantucketwhaler.com* *4 rooms, 6 suites* *In-room: kitchen (some), DVD, Wi-Fi. In-hotel: no kids under 12* *AE, MC, V* *Closed Dec.–Mar.* ✥ *B3.*

¢–$ **Nesbitt Inn.** The last real deal left in town, this homey Victorian has been in the same family since 1914. Fourth-generation proprietors Joanne and Steve Marcoux are so nice, and the rates so reasonable, that you're willing to overlook the shared baths and gently worn furnishings. Here you'll find the authentic, pre-glitz Nantucket. **Pros:** no pretense; true island spirit. **Cons:** busy street; small rooms. ✉ *21 Broad*

St. ☎ *508/228–0156* 🛏 *14 rooms, 3 apartments* ☖ *In-room: a/c (some), Wi-Fi* ▭ *MC, V* ☉ *Closed Jan.–early May* ⍦ *CP* ⚓ *B3.*

$–$$ 🛌 **The Periwinkle.** Sara Shlosser-O'Reilly's B&B (which extends to another house and a Brant Point cottage) has panache. Rooms range from affordable singles to nice-size quarters with canopied beds and harbor views. In one especially pretty setting, the blue-ribbon pattern of the wallpaper matches the cushions and canopy: it's like living in a nicely wrapped gift. **Pros:** central location; heavenly baking aromas; garden for lounging. **Cons:** usual town noises. ✉ *7–9 N. Water St., Box 1816* ☎ *508/228–9267* ⊕ *www.theperiwinkle.com* 🛏 *16 rooms, 1 cottage* ☖ *In-room: a/c, refrigerator, DVD (some), Wi-Fi* ▭ *D, MC, V* ⍦ *CP* ⚓ *B3.*

$$–$$$ 🛌 **Pineapple Inn.** No expense was spared in retrofitting this 1838 Greek
★ Revival captain's house for its new role as pamperer. It's decorated with impeccable taste, with down quilts and marble-finished baths. Breakfast is served in a formal dining room or beside the garden fountain. Whaling captains displayed a pineapple on their stoops upon completion of a successful journey, signaling the neighbors to come celebrate; here that spirit prevails daily—as it does at three in-town sister properties (The Summer House Fair Street, The Summer House India Street, and the 29 Fair Street Inn), comprising 48 rooms all told, operated under the auspices of the splendid Summer House out in 'Sconset—where all guests enjoy full beach and pool privileges. **Pros:** true elegance; quiet location; cushy quarters. **Cons:** some small rooms; communal breakfasts (not everyone's cup of cappuccino). ✉ *10 Hussey St.* ☎ *508/228–9992* ⊕ *www.pineappleinn.com* 🛏 *12 rooms* ☖ *In-room: a/c, Wi-Fi* ▭ *AE, MC, V* ☉ *Closed mid-Dec.–late Apr.* ⍦ *CP* ⚓ *B4.*

$–$$ 🛌 **Safe Harbor.** The name is apt: young ones *and* pets are welcome at
☺ this homey B&B with an enviable location mere steps from Children's Beach. Most of the antique-accoutered rooms have water views; some have private decks. Everyone's welcome to sit on the wide front porch and enjoy the ocean breezes. Innkeeper Michael Kopko—who's a town selectman and thus knows everyone and everything—outdoes himself daily in the art of creative muffinry. **Pros:** family-friendly; well cared for. **Cons:** noise from Children's Beach; boat-launch traffic. ✉ *2 Harborview Way* ☎ *508/228–3222* ⊕ *www.beesknees.net/safeharbor* 🛏 *5 rooms* ☖ *In-room: a/c, Wi-Fi. In-hotel: some pets allowed* ▭ *AE, MC, V* ☉ *Closed Jan.–mid-Apr.* ⍦ *CP* ⚓ *C2.*

$$–$$$ 🛌 **Seven Sea Street Inn.** If this red-oak post-and-beam B&B looks awfully well preserved, that's because it was custom-built in 1987. Decked out in Early American style (decorative stenciling, fishnet-canopy beds, braided rugs), it offers the ambience of antiquity without all the creaky drawbacks. The deluxe suite, with its cathedral ceiling, full kitchen, gas fireplace, and harbor view, warrants a leisurely stay. Two satellite buildings up your odds of booking a room. **Pros:** quiet side street; central location; handsome decor. **Cons:** some rooms smallish. ✉ *7 Sea St.* ☎ *508/228–3577* ⊕ *www.sevenseastreetinn.com* 🛏 *13 rooms, 2 suites* ☖ *In-room: a/c, refrigerator, DVD, Wi-Fi. In-hotel: some pets allowed, no kids under 5* ▭ *AE, D, MC, V* ⍦ *CP* ⚓ *C2.*

$$ 🛌 **Ships Inn.** This 1831 home exudes history: it was built for whal-
★ ing captain Obed Starbuck on the site of the birthplace of abolitionist

Lucretia Mott. Guest rooms, named for the ships Starbuck commanded, are furnished with period antiques and pretty wallpapers. In the basement is a restaurant of the same name (delighted murmurings waft up), which generates a wonderful Continental breakfast and afternoon tea. **Pros:** large rooms; handsome decor. **Cons:** on busy street. ⊠ *13 Fair St.* 🕾 *508/228–0040* ⊕ *www.shipsinnantucket.com* ⤳ *10 rooms.* ⚐ *In-room: a/c, refrigerator. In-hotel: restaurant, bar, no kids under 8* ▤ *AE, D, MC, V* ☺ *Closed late Oct.–late May* ❏ *CP* ✛ *B5.*

$$$–$$$$
Fodor's Choice
★

🏨 **Union Street Inn.** Ken Withrow worked in the hotel business, Deborah Withrow in high-end retail display, and guests get the best of both worlds. This 1770 house, a stone's throw from the bustle of Main Street, has been respectfully yet lavishly restored. Guests are treated to Frette linens, plump duvets, and lush robes (the better to lounge around in, my dear), as well as a full gourmet breakfast served on the tree-shaded garden patio—or in bed. Several rooms have that ultimate accessory for rekindling romance: a wood-burning fireplace. **Pros:** pampering by pros; pervasive good taste. **Cons:** bustle of town; some small rooms. ⊠ *7 Union St.* 🕾 *508/228–9222* ⊕ *www.unioninn.com* ⤳ *12 rooms* ⚐ *In-room: a/c, Wi-Fi. In-hotel: no kids under 12* ▤ *AE, MC, V* ❏ *BP* ✛ *C4.*

$$$–$$$$
🏨 **Vanessa Noel Hotel.** Shoe designer—and island summerer—Vanessa Noel's namesake hotel is a living catalog of trendy decor: each of the eight rooms in this 1847 house (some admittedly as small as shoe boxes) boasts Armani Casa bedside tables, Philippe Starck bathroom fixtures, Frette linens, and Bulgari toiletries. Though the concept might seem at odds with the island aesthetic, you'd be hard-pressed to name a hotel with these touches outside a metropolis. Distinguished by its grass window boxes, it features milk-painted walls, hemp shower curtains, and ayurvedic body products. Rooms in the latter are slightly less pricey. **Pros:** centrally located; glamour quotient. **Cons:** street noise. ⊠ *5 Chestnut St., at Centre St.* 🕾 *508/228–5300* ⊕ *www.vanessanoelhotel.com* ⤳ *18 rooms* ⚐ *In-room: a/c, Wi-Fi. In-hotel: bar, no kids under 12.* ▤ *AE, D, MC, V* ✛ *B3.*

$$$–$$$$
🏨 **Veranda House.** A fixture since the early 1880s, this lodging has tiers of balconies taking in the sweeping harbor vistas. The exterior may look unchanged, but the rooms got a makeover that introduced Frette linens, Simon Pearce lamps, Italian-tile rainfall showers, and the like. The buffet breakfasts are equally lush, featuring fresh-baked pastries and artisanal cheeses, and conviviality is encouraged via afternoon tea and biweekly wine-and-cheese receptions. A thoughtful "beach concierge" service means you don't have to tote your own towels, chairs, and umbrellas. A trio of less insistently stylish cottages is available for families with children. **Pros:** central but quiet location; impeccable condition. **Cons:** decor a bit garish (for Nantucket); pricey (though not for Nantucket). ⊠ *3 Step La., Box 1112* 🕾 *508/228–0695* ⊕ *www. theverandahouse.com* ⤳ *14 rooms, 4 suites* ⚐ *In-room: DVD, Wi-Fi. In-hotel: no kids under 10 (in inn rooms)* ▤ *AE, D, MC, V* ☺ *Closed late Oct.–mid-May* ❏ *CP* ✛ *B3.*

$$$$
🏨 **White Elephant.** The White Elephant, a 1920s behemoth right on Nantucket Harbor, seems determined to keep raising the bar in service and style. The complex—a main building plus a cluster of cottages with

breezy country-chic decor—hugs the harbor, leaving just enough room for a sweep of emerald lawn and the veranda of the hotel's in-house restaurant, the Brant Point Grill. Prices are lofty but, for the echelon it attracts, not all that extreme. The afternoon port-and-cheese reception offers a chance to hobnob. **Pros:** on the harbor; elegant design. **Cons:** can be snooty; expensive. ⊠ *50 Easton St., Box 1139* ☎ *508/228–2500* ⊕ *www.whiteelephanthotel.com* ⤴ *22 rooms, 31 suites, 11 cottages* ☒ *In-room: a/c, safe, refrigerator, DVD, Wi-Fi. In-hotel: restaurant, room service, bar, gym, spa, laundry service* ☐ *AE, D, DC, MC, V* ☾ *Closed early Dec.–late Apr.* ⦿ *BP* ✛ *D2.*

OUTSIDE NANTUCKET TOWN

For the location of these lodgings, see the Where to Eat and Stay Outside Nantucket Town map later in the chapter.

$$$$ **Cliffside Beach Club.** Which way to the beach? You're on it: this snazzily updated 1920s beach club stakes its claim with a flotilla of colorful umbrellas—somewhat miffing natives, who consider sand rights anathema. Local politics aside, this is one prime chunk of gentle bay beach, and the complex makes the most of its site, with a gorgeous cathedral-ceiling lobby decorated with hanging quilts, and rooms of every size and shape enhanced by island-made modern furnishings. Best of all, the fine restaurant Galley Beach serves as de facto concession stand. **Pros:** on beach; good restaurant. **Cons:** overentitled guests. ⊠ *46 Jefferson Ave., Box 449* ☎ *508/228–0618* ⊕ *www.cliffsidebeach.com* ⤴ *21 rooms, 4 suites, 1 apartment, 1 cottage* ☒ *In-room: safe, kitchen (some), refrigerator, DVD, Wi-Fi. In-hotel: restaurant, bar, pools, gym, beachfront* ☐ *AE* ☾ *Closed Nov.–May* ⦿ *CP.*

¢ **Robert B. Johnson Memorial Hostel.** One of the country's most picturesque hostels, this Hostelling International facility occupies a former 1873 lifesaving station—known as "The Star of the Sea"—right on Surfside Beach, a 3½-mi ride from town on the bike path (or via shuttle). Dorm rooms come in male, female, and coed configurations; the five-bed private room, which is wheelchair-accessible, tends to book quickly. Common areas include a kitchen, where a complimentary breakfast is offered. There's no lockout (customary at many urban hostels) and—huzzah—no curfew. Reservations are always a good idea, and essential in high season. **Pros:** super-cheap; on Nantucket's best beach. **Cons:** little privacy; no frills. ⊠ *31 Western Ave.* ☎ *508/228–0433* ⊕ *www. capecod.hiusa.org* ⤴ *44 dorm-style beds, 1 room* ☒ *In-room: no a/c, no phone, no TV. In-hotel: Wi-Fi hotspot, no kids under 18* ☐ *MC, V* ☾ *Closed late Sept.–late May* ⦿ *CP.*

NIGHTLIFE AND THE ARTS

Other than in-season charity galas and year-round community fundraisers (islanders look out for their own), the phrase "Nantucket nightlife" verges on oxymoronic. If it's glitz and nonstop action you're after, better stick to the mainland. On the other hand, if you like live music, you will rarely go wanting.

For listings of events, see the *Inquirer and Mirror* (⊕ *www.ack.net*), the *Nantucket Independent* (⊕ *www.nantucketindependent.com*), and

Yesterday's Island (⊕ *www.yesterdaysisland.com*). Also invaluable for up-to-the-minute events listings: Gene Mahon's blog, "Mahon about Town" (⊕ *www.mahonabouttown.wordpress.com*).

FILM

The **Nantucket Film Festival** (☎ *508/325–6274* ⊕ *www.nantucket-filmfestival.org*), held each June, emphasizes the importance of strong scripts. The final playlist—about two dozen short and feature-length films—always includes a few world premieres, and many selections have gone on to considerable commercial success. Shows tend to sell out, so it's best to buy online, well ahead.

The **Starlight Theatre** (✉ *1 N. Union St.* ☎ *508/228–4435* ⊕ *www. starlightnantucket.com*) is a small screening room appended to a café of the same name. It presents two shows nightly in season, plus rainy-day matinees.

MUSIC

The **Nantucket Island Academy of Music** (✉ *62 Centre St.* ☎ *No phone* ⊕ *www.niamusic.com*), led by internationally acclaimed soprano Greta Feeney, offers classes and mounts concerts.

Founded in 1959, **Nantucket Musical Arts Society** (☎ *508/228–1287*) mounts concerts—mostly classical, occasionally jazz—by internationally acclaimed musicians at the First Congregational Church Tuesday evenings at 8:30 July through August.

The **Nantucket School of Music** (✉ *11 Centre St.* ☎ *508/228–3352* ⊕ *www. ackmusic.com*), chaired by cellist Mollie Glazer, arranges classes and concerts featuring domestic and imported talent; choristers of all levels are welcome.

The **Noonday Concert Series** (✉ *Unitarian Universalist Church, 11 Orange St.* ☎ *508/228–5466*), Thursday at noon in July and August, brings in visiting performers and also showcases outstanding local musicians. Concerts range from bluegrass to classical.

BARS AND CLUBS

At the White Elephant's **Brant Point Grill** (✉ *50 Easton St.* ☎ *508/325–1320 or 800/445–6574* ⊕ *www.brantpointgrill.com*), the patrons are patently moneyed and the setting is country-elegant. A jazz-standards soloist or combo provides atmosphere (and takes requests).

The **Chicken Box** (*The Box*✉ *14 Dave St.* ☎ *508/228–9717*) rocks! Live music—including some big-name bands—plays six nights a week in season, and weekends throughout the year.

The **Club Car Lounge** (✉ *1 Main St.* ☎ *508/228–1101*) is an actual club car, salvaged from the narrow-gauge railroad that once served 'Sconset. These days it makes a convivial piano bar, where requests and sing-alongs are encouraged.

At **Galley Beach** (✉ *54 Jefferson Ave., at Cliffside Beach* ☎ *508/228–9641*) you can sip mojitos among a moneyed throng as piano riffs mix with the rhythm of gentle surf.

At **Lola 41** (⊠ *15 Beach St.* ☎ *508/ 325–4001* ⊕ *www.lola41.com*) gorgeously maintained socialites and their consorts socialize over sake and sushi.

The **Muse** (⊠ *44 Surfside Rd.* ☎ *508/ 228–6873* ⊕ *www.muse.com*) hosts bands (including the occasional big-name act) year-round. The crowd— the barnlike space can accommodate nearly 400—can get pretty wild.

Cineastes and sociable sorts claim the bar stools and patio tables at the **Starlight Café** (⊠ *1 N. Union St.* ☎ *508/228–4479*), which adjoins the Starlight Theatre; singer-songwriters serenade in season.

THEATER

Theatre Workshop of Nantucket (⊠ *Methodist Church, 2 Centre St.* ☎ *508/228–4305* ⊕ *www.theatreworkshop.com*), a community theater founded in 1956, stages plays, musicals, and readings year-round.

> ### MICHELANGELO ON THE BEACH
>
> Buddhas, dragons, mermaids, and, of course, whales invade Jetties Beach during the annual Sandcastle & Sculpture Day in mid-August. Creative concoctions such as porpoises, submarines, spaceships, flowers, and the famous lightship baskets—creatively crafted out of sand, shells, seaweed, and even beach litter—contend for prizes. Anyone can stake out a patch of sand, though registration is required if you're digging to win: forms are available at the Nantucket Chamber of Commerce office, at Zero Main Street.

BEACHES, SPORTS, AND THE OUTDOORS

BEACHES

A calm area by the harbor, **Children's Beach** (⊠ *Off Harbor View Way*) is within blocks of the center of town and a perfect spot for small children. The beach has a grassy park with benches, a playground, lifeguards, a café, picnic tables, showers, and restrooms. The Nantucket Park & Recreation Commission puts on free Thursday and Sunday evening concerts and offers tie-dyeing classes Friday at noon mid-July through August.

Cisco Beach (⊠ *Hummock Pond Rd., South Shore*) has heavy surf and lifeguards, but no food or restrooms. It's not easy to get to or from Nantucket Town: it's 4 mi from town and there are no bike paths, so you'll have to ride in the road, walk, drive, or take a taxi. Also, the dunes are severely eroded, so getting down onto the beach can be difficult. Still, the waves make it a popular spot for surfers.

Dionis Beach (⊠ *Eel Point Rd.*) is, at its entrance, a narrow strip of sand that turns into a wider, more private strand with high dunes and fewer children. The beach has a rocky bottom and calm, rolling waters; there are lifeguards on duty and restrooms with showers. Take the Madaket Bike Path to Eel Point Road, about 3 mi west of town.

★ A short bike- or shuttle-bus ride from town, **Jetties Beach** (⊠ *Bathing Beach Rd., 1½ mi northwest of Straight Wharf*) is a popular family beach because of its calm surf, lifeguards, bathhouse, restrooms, and snack bar. It's a good place to try out water toys: kayaks, sailboards, and Day Sailers are rented in summer. On shore it's a lively scene, with playground and volleyball nets on the beach and adjacent public tennis courts. There is a boardwalk to the beach (special wheelchairs are available). You'll have a good view of passing ferries—and an even better one if you clamber out on the jetty itself (careful, it's slippery).

Madaket Beach (⊠ *Off Madaket Rd., Madaket*) can be reached by shuttle bus from Nantucket Town or the Madaket Bike Path (5 mi from Upper Main Street); it has lifeguards and restrooms, and a small market and casual restaurant are located nearby. Madaket is known for challenging surf (beware of the rip currents: should you get swept away, swim parallel to shore until the pull abates) and unbeatable sunsets.

Fodor'sChoice ★ **Surfside Beach** (⊠ *Surfside Rd., South Shore*), accessible via the Surfside Bike Path (3 mi) or shuttle bus, is the island's most popular surf beach. This wide strand of sand comes fully equipped—with lifeguards, restrooms and showers, a snack bar, and beach wheelchairs. It draws teens and young adults as well as families and is great for kite flying and, after 5 PM, surf casting.

BICYCLING

The best way to tour Nantucket is by bicycle. Nearly 30 mi of paved bike paths wind through all types of terrain from one end of the island to the other: for details, consult the maps posted by Wheels, Heels, and Pedals (⊕ *www.wheelsheelsandpedals.com*), which supports alternative modes of transportation. It is possible to bike around the entire island in a day—should you tire, you and your bike are welcome aboard the in-season Nantucket Regional Transit Authority (NRTA) buses. The main bike routes start within ½ mi of town (warning: that first stretch can be dauntingly congested). All of them are well marked and lead—eventually—to popular beaches. The paths are also perfect for runners and bladers—but not mopeds, which must remain on the road (to the frustration of impatient drivers). Note that Nantucket requires bike riders 12 and under to wear a helmet.

The easy 3-mi **Surfside Bike Path** leads to Surfside, the island's premier ocean beach. A drinking fountain and rest stop are placed at about the halfway point.

The **Milestone Bike Path**, a straight shot linking Nantucket Town and 'Sconset, is probably the most monotonous of the paths but can still be quite pleasant. It's about 7 mi; paired with the scenic Polpis Path, it becomes a 16-mi island loop.

At 1.2 mi, the **Cliff Road Path**, on the north shore, is one of the easiest bike paths, but it's still quite scenic, with gentle hills. It intersects with the Eel Point and Madaket paths.

The **Eel Point/Dionis Beach Path** starts at the junction of Eel Point Road and Madaket Road and links the Cliff Road and Madaket bike paths to Dionis Beach. It's less than a mile long.

The 9-mi **Polpis Road Path**. skirts scenic bays and bogs as it wends its way toward 'Sconset; it intersects with Milestone Path east of the rotary.

The **Madaket Path** starts at the intersection of Quaker and Upper Main Street and follows Madaket Road out to Madaket Beach on the island's west end, about 6 mi from the edge of Nantucket Town. About one-third of the way, you could turn off onto Cliff Road Path or the Eel Point/Dionis Beach Path.

BIKE SHOPS **Island Bike & Sport** (⊠ *25 Old South Rd.* ☎ *508/228–4070* ⊕ *www. islandbike.com*), though located mid-island, offers free delivery.

Nantucket Bike Shop (⊠ *4 Broad St., Steamboat Wharf* ⊠ *Straight Wharf* ☎ *508/228–1999 or 800/770-3088 for both locations* ⊕ *www. nantucketbikeshop.com*), open April through October, rents bicycles and mopeds (not only perilous on Nantucket's sandy, bumpy roadways, but anathema to locals, so don't be surprised if you get some dirty looks). Ask about free delivery and pickup.

Young's Bicycle Shop (⊠ *6 Broad St., Steamboat Wharf* ☎ *508/228–1151* ⊕ *www.youngsbicycleshop.com*), established in 1931, rents bicycles, including tandems and children's equipment; weekly rates are available. Knowledgeable third-generational Harvey Young and staff will send you off with everything you need—an excellent touring map, a helmet, a quaint little Portuguese handlebar basket—*and* offer roadside assistance in case of mishap (or overconfidence regarding one's skills and/or endurance).

BIRD-WATCHING

Hundreds of species flock to the island's moors, meadows, and marshes over the course of a year. Birds that are rare in other parts of New England thrive here, because of the lack of predators and the abundance of wide-open, undeveloped space (currently about 60% of the island). Almost anywhere outside town you're sure to see interesting birdlife, not just in migratory season but year-round. Set up your spotting scope near the salt marsh at Eel Point any time of year and you're bound to see shorebirds feeding—low tide is the best time. Endangered piping plovers and least terns nest on the ocean side in spring. Folger's Marsh, about 3 mi east of town, and the Harbor Flats, at the end of Washington Street on the eastern edge of town, are also good shorebird-watching sites. Inland, a walk through Sanford Farm from Madaket Road to the south shore, traversing upland, forest, heath, and shore habitats, will bring you in range of Savannah sparrows, yellow warblers, osprey, and red-tailed hawks, the island's most common raptor. Be on the lookout for the protected Northern harrier. For woodland species, check out the trails through Windswept Cranberry Bog or the Masquetuck Reservation near Polpis Harbor.

Eco Guides: Strong Wings (⊠ *9 Nobadeer Farm Rd.* ☎ *508/228–1769* ⊕ *www. strongwings.org*) leads birders on hikes, bike rides, or casual strolls.

The **Maria Mitchell Association** (*MMA* ⊠ *4 Vestal St.* ☎ *508/228–0898* ⊕ *www.mmo.org*) leads marine-ecology field trips and nature and bird walks in season.

BOATING

In July and August, Nantucket is *the* place to study, close up, some of the world's most splendid yachts—and the well-to-do people who own and sail them. Don't be surprised if you see yachts with piggyback motor launches, automobiles, and helicopters. Some spend only a few days here, perhaps en route from the Mediterranean or the Caribbean. If you don't happen to own a floating palace, you can still hit the water—Nantucket has plenty of boat charters, rentals, and scenic cruises.

☾ ★ The **Endeavor** (✉ *Slip 1015, Straight Wharf* ☎ *508/228–5585* ⊕ *www. endeavorsailing.com*), a charter replica Friendship sloop, makes four 1½-hour trips into the sound daily in season (including a sunset cruise). Private charters and special themed trips for children can be arranged.

Nantucket Community Sailing (✉ *4 Winter St.* ☎ *508/228–6600* ⊕ *www. nantucketcommunitysailing.org*) rents Sunfish sailboats, sailboards, and kayaks at Jetties Beach (Memorial Day to Labor Day); it also has youth and adult instructional sailing programs, as well as adaptive water-sport clinics for disabled athletes. NCS's Outrigger Canoe Club—a Polynesian tradition—heads out several evenings a week (depending on interest) in season.

Sea Nantucket (✉ *Washington St. Ext., ¼ mi southeast of Commercial Wharf* ☎ *508/228–7499* ⊕ *www.seanantucketkayak.com*) rents kayaks and small sailboats by the hour or half day at the vest-pocket Francis Street Beach; they'll also deliver to the embarkation point of your choosing.

Shearwater Excursions (✉ *Slip 1011, Straight Wharf* ☎ *508/228–7037* ⊕ *www.explorenantucket.com*) mounts ecotours aboard a 50-foot power catamaran. One year-round option is a 2½-hour trip to view Muskeget Island's thousands of resident gray seals. Whale watches, which take six hours, head out thrice weekly in season: Captain Blair Perkins guarantees a sighting, which means that if no sea mammals show up, you can go again for free.

FISHING

Surf fishing is very popular on Nantucket, especially in late spring when bluefish are running (the best place to go after them is Great Point). Freshwater fishing is also an option at many area ponds.

A permit is required for shellfishing, specifically foraging for littleneck and cherrystone clams, quahogs, scallops, oysters, steamers, and mussels. You can pick one up—along with tips on where and how to get the best catch—**at the Marine and Coastal Resources Department** (✉ *34 Washington St.* ☎ *508/228–7261*).

Captain Peter Kaizer, a former commercial fisherman (and off-duty innkeeper), guarantees a good catch aboard the **Althea K** (☎ *508/228–3471* ⊕ *www.altheaksportfishing.com*); he also offers whale-watching and charter cruises.

Captain Tom's Charters (✉ *Public Landing, Madaket* ☎ *508/228–4225* ⊕ *www.captaintomscharters.com*) win consistent "best of" awards for Tom Mleczko's hands-on expertise. Choose among rips, bars, surf, open water, and flats (the latter for the added challenge of sight fishing with fly rods).

FITNESS CLUBS

The Nantucket Health Club (✉ *10 Young's Way* ☎ *508/228–4750* ⊕ *www. nantuckethealthclub.com*) has StairMasters, Lifecycles, treadmills, rowers, Airdyne bikes, New Generation Nautilus, and free weights; aerobics, Spinning, and yoga classes; and personal trainers. You can get a short-term pass—day, week, or month—that covers the machines plus fitness classes (with the exception of Spinning).

HIKING

Nantucket has 82 mi of beaches, and though almost 97% of the shoreline is privately owned, it's a point of pride that nearly all of it is open for public use. Distinctive ecosystems on the island include hardwood forests, salt marshes, cranberry bogs, freshwater ponds, and coastal heathlands, and sand-plain grassland (together with nearby Tuckernuck Island and Martha's Vineyard, the island holds more than 90% of the acreage of the rare latter category *worldwide*). The island is home to a huge number of deer; significant colonies of harbor seals, gray seals, and harbor porpoises; and turtles, frogs, rabbits, voles, and other reptiles and small field mammals.

Nearly all of the 8,900 acres maintained by the **Nantucket Conservation Foundation** (⌧ *118 Cliff Rd.* ☎ *508/228–2884* ⊕ *www. nantucketconservation.com*) are open to the public; though only a few trails are marked, you can feel free to wander knowing that you can't get lost—if you keep going in one direction, you're bound to hit a road or a beach eventually. The foundation, open weekdays 8 AM to 5 PM, puts out maps and informative brochures on the most popular hiking spots. Be aware that ticks and the attendant threat of Lyme and other tick-borne diseases are a serious problem here.

A 5- to 10-minute bike ride from Nantucket Town on the way to Madaket, the **Sanford Farm, Ram Pasture, and the Woods** (⌧ *Madaket Rd. between Milford and Cliff Rds.*) comprises 300 acres that were saved from developers by the Nantucket Conservation Foundation in 1971. The southern edge of the property borders the ocean.

The **Tupancy Links** (⌧ *165 Cliff Rd., 1¼ mi west of town*) runs between the Cliff Road bike path and Nantucket Sound. It's a smaller property that passes mainly through grassland populated by plants like false heather, oxeye daisy, and Queen Anne's lace, and it provides wonderful views once you reach the overlook at the water's edge.

SHOPPING

The historic center of town doubles as the commercial district: shops are concentrated primarily in the grid formed by Main, Centre, Broad, and Easy streets, with a few shops trailing off along the periphery. The former boathouses of Straight Wharf and Old South Wharf, retrofitted as shops and galleries, also attract well-heeled browsers. The necessities of island life—hardware, office supplies, etc.—tend to be clustered mid-island, where new stores offering nonessentials are gradually making inroads as well.

Most of Nantucket's shops are seasonal, opening in time for the Daffodil Festival in late April and closing soon after Christmas Stroll in early December; a hardy few stay open year-round and often offer rather astounding bargains off-season. On summer weekends, many shops stay open late (until 9 or 10). Most galleries hold their openings on Friday evening.

ANTIQUES

In business since 1974, **Lynda Willauer Antiques** (✉ *2 India St.* ☎ *508/228–3631* ⊕ *www.lyndawillauerantiques.com*) has amassed a stellar cache of American and English furniture, plus fine collectibles, including Chinese export porcelain and majolica.

★ **Nantucket Country** (✉ *38 Centre St.* ☎ *508/228–8868* ⊕ *www.nantucketcountryantiques.com*) has an especially rich inventory of quilts and flags; another specialty—in addition to maritime and "Nantucketiana," such as artifacts related to artist Tony Sarg—is antique children's toys.

Nantucket House Antiques (✉ *2 S. Beach St.* ☎ *508/228–4604* ⊕ *www.nantuckethouse.com*) displays a wealth of well-chosen artifacts, in inspired aggregations; the owners are interior decorators.

> **PETTICOAT ROW**
>
> During the whaling era—a time when women were generally considered better seen than heard—a large portion of the Centre Street shops in town were almost completely run by female merchants. The area is known to this day as Petticoat Row. Women have always played a strong role in Nantucket's history, partly because of the Quaker philosophy of gender equality and partly because on whaling expeditions men could be gone for years at a time. They became leaders in every arena, from religion to business.

Nina Hellman Marine Antiques & Americana (✉ *48 Centre St.* ☎ *508/228–4677* ⊕ *www.nauticalnantucket.com*) carries scrimshaw, whaling artifacts, ship models, instruments, and other marine antiques, plus folk art and Nantucket memorabilia. Charles Manghis, a contemporary scrimshaw artist, demonstrates and exhibits his craft here.

Fodor's Choice ★ **Rafael Osona Auctions** (✉ *American Legion Hall, 21 Washington St.* ☎ *508/228–3942* ⊕ *www.rafaelosonaauction.com*) holds auctions of fine antiques most Saturday mornings from Memorial Day weekend to early December; the items—furniture, decorative accessories, art, jewelry, and more—are previewable two days in advance.

Established in 1927, **Sylvia Antiques** (✉ *15 Main St.* ☎ *508/228–0960* ⊕ *www.sylviaantiques.com*) retains the richest stash of island-related antiquities.

ART GALLERIES

The **Artists' Association of Nantucket** (✉ *19 Washington St.* ☎ *508/228–0772* ⊕ *www.nantucketarts.org*) is the best place to get an overview of the work being done on-island; many members have galleries of their own.

The **Gallery at Four India** (✉ *4 India St.* ☎ *508/228–8509* ⊕ *www.galleryatfourindia.com*) is a quiet, spacious refuge, with highly sought-after American and marine paintings dating from the 1850s to 1940s, plus a small sampling of contemporary realism.

Quidley & Company (✉ *26 Main St.* ☎ *508/228–4300* ⊕ *www.quidleyandco.com*) specializes in high-end marine art.

★ The **South Wharf Gallery** (✉ *3 India St.* ☎ *508/228–0406* ⊕ *www.southwharfgallery.com*) has been showing top local work since 1978.

Nantucket Reds

Bermuda has its shorts, Fiji its sarongs. Nantucket's totemic clothing items are made of cotton dyed red so as to fade to a dull salmon shade. The reds were something of a secret code until they were singled out by *The Official Preppy Handbook* in 1980: "By their pink shirts ye shall know them" might be the watchwords for Nantucketers among the worldwide sailing community.

Now reds are as site-specific as Martha's Vineyard's Black Dog line (attempting to compete, in vain, with a satellite shop on Straight Wharf).

The principal purveyor of Nantucket reds is Murray's Toggery Shop on Main Street, which has catered to conservative dressers since the early 1900s. (Roland Macy worked here at his father's shop in the early 1800s before setting off to rewrite retailing history.) From baby togs to tote bags, you'll find everything you could want here in the way of reds. But for that weathered look that sets them off so well, you'll have to get out on the water.

BOOKS

Check the Nantucket Room at the back of **Mitchell's Book Corner** (⊠ *54 Main St.* ☎ *508/228–1080* ⊕ *www.mitchellsbookcorner.com*) for regional titles. The front is filled with an astute sampling covering a broad range of categories.

Nantucket Bookworks (⊠ *25 Broad St.* ☎ *508/228–4000* ⊕ *www. nantucketbookworks.com*) carries an extensive inventory, with an emphasis on literary works and Nantucket-specific titles, as well as children's books and gift items.

CLOTHING

Cheryl Fudge Designs (⊠ *23 Federal St.* ☎ *508/228–9860* ⊕ *www. cherylfudge.com*) makes one-off updates of vintage clothing (such as Hermes scarves revamped as wrap pants).

★ **Current Vintage** (⊠ *4 Easy St.* ☎ *508/228–5073* ⊕ *www.currentvintage-nantucket.com*) offers an unusual (perhaps unique) blend of inventory: vintage designer clothing *and* wine. Consider it one-stop shopping for the well-dressed oenophile.

Eye of the Needle (⊠ *14 Federal St.* ☎ *508/228–1923*) is a microcosm of urban fashion trends, playfully leavened.

The splashy resort wear that Lilly Pulitzer introduced in the '60s is enshrined at **In the Pink** (⊠ *5 S. Water St.* ☎ *508/228–0569* ⊕ *www. lillyshop.com*).

Murray's Toggery Shop (⊠ *62 Main St.* ☎ *508/228–0437* ⊕ *www. nantucketreds.com*) can claim credit for introducing the signature "Nantucket reds"—now available in a range of styles for men, women, and children.

Something about the Nantucket lifestyle prompts hat hunger. **Peter Beaton** (⊠ *16½ Federal St.* ☎ *508/228–8456* ⊕ *www.peterbeaton.com*) shows an international array of beauties, all customizable with special trim.

Summering designer Vanessa Noel (✉ *5 Chestnut St.* ☎ *508/228–5300* ⊕ *www.vanessanoel.com*) creates ultraglam shoes—they're expensive, to be sure, but fans gladly toe the line.

Island loyalties might be tested, but the **Vineyard Vines** (✉ *2 Harbor Sq.* ☎ *508/325–9600* ⊕ *www.vineyardvines.com*) line—from flip-flops to bathing trunks, not to mention the ties that started it all—is just so irresistibly preppy, resistance is futile.

Fodor's Choice ★ The inviting windows of **Vis-a-Vis** (✉ *34 Main St.* ☎ *508/228–5527* ⊕ *www.visavisnantucket.com*) display relaxed-luxe women's fashions amid antique home furnishings, some of which, including hooked rugs, quilts, and collectibles, are also for sale.

CRAFTS

Claire Murray (✉ *16 Federal St.* ☎ *508/228–1913 or 800/252–4733* ⊕ *www.clairemurray.com*) carries the designer's Nantucket-themed and other hand-hooked rugs and rug kits, quilts, and knitting and needlework kits.

Erica Wilson Needle Works (✉ *25 Main St.* ☎ *508/228–9881* ⊕ *www.ericawilson.com*) embodies the enthusiasms of the famous British-born designer, an island resident since 1958. In addition to her own embroidery and needlepoint kits, the store carries winning clothing and accessories for women.

The **Four Winds Craft Guild/Sylvia Antiques** (✉ *15 Main St.* ☎ *508/228–9623* ⊕ *www.sylviaantiques.com*) has showcased local folk arts, including scrimshaw and lightship baskets (old and new), ship models, and duck decoys, since 1927.

★ **Nantucket Looms** (✉ *51 Main St.* ☎ *508/228–1908* ⊕ *www.nantucketlooms.com*) stocks luscious woven-on-the-premises textiles and chunky Susan Lister Locke jewelry, among other adornments for self and home.

JEWELRY

Diana Kim England, Goldsmiths (✉ *56 Main St.* ☎ *508/228–3766* ⊕ *www.dianakimengland.com*) has created an elegant contemporary line featuring unusual gems such as tourmaline, chalcedony, and tanzanite.

The **Golden Basket** (✉ *18B Federal St.* ☎ *508/582–8205* ⊕ *www.thegoldenbasket.com*) was founded in 1977 by designer Glenaan M. Elliott, who fashioned the first miniature lightship basket. Other popular motifs include starfish and shells.

Jola Jewelry Designs (✉ *29 Centre St.* ☎ *508/325–6999*) is a jewel box—the tiny, lovely atelier of Polish-born goldsmith Jolanta Gutnik, who creates "passionate statements" using unusual stones and rare pearls.

Little Miss Drama (✉ *12 Old South Wharf* ☎ *508/325–1937*) is the brainchild of actress Pamela Diem Willis, who fashions fun, funky pieces out of chunky semiprecious stones.

Trianon/Seaman Schepps (✉ *47 Main St.* ☎ *508/325–5806* ⊕ *www.seamanschepps.com*) carries contemporary work—including some pieces incorporating Nantucket shells and sand—as well as the mostly nature-motif Seaman Schepps line, established in 1904.

MARKETS

★ **Bartlett's Farm** (✉ *33 Bartlett Farm Rd.* ☎ *508/228–9403* ⊕ *www. bartlettsoceanviewfarm.com*) encompasses 100 acres overseen by eighth-generation Bartletts. Healthy, tasty prepared foods—within a mini-supermarket—add incentive to visit. If you're not up for the trek, a produce truck is parked on Main Street through the summer.

"**Sconset Market** (✉ *4 Main St.* ☎ *508/228–9915*), though strictly seasonal, is well stocked with basics and gourmet comestibles alike.

TOYS

Carrying plenty of its namesake items in various sizes and shapes, the **Toy Boat** (✉ *41 Straight Wharf* ☎ *508/228–4552* ⊕ *www.thetoyboat. com*) also sells other high-quality toys for youngsters, including Nantucket mermaids, and children's books based on local themes (look for Joan Aiken's classic *Nightbirds on Nantucket*).

WINE

Leslie-Ann Sheppard stocks **The Cellar** (✉ *1 Windy Way* ☎ *508/228– 9123* ⊕ *www.thecellarnantucket.com*) with personal picks priced modestly and on up—way up. You can sample the wares at free Saturday afternoon tastings.

The miniconglomerate of **Cisco Brewers, Nantucket Vineyard, and Triple Eight Distillery** (✉ *5 Bartlett Farm Rd.* ☎ *508/325–5929* ⊕ *www. ciscobrewers.com*) makes boutique beers, wine, and vodka on-site.

7

SIASCONSET AND WAUWINET

★ *7 mi east of Nantucket Town.*

First a fishing outpost and then an artists' colony (Broadway actors flocked here, starting in the late 19th century), Siasconset—or 'Sconset, in the local vernacular—is a charming cluster of rose-covered cottages linked by driveways of crushed clamshells; at the edges of town, the former fishing shacks give way to magnificent sea-view mansions. The small town center consists of a market, post office, café, lunchroom, and liquor store–cum–lending library.

The tiny settlement of Wauwinet, a few miles north, is a hamlet of beach houses on the northeastern end of Nantucket. But early European settlers found the neck of sand above it to be the easiest way to get to the ocean for fishing. Instead of rowing around Great Point, fishermen would go to the head of the harbor and haul their dories over the narrow strip of sand and beach grass separating Nantucket Harbor from the ocean. Hence the name for that strip: the haulover.

EXPLORING

Altar Rock. Altar Rock Road, a dirt track about 3 mi west of the Milestone Road Rotary on Polpis Road, leads to the island's highest point, Altar Rock (elevation 101 feet), from which the view is spectacular. The hill overlooks approximately 4,000 acres of coastal heathland (a rare habitat) laced with paths leading in every direction.

Nantucket Shipwreck & Lifesaving Museum. This replica 1874 Life Saving Service showcases the island's maritime history—including the stories of hundreds of lives saved in an era when a foundering ship nearly always meant certain death. The collection includes original rescue equipment and boats, artifacts recovered from the *Andrea Doria* wreck, and photos and accounts of daring rescues. ⊠ *158 Polpis Rd., Siasconset* ☎ *508/228–2505* ⊕ *www.nantucketshipwreck.org* ⬚ *$5* ☉ *Mid-May–mid-Oct., daily 10–4.*

Sankaty Head Lighthouse. This red-and-white-striped beacon overlooking the ever-encroaching sea on one side and the Scottish-looking links of the private Sankaty Head Golf Club on the other was rescued—i.e., moved—from the brink in 2007. It's not open to the public. ⊠ *Baxter Rd., Siasconset.*

QUICK BITES
For a great picnic in 'Sconset, stop at **Claudette's** (⊠ *Post Office Sq., Siasconset* ☎ *508/257–6622*) for a box lunch to go, or dig right in on the shady patio. It's open mid-May through mid-October.

Sesachacha Pond. This kettle pond (pronounced *Sah*-kah-cha) off Polpis Road is a good spot for bird-watching. It's circled by a walking path that leads to an Audubon wildlife area and is separated from the ocean by a narrow strand on its east side. The vantage point from the pond provides a good view of Sankaty Head Lighthouse.

Siasconset Casino. Despite its name, this property dating to 1899 has never been a gambling site—the meaning of casino was broader back when it was built—but was instead used from the beginning as a theater venue, particularly during the actors'-colony heyday, and as a gathering place. The casino serves primarily as a private tennis club and as an informal movie house open to the public. ⊠ *New St., Siasconset* ☎ *508/257–6661* ⊕ *www.sconsetcasino.com.*

Windswept Cranberry Bog. Throughout the year, the 105-acre conservation area off Polpis Road is a beautiful tapestry of greens, reds, and golds—and a popular hangout for many bird species. The bog is especially vibrant in mid-October, when the cranberries are harvested amid a festival with hayrides, bog tours, and cranberry product samples. A map is available from the **Nantucket Conservation Foundation** (⊠ *118 Cliff Rd., Nantucket Town* ☎ *508/228–2884* ⊕ *www.nantucketconservation.com*).

WHERE TO EAT

$$$
NEW AMERICAN ✗ **The Chanticleer.** A beloved institution for several decades, this rose-covered landmark has benefited from the new reign of owner Susan Handy (of Black-Eyed Susan's in town). The setting and service remain as elegant as ever, but chef Jeff Worster's haute-brasserie menu is looser and livelier. World-cuisine elements seep in—the ginger aioli jazzing up a "cocktail" of mango and lobster—but solid French technique supports the expert execution of such classics as a local flounder meunière. The outdoor tables, tucked beneath flowery pergolas, remain the most coveted perch. ⊠ *9 New St., Siasconset* ☎ *508/257–4499* ⊕ *www.thechanticleer.net* ▭ *AE, MC, V* ☉ *Closed mid-Oct.–late May.*

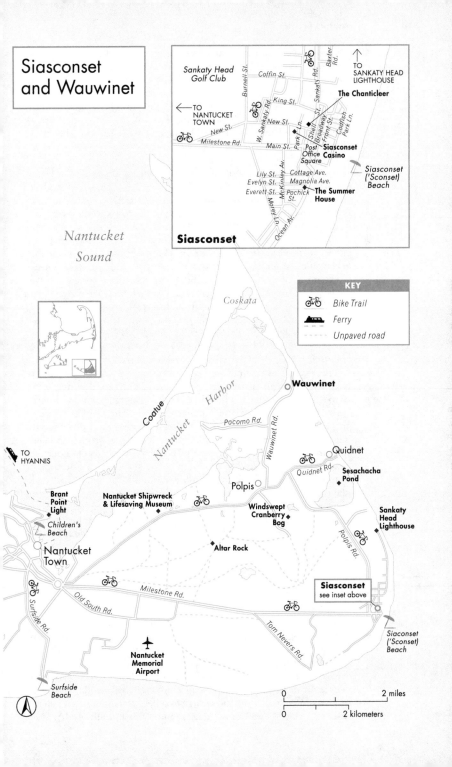

Siasconset and Wauwinet

Siasconset

Sankaty Head Golf Club

Coffin St.

Burnell St.

Sankaty Rd.

Baxter Rd.

↑ TO SANKATY HEAD LIGHTHOUSE

King St.

The Chanticleer

← TO NANTUCKET TOWN

W. Sankaty Rd.

New St.

New St.

Milestone Rd.

Main St.

Park Ln.

Shell St.

Broadway

Front St.

Codfish Park Ln.

Siasconset Casino

Post Office Square

Lily St.

Evelyn St.

Everett St.

McKinley Av.

Cottage Ave.

Magnolia Ave.

Pochick St.

Morey Ln.

Ocean Av.

The Summer House

Siasconset ('Sconset) Beach

Nantucket Sound

KEY

🚲 *Bike Trail*

⛴ *Ferry*

--- *Unpaved road*

Coskata

Harbor

Wauwinet

Coatue

Pocomo Rd.

Wauwinet Rd.

Nantucket

Quidnet

Quidnet Rd.

Sesachacha Pond

TO HYANNIS

Brant Point Light

Nantucket Shipwreck & Lifesaving Museum

Children's Beach

Polpis

Windswept Cranberry Bog

Nantucket Town

Surfside Rd.

Old South Rd.

Milestone Rd.

Altar Rock

Polpis Rd.

Sankaty Head Lighthouse

Siasconset see inset above

Tom Nevers Rd.

Siasconset ('Sconset) Beach

Nantucket Memorial Airport

Surfside Beach

0   2 miles

0   2 kilometers

$$ ✕ **Sconset Cafe.** This tiny, tasteful restaurant at the Sconset Rotary is so
AMERICAN low key you'd swear it was a private club. Owner Cindy Nelson looks
★ after each of the guests (mostly loyalist locals) as solicitously as any
dinner party hostess; her husband, Rolf, turns out superb cuisine from
a kitchen possibly smaller than yours at home. Every dish dazzles, from
a refreshing salad of watermelon and feta with mint to a perfectly—
which is to say, barely—seared slab of salmon with a lemon-vodka glaze,
plunked atop gaudy beet and goat cheese risotto. The café—a hand-
some retreat in beachy beige with exuberant black-and-white photos—is
also a prime breakfast spot. The Nelsons make what has got to be the
world's best granola. ⊠ *8 Main St., Siasconset* ☎ *508/257–4008* ⊕ *www.
sconsetcafe.com* ⊟ *No credit cards* ⊘ *Closed late Sept.–late May.*

$$ ✕ **The Summer House.** An integral element of the rose-canopied complex
NEW AMERICAN of shingled shacks that epitomizes 'Sconset, the Summer House's main
★ dining room is awash in white wicker and exuberant floral displays;
pianist Jamie Howarth keeps the mood buoyant. As the latest star chef
in residence, Todd English has kept his more playful leanings in check:
the menu is on the staid side, as befits the audience (spotted one evening: three generations sporting a rainbow of Izods). It's in the gorgeous
Beachside Bistro down below that the fun stuff is stashed: exemplary
fried clams (whole-bellied, of course) and a swell trio of tacos. Throw
in a moonrise and you've got one magical night. ⊠ *17 Ocean Ave., Siasconset* ☎ *508/257–9976* ⊕ *www.thesummerhouse.com* ⌂ *Reservations
essential* ⊟ *MC, V* ⊘ *Closed mid-Oct.–mid-May.*

$$$$ ✕ **Topper's.** The Wauwinet—a lavishly restored 19th-century inn on
NEW AMERICAN Nantucket's northeastern shore—is where islanders and visitors alike
★ go to experience utmost luxury. Many take advantage of the *Wauwinet
Lady* (a complimentary launch docked at the White Elephant, a sister
property) to frame the journey with a scenic harbor tour; jitney service
is also offered. In a creamy-white dining room awash with lush linens
and glorious flowers, Chef David Daniel presents exquisite bouchées
underscored by Rothko-like swaths of rarefied sauces. The prices might
seem almost reasonable were it not for portions that tend to tapas scale
(the rigatoni with house-cured pork belly, though delectable, consists
of about five bites). But you can always fill up on the bread basket
(featuring luscious brown bread) and follow up with an exquisite, if
minuscule, dessert. ⊠ *120 Wauwinet Rd., Wauwinet* ☎ *508/228–8768*
⊕ *www.toppersrestaurant.com* ⌂ *Reservations essential* ⊟ *AE, D, DC,
MC, V* ⊘ *Closed Nov.–Apr.*

WHERE TO STAY

$$$–$$$$ ⌂ **The Summer House.** Perched on a bluff overlooking 'Sconset Beach, this
Fodor'sChoice cluster of rose-covered cottages—cobbled from salvage in the 1840s—
★ epitomizes Nantucket's enduring allure. The rooms, though small, are
intensely romantic, with lace coverlets and pale pine armoires; most have
marble baths with whirlpool tubs, and one has a fireplace. Contempla-
tive sorts can claim an Adirondack chair on the lawn. Others may want
to race down to the beach, perhaps enjoying lunch beside the heated
pool en route. **Pros:** romantic setting; excellent restaurants; pool on the
beach. **Cons:** cottages can be snug; sounds of restaurant revelry. ⊠ *17*

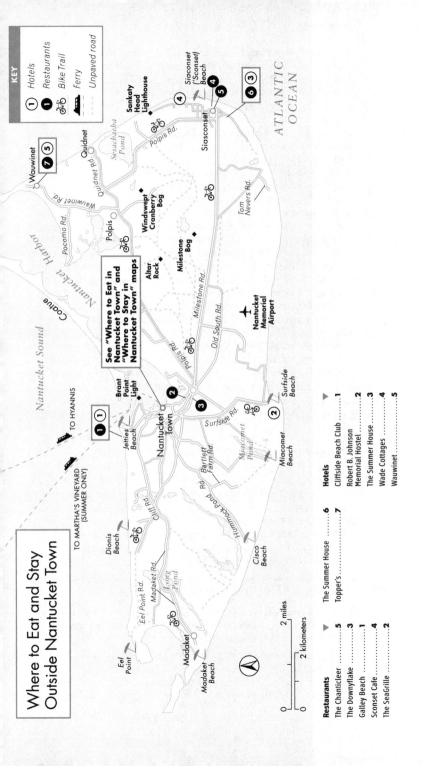

Where to Eat and Stay
Outside Nantucket Town

Nantucket Sound

TO HYANNIS

TO MARTHA'S VINEYARD
(SUMMER ONLY)

Coatue

Nantucket Harbor

Jetties Beach

Dionis Beach

Eel Point

Eel Point Rd.

Madaket Rd.

Cliff Rd.

Long Pond

Madaket

Madaket Beach

Cisco Beach

Hummock Pond

Bartlett Farm Rd.

Miacomet Pond

Miacomet Beach

Cisco Beach

Brant Point Light

Nantucket Town

See "Where to Eat in Nantucket Town" and "Where to Stay in Nantucket Town" maps

Surfside Rd.

Polpis Rd.

Old South Rd.

Nantucket Memorial Airport

Surfside Beach

Altar Rock

Milestone Bog

Milestone Rd.

Windswept Cranberry Bog

Polpis

Pocomo Rd.

Quidnet Rd.

Quidnet

Wauwinet Rd.

Wauwinet

Sesachacha Pond

Polpis Rd.

Tom Nevers Rd.

Sankaty Head Lighthouse

Siasconset ('Sconset)

Siasconset

Siasconset ('Sconset) Beach

ATLANTIC OCEAN

KEY

- **1** Hotels
- **1** Restaurants
- 🚲 Bike Trail
- ⛴ Ferry
- - - - Unpaved road

0 — 2 miles
0 — 2 kilometers

Restaurants ▶

The Chanticleer	**5**
The Downyflake	**3**
Galley Beach	**1**
Sconset Cafe	**4**
The SeaGrille	**2**
The Summer House	**6**
Topper's	**7**

Hotels ▶

Cliffside Beach Club	**1**
Robert B. Johnson Memorial Hostel	**2**
The Summer House	**3**
Wade Cottages	**4**
Wauwinet	**5**

Ocean Ave., Siasconset ☎ 508/257–4577 ⊕ www.thesummerhouse.com
➦ 10 rooms ☖ In-room: a/c, Wi-Fi. In-hotel: 2 restaurants, bars, pool,
beachfront ▤ AE, MC, V ☺ Closed Nov.–late Apr. ▮◎▮ CP.

$$–$$$ ▧ **Wade Cottages.** This 'Sconset complex of apartments, and cottages
☺   couldn't be better situated for beach aficionados. The buildings, in the
same family since the 1920s, are arranged around a central lawn with a
great ocean view. Furnishings tend to be of the somewhat worn beach-
house school, but you'll be too busy—and happy—to waste a moment
critiquing. **Pros:** dazzling view; great for families. **Cons:** more family-
oriented than romantic. ⊠ *Shell St., Siasconset ☎ 508/257–6308 ⊕ www.*
wadecottages.com ➦ 5 apartments, 1 cottage ☖ In-room: no a/c. In-hotel:
laundry facilities ▤ AE, MC, V ☺ Closed mid-Oct.–late May ▮◎▮ CP.

$$$$ ▧ **The Wauwinet.** This resplendently updated 1850 resort straddles a
Fodor's Choice   "haulover" poised between ocean and bay—which means beaches
★   on both sides. Head out by complimentary van or launch to partake
of utmost pampering (the staff-to-guest ratio exceeds one-on-one).
Optional activities include sailing, water-taxiing to a private beach
along Coatue, and touring the Great Point nature preserve by Land
Rover. Of course, it's tempting just to stay put, what with the cushy
country-chic rooms (lavished with Pratesi linens) and a splendid restaurant, Topper's. **Pros:** solicitous staff; dual beaches; peaceful setting.
Cons: distance from town; overly chichi. ⊠ *120 Wauwinet Rd., Wau-*
winet ☎ 508/228–0145 ⊕ www.wauwinet.com ➦ 32 rooms, 5 cottages
☖ In-room: a/c, safe, DVD, Wi-Fi. In-hotel: restaurant, room service,
bar, tennis courts, spa, beachfront, water sports, bicycles, no kids under
12 ▤ AE, DC, MC, V ☺ Closed Nov.–Apr. ▮◎▮ BP.

NIGHTLIFE AND THE ARTS

THE ARTS

The **Siasconset Casino** (⊠ *New St., Siasconset ☎ 508/257–6661*) shows
first-run movies, auditorium-style, Tuesday, Thursday, and Sunday evenings at 8:30, June through Labor Day. Old hands know to bring pillows to cushion the folding chairs.

NIGHTLIFE

The bar at the **Summer House** (⊠ *17 Ocean Ave., Siasconset ☎ 508/257–*
9976) is hands down the most romantic spot for a cocktail on-island.
Pianist Jamie Howarth entertains devotees, who cluster around the bar
or claim comfortable armchairs.

BEACHES, SPORTS, AND THE OUTDOORS

Siasconset Beach (⊠ *End of Milestone Rd., Siasconset*) has a lifeguard
(the surf runs moderate to heavy) but no facilities; restaurants and
restrooms are in the nearby village.

The 6.5-mi **Sconset Bike Path** starts at the rotary east of Nantucket Town
and parallels Milestone Road, ending in 'Sconset. It is mostly level, with
some gentle hills. Slightly longer (and dippier) the 9-mi Polpis Road
Path, veering off to the northeast, is far more scenic and leads to the
turnoff to Wauwinet.

Travel Smart Cape Cod, Nantucket & Martha's Vineyard

WORD OF MOUTH

"As a lover of visiting Martha's Vineyard year round, I can vouch for the beauty of the fall season on the island. The crowds have departed, the weather is (generally) temperate, restaurants and shops are open, and the natural beauty of the island is most enjoyable. Unless you wish to sun and swim, the only things unlikely in the fall; many consider it the very best time to visit the Cape and the Islands. And, it's entirely possible early October will allow for swimming."

— portiaperu

GETTING HERE AND AROUND

▮ AIR TRAVEL

Most long-distance travelers visiting Cape Cod head to a major gateway, such as Boston or Providence, Rhode Island, and then rent a car to explore the region. Flying time to Boston or Providence is 1 hour from New York, 2½ hours from Chicago, 6 hours from Los Angeles, and 3½ hours from Dallas.

Boston's Logan International Airport is one of the nation's most important domestic and international airports, with direct flights from all over North America and Europe (as well as other continents). Providence's efficient T.F. Green Airport receives very few international flights (mostly from Canada), but offers a wide range of direct domestic flights to East Coast and Midwest destinations; it serves the western United States to a lesser extent. Discount carrier Southwest also flies out of Providence, which helps keep fares down.

Another option is connecting from a major airport to one of the two airports on the Cape, the most popular being Barnstable Municipal Airport in Hyannis, which has direct service to Boston, Providence, and New York (LaGuardia), as well as to Martha's Vineyard and Nantucket. The other, Provincetown Airport, has direct flights to Boston. Flying to either of these smaller airports can be costly, especially during busy times in summer, but it can also save you plenty of time. There are also numerous flights to Nantucket and Martha's Vineyard from Hyannis, Boston, New Bedford, and Providence, and you can fly between Nantucket and Martha's Vineyard as well.

Airlines and Airports Airline and Airport Links.com (⊕ www.airlineandairportlinks.com) has links to many of the world's airlines and airports.

Airline-Security Issues Transportation Security Administration (⊕ www.tsa.gov) has answers for almost every question that might come up.

AIRPORTS

The major gateways to Cape Cod are Boston's Logan International Airport (BOS) and Providence's T.F. Green Airport (PVD). Smaller airports include the Barnstable (HYA), Martha's Vineyard (MVY), Nantucket (ACK), New Bedford (EWB), and Provincetown (PVC) municipal airports.

Airport Information Airline and Airport Links.com (⊕ www.airlineandairportlinks.com) has links to many of the world's airlines and airports. Boston: **Logan International Airport** (☏ 617/561–1806 or 800/235–6426 ⊕ www.massport.com/logan). Hyannis: **Barnstable Municipal Airport** (☏ 508/775–2020 ⊕ www.town.barnstable.ma.us). Martha's Vineyard: **Martha's Vineyard Airport** (☏ 508/693–7022 ⊕ www.mvyairport.com). Nantucket: **Nantucket Memorial Airport** (☏ 508/325–5300 ⊕ www.nantucketairport.com). New Bedford: **New Bedford Regional Airport** (☏ 508/991–6161 ⊕ www.newbedford-ma.gov). Providence: **T.F. Green Airport** (☏ 401/691–2471 ⊕ www.pvdairport.com). Provincetown: **Provincetown Airport** (☏ 508/487–0241 ⊕ www.provincetown-ma.gov).

TRANSFERS BETWEEN AIRPORTS

Cape Destinations, White Tie Limousines, and Limos to Logan provide chartered limo service from Boston and Providence to the Cape; call ahead for reservations. Rates vary greatly, depending on your Cape destination, which airport you're flying into, and what kind of car or van you book.

Limousine Agencies Cape Destinations (☏ 866/760–2555 ⊕ www.capedestinations.com). **Limos to Logan** (☏ 508/771–1000 ⊕ www.capecodlimo.com). **White Tie Limousines** (☏ 508/548–1066 ⊕ www.whitetielimo.com).

FLIGHTS

All of the nation's major airlines—as well as many international airlines—serve Boston's Logan International Airport, and all major national carriers serve Providence. Hyannis's Barnstable Municipal Airport is serviced by US Airways Express (with service to Boston and NYC's LaGuardia), Nantucket Airlines, Island Airlines, and Nantucket Shuttle (all with service to Nantucket), and Cape Air (with service to Boston, Providence, Nantucket, and Martha's Vineyard); Provincetown Airport is serviced by Cape Air (with service to Boston).

Smaller Airlines **Cape Air** (☎ 508/771–6944 or 866/227–3247 ⊕ www.flycapeair.com). **Island Airlines** (☎ 508/228–7575 or 800/248–7779 ⊕ www.islandair.net). **Nantucket Airlines** (☎ 508/228–6234 or 800/635–8787 ⊕ www.nantucketairlines.com).**Nantucket Shuttle Airlines** (☎ 508/771–2711 ⊕ www.nantucketshuttle.net) **US Airways Express** (☎ 800/428–4322 ⊕ www.usairways.com).

▌ BIKE TRAVEL

Biking is very popular on Cape Cod and the islands, which have an abundance of excellent bike trails, some of them as busy as the region's roads in summer. Note that Massachusetts law requires children under 13 to wear protective helmets while riding a bike, even as a passenger. *For information on trails, maps, and rentals, see listings for specific towns.*

Bike Maps **Rubel Bike Maps** (✉ Box 401035, Cambridge, MA ⊕ www.bikemaps.com).

▌ BOAT AND FERRY TRAVEL

Ferries are a great way to get from the mainland to Provincetown, Martha's Vineyard, and Nantucket. There are also some interisland ferries available. All ferry companies provide parking lots where you can leave your car for $10 to $15 per night. With recent rising fuel costs, many carriers have instituted additional fees; expect to pay an extra $3–$5 over the cost of the actual ticket.

FERRIES TO PROVINCETOWN

Bay State Cruise Company offers both standard and high-speed ferry service between Commonwealth Pier in Boston and MacMillan Wharf in Provincetown. High-speed service runs a few times daily from late May through mid-October and costs $79 round-trip; the ride takes 90 minutes. Slower service runs Saturday only from late June through early September and costs $44 round-trip; the ride takes three hours. On either ferry, the round-trip charge for bikes is $12.

Boston Harbor Cruises also offers high-speed service several times daily from mid-June to early September, with more-limited service mid-May to mid-June and early September to mid-October. Rates are $79 round-trip and $12 for bikes.

Capt. John Boats runs a seasonal ferry between Plymouth and Provincetown, with daily service from late June through early September and weekend service from mid-June. The boat departs from State Pier (near the *Mayflower II*) in Plymouth and docks at MacMillan Wharf in Provincetown. The trip takes approximately 90 minutes. A round-trip ticket costs $40, and bikes cost $5.

Boat and Ferry Lines **Bay State Cruise Company** (☎ 877/783–3779 ⊕ www.baystatecruisecompany.com). **Boston Harbor Cruises** (☎ 617/227–4321 or 877/733–9425 ⊕ www.bostonharborcruises.com). **Capt. John Boats** (☎ 508/747–2400 or 800/225–4000 ⊕ www.provincetownferry.com).

FERRIES TO MARTHA'S VINEYARD

The Steamship Authority runs the only car ferries, which make the 45-minute trip from Woods Hole to Vineyard Haven year-round and to Oak Bluffs from late May through mid-October. There are several runs per day, but fewer during the off-season. In summer and on autumn weekends, you *must* have a reservation if you want to bring your car (passenger reservations are never necessary). You should make car reservations as far ahead as possible; in season the reservations office is open daily 8 AM to 5 PM, with extended phone hours in summer and during busy times from 7 AM to 9 PM. You can also make car reservations online. One-way passenger fare year-round is $7.50; bicycles are $3. The one-way cost for a car in season (April–October) is $67.50; off-season, cars cost $42.50.

The *Island Queen* makes the 35-minute trip from Falmouth Harbor to Oak Bluffs from late May through early October. Ferries run multiple times a day from mid-June through early September, with less frequent (but still daily) service in spring and fall; call for schedules. Round-trip fare is $18; bikes are $6. Only cash and traveler's checks are accepted for payment.

The Vineyard Fast Ferry offers high-speed passenger service from North Kingstown, Rhode Island (just a half hour south of Providence and a half hour northwest of Newport) to Martha's Vineyard. The ride takes 95 minutes, making this a great option for those flying in to T.F. Green Airport, just south of Providence. Service runs from late May through early October and costs $49 each way ($7 for bikes).

Hy-Line offers both high-speed and conventional ferry service from Hyannis. The conventional ferries offer a 95-minute run from Hyannis to Oak Bluffs late May to mid-October. One-way fare is $21.50; bicycles cost $6. The high-speed runs from May through October, takes 55 minutes, and costs $36 each way; it costs $6 for bikes. The parking lot fills up in summer, so call to reserve a parking space in high season. From June to mid-September, Hy-Line's Around the Sound cruise makes a one-day round-trip from Hyannis with stops at Nantucket and Martha's Vineyard ($79.50). For interisland travel, Hy-Line operates a daily ferry from mid-June to mid-September. The 70-minute trip between Oak Bluffs and Nantucket costs $34 one-way and $6 for bikes.

The New England Fast Ferry Company makes the hour-long trip by high-speed catamaran from New Bedford to Oak Bluffs and Vineyard Haven from mid-May to late November several times daily (less frequently in spring and fall). One-way is $36, and bicycles are $6.

Boat and Ferry Information Hy-Line (☎ 508/778–2600 or 800/492–8082 ⊕ www.hylinecruises.com). **Island Queen** (☎ 508/548–4800 ⊕ www.islandqueen.com). **New England Fast Ferry** (☎ 866/683–3779 ⊕ www.nefastferry.com). **Steamship Authority** (☎ 508/477–8600 information and car reservations, 508/693–9130 on the Vineyard ⊕ www.steamshipauthority.com). **Vineyard Fast Ferry** (☎ 401/295–4040 ⊕ www.vineyardfastferry.com).

FERRIES TO NANTUCKET

The Steamship Authority runs car-and-passenger ferries from Hyannis to Nantucket year-round, a 2¼-hour trip. There's also high-speed passenger ferry service, which takes only an hour, from late March through late December. One-way passenger fare is $16.50, and bicycles are $6. Cost for a car traveling one-way April through October is $190, November through March, $130. One-way high-speed passenger ferry fare is $32.50, with bicycles $6.

Hy-Line's high-end, high-speed *Grey Lady* ferries run between Hyannis and Nantucket year-round in an hour. Such speed has its downside in rough seas—lots of bucking and rolling that some find nauseating. Seating ranges from benches on the upper deck to airline-like seats in side rows of the cabin to café-style tables and chairs in the cabin front. Make reservations in advance, particularly during the summer months or for holiday travel. One-way fare is $39, and bicycles are $6.

Hy-Line's slower ferry makes the roughly two-hour trip from Hyannis between late May and mid-October. The M/V *Great Point* offers a first-class section ($28 one-way) with a private lounge, restrooms, upholstered seats, carpeting, complimentary Continental breakfast or afternoon cheese and crackers, a bar, and a snack bar. Standard one-way fare is $21.50, and bicycles are $6.

From Harwich Port, the Freedom Cruise Line runs express high-speed 75-minute ferries to Nantucket between early June and late September, allowing you to explore the rose-covered isle without having to brave the crowds of Hyannis. Another plus is that for day trips to Nantucket, parking is free. Round-trip fare is $70 ($39 one-way), $12 for bikes. Sightseeing and seal cruises are also offered daily.

Boat and Ferry Information Freedom Cruise Line (☎ *508/432–8999* ⊕ *www. nantucketislandferry.com*). **Hy-Line** (☎ *508/778–2600 or 800/492–8082* ⊕ *www. hylinecruises.com*). **Steamship Authority** (☎ *508/477–8600 or 508/495–3278* ⊕ *www. steamshipauthority.com*).

▌ BUS TRAVEL

ON CAPE COD

Traveling to Cape Cod by bus is doable, but only if you're planning on arriving at your destination and staying there. A car is a must in most parts of the Cape. The one exception is Provincetown, where the streets are narrow, parking is a hassle, and all the sights are within walking distance.

Local beach shuttles and trolleys are a great option when you don't want to pay for beach parking or you'd just rather leave your car at your hotel.

The Cape Cod Regional Transit Authority operates several bus services that link Cape towns. All buses are wheelchair-accessible and equipped with bike racks. The SeaLine runs along Route 28 Monday through Saturday between Hyannis and Woods Hole (one-way fare $3.50 from Hyannis to Woods Hole; shorter trips cost less), with stops including Mashpee Commons, Falmouth, and the Woods Hole Steamship Authority docks.

The SeaLine connects in Hyannis with the Plymouth & Brockton line as well as the Barnstable Villager, another bus line that runs along Route 132 between Hyannis and Barnstable Harbor, stopping at the Cape Cod Mall. It also connects with the Hyannis Villager, which runs through Hyannis. The driver will stop when signaled along the route.

The H2O Line offers daily regularly scheduled service year-round between Hyannis and Orleans along Route 28. The Hyannis–Orleans fare is $3.50; shorter trips are less. Buses connect in Hyannis with the SeaLine, the Barnstable Villager, and Plymouth & Brockton lines.

The b-bus is composed of a fleet of minivans that will transport passengers door to door between any towns on the Cape. You must register in advance to use the b-bus service (you also pay in advance); phone the Cape Cod Regional Transit Authority 11 AM to 5 PM on weekdays to sign up. After you are enrolled, call for reservations from 8 to 5 on weekdays; reservations may be made up to a week in advance. Service runs seven days a week, year-round. The cost is $3 per ride plus 10¢ per mile.

The Flex bus runs between Harwich Port and Truro (from which free transfers are available to Provincetown, late May through mid-October), with stops in Brewster, Orleans, Eastham, and Wellfleet. All one-way fares are $2, and buses run Monday to Saturday year-round.

The Cape Cod Regional Transit Authority also runs the seasonal trolleys in Falmouth, Mashpee, Hyannis, Yarmouth, and Dennis. Fares and times vary.

On the Outer Cape, Cape Cod Regional Transit Authority's Provincetown Shuttle serves North Truro and Provincetown daily from late May through mid-October, with more-limited service in late fall and early spring, and no service in winter. The route begins at Dutra's Market in Truro and continues to Provincetown along Route 6A; it stops wherever a passenger or roadside flagger dictates. Once in Provincetown, the shuttle continues up Bradford Street, with alternating trips to Herring Cove Beach and Pilgrim Park as well as summertime service up to Provincetown Airport and Race Point Beach. It runs every 20 minutes and is outfitted to carry bicycles. The service is popular and reasonably priced ($2 for a single fare, $6 for a day pass).

ON NANTUCKET AND MARTHA'S VINEYARD

Traffic can be brutal on Nantucket and Martha's Vineyard, but both have excellent bus systems. Most visitors won't need a car at all; buses are frequent enough and cost so little that convenience far outweighs the trouble and cost of bringing your own car. The big buses of the Martha's Vineyard Transit Authority (VTA) provide regular service to all six towns on the island, with frequent stops in peak season and quite limited service in winter. The fare is $1 per town, including the town of departure. One-day ($6), three-day ($15), and one-week ($25) passes can be purchased on the bus and at Steamship Authority terminals.

The Nantucket Regional Transit Authority (NRTA) runs shuttle buses in town and to Madaket, mid-island areas (including the airport, 'Sconset, Surfside Beach, and Jetties Beach). Service is available late May to early September. Fares are $1 to $2, depending on the route. Passes cost $7 for one-day, $12 for three days, and $20 for one week.

Bus Information Cape Cod Regional Transit Authority (☎ 508/790–2613 or 800/352–7155 ⊕ www.capecodtransit.org). **Martha's Vineyard Transit Authority** (☎ 508/693–9440 ⊕ www.vineyardtransit.com). **Nantucket Regional Transit Authority** (☎ 508/228–7025 ⊕ www.shuttlenantucket.com). **Plymouth & Brockton Street Railway** (☎ 508/746–0378 ⊕ www.p-b.com).

BUS TRAVEL TO AND FROM CAPE COD

From Boston, Peter Pan Bus Lines serves Bourne, Falmouth, and Woods Hole. The Plymouth & Brockton Street Railway buses travel all the way to Provincetown from Boston and Logan International Airport, with stops en route at a number of towns throughout the Cape, including Plymouth, Sagamore, Barnstable, Hyannis, Orleans, Eastham, Wellfleet, and Truro.

Bus Information Peter Pan Bus Lines (☎ 508/548–7588 or 888/751–8800 ⊕ www.peterpanbus.com). **Plymouth & Brockton Street Railway** (☎ 508/746–0378 ⊕ www.p-b.com).

■ CAR TRAVEL

ON CAPE COD

To reach Cape Cod from Boston (60 mi), take Interstate 93 south, then Route 3 south, and cross the Sagamore Bridge, which puts you onto U.S. 6, the Cape's main artery, leading toward Hyannis and Provincetown. From western Massachusetts, northern Connecticut, and upstate New York, take Interstate 84 east to the Massachusetts Turnpike (Interstate 90) and take Interstate 495 south to the Bourne Bridge. From New York City and southern Connecticut and Rhode Island, take Interstate 95 north toward Providence, where you pick up Interstate 195 east (toward Fall River–New Bedford) to Route 25 east to the Bourne Bridge. From the Bourne Bridge you can take Route 28 south to Falmouth and Woods Hole (about 15 mi), or—as you approach the Bourne Bridge—follow signs to U.S. 6 if you're headed elsewhere on the Cape.

Driving times can vary widely, depending on traffic. In good driving conditions you can reach the Sagamore Bridge from Boston in about 1½ hours, the Bourne Bridge from New York City in about 5 hours.

On summer weekends, when more than 100,000 cars a day cross each bridge, make every effort to avoid arriving in late afternoon. Give yourself extra time if you're driving to any of the ferry terminals to Nantucket and Martha's Vineyard. U.S. 6 and Route 28 are heavily congested eastbound on Friday evening, westbound on Sunday afternoon, and in both directions on Saturday, when many rental homes change hands. On the north shore, the Old King's Highway—Route 6A—parallels U.S. 6 and is a scenic country road passing through occasional towns.

When you're in no hurry, use back roads—you won't get there any faster, but they're less frustrating and much more rewarding. Heading from the Bourne Bridge toward Falmouth, Route 28A is a prettier alternative to Route 28, and Sippewisset Road meanders near Buzzards Bay between West Falmouth and Woods Hole.

Driving to Provincetown from other points on the Cape is mostly a scenic adventure. The wooded surrounds of Truro break into a breathtaking expanse of open water and sand dunes, with the skyline of Provincetown beyond. The busiest time is early morning—especially on days when the sun is reluctant to shine—when it seems that everyone on Cape Cod is determined to make it to Provincetown. Traffic is heaviest around Wellfleet. Except during the traffic-heavy season, you'll find the drive from Wellfleet to Provincetown beautiful and only 25 minutes in duration.

Traffic delays often result from congestion at the Sagamore and Bourne bridges, but a "flyover" road connecting the Sagamore Bridge to Route 3 has greatly reduced the traffic jams.

ON THE ISLANDS

Traffic can be a challenge on the islands, especially in season. Nantucket is small enough that you can easily get around on foot or by public transportation. On Martha's Vineyard, it can be handy to have a car if you want to travel freely among the different towns. Bringing a car over on the ferry in summer requires reservations far in advance, costs almost double what it does off-season, and necessitates standing in long lines—it's sometimes easier and more economical to rent a car once you're on the island. Consider public transportation and taxis if you're only making a few trips to different parts of the island, which has very good bus service that can get you to just about every major sight, village, and beach.

PARKING

Parking, in general, is a great challenge across much of Cape Cod and the islands from mid-June through early September, when lots are full and street parking impossible to find. Popular and congested downtowns such as Falmouth, Provincetown, Hyannis, Oak Bluffs, Nantucket Town, and Chatham tend to prove especially tough. Anytime you can walk, bike, or cab it somewhere, or you're able to travel in one car instead of two or more, do so. Off-season, parking is rarely a problem anywhere on the Cape or islands.

RULES OF THE ROAD

In Massachusetts, highway speed limits are 55 MPH near urban areas, 60 or 65 MPH elsewhere. Speed limits on U.S. 6 on the Cape vary as it changes from four lanes to two lanes. Radar detectors are legal in Massachusetts.

Massachusetts permits a right turn on a red light unless a sign says otherwise. When you approach one of the Cape's numerous rotaries (traffic circles), note that the vehicles already in the rotary have the right of way and that those vehicles entering the rotary must yield. Be careful: some drivers forget (or ignore) this principle.

Massachusetts law requires that drivers strap children under age 5 (or under 40 pounds) into approved child-safety seats. Kids ages 5 to 12 must wear seat belts. Drivers (but not other passengers over age 12) are legally required to wear seat belts, but they can be ticketed for not wearing them only if they're pulled over for some other reason.

Local Car-Rental Resources

Rent-A-Wreck of Hyannis	508/771–9667 or 888/486–1470	www.rentawreck.com
MARTHA'S VINEYARD AGENCIES		
A-A Island	508/627–6800 or 800/627–6333	www.mvautorental.com
Adventure Rentals	Beach Rd., Vineyard Haven, 508/693–1959	www.islandadventuresmv.com
NANTUCKET AGENCIES		
Affordable Rentals	6 S. Beach St., Nantucket, 508/228–3501 or 877/235–3500.	www.affrentals.com
Nantucket Island Rent A Car	Nantucket Memorial Airport, 508/228–9989 or 800/508–9972	www.nantucketislandrentacar.com
Nantucket Windmill	Nantucket Memorial Airport, 508/228–1227 or 800/228–1227	www.nantucketautorental.com

CAR RENTAL

When you reserve a car, ask about cancellation penalties, taxes, drop-off charges (if you're planning to pick up the car in one city and leave it in another), and surcharges (for being under or over a certain age, for additional drivers, or for driving across state or country borders or beyond a specific distance from your point of rental). All these things can add substantially to your costs. Request car seats and extras such as GPS when you book.

Rates are sometimes—but not always—better if you book in advance or reserve through a rental agency's Web site. There are other reasons to book ahead, though: for popular destinations, during busy times of the year, or to ensure that you get certain types of cars (vans, SUVs, exotic sports cars).

In Massachusetts you must be 21 to rent a car, and rates may be higher if you're under 25. When picking up a car, non–U.S. residents will need a reservation voucher (for prepaid reservations made in the traveler's home country), a passport, a driver's license, and a travel policy that covers each driver.

Base rates in Boston begin at $25 to $40 a day and $170 to $250 a week for an economy car with air-conditioning, automatic transmission, and unlimited mileage; rates tend to be slightly lower out of Providence and slightly higher out of Hyannis, but much depends on availability, which changes regularly. Rates on Cape Cod will be higher than those in Boston; and even more expensive on the islands. Keep in mind that taxes and a variety of surcharges typically add 30% to 40% to your total bill.

You can book car rentals on Martha's Vineyard through the Woods Hole ferry terminal free phone. A handful of local agencies, listed below, have rental desks at the airport. The cost is $100 to $150 per day for a sedan. Renting a four-wheel-drive vehicle costs around $160 per day (seasonal prices fluctuate widely).

If you're determined to rent a car while on Nantucket, be sure to book early. Expect to spend about $100 a day during high season.

ESSENTIALS

▮ ACCOMMODATIONS

Accommodations on the Cape and islands range from campsites to bed-and-breakfasts to luxurious self-contained resorts offering all kinds of sporting facilities, restaurants, entertainment, services (including business services and children's programs), and all the assistance you'll ever need in making vacation arrangements.

Because real-estate prices have skyrocketed throughout the region in the past few years, many motels and hotels have been developed into more lucrative condominiums, and quite a few B&Bs have been sold and converted back to private homes. The effect is that the Cape has fewer lodging options than it has had in years, and lodging rates have risen a bit, too. That said, there are still plenty of overnight options.

Single-night lodgings for those just passing through can be found at countless tacky but cheap and conveniently located roadside motels or at chain hotels; these places often have a pool, TVs, or other amenities to keep children entertained in the evening. Bear in mind that many Cape accommodations, even simple motels, have two-, three-, and even four-night minimum stays on weekends in high season, generally from around Memorial Day through Labor Day. It's still worth checking with a property to see if you can stay for fewer days, especially if you're planning to come out for a last-minute visit, but be warned that finding a single-night accommodation on a late June, July, or August weekend can prove extremely challenging.

Because of extremely high demand for accommodations on the islands, it's best to reserve especially well in advance when planning a stay on Nantucket or Martha's Vineyard, especially from June through early September. If you're looking to visit during the summer months or over a popular weekend, such as the Nantucket Daffodil Festival in late April or Christmas Stroll, it's not a bad idea to book a full year in advance. Most inns on the islands require prepayment or nonrefundable deposits as well as three-night (or more) minimums in summer. And rates can be very high, averaging $250 a night or more on Nantucket and only slightly less on Martha's Vineyard.

Families may want to consider condominiums, cottages, and efficiencies, which offer more space; living areas; kitchens; and sometimes laundry facilities, children's play areas, or children's programs. Especially as single-night lodging options on the Cape diminish in number, this is an increasingly popular option, although many condo and cottage rentals have one-week minimum stays, especially in summer.

The lodgings we list are the cream of the crop in each price category. We always list the facilities that are available—but we don't specify whether they cost extra: when pricing accommodations, always ask what's included and what costs extra.

▮TIP➔ Assume that hotels operate on the European Plan (EP, no meals) unless we specify that they use the Breakfast Plan (BP, with full breakfast), Continental Plan (CP, Continental breakfast), Full American Plan (FAP, all meals), or Modified American Plan (MAP, breakfast and dinner).

APARTMENT AND HOUSE RENTALS

Many travelers to the Cape and the islands rent a house if they're going to stay for a week or longer rather than stay at a B&B or hotel. These can save you money; however, some rentals are luxury properties, economical only when your party is large. Many local real-estate agencies deal with rentals, and most specialize in a specific area. Be sure to book a property well in advance of your trip: prime properties are often rented out to the same people year after year. Rental choices are often more abundant in the smaller, quieter towns, such as Yarmouth, Chatham, Wellfleet, and Truro, or Up-Island on Martha's Vineyard. One-bedroom rentals on the Cape range from $500 to $1,000 per week, depending mainly on the proximity to water and views. Expect rentals on both Martha's Vineyard and Nantucket to be significantly higher than those on the Cape, simply because there are fewer options.

BED-AND-BREAKFASTS

Bed-and-breakfast inns have long been very popular on Cape Cod and the islands. Many of them occupy stately old sea captains' homes and other 17th-, 18th-, and 19th-century buildings; others are in newer homes.

In many cases, B&Bs are not appropriate for families—noise travels easily, rooms are often small, and the furnishings are often fragile—so be sure to ask. Many B&Bs do not provide phones or TVs in guest rooms, some are not air-conditioned, and all prohibit smoking indoors (some allow smoking on the grounds).

In summer you should reserve lodgings as far in advance as possible—several months for the most popular inns. Off-season, rates are much reduced, and you may find that it's easier to get to know your innkeeper.

Numerous B&B reservation agencies can aid you in choosing an inn. Classic Historic Inns of Cape Cod Bay offers a listing of distinctive and lovely inns along the Cape Cod Bay side of the Cape; many are carefully restored historic properties. One event of note sponsored by the inns is the annual Halloween murder mystery weekend.

Reservation Services Bed & Breakfast.com (☏ 512/322–2710 or 800/462–2632 ⊕ www. bedandbreakfast.com). **Bed & Breakfast Inns Online** (☏ 800/215–7365 ⊕ www.bbonline. com). **BnB Finder.com** (☏ 888/469–6663 ⊕ www.bnbfinder.com).

Reservation Services on the Cape Bed and Breakfast Cape Cod (☏ 508/255–3824 or 800/541–6226 ⊕ www. bedandbreakfastcapecod.com). **Cape Cod Rentals** (☏ 800/896–4606 ⊕ www.capecodrentals. com). **Classic Historic Inns of Cape Cod Bay** (⊕ www.historiccapecodbay.com).

Reservation Services on the Islands Martha's Vineyard and Nantucket Reservations (☏ 508/693–7200 ⊕ www.mvreservations.com). **Nantucket Accommodations** (☏ 508/228–9559 ⊕ www.nantucketaccommodation.com). **Nantucket Concierge** (☏ 508/228–8400 ⊕ www.nantucketconcierge.com).

CAMPING

There are many private and state-park camping areas on Cape Cod. For additional details on camping in specific areas, look for the 🏕 icon in that area's Where to Stay section.

HOME EXCHANGES

With a direct home exchange you stay in someone else's home while they stay in yours. Some outfits also deal with vacation homes, so you're not actually staying in someone's full-time residence, just their vacant weekend place.

Exchange Clubs Home Exchange.com (☏ 800/877–8723 ⊕ www.homeexchange. com); $9.95 per month for a one-year online listing.

❚ BEACHES

In season, you must pay to park at public beaches. Parking at "restricted" beaches is available only to residents and to visitors with permits. If you're renting a house, you can purchase a weekly beach permit; contact the local town hall for details. Walkers and cyclists do not need permits to use restricted beaches. The official season generally begins the last weekend in June and ends on Labor Day. Note that the lots are often open to all early in the morning (before 8) and late in the afternoon (after 4 or 5), even at resident beaches in season.

❚ EATING OUT

The restaurants we list are the cream of the crop in each price category. Note that ordering a lobster dinner, which can be far more expensive than other menu items, may push your meal into a higher price category than the restaurant's price range shows.

CUTTING COSTS

Even the best of the region's restaurants offer slightly scaled-down portions of pricier dinner menus during lunchtime. Any time of day, you can indulge in fresh local seafood and clambakes at seat-yourself shanties for a much lower price than their fine-dining counterparts. Often the tackier the decor (plastic fish on the walls), the better the seafood. These laid-back local haunts usually operate a fish market on the premises and are in every town on the Cape.

WINES, BEER, AND SPIRITS

Massachusetts is not a major wine-growing area, but Westport Rivers Winery in Westport and the Cape Cod Winery in East Falmouth produce respectable vintages. The family that owns Westport Rivers also runs the local Buzzards Bay Brewing Co. Wines from Truro Vineyards of Cape Cod are local favorites.

In Massachusetts, you can generally buy alcoholic beverages (wine, beer, and spirits) in liquor stores, known locally as package stores. A few exceptions allow some grocery stores to sell wine and beer. All of the towns on Martha's Vineyard except Oak Bluffs and Edgartown are "dry" and don't sell alcohol. Restaurants in these dry towns encourage diners to bring their own wine or beer; a corkage fee is usually charged for each bottle.

❚ EMERGENCIES

Cape Cod Hospital has a 24-hour emergency room. For rescues at sea, call the Coast Guard. Boaters should use Channel 16 on their radios.

Emergency Services Ambulance, fire, police (☎ *911 or dial township station*). **Coast Guard** (☎ *508/888–0335 in Sandwich and Cape Cod Canal, 508/945–0164 in Chatham, 508/487–0070 in Provincetown* ⊕ *www.uscg.mil*).

Hospitals Cape Cod Hospital (⊠ *27 Park St., Hyannis* ☎ *508/771–1800 or 877/227–3263* ⊕ *www.capecodhealth.org*). **Falmouth Hospital** (⊠ *100 Ter Heun Dr., Falmouth* ☎ *508/548–5300 or 877/227–3263* ⊕ *www.capecodhealth.org*). **Martha's Vineyard Hospital** (⊠ *1 Hospital Rd., Oak Bluffs* ☎ *508/693–0410* ⊕ *www.marthasvineyardhospital.com*). **Nantucket Cottage Hospital** (⊠ *57 Prospect St., Nantucket* ☎ *508/825–8100* ⊕ *www.nantuckethospital.org*).

24-Hour Pharmacies CVS Falmouth (⊠ *105 Rte. 28, Falmouth* ☎ *508/540–4307*). **CVS Hyannis** (⊠ *176 North St., Hyannis* ☎ *508/775–8462*). **CVS South Yarmouth** (⊠ *976 Main St., South Yarmouth* ☎ *508/398–8800*).

❚ GAY AND LESBIAN TRAVEL

Provincetown, at the tip of the Cape, is one of the East Coast's leading lesbian and gay seaside destinations, and it also has a large year-round lesbian and gay community. Dozens of P-town establishments, from B&Bs to bars, cater specifically to lesbian and gay visitors, and all of the town's restaurants are gay-friendly; many are gay-owned and -operated. Hyannis has Cape Cod's sole gay bar outside P-town, but attitudes throughout Cape Cod tend to be extremely accepting and tolerant toward gays and lesbians. Martha's Vineyard, although lacking any gay-specific nightlife, has a number of gay-friendly businesses and accommodations and has become increasingly popular as a gay vacation spot in recent years. Nantucket is also quite tolerant but has less of a gay following than the Vineyard.

▮ HEALTH

LYME DISEASE

Lyme disease, so named for its having been first reported in the town of Lyme, Connecticut, is a potentially debilitating disease carried by deer ticks, which thrive in dry, brush-covered areas, especially on Cape Cod. Always use insect repellent; it's imperative that you protect yourself from ticks from early spring through summer. To prevent bites, wear light-color clothing and tuck pant legs into socks. Look for black ticks about the size of a pinhead around hairlines and the warmest parts of the body. If you have been bitten, consult a physician, especially if you see the telltale bull's-eye bite pattern. Influenza-like symptoms often accompany a Lyme infection. Early treatment is imperative.

PESTS AND OTHER HAZARDS

Cape Cod's greatest insect pest is mosquitoes, which are at their worst after snowy winters and wet springs. The best protection is repellent containing DEET. A particular pest of coastal areas, especially salt marshes, is the greenhead fly. Their bite is nasty, and they are best repelled by a liberal application of Avon Skin So Soft. The fly is most active mid-July to early August.

Poison ivy is a pervasive vinelike plant, recognizable by its leaf pattern: three shiny green leaves together. In spring new poison-ivy leaves are red; likewise, they can take on a reddish tint as fall approaches. The oil from these leaves produces an itchy skin rash that spreads with scratching. If you think you may have touched some leaves, wash as soon as you can with soap and cool water.

SHELLFISHING

Cape Cod attracts seafood lovers who enjoy harvesting their own clams, mussels, and even lobsters; permits are required, and casual harvesting of all shellfish is strictly forbidden. Amateur clammers should be aware that some New England shellfish beds are periodically visited by red tides, during which microorganisms can render shellfish (excluding lobsters, scallops, and all fin fish) poisonous. To keep abreast of the situation, inquire when you apply for a license (usually at local town halls) and pay attention to red-tide postings as you travel.

Lyme Disease Info **Massachusetts Department of Public Health** (☎ 866/627–7968 ⊕ www.state.ma.us/dph). **National Centers for Disease Control and Prevention** (☎ 800/232–4636 ⊕ www.cdc.gov).

▮ HOURS OF OPERATION

Hours on the Cape and the islands can sometimes differ from those elsewhere in New England, as many businesses and attractions are open only seasonally or have limited hours during the quieter months, from mid-fall to mid-spring. Within the region, shops and other businesses in the towns near the Cape as well as on the Upper Cape and even as far out as Barnstable and Hyannis tend to be less seasonal, catering to the larger year-round populations in those areas. The farther out you go, toward the Lower Cape and Outer Cape and on the islands, the more likely you are to encounter businesses that close or keep shorter hours off-season.

MUSEUMS AND SIGHTS

Museum and attraction hours vary widely from place to place and from season to season. Some places are staffed by volunteers and have limited hours (open just a few hours a day several days a week) even in summer, although major museums and attractions are generally open daily in summer. Always check the hours of a place you plan to visit ahead of time.

SHOPS

Banks are usually open weekdays from 9 to 5 and Saturday mornings. The post office is open from 8 to 5 weekdays and often on Saturday morning. Shops in more heavily settled areas, particularly in indoor and strip malls, typically open at 9 or 10 daily and stay open until anywhere from 6 PM to 10 PM on weekdays and Saturday, and until 5 or 6 on Sunday. Hours vary greatly, so call ahead when in doubt.

On major roads and in some densely populated areas, you'll usually find at least one or two pharmacies and gas stations open 24 hours. Throughout the region, most bars and discos stay open until 1 AM.

▮ MONEY

Prices throughout this guide are given for adults. Substantially reduced fees are almost always available for children, students, and senior citizens.

CREDIT CARDS

Throughout this guide, the following abbreviations are used: **AE**, American Express; **D**, Discover; **DC**, Diners Club; **MC**, MasterCard; and **V**, Visa.

▮ PACKING

Only a few Cape Cod and island restaurants require a jacket and tie, as do some dinner cruises; the area prides itself on informality. Do pack a sweater or jacket, even in summer, for nights can be cool. *For suggested clothing to minimize bites from deer ticks and to prevent Lyme disease, see Health.* Perhaps most important of all, don't forget a swimsuit (or two).

▮ TAXES

The state hotel tax varies from town to town and can be up to 11.7%.

SALES TAX

Massachusetts state sales tax is 6.25%.

▮ TIME

Cape Cod is in the eastern standard time zone. When it is noon in Cape Cod, it is 9 AM in Los Angeles, 11 AM in Chicago, 5 PM in London, and 3 AM the following day in Sydney.

▮ TIPPING

The customary tipping rate for taxi drivers is 15% to 20%, with a minimum of $2. Bellhops—a relative rarity on Cape Cod's more casual lodging scene—are usually given $2 per bag in luxury hotels, $1 per bag elsewhere. Hotel maids should be tipped $2 per day of your stay. Waiters should be tipped 15% to 20%, though at higher-end restaurants, a solid 20% is more the norm. Many Cape Cod restaurants add a gratuity to the bill for parties of six or more. Ask what the percentage is if the menu or bill doesn't state it. Tip $1 per drink you order at the bar, though if at an upscale establishment, those $15 martinis might warrant a $2 tip.

▮ VISITOR INFORMATION

ON-LINE TRAVEL TOOLS

For general information, visit the Cape Cod Chamber of Commerce online at ⊕ *www.capecodchamber.org*. Other resources include the Cape Cod Information Center (⊕ *www.allcapecod.com*) and Cape Cod Online, the Web site of the *Cape Cod Times* (⊕ *www.capecodonline.com*).

TRANSPORTATION

SmarTraveler (⊕ *www.smartraveler.com*) provides real-time updates on traffic conditions on Cape Cod (just click on the link for Boston, and you'll find a further link to Cape Cod). You can look at live Web-cam pictures of the Bourne and Sagamore bridges at the Cape Cod USA site (⊕ *www.capecodlivecam.com*), as well as Web-cam pictures of Commercial Street in Provincetown, the harbor in Hyannis, and the beach at Wellfleet. A great resource for travelers is Smart Guide (⊕ *www.smartguide.org*), which updates travel alerts, provides maps, and tips for those coming to the Cape and islands.

For Cape Cod bus and trolley schedules, check with the Cape Cod Regional Transit Authority (⊕ *www.capecodtransit. org*). The transportation information site of the Cape Cod Commission (⊕ *www. gocapecod.org*) has links to transportation providers, updates on transportation-related construction projects, and information on bicycling and walking, including updates on the Cape Cod Rail Trail. Visit the Cape Cod Bike Guide (⊕ *www.capecodbikeguide.com*) for trail listings and general information about biking in the area. The Massachusetts Bicycle Coalition (⊕ *www.massbike.org*) has information for bicyclists. Rails-to-Trails Conservancy (⊕ *www.railtrails. org*) provides general information about rail trails, such as the Cape Cod Rail Trail.

Island ferry information and schedules are available online from the Steamship Authority (⊕ *www.steamshipauthority. com*) and from Hy-Line (⊕ *www. hylinecruises.com*). For information on the Boston-to-Provincetown ferries, visit the site of Bay State Cruise Company (⊕ *www.baystatecruisecompany. com*) or Boston Harbor Cruises (⊕ *www. bostonharborcruises.com*).

DISABILITY ACCESS

The Directory of Accessible Facilities lists accessible recreational facilities in Massachusetts (⊕ *www.mass.gov/dcr/ universal_access/index.htm*). Cape Cod Disability Access Directory (⊕ *www. capecoddisability.org*) has useful information about facilities on Cape Cod.

VISITOR INFORMATION OFFICES

Before you go, contact the state's office of tourism and the area's chambers of commerce for general information, seasonal events, and brochures. For specific information on Cape Cod's state forests and parks, the area's farmers' markets and fairs, or wildlife, contact the special-interest government offices below. You can also check Web sites on the Internet.

When you arrive, stop by the local chamber of commerce for additional information—each chamber is stocked with local brochures and produces a comprehensive annual guidebook on each town.

General Cape Contacts **Cape Cod Chamber of Commerce** (✉ *5 Shoot Flying Hill Rd., Centerville* ☎ *508/362-3225 or 888/332-2732* ⊕ *www.capecodchamber.org*). **Cape Cod National Seashore** (☎ *508/349-3785* ⊕ *www.nps.gov/caco*).

General Islands Contacts **Martha's Vineyard Chamber of Commerce** (✉ *Beach Rd., Box 1698, Vineyard Haven* ☎ *508/693-0085 or 800/505-4815* ⊕ *www.mvy.com*). **Nantucket Chamber of Commerce** (✉ *Zero Main St., Nantucket* ☎ *508/228-1700* ⊕ *www. nantucketchamber.org*).

Massachusetts Contacts **Department of Conservation and Recreation** (☎ *617/626-1250* ⊕ *www.mass.gov/dcr*). **Department of Fish and Game** (☎ *508/626-1500* ⊕ *www. state.ma.us/dfwele*). **Massachusetts Office of Travel & Tourism** (✉ *10 Park Plaza, Suite 4510, Boston* ☎ *800/227-6277* ⊕ *www. massvacation.com*).

INDEX

NOTES

NOTES

ABOUT OUR WRITERS

Sandy MacDonald, who updated Nantucket for this edition, has summered on the island since 1990. A seasoned travel writer, she has written several New England guidebooks and has also contributed to national magazines. While on Nantucket, she enjoys acting and singing with local companies, and working with the Miacomet Conservation Association to protect Nantucket's unique and fragile environment.

As the editor of *Cape Cod Life* magazine for nearly a decade, **Janice Randall Rohlf** got to know the Cape and Islands inside and out. A native New Englander, she has lived in Bourne for 15 years and is currently a freelance writer and editor for a number of regional and national magazines. Janice updated the Upper Cape chapter of this edition.

Laura V. Scheel updated the Experience, Mid Cape, Lower Cape, Outer Cape, and Martha's Vineyard chapters of this edition. She has written frequently for Fodor's, contributing to titles such as *Fodor's Maine Coast* and *Fodor's New England.* When not writing about travel, history, and the arts, she raises oysters in Wellfleet on the Outer Cape.